September 2001–August 2002

TARBELL'S

KJV & NRSV Lesson Commentary

BASED ON THE INTERNATIONAL SUNDAY SCHOOL LESSONS

PASTOR JEFF WALLACE

D1258422

COOK COMMUNICATIONS MINISTRIES CURRICULUM
COLORADO SPRINGS, COLORADO/PARIS, ONTARIO

TARBELL'S KJV & NRSV LESSON COMMENTARY © 2001 Cook
Communications Ministries, 4050 Lee Vance View, Colorado Springs, CO 80918, U.S.A.
All rights reserved. Printed in U.S.A. May not be reproduced without permission. Lessons
based on International Sunday School Lessons: the International Bible Lessons for
Christian Teaching, © 1998 by the Committee on the Uniform Series.

Editor: Dan Lioy

Senior Editor: Doug Schmidt

Bible Editor: Jim Townsend, Ph.D.

Cover Design by Jeffrey P. Barnes

Cover photography © 1998 by Dan Stultz

All Scripture quotations are from the King James Version or the New Revised Standard
Version of the Bible. Scripture quotations from THE NEW REVISED STANDARD VER-
SION OF THE BIBLE, © 1989 by the Division of Christian Education, National Council
of the Churches of Christ in the United States of America, are used by permission. All
rights reserved.

All Scripture quotations in the author's material, unless otherwise noted, are from the
New Revised Standard Version of the Bible.

ISBN: 0-7814-5612-6

CONTENTS

■

SEPTEMBER, OCTOBER, NOVEMBER 2001
JESUS' MINISTRY

UNIT I: PERFORMING MIRACLES

UNIT II: TRUTH IN PARABLES

UNIT III: THE SERMON ON THE MOUNT

■

DECEMBER 2001, JANUARY, FEBRUARY 2002
LIGHT FOR ALL PEOPLE

UNIT I: GOD'S SERVANT WILL BRING LIGHT

UNIT II: GOD'S PEOPLE WILL WALK IN LIGHT

UNIT III: GOD'S GRACE IS FOR ALL PEOPLE

CONTENTS

■

The time had come for the Israelite children to cross over into the long-awaited promised land. Moses, who would only view the land from the other side of the Jordan, had been conversing with God. Having told Moses that he would never set foot in Canaanland, the Lord instructed this great leader to charge Joshua, and encourage and strengthen him, because it was he who would cross over at the head of this people and who would secure their possession of the land that he would see (Deut. 3:28).

Even though we're not leading some two million people into uncharted territory, standing before and leading a Sunday school class can be rather daunting. And just like Joshua, we need to be encouraged and strengthened for such a task. Certainly the Lord provides the measure of encouragement and strength that we truly need. But it sure is nice to receive encouragement from and draw on the strength of those with whom we serve in the church!

We live at a time when we seem to be spending increasing amounts of time at our computers and on the Internet. Technology has vastly increased the methods by which we can communicate. But e-mail can't replace sipping a cup of tea while sitting on the front porch with a friend. Computers can't replace a well-timed hug offering consolation or support. And no amount of technology can replace the encouraging words shared between brothers and sisters in Christ.

Sure, make the most of the technology available to you. But don't lose that personal touch. Instill confidence in a dear friend with a face-to-face word of encouragement. Inspire a fellow teacher with a phone call. Spur on your students' walk with Christ by joining alongside them on their journey.

Forever in His service,
Jeffery Scott Wallace

A Note of Appreciation

To my congregation, who ministers to me more than I could ever minister to them; to Dad, Mom, and Bub, whose love and support have always been as solid as the Rock of Gibraltar; to Nathaniel and Gracie, who still bring joy to all the seasons of my life; and to Jill, my best friend, my wife, and my partner on the pilgrimage.

Sunday school materials from the following denominations and publishers follow the International Sunday School Lesson outlines (sometimes known as the Uniform Series). Because *Tarbell's KJV & NRSV Lesson Commentary* follows the same ISSL outlines, you can use *Tarbell's* as an excellent teacher resource to supplement the materials from these publishing houses.

Denominational:
>   Advent Christian General Conference—*Adult*
>   American Baptist (Judson Press)—*Adult*
>   Church of God in Christ (Church of God in Christ Publishing House)—*Adult*
>   Church of Christ Holiness—*Adult*
>   Church of God (Warner Press)—*Adult*
>   Church of God by Faith—*Adult*
>   National Baptist Convention of America (Boyd)—*All ages*
>   National Primitive Baptist Convention—*Adult*
>   Progressive National Baptist Convention—*Adult*
>   Presbyterian Church (U.S.A.) (Bible Discovery Series—Presbyterian Publishing House or P.R.E.M.)—*Adult*
>   Southern Baptist (Baptist Sunday School Board)—*All ages*
>   Union Gospel Press—*All ages*
>   United Holy Church of America—*Adult*
>   United Methodist Church (Cokesbury)—*All ages*

Nondenominational:
>   Cook Communications Ministries—*Adult*
>   Echoes Sunday School Literature—*Adult*
>   Standard Publishing—*Adult*
>   Urban Ministries—*All ages*

JESUS' MINISTRY

THE FIRST MIRACLE

BACKGROUND SCRIPTURE: John 2:1-11
DEVOTIONAL READING: Psalm 77:11-15

KEY VERSE: Jesus did this, the first of his signs, in Cana of Galilee,
and revealed his glory; and his disciples believed in him. John 2:11.

KING JAMES VERSION

JOHN 2:1 And the third day there was a marriage in Cana of Galilee; and the mother of Jesus was there:

2 And both Jesus was called, and his disciples, to the marriage.

3 And when they wanted wine, the mother of Jesus saith unto him, They have no wine.

4 Jesus saith unto her, Woman, what have I to do with thee? mine hour is not yet come.

5 His mother saith unto the servants, Whatsoever he saith unto you, do it.

6 And there were set there six waterpots of stone, after the manner of the purifying of the Jews, containing two or three firkins apiece.

7 Jesus saith unto them, Fill the waterpots with water. And they filled them up to the brim.

8 And he saith unto them, Draw out now, and bear unto the governor of the feast. And they bare it.

9 When the ruler of the feast had tasted the water that was made wine, and knew not whence it was: (but the servants which drew the water knew;) the governor of the feast called the bridegroom,

10 And saith unto him, Every man at the beginning doth set forth good wine; and when men have well drunk, then that which is worse: but thou hast kept the good wine until now.

11 This beginning of miracles did Jesus in Cana of Galilee, and manifested forth his glory; and his disciples believed on him.

NEW REVISED STANDARD VERSION

JOHN 2:1 On the third day there was a wedding in Cana of Galilee, and the mother of Jesus was there. 2 Jesus and his disciples had also been invited to the wedding. 3 When the wine gave out, the mother of Jesus said to him, "They have no wine." 4 And Jesus said to her, "Woman, what concern is that to you and to me? My hour has not yet come." 5 His mother said to the servants, "Do whatever he tells you." 6 Now standing there were six stone water jars for the Jewish rites of purification, each holding twenty or thirty gallons. 7 Jesus said to them, "Fill the jars with water." And they filled them up to the brim. 8 He said to them, "Now draw some out, and take it to the chief steward." So they took it. 9 When the steward tasted the water that had become wine, and did not know where it came from (though the servants who had drawn the water knew), the steward called the bridegroom 10 and said to him, "Everyone serves the good wine first, and then the inferior wine after the guests have become drunk. But you have kept the good wine until now." 11 Jesus did this, the first of his signs, in Cana of Galilee, and revealed his glory; and his disciples believed in him.

BACKGROUND

The apostle John knew that Jesus was no mere man. John recognized Him as divinity in human flesh. Having been one of the inner circle of the three disciples who were most intimate with Jesus, John testified in his Gospel that Jesus was *in the beginning* (John 1:1), was *with God*, and *was God. All things came into being through him, and without him not one thing came into being* (1:3). Yes, John knew Jesus as a man. But John also came to know Jesus as a vital member of the powerful, creative Godhead. That's why John portrayed Jesus as having control over all things—both natural and supernatural.

From the beginning verses of his Gospel, John—a devoted follower of Jesus and an eyewitness of His miracles—emphasized as one of his major themes the Savior's mastery over all creation. John's chief means of doing so was to describe in detail seven *signs* (2:11), or attesting miracles, that Jesus performed.

Jesus' turning water into wine revealed Him as the source of life (2:1-12). The healing of the royal official's son showed Jesus to be master over distance (4:46-54). The healing of the invalid at the pool of Bethzatha revealed Jesus as the master over time (5:1-17). The feeding of over 5,000 showed Jesus to be the Bread of Life (6:1-14). Jesus' walking on water and stilling the storm revealed Him as master over nature (6:15-21). The healing of the man blind from birth showed Jesus to be the Light of the World (9:1-41). And the raising of Lazarus from the dead revealed that Jesus has power over death (11:17-45).

John was not only keenly aware of the Jewish culture of the day, but he also had a good grasp of Palestinian geography. For instance, in recording Jesus' first miracle in Cana of Galilee, John talked about a place that is not mentioned in the other Gospels (2:1). Moreover, the apostle's attention to detail was meticulous. For example, John discussed how, after Jesus' baptism in the Jordan River, He called several people to be His disciples (1:35-51).

This week's lesson introduces us to the first of seven miracles recorded by John. While Jesus, along with His disciples, joined in the celebration of a wedding feast in Cana, the host of the feast edged toward a potentially grave social embarrassment: running out of wine for his guests. But Jesus demonstrated both His concern for the celebration's participants and His dominion over nature by miraculously turning water into wine.

NOTES ON THE PRINTED TEXT

Jesus came to the earth to provide salvation for the lost (Matt. 1:21). Interestingly, though, He began His public ministry by attending a wedding and taking part in its festivities. The wedding occurred in Cana of Galilee. The exact location of this spot is unclear, though we do know that it was the home of Nathanael (John 21:2). Jesus' mother was in attendance at the wedding (2:1), and both Jesus and His disciples had *been invited* (2:2).

Weddings in first-century Palestine were typically week-long festivals. Day after day, banquets would be prepared for many guests, with daily celebrations of the married couple's new life together. In most cases, the whole village was invited—and everyone who was invited was expected to come. It was considered an insult to refuse an invitation (Matt. 22:1-14; Luke 14:16-24).

To accommodate so many people, careful planning was imperative. After all, for a host to run out of wine during a wedding festival was more than embarrassing; it crossed the line of the unwritten but well-rehearsed rules of hospitality. Oddly, though, the host of the wedding in Cana somehow failed to plan for enough wine to satisfy the number of guests in attendance; consequently, *the wine gave out* (John 2:3). By reporting this social calamity to Jesus, Mary was not likely asking Him to perform a miracle. Probably she was hoping that Jesus would simply solve the problem by tracking down some more wine.

Jesus' response to His mother may seem difficult to understand: *"Woman, what concern is that to you and to me? My hour has not yet come"* (2:4). But it should be noted that the Greek noun rendered *woman* was a term of solemn and respectful address. While it was an unusual way of referring to one's mother, it was typically used with affection. The question about whose concern the dearth of wine was and the statement regarding Jesus' hour having not yet come seem to suggest that the time of His self-disclosure as the Messiah would be determined only by God the Father, not by Jesus Himself and certainly not by Mary, His mother.

Still, Mary depended on Jesus' involvement to solve the problem. Having lost her husband by this time—as tradition holds—it is likely that Mary had grown used to asking Jesus' help under such conditions. Apparently sensing His willingness to help, she told the host's servants to do *"whatever he tells you"* (2:5).

Sitting nearby were *six stone water jars for the Jewish rites of purification* (2:6). These vessels were for ceremonial cleaning, not for personal hygiene. The Mosaic law prescribed that people became symbolically unclean by touching objects of daily life. So before eating, the Jews would pour water over their hands to cleanse them. Jesus moved to solve the potentially embarrassing situation of the wedding host by instructing the servants to *"Fill the jars with water." And they filled them up to the brim* (2:7). When full, the water jars could hold between 20 and 30 gallons of liquid.

No mention is made of Jesus waving His hand over the jars. Nor is there any statement of His praying to the Father to ask Him to change the water to wine.

Jesus simply instructed the servants to fill the jars with water, and at some point after they had done so, the water was transformed to wine.

Jesus told the servants to draw out some of the liquid from the jar and to take it to the chief steward for tasting (2:8). When the headwaiter sampled the wine, he seemed both relieved and happy that a social disaster had been averted and that more wine had been made available (2:9). Still, the exceptional taste led him to exclaim: *"Everyone serves the good wine first, and then the inferior wine after the guests have become drunk. But you have kept the good wine until now"* (2:10).

Jesus' miracle (the first one recorded in John's Gospel) made quite an impression. It *revealed his glory; and his disciples believed in him* (2:11). As one of those believing disciples in attendance, John referred to this and others of Jesus' miracles as *signs*, emphasizing the significance of Jesus' action rather than the marvel of the miracle itself. Indeed, Jesus' miracles were not just wonders meant to astound, but also *signs* meant to demonstrate God's power. By turning water into wine, Jesus revealed Himself as the source of life and disclosed to His disciples the way He would go about His ministry, namely, by helping those in need and (thereby) validating God's love for all people.

SUGGESTIONS TO TEACHERS

Jesus' first miracle was not performed to save someone's life, but rather to help someone out of a distressing, discouraging, and potentially embarrassing situation. Surely your students can relate to this type of predicament. Complete and strategic plans are made. Every base seems to be covered. Every person and object is accounted for. The list has been checked and double-checked. But then something creeps up unexpectedly and surprises the hosts, and they find themselves on the brink of some social disaster!

Such a situation has become commonplace in our information-saturated society. We have so much to think about, to remember, and to do. And despite our plans and checklists, sometimes life deals us blindsided blows—some of them minor, some of them major—that we never would have guessed were coming.

1. IN STEPS JESUS! There isn't a problem that can arise that Jesus doesn't care about. And there isn't a problem that can arise that His grace—His unmerited favor—won't see us through. The Son of God was concerned enough about the potential social embarrassment of a wedding host to rescue him. Jesus' desire was for the wedding feast to go well, and His involvement assured the feast's success. Jesus' involvement in our lives assures our eternal success.

2. KEEP BELIEVING. As a friend of the host, Mary wanted to help. She turned to Jesus, hoping He would have a solution. Instead, she received an answer from Him that seems difficult to understand. Nonetheless, she kept trusting Him to do what He deemed best. We often take our problems to Christ sure of how He should take care of them. But then He comes up with a completely different plan. We need to learn to submit to Him and allow Him to deal with the problem. We also find ourselves in situations that are hard to understand, but we must keep trusting Him to work out trying situations in a way that will display His glory.

3. FROM ORDINARY TO EXTRAORDINARY. Under Jesus' domain, ordinary water became the most extraordinary, best-tasting wine at the wedding festival. Our lives, too, move from the ordinary to the extraordinary when we submit to Jesus' control over us.

4. TAKE FIVE. Many people refuse to step back from their important work to enjoy a warm celebration. Not so with Jesus. He gladly attended the wedding feast because people were there, and one of Jesus' purposes was to be with people. We all need time set aside for work and for carrying out our mission in life. But we also need time set aside for rest, for celebration, and for simply enjoying the presence of other people.

<hr>

FOR ADULTS

■ TOPIC: Seeing Is Believing

■ QUESTIONS: 1. Why do you think Mary approached Jesus, who had not yet performed any miracles, about the wedding host's running out of wine? 2. Why did Jesus' turning the water into wine give rise to the disciples' belief? 3. In what way did Jesus' performance of this miracle reveal His glory? 4. How has Jesus turned some ordinary aspect of your life into something extraordinary? 5. Do you find it hard to keep trusting in Jesus when you find yourself in a situation that you don't understand? How do you maintain your faith during those times?

■ **ILLUSTRATIONS:**

Miracle of the Master Carpenter. Cheryl Walterman Stewart, in the book *Chicken Soup for the Christian Family Soul*, tells about her Grandpa Nybakken, who worked as a carpenter. On a cold Chicago Saturday, he was building some crates for the clothes his church was sending to an orphanage in China. On his way home, he reached into his shirt pocket to find his glasses, but they were gone. He drove back to the church to look for them, but his search proved fruitless.

Mentally going over all that he had done that morning, Nybakken realized that the glasses had probably slipped out of his pocket and fallen into one of the crates that he had nailed shut. His brand-new glasses were heading for China!

The Great Depression was at its height, and Nybakken had six children. He had spent 20 dollars for those glasses that same morning. "It's not fair," he told God when he figured out what had happened. "I've been very faithful in giving of my time and money to Your work, and now this."

Several months later, the director of the Chinese orphanage was on furlough in the United States. While visiting the churches that supported him, he came to speak one Sunday night at Nybakken's small congregation. The missionary began by thanking the people for their faithfulness in supporting the orphanage.

"But most of all," the director said, "I must thank you for the glasses you sent last year. You see, the Communists had just swept through the orphanage, destroying everything, including my glasses. I was desperate. Even if I had the money, there was simply no way of replacing those glasses. Along with not being able to see well, I experienced headaches every day, so my co-workers and I were much in prayer about this. Then your crates arrived. When my staff removed the covers, they found a pair of glasses lying on top. Folks, when I tried on the glasses, it was as though they had been custom-made just for me! I want to thank you for being a part of that."

The congregation listened, happy for the miraculous glasses. But they thought the missionary must have confused their church with another one. There were no glasses on their list of items to be sent overseas. But sitting quietly in the back, with tears streaming down his face, an ordinary carpenter realized that the Master Carpenter had used him in an extraordinary way.

A Transformed Outlook. Daren used to be a butcher in a large grocery store. As a matter of fact, he's still a butcher in the same large grocery store. But something is vastly different about Daren and about the way he sees his job. Before, he saw his work as merely a way to earn a paycheck. For the most part, his job was mundane and boring. It was ordinary.

But when Daren committed his life to Christ, everything began to change. Over time, he sensed that his job was being transformed, even though his duties were the same as before. He began to sense a purpose in his work. He began to have a new excitement about going in to work every day. His was no longer an *ordinary* job; his had become an *extraordinary* ministry.

Daren gives credit where credit is due: to Jesus. The Savior had transformed Daren, and therefore had even transformed Daren's attitude toward his work. Jesus took the ordinary and turned it into something extraordinary. Daren now rejoiced over what Christ was doing in his life.

Believing to Understand. Saint Anselm of Canterbury (1033–1109) was one of the originators of medieval scholastic philosophy. His combination of personal enthusiasm and well-studied theology led his contemporaries to look up to him as a spiritual guide. Today, of course, he is most often remembered for his acceptance of rational inquiry into the mysteries of the Christian faith.

In his *Proslogium*, Saint Anselm explained how belief must precede understanding: "For I do not seek to understand that I may believe, but I believe in order to understand. For this I believe—that unless I believe, I should not understand." This statement echoes what Paul wrote in 2 Corinthians 5:7, *for we walk by faith, not by sight*. The apostle likewise declared in Romans 8:25, *But if we hope for what we do not see, we wait for it with patience*. Thankfully, we have the Spirit of God to *help us in our weakness* (8:26).

■ **TOPIC:** Seeing Is Believing

■ **QUESTIONS:** 1. Why do you think Jesus went about solving problems in the manner that He did? 2. Why do you think Jesus performed His first miracle at a wedding feast? 3. Think back over the miracles Jesus performed. Which would you have chosen for Him to perform first? Why? 4. When, if ever, do you feel like Jesus stepped in to rescue you from a potentially embarrassing situation? 5. How does it make you feel to know that the Creator of the universe cares about how a wedding feast comes off?

■ **ILLUSTRATIONS:**

Audacious Answer to an Audacious Prayer. Helen Roseveare, an English medical missionary serving in Zaire, tells about a night when her medical team did all they could to try to save a mother in the labor ward. Despite their efforts, the mother died, leaving them with a premature baby and a crying two-year-old girl. Not having an incubator—or the electricity to run an incubator—Roseveare knew the team would have trouble keeping the baby alive.

Roseveare sent one of the student midwives for a box and cotton wool to wrap the baby. Another student was sent to stoke the fire and fill a hot water bottle. But the second student returned in distress to tell Roseveare that in filling the bottle—the last one—it had burst. "All right," she said, "put the baby as near the fire as you safely can; sleep between the baby and the door to keep it free from drafts. Your job is to keep the baby warm."

The following day, Roseveare went to pray with the orphanage children. She told them about the newborn, explaining the medical team's problem about keeping the baby warm enough and mentioning the hot water bottle. She also told the children about the baby's sister, who continued to cry because her mother had died. During the prayer time, 10-year-old Ruth prayed with the usual blunt conciseness of African children: "Please, God, send us a water bottle. It'll be no good tomorrow, God, as the baby will be dead. So please send it this afternoon."

While Roseveare gasped at the audacity of the prayer, Ruth added, "And while You are about it, would You please send a dolly for the little girl, so she'll know You really love her?" Roseveare confesses that she didn't believe God could answer Ruth's prayer. The only way God could answer it would be by sending Roseveare a parcel from England. She had been in Zaire for almost four years at that time and had never received a parcel from home. And if someone did send her a parcel, who would put in a hot water bottle?

Halfway through the afternoon, while Roseveare was teaching in the nurses' training school, a message was sent that there was a car at her front door. When Roseveare returned home, there was a 22-pound parcel on the open porch. She testifies that she could already feel the tears pricking her eyes.

Knowing she shouldn't open the parcel alone, Roseveare sent for the orphanage children. Together they pulled off the string, carefully undoing each knot. Some 40 pairs of eyes were glued on the cardboard box. From the top, Roseveare lifted out brightly colored, knitted jerseys. Eyes sparkled as she gave them out. Then there were the knitted bandages for the leprosy patients, and the children looked a little bored. Then came raisins and other dried fruit. Then, as Roseveare put her hand in again, she grasped and pulled out a brand new rubber hot water bottle! Crying now, she knew that she had not asked God to send it, for she hadn't truly believed that He could.

Ruth was in the front row of the children. She rushed forward, crying out, "If God has sent the bottle, He must have sent the dolly too!" Rummaging down to the bottom of the box, she pulled out the small, beautifully dressed dolly. Ruth's eyes shown bright. She had never doubted. Looking at Roseveare, she asked, "Can I go over with you, Mummy, and give this dolly to that little girl, so she'll know that Jesus really loves her?"

Packed by Roseveare's former Sunday school class, that parcel had been on its way for five months. The class's leader had obeyed God's prompting to send a hot water bottle, and one of the girls had put in a dolly for an African girl—five months before—in answer to the believing prayer of a ten-year-old to bring it "that afternoon." Isaiah 65:24 says, *Before they call I will answer, while they are yet speaking I will hear.*

Do Whatever He Tells You. A teacher in North Carolina followed her Lord's will even though her obedience seemed ludicrous to some people at the time. Jane Smith, 42, a science teacher at a local middle school, donated her own kidney to one of her students. She was discharged from the regional hospital on April 17, 2000, three days after surgeons removed her left kidney and gave it to 15-year-old Michael Carter.

Deborah Evans, Michael's mother, said Smith was an answer to prayer. "I've had to teach Michael about faith," Evans said. The child, born with renal dysplasia, began dialysis treatments in the summer of 1999 after a kidney failed, and endured two surgery postponements because of infections. Evans told a reporter, "Even in his bad days, he would say, 'Mommy, I'm still praying.' I think Michael has developed a very special relationship with Christ."

Smith learned about Michael's need for a kidney on the school playground, when she suggested he pull up his baggy pants so he could run better. Michael told her that he was undergoing dialysis treatments, that baggy pants were comfortable, and that he needed a transplant. Smith said, "I have two, do you want one?" She reminisced, "It was one of those moments in your life that you know it was the right thing."

Evans at first couldn't believe Michael when he relayed his teacher's offer. But the child insisted. God proved that Michael was correct and honored his unwavering faith.

2

NATURE MIRACLES

BACKGROUND SCRIPTURE: Matthew 8:23-27; 14:14-21
DEVOTIONAL READING: John 6:28-40

KEY VERSE: They were amazed, saying, "What sort of man is this,
that even the winds and the sea obey him?" Matthew 8:27.

KING JAMES VERSION

MATTHEW 8:23 And when he was entered into a ship, his disciples followed him.

24 And, behold, there arose a great tempest in the sea, insomuch that the ship was covered with the waves: but he was asleep.

25 And his disciples came to him, and awoke him, saying, Lord, save us: we perish.

26 And he saith unto them, Why are ye fearful, O ye of little faith? Then he arose, and rebuked the winds and the sea; and there was a great calm.

27 But the men marvelled, saying, What manner of man is this, that even the winds and the sea obey him! . . .

14:14 And Jesus went forth, and saw a great multitude, and was moved with compassion toward them, and he healed their sick.

15 And when it was evening, his disciples came to him, saying, This is a desert place, and the time is now past; send the multitude away, that they may go into the villages, and buy themselves victuals.

16 But Jesus said unto them, They need not depart; give ye them to eat.

17 And they say unto him, We have here but five loaves, and two fishes.

18 He said, Bring them hither to me.

19 And he commanded the multitude to sit down on the grass, and took the five loaves, and the two fishes, and looking up to heaven, he blessed, and brake, and gave the loaves to his disciples, and the disciples to the multitude.

20 And they did all eat, and were filled: and they took up of the fragments that remained twelve baskets full.

21 And they that had eaten were about five thousand men, beside women and children.

NEW REVISED STANDARD VERSION

MATTHEW 8:23 And when he got into the boat, his disciples followed him. 24 A windstorm arose on the sea, so great that the boat was being swamped by the waves; but he was asleep. 25 And they went and woke him up, saying, "Lord, save us! We are perishing!" 26 And he said to them, "Why are you afraid, you of little faith?" Then he got up and rebuked the winds and the sea; and there was a dead calm. 27 They were amazed, saying, "What sort of man is this, that even the winds and the sea obey him?" . . .

14:14 When he went ashore, he saw a great crowd; and he had compassion for them and cured their sick. 15 When it was evening, the disciples came to him and said, "This is a deserted place, and the hour is now late; send the crowds away so that they may go into the villages and buy food for themselves." 16 Jesus said to them, "They need not go away; you give them something to eat." 17 They replied, "We have nothing here but five loaves and two fish." 18 And he said, "Bring them here to me." 19 Then he ordered the crowds to sit down on the grass. Taking the five loaves and the two fish, he looked up to heaven, and blessed and broke the loaves, and gave them to the disciples, and the disciples gave them to the crowds. 20 And all ate and were filled; and they took up what was left over of the broken pieces, twelve baskets full. 21 And those who ate were about five thousand men, besides women and children.

Monday, September 10	Mark 2:1-12	*Healed Because of His Friends' Faith*
Tuesday, September 11	John 9:1-12	*A Blind Man Is Healed*
Wednesday, September 12	Mark 5:1-15	*Healing the Gerasene Demoniac*
Thursday, September 13	Mark 5:21-24, 35-43	*Healing Jairus's Daughter*
Friday, September 14	Mark 5:25-34	*The Faith That Makes You Well*
Saturday, September 15	Mark 9:17-29	*Healing That Comes Only through Prayer*
Sunday, September 16	Mark 3:1-6	*Healing a Man with a Withered Hand*

BACKGROUND

Matthew, also known as Levi, was a Jew who collected taxes for the Roman government. His career placed him among the most hated and despised men of all Palestine. But Matthew's life was changed when Jesus saw him at his tax collector's booth and issued him the call to *"Follow me"* (Matt. 9:9). Jesus and his other disciples later dined at Matthew's home along with *many tax collectors and sinners* (9:10). When the Jewish religious leaders learned about this, they questioned why Jesus would associate with such people. Jesus responded to their inquiry by saying, *"Those who are well have no need of a physician, but those who are sick. Go and learn what this means, 'I desire mercy, not sacrifice.' For I have come to call not the righteous but sinners"* (9:12-13).

Years after becoming a follower of Christ, Matthew wrote his Gospel to his fellow Jews. Matthew demonstrated that Jesus is the Jewish nation's long-awaited Messiah and showed that He is the King to whom God has given power and authority to redeem and judge humankind. Many of Matthew's fellow Jews did not recognize Jesus as the Messiah because His kingship was not what they had expected. So Matthew emphasized Jesus' authority by telling about His miraculous control over nature as well as His healing the sick and demon-possessed and raising the dead. Matthew pointed out that Jesus died on the cross and rose from the dead so that the lost might be freed from sin's oppression. Matthew's Gospel, which is filled with messianic language, forms the connecting link between the Old and New Testaments due to its emphasis on Jesus' fulfillment of prophecy.

After summarizing Jesus' public ministry of teaching, preaching, and healing (chap. 4) and introducing His teaching ministry (chaps. 5—7), Matthew began to chronicle other deeds that Jesus performed (chap. 8). Many of Jesus' sermons and miracles took place on the Sea of Galilee or along its shore. This body of water, sometimes called the Sea of Gennesaret, the Sea of Tiberias, or the Sea of Chinnereth, was known for its sudden and violent storms. The pear-shaped lake, which is eight miles wide and thirteen miles long, lies 680 feet below sea level and is 150 feet deep in some places. The high hills that surround it are cut with deep ravines that can act like great funnels drawing turbulent winds from the heights down onto the lake without warning.

Jesus rescued His disciples in two such storms on the lake (8:23-27; 14:22-33), took walks along its shore (4:18), and sometimes taught large crowds from a boat anchored near the shore (13:2). During the first century A.D., the Sea of Galilee was known for its rich fishing industries, which gave rise to nine large, thriving cities around the lake. In fact, four of Jesus' disciples were men who had earlier made careers from fishing in the lake.

NOTES ON THE PRINTED TEXT

During the time of Christ, Galilee was a densely populated region. Its boundaries only covered a little more than 1,000 square miles, yet it had more than 200 towns with populations of 15,000 or more. Many of these towns and cities were built near the shore of the Sea of Galilee, and transportation by boat was often the quickest means to get from town to town—though not always the safest.

The ancient historian Josephus wrote that there were usually more than 300 fishing boats on the Sea of Galilee at one time. And because at least four of Jesus' disciples were fishermen, it is likely that the vessel they used to cross the sea was a fishing boat. Powered both by oars and sails, the boat was large enough to comfortably hold both Jesus and His 12 disciples.

While the group was journeying across the lake, a sudden *windstorm arose on the sea, so great that the boat was being swamped by the waves* (Matt. 8:24). When Jesus and His disciples launched into the sea, it was probably calm. Now they were caught without warning in a storm that stirred the water into what may have been violent 20-foot waves. During such a storm, the fishermen would have taken down the sails to keep them from ripping and to make the boat easier to control. Yet while all this activity was taking place, Jesus continued to sleep.

By this time the disciples had witnessed several of Jesus' miracles, but the knowledge of His awesome powers was offset by their awareness that the storm was endangering their lives. So they awoke Jesus, telling Him, *"Lord, save us! We are perishing!"* (8:25). Before addressing the problem of the winds and the waves, Jesus first questioned His disciples' fear and lack of faith. Then He *rebuked* (8:26) this violent force of nature in the same way He would also rebuke demonic powers (17:18). Immediately upon Jesus' rebuke, *there was a dead calm* (8:26). Now having seen Jesus miraculously control the forces of nature, the disciples *were amazed, saying, "What sort of man is this, that even the winds and the sea obey him?"* (8:27).

As news continued to get out about Jesus' miracles, He could rarely go any place where there wasn't a crowd waiting for Him. Such was the case when He sought to get away for some solitude after learning about John the Baptist's beheading (14:13). Taking a boat to a remote area, Jesus was followed along the edge of the lake by crowds on foot.

When [Jesus] went ashore, he saw a great crowd (14:14). Then, putting aside

His own need for privacy, *he had compassion for them and cured their sick*. As evening came and the time for dinner had already passed, the disciples came to Jesus with the request that He *send the crowds away so that they may go into the villages and buy food for themselves* (14:15). Jesus surprised the disciples by telling them that there was no need for the crowd to leave. He instructed His followers to *give [the people] something to eat* (14:16).

According to John 6:1-13, Andrew (the brother of Simon Peter and one of Jesus' 12 disciples) brought a boy's lunch consisting only of *five loaves and two fish* (Matt. 14:17). Jesus arranged the crowd in an orderly fashion, took the meager portion that was provided (14:18), and then *looked up to heaven, and blessed and broke the loaves* (14:19). At some point as the disciples distributed the food, they realized that another miracle was occurring.

And all ate and were filled (14:20). The number of men—about 5,000—was listed separately from the women and children because the Jewish culture of the day prescribed that these groups eat apart from each other when in public. Thus. it is possible that Jesus fed as many as 15,000 that day with a boy's lunch (14:21).

SUGGESTIONS TO TEACHERS

The *American Heritage Dictionary of the English Language* defines the word "master" in several ways. Among them are "one that has control over another or others"; "one who has control over or ownership of something"; "the captain of a merchant ship (also called master mariner)"; and "one whose teachings or doctrines are accepted by followers." *Didaskalos* is the Greek noun that is used throughout the Gospels to refer to an instructor or a master teacher. In fact, it is commonly translated "master," "teacher," or "instructor."

Through Jesus' calming of the storm and His feeding of over 5,000 people, He revealed His mastery over nature. Indeed, as the Son of God, Jesus makes magnificent use of natural things in supernatural ways. And His eternal power, care, and concern make Him the most qualified person to be the Master of our lives.

1. MASTER OF THE STORM. Physical, mental, emotional, and spiritual "storms" often barge into our lives and, like the disciples, a sudden burst of fear can chase away our faith. Of all times, this is when we must call on Jesus to renew our faith. Through faith we come to understand who God really is. We also begin to realize that He who brings calm to the storms of nature can also bring calm to the storms of our hearts.

2. MASTER OF COMPASSION. Certainly Jesus performed miracles for different reasons. Some were performed to teach important truths, and some were done as signs of His messianic identity. But in this week's lesson we see that Jesus healed people because *he had compassion for them* (Matt. 14:14). Jesus was a loving, caring, and concerned person. Of course, He still is. He knows and understands our suffering and our hurts. And when the time is right, His compassion will bring about the restoration we need.

3. MASTER OF PROVISION. One of our most basic life needs is for physical nourishment. This was also true for the crowds mentioned in this week's lesson. The disciples wanted to force them to go *into the villages* (14:15)—and away from Jesus—to buy some food for themselves. Jesus' plan, however, was to provide for their need. Because of Him, the people *all ate and were filled* (14:20).

4. MASTER OF THE MEAGER. The disciples were only able to collect five barley loaves and two fish—barely enough food to feed a boy. But in the hands of Jesus, what was insufficient became more than enough. Our talents and skills may seem to us to be insufficient and meager, but He can make use of and expand upon anything that we devote to His service. In His hands, the meager is multiplied!

FOR ADULTS

■ **TOPIC:** Filling Our Needs

■ **QUESTIONS:** 1. Why would the disciples—having seen other miracles that Jesus performed—panic during the storm, especially when they knew that Jesus was on the boat with them? 2. Do you think Jesus was overly harsh toward His disciples when He asked them, *"Why are you afraid, you of little faith?"* (Matt. 8:26). Explain your answer. 3. What, if anything, did Jesus teach His disciples by rebuking the violent storm? 4. How has Jesus brought calm and serenity to your life at times when you were most troubled? 5. How has Jesus stretched your resources beyond what you would have imagined?

■ **ILLUSTRATIONS:**

Count on the Storms. Before former news anchor John Chancellor succumbed to cancer, he observed in an interview: "If you want to make God laugh, tell God your plans." One of the things you can count on in this life is storms; you just can't plan when they'll occur.

Physical storms will assault your body and make you weak. Mental storms will assault your brain and make you unsure about your decisions. Emotional storms will assault your heart and make you wonder if your feelings have slipped into chaos. Even spiritual storms will assault your soul and make you question your long-held faith. But always remember that God has a purpose in the storms that come your way. It may be to increase your trust in Him; it may be to show you His power; or it may be to remind you that He, alone, is in control.

Running to Jesus. Looking westward outside my window, I saw skies a color that I've never seen them before—a ghoulish gray and pale green. In the distance, the tall trees waved back and forth as the strong winds ripped past them. Heavy rains pounded my windows. I turned the radio on to a local Christian station, waiting for a report from the National Weather Service. Only a few seconds passed before I heard a loud beep on the radio, letting me know a warning was being announced:

"A tornado watch and a severe thunderstorm warning has been issued!" Before the warning could be finished, however, the signal was interrupted. The sound of static now coming from my radio was comparable to the sound of the heavy winds and rain outside. I could feel it. Fear was rising within me. Remembering that I believe Jesus to be right here in the house with me, I prayed. I simply reminded the Lord—and myself—that my trust was in Him, and I asked Him to keep me safe from harm.

In one sense, I can't blame the disciples for being afraid in a violently rocking boat with 20-foot waves crashing around them. At least they knew to whom to go for safety. As His disciples, may we, too, go running to Jesus anytime we're afraid!

Making Use of the Meager. Wishing to encourage her young son's progress on the piano, a mother took her boy to a concert by the great Polish pianist Ignace Jan Paderewski. After they were seated in the concert hall, the mother spotted a friend in the audience and walked down the aisle to greet her. Seizing the opportunity to search the wonders of the auditorium, the little boy rose and eventually explored his way through a door marked NO ADMITTANCE.

When the house lights dimmed and the concert was about to begin, the mother returned to her seat and discovered that her child was missing. Suddenly, the curtains parted and spotlights focused on the impressive Steinway piano on stage. In horror, the mother saw her little boy sitting at the keyboard, innocently picking out "Twinkle, Twinkle, Little Star." At that moment, the great piano master made his entrance, quickly moved to the piano, and whispered in the boy's ear, "Don't quit. Keep playing."

Then leaning over, Paderewski reached down with his left hand and began filling in a bass part. Soon his right arm reached around to the other side of the child and he added a running obligatio. Together, the old master and the young novice transformed a frightening situation into a wonderfully creative experience. The audience was so mesmerized that, by the end of the concert, they were hard-pressed to recall what other compositions the great master had played; "Twinkle, Twinkle, Little Star" was foremost in their minds.

And that is how God makes use of our meager resources. We are the young novices; He is the Master. Five loaves and a couple of fish wouldn't go far among a crowd of thousands. But because a little boy offered all he had, Jesus turned the *meager* into a *miracle*.

What we can accomplish on our own is hardly noteworthy. We try our best, but the results aren't exactly graceful, flowing music. But when the hand of the Master gets involved, our life's work can become truly beautiful and magnificent. It's no wonder Paul could say, *Now to him who by the power at work within us is able to accomplish abundantly far more than all we can ask or imagine, to him be the glory in the church and in Christ Jesus to all generations* (Eph. 3:20-21).

■ **TOPIC:** Changing the Rules

■ **QUESTIONS:** 1. Do you think fear leads to a lack of faith, or does a lack of faith cause fear? Explain your answer. 2. What, if anything, did Jesus teach His disciples by sleeping through the violent storm? 3. What effect would a miracle like the calming of the storm have had on Jesus' disciples? 4. How does it make you feel to know that Jesus has compassion for needy people? 5. In what ways does Jesus continue today to feed the hungry and needy?

■ **ILLUSTRATIONS:**

Nothing to Fear. In a scene from the movie *Star Wars Episode I: The Phantom Menace*, the Jedi Council is interviewing young Anakin Skywalker to determine whether this boy with special abilities should be trained to become a Jedi knight. At one point, Master Jedi Yoda expresses to Anakin that "I sense much fear in you," and clarifies his feeling by adding, "Fear losing your mother, do you?" Anakin responds by asking, "What's that got to do with anything?" Yoda answers Anakin's question with one of the favorite lines from the movie: "Everything! Fear leads to anger; anger leads to hate; hate leads to suffering."

When the disciples were faced with a dangerous storm on the Sea of Galilee, their immediate fear caused their faith to virtually disappear. On the other hand, it is possible that their lack of faith allowed their fear to overcome them. But whatever the case, faith cannot survive in a climate of fear, nor can fear survive in a climate of faith.

Mo' Trust, No Fear. The catch phrase of the popular *X Files* TV show declares, "Trust no one; fear everything." Bumper stickers scream the opposing messages, "No Fear" and "Fear This!" In reality, it is hard to imagine a life lived in which no one is trusted and everything is feared. And yet, trust is hard to come by today, and fear seems to be on the increase.

Parents don't trust their kids, and kids don't trust their parents. Politicians in one party don't trust those in another party, and vice versa. The elderly don't trust the young, and the young don't trust the elderly. Regardless of age, everyone seems afraid of being left out or found out, of running out of money or prestige or status, of being expected to accomplish the impossible, or of being ostracized as a failure. In the ongoing battle between trust and fear, fear sometimes seems to be winning out.

But in the midst of this strife, Jesus calls out a question to us: *"Why are you afraid, you of little faith?"* (Matt. 8:26). Put your faith in the one who calms storms and hearts and feeds stomachs and minds. Trust Jesus, and fear little else.

God in Charge. A young man walked into a recruiting station and asked to reenlist. When asked why he was returning to the armed forces, the man replied:

"There's no one in charge on the outside." Though it may seem that the world's spinning out of control, God is still in charge. In the midst of the storms, in the midst of the starving masses, God is there offering both His comfort and His compassion. He is in control.

God's Voice. She was a 12-year-old girl at Franklin Graham's crusade in Cape Town, South Africa. She listened intently to every word the son of Billy Graham spoke. When Franklin asked those in the crowd who wished to commit themselves to Christ to come forward, the girl left her seat. She had heard God's voice calling her.

Are you sensitive to God's voice calling you? Jesus said that the Spirit would testify to each of us. Have you heard the Spirit speak God's word? If not, be tuned in as that 12-year-old girl was in Cape Town.

HEALING MIRACLES

BACKGROUND SCRIPTURE: Mark 3:1-6; John 9:1-12
DEVOTIONAL READING: John 4:46-54

3

KEY VERSE: [Jesus] said to the man, "Stretch out your hand."
He stretched it out, and his hand was restored. Mark 3:5.

KING JAMES VERSION

MARK 3:1 And he entered again into the synagogue; and there was a man there which had a withered hand.

2 And they watched him, whether he would heal him on the sabbath day; that they might accuse him.

3 And he saith unto the man which had the withered hand, Stand forth.

4 And he saith unto them, Is it lawful to do good on the sabbath days, or to do evil? to save life, or to kill? But they held their peace.

5 And when he had looked round about on them with anger, being grieved for the hardness of their hearts, he saith unto the man, Stretch forth thine hand. And he stretched it out: and his hand was restored whole as the other.

6 And the Pharisees went forth, and straightway took counsel with the Herodians against him, how they might destroy him. . . .

John 9:1 And as Jesus passed by, he saw a man which was blind from his birth.

2 And his disciples asked him, saying, Master, who did sin, this man, or his parents, that he was born blind?

3 Jesus answered, Neither hath this man sinned, nor his parents: but that the works of God should be made manifest in him.

4 I must work the works of him that sent me, while it is day: the night cometh, when no man can work.

5 As long as I am in the world, I am the light of the world.

6 When he had thus spoken, he spat on the ground, and made clay of the spittle, and he anointed the eyes of the blind man with the clay,

7 And said unto him, Go, wash in the pool of Siloam, (which is by interpretation, Sent.) He went his way therefore, and washed, and came seeing.

8 The neighbours therefore, and they which before had seen him that he was blind, said, Is not this he that sat and begged?

9 Some said, This is he: others said, He is like him: but he said, I am he.

10 Therefore said they unto him, How were thine eyes opened?

11 He answered and said, A man that is called Jesus made clay, and anointed mine eyes, and said unto me,

Go to the pool of Siloam, and wash: and I went and washed, and I received sight.

12 Then said they unto him, Where is he? He said, I know not.

NEW REVISED STANDARD VERSION

MARK 3:1 Again he entered the synagogue, and a man was there who had a withered hand. 2 They watched him to see whether he would cure him on the sabbath, so that they might accuse him. 3 And he said to the man who had the withered hand, "Come forward." 4 Then he said to them, "Is it lawful to do good or to do harm on the sabbath, to save life or to kill?" But they were silent. 5 He looked around at them with anger; he was grieved at their hardness of heart and said to the man, "Stretch out your hand." He stretched it out, and his hand was restored. 6 The Pharisees went out and immediately conspired with the Herodians against him, how to destroy him. . . .

JOHN 9:1 As he walked along, he saw a man blind from birth. 2 His disciples asked him, "Rabbi, who sinned, this man or his parents, that he was born blind?" 3 Jesus answered, "Neither this man nor his parents sinned; he was born blind so that God's works might be revealed in him. 4 We must work the works of him who sent me while it is day; night is coming when no one can work. 5 As long as I am in the world, I am the light of the world." 6 When he had said this, he spat on the ground and made mud with the saliva and spread the mud on the man's eyes, 7 saying to him, "Go, wash in the pool of Siloam" (which means Sent). Then he went and washed and came back able to see. 8 The neighbors and those who had seen him before as a beggar began to ask, "Is this not the man who used to sit and beg?" 9 Some were saying, "It is he." Others were saying, "No, but it is someone like him." He kept saying, "I am the man." 10 But they kept asking him, "Then how were your eyes opened?" 11 He answered, "The man called Jesus made mud, spread it on my eyes, and said to me, "Go to Siloam and wash.' Then I went and washed and received my sight." 12 They said to him, "Where is he?" He said, "I do not know."

Monday, September 17	Matthew 11:25-30	*The Weary Can Come to Jesus*
Tuesday, September 18	Luke 7:11-17	*A Son Is Restored to His Mother*
Wednesday, September 19	Matthew 12:15-21	*God's Chosen Servant*
Thursday, September 20	Matthew 12:22-28	*He Heals by Whose Authority?*
Friday, September 21	Matthew 15:1-9	*Breaking the Tradition of the Elders*
Saturday, September 22	Matthew 15:10-20	*The Things That Defile a Person*
Sunday, September 23	Matthew 15:21-31	*A Woman of Great Faith*

BACKGROUND

The Gospel of Mark was probably the first Gospel to be written; all but 31 verses of Mark are quoted in the other two Synoptic Gospels (namely, Matthew and Luke). Of the four Gospels, Mark's is the one that reads most like a series of newspaper accounts. Information about Jesus' activities take prominence in this Gospel, especially as the writer described one event in quick detail and then moved on to the next, often introducing the upcoming action with words like *Again he entered* (3:1), *Jesus departed* (3:7), *He left that place and came* (6:1), and *Then he went about* (6:6).

Perhaps it was this bent toward action that led Mark to record practically as many miracles as the longer Gospels of Matthew and Luke. As Mark wrote to the Christians in Rome, he portrayed Jesus—*the Son of God* (1:1)—as a man of both power and action.

John, on the other hand, recorded only seven miracles, six of which are unique among the four Gospels. Like Mark, John portrayed Jesus as a man of power. But unlike Mark, more of John's emphasis was on Jesus' embodiment of the truth. As such, John more readily wrote about Jesus' teaching and preaching, about His training of the disciples, about His conversations with those of both high and low stature, and about His confrontations with the religious leaders of the day.

In this week's lesson we will consider the healing of the man with a withered hand and the healing of a man born blind. In both of these accounts, the opposition of the Pharisees plays a pronounced role. The Pharisees were a Jewish religious group that zealously followed the Old Testament laws in addition to their own traditions. They had maintained and had grown used to a high degree of respect in their respective communities. Fairly early in Jesus' ministry, the Pharisees turned against Him, especially when Jesus began to question their focused desire for status and personal gain. Of course, the religious leaders were also jealous of Jesus' authoritative teaching, His rising popularity, and His miracles.

The Pharisees' chief condemnation of Jesus arose because He did not follow their very strict laws and traditions of keeping the Sabbath. They objected when Jesus healed on the Sabbath, considering such healings as work. Jesus, in turn, condemned their wrong attitudes—especially their putting more emphasis on keeping rules than on loving people. And so, typically, Jesus and the Pharisees found themselves moving into conflict after conflict.

NOTES ON THE PRINTED TEXT

Both of the healing miracles covered in this week's lesson took place on the Sabbath, the weekly day of rest and worship for the Jews. In the few centuries prior to Jesus, Jewish scribes tried to clarify what could and could not be done on the Sabbath. These legal experts created a long list of rules to show what constituted work and what did not. Among the activities described as work—and therefore, forbidden activities for the Sabbath—was tying a knot with both hands (though tying a knot with one hand was perfectly acceptable), building a fire, cooking a meal, sewing of any kind, and plowing or reaping. Because healing constituted the work of a physician, that, too, was forbidden.

Jesus dealt with this issue when He healed the man with the withered hand. He and His disciples had plucked grain for food while walking through some fields, bringing about the strict condemnation of the Pharisees. Jesus' response to their accusations certainly infuriated them even more: *The sabbath was made for humankind, and not humankind for the sabbath; so the Son of Man is lord even of the sabbath* (Mark 2:27-28).

Apparently a short time after this—on the Sabbath—Jesus went to a synagogue in Galilee (3:1). Tradition holds that the man with a withered hand who was there that day was a plasterer, to whom the use of both hands was particularly important. (Whether this tradition is true remains unclear.) The man's disease had left him powerless to do work—that is, until he received the healing touch of Jesus. The Pharisees in attendance clearly acknowledged Jesus' power to perform miracles, for after Jesus entered the synagogue, *They watched him to see whether he would cure him on the sabbath* (3:2). But their motive, despite their awareness, was so *that they might accuse him.*

After Jesus told the man with the withered hand to *"Come forward"* (3:3), the Savior turned His attention to the Pharisees. Knowing they were ready to accuse Him for any slight infraction of their tradition, Jesus asked them which was better, to preserve life by healing—even on the Sabbath—or to destroy life by refusing to heal (3:4-5)? The question was ironic in that the Pharisees were waiting for Jesus to make the one wrong move that would propel them to conspire *with the Herodians against him, how to destroy him* (3:6). The Herodians were a secular political party that took their name from Herod Antipas and strongly supported Roman rule (as opposed to the Pharisaic viewpoint).

Jesus' anger rose because of the Pharisees' uncaring attitudes. By failing to answer His question, they proved that they cared less for the man's welfare and more for their empty religious traditions. Perhaps most of all, they cared about coming up with a conspiracy by which they could see Jesus put to death. Although Jesus *was grieved at their hardness of heart* (3:5), He still showed compassion toward the man with the withered hand by restoring him to health.

In another episode involving controversy, Jesus and His disciples had returned to Jerusalem for the Feast of Dedication. As they were walking, they encountered *a man blind from birth* (John 9:1). According to many of the Jewish rabbis of the day, suffering was attributed to some sin, and that sin could even be committed by a child in the womb. So upon seeing the blind man, the disciples asked Jesus whose sin had led to the man's blindness (9:2). Jesus denied the whole line of rabbinical thinking and instead, shifted the attention of His disciples from cause to purpose. The purpose of the man's blindness, the Savior explained, was to provide an opportunity for the power of God to be seen in him (9:3-4).

Having pointed out to His followers that *"As long as I am in the world, I am the light of the world"* (9:5), Jesus *spat on the ground and made mud with the saliva* (9:6). In those days, people considered mud to have medicinal value. The Savior then rubbed the mud on the blind man's eyes and told him to wash in the Pool of Siloam, which was located on the southern end of the main ridge on which Jerusalem was built (9:7).

Then [the man] went and washed and came back able to see. When the *neighbors and those who had seen him before* (9:8) questioned him, they realized that he was formerly the blind beggar they had grown accustomed to seeing in the city. They asked how he had gained his sight. Some thought the man was the former blind beggar, while others thought he wasn't.

In the midst of debate, the man kept insisting that he was the same person (9:9). When questioned about his experience, the former blind beggar told those listening what Jesus had done for him (9:10-11). And when asked where Jesus might be, the man said he didn't know (9:12).

SUGGESTIONS TO TEACHERS

As God incarnate and the Light of the world, Jesus' great aim was to reveal to humankind the character of God—His compassion, His mercy, His grace, His love, and His purpose. Along the way, though, Jesus not only revealed God's character, but also exposed some of the sinful traits inherent in the human condition. Thus, in the accounts of two healing miracles studied in this week's lesson, we see how Jesus both reveals some of the extraordinary traits of God and, at the same time, exposes a few of the ignoble traits of fallen humanity.

1. **EXPOSED ATTITUDES.** Selfishness skews our vision of reality. The Pharisees knew enough about the Hebrew Scriptures to have recognized Jesus as the Messiah, but their bloated sense of self wouldn't allow it. Attainment of position and status became their all-encompassing motive and blinded them to the truth. And when Jesus exposed their attitudes, they began to look for ways to turn the people against Him, and eventually, to have Him killed.

2. **EXPOSED TRADITIONS.** Our petty humanmade rules and codes can conceal from us the love and compassion of God. When tradition is exalted above all

else, it becomes idolatry. The Pharisees' system of empty rules—the traditions they attached to the Mosaic law—had become their guiding set of principles and replaced the Spirit of God. But Jesus refused to allow meaningless tradition to hinder His demonstration of God's compassion. He taught that the Sabbath was made for human beings, not the other way around (Mark 2:27-28).

3. REVEALED ANGER. Jesus *looked around at them with anger; he was grieved at their hardness of heart* (3:5). Having the heart of God, Jesus got angry over what angered God, such as blatant stubbornness and unconcern. Anger itself is not wrong. It depends on what makes us angry and what we do with the emotion. The response of the Pharisees both angered and grieved Jesus, which shows His concern and compassion even toward those who had none.

4. REVEALED SUFFERING. Jesus put the blind man's suffering, which was no fault of his own, to good use. Jesus healed the man, and by so doing taught about faith and glorifying God. We know that good behavior is not always rewarded and that bad behavior is not always punished; innocent people do suffer. But regardless of the reason for the suffering, Jesus has the power to help us deal with it and to use it for the glory of God. May we seek strength through our suffering and pray that God will be glorified in the process.

5. REVEALED LIGHT. Just as Jesus brings sight to blindness, He brings light to darkness. He lights the path that lies before us so that we can see how to live (John 1:4-5).

FOR ADULTS	■ **TOPIC:** Restoring Wholeness

■ **QUESTIONS:** 1. What do you think was the underlying cause of the Pharisees' opposition to Jesus? 2. How can some of our long-held traditions possibly get in the way of God's concern and compassion? 3. What are some of the attitudes held today that you think would anger Jesus? 4. Have any physical or emotional handicaps ever turned into an opportunity for God to demonstrate His power in you? Explain your answer. 5. Do you think sin and suffering are ever related today? Explain your answer.

■ **ILLUSTRATIONS:**

Healing Attitudes. In April of 2000, the Far East Broadcasting Company reported how a witch doctor in Uganda had become a Christian. The man had warned Walter Karanja, an engineer who started a church among his co-workers in Masindi, to stop talking about Christ.

Finally the witch doctor burst wild-eyed into the church while Karanja was preaching. "Jesus of Walter, do not kill me!" he screamed. When Karanja asked him why he was so afraid, the witch doctor said that he and his followers had hated the church. "I have told them to use their powers to destroy you," he said.

"I know," Karanja replied, "but I am still here."

"Why is your power stronger than mine? Why have you and your God not killed me?" the witch doctor asked.

Karanja explained that his God, "the God of the universe," not only is all-powerful but also loving. When the man asked to know more, Karanja presented the Gospel to him. The witch doctor became a Christian and changed his name to John. A few days later he was baptized, and then he burned his witchcraft paraphernalia. News spread quickly, for he had been a prominent and feared leader. Clearly, the Gospel has the power to heal attitudes as well as bodies!

Eyes of Our Hearts. Lloyd J. Ogilvie, in his book *Enjoying God,* writes, "One of the most astounding achievements in ophthalmological surgery is the implanting of a lens in a human eye. After a friend of mine had this surgery in both eyes, and the bandages were removed, he exclaimed, 'How wonderful to have new eyes!'

"Our hearts have eyes. . . . Before conversion, our 'inner eyes' are clouded over with cataracts blocking our vision. We cannot see ourselves, others, and life in the clear light of truth. Nor can we behold God's true nature or see the beauty of the world that He's given us to enjoy. We are spiritually blinded.

"Conversion begins the healing of our heart-eyes by removing our spiritual cataracts. We understand what the cross means for our forgiveness, but we still do not perceive all that the Lord has planned for us and the power He has offered to us. We need a supernatural lens implant in the eyes of our hearts. Paul calls this lens the 'Spirit of wisdom and revelation,' . . . The Spirit is the lens for the eyes of our hearts."

Light in the Darkness. The seventeenth-century English politician Samuel Pepys was in a position to meet the most outstanding personalities of his day. As such, he wrote about those personalities and himself in his *Diary*, which he penned in shorthand between 1660 and 1669. At the age of 36, he learned that he was losing his eyesight. His last entry in his *Diary*—34 years before his death—were these words: "And so I betake myself to that course, which is almost as much as to see myself go into my grave; for which, and all the discomforts that will accompany my being blind, the good God prepare me!"

Unlike the man born blind whom Jesus healed so that he could see (John 9:1-7), Pepys thrived on his vision and was devastated to lose his sight. Still, in the midst of his devastation, he asked God to prepare him by being his light in the darkness.

FOR YOUTH

■ TOPIC: A Healing Word

■ QUESTIONS: 1. What do you think caused the Pharisees to be so opposed to Jesus? 2. What were some of their attitudes that you think upset Jesus? 3. What kinds of attitudes in our life might get in the way of

God's concern and compassion for others? 4. Do you think Jesus really understood the blind man's predicament? Explain your answer. 5. In what ways does sin and wrongdoing lead to suffering today?

■ **ILLUSTRATIONS:**

Bearing the Burden. Josh and Karen Zarandona tell the story of Brenda, a young woman who went rock climbing even though she was very scared. Despite her fear, she put on the gear, took a hold on the rope, and started up the face of a tremendous granite cliff. Brenda got to a ledge where she could take a breather when the safety rope snapped against her eye and knocked out her contact lens.

There Brenda was on a granite ledge, with hundreds of feet of rock above and below her. She perused the area closely, hoping the lens had landed on the ledge, but it just wasn't there. Her precarious position and blurry vision caused her to grow desperate and become upset. That's when Brenda remembered to pray to the Lord for help in finding her contact lens. When she got to the top, a friend examined her eye and her clothing for the lens, but there was none to be found. Brenda sat down, despondent, with the rest of the party, waiting for the rest of them to make it up the face of the cliff.

Brenda looked out across range after range of mountains, thinking about the Bible verse that says, *"the eyes of the LORD range throughout the entire earth, to strengthen those whose heart is true to him"* (2 Chron. 16:9). Brenda thought, "Lord, You can see all these mountains. You know every stone and leaf, and You know exactly where my contact lens is. Please help me."

Finally, the group walked down the trail to the bottom. There they found a new party of climbers just starting up the face of the cliff. One of them shouted out, "Hey, you guys! Anybody lose a contact lens?" That would be startling enough, but the climber saw it on the back of an ant! An ant was moving slowly across the face of the rock, carrying it.

Brenda's father is a cartoonist. When she told him the incredible story of the ant, the prayer, and the contact lens, he drew a picture of an ant lugging that contact lens with the words, "Lord, I don't know why You want me to carry this thing. I can't eat it, and it's awfully heavy. But if this is what You want me to do, I'll carry it for You."

Jesus told His disciples that there was no sinful cause for the blindness of the beggar's eyes. Rather, he had been born blind so that the power of God, as seen in the working of a miracle, could be displayed in him (John 9:3). Bearing a burden for the Lord calmly and patiently carries the purpose of glorifying God.

Sustenance for the Struggle. Gilbert was eight years old and had been in the Cub Scouts only a short time. During one of his meetings, he was handed a sheet of paper, a block of wood, and four tires, and he was told to return home and give the items to "Dad." That was not an easy task for Gilbert to do. His dad was not receptive to doing things with his son. But Gilbert tried. Dad read the paper and scoffed at the idea of making a pinewood derby car with his young, eager son. The block of wood remained untouched as the weeks passed.

Finally, Gilbert's mom stepped in to see if she could figure it out. The project began. Having no carpentry skills, she decided it would be best if she simply read the directions and let Gilbert do the work. And he did. She read aloud the measurements and the rules of what they could and couldn't do.

Within days Gilbert's block of wood was turning into a pinewood derby car. It was a little lopsided, but it looked great—at least through his mom's eyes. Gilbert had not seen any of the other kids' cars and was feeling proud of his "Blue Lightning." It's the sort of pride that comes with knowing you did something on your own.

Then the big night came. With Gilbert's blue pinewood derby in his hand and pride in his heart, he headed to the big race. Once there the little one's pride turned to humility. Gilbert's car was obviously the only car made entirely on his own. All the other cars were a father-son partnership, with cool paint jobs and sleek body styles made for speed.

A few of the boys giggled as they looked at Gilbert's lopsided, wobbly, unattractive vehicle. To add to the humility Gilbert was the only boy without a man at his side. A couple of the boys who were from single parent homes at least had an uncle or grandfather by their side. Gilbert had his mom.

As the race began, it was done in elimination fashion. Competitors kept racing as long as they were winning. One by one the cars raced down the finely sanded ramp. Finally it was between Gilbert and the sleekest, fastest looking car there. As the last race was about to begin, this wide-eyed, shy eight-year-old asked if they could stop the race for a minute because he wanted to pray. The race stopped.

Gilbert hit his knees clutching his funny looking block of wood between his hands. With a wrinkled brow he set to converse with his heavenly Father. Gilbert prayed in earnest for a very long minute and a half. Then he stood with a smile on his face and announced, "Okay, I'm ready!"

As the crowd cheered, a boy named Tommy stood with his father as their car sped down the ramp. Gilbert stood with his heavenly Father in his heart. The lad watched as his block of wood wobbled down the ramp with surprisingly great speed and rushed over the finish line a fraction of a second before Tommy's car.

Gilbert leaped into the air with a loud "Thank You!" as the crowd roared in approval. The Scout Master came up to Gilbert with microphone in hand and asked the obvious question, "So you prayed to win, huh, Gilbert?" To which he answered, "Oh, no sir. That wouldn't be fair to ask God to help me beat someone else. I just asked Him to make it so I don't cry when I lose."

Youth seem to have a wisdom far beyond us. Gilbert didn't ask God to win the race, and he didn't ask God to fix the outcome; rather, Gilbert asked God to give him strength in the outcome. When Gilbert first saw the other cars, he didn't cry out to God, "No fair, they had a father's help." No, he went to his heavenly Father for strength.

Like the Pharisees, perhaps we spend too much of our time building up ourselves—too much of our prayer time asking God to rig the race and to make us number one, or too much time asking God to remove us from the struggle, when we should be seeking God's strength to get through the struggle. Gilbert didn't pray to win and thus hurt someone else. Rather, he prayed that God would supply the grace to lose with dignity.

Gilbert, by stopping the race to speak to his heavenly Father, also showed the crowd that he wasn't there without a "Dad"; rather, his heavenly Father was most definitely there with him. Yes, Gilbert walked away a winner that night, with his heavenly Father at his side.

Did you know that there are 40 million children living on the streets of Latin America and over 1.5 million children on the streets of Manila in the Philippines? A lost generation to their countries. Lost to Christ.

Cross-cultural books that teach about God and his love for children are most effective and are used as a means of evangelizing and discipling children in the care of street children ministries. Cook Communications Ministries International *has literature that can mean the difference between utter hopelessness or a life full of meaning.*

To learn more about the global ministry projects of Cook Communications Ministries International, you can visit their web site at www.ccmi.org or call 1-800-323-7543.

MOTHER'S FAITH

BACKGROUND SCRIPTURE: Matthew 15:21-31
DEVOTIONAL READING: Luke 4:16-21

KEY VERSE: Jesus answered her, "Woman, great is your faith! Let it be done for you as you wish." And her daughter was healed instantly. Matthew 15:28.

4

KING JAMES VERSION

MATTHEW 15:21 Then Jesus went thence, and departed into the coasts of Tyre and Sidon.

22 And, behold, a woman of Canaan came out of the same coasts, and cried unto him, saying, Have mercy on me, O Lord, thou Son of David; my daughter is grievously vexed with a devil.

23 But he answered her not a word. And his disciples came and besought him, saying, Send her away; for she crieth after us.

24 But he answered and said, I am not sent but unto the lost sheep of the house of Israel.

25 Then came she and worshipped him, saying, Lord, help me.

26 But he answered and said, It is not meet to take the children's bread, and to cast it to dogs.

27 And she said, Truth, Lord: yet the dogs eat of the crumbs which fall from their masters' table.

28 Then Jesus answered and said unto her, O woman, great is thy faith: be it unto thee even as thou wilt. And her daughter was made whole from that very hour.

29 And Jesus departed from thence, and came nigh unto the sea of Galilee; and went up into a mountain, and sat down there.

30 And great multitudes came unto him, having with them those that were lame, blind, dumb, maimed, and many others, and cast them down at Jesus' feet; and he healed them:

31 Insomuch that the multitude wondered, when they saw the dumb to speak, the maimed to be whole, the lame to walk, and the blind to see: and they glorified the God of Israel.

NEW REVISED STANDARD VERSION

MATTHEW 15:21 Jesus left that place and went away to the district of Tyre and Sidon. 22 Just then a Canaanite woman from that region came out and started shouting, "Have mercy on me, Lord, Son of David; my daughter is tormented by a demon." 23 But he did not answer her at all. And his disciples came and urged him, saying, "Send her away, for she keeps shouting after us." 24 He answered, "I was sent only to the lost sheep of the house of Israel." 25 But she came and knelt before him, saying, "Lord, help me." 26 He answered, "It is not fair to take the children's food and throw it to the dogs." 27 She said, "Yes, Lord, yet even the dogs eat the crumbs that fall from their masters' table." 28 Then Jesus answered her, "Woman, great is your faith! Let it be done for you as you wish." And her daughter was healed instantly.

29 After Jesus had left that place, he passed along the Sea of Galilee, and he went up the mountain, where he sat down. 30 Great crowds came to him, bringing with them the lame, the maimed, the blind, the mute, and many others. They put them at his feet, and he cured them, 31 so that the crowd was amazed when they saw the mute speaking, the maimed whole, the lame walking, and the blind seeing. And they praised the God of Israel.

HOME BIBLE READINGS

BACKGROUND

By visiting the Phoenician cities of Tyre and Sidon, Jesus had left the largely Jewish region of Galilee and entered into predominantly Gentile territory. The persistent Canaanite woman of that district who came to Jesus begging for her daughter's healing was a descendant of the pagan population of Palestine. During the time of the Judges (beginning around 1375 B.C.), the Canaanites were the principal enemies of the Israelites; these were the people the Israelites chiefly sought to drive out of the land.

The Canaanites were descendants of Canaan, the son of Ham (Gen. 10:6, 15-20), and most likely lived in the region some 800 years before the Israelites crossed the Jordan River and began battling the various indigenous tribes. The Canaanites included the Hittites, the Jebusites, the Amorites, and the Hivites (to name a few groups of people; 15:19-20). They lived in well-developed cities, each with its own king and army. Most of the Canaanites were polytheistic, with their idols being Baal, Dagon, and Asherah, to which numerous temples were erected.

God had called upon the Israelites to conquer and drive out the Canaanites before they could live peacefully in the land. But the Israelites neither completely conquered them nor drove them from the land (Judg. 1:28).

Although the Canaanite woman in Matthew 15:21-28 was from a different ethnic background than the Jews, she apparently knew enough about the Jewish faith—and had enough insight into the Jews longing for their Messiah—to recognize Jesus as the fulfillment of the messianic prophecies. Jesus' reference to the Canaanite woman's people as *the dogs* (15:26) was not necessarily a derogatory term. *Dog* was a common Jewish word for the Gentiles and was based on their making no distinction between clean and unclean foods; in essence, when it came to eating, the Gentiles used about as much discretion as a pack of hungry dogs. Many Bible scholars also point out that the Greek *kynarion*—the term Jesus used—referred to house dogs or little puppies, not to wild, scavenging beasts.

NOTES ON THE PRINTED TEXT

Jesus said that His primary mission was to call the Jews back to God. But in making the trip to Tyre and Sidon, He consciously put Himself in a position to minister to people other than the Jews, like the Canaanite woman.

Even as a Gentile, this woman had apparently heard about Jesus and His message and ministry. Upon meeting Him, she spoke to Him as the Jewish Messiah and seems to have personally accepted the segments of His message that she had heard. And though Jesus restated that His mission was to *"the lost sheep of the house of Israel"* (Matt. 15:24), in the end, He made little distinction between His mission to the Jews and His willingness to respond to faith wherever He found it, such as in this Canaanite woman.

After leaving Gennesaret in Galilee, Jesus traveled about 50 miles northwest to *the district of Tyre and Sidon* (15:21). Upon Jesus' arrival in the region, the Canaanite woman kept begging Him to *"Have mercy on me, Lord, son of David; my daughter is tormented by a demon"* (15:22). The woman's persistent shouting brought no response from Jesus, but it evidently irritated His disciples, for they urged Him to *"Send her away, for she keeps shouting after us"* (15:23). By not asking Jesus to grant her request, the disciples showed little compassion or sensitivity to the woman's needs.

Having heard His disciples' desire to send the woman away, Jesus addressed her by explaining that His mission was *"to the lost sheep of the house of Israel"* (15:24). Jesus' statement here does not contradict His desire to save both Jews and Gentiles (Matt. 28:19; Rom. 15:9-12). Rather, He meant that the Jews were to become the first agents through whom He would extend His Gospel throughout the world (Rom. 1:16).

At this point the woman fell to her knees and begged, *"Lord, help me"* (Matt. 15:25). To those of us reading this passage today, Jesus' response seems sharp: *"It is not fair to take the children's food and throw it to the dogs"* (15:26). The debate surrounding Jesus' intention still continues. Perhaps Jesus was testing the woman's faith; perhaps He was using the situation as an opportunity to teach that faith is available to everyone; perhaps He was reflecting the Jews' attitude so as to contrast it with His own; or perhaps He was emphasizing, again, that the Gospel was to be given first to the Jews.

Whichever was the case, the woman was not offended and did not argue. Instead, she used Jesus' choice of words to renew her request: *"Yes, Lord, yet even the dogs eat the crumbs that fall from their masters' table"* (15:27). The woman's answer—and her faith—greatly impressed Jesus: *"Woman, great is your faith! Let it be done for you as you wish"* (15:28). This was not the first time Jesus had commended the faith of a Gentile. When a humble centurion had asked for healing for his servant, Jesus responded, *"Truly I tell you, in no one in Israel have I found such faith"* (8:10). And just like the centurion's servant, the Canaanite woman's daughter was healed without Jesus ever seeing or touching her.

Upon Jesus' return to the region around the Sea of Galilee, huge crowds brought to Him their friends and family members who were lame, blind, crippled, and mute (to name a few physical ailments; 15:29). *They put them at his feet, and he cured them, so that the crowd was amazed when they saw the mute speaking, the maimed whole, the lame walking, and the blind seeing. And they praised the God of Israel* (15:30-31).

SUGGESTIONS TO TEACHERS

The Canaanite woman had faith in Jesus. She believed that He could heal her daughter. So regardless of her own heritage and background and regardless of the fact that she was not Jewish, she took her need to Jesus and persisted in her petition and in her faith. And Jesus rewarded the woman because of her faith. Faith is described as *the assurance of things hoped for, the conviction of things not seen. Indeed, by faith our ancestors received approval* (Heb. 11:1-2).

1. KEEP THE FAITH. Persist in your faith. Don't allow put-downs or persecutions or pity to diminish your faith. God responds to faith, and He rewards faith. No matter who it is, no matter what your background, and no matter what your past, the Bible reminds us time and again that God responds to faith. He gives His approval to us because of our faith.

2. OVERCOMING ANNOYANCE. No doubt, the Canaanite woman annoyed Jesus' disciples. Their response to her persistent requests was to get rid of her. We can become so preoccupied with how we want things to go that we overlook some of the obvious needs around us—be they physical, mental, emotional, or spiritual. Jesus demonstrated sensitivity to the persistent pleas of a Canaanite woman. As we become more like Jesus, may we, too, be sensitive to needy, hurting people around us—even if doing so feels like an inconvenience. May we seize the opportunity to minister to the real needs of others.

3. HEALING HAPPENS. Because of their faith in Jesus, vast crowds brought to Him their infirm, and Jesus healed them. It is still possible for us to take to Him those near and dear to us who need His healing touch. Yes, but how? It's through prayer. By praying for them, we lay our loved ones at the feet of Jesus just as those did who sought His healing almost 2,000 years ago.

4. PRAISE: THE PROPER RESPONSE. Jesus' desire was that God receive praise for His great and mighty deeds. When God has stepped in on our behalf—when He has brought us through a difficult situation or blessed us with good things—our response ought always be to thank and praise Him.

FOR ADULTS

■ TOPIC: Persisting in Faith

■ QUESTIONS: 1. Why do you think Jesus went to the region of Tyre and Sidon rather than stay in Israel? 2. Imagine yourself in the Canaanite woman's situation. When Jesus told you that His primary mission was to people other than yourself, would you have walked away feeling excluded, would you have gotten angry and told Him off, or would you have persisted with your request? Explain your answer. 3. Why do you think Jesus answered the woman's request by saying, "*It is not fair to take the children's food and throw it to the dogs*" (Matt. 15:26)? 4. Why did Jesus commend the woman's great faith? 5. What do you do to continually strengthen your faith?

■ ILLUSTRATIONS:

Nine Minutes to Keep the Faith. On the last day of January, 2000, Alaska Airlines Flight 261, en route from Puerto Vallarta to San Francisco, crashed in the Pacific Ocean 20 miles from the California shore. All 83 passengers and 5 crew members were killed. According to the *San Francisco Examiner*, the board responsible for investigating the accident reported that the aircraft had suddenly dropped 7,000 feet, then remained stable for 9 minutes before it fell 18,000 feet in the final minute.

An airline pilot familiar with the investigation said that he had listened to the cockpit recording of what happened during the flight's last minutes. The pilot said that during that time, Linda Knight explained the Gospel to the other passengers using the intercom. Shortly before the crash, Linda led them in prayer to God for the forgiveness of their sins.

Pilots who have reviewed the report say that there is no plausible technical explanation for the fact that the aircraft remained relatively stable for those nine minutes. Perhaps it was God's timing and God's love that allowed the plane to remain in the air long enough for Linda to explain the Gospel. And like the Canaanite woman, Linda persistently kept her faith to the end.

Right Place at the Right Time. Three months after their victory over the Tennessee Titans, the Super Bowl champions took the field again to talk about God. Kurt Warner and three other Saint Louis Rams players told stories about their personal struggles and their relationship with Jesus Christ to a crowd of 25,000 at the Trans World Dome in Saint Louis.

"If you give your life to Jesus Christ, He's going to put you in the right place at the right time to touch lives," said Warner. He is the Rams' quarterback who eight years prior to leading the Rams to the Super Bowl was stocking shelves in a grocery store and collecting food stamps to help feed his family.

The players took turns telling their stories of overcoming injuries, poverty, and doubt. Tight end Ernie Conwell told how he played for three losing seasons with the Rams, then was injured and had to sit out most of the 1999 winning season, but went on to make a big catch in the Super Bowl. "It took a lot of strength to get me through. But I knew God had a plan for my life," Conwell said.

Defensive end Kevin Carter said people always called him an underachiever, and he has been plagued by injuries. "God allowed me to tap into the greatness of His power," said Carter, who led the NFL in quarterback sacks for the 1999 season.

Linebacker Mike Jones had told his wife he wanted to be a "warrior for Christ." He said to the crowd, "As you can see, I'm not the biggest, I'm not the fastest,

I'm not the strongest person to play in the NFL. And you can say the same thing about one of my heroes, David. David wasn't the biggest or the strongest, but he had the faith in God to get him through."

Warner helped to put the event together after he told his pastor about wanting to do something "where I could touch a lot of people at one time." Warner's pastor enlisted 87 other churches, and together they raised hundreds of thousands of dollars, organized 1,500 volunteers, rented the Dome, signed some prominent Christian musicians, and built a stage with an audio system and four video screens in six weeks. Victory 2000 was free to the public. Clearly, God rewards persistent faith!

Faith in Practice. When a nightclub opened on Main Street, the only church in that small town organized an all-night prayer meeting. The members asked God to burn down the club. Within a few minutes, lightning struck the club, and it burned to the ground. The owner sued the church, which denied responsibility. After hearing both sides, the judge said, "It seems that wherever the guilt may lie, the nightclub owner believes in prayer, while the church doesn't."

FOR YOUTH	■ TOPIC: Mothers Are Like That

■ **QUESTIONS:** 1. Do you think Jesus was intentionally putting Himself where He was needed by going to the region of Tyre and Sidon? Explain your answer. 2. Do you think your parents would have been as persistent in seeking your healing as this Canaanite woman was in seeking her daughter's healing? Explain your answer. 3. What do you think was Jesus' point in talking about the Jews as "children" and about the Gentiles as "dogs"? 4. How have you seen faith in God bring about great results in your life and the lives of others? 5. What can you do to build up your faith?

■ **ILLUSTRATIONS:**

Making the Best of a Bad Situation. For Sparky, school was all but impossible. He failed every subject in the eighth grade. He flunked physics in high school, getting a grade of *zero*. Sparky also flunked Latin, algebra, and English. He didn't do much better in sports. Although he did manage to make the school's golf team, he lost the only important match of the season. There was a consolation match, but he lost that too.

Throughout his youth, Sparky was awkward socially. He was not actually disliked by the other students; no one cared that much. He was astonished if a classmate ever said hello to him outside of school hours. There's no way to tell how he might have done at dating. Sparky never once asked a girl to go out in high school. He was too afraid of being turned down.

Sparky seemed like a loser. So he rolled with the circumstances. Sparky had made up his mind early in life that if things were meant to work out, they would.

Otherwise he would content himself with what appeared to be his inevitable mediocrity.

However, one thing was important to Sparky: drawing. He was proud of his artwork. Of course, no one else appreciated it. In his senior year of high school, he submitted some cartoons to the editors of the yearbook. The cartoons were turned down. Despite this particular rejection, Sparky was so convinced of his ability that he decided to become a professional artist.

After completing high school, he wrote a letter to Walt Disney Studios. He was told to send some samples of his artwork, and the subject for a cartoon was suggested. Sparky drew the proposed cartoon. He spent a great deal of time on it and on all the other drawings he submitted. Finally, the reply came from Disney Studios. He had been rejected once again. *Another loss for the loser.*

So Sparky decided to write his own autobiography in cartoons. He described his childhood self—a little boy loser and chronic underachiever. The cartoon character would soon become famous worldwide. For Sparky, the boy who had such a lack of success in school and whose work was rejected again and again, was Charles Schulz, who passed away in 2000 at the age of 77. He created the "Peanuts" comic strip and the little cartoon character whose kite would never fly and who never succeeded in kicking a football—Charlie Brown.

Charles Schulz and Charlie Brown are a little like the Canaanite woman whom Jesus told, *"It is not fair to take the children's food and throw it to the dogs"* (Matt. 15:26). Despite this remark, she made the best of the situation and kept the faith.

Valuable to God. A well-known speaker opened his seminar by holding up a $20 bill. In the room of 200, he asked, "Who would like this $20 bill?"

Hands shot up! The man said, "I am going to give this $20 to one of you but first, let me do this." Then he crumpled up the dollar bill. The speaker then asked, "Who still wants it?" Still the hands went up in the air. "Well," he replied, "what if I do this?" And he dropped it to the floor and ground it with his shoe. He picked it up, now all crumpled and dirty. "Now, who still wants it?" Still the hands went into the air.

"My friends," he said, "you have all learned a very valuable lesson. No matter what I did to the money, you still wanted it because it did not decrease in value. It was still worth $20. Many times in our lives, we are crumpled, dropped, and ground into the dirt by the decisions we make and by the circumstances that come our way. We feel as though we are worthless. But no matter what has happened or what will happen, you will never lose your eternal, God-given value."

Good Name for a Child. Butch O'Hare was a fighter pilot assigned to an aircraft carrier in the Pacific Ocean. Once, when his entire squadron was assigned to fly a particular mission, he looked at his fuel gauge after he was airborne and realized that someone had forgotten to top off his fuel tank. Because of this, he would not have enough fuel to complete his mission and get back to his ship. His flight leader told him to leave formation and return. As he was returning to the mother ship, he could see a squadron of Japanese Zeros heading toward the fleet to attack. And with all the fighter planes gone, the fleet was almost defenseless. His was the only opportunity to distract and divert them.

Single-handedly, O'Hare dove into the formation of Japanese planes and attacked them. The American fighter planes were rigged with cameras, so that as they flew and fought, the pictures that were taken helped pilots learn more about the terrain and enemy maneuvers. O'Hare dove at them and shot until all his ammunition was gone, and then he dove at them trying to clip off a wing or tail or anything that would make the enemy planes unfit to fly. He did anything he could to keep them from reaching the American ships.

Finally, the Japanese squadron took off in another direction, and Butch O'Hare and his fighter, both badly shot up, limped back to the carrier. He told his story, but not until the film from the camera on his plane was developed did they realize the extent to which he tried to protect his fleet. He was recognized as a hero and given one of the nation's highest military honors. Later, Chicago's O'Hare International Airport was named for him.

Prior to this time in Chicago, there was a man called "Easy Eddie," who worked as an attorney for the gangster Al Capone. Easy Eddie had managed to keep Al Capone out of jail despite all his crimes. To show his appreciation, Capone paid him very well. Easy Eddie not only earned big money, but also he would get extra things, like a residence that took up nearly an entire Chicago city block. His house was fenced, and he had live-in help and all the conveniences of the day.

Easy Eddie had a son. He loved his son and gave him all the best things while he was growing up: clothes, cars, and a good education. And because Easy Eddie loved his son, he tried to teach him right from wrong. But one thing he couldn't give his son was a good name—or a good example. Easy Eddie decided that this was much more important than all the riches he had been given. So he went to the authorities in order to rectify the wrongs he had done. In order to tell the truth, it meant he must testify against Al Capone, and he knew that Al Capone would do his best to have him killed. But Easy Eddie wanted most of all to try to be an example and do the best he could to give back to his son a good name. So he testified. Within the year, he was shot and killed on a Chicago street.

These two accounts might sound unrelated, but they're not. Butch O'Hare was Easy Eddie's son. Like the Canaanite woman who was looking out for her daughter—hoping that Jesus would heal her—Easy Eddie looked out for his son, hoping he (Easy Eddie) could pave the way for his son to have a good name.

RAISING OF LAZARUS

BACKGROUND SCRIPTURE: John 11:1-44
DEVOTIONAL READING: John 11:17-27

KEY VERSES: Jesus said to her, "I am the resurrection and the life. Those who believe in me, even though they die, will live, and everyone who lives and believes in me will never die." John 11:25-26.

5

KING JAMES VERSION

JOHN 11:1 Now a certain man was sick, named Lazarus, of Bethany, the town of Mary and her sister Martha.

2 (It was that Mary which anointed the Lord with ointment, and wiped his feet with her hair, whose brother Lazarus was sick.)

3 Therefore his sisters sent unto him, saying, Lord, behold, he whom thou lovest is sick.

4 When Jesus heard that, he said, This sickness is not unto death, but for the glory of God, that the Son of God might be glorified thereby.

5 Now Jesus loved Martha, and her sister, and Lazarus.

6 When he had heard therefore that he was sick, he abode two days still in the same place where he was. . . .

11 These things said he: and after that he saith unto them, Our friend Lazarus sleepeth; but I go, that I may awake him out of sleep.

12 Then said his disciples, Lord, if he sleep, he shall do well.

13 Howbeit Jesus spake of his death: but they thought that he had spoken of taking of rest in sleep.

14 Then said Jesus unto them plainly, Lazarus is dead.

15 And I am glad for your sakes that I was not there, to the intent ye may believe; nevertheless let us go unto him. . . .

38 Jesus therefore again groaning in himself cometh to the grave. It was a cave, and a stone lay upon it.

39 Jesus said, Take ye away the stone. Martha, the sister of him that was dead, saith unto him, Lord, by this time he stinketh: for he hath been dead four days.

40 Jesus saith unto her, Said I not unto thee, that, if thou wouldest believe, thou shouldest see the glory of God?

41 Then they took away the stone from the place where the dead was laid. And Jesus lifted up his eyes, and said, Father, I thank thee that thou hast heard me.

42 And I knew that thou hearest me always: but because of the people which stand by I said it, that they may believe that thou hast sent me.

43 And when he thus had spoken, he cried with a loud voice, Lazarus, come forth.

44 And he that was dead came forth, bound hand and foot with graveclothes: and his face was bound about with a napkin. Jesus saith unto them, Loose him, and let him go.

NEW REVISED STANDARD VERSION

JOHN 11:1 Now a certain man was ill, Lazarus of Bethany, the village of Mary and her sister Martha. 2 Mary was the one who anointed the Lord with perfume and wiped his feet with her hair; her brother Lazarus was ill. 3 So the sisters sent a message to Jesus, "Lord, he whom you love is ill." 4 But when Jesus heard it, he said, "This illness does not lead to death; rather it is for God's glory, so that the Son of God may be glorified through it." 5 Accordingly, though Jesus loved Martha and her sister and Lazarus, 6 after having heard that Lazarus was ill, he stayed two days longer in the place where he was. . . .

11 After saying this, he told them, "Our friend Lazarus has fallen asleep, but I am going there to awaken him." 12 The disciples said to him, "Lord, if he has fallen asleep, he will be all right." 13 Jesus, however, had been speaking about his death, but they thought that he was referring merely to sleep. 14 Then Jesus told them plainly, "Lazarus is dead. 15 For your sake I am glad I was not there, so that you may believe. But let us go to him." . . .

38 Then Jesus, again greatly disturbed, came to the tomb. It was a cave, and a stone was lying against it. 39 Jesus said, "Take away the stone." Martha, the sister of the dead man, said to him, "Lord, already there is a stench because he has been dead four days." 40 Jesus said to her, "Did I not tell you that if you believed, you would see the glory of God?" 41 So they took away the stone. And Jesus looked upward and said, "Father, I thank you for having heard me. 42 I knew that you always hear me, but I have said this for the sake of the crowd standing here, so that they may believe that you sent me." 43 When he had said this, he cried with a loud voice, "Lazarus, come out!" 44 The dead man came out, his hands and feet bound with strips of cloth, and his face wrapped in a cloth. Jesus said to them, "Unbind him, and let him go."

Monday, October 1	Matthew 13:24-30	*The Parable of the Weeds among the Wheat*
Tuesday, October 2	Matthew 13:36-43	*The Parable of the Weeds Explained*
Wednesday, October 3	Matthew 13:31-35, 44-46	*What the Kingdom of Heaven Is Like*
Thursday, October 4	Matthew 13:47-52	*More Kingdom Parables*
Friday, October 5	Mark 4:21-29	*The Parable of the Growing Seed*
Saturday, October 6	Matthew 13:1-13, 18-23	*The Parable of the Sower*
Sunday, October 7	Luke 15:1-10	*Jesus Told Them a Parable*

BACKGROUND

Over the course of Jesus' ministry, the village of Bethany became to Him a familiar place, and Lazarus, Martha, and Mary, as well as Simon the leper—all of whom resided in Bethany—became familiar faces. The village was only a short two-mile walk from Jerusalem and was even nearer to the Mount of Olives. Jesus often used the homes of His friends in Bethany as a stopping place for rest and relaxation before making His way back into Jerusalem. The village of Bethany still exists and is now called El-azariyeh, in honor of Lazarus.

Although the depth of Jesus' friendship with Simon is unclear, it is very clear that apart from His disciples, Lazarus, Martha, and Mary were among Jesus' closest friends. The three were siblings, had grown up together, and continued to live together in adulthood.

Upon Jesus' visits to this family's household, Martha typically served as the hostess, preparing and serving meals for Jesus and His disciples. And while Martha busied herself in the kitchen, Mary liked to sit with the disciples and listen to Jesus teach. Indeed, Mary was filled with such love for Jesus that on one occasion—sometime after He raised Lazarus from the dead—she poured expensive perfume on the Savior's feet and *wiped them with her hair* (John 12:3).

Lazarus and his sisters were by no means poor. Based on some of the minute descriptions of their home and surroundings, it seems they were quite wealthy compared to most of the people of that day. Some scholars also think Lazarus at times materially supported Jesus in His ministry. Whatever the case, Scripture clearly portrays the love Lazarus had for Jesus and Jesus' love for him. They ate together often and talked together often. They were, indeed, friends.

NOTES ON THE PRINTED TEXT

All of Jesus' "I am" statements recorded in the Gospel of John are great, but perhaps the greatest of all is the one in 11:25, *"I am the resurrection and the life. Those who believe in me, even though they die, will live."* The account of Jesus' raising Lazarus from the dead perfectly illustrates His bold statement. Jesus, who is the Creator of life, has power over life and death. And because He is *"the life,"* He can give eternal life to those who believe in Him.

Having been witnesses of Jesus' miraculous powers as well as having been His friends, Lazarus's sisters Mary and Martha sent urgent word to Jesus that *"he whom you love is ill"* (11:3). The sisters fully believed that Jesus could heal their brother, and they also fully expected an immediate response (11:1-2). By sending Jesus this urgent word, they hoped that He would drop whatever He was doing and immediately make His way back to Bethany.

When news of Lazarus's illness reached Jesus, He was preaching in the villages east of the Jordan River, likely in the region of Perea (11:6). A full day's journey of about 20 miles could have had Jesus at Lazarus's bedside. But Jesus did not leave immediately. Instead, He waited two days before crossing the Jordan, reentering the region of Judea, and making His way to Bethany—this despite the fact that *Jesus loved Martha and her sister and Lazarus* (11:5).

Jesus' delay would have seemed like a calloused response to the sisters' message had He not explained to His disciples that *"This illness does not lead to death; rather it is for God's glory, so that the Son of God may be glorified through it"* (11:4). But the message apparently did not reach Martha and Mary, who can be imagined looking over the horizon fully expecting Jesus' imminent return to Bethany. They likely knew that their message would reach Jesus within a day. They likely expected Jesus to begin His trip back to Bethany the next morning. One can imagine their heartbreak when Lazarus died with still no sign of Jesus' return.

As Jesus and His disciples were finally making the journey back to Bethany, He told them that Lazarus had *"fallen asleep"* (11:11), using a common description for death. Then He added, *"but I am going there to awaken him."* The disciples, misunderstanding the real meaning of Jesus' words, thought that if Jesus knew that Lazarus was getting rest, then he must be getting better (11:12-13). That's when Jesus *told them plainly, "Lazarus is dead"* (11:14). Jesus explained that if He had been with Lazarus during the final moments of his sickness, He might have healed him rather than allowing him to die. Jesus explained that He allowed Lazarus to die so that His power over death could be put on display for His disciples—*"so that you may believe"* (11:15).

Upon Jesus' arrival at the tomb of Lazarus, He was *again greatly disturbed* (11:38). The mourners who saw Jesus weeping thought His tears were due to having lost a dear friend; they didn't perceive that the tears were more over them than over Lazarus. Along with being troubled by their unbelief, He was also troubled by their criticism that *"Could not he who opened the eyes of the blind man have kept this man from dying?"* (11:37).

Lazarus had been in the grave for four days (indicating, again, that Jesus had taken His time getting back to Bethany from Perea). So when Jesus asked that the stone covering the entrance to the tomb be moved, Martha, again thinking practically, remarked that there would be *"a stench"* (11:39). But Jesus reminded

Martha that if she believed, she *"would see the glory of God"* (11:40), and she would also see the life-giving nature of the Son of God.

Jesus' brief prayer thanking God *"for having heard me"* (11:41) shows that the Father heard even Jesus' unspoken thoughts. But *"so that they may believe that you sent me"* (11:42), Jesus voiced His prayer of thanksgiving out loud *"for the sake of the crowd standing here."* Then, after Jesus called for Lazarus to come out of the tomb (11:43), the *dead man came out, his hands and feet bound with strips of cloth, and his face wrapped in a cloth* (11:44). As if to portray Lazarus's new-found deliverance from death, Jesus told those standing around him to *"Unbind him, and let him go"* (11:44).

SUGGESTIONS TO TEACHERS

Jesus had raised others from the dead, such as Jairus's daughter (Matt. 9:18-26; Mark 5:21-43; Luke 8:40-56) and a widow's son (Luke 7:11-17). But as described by John, Jesus' raising of Lazarus from the dead was His crowning miracle, and it led the religious leaders to begin plotting Jesus' death. A short time after raising Lazarus from the dead for the glory of God, Jesus would raise Himself from the dead for the glory of God. Thus Jesus not only has power over life and death, but He is also the giver of life—for the glory of God.

1. WHAT DRIVES GOD'S TIMING? When Jesus received news of Lazarus's illness, He waited two days before beginning His journey to Bethany, but His delay had a specific purpose. God, too, may seem—in our opinion—slow or neglectful to answer our prayers; but He is never late. Though He may seem to delay, He will meet our needs according to His own perfect sense of timing.

2. WHAT BRINGS GOD GLORY? To Martha and Mary, anxiously waiting for Jesus' arrival was a trial to endure, and their brother's death caused them to question Jesus' motives for delaying His return. But when Christians face a trial, they have the great potential of bringing glory to God, especially when they keep trusting Him in the midst of it. God has made a habit of masterfully bringing glorious good out of disastrously bad situations!

3. WHAT MAKES GOD GRIEVE? Jesus was greatly disturbed when He came to the tomb of Lazarus—to the point of even quietly weeping. The selfish criticism of Jesus for not making it back to Bethany in time to save Lazarus and the foolish disbelief and disregard for who He was both upset and bothered Him. Didn't the people have enough faith, even yet, to realize Jesus' power over life and death? Disbelief and disregard for Jesus still makes God grieve today.

4. WHAT CAUSES GOD'S RESPONSE? Jesus had told Martha that *"Those who believe in me, even though they die, will live, and everyone who lives and believes in me will never die. Do you believe this?"* (John 11:25-26). Jesus later reminded Mary, *"Did I not tell you that if you believed, you would see the glory of God?"* (11:40). Believing in Jesus will lead to God's response. He will do glorious things in response to belief.

FOR ADULTS

■ **TOPIC:** Believing and Living

■ **QUESTIONS:** 1. What was the purpose behind Jesus' delaying His trip to Bethany for two days? 2. What did Jesus mean when He called Himself *"the resurrection and the life"* (John 11:25)? 3. Put yourself in Martha's and Mary's place. How would you have felt when Jesus finally arrived? 4. Why do you think Jesus was *greatly disturbed* (11:38) when He came to the tomb of Lazarus, but not when He first heard that Lazarus was dead? 5. How might wholeheartedly trusting in God bring Him glory?

■ **ILLUSTRATIONS:**

Back from the Dead. A few days after my friend Ellarie had undergone hip replacement surgery, I went to the hospital with the intention of visiting and praying with her. Finding her room door closed, I gently knocked so as not to surprise or disturb her. No answer came from the other side of the door, so I quietly opened the door and this time, gently knocked on the wall of her room. Still no one spoke. I stepped back outside the door into the hallway to make sure that I was at the right room; then I walked back in, expecting to find her sleeping.

As I rounded the corner back into the room, nothing was to prepare me for the shock I saw. The bed sheet had been pulled completely over Ellarie's body. I could see the outline of her forehead, nose, and chin. My mind raced. *What happened? What could have gone wrong with a hip replacement surgery that caused her death?* As the surprised grief rose within me and as I stared at her sheet-covered body, I blurted out the words, "O Ellarie!"

At that moment Ellarie quickly flung the sheet from over her head. I was just getting used to the shock of her being dead when she shocked me again by being alive! She had pulled the sheet over her head to block a cold draft from blowing into her face and had been praying that someone would come into her room to help her.

What joy I experienced at that moment—at least after regaining my quite startled wits! This dear friend, whom I thought was dead, was alive. And after getting over the double initial shocks, I was overjoyed that her life had been "restored." Imagine the joy of Martha and Mary of having their brother restored from the grave.

From "Taps" to "Reveille." For Winston Churchill's funeral, which he planned himself for Saint Paul's Cathedral, many of the great hymns of the church were sung and portions of the Anglican liturgy recited. At the close of the service, a bugler, who had been stationed high in the dome of the cathedral, trumpeted the sad strains of "Taps," the military song played at funerals conveying the message that the day is done. After a few seconds of silence at the end of "Taps," another bugler, stationed on the other side of the cathedral's dome, played the notes of "Reveille," the military song telling soldiers that it's time to get out of bed and begin the day. Because Jesus is the resurrection and the life, the strains of "Taps" marking our deaths will barely be over when the music of "Reveille" will signal the beginning of a new and eternal life.

Out from the Clutches of Death. A Gospel message written on toilet paper saved a condemned man's life—in two ways. The man had been sentenced to die in a Chinese prison for stealing money, Hong Kong-based Sowers Ministry reported early in 2000. His brother, worried about the impending execution, consulted a Christian friend for advice, and became a Christian when he learned about Jesus' promise of life beyond the grave for those who believe in Him.

When the man visited his brother in jail, he handed him a note written on toilet paper, which was the only paper he had. It explained that he must put his faith in Christ to be forgiven for his sins. The inmate professed faith in Christ that day.

As other Christians prayed for this new believer's life to be spared, the Chinese authorities decided for undisclosed reasons to reduce his sentence! After serving a few more months time, he was placed on probation. But during those months, many other inmates in the prison became Christians because of his preaching. And his brother now leads a house church that ministers to prisoners.

FOR YOUTH

■ **TOPIC:** Alive Again!

■ **QUESTIONS:** 1. How would you feel if your best friend didn't make it at a time when you needed him or her the most? 2. Think about the saddest funeral you've ever attended. How did you feel while you were paying your last respects? 3. Have you ever felt like God was not listening to your prayers? If so, how did you deal with it? 4. Why would disbelief in Jesus and disregard for who He is grieve God? 5. What can you do in your life right now to bring glory to God?

■ **ILLUSTRATIONS:**

Death Be Not Proud. John Donne was a seventeenth-century poet, and as the dean of Saint Paul's Cathedral in London, possibly the most influential preacher of his day. One of his most often quoted poems is "Death Be Not Proud," in which he carries on a conversation with death:

> Death be not proud, though some have called thee
> Mighty and dreadful, for thou art not so,
> For those whom thou think'st thou dost overthrow,
> Die not, poor death, nor yet canst thou kill me. . . .
> One short sleep past, we wake eternally,
> And death shall be no more; death, thou shalt die.

No Fear of the Grave. In the March 1994 issue of the *New Oxford Review*, Henri J. M. Nouwen wrote an article explaining one family's overcoming their fear of the grave. The husband of a friend of his had died of a heart attack. His friend decided to keep her two young children away from her husband, Bob's, funeral, thinking it would be too hard for them to see their father's body put in the ground. For years after that death, the cemetery remained a fearful place for them.

Then one day, Nouwen's friend asked him to visit the grave with her, and she invited the children to come along. The oldest child was afraid to go, but the youngest one decided to go. When they came to the place where Bob was buried, the three of them sat down on the grass around the stone engraved with the words, "A Kind and Gentle Man."

Nouwen said, "Maybe one day we should have a picnic here. This is not only a place to think about death, but also a place to rejoice in our life. Bob will be most honored when we find new strength, here, to live." Nouwen admitted that at first it seemed a strange idea: to have a meal on top of a tombstone. But because Jesus promised life beyond the grave for those who believe in Him, Bob's absence from his family would only be for short time. Then they would all live together eternally. A few days later, Nouwen's friend took her elder child to the grave, the younger one having convinced his sister that there was nothing to fear about the place.

Rise from the Dead. Blanche Gwinn of Elizabethton, Tennessee, thought she had recently buried her son, John, a Vietnam war casualty, when there was a knock at her door. A representative from the U.S. Army had come to tell her there had been a terrible mistake. Her son was alive and well in Vietnam!

A few days later, Blanche gave her son a joyful welcome when the Army flew him home to the states for an immediate leave. To this day, Blanche still tells her story to almost everyone she meets. Seeing her son alive and well was like seeing a loved one "rise from the dead."

Martha and Mary saw their brother actually rise from the dead. When Jesus called for him to come out of the tomb, these sisters watched as he walked out still covered in his burial clothes.

PURPOSE OF PARABLES

BACKGROUND SCRIPTURE: Matthew 13:1-35
DEVOTIONAL READING: Matthew 13:18-23

KEY VERSES: "The reason I speak to them in parables is that 'seeing they do not perceive, and hearing they do not listen, nor do they understand.'" Matthew 13:13.

KING JAMES VERSION

MATTHEW 13:1 The same day went Jesus out of the house, and sat by the sea side.

2 And great multitudes were gathered together unto him, so that he went into a ship, and sat; and the whole multitude stood on the shore.

3 And he spake many things unto them in parables, saying, Behold, a sower went forth to sow;

4 And when he sowed, some seeds fell by the way side, and the fowls came and devoured them up:

5 Some fell upon stony places, where they had not much earth: and forthwith they sprung up, because they had no deepness of earth:

6 And when the sun was up, they were scorched; and because they had no root, they withered away.

7 And some fell among thorns; and the thorns sprung up, and choked them:

8 But other fell into good ground, and brought forth fruit, some an hundredfold, some sixtyfold, some thirtyfold.

9 Who hath ears to hear, let him hear.

10 And the disciples came, and said unto him, Why speakest thou unto them in parables?

11 He answered and said unto them, Because it is given unto you to know the mysteries of the kingdom of heaven, but to them it is not given.

12 For whosoever hath, to him shall be given, and he shall have more abundance: but whosoever hath not, from him shall be taken away even that he hath.

13 Therefore speak I to them in parables: because they seeing see not; and hearing they hear not, neither do they understand. . . .

34 All these things spake Jesus unto the multitude in parables; and without a parable spake he not unto them:

35 That it might be fulfilled which was spoken by the prophet, saying, I will open my mouth in parables; I will utter things which have been kept secret from the foundation of the world.

NEW REVISED STANDARD VERSION

MATTHEW 13:1 That same day Jesus went out of the house and sat beside the sea. 2 Such great crowds gathered around him that he got into a boat and sat there, while the whole crowd stood on the beach. 3 And he told them many things in parables, saying: "Listen! A sower went out to sow. 4 And as he sowed, some seeds fell on the path, and the birds came and ate them up. 5 Other seeds fell on rocky ground, where they did not have much soil, and they sprang up quickly, since they had no depth of soil. 6 But when the sun rose, they were scorched; and since they had no root, they withered away. 7 Other seeds fell among thorns, and the thorns grew up and choked them. 8 Other seeds fell on good soil and brought forth grain, some a hundredfold, some sixty, some thirty. 9 Let anyone with ears listen!"

10 Then the disciples came and asked him, "Why do you speak to them in parables?" 11 He answered, "To you it has been given to know the secrets of the kingdom of heaven, but to them it has not been given. 12 For to those who have, more will be given, and they will have an abundance; but from those who have nothing, even what they have will be taken away. 13 The reason I speak to them in parables is that 'seeing they do not perceive, and hearing they do not listen, nor do they understand.'" . . .

34 Jesus told the crowds all these things in parables; without a parable he told them nothing. 35 This was to fulfill what had been spoken through the prophet:

"I will open my mouth to speak in parables;
  I will proclaim what has been hidden from the
  foundation of the world."

Monday, October 8	Deuteronomy 15:7-11	*Your Neighbor in Need*
Tuesday, October 9	Luke 18:18-25	*Sell What You Have and Give It to the Poor*
Wednesday, October 10	Luke 9:57-62	*Follow Now, and Don't Look Back*
Thursday, October 11	Luke 10:17-24	*Things Hidden from the Wise*
Friday, October 12	Deuteronomy 6:4-9	*Love God*
Saturday, October 13	Leviticus 19:13-18	*Love Your Neighbor*
Sunday, October 14	Luke 10:25-37	*Who Is My Neighbor?*

BACKGROUND

Jesus often made use of parables when teaching His disciples and the large crowds that gathered to hear Him speak. Because of Jesus' apparent love for telling these parables and His masterful skill at doing so, author Madeleine L'Engle once briefly summed up the whole of the Savior's being by calling Him "the God who told stories."

A parable is a story that teaches a lesson. It compares something familiar to something unfamiliar. Each parable usually points out only one spiritual truth, enabling hearers to understand that truth by using everyday objects and relationships.

The story lines of Jesus' parables were easily understood by His listeners, but there were often times when He had to explain what they meant. His purpose in telling these stories was to compel those of His listeners who were truly searching for spiritual truth to discover it. For them, Jesus' simple stories were loaded with profound spiritual insight. At the same time, His parables tended to conceal spiritual truth from those too lazy, stubborn, or haughty to diligently seek it out. For them, Jesus' parables were little more than stories without meaning.

Jesus' favorite subject matter for His parables was the kingdom of God. In fact, the parable of the sower is a description of *"the secrets of the kingdom of heaven"* (Matt. 13:11)—what living under God's reign looks like, sounds like, feels like, and acts like. These "kingdom parables" are usually clearly introduced by Jesus' words, *"The kingdom of heaven may be compared to"* (13:24) or *"The kingdom of heaven is like"* (13:31, 33, 44, 45, 47).

NOTES ON THE PRINTED TEXT

Matthew 13 is devoted to a compilation of both the telling and the explaining of Jesus' kingdom parables. In each of these stories, Jesus dealt with both the presence and the anticipated fulfillment of the kingdom of God. The first and main story recorded in this chapter is the parable of the sower.

The occasion for Jesus' teaching arose when He walked down to the shore of the Sea of Galilee and an immense crowd gathered around Him and followed Him

(13:1-2). Jesus climbed into and sat down in a boat that was docked along the shore, and from there He *told them many things in parables* (13:3).

The parable of the sower is about a farmer who scatters many seeds over a plot of ground. He plants an abundance of seed, knowing that if he sows enough of it at the outset, he'll end up with a plentiful harvest. The sower knows from the outset that not all the seeds are going to fall on fertile ground; he also knows that not all the seeds that do sprout will grow to fruition. Nonetheless, he sows abundantly hoping to overcome the expected losses.

As the farmer sowed, some of the seeds fell on a footpath and were snatched up by birds. Others fell on shallow soil with underlying rock and wilted in the hot sun. Others fell among thorns and were choked out. But the really surprising part of Jesus' parable is not that some of the seeds flourish while others wither and die (13:4-7). The ear-catching shocker of this story lies in the overabundance of grain that the sower enjoys from those seeds that do prosper: *"Other seeds fell on good soil and brought forth grain, some a hundredfold, some sixty, some thirty"* (13:8).

Most first-century farmers expected a good harvest to yield 10 bushels of wheat for every bushel of seed planted. But in Jesus' parable, the farmer gets yields of outrageous proportions—30, 60, and even 100-fold increases! Underlying in Jesus' parable is the lesson that only divine power—only God's own hand—can bring about such incredible yields.

Though the disciples understood the simple story, it is not clear whether they or the crowd grasped the parable's meaning. Perhaps the disciples did because they did not ask Jesus to explain it, even though He later explained its meaning in detail (13:18-23). The disciples did, however, come to Jesus and ask, *"Why do you speak to them in parables?"* (13:10). Jesus answered their question by telling them that the privilege of understanding the secrets of the kingdom belonged to His followers. Such a privilege does not belong to those who refuse to believe (13:11). And thus *"to those who have, more will be given, and they will have an abundance; but from those who have nothing, even what they have will be taken away"* (13:12). Then, quoting Isaiah 6:9, Jesus pointed out the sad truth that those who are not willing to receive and believe His message will find the truth hidden from them (Matt. 13:13).

Jesus consistently used stories and illustrations like the parable of the sower when speaking to the crowds, and *without a parable he told them nothing* (13:34). Even Jesus' method of teaching had been prophesied in Psalm 78:2-3. As Matthew 13:35 says, *"I will open my mouth to speak in parables."*

SUGGESTIONS TO TEACHERS

It is true that the parable of the sower points out one primary spiritual truth, namely, that through the Gospel, God actively spreads the message of His kingdom throughout the world, and people will respond to it in varied ways. Only when one *"hears the word and understands it"* (Matt. 13:23) will the message take root, grow to maturity, and bear fruit in that person's life.

Still, as sowers in God's service, Christians are called to spread the message of the kingdom, to "*make disciples of all nations, baptizing them in the name of the Father and of the Son and of the Holy Spirit, and teaching them to obey everything that I have commanded you*" (28:19-20). As such, there are a few lessons that we might glean from this farmer's approach to sowing seeds.

1. SPREAD LOTS OF SEED! The sower in Jesus' parable did not sow his seed sparingly. He sowed abundantly, fully expecting a huge harvest. Whenever we can, at every possible opportunity, we ought to plant the seeds of God's kingdom in the minds and hearts of those around us. And the more seeds we plant, the better!

2. SPREAD GOOD SEED! Much of the seed that we'll sow will not be our words or explanations, but our actions and behaviors. Are our lives so directed by the Holy Spirit that others cannot help but see Jesus living within us? Our Christian walk—the way we conduct our lives—has immeasurable potential to impact others for the kingdom of God.

3. SPREAD SEED ON GOOD SOIL! Though it is best to sow our seed thickly and abundantly, we would do well to keep our eyes open for good soil into which to sow. Some are more diligently seeking the truths of the kingdom of God than others. Are we able to recognize these seekers? May we discipline ourselves to discern the best soil in which to plant our seeds.

4. SPREAD SEED WITH OTHER SOWERS! The more sowers there are, the more seeds that will get sown. When we join with other believers to sow the seeds of kingdom truth, we cover more ground, get the message to more people, better maximize our potential, and reap a greater harvest.

FOR ADULTS　　■ TOPIC: Hearing the Word

■ QUESTIONS: 1. Why do you think Jesus used parables as His chief teaching method? 2. What is Jesus really saying in the parable of the sower? 3. How might this parable help you understand what is happening in your own ministry? 4. Why is it that when it comes to understanding the kingdom of God, "*to those who have, more will be given, and they will have an abundance; but from those who have nothing, even what they have will be taken away*" (Matt. 13:12)? 5. In what ways can "*the cares of the world and the lure of wealth*" (13:22) choke out the message of the kingdom in one's life?

■ ILLUSTRATIONS:

Preparing the Soil. Eugene, the pastor of a rural church, was thrilled to have Steve, the pastor of one of the denomination's largest churches, come into town. The people of Eugene's church had high regard for Steve, and Eugene felt that having the preacher speak at his church would greatly inspire his small flock.

When the renowned minister arrived late in the morning, Eugene took him to the local diner for lunch. But when the waitress, who attended Eugene's church, brought the two men the food they had ordered, Steve immediately grew upset at how the food had been prepared and arranged on his plate. Loudly voicing his disapproval to the waitress, Steve left no opening for the waitress to address his accusations. Finally, the waitress picked up Steve's plate, and with tears streaming from her eyes, hurried back into the kitchen.

Eugene was so astounded at Steve's inconsideration that, for a moment, he was speechless. Then he leaned over the table toward Steve and said, "Pastor, I dare you to witness to our waitress about the love and mercy of Jesus when she comes back."

Sometimes our actions and behaviors prepare the soil into which we will plant the seeds of God's grace. At times, we have the potential to make the soil harder or softer, more or less willing to accept the message of God's kingdom.

Becoming Good Soil. Laura Schlessinger, the host of her own radio program called "Dr. Laura," states the following in her book *How Could You Do That?*: "What's the number one, most typically asked question on [my] internationally syndicated show? The caller usually wants to know this: 'Now that I've done all these things I shouldn't have done, how can I avoid the consequences I knew, but denied, and just hoped would not happen?'"

Schlessinger confesses that her pet peeve is "when callers protest that they are 'only human.' Only human? As if one's humanness were a blueprint for instinctive, reflexive reactions to situations, like in the rest of the animal kingdom. I see being 'human' as the unique opportunity to use our minds and wills to act in ways that elevate us above the animal kingdom."

Schlessinger then closes her point with an illustration from the film classic *The African Queen*. Humphrey Bogart as Charlie, the solitary sailor, tries to invoke the "only human" excuse when he attempts to explain his prior drunken evening. Katharine Hepburn as Rosie, the missionary, peers over her Bible and aptly retorts, "We were put on the earth to rise above nature."

It is time to allow the Holy Spirit to work in us to become "good soil," and then let the seeds that God has planted in our hearts take root, grow to maturity, and bear fruit.

Scattering Gospel Seeds. In May of 2000, a pastor in Russia scattered seeds for the kingdom of God by setting up a large tent in a Muslim region of the country. Within a few weeks, the services he was leading were drawing 3,000 people. Vladimir Silchuk then began preaching nightly, and most of the people who attended became Christians, he told *Religion Today*.

Silchuk's tent held about 1,000 people and was filled to capacity each night with many sitting outside. The meetings, which took place in the city of Ufa, in the Bashkortostan region, continued throughout the summer.

The region is home to the Tartar and Bashir people, who are of Mongolian descent and largely unreached with the Gospel. The region "has been an Islamic stronghold for many years," said Perry Hubick of Saskatchewan, Canada, a church elder who has ministered with Silchuk. "Many heard the Gospel for the very first time and responded to Christ."

FOR YOUTH

■ TOPIC: Get the Message?

■ QUESTIONS: 1. From the parable of the sower, what is the crop that the seed is supposed to produce? 2. Why do you think Jesus used this simple story to explain how people receive His message? 3. What would a parable like this one accomplish that a simple, straightforward discussion would not? 4. How would you explain this parable to urban gang members who don't know anything about sowing seed in a field? 5. What can you do to make sure that your life is "good soil" into which to sow the message of the kingdom?

■ ILLUSTRATIONS:

God's Employee. Russ Blowers is a minister who is active in his local Rotary Club. Each week at the Club's meetings, one of the members gives a brief statement about his job. When it was his turn, Russ told, in essence, a modern-day parable describing his role as a Christian under God's employ: "I'm with a global enterprise. We have branches in every country in the world. We have our representatives in nearly every parliament and boardroom on earth. We're into motivation and behavior alteration. We run hospitals, feeding stations, crisis pregnancy centers, universities, publishing houses, and nursing homes.

"We care for our clients from birth to death. We are into life insurance and fire insurance. We perform spiritual heart transplants. Our original Organizer owns all the real estate on earth plus an assortment of galaxies and constellations. He knows everything and lives everywhere. Our product is free for the asking. (There's not enough money to buy it.)

"Our CEO was born in a hick town, worked as a carpenter, didn't own a home, was misunderstood by His family, hated by enemies, walked on water, was condemned to death without a trial, and arose from the dead—and I talk with Him every day."

Sowing Abundantly. When a lot of seeds are scattered abundantly over a plot of ground, some of the seeds will fall on good soil. An Indonesian evangelist was trying to scatter seeds abundantly in May of 2000, when a couple of bandits tried to rob him. But the robbers ended up giving their lives to Christ.

The evangelist and his associates were returning from a conference in Jayapura, Indonesia, when the two gunmen stopped them. When the evangelist rolled down the window of the car to hand over their money, one of the associates told the bandits that they had just come from leading a seminar "about the kingdom of God."

"Why don't you hold a seminar here?" one of the bandits said. "Then we can be freed from our drinking." The evangelist got out of the car and explained what sin is and the need to trust in Christ for forgiveness and to be freed from alcoholism. The young man knelt in the middle of the road to pray, and when he stood, "his deliverance was visible," the evangelist said. "His body relaxed noticeably." Another member of the gang also asked to become a Christian.

Seeds of Revival. During one week back in the year 2000, more than 27,100 people were baptized by Christians in Peru. The baptisms, performed throughout the country, accompanied the Impacto 2000 outreach program held at San Marcos Stadium in Lima by evangelist Alejandro Bullon. The program appeared live on television, cable, and satellite broadcasts in Peru and in the Spanish-speaking areas of South and Central America.

"This shows that no one knows what God will do," said pastor Raul Gomez, the leader of a local church in Peru. "Jesus just said go and make disciples. That's what we as pastors and lay members are continuing to do through small groups studying the Bible together."

"This event well illustrates the amazing church growth here in Peru and throughout South America," said Jan Paulsen, president of a large church organization. "For my wife, Kari, and myself, this has been a truly astonishing experience to see the Holy Spirit working in so many ways."

Bullon, a native of Peru, said the baptisms were a result of the whole church working together to reach friends and neighbors. "Christ is waking us up, and the Holy Spirit is preparing His church," he said. "This is the result of the personal enthusiasm of lay members. Even my 75-year-old mother is out looking for people to study with and to invite to the meetings. I can't give 50,000 Bible studies, but the members can. I just preach and give the call. Together we can do great things for God."

THE GOOD SAMARITAN

BACKGROUND SCRIPTURE: Luke 10:25-37

DEVOTIONAL READING: Deuteronomy 15:7-11

KEY VERSES: [Jesus asked,] "Which of these three, do you think, was a neighbor to the man who fell into the hands of the robbers?" [The lawyer] said, "The one who showed him mercy." Luke 10:36-37.

KING JAMES VERSION

LUKE 10:25 And, behold, a certain lawyer stood up, and tempted him, saying, Master, what shall I do to inherit eternal life?

26 He said unto him, What is written in the law? how readest thou?

27 And he answering said, Thou shalt love the Lord thy God with all thy heart, and with all thy soul, and with all thy strength, and with all thy mind; and thy neighbour as thyself.

28 And he said unto him, Thou hast answered right: this do, and thou shalt live.

29 But he, willing to justify himself, said unto Jesus, And who is my neighbour?

30 And Jesus answering said, A certain man went down from Jerusalem to Jericho, and fell among thieves, which stripped him of his raiment, and wounded him, and departed, leaving him half dead.

31 And by chance there came down a certain priest that way: and when he saw him, he passed by on the other side.

32 And likewise a Levite, when he was at the place, came and looked on him, and passed by on the other side.

33 But a certain Samaritan, as he journeyed, came where he was: and when he saw him, he had compassion on him,

34 And went to him, and bound up his wounds, pouring in oil and wine, and set him on his own beast, and brought him to an inn, and took care of him.

35 And on the morrow when he departed, he took out two pence, and gave them to the host, and said unto him, Take care of him; and whatsoever thou spendest more, when I come again, I will repay thee.

36 Which now of these three, thinkest thou, was neighbour unto him that fell among the thieves?

37 And he said, He that shewed mercy on him. Then said Jesus unto him, Go, and do thou likewise.

NEW REVISED STANDARD VERSION

Luke 10:25 Just then a lawyer stood up to test Jesus. "Teacher," he said, "what must I do to inherit eternal life?" 26 He said to him, "What is written in the law? What do you read there?" 27 He answered, "You shall love the Lord your God with all your heart, and with all your soul, and with all your strength, and with all your mind; and your neighbor as yourself." 28 And he said to him, "You have given the right answer; do this, and you will live."

29 But wanting to justify himself, he asked Jesus, "And who is my neighbor?" 30 Jesus replied, "A man was going down from Jerusalem to Jericho, and fell into the hands of robbers, who stripped him, beat him, and went away, leaving him half dead. 31 Now by chance a priest was going down that road; and when he saw him, he passed by on the other side. 32 So likewise a Levite, when he came to the place and saw him, passed by on the other side. 33 But a Samaritan while traveling came near him; and when he saw him, he was moved with pity. 34 He went to him and bandaged his wounds, having poured oil and wine on them. Then he put him on his own animal, brought him to an inn, and took care of him. 35 The next day he took out two denarii, gave them to the innkeeper, and said, 'Take care of him; and when I come back, I will repay you whatever more you spend.' 36 Which of these three, do you think, was a neighbor to the man who fell into the hands of the robbers?" 37 He said, "The one who showed mercy." Jesus said to him, "Go and do likewise."

7

HOME BIBLE READINGS

BACKGROUND

Racial prejudice and a history of animosity fueled an intense rivalry between the Jews and Samaritans. The Samaritans, who lived in the province of Samaria between Judea and Galilee, considered themselves proper; but Jews living in the province of Judea did not think the Samaritans were following the true Jewish religion. Thus the rivalry bred a deep hatred between the two groups—a hatred that was present at least 400 years before Christ. The bitterness between them was so fierce that Jews traveling between Judea and Galilee tried never to go through Samaria, even if it meant an extra day's journey.

The history of this rivalry goes back to 722 B.C., when Assyria conquered the northern kingdom of Israel and sent many of the people from Samaria into exile. The Assyrians also relocated foreigners into this region. Eventually some of these immigrants married the Israelites whom the Assyrians left behind in Samaria.

In 586 B.C., Babylon overran the southern kingdom of Judah and deported many of its people to Babylon. Then, in 538 B.C., the first group of Jewish exiles were allowed to return to their homeland to rebuild the Jerusalem temple. Their presence initiated the conflict between the people of Judah (the Jews) and the people of Samaria (the Samaritans), for each group viewed the other with suspicion. The Jews (who prided themselves on their "pure" Jewishness) came to hate the Samaritans, and the Samaritans reciprocated with bitterness and resentment.

The detestation reached a point of no return when the Samaritans built their own temple on Mount Gerizim, a sanctuary meant to rival the Jews' temple in Jerusalem. Additionally, the two groups despised each other for what they considered the other's hybrid religion. Samaritans accepted only their Torah—the five books of Moses—as the true law of God, whereas the Jews considered the entire Old Testament as the inspired message of the Lord.

NOTES ON THE PRINTED TEXT

Jesus' parable of the good Samaritan is one of several that are recorded solely in the Gospel of Luke. Jesus told the story in response to a question. Rather than answering the query by granting a succinct definition of "neighbor," Jesus decided to illustrate His reply by spinning a tale about some familiar territory, some familiar characters, and their very unfamiliar actions.

Jesus had been praying and blessing His disciples when an expert in the Jewish law stood up in the crowd to test Him by asking Him a question: *"Teacher, . . . what must I do to inherit eternal life?"* (Luke 10:25). The lawyer was trying to discredit Jesus, perhaps thinking he could outwit the Savior in public debate. But Jesus immediately turned the tables on the legal expert. Instead of saying something that might sound like a contradiction of the law, Jesus asked the official, *"What is written in the law? What do you read there?"* (10:26).

The lawyer quoted two Old Testament passages (10:27): Deuteronomy 6:5, which emphasizes our love for God, and Leviticus 19:18, which emphasizes our love for humankind. Jesus affirmed the lawyer's response: *"You have given the right answer; do this, and you will live"* (Luke 10:28). But the lawyer asked an additional question to show that he knew what he was talking about: *"And who is my neighbor?"* (10:29).

Jesus responded with a story about a man who traveled from Jerusalem to Jericho. Those listening would have been familiar with that notorious stretch of road. The route was known for the beggars and thieves who camped nearby. They plundered travelers along the narrow, winding mountain road. In fact, that's what happened to the traveler in Jesus' story. He *"fell into the hands of robbers, who stripped him, beat him, and went away, leaving him half dead"* (10:30).

As the traveler lay on the ground fighting for his life, a Jewish priest came along. But seeing the beaten and bloodied victim, the priest made the decision not to help him; instead, the clergy-type walked to the other side of the road and passed by the injured man. A temple assistant (a Levite) also noticed the man, but he, too, decided not to get involved (10:31-32).

Finally, a Samaritan came along. Because of the Jewish-Samaritan rivalry, the Samaritan could have rationalized failing to assist the wounded traveler more easily than did the Jewish priest and temple assistant. But unlike them, the Samaritan, *"when he saw him, he was moved with pity"* (10:33), and took extensive action to help the hapless victim. The Samaritan bandaged the man's injuries, pouring on oil to ease the pain and wine to cleanse the wounds. He then *"put him on his own animal"* (10:34) and transported the man to an inn. Moreover, the Samaritan arranged to pay all the man's expenses for a lengthy stay at the inn (10:35).

In telling this story, Jesus did not answer the lawyer's question. Rather, the Savior presented him with an entirely different query: *"Which of these three, do you think, was a neighbor to the man who fell into the hands of the robbers?"* (10:36). The answer, of course, was clear, *"The one who showed him mercy"* (10:37). Jesus then told the lawyer to *"Go and do likewise."*

SUGGESTIONS TO TEACHERS

One of the Pharisees asked Jesus, *"Teacher, which commandment in the law is the greatest?"* He said to him, *"'You shall love the Lord your God with all your heart, and with all your soul, and with all your mind.' This is the greatest and first commandment. And a second is like it: 'You shall love your neighbor as yourself.' On these two commandments hang all the law and the prophets"* (Matt. 22:36-40). Jesus wants us to apply the principle of love to our lives—love both for God and for our fellow human beings. To be a good neighbor, we should look for opportunities to do the following.

1. GET LOVE. Love is both a choice and an attitude. Without it, selfishness takes control of our hearts, and we become more concerned about what might happen to us than about helping those who are in need. We should remember that *"No one has greater love than this, to lay down one's life for one's friends"* (John 15:13). God's love is the driving force that gets a good neighbor to take action.

2. GET INVOLVED. Our society is plagued with a lack of involvement. Like the priest and the temple assistant in Jesus' parable, there is a growing tendency to go out of our way to avoid getting involved. A good neighbor cannot cross to the other side of the road and leave a truly needy person without help. A good neighbor gets involved. A good neighbor stoops to help. A good neighbor sacrifices. And a good neighbor eases the pain.

3. GET MERCIFUL. There's never been, nor will there ever be, a human being for whom God did not show some measure of mercy. We're all the recipients of His mercy, so let's pass a little of it on! May we strive to offer compassionate treatment to those around us. And may God grant us and develop within us a disposition to be kind.

4. GET HELP. None of us can do all that needs to be done by ourselves. So when the task seems overbearing or too much to accomplish on our own, we should enlist the help of other good neighbors who, out of the love of their hearts, are more than willing to get involved and to show mercy.

5. GET NEIGHBORLY. A combination of love, involvement, mercy, and help makes for a good neighbor. And that's what Jesus has called us to be. We cannot become hermits and adequately love our neighbors. We have to get to know them. The lesson that Jesus taught—and the lesson that we must live—is that we become good neighbors by showing compassion and kindness to everyone we encounter.

For Adults

■ **Topic:** Being a Neighbor

■ **Questions:** 1. How might the priest and the temple assistant justify—or rationalize—not getting involved with the injured traveler? 2. What did the Samaritan sacrifice to get involved with the wounded traveler? What might the Samaritan have potentially sacrificed? 3. How do you think Jesus' hearers might have reacted when they learned that a Samaritan was the hero of the story, and not the priest or the Levite? 4. Do you think the lawyer's attitude was changed after he had heard Jesus' parable? Explain your answer. 5. In what ways can you show mercy to your fellow human beings?

Good Samaritans at the Battlefront. Although Russian soldiers fighting in Chechnya have been suspicious and leery of practically everyone other than their fellow soldiers, there is one group of people that they have learned to trust: the Salvation Army. Surly Russian soldiers in Chechnya have been polite to Salvation Army aid workers and have even pinned the organization's emblems to their own lapels.

The Salvation Army has been among the few international religious groups working in the war-torn region, according to a report from the Religion News Service. And the Salvation Army aid workers have a big job. The state-sponsored religious organization, which has backed the Russian invasion of Chechnya, has made little effort to send humanitarian aid. Even the United Nations has typically considered the area too dangerous to enter, and instead has helped some 215,000 refugees in neighboring Ingushetia.

In the meantime, the Salvation Army has acted as good Samaritans by delivering $100,000 in baby food every month to Chechen mothers and infants in devastated villages. A package containing juice, dry milk, porridge, and puree has been enough to feed a child for three weeks. Chechen children often are born underweight, and mothers traumatized by the war aren't producing breast milk, the Salvation Army's Geoff Ryan explained.

Nearly all the Salvation Army staff in Chechnya are Muslim. Ryan is the only Christian, and he is determined to make sure people know about the Salvation Army's religious identity. "I want to make sure it is clear right up front that we are a Christian organization," he said. More than 40,000 pocket calendars clearly stating the organization's Christian principles have been given out.

Trashing Overlooked Human Beings. In an Indianapolis newspaper some years ago was this headline: "Homeless Woman Crushed with Trash." It seems that a homeless woman crawled into a dumpster to sleep, was loaded into a truck, compressed with the trash, and arrived at the incinerator, dead. They found her by her white tennis shoes and red windbreaker. Nearby residents had seen her climb into the dumpster, but when they heard the truck begin to grind, they did not warn the driver in time.

Accounts of the homeless being crushed—even crushed to death in trash bins—have actually become commonplace. It happened in Denver at least twice during the 1990s, in Washington once, in Los Angeles once, and in Atlanta once (just to name some incidents). How tragic it is that overlooked human beings are being gathered up with the trash!

Do Something. Theodore Roosevelt, the twenty-sixth president of the United States, seemed to always display a vigorous determination to get involved. He was Assistant Secretary of the Navy in 1898 when the Spanish-American War broke out, and he resigned that post to form the Rough Riders, a volunteer cavalry group that was to become famous for its charge up San Juan Hill in Cuba. An advocate of a venturesome foreign policy, Roosevelt effected the construction of the Panama Canal, won the Nobel Peace Prize for his successful intervention in the Russo-Japanese War, and dispatched the U.S. Fleet on a round-the-world tour.

Roosevelt's famous motto was "Speak softly and carry a big stick." But he had another motto that he wrote as advice to himself and others but that sounds as if it could have come from the mouth of the good Samaritan: "In a moment of decision, the best thing you can do is the right thing to do. The worst thing you can do is nothing."

	■ **TOPIC:** Who's My Neighbor?
FOR YOUTH	■ **QUESTIONS:** 1. Why did Jesus respond to the lawyer's question with a story instead of a straight answer? 2. What might have

caused the Samaritan to stop and help, while the others *"passed by on the other side"* (Luke 10:31-32)? 3. What is it that really made the Samaritan good? 4. How does your conscience feel when you avoid helping someone who might really need assistance? How does it feel after you've stopped to help? 5. Who are the people that might classify as your "neighbors"?

■ **ILLUSTRATIONS:**

Keeping to Ourselves. Our lack of involvement is showing up on a lot of fronts. Back in the 1970s, we bemoaned the death of Kitty Gennovese, who was murdered on the streets of New York in plain view of scores of people in a nearby apartment bu¹lding. During the incident, no one tried to stop the murder or even call the police.

Still today many scholars worry that we're becoming more and more isolated. One professor illustrates our increasing seclusion by pointing out what is happening to bowling. In his book, *Bowling Alone: America's Declining Social Capital,* Harvard political scientist Robert D. Putnam tells how more Americans are bowling than ever before. But bowling in organized leagues has plummeted. According to his statistics, "Between 1980 and 1993, the total numbers of bowlers in the United States increased by 10 percent, while league bowling decreased by 40 percent."

Putnam uses bowling only as an analogy of what is happening throughout our society. Fewer people are volunteering their time to work with churches and social agencies; fewer people are becoming members of social clubs; and more people are keeping to themselves. "Where once we played together, ate pizza together, kept score together, drank Coke together, while building up the social capital and trust necessary among members of a community that could bring about greater civic involvement, today we bowl alone."

Stranger in Need. In his book, *The Samaritan's Imperative*, Michael J. Christensen cites a story about two monks walking back to their monastery in the freezing cold. As they cross a bridge, the two monks hear a man calling for help in the ravine below. They want to stop, but they know they must reach the monastery before sunset or they will freeze to death. The first monk chooses to risk the danger of the cold in order to help another to safety. He climbs down into the ravine, gathers the wounded man into his arms, and slowly makes his way back to the monastery. The second monk has already gone on ahead, determined to get back safely before sunset.

Night comes, and with it, the bitter cold. As the first monk nears the monastery, he stumbles over something in the middle of the road. To his sorrow, it is the body of his spiritual brother who had gone on alone and had frozen to death. In seeking to save his life, he had lost it. But the compassionate monk, willing to lose his life, was kept warm by the heat exchanged from carrying the stranger in need.

Whom Shall I Send? Both Bob and Deloris are very active at the church I pastor, but if the truth be told, Deloris is more active than Bob. In fact, Deloris is more active than just about anyone else I know! When someone is needed to lead a Bible study for the kids, Deloris is there with an open Bible. When someone needs food, Deloris collects it and delivers it. When someone needs good Christian counsel, Deloris is there to give it in a heartbeat. When someone desires prayer, Deloris is on her knees beside him or her, praying fervently for that person. She is the perennial good Samaritan.

Just watching Deloris go sometimes saps Bob—and the rest of us—of energy. So you can imagine our stares when we were asking for volunteers to help with our children's church, and we saw Bob's hand shoot up before Deloris's. With his hand still in the air and our eyes glued on him, Bob, quoting his own version of Isaiah 6:8, said, "Here am I, Lord. Send Deloris!"

PARABLES ON PRAYER

BACKGROUND SCRIPTURE: Luke 18:1-14
DEVOTIONAL READING: Genesis 32:22-30

KEY VERSES: Jesus told them a parable about their
need to pray always and not to lose heart. Luke 18:1.

KING JAMES VERSION

LUKE 18:1 And he spake a parable unto them to this end, that men ought always to pray, and not to faint;

2 Saying, There was in a city a judge, which feared not God, neither regarded man:

3 And there was a widow in that city; and she came unto him, saying, Avenge me of mine adversary.

4 And he would not for a while: but afterward he said within himself, Though I fear not God, nor regard man;

5 Yet because this widow troubleth me, I will avenge her, lest by her continual coming she weary me.

6 And the Lord said, Hear what the unjust judge saith.

7 And shall not God avenge his own elect, which cry day and night unto him, though he bear long with them?

8 I tell you that he will avenge them speedily. Nevertheless when the Son of man cometh, shall he find faith on the earth?

9 And he spake this parable unto certain which trusted in themselves that they were righteous, and despised others:

10 Two men went up into the temple to pray; the one a Pharisee, and the other a publican.

11 The Pharisee stood and prayed thus with himself, God, I thank thee, that I am not as other men are, extortioners, unjust, adulterers, or even as this publican.

12 I fast twice in the week, I give tithes of all that I possess.

13 And the publican, standing afar off, would not lift up so much as his eyes unto heaven, but smote upon his breast, saying, God be merciful to me a sinner.

14 I tell you, this man went down to his house justified rather than the other: for every one that exalteth himself shall be abased; and he that humbleth himself shall be exalted.

NEW REVISED STANDARD VERSION

LUKE 18:1 Then Jesus told them a parable about their need to pray always and not to lose heart. 2 He said, "In a certain city there was a judge who neither feared God nor had respect for people. 3 In that city there was a widow who kept coming to him and saying, 'Grant me justice against my opponent.' 4 For a while he refused; but later he said to himself, 'Though I have no fear of God and no respect for anyone, 5 yet because this widow keeps bothering me, I will grant her justice, so that she may not wear me out by continually coming.'" 6 And the Lord said, "Listen to what the unjust judge says. 7 And will not God grant justice to his chosen ones who cry to him day and night? Will he delay long in helping them? 8 I tell you, he will quickly grant justice to them. And yet, when the Son of Man comes, will he find faith on earth?"

9 He also told this parable to some who trusted in themselves that they were righteous and regarded others with contempt: 10 "Two men went up to the temple to pray, one a Pharisee and the other a tax collector. 11 The Pharisee, standing by himself, was praying thus, 'God, I thank you that I am not like other people: thieves, rogues, adulterers, or even like this tax collector. 12 I fast twice a week; I give a tenth of all my income.' 13 But the tax collector, standing far off, would not even look up to heaven, but was beating his breast and saying, 'God, be merciful to me, a sinner!' 14 I tell you, this man went down to his home justified rather than the other; for all who exalt themselves will be humbled, but all who humble themselves will be exalted."

HOME BIBLE READINGS

BACKGROUND

The element of surprise was one of the common characteristics of Jesus' parables that helped to make such an impact on His hearers. And having an unexpected hero or heroine was one of the ways Jesus always seemed to manage a surprise in His stories. For instance, in the parable of the good Samaritan (Luke 10:25-37), most of Jesus' hearers would have expected the hero to be either the priest or the Levite. Instead, they are turned into villains and the hero becomes—of all people—a Samaritan. In the parable of the prodigal son (15:11-32), most of Jesus' hearers would have expected the hero to be the son who stayed home, not the one who left home and squandered his inheritance.

In the two parables on prayer recorded in 18:1-14, Jesus again made use of the element of surprise. In the parable of the unjust judge, most of Jesus' listeners would have guessed the judge to be the hero of the story. After all, the Jews had tended to limit the times for prayer because they didn't want to weary God with their constant petitioning. (Three times a day was accepted as a maximum.) So they might have expected the judge to have the helpless, badgering widow cast out of his courtroom. Instead, the persistent widow becomes the heroine.

In the parable of the Pharisee and the tax collector, Jesus' hearers would be even more likely to jump to conclusions regarding the hero. In the culture of the day, the Pharisees were considered good and the tax collectors were thought to be evil. The Pharisees were the strictest, most religious, and one of the most influential group of Jews at the time. In contrast, the tax collectors were regarded as traitors who worked for the occupying Roman government. The Pharisee standing and praying in the temple was in his element, while the tax collector, an unlikely candidate for any religious exercises, stood off in a corner so as not to be noticed. The Pharisee had status and respect, but the tax collector had neither. Surely the Pharisee knew more about how to pray than the tax collector. But again, a sudden twist in Jesus' story revealed a surprise hero.

NOTES ON THE PRINTED TEXT

In both of these parables about prayer, Luke plainly stated Jesus' purpose for telling the stories. The parable of the unjust judge and the persistent widow is *about [the disciples'] need to pray always and not to lose heart* (Luke 18:1).

Jesus knew that when praying people see no sign of the answer they long for, it's easy for them to become discouraged. Thus this first parable encourages God's people to keep on praying. The parable of the Pharisee and the tax collector, on the other hand, is told for *some who trusted in themselves that they were righteous and regarded others with contempt* (18:9). Thus this second parable brings out the attitude in which God's people should pray.

Jesus did not paint a glowing picture of the unjust judge. As the Savior described him, the judge was apathetic toward God as well as being unconcerned about the needs of others or even about their opinion of him. A destitute widow constantly petitioned this haughty judge (18:2-3). Along with orphans, widows were among the most helpless and vulnerable people in first-century society, for they had no family to uphold their causes. For a while the judge tried to ignore the widow, but she kept coming back, making use of her one strong character trait: persistence (18:4). After repeatedly hearing her make requests for fair treatment in court, the judge finally did as she asked for no greater reason than "*that she may not wear me out by continually coming*" (18:5).

Jesus then pointed out the moral of the story (18:6). Since even a dishonest judge can sometimes act justly—especially under constant pressure—how much more should we expect God to "*grant justice to his chosen ones who cry to him day and night? Will he delay long in helping them? I tell you, he will quickly grant justice to them*" (18:7-8). Of course, the vindication spoken of here must be understood in terms of God's timing. At the right moment, according to God's timing, justice will be granted speedily. And when Jesus asked whether He would "*find faith on the earth*" (18:8) when He returns, He was not suggesting that there would be no true believers. Rather, the Savior was questioning how many He would find who had persisted in their faith.

Jesus' second parable about prayer centered on two men who were worshiping in the temple at the same time. The Pharisee's prayer was uttered in an attitude of immense pride. As if to impress God, the religious leader noted a list of vices that he abstained from and another list of devout practices in which he engaged. It's noteworthy that these pious practices go well beyond even that which was prescribed by the Mosaic law. What the Pharisee boasted about himself may have been completely true, but the attitude of his prayer was all wrong (18:9-12).

The tax collector's prayer was uttered under great conviction of sin. His sense of unworthiness prevented him from even lifting up his eyes toward heaven, and he kept beating his breast in a display of sorrow. Even as he begged for mercy, he recognized who and what he was. His prayer is simple: "*God, be merciful to me, a sinner!*" (18:13).

The tax collector's prayer is the one that God accepted. As Jesus put it, "*I tell you, this man went down to his home justified rather than the other*" (18:14). Jesus then underscored the principle of His story: "*for all who exalt themselves will be humbled.*" In essence, we have nothing we can boast about to God. By contrast, *"all who humble themselves will be exalted."* When we come to God in repentance and faith, we experience His forgiveness and restoration.

SUGGESTIONS TO TEACHERS

In both of the parables recorded in Luke 18:1-14, Jesus provided a model for us to emulate. On the one hand, we are to pray like the persistent widow, *to pray always and not to lose heart* (18:1). On the other hand, we are to pray like the tax collector, who trusted in God for his righteousness and regarded others with compassion (18:14). Looking to the widow and the tax collector as examples, we can also understand what Jesus desires of us.

1. PRAY CONSTANTLY. *Pray without ceasing* (1 Thess. 5:17). Of course, this doesn't mean that we spend all our waking hours on our knees in prayer. But it does mean that we should stay in an attitude of prayer throughout the day, realizing God's abiding presence within us always.

2. PRAY PERSISTENTLY. May we not grow weary or discouraged in our prayer lives. May we never give up. May we be strong in our resolve to keep praying. May we believe that God will answer in His time. May we keep our requests continually before God's throne.

3. PRAY FAITHFULLY. As the children of God, we can pray with faith that God will answer us. We can trust that the Lord will help us quickly, granting us justice and mercy, fullness of life, and eternal salvation.

4. PRAY HUMBLY. The Lord is God, and we're not. We cannot allow our pride to hone in on our prayers as the Pharisee did. We must realize—while praying and at all times—that left to our own volition, we are neither good nor righteous nor pure. Like the tax collector, our prayers should be marked by meekness and a submissive respect for the power and majesty of God.

5. PRAY EARNESTLY. Jesus doesn't want us to be casual about prayer, but rather earnest, serious, intentional, determined, and disciplined. Julian of Norwich said prayer "is yearning, beseeching, and beholding"—an activity that involves desiring, imploring, and communing with God. While it is doubtful that Jesus wants us to pester God, the Savior most certainly wants us to be diligent in lifting up our requests to Him in prayer.

6. PRAY DEPENDENTLY. Remember that we completely depend on God, and because we do, our prayers should acknowledge that fact. And there is nothing wrong with being wholly dependent on Him and full of desire for His gifts that bring us abundant life.

FOR ADULTS

■ **TOPIC:** Praying Effectively

■ **QUESTIONS:** 1. When God seems slow to answer your prayers, what do you do to keep from getting discouraged? 2. How is God like the judge in the parable of the persistent widow? How is He unlike the judge?

3. In what ways is the persistent widow a good model for our prayer lives? In what ways is she not a good model? 4. Do you think it is difficult to eliminate pride and selfishness from your prayers? Explain your answer. 5. What concepts do both of these parables teach us about God?

■ ILLUSTRATIONS:

Encouragement for the Discouraged. In the fictional movie classic, *It's a Wonderful Life*, countless prayers are being lifted up for George Bailey, a man who has sacrificed his dreams on numerous occasions so that he could serve his family and community of Bedford Falls. His Uncle Billy's misplacement of $8,000 has led to a warrant being issued for his arrest, and George, now feeling as though his family would be better off with the proceeds of his life insurance than they would be with him alive, contemplates suicide.

As God entertains the stampede of prayers from George's family and friends, He sends for an angel named Clarence to attempt to show George that his is "a wonderful life." As Clarence begins to take note of his instructions, he asks, "What's the matter with him? Is he sick?" God responds by saying, "Worse. He's *discouraged*."

Discouragement can be a terrible feeling. But even though trials and difficulties rail at us, and even though it sometimes seems as if God doesn't hear our prayers, Jesus encourages us not to lose heart when we're praying. God will prove Himself trustworthy.

Hope and Pray. As vice president, George Bush represented the United States at the funeral of former Soviet leader Leonid Brezhnev in 1982. Bush said he was deeply moved by a silent protest carried out by Brezhnev's widow. She stood motionless by the coffin until seconds before it was closed. Then, just as the soldiers touched the lid, Brezhnev's wife performed an act of great courage and hope, a gesture that must surely rank as one of the most profound acts of civil disobedience ever committed: she reached down and made the sign of the cross on her husband's chest.

There, in the citadel of secular, atheistic power, the wife of the man who had run it all hoped and prayed that her husband was wrong. She hoped and prayed that there was another life, and that the life was best represented by Jesus, who died on the cross and rose again so that the lost might be saved.

Prayer for Mom. Dylan had been misbehaving and was sent to his room. After a while he emerged and informed his mother that he had thought it over and had even said a prayer.

"Fine," said the pleased mother. "If you ask God to help you not misbehave, He will help you." "Oh, I didn't ask Him to help me not misbehave," Dylan said. "I asked Him to help you put up with me!"

FOR YOUTH ■ **TOPIC:** No Bragging Allowed

■ **QUESTIONS:** 1. Do you ever get discouraged when it seems that God is taking a long time to answer your prayers? What can help you get past the discouragement? 2. How do you feel about the unjust judge in Jesus' parable, and also about the persistent widow? 3. In what ways is the tax collector a good model for our prayer lives? In what ways is he not a good model? 4. Why is it always best for us to approach God with humility rather than arrogance? 5. What do these two parables tell us about the character of God?

■ **ILLUSTRATIONS:**

Never Far Away. My wife, Jill, had taken her mother shopping in a nearby city when I got the call to come to church to try to fix the copier. We had never left our kids, Nathaniel, 9, and Gracie, 7, at home by themselves before, but since the church was only a half-mile away, I thought that this would be a good opportunity to see how they'd do.

So I brought in Bonhoeffer, our collie, to be their guard dog, locked all the doors, and gave them strict instructions not to answer the phone, go to the door, or turn on any electrical appliances other than the television. I figured I'd only be gone for a few minutes.

But the copier took longer than I expected to fix, a phone call came in while I was at the church, and one person dropped by who had some questions about their faith. I had been at the church for well over an hour when I finally made it back home. As I pulled into the driveway, I noticed that someone had taped a yellow sheet to our front door. I assumed that someone had knocked on the door, the kids didn't answer just as they had been instructed, and that the visitor decided to leave me a note.

But as I walked down our front walk, I noticed that the writing looked as though it was a child's. As I reached the door, I could tell that it was Gracie's handwriting. As soon as I had left, she promptly wrote a note and taped it to our front door. The brief note announced for the world to see: "9-year-old and 7-year-old and 1-year-old [the 1-year-old being the dog] at home alone. Please do not kill us!"

When I stopped laughing, I realized that I had taken so many precautions and set up so many rules that Gracie had decided to place her trust in her sign during my absence. She had overlooked the fact that I was not far away, that if she needed me she could reach me by phone, and that I loved her enough to drop everything to rescue her from any kind of trouble.

God is never far away. We can reach Him at a moment's notice through prayer. And He loves us enough to drop everything to rescue us from trouble.

The Secret Heart of All Our Prayers. In Frederick Buechner's [BEEK-nuhrs] book *Wishful Thinking: A Seeker's ABC*, the author writes, "The God you call upon will finally come, and even if He does not bring you the answer you want, He will bring you Himself. And maybe at the secret heart of all our prayers, that is what we are really praying for." Prayer isn't a way for us to get everything we want. It is but one of the ways we express our intense desire for God's presence, power, and peace.

God's Way Is Best. God's grace—the good things He grants us that we don't deserve—are not always readily clear. That's brought out in a poem called "God's Way" by Kao Chung-Ming:

> I asked the Lord
> for a bunch of flowers
> but instead He gave me an ugly cactus
> with many thorns.
> I asked the Lord
> for some beautiful butterflies
> but instead He gave me
> many ugly and dreadful worms.
> I was threatened.
> I was disappointed.
> I mourned.
> But after many days,
> suddenly,
> I saw the cactus bloom
> with many beautiful flowers
> and those worms became
> beautiful butterflies
> flying in the wind.
> God's way is the best way.

THE SHEEP AND THE GOATS

BACKGROUND SCRIPTURE: Matthew 25:31-46
DEVOTIONAL READING: 1 John 4:7-21

KEY VERSE: [Jesus said] "Just as you did it to one of the least of these who are members of my family, you did it to me." Matthew 25:40.

KING JAMES VERSION

MATTHEW 25:31 When the Son of man shall come in his glory, and all the holy angels with him, then shall he sit upon the throne of his glory:

32 And before him shall be gathered all nations: and he shall separate them one from another, as a shepherd divideth his sheep from the goats:

33 And he shall set the sheep on his right hand, but the goats on the left.

34 Then shall the King say unto them on his right hand, Come, ye blessed of my Father, inherit the kingdom prepared for you from the foundation of the world:

35 For I was an hungred, and ye gave me meat: I was thirsty, and ye gave me drink: I was a stranger, and ye took me in:

36 Naked, and ye clothed me: I was sick, and ye visited me: I was in prison, and ye came unto me.

37 Then shall the righteous answer him, saying, Lord, when saw we thee an hungred, and fed thee? or thirsty, and gave thee drink?

38 When saw we thee a stranger, and took thee in? or naked, and clothed thee?

39 Or when saw we thee sick, or in prison, and came unto thee?

40 And the King shall answer and say unto them, Verily I say unto you, Inasmuch as ye have done it unto one of the least of these my brethren, ye have done it unto me.

41 Then shall he say also unto them on the left hand, Depart from me, ye cursed, into everlasting fire, prepared for the devil and his angels:

42 For I was an hungred, and ye gave me no meat: I was thirsty, and ye gave me no drink:

43 I was a stranger, and ye took me not in: naked, and ye clothed me not: sick, and in prison, and ye visited me not.

44 Then shall they also answer him, saying, Lord, when saw we thee an hungred, or athirst, or a stranger, or naked, or sick, or in prison, and did not minister unto thee?

45 Then shall he answer them, saying, Verily I say unto you, Inasmuch as ye did it not to one of the least of these, ye did it not to me.

NEW REVISED STANDARD VERSION

MATTHEW 25:31 "When the Son of Man comes in his glory, and all the angels with him, then he will sit on the throne of his glory. 32 All the nations will be gathered before him, and he will separate people one from another as a shepherd separates the sheep from the goats, 33 and he will put the sheep at his right hand and the goats at the left. 34 Then the king will say to those at his right hand, 'Come, you that are blessed by my Father, inherit the kingdom prepared for you from the foundation of the world; 35 for I was hungry and you gave me food, I was thirsty and you gave me something to drink, I was a stranger and you welcomed me, 36 I was naked and you gave me clothing, I was sick and you took care of me, I was in prison and you visited me.' 37 Then the righteous will answer him, 'Lord, when was it that we saw you hungry and gave you food, or thirsty and gave you something to drink? 38 And when was it that we saw you a stranger and welcomed you, or naked and gave you clothing? 39 And when was it that we saw you sick or in prison and visited you?' 40 And the king will answer them, 'Truly I tell you, just as you did it to one of the least of these who are members of my family, you did it to me.' 41 Then he will say to those at his left hand, 'You that are accursed, depart from me into the eternal fire prepared for the devil and his angels; 42 for I was hungry and you gave me no food, I was thirsty and you gave me nothing to drink, 43 I was a stranger and you did not welcome me, naked and you did not give me clothing, sick and in prison and you did not visit me.' 44 Then they also will answer, 'Lord, when was it that we saw you hungry or thirsty or a stranger or naked or sick or in prison, and did not take care of you?' 45 Then he will answer them, 'Truly I tell you, just as you did not do it to one of the least of these, you did not do it to me.'"

9

BACKGROUND

At the close of Matthew 24, Jesus, while teaching His disciples on the Mount of Olives, told a parable contrasting the reward given to a master's faithful servants with the punishment meted out to his unfaithful servants. As Jesus continued teaching His disciples about His second coming, Matthew recorded three more parables on the same theme: that the faithful will be rewarded and the unfaithful punished.

In Jesus' parable of the 10 bridesmaids, the wise young women who remain prepared for the bridegroom's return take part in the marriage feast, while the foolish young women who fail to prepare themselves are excluded from the feast (25:1-13). In Jesus' parable of the talents, the two servants who invest and make gains on their talents are rewarded with more, while the worthless servant who buried his talent is thrown into the outer darkness (25:14-30). And in Jesus' parable of the sheep and the goats, those who respond to the needs of people around them inherit the kingdom, while those who fail to respond suffer the condemnation awaiting the devil and his angels (25:31-46).

The clear-cut distinction between each of the two groups reminds us of the parable with which Jesus closed His Sermon on the Mount, namely, about the wise man who built his house on a rock and the foolish man who built his house on the sand (7:24-27). The distinction also reminds us of Jesus' frequent warning: *"For the Son of Man is to come with his angels in the glory of his Father, and then he will repay everyone for what has been done"* (16:27).

The separation of sheep and goats would have sounded quite familiar to anyone in Palestine who had worked with both kinds of animals. During the day, sheep and goats were allowed to graze together; but at nightfall they were usually separated because sheep prefer the open night air while goats need the warmth of shelter. Of course, the shepherd stayed with the sheep through the night to protect them, and because he spent more time with them than he did the goats, his fondness for the sheep typically rose above that of his fondness for the goats. The sheep had a way of becoming familiar to him, and they depended on him for their safety. Thus would Jesus say, *"The one who enters by the gate is the shepherd of the sheep. The gatekeeper opens the gate for him, and the sheep hear his voice. He calls his own sheep by name and leads them out. When he has brought out all his own, he goes ahead of them, and the sheep follow him because they know his voice"* (John 10:2-4).

NOTES ON THE PRINTED TEXT

Sheep are mentioned more often in the Bible than any other animal. Kept more for their milk and wool than for their meat, they needed pasture and water, so the shepherd and his household moved with the sheep from place to place. Goats, of course, are also mentioned frequently in the Bible. These animals were an important source of milk and meat. Their hair was made into clothing and their skins into containers for water and wine.

Goats were viewed as a lesser animal than sheep perhaps because the Old Testament law prescribed that people's sins be placed upon a goat—the scapegoat—and sent away from the camp into the wilderness (Lev. 16:8-10). In the parable recorded in Matthew 25:31-46, the sheep represent the righteous, who demonstrate the reality of their faith by their actions. The goats, in contrast, represent the wicked, who demonstrate the reality of their unbelief by their actions.

Jesus was emphatic about the certainty of His second coming. He declared that He would come *"in his glory, and all the angels with him, [and] then he will sit on the throne of his glory"* (25:31). Following Jesus' return, all the nations will be gathered into His presence for a time of judgment, which will take place *"as a shepherd separates the sheep from the goats"* (25:32).

When this judgment will take place is debated, but two views are worth mentioning. One group says this judgment will occur at the end of the age at the great white throne (Rev. 20:11-15). At that time, the determination will be made as to who will enter the eternal kingdom of the saved and who will be relegated to eternal punishment in hell. Another group says this judgment will occur when Jesus comes to set up a kingdom on earth. At that time, the determination will be made as to who will enter His kingdom based on the way they treated *"these who are members of my family"* (Matt. 25:40) during the preceding time of great distress (24:15-22).

Who are these members of the King's family? Some say they are all Christians; others say they are the Jews; still others say they are suffering people everywhere. But debating the identity of these members of the King's family is similar to the lawyer's testing Jesus with the question, *"And who is my neighbor?"* (Luke 10:29). The point of the parable of the sheep and goats, like the point of the parable of the good Samaritan, is not so much concerned with the "who" but rather with the "what." In other words, God wants us to reach out to others in need.

For the sheep on Jesus' right-hand side (the place of honor; Matt. 25:33), the King will offer an invitation to *"inherit the kingdom prepared for you from the foundation of the world"* (25:34). The reason the King will give for His invitation is that the righteous loved and took care of Him when He was in need. But those who are rewarded won't be able to recall a time when they did this for the King

(25:35-39). Then the king will tell them that *"just as you did it to one of the least of these who are members of my family, you did it to me"* (25:40). Thus the divine blessing will be given to those who served with no thought of getting a reward. Their service arose out of their love and concern for others.

For the goats on Jesus' left-hand side (the place of dishonor), the King will send them away *"into the eternal fire prepared for the devil and his angels"* (25:41). The reason the King will give for this decision is that they failed to look after Him when He was in need. The condemned, however, won't be able to recall a time when they failed to help Him (25:42-44). Then the King will tell them that *"just as you did not do it to one of the least of these, you did not do it to me"* (25:45). The wicked will be sentenced to eternal punishment because they showed by their actions that they worshiped and served themselves (25:46).

SUGGESTIONS TO TEACHERS

Though we may be unaware of it at the time, when we minister to the deprived and dispossessed, we are, indeed, ministering to the Lord. Still, even ministering to the Lord does not earn us our salvation. The New Testament teaches that our deeds of kindness in and of themselves cannot secure us everlasting life. Yet Scripture also teaches that when faith is real, it must, of necessity, express itself through a lifestyle of concern for others. For example, the Book of James reminds us that *faith by itself, if it has no works, is dead* (2:17). Thus, if our commitment to God is real, it will show in our actions. Clearly, then, our serving and meeting the needs of others is not a substitute for our faith in Christ, but rather an affirmation of our trust in Him.

1. ACTS OF MERCY. Jesus' parable of the sheep and the goats describes acts of mercy we all can do every day—feeding the hungry, giving drinks to the thirsty, welcoming strangers, clothing the naked, taking care of the sick, and visiting the imprisoned. None of these deeds of kindness depend on our being wealthy, skillful, or intelligent. They are simple acts of mercy and compassion that are freely received just as much as they are freely given.

2. ACTS OF BELIEF. The most genuine evidence of our belief in Christ is in the way we act, especially toward those who can use our help. Jesus calls us to treat others as if they were Him. Of course, carrying out this mandate is no easy task. But what we do for others demonstrates what we really think about Jesus' words: *"Truly I tell you, just as you did it to one of the least of these who are members of my family, you did it to me"* (Matt. 25:40).

3. ACTS OF CONCERN. God looks for us to have sincere, heartfelt concern for our fellow human beings, and especially so for our brothers and sisters in Christ. Because of the command to *"love your neighbor as yourself"* (22:39), we have no excuse to neglect those around us who have deep needs. And we cannot hand over the responsibility of caring and helping to our government or even to our church. Jesus demands our personal involvement in caring for others' needs.

| FOR ADULTS | |

■ **TOPIC:** Serving Christ by Serving Others

■ **QUESTIONS:** 1. Do you consider Jesus' story more of a parable or more of a prophecy? Explain your answer. 2. Why do you think the King waited until the scene of the judgment to separate the sheep from the goats? 3. In what ways are those who carry out these acts of mercy similar to those who don't? In what ways are they different? 4. Who do you think are *"the least of these"* (Matt. 25:40) mentioned in Jesus' parable? 5. What does His parable teach us about our Christian responsibility to others in need?

■ **ILLUSTRATIONS:**

I Was Thirsty, and You Gave Me Milk. Dan West, a Christian relief worker in Spain during the Spanish Civil War, was handing out cups of powdered milk to a long line of hungry children on both sides of the conflict. All too often, the milk ran out before the line ended. As a farmer, Dan's response was practical. "Wouldn't it be better," he reasoned, "to supply families with an ongoing source of nutritious milk so that parents could feed their children themselves without having to depend on powdered milk from abroad?"

When Dan shared his idea back home in Indiana, his friends agreed. "I'll give a calf, if someone else will raise her," one person said. Soon afterward, the first boatload of heifers sailed in 1944, not to Spain, because the war there was soon over, but rather to Puerto Rico. And right from the start, families who received the heifers made a commitment to pass on their gift animal's first female offspring to another family in need.

In the 57 years since then, a parade of animals—some familiar (like goats, cows, chickens, sheep, and rabbits) and some exotic (like camels, water buffalo, llamas, and guinea pigs)—has circled the world. The oldest U.S. hunger organization, Heifer Project International, has helped more than 23 million people in 110 countries move toward self-reliance.

Showing That We Care. In one of the uplifting stories in *Chicken Soup for the Soul at Work*, Rick Phillips, a management trainer for the Circle K Corporation, tells about how hard it is to retain quality employees. During the management seminars that he leads, he asks the participants, "What has caused you to stay long enough to become a manager?" At one of his seminars, Cynthia, a new manager, slowly answered with her voice almost breaking, "It was a $19 baseball glove."

Cynthia told the group that she originally took a Circle K clerk job as an interim position while she looked for something better. On her second or third day behind the counter, she received a phone call from her nine-year-old son, Jessie. He needed a baseball glove for Little League. She explained that as a single mother, money was very tight, and her first check would have to go for paying bills. Perhaps she could buy his baseball glove with her second or third check.

When Cynthia arrived for work the next morning, Patricia, the store manager, asked her to come to the small room in back of the store that served as an office. Cynthia wondered if she had done something wrong or left some part of her job incomplete from the day before. She was concerned and confused.

Patricia handed her a box. "I overheard you talking to your son yesterday," she said, "and I know that it's hard to explain things to kids. This is a baseball glove for Jessie because he may not understand how important he is, since you have to pay bills before you can buy gloves. You know we can't pay good people like you as much as we would like to; but we do care, and I want you to know you are important to us."

The thoughtfulness, empathy, and love of this convenience store manager demonstrates vividly that people remember more how much an employer cares than how much the employer pays. And what an important lesson to be learned for the price of a Little League baseball glove!

God Blesses the Cheerful Giver. Some years ago a church in northern California decided to give away its building fund—and it received an even bigger blessing. The congregation had raised $120,000 toward its multimillion dollar sanctuary when pastor David heard about the needs of another ministry in Los Angeles, California. The center had bought the former Queen of Angels Hospital in the city and was refurbishing nine buildings as a massive center for its ministry.

David sensed that God wanted the building fund money to go to that undertaking, not to his church. So he received approval from his congregation in 1997, and soon afterward he was presenting a check for $120,000 to pastor Tommy, who was developing the center along with his son Matthew.

But soon after David gave away the building fund money, new and more money began pouring into his church's building project. Donations came in from unexpected sources, such as nonprofit foundations, other ministries, as well as private individuals. David and his congregation dedicated their new multimillion dollar facility to the Lord on Easter Sunday of 2000. And they moved into the facility debt-free!

Starting to Get Better. Pastor Duane Windemiller tells about how years ago he was conducting a funeral at a church in New Hampshire. The funeral was for an old family physician who had lived 102 years. A woman stood up in the middle of the service and, with tears making tracks down her face, said, "Whenever we heard his old Model T turning into our yard, we started to get better."

"Yes!" In a 1998 *Our Daily Bread* devotional, it was noted that "on April 19, 1995, a bomb destroyed the federal building in Oklahoma City, killing 169 people. On the same day, an Ohio couple, Julie and Bruce Madsen, set out on a cross-country odyssey to write a book about hope and goodness in America.

"In their search, the Madsens found stories of hope in the lives of ordinary people responding to adversity and tragedy. For example, a minister leads prayer vigils at the site of every murder in his midwestern city, and a physician has devoted his career to helping the homeless. 'By their fruits you will know them,' Julie wrote in one of her stories. She wondered, 'Do we leave people feeling uplifted, or drained and downhearted?'

"If the Madsens had met you or me, would they have discovered a story of hope? If Christ is at work in and through us, the answer can be a resounding 'Yes!'"

FOR YOUTH

■ TOPIC: On the Other Hand . . .

■ QUESTIONS: 1. What do you think was the King's reason for separating the sheep from the goats? 2. How are the sheep and the goats alike? How are they different? 3. Why do you think Jesus called those needing help *"the least of these who are members of my family"* (Matt. 25:40)? 4. How might the thought of serving Jesus help you serve people you wouldn't normally reach out to? 5. How have those whom you've helped with acts of kindness reminded you of Jesus?

■ **ILLUSTRATIONS:**

Seeing the Face of Christ. In a 1997 *Sojourners* article, Jim Forest writes how for six years Dorothy Day looked for a way to connect her social conscience with her religious conversion. Finally, her search gave birth to a relief movement in May 1933. Originally it was just a newspaper, but within weeks of the paper's publication, the first house of hospitality—her apartment—came into being simply because Dorothy couldn't turn away a homeless woman who had seen the paper and came asking for help. Today there are nearly 175 houses of hospitality, not to mention the many more places of welcome that wouldn't exist had it not been for Dorothy Day's struggle to live her faith with directness and simplicity.

At the core of Dorothy's life was her experience of ultimate beauty—Christ's face hidden in the faces of America's human castoffs. "Those who cannot see the face of Christ in the poor," she used to say, "are atheists indeed."

Pass on the Kindness. In a little poem called "Pass It On," Henry Burton wrote:

Have you had a kindness shown?
Pass it on;
'Twas not given for thee alone,
Pass it on;
Let it travel down the years,
Let it wipe another's tears,

'Till in Heaven the deed appears—
Pass it on.

Aim at Heaven. C. S. Lewis knew that for us to be effective Christian servants, we must keep our eyes on Jesus and we must keep as our goal the kingdom of heaven. He has been quoted as saying, "If you read history, you will find that the Christians who did the most for the present world were just those who thought most of the next. The apostles themselves, who set on foot the conversion of the Roman Empire, the great people who built up the Middle Ages, the English evangelicals who abolished the slave trade, all left their mark on earth, precisely because their minds were occupied with heaven. It is since Christians have largely ceased to think about the other world that they have become so ineffective in this one. Aim at heaven and you will get earth 'thrown in.' Aim at earth and you will get neither."

Being Happy with God. Mother Teresa taught those who joined her in her mission to minister to the destitute and dying of India that "being happy with God means loving as He loves, helping as He helps, giving as He gives, serving as He serves, rescuing as He rescues, being with Him 24 hours, touching Him in His distressing disguise."

Rewards and Responsibilities

BACKGROUND SCRIPTURE: Matthew 5:1-16
DEVOTIONAL READING: Psalm 24

KEY VERSES: "Let your light shine before others, so that they may see your good works and give glory to your Father in heaven." Matthew 5:16.

KING JAMES VERSION

MATTHEW 5:1 And seeing the multitudes, he went up into a mountain: and when he was set, his disciples came unto him:

2 And he opened his mouth, and taught them, saying,

3 Blessed are the poor in spirit: for theirs is the kingdom of heaven.

4 Blessed are they that mourn: for they shall be comforted.

5 Blessed are the meek: for they shall inherit the earth.

6 Blessed are they which do hunger and thirst after righteousness: for they shall be filled.

7 Blessed are the merciful: for they shall obtain mercy.

8 Blessed are the pure in heart: for they shall see God.

9 Blessed are the peacemakers: for they shall be called the children of God.

10 Blessed are they which are persecuted for righteousness' sake: for theirs is the kingdom of heaven.

11 Blessed are ye, when men shall revile you, and persecute you, and shall say all manner of evil against you falsely, for my sake.

12 Rejoice, and be exceeding glad: for great is your reward in heaven: for so persecuted they the prophets which were before you.

13 Ye are the salt of the earth: but if the salt have lost his savour, wherewith shall it be salted? it is thenceforth good for nothing, but to be cast out, and to be trodden under foot of men.

14 Ye are the light of the world. A city that is set on an hill cannot be hid.

15 Neither do men light a candle, and put it under a bushel, but on a candlestick; and it giveth light unto all that are in the house.

16 Let your light so shine before men, that they may see your good works, and glorify your Father which is in heaven.

NEW REVISED STANDARD VERSION

MATTHEW 5:1 When Jesus saw the crowds, he went up the mountain; and after he sat down, his disciples came to him. 2 Then he began to speak, and taught them, saying:

3 "Blessed are the poor in spirit, for theirs is the kingdom of heaven.

4 "Blessed are those who mourn, for they will be comforted.

5 "Blessed are the meek, for they will inherit the earth.

6 "Blessed are those who hunger and thirst for righteousness, for they will be filled.

7 "Blessed are the merciful, for they will receive mercy.

8 "Blessed are the pure in heart, for they will see God.

9 "Blessed are the peacemakers, for they will be called children of God.

10 "Blessed are those who are persecuted for righteousness' sake, for theirs is the kingdom of heaven.

11 "Blessed are you when people revile you and persecute you and utter all kinds of evil against you falsely on my account. 12 Rejoice and be glad, for your reward is great in heaven, for in the same way they persecuted the prophets who were before you.

13 "You are the salt of the earth; but if salt has lost its taste, how can its saltiness be restored? It is no longer good for anything, but is thrown out and trampled under foot.

14 "You are the light of the world. A city built on a hill cannot be hid. 15 No one after lighting a lamp puts it under the bushel basket, but on the lampstand, and it gives light to all in the house. 16 In the same way, let your light shine before others, so that they may see your good works and give glory to your Father in heaven."

10

Monday, November 5	Galatians 3:19-29	*The Law in Perspective*
Tuesday, November 6	Luke 11:37-52	*Burdensome Laws Are Barriers to Faith*
Wednesday, November 7	Luke 12:1-7	*Hypocrisy Doesn't Work*
Thursday, November 8	Matthew 5:21-26	*Murder, Anger, or Reconciliation*
Friday, November 9	Matthew 5:27-37	*Lust: Adultery in the Heart*
Saturday, November 10	Matthew 5:38-48	*Be Perfect*
Sunday, November 11	Matthew 5:17-20	*Fulfilling, Not Abolishing, the Law*

BACKGROUND

The Gospel of Matthew places a special emphasis on the teaching of Jesus, and it does so in a way that is unique. One of the interesting features of Matthew's writing is that he grouped Jesus' teaching into five distinct sections. The Sermon on the Mount (chapters 5—7) is the first of these sections. The second section appears in chapter 10, in which Jesus instructed His disciples about their mission of spreading the Gospel. The third section appears in chapter 13, in which Jesus told parables about the kingdom of God. The fourth section appears in chapter 18, in which Jesus taught about life in the Christian community. And the fifth section appears in chapters 23—25, in which Jesus taught about His second coming and judgment.

A straightforward reading of Matthew 4:1—5:2 gives the impression that Jesus taught the Sermon on the Mount during the first year of His public ministry. Likewise, a straightforward reading of 5:1—7:29 suggests that Jesus delivered His sermon at one time in one location.

Despite this impression, the relation between the Sermon on the Mount recorded in Matthew and the Sermon on the Plain recorded in Luke 6:17-49 remains unclear. Only a portion of the first appears in the second, and 34 of the verses in Matthew's sermon occur in different contexts in Luke. Apparently Jesus repeated some of His weightier sayings in different forms, with varied application, to meet the need of the situation.

Observations such as these have led some to argue that the Sermon on the Mount is a compilation of various teachings that were given on different occasions in several places. According to this view, Luke presented an abbreviated version of the longer sermon recorded in Matthew. Matthew either took a single sermon and expanded it with other relevant teachings of Christ, or he took numerous teachings of Jesus and weaved them into a coherent, thematically related unit.

Those who say the Sermon on the Mount and the Sermon on the Plain are the same argue that the differences between the two discourses can be accounted for or harmonized. It is also maintained that the similarity of the beginnings, endings, and subject matter strengthens the impression that the two passages represent the same discourse.

Despite the differences of opinion, there are some broad conclusions that can be drawn. First, an examination of Matthew 5:1—7:29 reveals that it is not a mere patchwork of isolated and unrelated sayings. Rather it reads as a seamless whole. Thus, one should study the passage as a complete literary unit. Second, one should consider the sermon to be an accurate and reliable account of what Jesus taught. This remains true regardless of whether this discourse was given at one time or represents material He repeated numerous times under a variety of circumstances.

NOTES ON THE PRINTED TEXT

Matthew 5—7 is called the Sermon on the Mount because Jesus delivered this series of messages on one of the gently sloping hillsides at the northwest corner of the Sea of Galilee, probably not far from Capernaum. As Jesus' popularity soared, huge crowds began to follow Him (5:1-2). His disciples could easily have been tempted to feel proud, prestigious, and possessive. Perhaps that's why Jesus warned them about the challenges they faced. He told them that instead of expecting fame and fortune, they should expect to mourn, face hunger, and be persecuted. And though their reward may not come in this life, Jesus assured them that they would reap rich heavenly rewards for embodying certain spiritual qualities (5:3-12).

The Beatitudes are the first section of the Sermon on the Mount. The Beatitudes are named from the Latin word *beatitudo,* a term that refers to a state of joy or bliss. The Beatitudes are a list of both the responsibilities and blessings of discipleship. In His discourse, Jesus implied much more than just being happy. Worldly joy is a fleeting emotion that's dependent on one's outward circumstance. Blessedness, however, is a deep-seated, long-lasting spiritual joy that comes from God and is independent of one's outward circumstances.

Each beatitude recorded in 5:3-12 seems to clash with some worldly value. For instance, our need for God clashes with our longing for personal independence; our mourning clashes with our desire for happiness at any cost; and the call to be gentle and lowly clashes with our innate craving for power. Clearly, Jesus neither wanted nor expected His disciples to be like everybody else. Of course, He knew that by them being different, they would face intense opposition, especially in the form of persecution. Nevertheless, those who cultivated these spiritual qualities were promised eternal blessings.

"The poor in spirit" (5:3)—those who humbly acknowledge their spiritual need—are blessed because they will receive as a gift the kingdom of heaven. *"Those who mourn"* (5:4)—those who grieve over their spiritual poverty—are blessed because God will forgive and comfort them. *"The meek"* (5:5)—those who humbly submit to God—are blessed because they are promised the earth as an inheritance.

"Those who hunger and thirst for righteousness" (5:6)—those who earnestly long for all that God offers and requires—are blessed because God will satisfy

their desire for salvation. *"The merciful"* (5:7)—those who show kindness and forgiveness to the undeserving—are blessed because they will receive from God the compassion they've shown to people. *"The pure in heart"* (5:8)—those whose lives are marked by virtue and integrity—are blessed because they will enjoy an intimate relationship with the living God.

"The peacemakers" (5:9)—those who work for peace in their families, schools, churches, businesses, and communities—are blessed because they will be known as spiritual children in God's heavenly family. *"Those who are persecuted for righteousness' sake"* (5:10-12)—those who suffer for truth, uprightness, and goodness—are blessed because they will receive the divine kingdom.

It is clear from this teaching of Jesus that position, authority, and money are simply not important in His kingdom. What is important is His followers' faithful and humble obedience. Such a message would have challenged the proud and legalistic religious leaders of the day.

Jesus summed up the Beatitudes by reminding His disciples that their character, integrity, and way of living should stand out from the rest of the world. As *"the salt of the earth"* (5:13) and *"the light of the world"* (5:14), they were to be a positive moral influence, that is, a reflection of God's love. Also, they were to radiate the knowledge and presence of God to people living in spiritual darkness or ignorance (5:15).

Given these statements, it's not surprising why Jesus told His disciples to *"let your light shine before others"* (5:16). He wanted the unsaved to see the good works that God's grace had produced in the lives of believers. As a result, the lost might be drawn to God's saving power.

Suggestions to Teachers

Jesus longs for us to both have and demonstrate the spiritual qualities He possesses. There are some virtues that we would really like to have; yet we find them difficult to possess and express. There are other qualities that seem undesirable to us, for they run counter to our own worldly values.

In either case, Jesus still wants us to be different, to be a purifying agent in a sinful world, to be *"the salt of the earth"* (Matt. 5:13). He also yearns for us to stand out like *"a city built on a hill"* (5:14). If we accept Jesus' offer of love, grace, and mercy, He will empower us to be a source of spiritual *"light to all in the house"* (5:15). When this is consistently true for us, there are certain virtues that will become increasingly evident in our lives.

1. BE DISTINCTIVE. Living for God sometimes means being different from the people of the world. We have to be willing to love when others hate, to give when others take, and to help when others abuse. But by giving up our own rights in order to serve other people, we'll one day receive the eternal rewards God has in store for us.

2. BE HUMBLE. Reflecting Jesus' humility isn't easy, especially when the world around us is grasping for power and pride. Admittedly, though our Christian faith may make us unpopular, it sometimes can actually bring us a certain measure of attention. At those times, if we don't remember who we are and who God is, we can easily find ourselves using our Christian notoriety to promote our own personal interests.

3. BE UNPOPULAR. Surely there will be times when our Christian lifestyle will cause us to be alienated from and ostracized by others. Remember that we were forewarned; but we're also promised a heavenly reward for living for Jesus.

4. BE NOTICED. The only way we'll ever get *"persecuted for righteousness' sake"* (Matt. 5:10) is if it becomes known that we're followers of Christ. We can't always run and hide from the truth that we belong to God. In fact, our being verbally, emotionally, and even physically persecuted proves that we are being faithful to our Lord.

5. BE SALTY. In ancient times, people used salt to season and preserve their food and to bring out its flavor. In a figurative sense, we need to have a wholesomeness about us that enables us to be a blessing and a moral preservative in the world. Otherwise, if we become too much like the world, we become morally insipid.

6. BE SHINY. We are not *the* light of the world; Jesus fulfills that role. But we are lesser *lights* in the world, reflecting His presence and purity in the same way that the moon, in the dark night sky, reflects the radiance of the sun. Thus, if we live for Christ, we will shine like lights, showing others what Jesus is like. May we be beacons for the Lord, shining our light to the rest of the world!

FOR ADULTS

■ **TOPIC:** Finding Supreme Happiness
■ **QUESTIONS:** 1. In what ways do all of the Beatitudes relate to each other? 2. How do each of the Christian spiritual qualities relate to the promise that follows it? 3. Which of the Beatitudes do you think is the easiest to carry out? Which is the hardest? 4. In what ways would fulfilling the Beatitudes help us to be "salt" and "light" in the world? 5. How has your Christian faith given you contentment with life?

■ **ILLUSTRATIONS:**

How to Live. A psychiatrist and a student of Sigmund Freud, James Tucker Fisher, closed his book called *A Few Buttons Missing: The Case Book of a Psychiatrist* (which he co-wrote with Lowell S. Hawley) with this final note:

"I dreamed of writing a handbook that would be simple, practical, easy to understand, and easy to follow. It would tell people how to live—what thoughts and attitudes and philosophies to cultivate and what pitfalls to avoid, in seeking mental health. I attended every symposium . . . possible, . . . and took notes on the wise words of teachers and my colleagues who were leaders in the field.

"And then quite by accident, I discovered that such a work had already been completed. . . . If you were to take the sum total of all the authoritative articles ever written by the most qualified of psychologists and psychiatrists on the subject of mental hygiene—if you were to combine them and refine them and cleave out the excess verbiage . . . you would have an awkward and incomplete summation of the Sermon on the Mount."

When People Revile You and Persecute You. During World War II, when the Nazi armies were in almost every country of Europe, King Christian of Denmark stubbornly resisted them. His country was quite small compared to the powerful Third Reich, and the king knew he could not win on the battlefield, but he still put up a valiant moral struggle.

One day he observed a Nazi flag flying above one of his public buildings. He reminded the German commander that this was contrary to the treaty between the two nations. Then he told the occupying forces, "The flag must be removed before twelve o'clock; otherwise I will send a soldier to remove it."

At five minutes before noon, the flag was flying, and the king announced that he was sending a soldier to take it down. "The soldier will be shot," the Nazi officer replied. Then King Christian calmly said, "I think I should tell you that I will be that soldier."

Blessed Are the Peacemakers. William Penn's colony of Pennsylvania pioneered two experiments. The first was the Quaker guarantee of total freedom of conscience. The second was its security system. Unguarded by fort or by soldier, the colony protected itself from attack by a just social policy that treated native Americans fairly and as friends. For 70 years the colony was absolutely safe, its borders respected and its people unharmed. But all this changed in 1756, when the British government ordered the colony to bear arms against the French, which drove the Quakers from power and the colony into the Seven Years' War.

FOR YOUTH

■ TOPIC: The Good Life!

■ QUESTIONS: 1. What do you think it means to be *"poor in spirit"* (Matt. 5:3)? 2.What erroneous ideas might people have about meekness (vs. 5)? 3. What would you say it means to be *"pure in heart"* (vs. 8)? How is this possible in our age of materialism and vice? 4. Why is it possible to rejoice when we are persecuted? 5. How do the promises of the Beatitudes compare with what most people in the world really value?

■ ILLUSTRATIONS:

For Righteousness' Sake. The day after the funeral for Cassie Bernall, who was gunned down in the Columbine, Colorado, school shooting, Amy Goldstein of

The *Washington Post* wrote, "For her funeral yesterday morning, friends of Cassie Bernall had stitched together a video, interspersing their remembrances of the Columbine High School junior with photographs of the young woman with long blond hair, a wide smile, and slender cross at her throat.

"'Her eyes shone with Christ's light,' one of the friends said in the video.

"'Cassie was one of the strongest Christians I've ever known,' said another friend. 'I knew that she was so willing to die for Christ.'

"Added a third: 'I just thank God she went out . . . a martyr. She went out dying for what she believed.'

"As the first jolt of tragedy has begun yielding to a deeper search for meaning, the deaths of at least a few of Littleton's dozen murdered teenagers are being understood—locally and in churches across the United States—through the prism of Christianity. As the identities of the victims began to seep out last week, it became evident that some apparently had been selected by Eric Harris and Dylan Klebold, the gun-wielding pair who rampaged the school, because of their fervent religious faith."

Salt of the Earth. A television news director says God gave her a job to do. "I have no problem seeing myself as a missionary," Paula Madison of WNBC in New York said in a 2000 interview. "I genuinely believe God put me here for a reason. I see myself as an agent of change for the better."

Madison has downplayed sensationalism. Since taking the job back in 1996, she has looked for stories about "the least among us." And she has increased religion coverage, hoping to prove that if she can set a different tone and still be successful, other stations will follow. She attained that goal in 1999 when News Channel 4 finished first among local newscasts in the ratings for the first time in 16 years.

In addition to assigning reporters, Madison, 47, selects off-screen personnel, and sets the tone, discipline, and style of the newsroom. She says she prays every day that she and the reporters she assigns to stories will exercise good judgment, wisdom, and sensitivity. "I want measured, reasonable discourse," she said.

In the Same Way They Persecuted the Prophets. When Mother Teresa first began her work among the dying on the streets of Calcutta, India, she was obstructed at every turn by government officials and orthodox Hindus, who were suspicious of her motives and used their authority to harass her and frustrate her efforts. She and her colleagues were insulted and threatened with physical violence.

One day a shower of stones and bricks rained down on the women as they tried to bring the dying to their humble shelter. Eventually Mother Teresa dropped to her knees before the mob. "Kill me!" she cried in Bengali, her arms outstretched in a gesture of crucifixion, "and I'll be in heaven all the sooner." The rabble withdrew, but soon the harassment increased with even more irrational acts of violence, and louder demands were made of officials to expel the foreigner.

One morning, Mother Teresa noticed a gathering of people outside the nearby Kali Temple, one of the holy places for Hindus in Calcutta. As she drew closer, she saw a man stretched out on the street with turned-up eyes and a face drained of blood. A triple braid denoted that he was of the Brahman caste, not of the temple priests. No one dared to touch him, for people recognized he was dying from cholera.

Mother Teresa went to him, bent down, took the body of the Brahman priest in her arms, and carried him to her shelter. Day and night she nursed him, and eventually he recovered. Over and over again he would say to the people, "For 30 years I have worshiped a Kali of stone. But I have met in this gentle woman a real Kali, a Kali of flesh and blood." Never again were stones thrown at Mother Teresa and her colleagues.

"But I Say to You"

BACKGROUND SCRIPTURE: Matthew 5:17-48
DEVOTIONAL READING: Amos 5:4-15

KEY VERSES: "Do not think that I have come to abolish the law or the prophets; I have come not to abolish but to fulfill." Matthew 5:17.

KING JAMES VERSION

MATTHEW 5:17 Think not that I am come to destroy the law, or the prophets: I am not come to destroy, but to fulfil.

18 For verily I say unto you, Till heaven and earth pass, one jot or one tittle shall in no wise pass from the law, till all be fulfilled.

19 Whosoever therefore shall break one of these least commandments, and shall teach men so, he shall be called the least in the kingdom of heaven: but whosoever shall do and teach them, the same shall be called great in the kingdom of heaven.

20 For I say unto you, That except your righteousness shall exceed the righteousness of the scribes and Pharisees, ye shall in no case enter into the kingdom of heaven. . . .

38 Ye have heard that it hath been said, An eye for an eye, and a tooth for a tooth:

39 But I say unto you, That ye resist not evil: but whosoever shall smite thee on thy right cheek, turn to him the other also.

40 And if any man will sue thee at the law, and take away thy coat, let him have thy cloke also.

41 And whosoever shall compel thee to go a mile, go with him twain.

42 Give to him that asketh thee, and from him that would borrow of thee turn not thou away.

43 Ye have heard that it hath been said, Thou shalt love thy neighbour, and hate thine enemy.

44 But I say unto you, Love your enemies, bless them that curse you, do good to them that hate you, and pray for them which despitefully use you, and persecute you;

45 That ye may be the children of your Father which is in heaven: for he maketh his sun to rise on the evil and on the good, and sendeth rain on the just and on the unjust.

46 For if ye love them which love you, what reward have ye? do not even the publicans the same?

47 And if ye salute your brethren only, what do ye more than others? do not even the publicans so?

48 Be ye therefore perfect, even as your Father which is in heaven is perfect.

NEW REVISED STANDARD VERSION

MATTHEW 5:17 "Do not think that I have come to abolish the law or the prophets; I have come not to abolish but to fulfill. 18 For truly I tell you, until heaven and earth pass away, not one letter, not one stroke of a letter, will pass from the law until all is accomplished. 19 Therefore, whoever breaks one of the least of these commandments, and teaches others to do the same, will be called least in the kingdom of heaven; but whoever does them and teaches them will be called great in the kingdom of heaven. 20 For I tell you, unless your righteousness exceeds that of the scribes and Pharisees, you will never enter the kingdom of heaven. . . .

38 "You have heard that it was said, 'An eye for an eye and a tooth for a tooth.' 39 But I say to you, Do not resist an evildoer. But if anyone strikes you on the right cheek, turn the other also; 40 and if anyone wants to sue you and take your coat, give your cloak as well; 41 and if anyone forces you to go one mile, go also the second mile. 42 Give to everyone who begs from you, and do not refuse anyone who wants to borrow from you.

43 "You have heard that it was said, 'You shall love your neighbor and hate your enemy.' 44 But I say to you, Love your enemies and pray for those who persecute you, 45 so that you may be children of your Father in heaven; for he makes his sun rise on the evil and on the good, and sends rain on the righteous and on the unrighteous. 46 For if you love those who love you, what reward do you have? Do not even the tax collectors do the same? 47 And if you greet only your brothers and sisters, what more are you doing than others? Do not even the Gentiles do the same? 48 Be perfect, therefore, as your heavenly Father is perfect."

HOME BIBLE READINGS

BACKGROUND

Seven times in the Gospels the phrase "the law and the prophets" is mentioned as a cohesive unit; four of those times occur in Matthew, and two of those appear in the Sermon on the Mount. Among the Gospels only Mark does not include the phrase. Every time Matthew and Luke mention it, Jesus Himself spoke the words. The only time in the Gospels when Jesus did not utter the phrase, it was still used in reference to Him: *Philip found Nathanael and said to him, "We have found him about whom Moses in the law and also the prophets wrote, Jesus son of Joseph from Nazareth"* (John 1:45).

The phrase *"the law [and] the prophets"* (Matt. 5:17) referred to the whole of the Hebrew Scriptures—the Mosaic law (which consists of the first five books of the Old Testament) and the Old Testament prophets (which refers not only to both the so-called major and minor prophets but also the historical books). To the pious Jew, *"the law [and] the prophets"* was perfect and unchangeable. And by Jesus' own admission, He did not come to do away with the inspired and sacred Hebrew writings, but rather to bring out by His own teaching and actions the quality of life they were intended to foster in God's people.

And yet, to many of the religious leaders of Jesus' day, His life and ministry appeared to diminish the law. For instance, they censured Him for healing on the Sabbath and failing to observe their pet rituals. Despite their negative opinions, Jesus made it clear that His goal was not to *"abolish the law or the prophets; I have come not to abolish but to fulfill."* Thus, Jesus did not speak against the law itself, but rather against the abuses and excesses to which it had been subjected. He was trying to bring people back to the law's original purpose.

In the Old Testament, there were three categories of the law: ceremonial, civil, and moral. The ceremonial laws related specifically to Israel's worship, such as the instructions for offerings in Leviticus. Since their primary purpose was to point to Jesus' shedding His blood for the sins of the world, they were no longer necessary after Jesus' death and resurrection. But though we no longer follow these ceremonial guidelines, such as offering animal sacrifices, we are still bound by the principles behind them—to worship and love our God and *to present [our] bodies as a living sacrifice, holy and acceptable to God, which is [our] spiritual worship* (Rom. 12:1).

The civil law applied to daily living in Israel, such as the miscellaneous regulations recorded in Deuteronomy 23:9—25:19. Because our society is so radically different from the time when God revealed the Mosaic law, we cannot specifically follow all these guidelines. But again, the principles of living civilly underlying these laws are timeless and ought to guide both our personal and social conduct.

The moral law, such as the Ten Commandments, is the direct command of God and required strict obedience. These laws reveal the holy nature and the will of God. Many believe either some or all of these commandments still apply today.

Though the Mosaic law was given specifically to Israel, it rests on eternal moral principles that are consistent with God's character. Thus it is a summary of fundamental and universal moral standards. It expresses the essence of what God requires of people. That's why when God judges, He can be impartial in His dealings with everyone (Rom. 2:12).

NOTES ON THE PRINTED TEXT

Matthew 5:17 is one of several purpose statements that Jesus made. (For two other examples, see Luke 4:18-21 and John 10:10.) He declared that His purpose was to fulfill *"the law [and] the prophets"* (Matt. 5:17). At the point when Jesus made this statement, the religious leaders had, over time, turned God's commands into a confusing mass of rules. That's why Jesus sought to reemphasize the original purpose the Lord had intended for the Mosaic law. Jesus also sought to help God's people obtain a clearer understanding of the law.

Though Jesus railed against the abuses and excesses of the religious leaders' interpretations of the law, He did not dilute it. In fact, He declared that *"not one letter, not one stroke of a letter, will pass from the law until all is accomplished"* (Matt. 5:18). In essence, no part of God's will for His people would be altered. Clearly, despite what His critics said, Jesus refused to undermine in any way God's revelation through Moses. The Savior affirmed that the law was from God and thus to be obeyed. Indeed, to break even the least significant of these commands and to lead others to do the same was to *"be called least in the kingdom of heaven"* (5:19). On the other hand, to obey them and to encourage others to do the same was to be acknowledged as *"great in the kingdom of heaven."*

Both *"the scribes and the Pharisees"* (5:20) scrupulously and exactingly observed the Mosaic law—at least outwardly. Their weakness was that they refused to allow God to change their hearts and attitudes. They also failed to show compassion to their fellow human beings. Sadly, the religious leaders made an outward show of their piety while transgressing the original intent of the law. It's no wonder Jesus viewed them as spiritual frauds who deserved to be condemned. Despite their piety, not even they were sufficiently good to merit God's approval. It's sobering to learn that *"unless your righteousness exceeds that of the scribes and Pharisees, you will never enter the kingdom of heaven."*

At this point, Matthew recorded five of Jesus' *"You have heard that it was said"* (5:21, 27, 33, 38, 43) statements. The Savior's intent was to contrast the religious leaders' wrongheaded understanding of the Mosaic law with the true intent behind it.

One of the oldest laws in the world was based on the principle of equal retaliation. Found three times in the Old Testament (Exod. 21:24; Lev. 24:20; Deut. 19:21), the intent of this civil law was to put limits on vengeance—in essence, to make the punishment fit the crime. Tragically, some of Israel's religious leaders used the law to excuse their vendettas against others. Jesus declared that God wanted His people to be characterized by humility and patience.

To illustrate His point, Jesus told His followers that if a person slapped them on the right cheek, they were to turn the other cheek so that person might slap it, if he or she so desired (5:39). His followers were to *"give [their] cloak as well"* (5:40) when someone demanded their tunic, to go *"the second mile"* (5:41) when a Roman soldier forced them to go one, and to give *"to everyone who begs from you"* (5:42). At issue here was being just and merciful. Instead of demanding their own rights, Jesus' followers were to give them up freely. Such, of course, was only possible to do in God's strength.

Leviticus 19:18 says *you shall love your neighbor as yourself.* Although no Old Testament command called for the Israelites to hate their enemies, some of the teachers of the law in Jesus' day argued that the command to *"love your neighbor"* (Matt. 5:43) implied permission to hate their enemies. Jesus undermined this false teaching by declaring that God's people were to love their enemies—even their persecutors—as well as their friends. Jesus called on His disciples to love their enemies not merely with feelings but also with actions that were in their enemies' best interests, such as praying for them (5:44).

In this way Christians were to show themselves to be children of their heavenly Father. After all, God *"makes his sun rise on the evil and on the good"* (5:45). His favor extends to all people. So to be like Him—to *"be perfect . . . as your heavenly Father is perfect"* (5:48)—Christians were to show kindness to friend and foe alike (5:46-47).

There is no eternal reward in loving only those who love us. Also, there is nothing extraordinary about being courteous only to our friends. What God requires is that we have an active concern for people everywhere, regardless of how they treat us. To love both our neighbors and our enemies is to display a family likeness with God.

Suggestions to Teachers

Jesus' command for us to *"be perfect"* (Matt. 5:48) is both a directive and a reminder. We are told to have the same kind of love for our fellow human beings that is described in verses 38-47. *"Be perfect"* is also a reminder that God loves all people without partiality. Of course, we'll never be perfect in the sense that God is, but we should strive to love everyone as He does. Also, obedience to such a command requires the transforming work of the Holy Spirit. We cannot love others as Jesus does apart from the grace of God.

1. TO OBEY IS TO HAVE THE RIGHT ATTITUDE. First Samuel 15:22-23 records the prophet Samuel's words to Saul after the king had chosen to offer ritual sacrifices instead of obeying a direct command from the Lord: *"Has the LORD as great delight in burnt offerings and sacrifices, as in obeying the voice of the LORD? Surely, to obey is better than sacrifice, and to heed than the fat of rams. For rebellion is no less a sin than divination, and stubbornness is like iniquity and idolatry."* Jesus longs for our loving obedience far more than our absent-minded religious formalities and ceremonies. It's not so much that these activities are unimportant as it is that we have the proper reasons and attitudes for performing them.

2. TO OBEY IS TO HELP OTHERS OBEY. God wants us to go beyond telling and encouraging others to obey Him. He wants us to help others obey Him by obeying Him ourselves and by being an example of obedience.

3. TO OBEY IS TO LOVE GOD. Real obedience cannot happen apart from our love for God. In fact, our obedience demonstrates our love for Him. It's no wonder that Jesus said, *"They who have my commandments and keep them are those who love me; and those who love me will be loved by my Father, and I will love them and reveal myself to them"* (John 14:21).

4. TO OBEY IS TO BE GOD-CENTERED. The religious leaders of Jesus' day obeyed God outwardly, but they did so because it would enhance their status among the people. Their obedience was self-centered. Jesus said our obedience should be God-centered, based on our reverence for Him. We're to follow His will, not seek the approval of those who may be watching us.

5. TO OBEY IS TO LIVE BY THE PRINCIPLES BEHIND THE LAW. Jesus' teaching went beyond a ritualistic obedience to the law. He taught that we should obey the "spirit of the law," namely, the principles behind the law and the purpose for which God gave the law.

6. TO OBEY IS TO TRUST GOD. We are not left to our own devices when it comes to obeying God. The Lord, through His Spirit, helps us to obey Him. We cannot obey by ourselves; rather, our obedience comes from God working in us.

FOR ADULTS

■ TOPIC: Fulfilling the Commandments

■ QUESTIONS: 1. Why do you think Jesus felt the need to explain His stance on *"the law [and] the prophets"* (Matt. 5:17)? 2. In what ways do Jesus' teachings fulfill *"the law [and] the prophets"*? 3. In what ways did the righteousness of the Pharisees fall short of true obedience to the law? 4. How do the guidelines of the Old Testament apply to us today? 5. According to 5:48, in what sense does God want us to be perfect?

Love Your Enemies. On the morning of November 8, 1987, Gordon Wilson took his daughter Marie to a parade in the town of Enniskillen, Northern Ireland. As Wilson and his 20-year-old daughter stood beside a brick wall waiting for English soldiers and police to come marching by, a bomb planted by terrorists exploded from behind, and the brick wall tumbled down on them.

The blast instantly killed six people and pinned Gordon and Marie beneath several feet of bricks. Gordon's arm and shoulder were severely injured. Unable to move, he felt someone take hold of his hand. It was Marie.

"Is that you, Dad?" she asked.

"Yes, Marie," Gordon answered. Though her voice was belabored, he could hear her over the screams of several people.

"Are you all right?" Gordon asked her.

"Yes," she said.

As Gordon felt his daughter's grip beginning to loosen, again and again he asked if she was all right. Each time she said yes. Finally, Marie said, "Daddy, I love you very much." Those were her last words. Four hours later she died in the hospital of severe spinal and brain injuries.

Later that evening, a British Broadcasting Company reporter requested permission to interview Gordon. After Gordon described what had happened, the reporter asked, "How do you feel about the guys who planted the bomb?"

"I bear them no ill will," Gordon replied. "I bear them no grudge. Bitter talk is not going to bring Marie back to life. I shall pray tonight and every night that God will forgive them."

Many asked Gordon, who later became a senator in the Republic of Ireland, how he could say such a thing, how he could forgive such a horrendous act. Gordon explained, "I was hurt. I had just lost my daughter. But I wasn't angry. Marie's last words to me—words of love—had put me on a plane of love. I received God's grace, through the strength of His love for me, to forgive." And for years after this tragedy, Gordon continued to work for peace in Northern Ireland.

Pray for Them Who Despitefully Use You. A woman called the pastor's office, asking the minister to come to her home to pray for her ill husband. The pastor didn't recognize her voice, so he asked her name.

"This is Orlean Weathers," she said.

"Mrs. Weathers," the pastor said, "I'm sorry, but I don't believe I know you. Have you attended our church?"

"Oh, no," she said. "I attend Reverend Morgan's church over on the other side of town."

"Well," the pastor responded, "don't you think you ought to call Reverend Morgan to come and pray with your husband?"

"No, sir. I couldn't do that," she said. "What my husband has is contagious."

But I Say unto You. In 1777, George Washington's army faced a winter of cold and bleak inactivity on a small mountain near Morristown, New Jersey. The general sensed the restlessness of his men, and so he ordered a stockade built around the encampment immediately. He also doubled the perimeter guard. Work started right away and rumors abounded about how near the enemy might be and whether the stockade would be finished on time.

In the spring, even though the fortifications were not finished, Washington ordered a move. Thinking they were about to be overrun by the enemy, the soldiers did a rapid deployment. Leaving the unfinished fortification, they marched—not to defeat—but to victory over nearby English forces. It was only history that gave the unfinished fort its name: Fort Nonsense.

God, in His inscrutable wisdom, sometimes sends us to do tasks that we don't fully understand, that don't make a lot of earthly sense. But He asks us to work at them, not for the immediate necessity of their completion, but for the good of our character and the good of our souls, especially as He leads us on to higher things.

FOR YOUTH

■ TOPIC: Love My Enemy?

■ QUESTIONS: 1. Why should we be just as concerned about obeying God in our attitudes (which people can't see) as we are about obeying God through our actions (which people can see)? 2. Do you think Jesus, through His teaching about the Mosaic law, makes it easier or harder to obey the law? Explain your answer. 3. What do you think was the original intent of the law about *"an eye for an eye"* (Matt. 5:38) and *"a tooth for a tooth"*? 4. What inner quality do you think Jesus desires for believers? 5. In what ways can believers depend on God to help them obey Him?

■ ILLUSTRATIONS:

Pray for Them Who Persecute You. Chris Carrier of Coral Gables, Florida, was abducted when he was 10 years old. His kidnappers, angry with the boy's family, burned him with cigarettes, stabbed him numerous times with an ice pick, shot him in the head, and left him to die in the Everglades. Remarkably, the boy survived, though he lost sight in one eye. No one was ever arrested.

Finally, 22 years later, a man confessed to the crime. Chris, by then a youth minister at a nearby church, went to see him. He found the man, a 77-year-old ex-convict, frail and blind, living in a Miami Beach nursing home. Chris began visiting often, reading to the ex-convict from the Bible and praying with him. The ministry of Chris opened the door for the man to make a profession of faith in Jesus Christ.

No arrest was forthcoming, for the statute of limitations on the crime was long past. And the statute of limitations had also run out on Chris's hatred and bitterness. He said, "While many people can't understand how I could forgive my kidnapper, from my point of view I couldn't *not* forgive him. If I'd chosen to hate him all these years, or spent my life looking for revenge, then I wouldn't be the man I am today, the man my wife and children love, the man God has helped me to be."

I studied intently the photograph, in *Leadership Journal*, of Chris holding his kidnapper's hand and praying with him as he lay in a nursing home bed. When I think about the absence of hatred, when I think about the presence of forgiveness, and when I think about Jesus' command to love your enemies, I think about that picture.

I'm Diving In! I recently ran across the anonymous quote, "We're not in this to test the waters; we are in this to make waves." What an excellent idea for the believer who wants to fulfill Christ's call to impact this world. We're not called to be like everybody else. We're not called to go with the flow. We are called to be different, to act different, and to talk different. We shouldn't resign ourselves to simply testing the waters. We should do what Steven Curtis Chapman's hit song of 1999 says:

I'm diving in, I'm going deep in over my head, I want to be
Caught in the rush, lost in the flow, in over my head, I want to go
The river's deep, the river's wide, the river's water is alive
So sink or swim, I'm diving in!

Be Careful! One day Francis of Assisi and Brother Leo were out walking together. Suddenly Brother Leo called out, "Brother Francis!"

"Yes, I am Brother Francis," came the reply.

"Be careful, Brother Francis! People are saying remarkable things about you! Be careful."

And Francis of Assisi replied, "My friend, pray to the Lord that I may succeed in becoming what people think I am."

CONCERNING TREASURES

BACKGROUND SCRIPTURE: Matthew 6
DEVOTIONAL READING: Philippians 4:4-9

KEY VERSES: [Jesus said] "Strive first for the kingdom of God and his righteousness, and all these things will be given to you as well. So do not worry about tomorrow." Matthew 6:33-34.

KING JAMES VERSION

MATTHEW 6:19 Lay not up for yourselves treasures upon earth, where moth and rust doth corrupt, and where thieves break through and steal:

20 But lay up for yourselves treasures in heaven, where neither moth nor rust doth corrupt, and where thieves do not break through nor steal:

21 For where your treasure is, there will your heart be also. . . .

25 Therefore I say unto you, Take no thought for your life, what ye shall eat, or what ye shall drink; nor yet for your body, what ye shall put on. Is not the life more than meat, and the body than raiment?

26 Behold the fowls of the air: for they sow not, neither do they reap, nor gather into barns; yet your heavenly Father feedeth them. Are ye not much better than they?

27 Which of you by taking thought can add one cubit unto his stature?

28 And why take ye thought for raiment? Consider the lilies of the field, how they grow; they toil not, neither do they spin:

29 And yet I say unto you, That even Solomon in all his glory was not arrayed like one of these.

30 Wherefore, if God so clothe the grass of the field, which to day is, and to morrow is cast into the oven, shall he not much more clothe you, O ye of little faith?

31 Therefore take no thought, saying, What shall we eat? or, What shall we drink? or, Wherewithal shall we be clothed?

32 (For after all these things do the Gentiles seek:) for your heavenly Father knoweth that ye have need of all these things.

33 But seek ye first the kingdom of God, and his righteousness; and all these things shall be added unto you.

34 Take therefore no thought for the morrow: for the morrow shall take thought for the things of itself. Sufficient unto the day is the evil thereof.

NEW REVISED STANDARD VERSION

MATTHEW 6:19 "Do not store up for yourselves treasures on earth, where moth and rust consume and where thieves break in and steal; 20 but store up for yourselves treasures in heaven, where neither moth nor rust consumes and where thieves do not break in and steal. 21 For where your treasure is, there your heart will be also. . . .

25 "Therefore I tell you, do not worry about your life, what you will eat or what you will drink, or about your body, what you will wear. Is not life more than food, and the body more than clothing? 26 Look at the birds of the air; they neither sow nor reap nor gather into barns, and yet your heavenly Father feeds them. Are you not of more value than they? 27 And can any of you by worrying add a single hour to your span of life? 28 And why do you worry about clothing? Consider the lilies of the field, how they grow; they neither toil nor spin, 29 yet I tell you, even Solomon in all his glory was not clothed like one of these. 30 But if God so clothes the grass of the field, which is alive today and tomorrow is thrown into the oven, will he not much more clothe you—you of little faith? 31 Therefore do not worry, saying, 'What will we eat?' or 'What will we drink?' or 'What will we wear?' 32 For it is the Gentiles who strive for all these things; and indeed your heavenly Father knows that you need all these things. 33 But strive first for the kingdom of God and his righteousness, and all these things will be given to you as well.

34 "So do not worry about tomorrow, for tomorrow will bring worries of its own. Today's trouble is enough for today."

12

Monday, November 19	Luke 6:27-36	*Love Your Enemies*
Tuesday, November 20	Luke 6:37-42	*Do Not Judge*
Wednesday, November 21	Luke 13:22-30	*Enter through the Narrow Door*
Thursday, November 22	Romans 13:8-14	*Love Fulfills the Law*
Friday, November 23	Romans 14:1-8	*Welcome the Weak*
Saturday, November 24	Matthew 7:1-12	*Ask, Search, and Knock*
Sunday, November 25	Matthew 7:13-29	*Who Will Enter?*

BACKGROUND

When students of the Bible think about Jesus' teachings, parables, and sermons, they usually assume that He spent the bulk of His time talking about God, love, or salvation. But in reality, the two subjects He focused most of His attention on were first, the kingdom of God, and second, money.

In Jesus' teaching about money, which Bible scholars say encompassed nearly one-sixth of His words recorded in the Gospels, Jesus spoke against miserly hoarding and in favor of compassionate distribution. He didn't want His followers' relationship with wealth to take priority over their relationship with God. So typically, the primary focus of the Savior's teaching was on His disciples sharing whatever they possessed with the less fortunate.

Jesus operated under the assumption that all our wealth and possessions actually belong to God. And because everything belongs to Him, we have been set up in the role of "stewards" in which we care for and distribute those certain portions over which we have "stewardship." Incidentally, the Greek word commonly translated "steward" is *oikonomos*, a term that means "house-supervisor," "manager," or "overseer." When originally translated into English, however, the word "steward" was "styward," meaning "the keeper of pigs."

In Matthew 6:19-34, Jesus taught that our earthly stewardship directly relates to our heavenly stewardship. He also declared that, while living on earth, we should be stewards of or investors in heavenly treasures for our life after death. For instance, when Luke recorded the negative version of this same statement— *"So it is with those who store up treasures for themselves but are not rich toward God"* (Luke 12:21)—he placed it at the end of one of Jesus' parables to emphasize how riches can get in the way of spiritual gain.

Of course, it is a natural tendency for human beings to be concerned about having sustenance and possessions for everyday life. But that concern easily erupts into worry, especially when we place more of our trust in possessions than in God, or when we allow our possessions to dominate our lives.

Understandably, Jesus condemned both worry and the love of money as a lack of trust in God. Indeed, He called upon His followers to live contentedly with whatever they have, for they, unlike the rest of the world, have chosen as most important what is eternal and lasting over that which is fading and being used up. With Paul they can genuinely say, *I have learned to be content with whatever I have* (Phil. 4:11).

NOTES ON THE PRINTED TEXT

Jesus knew the tendency of people to be selfish, to look out for themselves, and to stockpile goods for their own welfare. He thus declared, *"Do not store up for yourselves treasures on earth"* (Matt. 6:19). Why? It's because they will eventually be destroyed. The main concern of believers was not to amass earthly wealth and security. Rather, Jesus said, they were to *"store up for yourselves treasures in heaven"* (6:20), where the uncertainties of earthly life could not affect them.

Jesus was making a clear contrast between heavenly values and earthly values. The believers' highest priority should be to that which does not fade, cannot be stolen or used up, and never wears out. Through faithfulness to God, along with kindness and goodness to others, the believers' goal is to store up for themselves treasures in heaven, for only these have eternal value.

Although Jesus used an investment analogy, He did not mean that storing treasures in heaven was limited to the giving of one's income to the work of the Lord. These *"treasures in heaven"* were accomplished by all the believers' acts of obedience to God. There is a sense in which giving our money to God's work is like investing in heaven. But we should seek to please God not only in our giving but also in fulfilling His purposes in whatever we do. Our *"treasures in heaven"* consist of anything we do in this earthly life that has eternal value.

In urging His disciples to trust God and to labor for those things with eternal value, Jesus noted that *"where your treasure is, there your heart will be also"* (6:21). In essence, where we invest our time, talents, and resources is a barometer of what concerns us the most (Luke 12:34).

Because of the multiple ill effects of worry, Jesus also told His disciples not to be anxious about those needs that God promises to supply. Specifically, Jesus mentioned *"what you will eat or what you will drink, or about your body, what you will wear"* (Matt. 6:25). Those who have placed their trust in God need not be anxious about obtaining sufficient food, drink, or clothing. Certainly these items are necessary to survive, but obtaining them should never become the all-consuming goal of our lives.

The one who created us knows that worry can never satisfy our needs and can literally destroy our peace. Perhaps this is why Jesus stressed the Lord's intimate familiarity with our needs. God can be trusted to supply whatever we need to serve Him effectively (Phil. 4:19). The main reason, then, we should not worry is that God cares about us. If He provides for the birds and the lilies and the grass, all the more so will He care and provide for us, whom He has created in His image (Gen. 1:26-27). In fact, Matthew 6:25-34 suggests seven reasons not to worry.

First, God can be trusted with even the most minute details of our lives (6:25). Second, worrying about the future impedes what we do today (6:26). Third, worrying does us more harm than good (6:27). Fourth, God provides for those who completely depend on Him (6:28-30). Fifth, worrying shows a lack of faith in and dependence on God (6:31-32). Sixth, worrying distracts us from tackling the real challenges God wants us to pursue (6:33). And seventh, living one day at a time keeps worry from overtaking us (6:34).

All kinds of people, possessions, goals, and desires will compete for our top priority. And any of these can knock God out of first place, especially if we do not daily choose to give Him first place in every area of our lives. That's why Jesus made the crux of His message to *"strive first for the kingdom of God and his righteousness, and all these things will be given to you"* (6:33). Above all else, Jesus wants the kingdom of God to be our primary concern. When we put God's work first and do what He wants, He truly will have foremost priority in our lives. We will be filling our thoughts with the same desires as His, and we will be modeling our character after His.

SUGGESTIONS TO TEACHERS

To make sure that the kingdom of God—and not anything else—remains the foremost priority in our lives, there are a few things we should and should not be doing.

1. SERVE GOD, NOT MONEY. Ours is a materialistic society in which most people serve money—whether or not they admit it. They prove that they serve money over God by spending all their waking hours collecting and storing it. And even if they don't somehow lose their money, they will eventually die and leave it behind. It is far better for us to serve our eternal God. Our commitment to Him and to spiritual matters ought to far outweigh our desire for money and what we can buy with it.

2. INVEST IN HEAVEN, NOT IN EARTH. Think eternal. Act eternal. Invest eternal. Be eternal. In the end, nothing will be left except what we've invested for God and the furtherance of His kingdom.

3. PLAN, DON'T WORRY. The old adage says, "Those who fail to plan, plan to fail." Jesus' teaching implied that planning for tomorrow is time wisely invested. In contrast, worrying about tomorrow is time foolishly wasted. Careful planning is thinking ahead about goals and steps and schedules, all while trusting God's guidance. When done well, planning can even help alleviate worry. Worrying, on the other hand, causes us to misplace our trust, and we find it difficult to depend on God. How tragic it is when we let worries about tomorrow affect our moment-by-moment relationship with God!

4. TRUST GOD, NOT YOUR POSSESSIONS. Our possessions will come and go, but our God is here to stay. So let us trust Him exclusively and put our possessions to use for His kingdom.

5. GIVE, DON'T HOARD. Remember that *the love of money is a root of all kinds of evil, and in their eagerness to be rich some have wandered away from the faith and pierced themselves with many pains* (1 Tim. 6:10). By developing the habit of giving generously to the Lord's work, we prove to God—and to ourselves—that we control our possessions and not the other way around. May we become more fascinated with giving to the kingdom of God and less fascinated with all that we might hoard for ourselves.

6. BE CONCERNED, DON'T WORRY. While we are commanded to be concerned, we are also commanded not to worry. What's the difference? Concern moves us to action, while worrying immobilizes us. Concern prompts us to help others, while worrying negatively affects the way we treat others. Concern increases our productivity, while worrying disrupts our productivity. Concern leads us to our trust in God, while worrying undermines our trust in Him.

FOR ADULTS	■ TOPIC: Worrying Needlessly ■ QUESTIONS: 1. What is the link between your treasure and your heart? 2. What do you think it means to *"strive first for the king-*

dom of God and his righteousness" (Matt. 6:33)? 3. Why is it important to make God, not money, our master? 4. What do you think Jesus really meant when He said *"do not worry about tomorrow"* (6:34)? 5. What would you say are some of the ill effects of worrying?

■ **ILLUSTRATIONS:**

Rich toward God. The Marquis de Lafayette was a French general and politician who was extremely rich and fit into the highest French social class. He assisted George Washington in the American Revolution, and then he returned to France and resumed his life as the master of several estates.

In 1783, the harvest was a poor one, but the workers of Lafayette's farms still somehow managed to fill his barns with wheat. "The bad harvest has raised the price of wheat," said one of his workers. "This is the time to sell." Lafayette thought about all the hungry peasants in the surrounding villages. Then he said, "No. This is the time to give."

Lafayette had an opportunity to store up treasures for himself, but decided instead to offer his wealth to the poor. This act did not impoverish him, but instead made him rich—rich toward God. Such generosity is good planning for anyone who wants to store up treasures in heaven.

Coming Up Empty. Magazine editor Lewis Lapham, in his book, *Money and Class in America*, tells the story of a chance encounter with a Yale University classmate who had become a New York businessman. The two ran into each other about 30 years after their college graduation, and the businessman immediately began to cry on Lapham's shoulder.

"I'm nothing," the man said. "You understand that, nothing. I earn $250,000 a year, but it's nothing, and I'm nobody."

The businessman's despair struck Lapham as being rather grotesque. After all, if the average American family of four earns an annual income in the tens of thousands of dollars, how could this person possibly feel deprived? But when the businessman listed his expenses—a Park Avenue apartment, private school tuitions, taxes, salaries for a maid and a part-time laundress—the total came to $300,400. He was clearly going broke on an income of $250,000 a year!

"As it is," said the businessman, "I live like an animal. I eat tuna fish out of cans and hope that when the phone rings it isn't somebody dunning me for a bill." He might have been pulling down a quarter of a million dollars a year, but according to Lapham, he "had the look of a man who was being followed by the police." He had put his treasures where his heart was, and had come up empty.

Lessen Your Load. In Noah BenShea's book, *Jacob's Journey: Wisdom to Find the Way, Strength to Carry On,* a rich man comes to Jacob, the baker, and asks him, "When others turn to me for help, what should I say?"

"Say, thank you," Jacob replied, toying with a leaf that had fallen from a tree.

"What?" said the man. "Why should I say 'thank you'?" His voice grew louder as if to boost his confidence. "What can the poor give me?"

"Have you ever met a man whose success is not also a burden?" said Jacob. "Charity allows you to lessen your load. In this way, having less can add to your life!"

Now the stranger's voice took a new tone. "I feel like a fool," he said.

"No," responded Jacob. "A fool is one who knows too much to learn anything."

FOR YOUTH

■ TOPIC: Hidden Treasures

■ QUESTIONS: 1. Why is it far wiser to store up treasures in heaven rather than on earth? 2. Why is our heart an accurate indicator of what we treasure most? 3. What is worry, and why is it futile? 4. What lessons about trust can we learn by observing nature? 5. What is the difference between worry and proper concern for the future?

■ ILLUSTRATIONS:

Giving and Storing. Pastor Gary tells how, four years ago, a group of middle-school youth from his church in the northwest part of the United States visited different neighbors to collect food for the local food bank. Of course, an added task was extending an invitation to people to attend pastor Gary's church.

In only one hour, the entire group collected more than 760 pounds of food. The youth returned to the church joyful at the generosity of so many people and amazed at what God had accomplished through them.

Then, over pizza, the youth and their parents traded stories. One of the parents told how some youth from the church had knocked on the doors of several lovely homes with nice cars in the driveway where the occupants exclaimed, "We really don't have any extra food to share!" Then one of the other occupants bellowed, "You've got to be kidding!" A teacher friend of pastor Gary calls that "poor talk." In other words, it's when "people of means" pretend they are just getting by.

Giving and seeing that others are fed and taken care of is one of the ways that we can store up for ourselves treasures in heaven.

No Fear of Death. One of my favorite storytellers is the author Robert Fulghum. He's written several best-selling books, beginning with one called *All I Really Need to Know I Learned in Kindergarten*. More than 15,000,000 copies of his books are in print, in more than 25 languages, and in nearly 100 countries. Needless to say, he has done very well financially.

In an interview six years ago with a Christian magazine called *The Door*, Fulghum reports that since his success, people are always saying, "Well, you must have a big house and a big car." And he responds, "No, I have the same house, same car, same friends, same wife." Fulghum admits to being on guard against all kinds of greed, and is committed to serving God, not money.

Of course, fame is a challenge, Fulghum admits, "and the challenge is to be a good steward with this kind of authority and power—especially with the economics." So one year he did a book tour, and used it to raise $670,000 for a number of good causes. "I don't think I should be given extra credit for doing that," he says. "I think you should think ill of me if I didn't do that."

Death doesn't scare Fulghum. In fact, in one of his books is a picture of the grave he has already picked out, and he likes to visit it. It reminds him to live in a way that is laying up for himself treasures in heaven. And when Fulghum sees the grave, he says to himself, "Don't get lost here. Know where you're going."

Those who find ways to serve God have discovered the right path. They don't have to fear death, for they know where they're going. Their treasure is waiting for them in heaven, not in an earthly bank account, an estate, or in stocks and bonds.

Ready to Die. In her book, *I Heard the Owl Call My Name*, Margaret Craven tells the story of a cleric's visit to a young minister serving a tribe of Native Americans in British Columbia. The cleric knew and loved this tribe, and enjoyed their feasting and dancing. At the end of his visit he tried to describe his feelings to the minister.

"Always when I leave the village," the cleric said slowly, "I try to define what it means to me, why it sends me back to the world refreshed and confident. Always I fail. It is so simple, it is difficult. When I try to put it into words, it comes out one of those unctuous, over-pious platitudes at which clerics are expected to excel."

They both laughed.

"But when I reach here and see the great scar where the inlet side [of the river] shows its bones, for a moment I know."

The minister asked, "What, my lord?"

"That for me it has always been easier here, where only the fundamentals count, to learn what every man must learn in this world."

"And that, my lord?"

"Enough of the meaning of life to be ready to die."

DO UNTO OTHERS

BACKGROUND SCRIPTURE: Matthew 7
DEVOTIONAL READING: Romans 13:8-14

KEY VERSES: "In everything do to others as you would have them do to you; for this is the law and the prophets." Matthew 7:12.

KING JAMES VERSION

MATTHEW 7:1 Judge not, that ye be not judged.

2 For with what judgment ye judge, ye shall be judged: and with what measure ye mete, it shall be measured to you again.

3 And why beholdest thou the mote that is in thy brother's eye, but considerest not the beam that is in thine own eye?

4 Or how wilt thou say to thy brother, Let me pull out the mote out of thine eye; and, behold, a beam is in thine own eye?

5 Thou hypocrite, first cast out the beam out of thine own eye; and then shalt thou see clearly to cast out the mote out of thy brother's eye. . . .

12 Therefore all things whatsoever ye would that men should do to you, do ye even so to them: for this is the law and the prophets.

13 Enter ye in at the strait gate: for wide is the gate, and broad is the way, that leadeth to destruction, and many there be which go in thereat:

14 Because strait is the gate, and narrow is the way, which leadeth unto life, and few there be that find it.

15 Beware of false prophets, which come to you in sheep's clothing, but inwardly they are ravening wolves.

16 Ye shall know them by their fruits. Do men gather grapes of thorns, or figs of thistles?

17 Even so every good tree bringeth forth good fruit; but a corrupt tree bringeth forth evil fruit.

18 A good tree cannot bring forth evil fruit, neither can a corrupt tree bring forth good fruit.

19 Every tree that bringeth not forth good fruit is hewn down, and cast into the fire.

20 Wherefore by their fruits ye shall know them.

NEW REVISED STANDARD VERSION

MATTHEW 7:1 "Do not judge, so that you may not be judged. 2 For with the judgment you make you will be judged, and the measure you give will be the measure you get. 3 Why do you see the speck in your neighbor's eye, but do not notice the log in your own eye? 4 Or how can you say to your neighbor, 'Let me take the speck out of your eye,' while the log is in your own eye? 5 You hypocrite, first take the log out of your own eye, and then you will see clearly to take the speck out of your neighbor's eye. . . .

12 "In everything do to others as you would have them do to you; for this is the law and the prophets.

13 "Enter through the narrow gate; for the gate is wide and the road is easy that leads to destruction, and there are many who take it. 14 For the gate is narrow and the road is hard that leads to life, and there are few who find it.

15 "Beware of false prophets, who come to you in sheep's clothing but inwardly are ravenous wolves. 16 You will know them by their fruits. Are grapes gathered from thorns, or figs from thistles? 17 In the same way, every good tree bears good fruit, but the bad tree bears bad fruit. 18 A good tree cannot bear bad fruit, nor can a bad tree bear good fruit. 19 Every tree that does not bear good fruit is cut down and thrown into the fire. 20 Thus you will know them by their fruits."

13

HOME BIBLE READINGS

BACKGROUND

When removed from its context, Jesus' injunction not to *"judge, so that you may not be judged"* (Matt. 7:1) seems like a relatively simple directive. On the surface it appears as if Jesus simply does not want us to be making determinations about the standing of other people with God. But when this verse is viewed within the context of another later passage in the Sermon on the Mount, matters get more complicated. How do we fulfill Jesus' command not to judge while at the same time put into practice the declaration *"you will know them by their fruits"* (7:16, 20)?

The Greek verb rendered "judge" is *krino* [KRIH-no], and it can carry varied meanings such as "to distinguish and decide" or "to conclude and condemn." Too often, when taken out of context, believers have assumed that Jesus does not want them to make moral evaluations about anyone or anything. But 7:15-20 makes it clear that this is not at all what Jesus intended. He warned that false prophets can be known by the fruit they bear. He thus urged His followers to form opinions about others based on careful consideration and discernment. He did not ask believers to lay aside their critical thought processes. Rather, He told them to resist the urge to speak harshly about others.

Clearly, Jesus wants us to be careful about the manner in which we do our "fruit-inspecting." The implication is that, while we are looking at others' fruit and making determinations about their Christian witness, others will be checking ours out as well and making the same type of determination.

Even while "fruit-inspecting," the Christian is not to judge self-righteously. The point is not to tear down another in order to build up oneself. Rather, we should humbly consider one another's standing with God by examining the outcome—the fruit—of each other's lives. And once the appropriate determination has been made, then will come the time to confront the person over those issues that are beneath the Christian standard.

The real issue, then, in 7:1 is engaging in unfair, hypocritical judgment. Jesus was referring to people who magnified the faults of others while excusing their own shortcomings. The Savior stressed that God would evaluate us by the same standard by which we evaluated others (7:2). The only way out of this dilemma is to leave eternal judgments with the Lord, who alone is fair in His assessments.

Perhaps it is our human nature that causes so many of us to pay much more attention to other people's faults than to our own shortcomings. Most of us would admit a natural tendency to evaluate others based on a rather lofty standard while lowering that standard considerably and cutting ourselves some slack when it comes to evaluating ourselves.

Jesus condemned doing this sort of thing (Matt. 7:1). He said that if we are guilty of a judgmental spirit, God will be as hard on us as we are on others. *"For with the judgment you make you will be judged, and the measure you give will be the measure you get"* (7:2).

To drive home His point, Jesus presented the ludicrous picture of a person with a long rafter protruding from his eye trying to extract a speck of sawdust from his neighbor's eye. Hypocrisy, of course, is Jesus' target here. "How hypocritical," we can imagine Jesus saying, "for one person to be obsessed with another's minor fault when he refuses to acknowledge his own huge moral defect!" (7:3-4). Then, attaching a label of immorality to such a person, Jesus declared, *"You hypocrite, first take the log out of your own eye, and then you will see clearly to take the speck out of your neighbor's eye"* (7:5).

The theme of these verses is in some ways summed up in what has come to be known as the Golden Rule. As Jesus had called for His disciples to give mercy as they would like to be given mercy (5:7) and to judge as they would want to be judged (7:1), now the Savior called for them to *"do to others as you would have them do to you"* (7:12).

In many cultures, the Golden Rule is found in a negative form. For instance, Confucius taught, "What you do not want done to yourself, do not do to others." And Isocrates [eye-SOCK-ruh-teez] said, "Whatever angers you when you suffer it at the hands of others, do not do it to others." But Jesus was the first to actually make the statement in a positive form: "to do" instead of "refraining from doing." To *"do to others"* does not allow us to be satisfied with doing nothing. The way Jesus stated the Golden Rule should move us to action on the behalf of others. It beckons us to do for other people all those things we would appreciate being done for us. In fact, Jesus said that this kind of vigorously active concern for others is a summation of the teaching of the *"law and the prophets."*

Once again, Jesus told His disciples that their character, integrity, and way of life should stand out from the rest of the world. After all, they are *"the salt of the earth"* (5:13) and *"the light of the world"* (5:14), and as such, they should strive to be a positive moral influence in the world. Jesus knew His teaching would be difficult to follow. Trials and tribulations certainly await those who commit to obeying Christ. Indeed, *"the gate is narrow and the road is hard that leads to life, and there are few who find it"* (7:14). Only a few travel the road of personal commitment and discipline.

There is an easier way to live, Jesus implied. Those who live for their own self-centered desires may find that their earthly life is practically effortless and comfortable. But at some point they will come to realize that *"the gate is wide and the road is easy that leads to destruction, and there are many who take it"* (7:13). Jesus made the choice clear. We can follow the crowd that takes the path of least resistance, or we can join the few who accept the demands of loyalty to Christ. The easy way leads to destruction, while the hard way leads to eternal life.

Jesus knew that false prophets would arise who would try to deceive His followers. So Jesus warned against those who would *"come to you in sheep's clothing"* (7:15), appearing to be one of the believing flock. But because *"inwardly [they] are ravenous wolves,"* they are driven by personal greed and will tear apart and ruin the true flock. Spiritual frauds do all this for their own personal gain.

Jesus said the false prophets can be recognized by their fruits (7:16). They may look like spokespersons for God, using religious language and looking very spiritual. But if their lives don't bear the good fruit of obedience to Christ, they are charlatans. Jesus said to identify these imposters by their fruit—simply by the way they live. If there are no grapes, you don't have a grapevine; if there are no figs, you don't have a fig tree. Similarly, if the lifestyle doesn't measure up to the claims, then the person is a pious fraud. And Jesus said we are to remove such a person's influence from our lives as radically as an orchard owner would cut down a fruitless tree. True prophets are not motivated by money, fame, or power. They are motivated by the desire to glorify God (7:17-20).

SUGGESTIONS TO TEACHERS

There's an ancient adage that says, "Like root, like fruit." Christian faith will produce ethical uprightness. In contrast, deplorable conduct is a sure indicator of decayed character.

1. JUDGE YOURSELF FIRST. We should make sure our heart is in the right place. And we should repent of any wrongdoing ourself before counseling someone else to do so. When we've dealt with the sinful habits in our own life, we'll be ready to lovingly and constructively assist our neighbors in dealing with their sinful habits.

2. EXAMINE YOUR MOTIVES. Rather than being predisposed toward criticizing others, we should examine our own motives. And we ought to take a look at our own conduct. We actually may be wanting to fault others for a habit that is rather pronounced in us! We should determine that our purpose is a win-win proposition that is for the betterment of both our neighbor and ourself—that the outcome will be that both of us grow closer to God.

3. ENCOURAGE FRUITFULNESS. We should get out of the habit of tearing others down. It is better to get into the habit of encouraging them to bear Christian fruit. We ought to acknowledge good behavior and be on the lookout for wrong behavior. We should do the latter by being discerning rather than negative. After all, our ultimate goal is to bear good fruit.

4. TAKE THE INITIATIVE. It usually isn't all that tough to hold back from hurting other people. It can be a lot more difficult to take the initiative to pitch in and do something good for them. Would we want others to take the initiative to help us out of a predicament? Then we should take the initiative to help them out of their predicaments, too.

5. TAKE THE HARD ROAD. The hard road is characterized by humility, sacrifice, and unselfishness. The easy road is characterized by egotism, indulgence, and selfishness. The hard road takes devotion and diligence. The easy road takes neither. The hard road leads to eternal life. The easy road leads to destruction. We should take the hard road, which paradoxically is easiest (Matt. 11:30).

6. INSPECT THE FRUIT. It's all right to check out others' fruit—as long as we don't mind them checking out ours. In fact, fruit inspection can be good for us and our fellow Christians as long as we make use of the inspections to encourage one another in the faith.

FOR ADULTS

■ **TOPIC:** Relating to Others

■ **QUESTIONS:** 1. What kind of judgment was Jesus condemning? 2. What did Jesus say summed up *"the law and the prophets"* (Matt. 7:12)? 3. What characterizes the narrow gate and the broad gate? 4. What was Jesus' intent in mentioning healthy trees and sickly trees? 5. Why is it important for us to be able to recognize spiritual frauds? 6. What do the words coming from our mouth indicate about what's in our heart?

■ **ILLUSTRATIONS:**

With the Judgment You Make. Bill had wild hair, wore jeans and a T-shirt with holes in it, and had no shoes. That was his wardrobe for his entire four years of college. He was kind of esoteric and extremely bright. Also, he had become a Christian while attending college.

Across the street from the campus was a very traditional church. The congregation wanted to develop a ministry to the college students, but the members weren't sure how to go about it. Then one day Bill decided to attend the church. He entered the building in his customary wardrobe.

Since the service had already started, Bill walked down the aisle looking for a seat. The church was packed, and Bill couldn't find a seat. As he moseyed around, the people were growing a bit uncomfortable, but no one said anything. Bill moved closer and closer to the pulpit and, when he realized there were no seats, he sat down on the floor in front of the first pew. By now, the congregation was really uptight, and the tension in the air was thick.

It was then that the minister realized that, from the back of the church, one of the older deacons had begun slowly making his way toward Bill. The deacon was in his eighties, had silver-gray hair, and was wearing a three-piece suit. He was a godly man, very elegant, very dignified, and very courtly. He shuffled down the aisle with a cane. As he slowly inched toward the college student, the congregation was thinking that they couldn't really blame the deacon for what he was about to do.

It took well over a minute for the deacon to reach Bill. The church was completely silent except for the clicking of the man's cane. All eyes were focused on him. Even the minister had held off on his sermon until the deacon had finished what he had planned to do.

Finally, the deacon reached the front of the sanctuary. Then the congregation watched in utter amazement as the elderly man dropped his cane on the floor. With great difficulty, he lowered himself and sat down next to Bill so that he wouldn't be alone. When the minister stepped behind the pulpit, he said, "What I'm about to preach, you will not remember for very long. But what you have seen here, you must never forget."

Do to Others. In *A Second Helping of Chicken Soup for the Soul*, Mike Buetelle tells that when he was in junior high, the eighth-grade bully punched him in the stomach. Not only did it hurt and make him angry, but the embarrassment and humiliation were almost intolerable. He desperately wanted to even the score. He planned to meet the bully by the bike racks the next day and let him have it.

For some reason, Mike made the mistake of telling his plan to his grandmother, Nana. She gave him one of her hour-long lectures. The lecture seemed like a drag, but among other things, Mike vaguely remembered her telling him that he didn't need to worry about the bully. She said, "Good deeds beget good results, and evil deeds beget bad results."

Mike told his Nana, in a nice way, that he thought she didn't understand his situation. Mike also told her that he did good things all the time, and that all he got in return was grief. But his Nana stuck to her guns, saying, "Every good deed will come back to you someday, and every bad thing you do will also come back to you."

It took Mike 30 more years to understand the wisdom of his Nana's words. She was living in a board-and-care home in southern California. Each Tuesday, Mike went by and took her out to dinner. He would always find her neatly dressed and sitting in a chair right by the front door. He vividly remembers their last dinner together before she went into the convalescent hospital. They drove to a nearby simple little family-owned restaurant. He ordered pot roast for Nana and a hamburger for himself.

The food arrived, and as Mike dug in, he noticed that his Nana wasn't eating. She was just staring at the food on her plate. Moving his plate aside, Mike took his Nana's plate, placed it in front of him, and cut her meat into small pieces. He then placed the plate back in front of her. As she very weakly forked the meat into her mouth, Mike was struck with a memory that brought instant tears to his eyes.

Forty years previously, Mike was a little boy sitting at the table. His Nana had always taken the meat on his plate and cut it into small pieces so he could eat it. It had taken 40 years, but the good deed had been repaid. Nana was right. "Every good deed you do will someday come back to you."

These Shall Still Bear Fruit. For my fortieth birthday, I received my all-time favorite pastor's birthday card. The cover had a drawing of a great oak tree with the words, "Pastor, if you were a tree, you'd be an oak." I opened the card to read "a little rough on the outside and surrounded by nuts, but solid and straight on the inside! Have a Great Birthday."

When I finished my chuckling, my eyes settled on this verse, also in the card, from Psalm 92:13-14, *[The righteous] are planted in the house of the LORD; they flourish in the courts of our God. In old age they still produce fruit; they are always green and full of sap.* Like the kind and considerate people who sent me the card, I hope and pray that I will always bear good fruit. As Jesus said in John 15:8, *"My Father is glorified by this, that you bear much fruit and become my disciples."*

FOR YOUTH

■ TOPIC: Take the High Road

■ QUESTIONS: 1. How is it possible to "inspect fruit" without being judgmental? 2. By what standard would you want others to evaluate you? 3. Have you ever had someone criticize the "speck" in your eye, all the while looking past the "log" in his or her own eye? How did that make you feel? 4. What are some of the things you've done for others that you wish someone would do for you? 5. Why do you think that *"the gate is narrow and the road is hard that leads to life"* (Matt. 7:14)?

■ ILLUSTRATIONS:

As You Would Have Them Do to You. Some years ago, *The Phoenix Sun* printed a piece that contained these words that sound like an expounding of the Golden Rule: "Live every day as if it were your last. Do every job as if you were the boss. Drive as if all other vehicles were police cars. Treat everybody else as if he or she were you."

In Sheep's Clothing. Asheville, North Carolina, has become the center of an unlikely spiritual clash. The city of 68,000, known as the home of Billy Graham and his training center, has also become "America's new freak capital;" according to a 2000 issue of the *Rolling Stone* magazine.

"The place overflowed with hippies, neo-hippies, punks, witches, and pagans," the magazine said. Asheville residents are not pleased with the new label for the city, located in the hills where Methodist revival preacher Francis Asbury rode his horse while spreading the Gospel during the second great awakening (a period of intense religious revival in the United States in the opening decades of the nineteenth century).

The situation came to a head when the mayor proclaimed the last week in October "Earth Religions Awareness" week, arousing anger among Christians for the city's support of paganism. About 3,000 Christians protested in front of city hall and asked the mayor also to proclaim it as "The Lordship of Christ" week. The mayor decided to rescind her earlier proclamation, which upset many of the local people who practice pagan religions.

A Bad Tree Cannot Bear Good Fruit. Why isn't the church—the body of Christ—bearing the kind of fruit that we ought to bear? In his book *America's Only Hope,* Anthony T. Evans (president of the Urban Alternative in Dallas, Texas) suggests what the problem might be.

"There's obviously nothing wrong with the Head of the church. Jesus is alive and well. . . . Our central nervous system, the Holy Spirit, is also fine. The Spirit is taking the Word and sending it through the body so the body knows what to do and has the power to do it. The problem lies in the body. The hands get the word from the Spirit, but they don't feel like moving. The feet don't feel like walking. The mouth doesn't feel like talking. As a result, the church stumbles around like a diseased body. Think of the message a sick church gives to the world."

LIGHT FOR ALL PEOPLE

THE SERVANT'S MISSION

BACKGROUND SCRIPTURE: Isaiah 49:1-7
DEVOTIONAL READING: Isaiah 49:8-13

KEY VERSE: "I will give you as a light to the nations,
that my salvation may reach to the end of the earth." Isaiah 49:6.

KING JAMES VERSION

ISAIAH 49:1 Listen, O isles, unto me; and hearken, ye people, from far; The LORD hath called me from the womb; from the bowels of my mother hath he made mention of my name.

2 And he hath made my mouth like a sharp sword; in the shadow of his hand hath he hid me, and made me a polished shaft; in his quiver hath he hid me;

3 And said unto me, Thou art my servant, O Israel, in whom I will be glorified.

4 Then I said, I have laboured in vain, I have spent my strength for nought, and in vain: yet surely my judgment is with the LORD, and my work with my God.

5 And now, saith the LORD that formed me from the womb to be his servant, to bring Jacob again to him, Though Israel be not gathered, yet shall I be glorious in the eyes of the LORD, and my God shall be my strength.

6 And he said, It is a light thing that thou shouldest be my servant to raise up the tribes of Jacob, and to restore the preserved of Israel: I will also give thee for a light to the Gentiles, that thou mayest be my salvation unto the end of the earth.

NEW REVISED STANDARD VERSION

ISAIAH 49:1 Listen to me, O coastlands,
 pay attention, you peoples from far away!
The LORD called me before I was born,
 while I was in my mother's womb he named me.

2 He made my mouth like a sharp sword,
 in the shadow of his hand he hid me;
he made me a polished arrow,
 in his quiver he hid me away.

3 And he said to me, "You are my servant,
 Israel, in whom I will be glorified."

4 But I said, "I have labored in vain,
 I have spent my strength for nothing and vanity;
yet surely my cause is with the LORD,
 and my reward with my God."

5 And now the LORD says,
 who formed me in the womb to be his servant,
to bring Jacob back to him,
 and that Israel might be gathered to him,
for I am honored in the sight of the LORD,
 and my God has become my strength—

6 he says,
"It is too light a thing that you should be my servant
 to raise up the tribes of Jacob
 and to restore the survivors of Israel;
I will give you as a light to the nations,
 that my salvation may reach to the end of the earth."

BACKGROUND

Isaiah is often referred to as "the prince of prophets" not only because of the way he portrayed God's future fulfillment of justice and redemption, but also because of the way he described the culmination of God's justice and redemption in the coming of the Messiah. Isaiah's prophecies were directed toward the nation of Judah during a precarious time in that southern kingdom's history.

Successive empires would look to both the land and people of Judah with the desire to conquer. First, the Assyrian empire overran the northern kingdom of Israel in 722 B.C. Then the Babylonians rose to power, and in 586 B.C., they conquered Judah, destroyed the temple and much of Jerusalem, and carried off into exile the nation's best and brightest people. Later, Persia conquered Babylon (in 539 B.C.) and thus ruled over Judah, too. And a little more than 200 years later, Alexander the Great and his battle-hardened Greek troops overpowered the Persians and gained control of the region.

Isaiah wrote his prophecies to call the nation of Judah back to God and to tell about the Lord's salvation through the Messiah. Isaiah also intended his prophecies to help the Jews, whether located in their own homeland or in exile, to maintain their faith in God in the midst of overwhelming disaster. During Isaiah's own lifetime (he is thought to have prophesied between 740 and 681 B.C.) the constantly menacing threat was the Assyrians. Because both the northern and southern kingdoms tended to trust in their own military might rather than in the power of God, Isaiah preached forcefully to both peoples and their rulers. But 18 years into Isaiah's prophetic work, the Assyrians conquered the northern kingdom of Israel.

As Isaiah continued his prophesying to the people and rulers of the southern kingdom of Judah, he foresaw even mightier empires than Assyria on the horizon. The people of Judah, he foretold, because of their lack of faith, would also fall to a power greater than the Assyrians. But even in the midst of the Israelites' devastation, God's eye would be watching over them. Isaiah prophesied that the land and the people would not always be ruled by brute force. In a future day God would send His Servant, the Messiah, who through faith and purity would both deliver and lead His chosen people. Under His righteous rule, peace, justice, and hope would endure for all time.

NOTES ON THE PRINTED TEXT

Isaiah, having prophesied in chapter 48 of the Israelites' deliverance from Babylonian captivity, in chapter 49 initiated a description of the way that the Lord would accomplish an even greater deliverance of His people than that from Babylon. At the right time—at the time of God's own choosing—He would deliver His people from the sin that had brought them into bondage in the first place. Thus this deliverance would exceed the greatness of God's deliverance of the Israelites from Egyptian bondage and from Babylonian bondage. God's chosen instrument for this great deliverance would be His righteous Servant (vss. 3-6), namely, the prophesied Messiah. Though He is first mentioned in 42:1-9, the Servant is the central focus of this week's Scripture text.

Earlier in the prophecy of Isaiah, "the servant of the Lord" was a more generic phrase for any person or nation who voluntarily served God. In fact, at several points, *my servant* (41:8) designated the entire nation of Israel. But Israel as the Lord's chosen messenger to the peoples of the world too often failed in its mission of outreach (42:19). And because of the nation's failure, the faithful servant is elsewhere described as a small portion of God's chosen people who continued to obey and follow Him, *the remnant of Israel* (10:20) and *the remnant of Jacob* (10:21). But the ultimate meaning of this "servant of the Lord" is found in what have come to be known as Isaiah's "servant songs" (42:1-9; 49:1-7; 50:4-11; 52:13—53:12). In these songs or poems, the ideal Servant can only be an individual whose suffering and death makes atonement possible for the lost (53:5-6). Thus this Servant of the Lord is God's perfect solution for humanity's greatest need. And such prophecy can only refer to Jesus Christ, God's own Son, who was completely committed to the Lord's redemptive mission for the world. In Christ, salvation is freely offered to both Jews and Gentiles.

Isaiah 49:1 contains a summons for the *coastlands* and *you peoples from far away* to listen to the calling and mission that God had given to His Servant. The far reaching scope of God's intended salvation through the Servant is directly portrayed. The Lord's Servant was called upon long before He was born, which indicates that His mission was not an afterthought, but rather a part of God's plan and purpose from eternity past. Some scholars say this verse is also a reference to Jesus' virgin birth.

The Servant, who was speaking for Himself through the prophet Isaiah, next described the ways in which God would equip Him for His mission. His *mouth like a sharp sword* (49:2) likely refers to His teaching. His being hidden in *the shadow of His hand* is descriptive of God's protection over Him. God making Him *a polished arrow* probably refers to God's using Him as the instrument for the deliverance from sin.

In 49:3 we encounter the first time the Servant quoted Himself directly. It is clear that the attitudes He was expressing are not those of the nation of Israel. Incarnate within this Servant was, however, an expression of what the nation of

Israel might have been had it wholeheartedly committed itself to God. Thus this individual Servant is the Messiah, through whom God would ultimately be glorified. In essence, the Servant would succeed where the nation of Israel failed.

"I have labored in vain, I have spent my strength for nothing and vanity" (49:4) might indicate that, from an earthly point of view, the Servant's mission would seem to be a failure. But His failure would not be like Israel's, who disobeyed God and fell short of its mission. Though the Servant would in no way be a failure to God, He would temporarily suffer failure in the eyes of many people. In an earthly sense, the Servant's mission would fall short of human expectations in that He *was despised and rejected by others; a man of suffering and acquainted with infirmity; and as one from whom others hide their faces he was despised, and we held him of no account* (53:3). And though He would not resort to human efforts to gain success, He would leave the outcome of His mission in His Father's hands.

More mission statements follow. The Servant is *to bring Jacob back to him, and that Israel might be gathered to him* (49:5) and *to raise up the tribes of Jacob and to restore the survivors of Israel* (49:6). This is not only a prophecy about the Servant's breaking the people's captivity in Babylon, but also a prophecy about the Servant's breaking the people's captivity to the power of sin. In both cases, the promise was that they would be released from captivity and delivered.

The latter part of 49:6 has sometimes been called "the Great Commission of the Old Testament." In response to the Servant's acknowledgement that *God has become my strength* (49:5), God the Father said that He would give the Servant *as a light to the nations, that my salvation may reach to the end of the earth* (49:6). Once again, the far-reaching scope of God's plan of redemption is put on display. The Servant is the one who would provide salvation through a sacrificial giving of Himself. Thus, the Servant's ministry would encompass people from all walks of life.

SUGGESTIONS TO TEACHERS

When we delve into a study of Isaiah's prophecy, we find several comparisons being made to get across its message about the Servant's mission. And we soon learn that things aren't always what they seem. In Isaiah 49:1-6, we find an old covenant that points to a new one, a grand success that initially looks like a hideous failure, a missionary nation that gets exiled because it refused to leave home, and a light that is a mirror-image reflection of the original.

1. WHEN AN OLD COVENANT LOOKS LIKE A NEW ONE. Hidden between the lines of these verses is a message about the nation of Israel's lackluster approach to its mission. God had made a covenant with Israel so that this chosen nation might show the rest of the world the rewards of intimacy with and obedience to the one true God. But when Israel either kept God to itself or forgot

Him completely, thus breaking the covenant, God turned to His Servant, His own Son, the Messiah, to see to it that the mission of proclaiming the news of His salvation *to the end of the earth* (Isa. 49:6) might be accomplished. Thus was established a new covenant for all who would believe.

2. WHEN SUCCESS LOOKS LIKE FAILURE. When Jesus hung on the cross, His lifeblood dripping to the ground, executed like a common criminal, it looked to the world as if His mission was a failure. But God turned what looked like a "failure" into a great success. Jesus' sacrificial death made a way for the lost to be saved.

3. WHEN A MISSIONARY LOOKS LIKE A HOMEBODY. In eternity past—before the Servant, Jesus Christ, was born—God had chosen Him to bring the light of the message of salvation to the whole world. Christ offered salvation to all nations, and His disciples began the missionary effort to take the Gospel to the ends of the earth. Today's missionary work continues Jesus' desire to take the light of the Gospel to all nations. But to fulfill His will, we cannot be homebodies. Though we may not be called or in the position to take His Gospel to the ends of the earth, we are all called and in the position to take the message of truth around the block to those who are near to us.

4. WHEN A REFLECTION LOOKS LIKE THE LIGHT. Jesus said, "*I am the light of the world. Whoever follows me will never walk in darkness but will have the light of life*" (John 8:12). And Jesus also said, "*You are the light of the world. A city built on a hill cannot be hid*" (Matt. 5:14). God's Servant, Jesus Christ, is the Light of the world. And as Christians, we are called to reflect His light of salvation wherever we encounter spiritual darkness.

FOR ADULTS	■ **TOPIC:** The Gift of Light

■ **QUESTIONS:** 1. In that the Servant's mouth was *like a sharp sword* (Isa. 49:2), how do you think He would speak to the people? 2. Why did the Lord refer to the Servant as *Israel* (49:3) in that He was speaking to Him as an individual? 3. How do the Servant's words in 49:4 contrast with the way in which He was received by the nation of Israel? 4. What promises did the Lord make to the Servant despite His prophesied discouragement? 5. In what ways would the Servant be *a light to the nations* (49:6)?

■ **ILLUSTRATIONS:**

In the Shadow of His Hand. Robert Browning wrote, "Life's a little thing!" But a little thing can mean a life—even two lives. Two young men realized this several years ago in downtown Denver. One of them says he and his friend saw something tiny and insignificant change the world, but no one else even seemed to notice.

It was one of those beautiful Denver days—crystal clear, no humidity, and not a cloud in the sky. The two young men decided to walk the 10 blocks to an outdoor restaurant rather than take the shuttle bus that runs up and down the mall. The tables of the restaurant were set appropriately on the grass infield, and many colorful pennants and flags hung limply overhead.

As the two young men sat outside, the sun continued to beat down on them, and it became increasingly hot. There wasn't a hint of a breeze, and heat radiated up from the tabletop. Nothing moved, except the waiters, of course. And they didn't move very fast, either.

After lunch the two young men started to walk back up the mall. They both noticed a mother and her young daughter walking out of a card shop toward the street. The mother was holding her daughter by the hand while reading a greeting card. It was immediately apparent that she was so engrossed in the card that she did not notice a shuttle bus moving toward her at a good clip. She and her daughter were one step away from disaster when one of the young men started to yell. He hadn't even gotten a word out when a breeze blew the card out of the mother's hand and over her shoulder. She spun around and grabbed at the card, nearly knocking her daughter over. By the time the mother picked up the card from the ground and turned back around to cross the street, the shuttle bus had whizzed by her. She never even knew what had almost happened.

To this day two things continue to perplex the young men about this event. First, where did that one spurt of wind come from to blow the card out of that mother's hand? This was perplexing to them, for there had not been a whisper of wind at lunch or during the long walk back up the mall.

Second, if the one young man had been able to get his words out, the mother might have looked up as she and her daughter continued to walk into the path of the bus. But it was the wind that made the mother turn back to the card—in the one direction that saved her life and that of her daughter. The passing bus did not create the wind. On the contrary, the wind came from the opposite direction. These two young men have no doubt that it was a breath from God protecting a mother and her child!

The awesomeness of this event, however, is that the mother never knew what had happened. As the two young men continued back to work, they wondered how God often acts in our lives—hiding us in the shadow of His hand—without our being aware. The difference between life and death can very well be a little thing. And amazing events often blow unseen through our lives.

Siberia: To the End of the Earth. Siberia in winter isn't April in Paris! But it was the right place at the right time for Russian Christians looking for a warm welcome several years ago.

Teams of Russian missionaries braved sub-zero temperatures to take the Gospel to the impoverished and spiritually bereft people of Siberia, Hannu Haukka of International Russian Radio/TV told *Religion Today*. The missionaries covered 9,000 miles and spoke in dozens of towns that dot the frozen tundra from the Siberian capital of Yakutsk to the Bering Sea. Many people became Christians in the towns. Residents thronged to see the visitors and hear what they had to say, since the isolated towns get few visitors and even fewer missionaries.

A tribal chief in Borulah called everyone who had a telephone and told them to invite their neighbors and come hear the missionaries speak. "The assembly hall was packed," the team leader said. "We spoke for two hours and nobody wanted to leave." When the missionaries invited people to trust in Christ, "everyone came forward. Now these people need a pastor to work with them."

Citizens begged a team of Christians traveling through Deputatsk to preach. The team had stopped to have its vehicle serviced when people noticed a sign on the bumper proclaiming the Gospel. "We too are human beings. Many of our townfolk want to hear about God," they said. The team held an impromptu service that ran late into the night. In Topolin, a "great spiritual hunger" caused services to extend for eight hours.

The rugged landscape and brutal climate isolates Siberians. Travel is difficult because of its few airports, nearly impassible roads, and swampy terrain. Winter is the best time to travel because swamps freeze, allowing vehicles to reach otherwise inaccessible places. Some towns are separated by hundreds of miles, but even nearby towns took hours to reach in the teams' four-wheel-drive vehicles. Such isolation makes Siberia one of the most spiritually desolate places in Russia, Haukka related. Poverty, spiritual oppression, and extended periods of winter darkness cause depression, alcoholism, and suicide.

Northern Siberia has "a big alcohol problem," said Stanislav Yefimov, a Yakut Eskimo who became a Christian through the broadcast ministry of IRR/TV. "People are continually drunk because they are looking for an escape from their problems," and others delve into witchcraft, he reported.

IRR/TV began Christian broadcasts to the Yakuts several years ago. It opened a facility to produce television programs in 15 languages all over Russia, including the Chinese and Mongolian borders, Caucasus Mountain region, and republics of the Commonwealth of Independent States (CIS). The ministry's Moscow training center teaches Christians how to produce radio and television broadcasts, which reach millions of Russians a week on 50 channels. Special broadcasts reach 70 million Muslims, 10 million Jews, and 17 million hearing-impaired people in Russia and the CIS.

Haukka, a Canadian minister, founded IRR/TV in Finland during the Soviet days. He signed a historic deal with Soviet television in 1989, which allowed the Christian Broadcast Network's Superbook animated Bible-on-video to be broadcast to the country. Some 200 million people saw the broadcast, and the response to a follow-up questionnaire was overwhelming. Here is a concrete way in which the Servant of the Lord continues to be *a light to the nations* (Isa. 49:6) and whose message of hope is reaching *to the end of the earth.*

■ TOPIC: Mission Possible!

■ QUESTIONS: 1. In what ways do you think God would hide the Servant *in the shadow of his hand* (Isa. 49:2)? 2. Have you ever felt like God was hiding you in the shadow of His hand? 3. In what ways does Jesus Christ fulfill this mission of being God's Servant? 4. In light of this Servant's mission, what do you think your mission is as a follower of the Servant? 5. What are some things you can continue to do to make sure that God's salvation *may reach to the end of the earth* (49:6)?

■ ILLUSTRATIONS:

On a Mission. Several years ago more than 30,000 college students prayed and worshiped together at a large park in Memphis, Tennessee. Organizers said almost 24,000 people had registered in advance and the rest arrived at the gate for the prayer rally, which was carried live on the Internet.

According to a Memphis newspaper, organizer Louie Giglio prayed, "From north, south, east, and west, we come to stand before You to affirm that You are our God. This day belongs to You. Everything belongs to You." Giglio is the founder of Passion Conferences and its daylong worship, music, and prayer service, called OneDay.

The students stood with their hands raised above their heads, praising God, or knelt in the field with their heads bowed, praying for revival, praying that the light of Jesus' salvation might extend to the end of the earth. "It was unbelievable—tens of thousands of students from all over the world spending the entire day on Saturday praising God and praying for revival in their generation," Jocelyn Scott, a Campus Crusade for Christ staff member who traveled from Edison, N.J., told *Religion Today*.

Students started arriving Thursday afternoon and pitched hundreds of tents. More than half camped out in the 4,600-acre park, event coordinator Matt Morris said. Rain threatened, but held off, and only a slight drizzle fell briefly on Saturday.

In between prayers and speeches, people listened to Christian music as they watched the broadcast on three giant screens. Hay-wagon shuttles transported participants around the park. Students added their individual artwork or written comments to a 40- by 50-foot banner, which was hoisted like a sail for all to see. Exhibitors from missions organizations were taking the names of interested students as fast as they could.

The event concluded on Sunday with a commissioning service during which students promised to spread the Gospel. More than 10 percent stood when asked to make a commitment to serve a year or more on a mission field. For months afterward, Morris was receiving hundreds of e-mails a day from students relating how they wanted to get involved in various ministries, pray, or reach out to someone with the Gospel.

Attitude the Key to Mission's Success. The attitude we take toward achieving our Christian mission will have much to do with whether we are a success or a failure in the end. A well-known preacher and writer named Chuck Swindoll has said this about attitude:

> The longer I live, the more I realize the impact of attitude on life. Attitude to me, is more important than facts, than the past, than education, than money, than circumstances, than failures, than successes, than appearance, or skill. It will make or break a company, a team, a church, a home, a relationship. The remarkable thing is that we have a choice every day regarding the attitude we will embrace for that day. We cannot change the inevitable. The only thing we can do is play on the one string we have, and that is our attitude. I am convinced that life is 10 percent what happens to me and 90 percent how I react to it. And so it is with you . . . you alone are in charge of your attitude.

THE PEACEFUL KINGDOM

BACKGROUND SCRIPTURE: Isaiah 11:1-9
DEVOTIONAL READING: Isaiah 12

KEY VERSE: The wolf shall live with the lamb, the leopard shall lie down with the kid, the calf and the lion and the fatling together, and a little child shall lead them. Isaiah 11:6.

KING JAMES VERSION

ISAIAH 11:1 And there shall come forth a rod out of the stem of Jesse, and a Branch shall grow out of his roots:

2 And the spirit of the LORD shall rest upon him, the spirit of wisdom and understanding, the spirit of counsel and might, the spirit of knowledge and of the fear of the LORD;

3 And shall make him of quick understanding in the fear of the LORD: and he shall not judge after the sight of his eyes, neither reprove after the hearing of his ears:

4 But with righteousness shall he judge the poor, and reprove with equity for the meek of the earth: and he shall smite the earth with the rod of his mouth, and with the breath of his lips shall he slay the wicked.

5 And righteousness shall be the girdle of his loins, and faithfulness the girdle of his reins.

6 The wolf also shall dwell with the lamb, and the leopard shall lie down with the kid; and the calf and the young lion and the fatling together; and a little child shall lead them.

7 And the cow and the bear shall feed; their young ones shall lie down together: and the lion shall eat straw like the ox.

8 And the sucking child shall play on the hole of the asp, and the weaned child shall put his hand on the cockatrice' den.

9 They shall not hurt nor destroy in all my holy mountain: for the earth shall be full of the knowledge of the LORD, as the waters cover the sea.

NEW REVISED STANDARD VERSION

ISAIAH 11:1 A shoot shall come out from the stump of Jesse,
and a branch shall grow out of his roots.

2 The spirit of the LORD shall rest on him,
the spirit of wisdom and understanding,
the spirit of counsel and might,
the spirit of knowledge and the fear of the LORD.

3 His delight shall be in the fear of the LORD.
He shall not judge by what his eyes see,
or decide by what his ears hear;

4 but with righteousness he shall judge the poor,
and decide with equity for the meek of the earth;
he shall strike the earth with the rod of his mouth,
and with the breath of his lips he shall kill the
wicked.

5 Righteousness shall be the belt around his waist,
and faithfulness the belt around his loins.

6 The wolf shall live with the lamb,
the leopard shall lie down with the kid,
the calf and the lion and the fatling together,
and a little child shall lead them.

7 The cow and the bear shall graze,
their young shall lie down together;
and the lion shall eat straw like the ox.

8 The nursing child shall play over the hole of the
asp,
and the weaned child shall put its hand on the
adder's den.

9 They will not hurt or destroy on all my holy
mountain;
for the earth will be full of the knowledge of
the LORD
as the waters cover the sea.

HOME BIBLE READINGS

BACKGROUND

Many Bible scholars believe that the prophet's description of the messianic King in Isaiah 11 was done to contrast the coming monarch's rule with that of King Ahaz of Judah. Ruling from 735 to 715 B.C., Ahaz was the twelfth king of Judah and one the nation's most wicked rulers. Isaiah was about five years into his prophetic ministry when Ahaz ascended the throne.

Ahaz's disregard for the one true God was shown by his evil actions, including sacrificing his own son to pagan gods and encouraging his people to likewise sacrifice their children. Ahaz also copied some of the pagan religious customs from the non-Jewish people within and on the fringes of the nation's land, and even went so far as to change the temple services, replacing the altar of burnt offering with a replica of the pagan altar he had seen in Damascus of Aram (2 Kings 16; 2 Chron. 28).

Ahaz also led his nation to turn its back on God by seeking to establish alliances with godless nations. Both the northern kingdom of Israel and Aram were under Assyria's control. When they united against Judah, they had hoped to force Ahaz and the southern kingdom of Judah to join their revolt against Assyria. But the plan backfired when Ahaz asked Assyria to come to his aid (Isa. 7:1-9).

Relying more upon the appeasement taxes paid out to Assyria than upon God to keep the Assyrians out of his land, Ahaz's scheme eventually failed. Though the king of Assyria did not conquer Judah, he did cause a great deal of trouble, and Ahaz lived to regret asking for Assyria's help. It's true that Israel fell to the Assyrians in 722 B.C. and that Ahaz remained on the throne in Jerusalem; but he and Judah's high priest were viewed by the people of their own land and by surrounding lands as weak and compromising. Both the political and religious systems of Judah were in shambles. The latter was especially so because Ahaz had made pleasing those in power the chief aim of the temple rituals.

As Judah suffered under King Ahaz's complete lack of faith and the nation's political and religious turmoil, the prophet Isaiah promised a coming King whose *delight shall be in the fear of the LORD* (11:3), one who would lead His people with *wisdom and understanding* (11:2) and with *righteousness* (11:4) and *faithfulness* (11:5). The role of this future King would remain unfulfilled until His coming as Jesus the Messiah.

NOTES ON THE PRINTED TEXT

The first nine verses of Isaiah 11 are considered a poem. In fact, the scholar Hans Wildberger called it the "pearl of Hebrew poetry." Within these verses are several sets of images and metaphors, like the shoot out of the stump and the branch out of the roots (11:1), the rod of the mouth and the breath of the lips (11:4), and righteousness as a belt around the waist (11:5).

Following these images and metaphors is a lovely description of a pastoral scene, where various pairs of animals—typically strongly opposed to each other—convey a picture of perfect peace. It's hard to imagine wolves resting with lambs, leopards lying down with young goats, and calves and lions eating together peacefully. But that's the way things are depicted during the Messiah's righteous, peaceful reign. By making use of these common images and metaphors, Isaiah encouraged his beleaguered people with a message of hope: *the earth will be full of the knowledge of the LORD as the waters cover the sea* (11:9).

This poem commences after a description of the downfall of the region's immense powers. Isaiah 10:33 portrayed how *the tallest trees will be cut down, and the lofty will be brought low.* This is a reference to the Assyrian Empire—an empire that, after conquering much of the Middle East (including Israel), would fall, never to rise again. Then in 11:1, the focus shifts to Judah, which many thought was nothing but a dried-up stump. Isaiah declared that a day was coming when the stump of Israel would flourish again; a new branch would sprout from the old root of Jesse's family line. The shoot growing from the stump refers to the promised Messiah. Far greater than the original tree, this shoot would bear much fruit and would rule forever.

The coming Messiah would be empowered by the Holy Spirit, who would endow Him with the *wisdom, understanding, counsel, might,* and *knowledge,* (11:2) necessary for Him to undertake and fulfill the purposes of God for His people. Because the Messiah's *delight shall be in the fear of the LORD* (11:3), His judgment would be fair and truthful. He would not judge simply on the basis of appearances or by what He heard, but with real discernment that arises out of His righteousness. It would be His word, not His military might, that provided the foundation for His authority.

Of course, the rulers of Isaiah's day lacked these qualities. Judah had grown ever more corrupt and was little more than a vassal state of the hostile, foreign powers that surrounded it, especially Assyria. Both the leadership of the nation and its people desperately needed a revival of righteousness, justice, and faithfulness—all qualities the future Messiah would possess. The people needed to turn from selfishness and show justice to the poor and the oppressed—actions the Messiah would perform (11:4).

In ancient times when people prepared for vigorous action, they tied up their loose, flowing garments with a belt. So when Isaiah said that *righteousness shall be the belt around his waist, and faithfulness the belt around his loins* (11:5), he was prophesying both the Messiah's active involvement in administering justice and the basis for His actions: righteousness and faithfulness.

The prophetic poem then describes what the reign of this Messiah would look like. It would be unlike anything ever experienced by humanity in that it would be perfect paradise—a time of perfect peace. Death and destruction would be defeated, and arrogance and pomp would no longer be mistaken for capable leadership. Even the animal kingdom would be at peace, and this peace would extend to such a degree that *a little child shall lead them* (11:6). Indeed, the peace of this age is reflected in the fact that children would go unharmed as they play with formerly ferocious animals.

Though it is clear that Christ came to bring peace to the human soul through His death and resurrection, it is also clear that not all of the prophecies of Isaiah 11 were fulfilled at Christ's first coming. For instance, nature has not yet returned to its intended balance and harmony: *For the creation waits with eager longing for the revealing of the children of God; for the creation was subjected to futility, not of its own will but by the will of the one who subjected it, in hope that the creation itself will be set free from its bondage to decay and will obtain the freedom of the glory of the children of God* (Rom. 8:19-21). Thus, this golden age is yet to come, and such perfect tranquility will be possible only when Jesus reigns over the earth.

In the meantime, God's chosen people—the nations of Israel and Judah—continued under the harsh dominion of surrounding nations. They needed to know and keep the faith that their one, true God was still in control despite their desperate situation. So in speaking of the coming Messiah and His kingdom of peace, Isaiah reminded his hearers that they *will not hurt or destroy on all my holy mountain* (Isa. 11:9). Because many of the pagans in power over the Israelites believed that their gods lived on the mountains, this was a way of saying that God would be eventually recognized as superior to the idols of all the other nations.

Although the word "Messiah" does not appear in Isaiah 11:1-9, the description of this coming ruler influences the way the New Testament describes Jesus the Messiah (Rom. 15:12; 2 Thess. 2:8; Rev. 19:11, 15). Isaiah, who had been a witness to the folly of Ahaz, and who with all of the house of Judah watched the armies of Sennacherib approach the walls of Jerusalem, may have foreseen then that the ax would eventually fall on the Davidic line. Sensing what was coming, Isaiah comforted Hezekiah, who followed Ahaz as king of Judah, by telling him, *The surviving remnant of the house of Judah shall again take root downward, and bear fruit upward* (2 Kings 19:30).

Isaiah wrote his prophetic poem to give assurance to future generations of a coming King who would emerge as a shoot from the stump of Jesse and would rule with righteousness and initiate unparalleled peace for His people. The consummation of His kingdom awaits a future glorious time, but presently He reigns in the hearts of those who submit to Him as Lord.

SUGGESTIONS TO TEACHERS

Isaiah earlier referred to the coming Messiah as the *Prince of Peace* (Isa. 9:6). In chapter 11, Isaiah showed what the Messiah's rule and dominion would look like. Indeed, His would be a kingdom of peace in which judgment would be fair and compassion would be actively poured out. This kingdom is already active in the hearts of His people, and so, with God's help, we can seek to exhibit the traits of His dominion to the world around us.

1. GIVE WHAT YOU'D LIKE TO GET. How often have we said, "It's just not fair"? We desperately long for fairness from other people, and so we ought also to show fairness to others. We rightfully get upset with those who base their judgments on appearance or false evidence or rumors, and so we ought also to refrain from judging others by such shaky and inadequate standards. Only Christ can be the perfectly fair judge; thus only as He governs our hearts can we learn to be as fair in our treatment of others as we expect them to be toward us.

2. GIVE A HELPING HAND. Righteousness and faithfulness would be the basis for the coming Messiah's vigorous action on behalf of His people. Isaiah said *with righteousness he shall judge the poor, and decide with equity for the meek of the earth* (11:4). These two basic concepts of the faith should be the basis for our vigorous action as well. The righteousness and faithfulness that God values is much more than just refraining from sin. It is actively turning toward others and offering them the help they need.

3. GIVE THOUGHT TO THE FACT THAT GOD IS IN CONTROL. "Desperate situations call for desperate measures," quipped Sir Winston Churchill. Although God's people were in a desperate situation, Isaiah reminded them that the behavior of nations is well within the realm of God's rule. God's plan was being fulfilled, and God's plan would be fulfilled. And the most critical part of His plan was a coming King, a promised Messiah, who would deliver His people and rule with justice. Beyond keeping our faith in God, we need to keep the faith that God is in control.

4. GIVE YOUR NATION THE BENEFIT OF PRAYER FOR REVIVAL. Just as in Judah the leadership of the nation and its people desperately needed a revival of righteousness, justice, and faithfulness, so, too, do we need revival. Be a part of making the conditions right for revival by seeking to live a holy life and praying that God would bless us with a spiritual reawakening.

FOR ADULTS

■ **TOPIC:** The Gift of Peace

■ **QUESTIONS:** 1. In what ways was Jesus' advent like *a shoot . . . come out from the stump of Jesse, and a branch . . . out of his roots* (Isa. 11:1)? 2. What evidence from Jesus' life demonstrates to you that He was the fulfillment of the prophecy of 11:2? 3. Why was it important that the coming Messiah's *delight . . . be in the fear of the LORD* (11:3)? 4. In what ways would

Jesus *judge the poor, and decide with equity for the meek of the earth* (11:4)?
5. How does seeking to follow the Lord also help us pursue righteousness and
faithfulness in our lives?

■ ILLUSTRATIONS:

To the Rescue. When I went downstairs at the parsonage one morning to brush
my teeth, I found my daughter Gracie sitting on our bed reading the back of a
novel. Curled up on the floor asleep was our little mutt of a puppy, Oreo. Feeling
a bit mischievous, I yanked the book from Gracie's hands and gently popped her
on the head with it.

Gracie let out one of her "Oh, Daddys!" which stirred Oreo from its slumber.
At that point, Gracie and I both knew we wanted to play this little game in which
I act like I'm pounding on her and she yells out like she's hurting—all to see how
our dog will react.

We'd never played that game with Oreo before, although we've played it
numerous times with our older and more mature collie, Bonhoeffer. Bonhoeffer
always steps right in when we play this game. The dog is very protective of its
boy and girl (my son, Nathaniel, and my daughter, Gracie). I'm certain that the
dog thinks of them as its sheep that it must both herd and protect! In fact, when
Nathaniel and I wrestle, Nathaniel yells out like he's being beaten to a pulp, and
Bonhoeffer zooms to his rescue, either grabbing a piece of my clothing and
pulling me away or clamping down on my arm and edging me off of Nathaniel.

Oreo didn't know this game, and Gracie and I were excited to see how the dog
would react. So I kept "pelting" Gracie with the book and she kept crying out for
help. At first, Oreo jumped up on all fours and said, "Boof!"—not a bark, just a
sound that a dog makes to ask what's going on. Then Oreo jumped up on the bed
to conduct a further investigation. It looked at me, then at Gracie, and then back
at me. It was clear that, as Oreo kept looking back and forth at us, it didn't know
what to do.

Then Gracie and I saw a light go on in Oreo's eyes. You could actually see it!
An idea flashed through that little dog's mind. It jumped down on the floor and
shot up the stairs at breakneck speed. Gracie and I listened, wondering what in the
world that little dog was up to. Was Oreo running from trouble? Was the dog
sticking its head in the sand so as to cast from its mind the conflict going on
downstairs? As we listened we could hear Oreo's footsteps dashing across the
floor upstairs. Then we heard the dog stop. For about three seconds, there was
silence. Then we heard the pound of Bonhoeffer jumping off the couch onto the
floor. Now two sets of dog footsteps were running across the floor.

Down the stairs came both dogs, Bonhoeffer leading the way and Oreo following at its side. We could hear Bonhoeffer growling all the way down the steps,
like it meant to put to a stop right then and there to any "violence" that may have
been taking place. At that point, Gracie and I were doubled over in laughter! But

the two of us still wonder how Oreo communicated to Bonhoeffer that there was trouble going on downstairs and that the dog's assistance was required immediately.

Oreo taught me something that morning. Sometimes—perhaps even most of the time—we are not big enough or strong enough or smart enough or wise enough to take care of a distressing situation by ourselves. There comes a time when we realize our lack of bigness, strength, knowledge, and wisdom, and we need to go get a peacemaker in the quickest place we can find it. Jesus the Messiah will one day bring perfect peace, and we can go to Him anytime to gain peace for our souls.

God Is in Control. Gladys Aylward, a missionary to China more than 50 years ago, was forced to flee when the Japanese invaded Yangcheng. But she could not leave her work behind. With only one assistant, she led more than 100 orphans over the mountains toward Free China. During her harrowing journey out of the war-torn city, Gladys grappled with despair as never before. After passing a sleepless night, she faced the morning with no hope of reaching safety. Then a 13-year-old girl in the group reminded her of their much-loved story of Moses and the Israelites crossing the Red Sea.

"But I am not Moses!" Gladys cried in desperation.

"Of course you aren't," the girl said, "but the Lord is still God."

When Gladys and the orphans made it through, they proved once again that no matter how inadequate we feel, the Lord is still God, and we can trust in Him.

Backed into a Corner. Richard Exley said, "Sometimes God has to allow us to be backed into a corner before we truly rely on Him." God's chosen people found themselves backed into that corner. As a powerful force kept them in that corner, they weakly cowered. But a promised Messiah gave them hope, a King who would lead them in righteousness and faithfulness and establish peace in their hearts—and free them from the bondage of their corner!

FOR YOUTH

■ TOPIC: Peace at Last!

■ QUESTIONS: 1. Why do you think Isaiah introduced the Messiah as a new shoot sprouting from the roots of an old stump? 2. Why is it important that the coming Messiah's judgment be based on righteousness and faithfulness? 3. Why was it necessary for the Messiah to have *the spirit of wisdom and understanding, the spirit of counsel and might, the spirit of knowledge and the fear of the LORD* (Isa. 11:2)? 4. How do you think Jesus demonstrated these traits in His life? 5. How would you describe a kingdom of perfect peace? What do you think it would look like? 6. What do you think is your responsibility for working to bring about Jesus' kingdom of peace?

Perfect Peace. "Maybe all dogs do go to heaven," reported *Newsweek* in 1998. But first, they might want to drop by the Episcopal Church of the Holy Trinity on Manhattan's Upper East Side, where parishioners and their pooches are regulars at Sunday morning services. As long as they behave, dogs and their masters are welcome to sit side by side and even accompany each other to the altar during Communion.

"It's like being with a family member," says Judith Gwyn Brown, who attended the early Sunday morning service with her puli sheepdog, Cordelia. "We both get a lot out of it."

But can a pet really be pious? Church spokesman Fred Burrell wouldn't touch the question, saying, "I don't think I'll go there."

So is this the peaceful kingdom prophesied in Isaiah? No. Perfect peace will come to all creation when Christ reigns supreme.

And a Little Child Will Lead Them. It was one of the hottest days of summer and the community had not seen rain in more than a month. The crops were dying. Cows had stopped giving milk. The creeks and streams were dried up. If the community didn't see some rain soon, as many as 10 farmers would be facing bankruptcy. One of those farmers was Matthew, along with his wife, Tara.

Every day Matthew and his brothers would go about the arduous process of trying to get water to the fields. Lately this process had involved taking a truck to the local water rendering plant and filling it up with water. But severe rationing had cut everyone off.

It was on this day that Tara says she learned the true lesson of sharing and witnessed the only miracle she believes she has seen with her own eyes. This miracle, in which she was shown the true character of God, came through the compassionate efforts of a little boy in a sunburned body.

Tara was in the kitchen making lunch for her husband and his brothers when she saw her six-year-old son, Billy, walking toward the woods. He wasn't walking with the usual carefree abandon of a youth but with a serious step. He was obviously walking with a great deal of effort, trying to be as still and as quiet as possible. Minutes after he disappeared into the woods, he came running out again, toward the house. Tara went back to making sandwiches, thinking that whatever task Billy had been doing was completed.

Moments later, however, Billy was once again walking in that slow purposeful stride toward the woods. This activity went on for an hour: walk carefully to the woods, run back to the house. Finally Tara couldn't take it any longer and she crept out of the house and followed Billy on his journey—being very careful not to be seen as he was obviously doing important work and didn't need his mother checking up on him.

Billy was cupping both hands in front of him as he walked, being very careful not to spill the water he held in them. Maybe two or three tablespoons were held in his tiny hands. Tara sneaked close as Billy went into the woods. Branches and thorns slapped his little face, but he did not try to avoid them. He had a much higher purpose.

As Tara leaned in to spy on Billy, she saw the most amazing site. Several large deer loomed in front of Billy. He walked right up to them. Tara almost screamed for him to get away. A huge buck with elaborate antlers was dangerously close. But the buck did not threaten him; he didn't even move as Billy knelt down. Then Tara saw a tiny fawn lying on the ground, obviously suffering from dehydration and heat exhaustion, lift its head with great effort to lap up the water cupped in Billy's hand.

When the water was gone, Billy jumped up to run back to the house. Tara hid behind a tree. She followed Billy back to the house to a spigot that had been shut off because of the water shortage. Billy opened it all the way up and a small trickle began to creep out. He knelt there, letting the drip slowly fill up his makeshift "cup," as the sun beat down on his little back.

Then it became clear to Tara—the trouble Billy had gotten into for playing with the hose the week before, the lecture he had received about the importance of not wasting water, and the reason he didn't ask his mother to help him.

It took almost 10 minutes for the drops to fill Billy's hands. When he stood up and began the trek back, Tara was there in front of him. Billy's eyes filled with tears. "I'm not wasting," was all he said. As he began his walk, Tara joined him—with a small pot of water from the kitchen. She let Billy tend to the fawn; she stayed away. It was Billy's job.

Again Tara stood on the edge of the woods watching the most beautiful heart she had ever known working so hard to save another life. Like the tears that rolled down her face, drops of water began to hit the parched ground. Then more drops. Then more. She looked up at the sky. It was as if God Himself was weeping with pride.

Tara says, "Some will probably say that this was all just a big coincidence. That miracles don't really exist. That it was bound to rain sometime. And I can't argue with that. I'm not going to try. All I can say is that the rain that came that day saved our farm, just like the actions of one little boy saved another life."

Peaceful Acceptance. Children with severe skin diseases continue to find acceptance at a Christian summer camp. These children, who are socially excluded because of their deformities, are accepted and make lifelong friends at Camp Knutson, near Cross Lake, Minnesota, run by Lutheran Social Services.

Most of the children have never been able to go to the beach or for a walk without getting stares or rude comments, *The Lutheran* magazine reported. Some are covered head-to-toe with bandages or use a wheelchair, and others require as much as five hours of medical treatment a day.

The campers get absorbed without self-consciousness in activities such as swimming, waterskiing, tubing, and horseback riding, or sitting around a campfire. These are big steps for the young people, who have been closely monitored since birth by parents and schools.

"All we believe in at Camp Knutson are compliments," camper and junior counselor Shauna Egesdal said. "No putdowns are allowed."

COMFORT FOR GOD'S PEOPLE

BACKGROUND SCRIPTURE: Isaiah 40:1-11
DEVOTIONAL READING: Isaiah 40:25-31

3

KEY VERSE: The grass withers, the flower fades;
but the word of our God will stand forever. Isaiah. 40:8.

KING JAMES VERSION

ISAIAH 40:1 Comfort ye, comfort ye my people, saith your God.

2 Speak ye comfortably to Jerusalem, and cry unto her, that her warfare is accomplished, that her iniquity is pardoned: for she hath received of the LORD's hand double for all her sins.

3 The voice of him that crieth in the wilderness, Prepare ye the way of the LORD, make straight in the desert a highway for our God.

4 Every valley shall be exalted, and every mountain and hill shall be made low: and the crooked shall be made straight, and the rough places plain:

5 And the glory of the LORD shall be revealed, and all flesh shall see it together: for the mouth of the LORD hath spoken it. . . .

8 The grass withereth, the flower fadeth: but the word of our God shall stand for ever.

9 O Zion, that bringest good tidings, get thee up into the high mountain; O Jerusalem, that bringest good tidings, lift up thy voice with strength; lift it up, be not afraid; say unto the cities of Judah, Behold your God!

10 Behold, the Lord GOD will come with strong hand, and his arm shall rule for him: behold, his reward is with him, and his work before him.

11 He shall feed his flock like a shepherd: he shall gather the lambs with his arm, and carry them in his bosom, and shall gently lead those that are with young.

NEW REVISED STANDARD VERSION

ISAIAH 40:1 Comfort, O comfort my people,
  says your God.
2 Speak tenderly to Jerusalem,
  and cry to her
that she has served her term,
  that her penalty is paid,
that she has received from the LORD's hand
  double for all her sins.
3 A voice cries out:
"In the wilderness prepare the way of the LORD,
  make straight in the desert a highway for our God.
4 Every valley shall be lifted up,
  and every mountain and hill be made low;
the uneven ground shall become level,
  and the rough places a plain.
5 Then the glory of the LORD shall be revealed,
  and all people shall see it together,
for the mouth of the LORD has spoken." . . .
8 The grass withers, the flower fades;
  but the word of our God will stand forever.
9 Get you up to a high mountain,
  O Zion, herald of good tidings;
lift up your voice with strength,
  O Jerusalem, herald of good tidings,
  lift it up, do not fear;
say to the cities of Judah,
  "Here is your God!"
10 See, the Lord GOD comes with might,
  and his arm rules for him;
his reward is with him,
  and his recompense before him.
11 He will feed his flock like a shepherd;
  he will gather the lambs in his arms,
and carry them in his bosom,
  and gently lead the mother sheep.

Home Bible Readings

Background

Isaiah 40 marks the beginning of what many Bible scholars consider the second half of the Book of Isaiah. Whereas the first 39 chapters generally carry the message of judgment for sin, the final 27 chapters of the book predominately bring a message of forgiveness, comfort, and hope, in which Israel is invited to return home from exile. Looking beyond Judah's imminent captivity, the prophet foresaw a day of salvation for God's people. Thus this section of Isaiah's prophecy is often called the "Book of Consolation."

In the first 39 chapters of Isaiah, God had threatened to punish Israel, Judah, and other nations for their unbelief, immorality, and idolatry. Because God is holy, He had required His people to treat others justly; but despite His kind treatment of them, even they had failed to treat others kindly (especially the disadvantaged). The Israelites' faith in God had for the most part degenerated into national pride and empty religious rituals. Finally God's promised retribution was fulfilled when Israel fell to the Assyrians (722 B.C.) and Judah fell to the Babylonians (586 B.C.).

However, once the fall of Israel and Judah had occurred, God promised comfort, deliverance, and restoration in His future Kingdom. The promised Messiah would rule over His faithful followers in the age to come, thus giving hope to the people of Israel and Judah.

The translation of the initial verses of Isaiah 40 from Hebrew into English can shroud the fact that God was speaking to a group, such as the heavenly hosts, and not to the prophet Isaiah alone. For instance, note that the Hebrew verb rendered "comfort" (40:1) is a plural-form command. It's an order given to a multitude, all of whom are given the same task—to collectively announce the end of the Babylonian exile. Also note that "comfort" is repeated twice to underscore that there would be an end of punishment and the coming of a new day of freedom. The promise of a brighter future could be found only in the faithfulness of God.

Thus the goal of this second section of Isaiah was to convince God's people that the Lord not only would allow them to return home, but also that He desired that they do so. The necessity of this message was mandated because not all the people of God would be unhappy in Babylon. Many of them would assimilate into the Babylonian culture. And for them, the prospect of returning to a homeland in ruins was not their idea of a bright future.

NOTES ON THE PRINTED TEXT

To persuade the future exiles that returning to their homeland was the will of God would require two things. First, they would have to be convinced that God had forgiven them for the sins that had led to their exile. Second, they would have to be convinced that they would be able to survive the journey.

Thus the words of comfort in Isaiah 40:1-2 addressed the first concern. God had repeatedly told the Israelites that if they departed from the exclusive worship of Him, they would forfeit their right to live in the promised land (Deut. 28:58-65; 2 Kings 17:7-20). Of course, prophets of God had also foretold that He would forgive those who repented and returned to Him in faith and obedience (Jer. 31:31-34; Ezek. 36:22-38; Hos. 14:1-7). In fact, Deuteronomy 30:1-5 promised that, even if the people were exiled as far away as the ends of the earth, God would still gather those who would truly desire to return. Thus for those who thought that the Exile would last forever, Isaiah 40:1-2 announced God's pardon.

The Lord commanded that His people be comforted with the announcement that they had *served [their] term* (40:2). He had pardoned them and now they were free to return to their homeland. Surely this would be an announcement beyond their comprehension. Judah still had about a century of trouble to experience before Jerusalem would fall, and then the nation would face about 70 years of exile. In the midst of this dire prognosis, God told Isaiah to speak tenderly to His chosen people.

Make straight in the desert a highway for our God (40:3) refers to preparing a road for the coming of a king. All obstacles were cleared off the road and the general direction of the route was straightened to make travel easier for the visiting monarch. An ancient Near Eastern custom was to send representatives ahead of a king to prepare the way for his visit. It is clear that the language in this verse refers to the coming Messiah. Indeed, John the Baptist used these words as he challenged the people to prepare themselves for the coming of the Lord (Matt. 3:3). That *every valley shall be lifted up, and every mountain and hill be made low; the uneven ground shall become level, and the rough places a plain* (Isa. 40:4) provides a picture of how this processional highway for the Lord's coming to Jerusalem would be prepared.

The glory of the LORD (40:5) would be revealed in that God would redeem His people from Babylon and all the nations would witness this deliverance. And ultimately, the glory of God's redemption would be seen in His Son, Jesus Christ, who would make salvation possible for the lost.

The kingdoms of the world and the people of those kingdoms *are grass, their constancy is like the flower of the field* (40:6). Even the immense power of kingdoms like Assyria and Babylon would soon vanish. They would wither and fade *when the breath of the LORD blows upon it* (40:7). In contrast to their temporary stay as world powers, the Word of God is permanent; it is eternal and unfailing. Thus when the plans and purposes of nations fail to prevail, the Word of God *will stand forever* (40:8).

Beyond being eternal, the Word of God is also *good tidings* (40:9) for those who hear it and have faith in it. After all, it is God's Word that promised His people that the Lord would lead them back to their homeland. It is God who promised to care for His people and redeem them.

In 40:10 and 11, God is characterized by both strength and gentleness. He is powerful as He *comes with might, and his arm rules for him* (40:10). And yet He is also gentle, pictured as a shepherd who cares for and guides his flock. The divine Shepherd cares for the most defenseless members of His flock. *He will gather the lambs in his arms, and carry them in his bosom, and gently lead the mother sheep* (40:11). A recurring prophetic theme is reinforced here—that the truly powerful nation is not the one with a strong military, but rather the one that relies on God's care and strength.

SUGGESTIONS TO TEACHERS

Regardless of our current circumstances, regardless of our stressful situations, and regardless of our times of trial and testing, God is in our presence. And when we commit to trusting and obeying Him, He promises us that His peace and comfort will remain with us.

1. COMFORT IN ADVERSITY. Not everyone is going to go along with or agree with our faith in and commitment to God. We will face opposition, and we will face adversity. And though we cannot avoid adversity, as we face it we can find and experience God's comfort. As long as we're living for Him, we will be able to find promises and encouragement in His Word and in His presence.

2. COMFORT IN TRIALS. We will face trials and sufferings that we cannot explain. There will seem to be no purpose or reason behind them. But though we are not immune to them, our faith need not be hindered by them. In the midst of trials and sufferings—even when our life seems to be falling apart—we can call on God to comfort us. And He will come to us *like a shepherd; he will gather the lambs in his arms, and carry them in his bosom, and gently lead the mother sheep* (Isa. 40:11).

3. COMFORT AGAINST THE FLOW. As believers, we will feel as though we are swimming upstream while striving to live the Christian life and obey God's Word. All around us, opinions and perceptions will change. We must remember that *the word of our God will stand forever* (40:8). Only in God's Word will we find lasting solutions to each of our problems and needs. Scripture truly is *a lamp to [our] feet and a light to [our] path* (Ps. 119:105).

4. COMFORT THROUGH REDEMPTION. At one time, our sin had separated us from God. We were trapped in sin's clutches and held captives as exiles from God. But our Redeemer, Jesus Christ, has delivered us! And because He has, we can find great comfort for our minds, hearts, and souls through Him and His mercy and grace.

■ TOPIC: The Gift of Comfort

■ QUESTIONS: 1. Why do you think God would issue words of comfort to Judah long before the nation was punished by being exiled to Babylon? 2. How would these words be of comfort to God's people who were facing hard times but had not yet faced the worst of times? 3. What does God say to the people to assure them that He will, indeed, forgive them? 4. What instructions were given for the people to prepare the way for the coming of their Messiah? 5. In what ways does the Word of God *stand forever* (Isa. 40:8)?

■ ILLUSTRATIONS:

Comfort for the Raging. Two shoppers in a supermarket got in a fistfight over who should be first in a newly opened checkout lane. An airline flight returned to a major American city after a passenger was accused of throwing a can of beer at a flight attendant and biting a pilot. One father in an eastern state beat another father to death in an argument over rough play at their sons' hockey practice. A high school baseball coach in the South turned himself in to face charges that he broke an umpire's jaw after a disputed call. All these events were reported by *USA Today* over the span of a few months.

"Bad tempers are on display everywhere," wrote reporter Karen S. Peterson. The media is constantly reporting incidents of road rage, airplane rage, biker rage, surfer rage, grocery store rage, and rage at youth sporting events. This had led scientists to say the United States is in the middle of an anger epidemic. This epidemic rattles both those who study social trends and parents who fear the country is at a cultural precipice.

"We have lost some of the glue holding our society together," Peterson quoted one parent as saying. "We have lost our respect for others. The example we are setting for our kids is terrible."

Experts searching for causes blame an increasing sense of self-importance, the widespread feeling that things should happen "my" way. Other factors, they say, include too little time, overcrowding, intrusive technology, and too many demands for change in a society hurtling into the twenty-first century. In the midst of our rage, we are desperately in need of comfort—and of a Comforter.

God for the Pressured. Lloyd J. Ogilvie, in his book *Life without Limits*, tells the story of a pastor who, in the space of one week, heard the following comments from various people:

A woman said, "I'm under tremendous pressure from my son these days. I can't seem to satisfy him, however hard I work. He really puts me under pressure."

A young man said, "My parents have fantastic goals for me to take over the family business. It's not what I want to do, but their pressure is unbearable."

A college woman said, "I'm being pressured by my boyfriend to live with him before we are married. You know . . . sort of try it out . . . to see if we are right for each other."

A husband said, "My wife is never satisfied. Whatever I do, however much I make, it's never enough. Life with her is like living in a pressure cooker with the lid fastened down and the heat on high."

A secretary said, pointing to her phone, "That little black thing is driving me silly. At the other end of the line are people who make impossible demands and think they are the only people alive."

A middle-aged wife said, "My husband thinks my faith is silly. When I feel his resistance to Christ, I wonder if I'm wrong and confused. As a result, I've developed two lives; one with him and one when I'm with my Christian friends."

An elderly woman said, "My sister thinks she has all the answers about the faith and tries to convince me of her point of view. I feel pressured to become her brand of Christian, but I keep thinking if it means being like her, I don't want it at all. When she calls, I just put the phone on my shoulder and let her rant on while I do other things. A half-hour later, she's still on the line blasting away, but I still feel pressure."

A young pastor at a clergy conference said, "I hardly know who I am anymore. There are so many points of view in my congregation, I can't please them all. Everyone wants to capture me for his camp and get me to shape the church around his convictions. The pressure makes me want to leave the ministry."

All of these persons have one thing in common. They are being pressured by other people and they are in need of comfort.

A Sign for Comfort. In the May 1999 *Washington Monthly*, Charles Peters asked, "Have you ever been guilty of an act of rudeness or inconsiderateness on the highway? I have. And I have often wanted to apologize immediately, but I haven't known what to do. Although there are many widely recognized gestures of anger on the road, e.g. the shaken fist or the extended middle finger, I don't know any way to say 'I'm sorry.' I've tried bobbing my head down or waving a hand but the meaning simply isn't clear. Too bad. I'm convinced a lot of road rage could be nipped in the bud if the original offender only knew how to say, 'The mistake was mine.'"

A confession of a mistake and an acknowledgement of forgiveness not only calms us down, but also brings comfort.

■ TOPIC: Better Days Ahead!

■ QUESTIONS: 1. Why was it important for God's people to hear comforting words from Him? 2. How do you think the people felt when God told the nation of Judah that *she has served her term, that her penalty is paid, that she has received from the LORD's hand double for all her sins* (Isa. 40:2)? 3. What do you think you would have done to *prepare the way of the LORD*

(40:3)? 4. How would the glory of the Lord be revealed through the coming of the Messiah? 5. What do you think is meant by the phrase *the word of our God will stand forever* (40:8)?

■ ILLUSTRATIONS:

Making Way for Better Days. Tens of thousands of teenagers clap to Christian music and jot notes from speakers every three years as part of the DC/LA conferences, sponsored by Youth for Christ. The last were held in the summer of 2000, and young people made serious decisions and learned to take risks for their faith. By making commitments to tell others about the forgiveness of Christ, they're making sure that better days lie ahead for their friends and family—and even acquaintances.

Being challenged to lead in their churches and schools is fine with many of the teens. Rather than running away from responsibility and risk, they have been looking for it, and just needed someone to direct them, Cari Allen of Youth for Christ told *Religion Today*. Even more so than in previous years, teens are saying, "this is the time, that they are ready to go and do something for Christ," said Allen, who has attended the conferences since 1985. "We tend to think of young people as the church of tomorrow, but I believe they are the church of today—and they need to act like it."

In Los Angeles, teens "in droves" said they "wanted to do something to make their lives count, do something positive and courageous for Christ," Allen said. The conference challenged them to start outreaches, Bible clubs, or prayer groups on their school campuses. The teens learned to take risks, and some practiced by going out into the streets and sharing their faith with strangers. In Los Angeles, 1,500 people were approached on beaches and in malls, and more than 100 became Christians, Allen said.

On the last night of the Los Angeles conference, speaker Reggie Dabbs told the teens to bow their heads and "decide whether they will go," Allen said. At the end of the prayer, Dabbs asked, "Will you?" At that, the teens "raised their arms and screamed at the top of their lungs, 'I'll go,'" Allen said. "I've never heard anything louder. I didn't see one kid sitting."

Most of those attending the conference were committed Christians, but some arrived as unbelievers who came for a good time but found that "God knocked them off their feet," Allen said.

Instructional sessions for adult leaders also took place. They were urged to reject the standard "youth group" model of entertainment and token ministry for a "youth ministry" model. There also was a time for the adults to "talk, laugh, and cry about what the kids are doing," Allen said.

Comfort for the Needy. In an attempt to bring comfort to Vietnamese children without parents, Christian workers are running an orphanage under difficult conditions in Vietnam. The religious group opened a home for children from the minority Cham population, according to Zenit, a Christian news agency. Bethany House, northeast of Ho Chi Minh City, houses 50 boys three- to nineteen-years old, many of whom have lost both parents. Cham fathers normally abandon their children and remarry if the mother dies, according to the news agency.

The orphans attend school and also are instructed in the faith. The Christian workers often are confronted by local authorities, since the Cham people embrace their own traditional religion, a local version of Hinduism, according to Zenit. However, some Cham adults have converted to Christianity and been baptized.

Comfort through Redemption. A year after brutally attacking a pastor, a gang member became a Christian. Patrick Shikanda Lokhotio apologized for attacking Timothy Njoya, pastor of a large Presbyterian church in Nairobi, Kenya, *Ecumenical News International* reported. Lokhotio beat Njoya with a wooden club outside the Parliament building on June 10, 1999, as the pastor led a political protest.

Lokhotio sought forgiveness from Njoya and his congregation in an address to the church July 3, 2000. Njoya publicly forgave him months ago and asked the authorities to stop criminal proceedings against him. Lokhotio said he was ashamed for "beating up a man of God," and promised to live a Christian lifestyle.

Lokhotio's change "shows God's miracles have worked in this church," Njoya said. Lokhotio had been a member of a youth gang. During his talk, he introduced six members of the gang who also have pledged to mend their ways. About 100 other members of the gang have said they will come to the church.

THE PRINCE OF PEACE

BACKGROUND SCRIPTURE: Isaiah 9:1-7; Luke 2:1-20
DEVOTIONAL READING: Luke 2:8-20

KEY VERSE: A child has been born for us, a son given to us;
authority rests upon his shoulders; and he is named Wonderful
Counselor, Mighty God, Everlasting Father, Prince of Peace. Isaiah 9:6.

4

KING JAMES VERSION

ISAIAH 9:2 The people that walked in darkness have seen a great light: they that dwell in the land of the shadow of death, upon them hath the light shined.

3 Thou hast multiplied the nation, and not increased the joy: they joy before thee according to the joy in harvest, and as men rejoice when they divide the spoil.

4 For thou hast broken the yoke of his burden, and the staff of his shoulder, the rod of his oppressor, as in the day of Midian.

5 For every battle of the warrior is with confused noise, and garments rolled in blood; but this shall be with burning and fuel of fire.

6 For unto us a child is born, unto us a son is given: and the government shall be upon his shoulder: and his name shall be called Wonderful, Counsellor, The mighty God, The everlasting Father, The Prince of Peace.

7 Of the increase of his government and peace there shall be no end, upon the throne of David, and upon his kingdom, to order it, and to establish it with judgment and with justice from henceforth even for ever. The zeal of the LORD of hosts will perform this.

NEW REVISED STANDARD VERSION

ISAIAH 9:2 The people who walked in darkness
have seen a great light;
those who lived in a land of deep darkness—
on them light has shined.

3 You have multiplied the nation,
you have increased its joy;
they rejoice before you
as with joy at the harvest,
as people exult when dividing plunder.

4 For the yoke of their burden,
and the bar across their shoulders,
the rod of their oppressor,
you have broken as on the day of Midian.

5 For all the boots of the tramping warriors
and all the garments rolled in blood
shall be burned as fuel for the fire.

6 For a child has been born for us,
a son given to us;
authority rests upon his shoulders;
and he is named
Wonderful Counselor, Mighty God,
Everlasting Father, Prince of Peace.

7 His authority shall grow continually,
and there shall be endless peace
for the throne of David and his kingdom.
He will establish and uphold it
with justice and with righteousness
from this time onward and forevermore.
The zeal of the LORD of hosts will do this.

Monday, December 24	Luke 2:8-14	*The Good News of Great Joy*
Tuesday, December 25	Luke 2:15-20	*All Who Heard Were Amazed*
Wednesday, December 26	Luke 2:25-35	*A Light for Revelation to the Gentiles*
Thursday, December 27	Isaiah 42:1-17	*The Servant of the Lord*
Friday, December 28	Isaiah 42:18-25	*Israel's Blindness*
Saturday, December 29	Isaiah 43:1-7	*God Has Called You by Name*
Sunday, December 30	Isaiah 43:8-13	*The Lord Is the Only Savior*

BACKGROUND

Old Testament priests, prophets, and kings were anointed with olive oil in ceremonies signifying their dedication and initiation into the work of God. Even the utensils used in the tabernacle and temple were anointed to show that they were set apart for God's use and purposes. In this regard, *Messiah* comes from a Hebrew term that means "anointed one." Its Greek counterpart is *Christos*, from which the word *Christ* comes. Messiah was one of the titles used by early Christians to describe who Jesus was.

God promised the people of Israel that He would send them His "anointed one" to bring peace and to establish His eternal kingdom. Isaiah, perhaps more than any other prophet, gave so many details about the coming of the Messiah. And though the prophet clearly foretold the Messiah's birth, life, and even death, many people misunderstood the Messiah's actual purpose. Because religious leaders emphasized the promised kingship of the coming Messiah, many expected a political leader who would help them overthrow the authority of civil powers that were oppressing God's people, such as Rome in the first century when Jesus came.

Instead, the Father sent His Son to give meaning to life on earth and for all eternity. Jesus came over six centuries after Isaiah's prophecy, and He came as a suffering Servant who would bring more than an earthly blessing. He came to bring all people—not only the Jews—an abundant spiritual life that would continue throughout eternity in heaven.

Thus God's Son would be the light that would pierce through and shine on a dark and sinful world. Jesus Christ would be the Lord's answer to a world filled with pride and arrogance. The coming of the Messiah would not establish a new political order, but rather fulfill the promise of an ideal King.

NOTES ON THE PRINTED TEXT

Portions of Isaiah 9 are filled with phrases that may have originally referred to a line of kings after David or perhaps may have been used in celebrating the accession of a specific Judean king. For example, Isaiah possibly heard some of these words at the celebration of Hezekiah's accession, and then heard them again from God when He described to the prophet the coming of the Messiah. But the Messiah would be what Judah's human kings had not been. The

Messiah would be the ideal King.

Isaiah 9 begins with a promise that *there will be no gloom for those who were in anguish* (9:1). Direct reference is then made to the tribes of Zebulun and Naphtali, two northern regions of Israel and two peoples that had most outrightly rejected God and had suffered greatly under the Assyrian invasion. Although these tribes had suffered contempt, *in the latter time he will make glorious the way of the sea, the land beyond the Jordan, Galilee of the nations* (9:1). Thus, into the darkest regions of the nation of Israel, God would shine *a great light; those who lived in a land of deep darkness—on them light has shined* (9:2). Other passages in Isaiah clarify that this "light" was not for the nation of Israel alone, but also *a light to the nations* (42:6; 49:6) of all the world.

Because of the deliverance and redemption that would be brought by the Messiah, Isaiah prophesied that the nation would exult in an increase of its joy and that the people will *rejoice before you as with joy at the harvest* (9:3). The prophet explained, *For the yoke of their burden, and the bar across their shoulders, the rod of their oppressor* (9:4) would be broken. As in 10:26-27, Isaiah foretold that God would destroy the Assyrian army as well as its oppressive yoke on His people. God referred to the way He engineered Gideon's victory over the hordes of Midianites and broke their dominion over Israel (Judg. 7:22-25) as an example of how He would work again in His people's behalf. And when this took place and the Messiah had established His kingdom, military equipment would no longer be needed. Indeed, they *shall be burned as fuel for the fire* (Isa. 9:5).

Isaiah foretold that *a child has been born to us, a son given to us* (9:6). The Messiah would be a royal son, a son of David. He would possess authority and power to rule over not only His own people, but also over all the people of the world. The prophet then attributed to the Messiah what are often called "throne names." Each of these titles consists of two elements. Unlike the name *Emmanuel*, these titles were different from typical Old Testament names. And yet, like other Old Testament names, the titles given to the Messiah would be reflective of His character.

The first throne name is *Wonderful Counselor* (9:6). This reveals the Messiah's character as a King who would determine and carry out an active ministry. (That ministry is spelled out in chapter 11.) In that He would give counsel that is truly wonderful and advice that is always right, He and His ministry would cause all the world to marvel.

The second throne name is *Mighty God* (9:6). This is the strongest of all the throne names. This title was always used for God and never used to refer to a man. Thus the prophet declared that the Messiah would be God in the flesh. He would be divine in might. He would be a powerful warrior in His people's behalf. He would be exceptional, distinguished, and without peer. He would be God incarnate.

The third throne name is *Everlasting Father*. The character portrayed in this name is that the Messiah would be timeless—that He alone would be the source of eternal life. And as a father, He would continually give His people fatherly love and care. He would be an enduring, compassionate provider and protector. Because He is God incarnate, He would be a true father to His people.

The fourth and last of the throne names is *Prince of Peace*. The Messiah would be of royal descent, and He would be a King who brings peace and prosperity. As the Prince of Peace, He would represent the best qualities of all of Israel's heroes. His rule would bring wholeness and well-being to both individuals and to society as a whole. His government would be characterized by justice and lasting peace.

The Messiah's *authority shall grow continually, and there shall be endless peace for the throne of David and his kingdom* (9:7). Despite the sins of kings like Ahaz, the Messiah would be a descendant of David who would rule in righteousness forever.

SUGGESTIONS TO TEACHERS

Though we may not have been stripped from our homes and taken off to a far country, we all still face violence and oppression on several fronts. And though we may not be longing for someone to make a way for us to return home, we all long for the Lord to deliver us from the quagmire of sinful habits, broken relationships, and the heavy burdens of despairing circumstances. We need only look to our Wonderful Counselor, our Mighty God, our Everlasting Father, and our Prince of Peace to find true and lasting joy for our lives.

1. PEACE THAT OVERCOMES SIN. Sin wreaks havoc on our lives. It diminishes our impact, harms our outlook, and dwindles our physical, mental, emotional, and spiritual health. In essence, sin violently attacks our lives and living. But with the birth of the Messiah comes a message of hope. He came to deliver all of us from our slavery to sin and to give us a peace that overcomes sin.

2. PEACE THAT OVERCOMES DARKNESS. Sometimes our society and culture make us feel like we are *the people who walked in darkness* (Isa. 9:2). But even in our time of great darkness, we have received God's promise of the Light who would shine on all of us, giving us peace for our weary souls.

3. PEACE THAT OVERCOMES DESPAIR. When we're in the depths of gloom and despair, we may fear that our sorrows and troubles will never come to an end. But we can take comfort in this promise. Although the Lord may not always spare us from troubles, if we follow Him wholeheartedly, He will lead us safely through them and give us peace in the midst of them.

4. PEACE THAT OVERCOMES VIOLENCE. When we receive, on a daily basis, the peace that only the Prince of Peace can bring, we can become instruments of His peace; we can become peacemakers. May we strive not only to harbor God's peace in our hearts, but also to carry His peace into situations where conflict and violence threaten the hearts—and even lives—of other people. Jesus said, *"Blessed are the peacemakers"* (Matt. 5:9).

■ **TOPIC:** The Gift of Wholeness

■ **QUESTIONS:** 1. In what ways were the people Isaiah was addressing walking in darkness? 2. What effect would seeing a great light have upon them? 3. How did the coming of the Messiah break *the yoke of their burden, and the bar across their shoulders, the rod of their oppressor* (Isa. 9:4)? 4. What kind of peace has the Prince of Peace brought into your life? 5. In what ways is the authority of Christ continuing to grow today?

■ **ILLUSTRATIONS:**

Keep the Christmas Story Simple. In his book *The Gift of Worship*, C. Welton Gaddy tells the story of when, at the beginning of the Christmas holidays one year, the renowned scholar and lecturer, Paul Tillich, went downtown in New York City to worship with a small congregation in a storefront church. The pastor was one of Tillich's students. Tillich listened with dismay as the young preacher related the Christmas story to a beleaguered group of uneducated people using the language of the lecture hall. He spoke eloquently of how "the divine transcendent had become immanent." After the service ended, the brilliant teacher, with tears in his eyes, approached his student. Tillich said, "Son, just tell them that God became a man in Jesus of Nazareth."

Making Peace. In an article called "Making Peace" in the Spring 2000 issue of *Yes!* authors Eran Fanenkel and John Marks wrote about how the war in the Balkans has reminded the world of how ethnic and religious tensions can lead to war, resulting in untold suffering and death. But what has not been reported, they said, is the story of Macedonia, where, although the same ethnic and religious conditions exist as in its Balkan neighbors, peace—not war—has broken out.

With a population of only 2.2 million, Macedonia is ethnically fragmented— Turks, Albanians, ethnic Macedonians, Serbs, and Vlachs. These various groups seldom interact with each other, and yet war has been avoided because they seem to have learned that collaboration serves them better than violence.

National will is one ingredient that has contributed to this attitude. Macedonia is governed by a coalition of interests. Although grievances exist, it has shown restraint in dealing with sensitive issues by recognizing that all will suffer if they resort to violence.

Nongovernmental agencies are another ingredient that has contributed to this attitude. These groups, such as Search for Common Ground, provided a wide range of technical, humanitarian, and developmental aid. Search for Common Ground, for example, has organized cross-ethnic teams reporting for the media. The organization simultaneously publishes articles in Macedonian, Turkish, Albanian, and Roma. Rather than being used as a tool for social fragmentation, the media is a forum for common interests.

Search for Common Ground has also produced television documentaries, provided educational resources for children, and sponsored cross-cultural "Eko-Patrols" to foster respect for the environment. Sometimes it doesn't seem like much, but in Macedonia, little is slowly becoming much. It's hard to put a price on peace.

Celebrating the Prince of Peace? It is somewhat sad that in our Christmas celebrations we all too often leave out celebrating the coming of Jesus—our Prince of Peace. We celebrate for celebration's sake, forgetting the reason and purpose behind the celebration. Perhaps the author Aldous [AWL-duss] Huxley had this in mind when he ended his book, *The Genius and the Goddess*, on a tragic note. The narrator sees the author to the door with the poignant parting words: "Drive carefully. This is a Christian country, and it's the Savior's birthday. Practically everybody you will see will be drunk."

FOR YOUTH

■ **TOPIC:** Birth of New Hope!

■ **QUESTIONS:** 1. How has Jesus been a great light to you? 2. How has Jesus been the Wonderful Counselor to you? 3. How has Jesus been the Mighty God to you? 4. How has Jesus been the Everlasting Father to you? 5. How has Jesus been the Prince of Peace to you?

■ **ILLUSTRATIONS:**

Christmas Prayer. In his "Advent Prayer of Confession," Israel Galindo prays the following:

> As we retell the Christmas story and wait for the celebration of Christmas Day, we marvel again that You would send the Baby to live here on this planet. For we learn early in life that it is painful to live here, on this planet of uncertainty; it can be hard here, Lord—and lonely, and meaningless; for our spirits grow cold; our hearts lose hope too easily; and it is painful, sometimes, even to love too much, or to care too deeply.
>
> So we wait, anxiously, for the birth of the Promised One who turns the darkness to light, removes the dreaded sting of death, and in His birth brings eternal hope. Our God, we confess now, as Your corporate church, that we often have been the cause of your pain. And so, in the words of our Jewish brethren, we pray . . .
>
> "For the sins which we have committed against Thee under stress or through choice, in stubbornness or in error, in the evil meditations of the heart, by word of mouth, by abuse of power, by exploiting and dealing treacherously with our neighbor, bear with us, pardon us, forgive us!"
>
> For this we pray in the name of the Child of Royal Birth, the Savior born unto us in the city of David: Jesus Christ, the Lord. Amen.

Merry Christmas, Anyway. Leonard Sweet has asked whether we need more evidence that Jesus needs His birthday back. Answering his own question, Sweet wrote about how when he started a spirituality newsletter called *SoulCafe*, he sent sample copies to a couple hundred thousand people whose names he purchased from a mass mailing list company.

On one of the responses Sweet received on the "No Postage Necessary" postcards was this scrawled message from Florida explaining the recipients' disinterest in the newsletter: "We're not Christians. Kindly keep Jesus to yourself. . . . Merry Christmas."

Room for Peace. In a sermon called, "Do You Believe the Angels?" James A. Harnish said the following:

> I've begun to think that, in one sense, the manger is a very small place. There isn't room in there for all the baggage we carry around with us. There's no room at the manger for our pious pride and self-righteousness. There's no room in the manger for our human power and prestige. There's no room at the manger for the baggage of past failure and unforgiven sin. There's no room at the manger for our prejudice, bigotry, and jingoistic national pride. There's no room for bitterness and greed. There is no room at the manger for anything other than the absolute reality of who and what we really are: very human, very real, very fragile, very vulnerable human beings who desperately need the gift of love and grace which God so powerfully desires to give.

JUSTICE FOR THE NATIONS

BACKGROUND SCRIPTURE: Isaiah 42:1-9
DEVOTIONAL READING: Isaiah 43:1-7

KEY VERSE: Here is my servant, whom I uphold, my chosen, in whom my soul delights; I have put my spirit upon him; he will bring forth justice to the nations. Isaiah 42:1.

KING JAMES VERSION

ISAIAH 42:1 Behold my servant, whom I uphold; mine elect, in whom my soul delighteth; I have put my spirit upon him: he shall bring forth judgment to the Gentiles.

2 He shall not cry, nor lift up, nor cause his voice to be heard in the street.

3 A bruised reed shall he not break, and the smoking flax shall he not quench: he shall bring forth judgment unto truth.

4 He shall not fail nor be discouraged, till he have set judgment in the earth: and the isles shall wait for his law.

5 Thus saith God the LORD, he that created the heavens, and stretched them out; he that spread forth the earth, and that which cometh out of it; he that giveth breath unto the people upon it, and spirit to them that walk therein:

6 I the LORD have called thee in righteousness, and will hold thine hand, and will keep thee, and give thee for a covenant of the people, for a light of the Gentiles;

7 To open the blind eyes, to bring out the prisoners from the prison, and them that sit in darkness out of the prison house.

8 I am the LORD: that is my name: and my glory will I not give to another, neither my praise to graven images.

9 Behold, the former things are come to pass, and new things do I declare: before they spring forth I tell you of them.

NEW REVISED STANDARD VERSION

ISAIAH 42:1 Here is my servant, whom I uphold,
my chosen, in whom my soul delights;
I have put my spirit upon him;
he will bring forth justice to the nations.

2 He will not cry or lift up his voice,
or make it heard in the street;

3 a bruised reed he will not break,
and a dimly burning wick he will not quench;
he will faithfully bring forth justice.

4 He will not grow faint or be crushed
until he has established justice in the earth;
and the coastlands wait for his teaching.

5 Thus says God, the LORD,
who created the heavens and stretched them out,
who spread out the earth and what comes from it,
who gives breath to the people upon it
and spirit to those who walk in it:

6 I am the LORD, I have called you in righteousness,
I have taken you by the hand and kept you;
I have given you as a covenant to the people,
a light to the nations,

7 to open the eyes that are blind,
to bring out the prisoners from the dungeon,
from the prison those who sit in darkness.

8 I am the LORD, that is my name;
my glory I give to no other,
nor my praise to idols.

9 See, the former things have come to pass,
and new things I now declare;
before they spring forth,
I tell you of them.

BACKGROUND

Isaiah 42:1-9 is the first of four "servant songs" in which the Servant—the Messiah—represents the nation of Israel in its ideal form. Though God had called Israel to be a kingdom of priests (Exod. 19:6), the nation had failed miserably in fulfilling its mission. At the appointed time, God would send His Son, the Messiah, who would not only serve as God's High Priest but also would atone for the sins of the world.

The other three servant songs may be found in Isaiah 49:1-7, 50:4-11, and 52:13—53:12. Through the course of these four poems, Isaiah described the mission and ultimately the suffering the Messiah would face as He fulfilled His God-given assignment. The first servant song, however, seems to purposefully keep obscure the identity of this Servant with whom God was so pleased. In other passages of Isaiah, the prophet apparently had no hesitation about naming these ambassadors of God—whether the servant be all Israel or a pagan Persian king named Cyrus (45:1). But in 42:1-9, the prophet kept the Servant's identity anonymous to the reader.

This servant song praises the qualities of justice and of mercy that are part of God's divine character and will be present in the Servant's character. Combined, justice and mercy are God's expression of power and compassion. As such, this song is seen by many scholars as the Servant's original call or commission. It opens with an expression of great exuberance and positive delight of the Lord for His Servant.

Some confusion about identifying the Servant of Isaiah 42:1-9 arises because of the prophet's clear identification of Cyrus as the servant in 41:2-3. But Cyrus would only be used of God—as a servant—to deliver the Jews from Babylonian oppression and exile. This Medo-Persian king—*a victor from the east* (41:2)—served God's purposes for a time, but he did not exhibit the whole character of God. The Servant of 42:1-9 is one whom God would *uphold, my chosen, in whom my soul delights; I have put my spirit upon him* (42:1). The language of this verse is much like that of the words proclaimed at the baptism of Jesus (Matt. 3:13-17). Because the Servant of Isaiah 42:1-9 does exhibit the whole character of God, it is clear that this a reference to the coming Messiah. He alone will *bring forth justice to the nations* (42:1).

NOTES ON THE PRINTED TEXT

The first lines of Isaiah 42:1-9 set apart God's Servant from any other servants, prophets, or kings. The focus here is upon God's chosen one, the one upon whom God promised to place His own Spirit. This Servant, the Messiah, would be God's own trusted envoy, His confidential representative. The Messiah would be powered by more than mere human energy. This Servant would be filled with a divine light that would give Him the strength to carry out the entire will of God. Specifically, the mission for which the Messiah would be enabled would be to *bring forth justice to the nations* (42:1).

In order to carry out His mission, the Servant would not have to be belligerent or loud. In fact, *He [would] not cry or lift up his voice, or make it heard in the street* (42:2). He would patiently bring God's teaching and the restoration of justice to the world. The Messiah's administration of justice would not be like those of other kings and rulers (namely, by crushing His oppressors and smashing all political opposition). Rather, He would turn the political, economic, and spiritual climate on its head by ushering in justice with a kinder and gentler approach. He would establish that justice quietly, gently, and peaceably—more like *a bruised reed* (42:3) than a whip, more like *a dimly burning wick* than a firebrand. Only through His own humility and compassion would the Messiah bring justice to the world. Like the child of 9:6-7 and the branch of 11:1-10, the Servant would respond to the coercive power of the world with the persuasive power of the Spirit.

Both the energy and the integrity that the Servant would bring to carrying out God's mission would persevere. He would not grow discouraged in seeing the mission to completion. As the embodiment of God's justice, the Messiah would *not grow faint or be crushed until he has established justice in the earth* (42:4), and that despite sure opposition. Isaiah pointed out that the Servant would suffer even as a part of His mission to restore justice (53:3-12). But no amount of pain or persecution would deter Him from fulfilling the mission God had given Him.

Whereas 42:1-4 are words God spoke to the people describing His Servant, verse 5 begins the words God spoke directly to His chosen Servant. The Lord began by touting His creative credentials. God acknowledged that He is the one *who created the heavens and stretched them out, who spread out the earth and what comes from it* (42:5). And as the Creator and Source of life, God had the full and complete right to appoint His Servant to establish justice throughout all the nations.

God called His Servant to be a *light to the nations* (42:6)—a reference extending beyond Israel's borders to the whole world. Indeed, God gave His Servant *as a covenant to the people*. Through Jesus, not only would a new covenant be mediated, but it would also be established in Him—in the shedding of His blood for the sins of the world. One segment of His mission of redemption would be to *open the eyes that are blind, to bring out the prisoners from the dungeon* (42:7). It is unlikely that the prophet meant this only in a literal sense. Rather it is the blindness, darkness, and bondage of sin that is mainly being referred to.

In the final verses of this servant song, God cast aside any doubt as to His own identity: *I am the LORD, that is my name; my glory I give to no other* (42:8). He is no mere idol; He is the Creator. Since idols did not create the world, idols cannot redeem it. But God can. And He promised to do so through His ideal Servant. He then validated His own promise by acknowledging that His past prophetic declarations had been fulfilled; thus what He now declared would also come true.

SUGGESTIONS TO TEACHERS

The initial step of becoming a servant of the Servant—a servant of Jesus Christ—is to trust Him with our whole hearts and with all our lives. Once we've come to trust Him to receive eternal life, we can follow Him, learning His ways and His outlook on both earthly life and spiritual life. Then, as we learn about Jesus' ways and outlook, we can begin to imitate Him, doing as He does, thinking as He thinks, and feeling as He feels.

1. TRUST THE SERVANT. The Servant of Isaiah 42:1-9 exhibited character traits such as gentleness, encouragement, justice, and truth. We find those same character traits in Jesus, especially as we develop our relationship with Him. Thus when we feel broken, bruised, or burned out in our spiritual life, we need to trust in the Lord to get us back on our feet. It is not the Servant's purpose to crush or destroy us; rather, His purpose is to save and protect us.

Jesus' constant presence gives us the strength we need to live out His will for us despite our circumstances. Because of His strength, we need not wrestle with frustration, anger, or fear. We have God's power working through us; we need only surrender to His gentle, just Servant.

2. FOLLOW THE SERVANT. As Christians, all of us should take our cue from the greatest of God's servants, Jesus the Messiah. He is the one who brought sight to the blind, healing to the sick, release to the captives, and a message of peace, salvation, and reconciliation. If we are looking for the one who is filled with God's light most fully, we need look no farther than Jesus. And we should follow Him. We've been given the opportunity to share in His mission. Indeed, God calls us to be servants of the Servant.

3. IMITATE THE SERVANT. God expects us as servants of the Servant to imitate Him—to grow ever more Christlike. As such, we, too, should stand for justice, as well as be His witnesses telling how He has broken the blindness, darkness, and bondage of sin. We can act boldly to change the status quo—to break the bonds that keep people trapped in prisons of ignorance, animosity, and despair. And we can imitate the Servant's loving attributes—gentleness, encouragement, justice, and truth—as we do so. Through God's Spirit, we can show such sensitivity to people around us, reflecting God's goodness and honesty to them. Such attributes are desperately needed in our world today.

■ TOPIC: The Gift of Justice

■ QUESTIONS: 1. How would you describe the Servant's relationship to God? 2. What attributes or character traits will the Servant possess? 3. Why will God's Servant *not cry out or lift up his voice* (Isa. 42:2)? 4. In what way will the promised Messiah actually bring justice to the nations? 5. What do you think God meant when He told the Servant *I have taken you by the hand and kept you* (42:6)?

■ ILLUSTRATIONS:

Waiting for a Savior. In his book *Sometimes Rough Roads Lead to Right Places*, Clark Cothern tells about a Christmas when his family encountered an unexpected house guest. A squirrel had fallen down their chimney into the wood burner stove in the basement of their Michigan home. Cothern writes:

> I thought if it knew we were there to help, I could just reach in and gently lift it out. Nothing doing. As I reached in . . . it began scratching about like a squirrel overdosed on espresso.
>
> We finally managed to construct a cardboard box "cage" complete with a large hole cut into one side, into which the squirrel waltzed when we placed the box against the wood burner's door. We let it out into the safety of our backyard.
>
> Later, I thought, "Isn't it funny how, before its redemption, our little visitor had frantically tried to bash its way out of its dark prison? It seemed that the harder it struggled in its own strength to get free, the more pain it caused itself."
>
> In the end, he simply had to wait patiently until one who was much bigger—one who could peer into his world—could carry him safely to that larger world where he really belonged. That is what we need the Lord to do for us.

Corporate Justice? The salaries of corporate chief executive officers (CEOs) have soared in recent years. CEOs on the brink of the new millennium were earning 209 times what they pay their average factory worker. In 1965, the multiple was 44. Sadly, these big raises often coincide with massive layoffs. Clearly, there is an issue of injustice here.

According to Charles Peters of *The Washington Monthly*, one CEO was paid $16.6 million in salary and bonuses in 1997. The company also announced plans to lay off 10 percent of its employees. It is clear that at least some of the dollars for executive salaries come from money saved by not paying workers. And, as "the big shots do better and better, the lot of the poor continues to head south." *The New York Times* reported that "the supply of low-rent apartments dropped by 900,000 in a recent four-year period, while the number of 'very low income families' grew by 370,000."

There is an inequality here that is not in line with God's plan for all His people. And there is something we can do to *faithfully bring forth justice* (Isa. 42:3). If we are a stockholder, we can raise our voice at an annual meeting—CEOs and corporate boards care a great deal about what stockholders think. And if we are a registered voter, we can let our representative know about our concern about the availability of affordable housing for the working poor—elected officials are very anxious to get our vote at the next election. And, of course, we can always pray that God will continue to *bring forth justice to the nations* (42:1). With our power from God, we can give a jolt to injustice.

Justice by Way of Reconciliation. As the death toll in Mexico's bloodstained southern state of Chiapas continued to rise in 1998, church leaders intensified their efforts toward peaceful reconciliation. So said Dean Alford in the *Christianity Today* article "Words Against Weapons: Evangelicals, Catholics Dialogue to Help Bring Peace to Violent Chiapas." Religious differences were an exacerbating part of the conflict, pitting one religious group against another. But starting in 1996, some church leaders launched a series of community-based dialogues between these Christian groups.

"When you get in a room and sit face-to-face, and each tell your stories, it's difficult to think of them as your enemy," says Ken Sehested, executive director of the Baptist Peace Fellowship of North America, which is involved in the dialogues. In order to build community, attendees serve meals and clean up the kitchen in mixed groups. Says one leader, "It's a very human thing and breaks down some barriers." Grass-roots church leaders are bringing invisible light to Chiapas as they work to break the bonds of religious animosity.

FOR YOUTH

■ TOPIC: Justice Rules!

■ QUESTIONS: 1. What was the mission of God's Servant? 2. How would the Messiah go about fulfilling this mission? 3. What type of character traits would be needed to fulfill such a mission? 4. In what way would the Servant be a covenant—or a contract—between God and His people? 5. Do you think Jesus fulfills this mission? Explain your answer.

■ ILLUSTRATIONS:

Waiting Like a Trapeze Flyer. In a sermon entitled "Waiting on God" (*Preaching Today #199*), John Ortberg related the following:

Not long before his death, Henri Nouwen wrote a book called *Sabbatical Journeys.* He writes about some friends of his who were trapeze artists, called the Flying Roudellas. They told Nouwen there's a special relationship between flyer and catcher on the trapeze. The flyer is the one that lets go, and the catcher is the one that catches. As the flyer swings high above the crowd on the trapeze, the moment comes when he must let go. He arcs out into the air. His job is to remain as still as possible and wait for the strong hands of the catcher to pluck him from the air.

One of the Flying Roudellas told Nouwen, "The flyer must never try to catch the catcher." The flyer must wait in absolute trust. The catcher will catch him, but he must wait.

Getting What We Don't Deserve. Denny Rydberg, the president of Young Life, shared the following story in the October 1999 edition of his ministry newsletter:

It was the first night of camp, and a group of tough kids from the city had hardly unpacked when the leaders received word about a theft. A work crew kid was missing a wallet, $35, and a watch. The next morning, Kirk, the intern from the city, found the empty wallet in his cabin. He immediately called his guys together and hit them with the hard facts.

"Man, you guys did exactly what society expected you to do. You just proved them right. And it's a shame. Now you've got 20 minutes to produce that money and the watch, or we're all going home." Kirk walked out and shut the door. He could hear the guys shouting at one another and scrambling around inside the cabin. In a moment, the door opened again, and the toughest kid in the crowd presented Kirk with the $35 and the watch. The money was already spent, but the kids had emptied their pockets and pooled their cash.

When the staff person came to pick up the stolen goods, someone asked, "Who did it?" Kirk replied, "We all did it. We're all guilty. We're in this together." The kids were shocked by Kirk's display of solidarity. Then he shut the cabin door and started to preach.

"Let's talk about grace," he said to the silent cabin. "Grace is getting something you don't deserve. God is going to correct you, but He's going to forgive you. Jesus is going to break you, but He's going to remake you. We all deserve to go home, but we're going to get to stay." It was only the first morning of camp, but God already had the undivided attention of 17 tough guys from the city.

A few nights later, Kirk invited the work crew kid who had been robbed to come to his cabin and to share his own experience of God's grace with the guys. After the young man left that night, Kirk said, "Now I'm going to say a prayer, and if any of you want to pray with me and give your lives to God, then just do it." By the end of the prayer, 17 baritone voices had cried out to Jesus Christ.

GOOD NEWS FOR ALL NATIONS

BACKGROUND SCRIPTURE: Isaiah 60—61
DEVOTIONAL READING: Isaiah 60:17-22

KEY VERSE: Arise, shine; for your light has come,
and the glory of the LORD has risen upon you. Isaiah 60:1.

KING JAMES VERSION

ISAIAH 60:1 Arise, shine; for thy light is come, and the glory of the LORD is risen upon thee.

2 For, behold, the darkness shall cover the earth, and gross darkness the people: but the LORD shall arise upon thee, and his glory shall be seen upon thee. . . .

3 And the Gentiles shall come to thy light, and kings to the brightness of thy rising.

61:1 The Spirit of the Lord GOD is upon me; because the LORD hath anointed me to preach good tidings unto the meek; he hath sent me to bind up the brokenhearted, to proclaim liberty to the captives, and the opening of the prison to them that are bound;

2 To proclaim the acceptable year of the LORD, and the day of vengeance of our God; to comfort all that mourn;

3 To appoint unto them that mourn in Zion, to give unto them beauty for ashes, the oil of joy for mourning, the garment of praise for the spirit of heaviness; that they might be called trees of righteousness, the planting of the LORD, that he might be glorified.

4 And they shall build the old wastes, they shall raise up the former desolations, and they shall repair the waste cities, the desolations of many generations.

NEW REVISED STANDARD VERSION

ISAIAH 60:1 Arise, shine; for your light has come,
and the glory of the LORD has risen upon you.
2 For darkness shall cover the earth,
and thick darkness the peoples;
but the LORD will arise upon you,
and his glory will appear over you.
3 Nations shall come to your light,
and kings to the brightness of your dawn. . . .
61:1 The spirit of the Lord GOD is upon me,
because the LORD has anointed me;
he has sent me to bring good news to the oppressed,
to bind up the brokenhearted,
to proclaim liberty to the captives,
and release to the prisoners;
2 to proclaim the year of the LORD'S favor,
and the day of vengeance of our God;
to comfort all who mourn;
3 to provide for those who mourn in Zion—
to give them a garland instead of ashes,
the oil of gladness instead of mourning,
the mantle of praise instead of a faint spirit.
They will be called oaks of righteousness,
the planting of the LORD, to display his glory.
4 They shall build up the ancient ruins,
they shall raise up the former devastations;
they shall repair the ruined cities,
the devastations of many generations.

6

BACKGROUND

The last section of the Book of Isaiah (chapters 56—66) is often seen as a new section because of the different themes that are introduced and also because many of the most prominent themes from chapters 40—55, including the theme of the Servant, are completely absent in chapters 56—66. Chapters 40—55 are comprised of an inspiring message that was meant to encourage the exiles to return to their homeland. In addition to foreseeing that God's people would endure the Babylonian exile, the prophet Isaiah also foresaw that the sins of Judah would be erased and the people's return home would be eminent.

Whereas chapters 56—59 of this last section of the prophetic book stressed the necessity for a righteous life and humanity's inability to produce such righteousness, the concluding section, beginning with chapter 60, emphasized God's ability to make His people righteous. It is, in essence, the climax of the book as a whole, for here Isaiah began to tell how God's people, who at one time sought their own prideful glory, would become repentant and put their trust back in the Lord. And as a result of their repentance, they would receive from God a glory that would never fade.

In chapter 61, Isaiah built upon some of the themes that he wrote about in chapters 40—55, except that he did not name them specifically. He did make one marvelous claim after another regarding the restoration of the nation of Israel in its homeland upon returning from Babylonian exile. The prophet also foresaw a time when the nation would rise out of its darkness and shine with God's glory. And when that occurred, so bright would be Israel's light that the Gentiles would be drawn to it. Thus all people would be drawn to Jerusalem to worship the Lord: *Strangers shall stand and feed your flocks, foreigners shall till your land and dress your vines; but you shall be called priests of the LORD, you shall be named ministers of our God* (61:5-6).

NOTES ON THE PRINTED TEXT

Though Zion as a nation had disobeyed God and had fallen into captivity as its divine punishment, God said *he will come to Zion as Redeemer, to those in Jacob who turn from transgression* (Isa. 59:20). With the covenant restored, with the Word of God in the mouths of God's people, and with the Spirit of the Lord upon them, a remnant of believers would be told to *Arise, shine* (60:1) and reflect the redeeming glory of the Lord. Though they had lived in a *thick darkness* (60:2)—in gloom and oppression as a result of their sin—*the Lord will arise upon you*. The analogy is to a sunrise that breaks the darkness of the night.

When God's *glory will appear over you*, from the nation would come a great light. And when that light appeared, all nations would be drawn to its brightness. Of course, the Messiah was the light that would rise from Zion (60:3). And even though the Messiah came for the Jews, He would also draw Gentiles to Himself because of His message of redemption and salvation for all the world. This prophecy has been partially fulfilled in Christ's first coming and will be completely fulfilled when He comes again.

The words of chapter 61 are those that Jesus read in the synagogue in Nazareth at the beginning of His ministry. Having read this prophecy about Himself and His mission, *he rolled up the scroll, gave it back to the attendant, and sat down. The eyes of all in the synagogue were fixed on him. Then he began to say to them, "Today this scripture has been fulfilled in your hearing"* (Luke 4:20-21). Based on Jesus' words, Isaiah 61 contains the prophetic words of the coming Messiah Himself. The language repeats the promise concerning the Servant in Isaiah 42:1— *Here is my servant, whom I uphold, my chosen, in whom my soul delights; I have put my spirit upon him*. Though the Servant is not mentioned by name in chapter 61, the Speaker of this prophecy made the claim that He is the one on whom God has poured out His Spirit. Therefore, the Speaker is the Servant and Messiah.

Not only has God placed His Spirit upon the Messiah, but He has also anointed Him *to bring good news to the oppressed, to bind up the brokenhearted, to proclaim liberty to the captives, and release to prisoners* (61:1). While it was not unusual for prophets to be anointed in the Old Testament, it was more typical for kings to be anointed. In this case, the Messiah was not only to be anointed as Israel's King but also as its Prophet. (The word *messiah* actually means "the anointed one.") To those who were living in exile, the mission of the Messiah gave them hope that the great and difficult task of reconstituting the nation, rebuilding its cities, and reconstructing the temple would be accomplished. The voice of the Messiah would be there to counsel them and authoritatively announce their eventual triumph.

The Messiah would go beyond proclaiming *the year of the LORD's favor* (61:2) to also proclaiming *the day of vengeance of our God*. Some Bible scholars believe that because of the events mentioned along with the phrase *the year of the LORD's favor*, what is being spoken of is the Year of Jubilee described in Exodus 21—23, Leviticus 25, Deuteronomy 15. But the Jubilee is not specifically mentioned, and it seems more likely that the passage simply extols the will of God to deliver and redeem His people from captivity.

As for *the day of vengeance of our God* (Isa. 61:2), Israel would have come full circle with regard to this concept. At first, God took vengeance on the enemies of

Israel. But after years of the nation's betraying God through the worship of idols, the prophet Amos announced that those who longed for the Lord to help them in battle would be dismayed to find that He now fought against Israel (Amos 5:18-27). In Isaiah 61:2, the prophet announced that God would once again fight for Israel, punishing its oppressors and allowing it to rebuild its ruined country. Zion would once again be restored to a position of respect and admiration among the nations.

Because of this promised restoration—*they shall build up the ancient ruins, they shall raise up the former devastations; they shall repair the ruined cities, the devastations of many generations* (61:4)—the Messiah promised comfort and provision *for those who mourn in Zion* (61:3). The redeemed and repentant people would be given a garland of victory instead of the ashes of mourning, the oil of rejoicing instead of death, and an attitude of praise instead of a weary spirit.

SUGGESTIONS TO TEACHERS

Although Isaiah 60 issues instructions for the attitudes of the Jews returning to their homeland and chapter 61 declares the mission of the coming Messiah, we may also apply these instructions, attitudes, and mission to our own lives and Christian witness.

1. ARISE, SHINE. Just as the nation of Israel was called upon to *arise, shine* (60:1) because its days of oppression were over, so we are called upon to rise and shine because our days of being oppressed by sin are over. Jesus said, *"You are the light of the world. A city built on a hill cannot be hid. No one after lighting a lamp puts it under the bushel basket, but on the lampstand, and it gives light to all in the house. In the same way, let your light shine before others, so that they may see your good works and give glory to your Father in heaven"* (Matt. 5:14-16).

2. THE LORD'S GLORY APPEARS OVER YOU. Because the people had been delivered from captivity, because they had been chosen and blessed by God, because God caused His glory to appear over them, they took on the appearance of the people of God. To the surrounding nations, they would be viewed as a people who worshiped the one true God and who were under His protection. We, too, when we're saved by the grace of God, should take on the appearance of God's people. The apostle Peter wrote, *But you are a chosen race, a royal priesthood, a holy nation, God's own people, in order that you may proclaim the mighty acts of him who called you out of darkness into his marvelous light* (1 Pet. 2:9).

3. NATIONS WILL COME TO YOUR LIGHT. God promised the nation of Israel that when its people committed their lives to Him and lived under His rule, the nations of the world would be drawn to their light, and thus drawn to God. The same is true for us. Isaiah prophesied, *You are my witnesses, says the LORD, and my servant whom I have chosen, so that you may know and believe me and understand that I am he* (Isa. 43:10).

4. PROCLAIM THE YEAR OF THE LORD'S FAVOR. It was the mission of the Messiah *to proclaim the year of the LORD's favor* (61:2). But as believers within the Body of Christ, we are to continue working toward the fulfillment of our Lord's mission: bringing *good news to the oppressed* (61:1), binding *up the brokenhearted*, proclaiming *liberty to the captives*, and announcing *release to the prisoners*. Yet as we long for the fulfillment of Christ's mission, we must patiently wait for God's timing. He is in control of history, and He weaves together all our lives into His plan.

FOR ADULTS

■ TOPIC: A Time for Building

■ QUESTIONS: 1. In what ways has your light come? 2. In what ways would the glory of the Lord appear over the people of Judah? 3. Why was it important that the Messiah be anointed to preach good news to the oppressed? 4. What good news does the Messiah bring for the oppressed, brokenhearted, and captive? 5. How would the Messiah bring comfort to the mourning exiles in Babylon?

■ ILLUSTRATIONS:

The Glory of the Lord Has Risen upon You. In his book, *The Bible Jesus Read*, Philip Yancey wrote the following:

> Out of their tortured history, the Jews demonstrate the most surprising lesson of all: You cannot go wrong personalizing God. God is not a blurry power living somewhere in the sky, not an abstraction like the Greeks proposed, not a sensual superhuman like the Romans worshiped, and definitely not the absentee watchmaker of the deists. God is "personal." He enters into people's lives, messes with families, shows up in unexpected places, chooses unlikely leaders, calls people to account. Most of all, God loves.

Good News Seeds. In the book *Parables*, Migan McKenna writes a story about a woman who wanted peace in the world and peace in her heart. But she was very frustrated. The world seemed to be falling apart. She would read the papers and get depressed.

One day the woman decided to go shopping, and she went into a mall and picked a store at random. She walked in and was surprised to see Jesus behind the counter. She knew it was Jesus because He looked just like the pictures she'd seen on religious cards and devotional pictures. The woman finally got up her nerve and asked, "Excuse me, are you Jesus?"

"I am."

"Do you work here?"

"No, I own the store."

"Oh, what do you sell here?"

"Just about everything," Jesus said. "Feel free to walk up and down the aisles, make a list, see what it is you want, and then come back and we'll see what we can do for you."

The woman did just that—walked up and down the aisles. There was peace on earth, no more war, no hunger or poverty, peace in families, no more drugs, harmony, clean air, and the careful use of resources. The woman wrote furiously. By the time she got back to the counter, she had a long list. Jesus took the list, skimmed through it, looked up at the woman and smiled. "No problem." And then He bent down behind the counter and picked out all sorts of things, stood up, and laid out the packets. The woman asked, "What are these?"

"Seed packets," Jesus said. "This is a catalog store."

The woman said, "You mean I don't get the finished product?"

"No, this is a place of dreams. You come and see what it looks like, and I give you the seeds. You plant the seeds. You go home and nurture them and help them to grow and someone else reaps the benefits."

"Oh," the woman said. And she left the store without buying anything.

Committed to the Messiah's Mission. When Julius Caesar landed on the shores of Britain with his Roman legions, he took a bold and decisive step to ensure the success of his military venture. Ordering his men to march to the edge of the Cliffs of Dover, he commanded them to look down at the water below. To their amazement, they saw every ship in which they had crossed the channel engulfed in flames. Caesar had deliberately cut off any possibility of retreat. Now that his soldiers were unable to return to the continent, there was nothing left for them to do but to advance and conquer! And that is exactly what they did.

That was the kind of commitment the Messiah had to His mission—no turning back. May we be so dedicated to His mission as well.

FOR YOUTH ■ TOPIC: A Light in the Night
■ QUESTIONS: 1. Why do you think God commanded Zion (Jerusalem) to arise and let its light shine? 2. Why might people who don't believe in Christ be drawn to His *light* (Isa. 60:3)? 3. In what ways did Jesus reveal that the Spirit of the Lord was upon Him? 4. What do you think is *the year of the LORD's favor* (61:2)? 5. What might be some tactful ways to comfort a hurting person who is doubting God's goodness?

■ **ILLUSTRATIONS:**

Nations Shall Come to Your Light. Businessman Harvey Mackay, who wrote the book *Swim with the Sharks*, told in a newspaper column about the importance of leaders being willing to do whatever kind of work is required. As an example of being willing to do anything on the factory floor, Mackay mentioned Philip Pillsbury of the Pillsbury milling family. Mackay wrote the following:

> The tips of three of his fingers were missing. . . . [That's] the unmistakable mark of a journeyman grain miller, albeit a somewhat less-than-dexterous one. Pillsbury had an international reputation as a connoisseur of fine foods and wines, but to the troops, his reputation as a man willing to do a hard, dirty job was the one that mattered . . . and you can be sure everyone was aware of it.

The best leaders, like Jesus Christ, see themselves as servants. The people that are greatest in the kingdom of God are those missing the tips of their fingers (so to speak).

Poet's Longing. Thomas Hardy's poem, "The Oxen," describes an old English rural folk legend in which the oxen are said to kneel in their stalls every Christmas Eve at the stroke of midnight in memory of Jesus' birth in Bethlehem. At the end of the poem, Hardy imagines someone telling him that in a remote farm the animals were kneeling that night. If he were invited to see this, the agnostic Hardy said he would "go with the person in the . . . hope that it might be so."

Perhaps you, like the poet Hardy, have wished that there might be some cause for hoping, some reason for worshiping, and some evidence for believing the truth of Christ's birth. Consider Luke 2:11, *"to you is born this day in the city of David a Savior, who is the Messiah, the Lord."*

The Father has come to us in the person of His Son, Jesus. And at the manger, God has reached out to us in love. All of us are residents of this planet where Jesus made His home! This is the reason for hoping, worshiping, and believing.

Proclaiming the Year of the Lord's Favor. *Religion Today* reported in 1999 that Christians who work in television and radio are launching an aggressive evangelistic campaign to reach millions of people in the Philadelphia area.

Forty professionals from almost every media outlet in Philadelphia, including NBC, ABC, CBS, and cable, are donating their time and expertise to produce and air top-quality Christian advertisements for television, radio, billboards, and the Internet. The group, which calls itself Mission Media: Delaware Valley, is under the auspices of the Urban Family Council, an educational and research organization. A similar advertising campaign was already underway in Boise, Idaho, and organizers there had provided ideas and inspiration for the Delaware Valley outreach.

The television ad campaign includes four phases. The first is meant to show that "the church loves you." It portrays the church as a relevant place to be, the cornerstone of society, and the best place to raise children. The second phase shows that there is a God. It is more intellectually aggressive, discussing evidences for the existence of God in the complexity and design of nature—from the stars to DNA. The third and fourth phases discuss fulfilled biblical prophecies to show that Jesus is God and that the Bible was inspired by God.

It is not for a lack of strength or accuracy that the Christian faith wanes in the United States. The fault lies in our failure to communicate the essential evidence and implications of the Gospel. The result is an entire generation of young people who fail to find the meaning of life.

SEEK THE LORD

BACKGROUND SCRIPTURE: Isaiah 55
DEVOTIONAL READING: Psalm 85:4-9

KEY VERSE: Seek the LORD while he may be found, call upon him while he is near. Isaiah 55:6.

KING JAMES VERSION

ISAIAH 55:1 Ho, every one that thirsteth, come ye to the waters, and he that hath no money; come ye, buy, and eat; yea, come, buy wine and milk without money and without price.

2 Wherefore do ye spend money for that which is not bread? and your labour for that which satisfieth not? hearken diligently unto me, and eat ye that which is good, and let your soul delight itself in fatness.

3 Incline your ear, and come unto me: hear, and your soul shall live; and I will make an everlasting covenant with you, even the sure mercies of David. . . .

5 Behold, thou shalt call a nation that thou knowest not, and nations that knew not thee shall run unto thee because of the LORD thy God, and for the Holy One of Israel; for he hath glorified thee.

6 Seek ye the LORD while he may be found, call ye upon him while he is near:

7 Let the wicked forsake his way, and the unrighteous man his thoughts: and let him return unto the LORD, and he will have mercy upon him; and to our God, for he will abundantly pardon.

8 For my thoughts are not your thoughts, neither are your ways my ways, saith the LORD.

9 For as the heavens are higher than the earth, so are my ways higher than your ways, and my thoughts than your thoughts.

NEW REVISED STANDARD VERSION

ISAIAH 55:1 Ho, everyone who thirsts,
    come to the waters;
and you that have no money,
    come, buy and eat!
Come, buy wine and milk
    without money and without price.
2 Why do you spend your money for that which is
    not bread,
    and your labor for that which does not satisfy?
Listen carefully to me, and eat what is good,
    and delight yourselves in rich food.
3 Incline your ear, and come to me;
    listen, so that you may live.
I will make with you an everlasting covenant,
    my steadfast, sure love for David. . . .
5 See, you shall call nations that you do not know,
    and nations that do not know you shall run to you,
because of the LORD your God, the Holy One of
    Israel,
    for he has glorified you.
6 Seek the LORD while he may be found,
    call upon him while he is near;
7 let the wicked forsake their way,
    and the unrighteous their thoughts;
let them return to the LORD, that he may have mercy
    on them,
    and to our God, for he will abundantly pardon.
8 For my thoughts are not your thoughts,
    nor are your ways my ways, says the LORD.
9 For as the heavens are higher than the earth,
    so are my ways higher than your ways
    and my thoughts than your thoughts.

7

BACKGROUND

Isaiah 55 is a hymn of joy and triumph celebrating the nation of Israel's restoration to its homeland. It closes the section of Isaiah beginning at chapter 40, all of which contains a message of inspiration that would encourage the exiles living in Babylon to return to Judah's cities, towns, and countrysides. The glorious message that the sins of Judah would be erased was proclaimed in these chapters by the prophet Isaiah.

As such, the hymn of chapter 55 is the climax of God's promise of salvation. And this promise is not only issued to the people of Israel, but it is also extended to all the people of the world. Indeed, as chapter 55 proclaims, God's gift of salvation is now freely offered to anyone who would humbly accept it. Everyone—Jew or Gentile—who is spiritually hungry and thirsty can now partake of God's grace and mercy, and they can do so freely.

The Bible makes clear in many ways that God welcomes all those who want to know Him. And Isaiah's invitation is one of the most brilliant explanations of how God yearns for people to come to Him. Best of all, the prophet made it clear that anyone can come without any special credentials. God welcomes the spiritually needy, not people who think they don't need Him.

NOTES ON THE PRINTED TEXT

Along with the summons for the exiles in Babylon to return to and restore their homeland is an invitation for all people to accept the salvation of the Lord. The invitation in Isaiah resembles the Beatitude in which Jesus said, "*Blessed are those who hunger and thirst for righteousness, for they will be filled*" (Matt. 5:6). In Isaiah 55:1, God beckoned, *everyone who thirsts, come to the waters; and you that have no money, come, buy and eat!* In this way God promised spiritual refreshment for everyone who had a spiritual thirst. Jesus, too, offered this "spiritual drink" when He said, "*those who drink of the water that I will give them will never be thirsty. The water that I will give will become in them a spring of water gushing up to eternal life*" (John 4:14).

That food, wine, and milk could be purchased with no money would be proof that good times were on the way for the exiled Jews (Isa. 55:1). Wine and milk were cultural symbols of abundance, enjoyment, and nourishment. Even the poorest of the returning exiles was promised a healthy portion of this abundance. Furthermore, and more importantly, God would pour out His salvation in abundance—and no purchase would be necessary. His salvation would be offered freely as a gift because the sacrifice of the Messiah had paid off humanity's sin debt in full (53:5-9). Thus salvation would be extended to all people; it could not be earned, only accepted with grateful hearts.

The question, *Why do you spend your money for that which is not bread, and your labor for that which does not satisfy?* (55:2), is apparently a reference to the pagan religious practices that God's people had adopted from both inhabitants of their land and later from invading foreigners. God had offered His people something infinitely greater—salvation through faith in Him. His great spiritual blessings are compared to a banquet where *rich food* is served. Faith in the one true God satisfies, while misplaced faith in pagan idols will never satisfy.

The *everlasting covenant* (55:3) was one made to David, to whom God promised an unending dynasty that would culminate in the coming of the Messiah. God's assurance of His *steadfast, sure love for David* was a divine guarantee that the life of the nation would be continued. This covenant with David promised a permanent homeland for the Israelites, no threat from pagan nations, and no wars (2 Sam. 7:10-11). But Israel failed to fulfill its part of the covenant to obey God and stay away from idols, and thus the nation was punished. Even so, God was ready to renew His covenant with His people.

Isaiah 55:5 returns to one of the major themes of the Old Testament—a theme that the people of Israel too often forgot. God had chosen them—and called them out—to be His representatives in the world. And as His representatives, they were to be His obedient servants. As God blessed His people, other peoples would yearn to follow their God and serve Him, and God would bless them as well. The Israelites were not to be exalted or excluded from other people, but rather to be examples to and impact others for the glory of God. This national purpose is restated as a reminder to God's people to be witnesses of His love and salvation: *You shall call nations that you do not know, and nations that do not know you shall run to you, because of the Lord your God, the Holy One of Israel, for he has glorified you.* God's purpose with His people then—and now—is that the nations might be drawn to the spiritual light that they reflect.

Therefore the people are told to *seek the LORD* (55:6) while the window of opportunity is open for them to do so—*while he may be found . . . while he is near.* But just as the people receive a call to seek the Lord, so they also receive a call to repentance: *let the wicked forsake their way, and the unrighteous their thoughts; let them return to the LORD* (55:7). Another promise is given to those who combine seeking the Lord with repentance: the Lord will *have mercy on them* and *will abundantly pardon.*

The salvation, grace, and mercy of the Lord are truly beyond comprehension. His purposes and intentions are greater and higher than ours. His ways and directions are greater and higher than ours. His knowledge and wisdom are far greater than any human's. He is both all-powerful and all-knowing. But He does reveal that part of Himself that He wants us to know through His Word. And His Word declares that, because of His love for us, He announces His offer of salvation to all humanity.

SUGGESTIONS TO TEACHERS

Many of us foolishly try to fit God into our mold—to make His plans and purposes conform to ours. But God says that His ways are higher than our ways and His thoughts higher than our thoughts (Isa. 55:9). He calls us to fit into His plans—not the other way around. In Isaiah 55, God gives a set of instructions that we would do well to follow if we are to secure our salvation in Him.

1. COME TO THE WATERS. Realize that God extends to us His offer of salvation through His Son, Jesus Christ. We have all sinned, and we need forgiveness for our sins. God offers His forgiveness to us freely through faith in His Son. Thus, all that is left for us is to go to the Lord—to His waters—and eagerly receive His nourishment for our souls.

2. LISTEN CAREFULLY TO ME. The Lord also calls us to repentance and obedience. He does not want us to be eating the stale bread crumbs of this world when we could be feasting on the fresh loaves at His table! Thus, He calls us to turn away from our sins and from living for ourselves and turn to obeying Him and living for Him.

3. SEEK THE LORD. Seek God's will for your life. Seek to do things His way. Seek to love the way He loves. Seek a personal relationship with Him through His Son, Jesus Christ. Break down any barriers that are keeping you from Him. And don't put it off. Seek Him *while he may be found* (Isa. 55:6), while He is diligently speaking to your heart.

4. CALL UPON THE LORD. Be sure to pray. Take time to talk to God. As Paul commanded in 1 Thessalonians 5:17, *Pray without ceasing.* Also, be sure to listen for God to guide you through His Word.

FOR ADULTS

■ **TOPIC:** Seek the Lord

■ **QUESTIONS:** 1. What do you think the water and food of Isaiah 55:1 actually represent? Why might water and food be used as an analogy? 2. What are some unsatisfying ways that you could spend your resources, like your time and money? 3. What do you think is the purpose of God's everlasting covenant with David? 4. Why was it important that *the wicked forsake their way, and the unrighteous their thoughts* (55:7)? 5. In what ways do you think God's ways and thoughts are higher than our ways and thoughts? 6. Why is it best for us to conform our plans and purposes to the will of God?

■ **ILLUSTRATIONS:**

For That Which Does Not Satisfy. In July of 1983, my family was in our first apartment between Knoxville and Maryville—an out of the way place called Louisville, Tennessee. My wife, Jill, waited until after we were married to get rid of some of my belongings. Jill knew all along that I had some stuff that she just didn't want in the same house that she lived in. I knew she loved me, but that doesn't mean she loved all my stuff.

There was the yellow beanbag, for instance. Somehow Jill just couldn't see how that would go in the same room with her Martha Washington sewing cabinet that her father had refinished for her. Then there were my old posters; Jill couldn't envision them hanging over her antique jelly cabinet. I suggested that we hang my black-and-white photograph of an Appalachian family—complete with barnwood frame—over her oak washstand. "No," she said sweetly. "I don't think that would do." So maybe my Mason fruit jar of Cocke County moonshine, given to me by the sheriff as a memento of my journalistic work, could sit on the oak washstand. But no! Jill's moss rose tea set got to sit on the washstand.

"Where are we gonna put my stuff?" I asked. "Some of this junk has a lot of sentimental value to me." Jill smiled at me, again sweetly and innocently. She didn't have to say it. I could read it in her eyes. *The dumpster wouldn't be such a bad place for it,* she was thinking. And so within months, most of my ugly, dilapidated, unsightly stuff was replaced by finely finished antiques from the shop of Jill's father. My stuff that didn't make it to the dumpster was relegated to the laundry room wall. *Perhaps Jill was secretly encouraging me to spend more time in there.*

The thing is, I don't recall, at least not after those first few months, ever missing my ugly stuff. I do, on the other hand, recall developing quite a fondness for the beautiful things that now decorated our home. To beautify the inside of your house, you have to get rid of some of the ugly stuff. Also, to fill your house with good things, you have to throw out some of the bad things. Likewise, to make room for the righteous, you must empty out the evil.

Let the Wicked Forsake Their Way. Four hundred witch doctors participated in an extraordinary church service. It was held several years ago at Christ the King in Kampala, Uganda, as the culmination of the work of missionary Ross Russo, who has traveled through rural areas urging people to turn to God, *All Africa News Agency* (AANA) said.

"Excitement mixed with surprise and disbelief" characterized the packed service as 15 of the witch doctors "gave testimonies of how they have been hoodwinking people," AANA said. The service, part of a three-day gathering, attracted the attention of the media, Christians, animists, and newspaper cartoonists, who depicted witch doctors from across Africa scampering to the church because "even Jesus entered the homes of sinners and tax collectors," AANA said.

Some people were afraid trouble would erupt between church leaders and the witch doctors, who dressed in wildcat and leopard attire with a red and yellow headband. But there was no acrimony. "It was a day of repentance, and the congregation was treated to a session of confessions and revelations of the past indulgences in 'human divine power.'"

The witch doctors told how they tricked ignorant and unsuspecting clients by changing their voices to assume the presence of a spirit or ghost. Eliya Kayiira, a witch doctor for 20 years and now a minister, described how drumming, singing, and the odor of a special herb during rituals weakens people and makes them think they are possessed. The banging of the shrine door and shrieking of ghosts arriving to solve the problems are tricks performed by the witch doctor, who sometimes severely beats his clients, he said.

"It is this fear of the witch doctor and his knowledge about the clients' affairs having been relayed to him by other clients who interact with the client that gives him power," Kayiira said. "Clients then pay for the services without hesitation to have their problems solved." Several witch doctors said they were lured into the trade by threats from another witch doctor that they would not otherwise recover from an illness.

FOR YOUTH

■ TOPIC: Something for Nothing

■ QUESTIONS: 1. What were the exiles being urged to do in Isaiah 55:1? Why would this have been difficult for them to carry out? 2. According to 55:2, what was the key to the spiritual prosperity of God's people? 3. What was the "everlasting covenant" (55:3) that God made with David and his descendants? 4. When would people of foreign nations flock to God's people? 5. Why did Isaiah warn the exiles not to delay in seeking the Lord?

■ ILLUSTRATIONS:

The Place of Memory. Miguel de Unamuno (1864–1936) was an influential Spanish writer. In his classic work entitled *Tragic Sense of Life*, he wrote the following about the importance of teaching our children to remember what God has done in the past: "Memory is the basis for individual personality, just as tradition is the basis of the collective personality of a people. We live in memory and by memory, and our spiritual life is at the bottom of the effort of our memory to persist, to transform itself into hope, the effort of our past to transform itself into our future."

Most Saluted Man in America. Richard Stans, according to William Safire, is the most saluted man in the United States. Safire points out that millions of school children place their right hands over their hearts to pledge allegiance to the flag, and to the republic for Richard Stans. Safire also claims that he has learned that many youngsters start the famous pledge by saying, "I pledge a legion to the flag," while others begin with, "I led the pigeons to the flag." The words, "one nation, indivisible," sometimes are corrupted into "One naked individual," or "One nation in a dirigible," or "One nation and a vegetable."

While we may smile at these childish misunderstandings of the words of the Pledge of Allegiance, we should note that many of our children have just as poor an understanding of what God's Word says. We have failed to teach our children well in many areas, and must heed the warning that the generation that forgets the truths of Scripture will spiritually perish.

Unwavering Commitment. The most famous and best-loved athlete Scotland ever produced was Eric Liddell. He was an internationally known rugby player and an Olympic gold medallist. The story of his refusal to run in the preliminary heats of the 100-meter dash at the Paris Olympics in 1924 was told in the movie entitled *Chariots of Fire.*

Liddell was a man who had an unswerving commitment to love the Lord and keep His commandments. While the race put him into a conflict with his fellow citizens, the leaders of his nation, the International Olympic Committee, his friends, and others, Liddell would not deviate from his stand.

Like Liddell, you will often be torn by conflicting allegiances to family, peers, and others. But like Liddell, you too can stand up to the world by relying on God's power. He will give you the strength to do what is right.

Revolution Ending. The so-called "sexual revolution" is slowing, and perhaps, even ending. Mark Judge of *Insight* magazine cites surveys (including one of 200,000 teens done by *USA Today*) that demonstrates a "decline" in sexual activity among teens. Literally thousands more young people are saying *no* to premarital sex, are waiting for marriage, and are returning to more traditional dating and courtship patterns.

A growing tide of problems, such as sexually transmitted diseases, AIDS, divorce, and a culture saturated with sex, plus a more affirmative effort by churches, has led a younger generation to adopt a different perspective on physical intimacy. As a follower of Christ, you will want to consider what the Bible teaches about this. Let your love for God and commitment to His Word be demonstrated by your efforts to remain chaste.

So Are My Ways Higher than Your Ways. In his book *Fresh Wind, Fresh Fire,* Jim Cymbala writes about how God is like a well—and no one has ever fathomed its depth. To go into the power of God is to plunge ever deeper and deeper into God's well. Every man or woman used by God has gone down into this vast reservoir.

Inside the well there is no cause for leaving or jumping out. Who will ever fathom the fullness of the love of God? Who will ever exhaust the richness of His mercy to fallen human beings? Who will ever understand the real power of God?

Monastic Method of Being Mindful. In the old European monasteries, one member was assigned to move throughout the abbey each day to the kitchens, the stables, the fields, the scriptorium, and every other place where members of the faith community were at work. This person was to tap each monk on the shoulder and ask, "Are you remembering God?"

Daily devotions and weekly worship are meant to do the same for us. What are you consciously doing each day to remind yourself of God in your life?

TRUE WORSHIP

BACKGROUND SCRIPTURE: Isaiah 58
DEVOTIONAL READING: Isaiah 58:10-14

KEY VERSE: Is not this the fast that I choose: to loose the bonds of injustice? Isaiah 58:6.

KING JAMES VERSION

ISAIAH 58:3 Behold, in the day of your fast ye find pleasure, and exact all your labours.

4 Behold, ye fast for strife and debate, and to smite with the fist of wickedness: ye shall not fast as ye do this day, to make your voice to be heard on high.

5 Is it such a fast that I have chosen? a day for a man to afflict his soul? is it to bow down his head as a bulrush, and to spread sackcloth and ashes under him? wilt thou call this a fast, and an acceptable day to the LORD?

6 Is not this the fast that I have chosen? to loose the bands of wickedness, to undo the heavy burdens, and to let the oppressed go free, and that ye break every yoke?

7 Is it not to deal thy bread to the hungry, and that thou bring the poor that are cast out to thy house? when thou seest the naked, that thou cover him; and that thou hide not thyself from thine own flesh?

8 Then shall thy light break forth as the morning, and thine health shall spring forth speedily: and thy righteousness shall go before thee; the glory of the LORD shall be thy rereward.

9 Then shalt thou call, and the LORD shall answer; thou shalt cry, and he shall say, Here I am.

NEW REVISED STANDARD VERSION

ISAIAH 58:3 Look, you serve your own interest on your fast day,
and oppress all your workers.

4 Look, you fast only to quarrel and to fight
and to strike with a wicked fist.
Such fasting as you do today
will not make your voice heard on high.

5 Is such the fast that I choose,
a day to humble oneself?
Is it to bow down the head like a bulrush,
and to lie in sackcloth and ashes?
Will you call this a fast,
a day acceptable to the LORD?

6 Is not this the fast that I choose:
to loose the bonds of injustice,
to undo the thongs of the yoke,
to let the oppressed go free,
and to break every yoke?

7 Is it not to share your bread with the hungry,
and bring the homeless poor into your house;
when you see the naked, to cover them,
and not to hide yourself from your own kin?

8 Then your light shall break forth like the dawn,
and your healing shall spring up quickly;
your vindicator shall go before you,
the glory of the LORD shall be your rear guard.

9 Then you shall call, and the LORD will answer;
you shall cry for help, and he will say, Here I am.

BACKGROUND

Although the closing chapters of Isaiah—including chapter 58—introduce us to the coming Messiah's program of peace for the world, the prophet still addressed the need for repentance of some of the past and present sins of the people. Intermingled with prophecies about both the Messiah's first coming and His second coming as the Lord, Judge, and King of the universe, are calls for the people to prepare themselves by growing in righteousness and holiness.

Thus Isaiah is told to *Shout out, do not hold back! Lift up your voice like a trumpet!* (58:1). The prophet was, again, to boldly and loudly denounce the sins of Israel and Judah. This time their sins were not of action or inaction, but rather of attitude. God wanted His people warned that, even though they delighted in seeking Him on a daily basis, they would be judged for making a mere show of their religion. Specifically, the Lord disapproved of their attitude and motivation toward fasting.

Fasting is the spiritual discipline of abstaining from food for various godly reasons. In its simplest form, fasting has, for the most part, been practiced to demonstrate the sincerity of our prayers. The Bible gives several reasons and occasions for fasting, such as when believers face periods of distress (2 Sam. 3:35; Ps. 35:13), when they are on the brink of a national crisis (2 Chron. 20:3; Ezra 8:21; Esth. 4:16), when they are making difficult spiritual decisions (Matt. 4:2; Acts 13:2), when they are hard-pressed to meet individual needs (Matt. 17:21), or when they are anticipating the return of Christ (Luke 5:35).

But for those who are addressed in Isaiah 58, fasting had become little more than a religious ritual, as had going to the temple every day or listening to the Scripture readings. Thus God, through the prophet Isaiah, contrasted what He considered a true fast with the type of fasting that was only a false external show of piety. He wanted His people to know that true worship was more than a religious ritual; true worship would lead them into a vital relationship with their God.

For believers today, true worship is the acknowledgment that God has done everything necessary through His Son. Thus, those who truly worship God claim Jesus as their Savior. It should come as no surprise that God will not settle for anything less.

NOTES ON THE PRINTED TEXT

Isaiah 58 opens with God instructing Isaiah to deliver another message to His people. This message is to chastise them for their rebellion and their sins. But as God speaks, it remains difficult to determine what rebellion and sins He is referring to. In fact, God almost seems to praise His people for the way they *seek me and delight to know my ways* (58:2). But then He said, *as if they were a nation that practiced righteousness and did not forsake the ordinance of their God.* The words *as if* begin the portrayal of a people who were diligently practicing their religious rituals, even though their hearts were still not right with God.

In 58:3, it is the people who get to voice their complaint against God, and they did so in the form of two questions. They wanted to know why the Lord had not been impressed with their fasting and why He had not noticed their acts of penance. Why hadn't their acts of self-denial and repentance brought them any special favors from God? God addressed their inquiry with a straightforward answer: *Look, you serve your own interest on your fast day, and oppress all your workers.* Thus God criticized their fasting and penance as outward forms of worship and not as an expression of their hearts.

God, who can see past one's exterior and see that person's attitude and motivation, knew that the people's religious practices were selfish and self-seeking. They were pursuing religion for their own sakes, not for the sake of God and others. In the people's minds, they still planned *to quarrel and to fight and to strike with a wicked fist* (58:4) after their acts of fasting and penance. Their religious rituals only served to make them feel better, as though they had been forgiven of their sins. And in this way their formal religion had become a substitute for their sincere commitment to God.

Such hypocritical religious activity was actually a hindrance to prayer. Indeed, God would not recognize acts of worship that were performed hypocritically: *Such fasting as you do today will not make your voice heard on high.* Fasting and other spiritual disciplines were not to be ends in themselves, but were intended to result in greater godliness in the people's relationship with the Lord and with others. If rites and rituals did not have that result, God expressed no interest in them (58:5).

Having pointed out what was wrong with the type of fasting and penance the people were practicing, God then expressed *the fast that I choose* (58:6). The kind of fasting God wanted from His people was to free those who are wrongly imprisoned, to stop oppressing those who worked for them, to share their food with the hungry, to welcome poor wanderers into their homes, and to give clothes to those who need them. To do so would reveal outward evidence of genuine inward righteousness. To do so would be to please God.

In return for pleasing God, He promised to heal, protect, and guide His people. Joy, prosperity, and salvation would be theirs. And *then you shall call, and the LORD will answer; you shall cry for help, and he will say, Here I am* (58:9).

SUGGESTIONS TO TEACHERS

John Wesley once said that "There is no holiness but social holiness." God has made it clear in His Word that a heart that is pure toward Him cannot be indifferent toward other human beings. It is in delivering others in Christ's name that we ourselves are delivered, for God repeatedly instructs us to worship Him by serving others. It is as Jesus said, *"Truly I tell you, just as you did it to one of the least of these who are members of my family, you did it to me"* (Matt. 25:40).

1. GET FORGIVENESS. God calls us to repentance when we harbor unforgiven sin in our heart and continue in a sinful lifestyle. All the religious rituals in the world won't get through to God until we accept His forgiveness and get our hearts right with Him.

2. HAVE COMPASSION. More than worshiping God repeatedly and correctly, more than even having the right doctrine, God yearns for us to have compassion for the oppressed, the poor, and the helpless. When we see their faces, He wants us to see the face of Jesus.

3. BE RESPONSIVE. Our worship of God must go beyond what we can obtain for ourselves. We should work at disciplining all of our desires—physical, mental, emotional, and spiritual—so that we can be more responsive to the needs of those around us. God is not interested in our worship if we are simply pursuing religion for ourselves and ourselves alone.

4. REACH OUT. Of course, it's true that we cannot be saved without faith in Christ, but the Bible says our faith lacks sincerity if it doesn't reach out to others (Jas. 1:27; 1 John 3:17-18). Fasting can certainly be beneficial spiritually and physically. But God desires that our fasting go beyond our own personal growth to acts of charity, generosity, justice, and kindness.

FOR ADULTS	■ **TOPIC:** True Worship

■ **QUESTIONS:** 1. In what ways were the people's view of fasting and God's view of fasting different? 2. In what ways might fasting be done to *serve your own interest* (Isa. 58:3)? 3. What might you do to *let the oppressed go free* (58:6) in your community? 4. Why do you think anyone would hide *from your own kin* (58:7)? 5. In what way are we worshiping God by giving to the needy?

■ **ILLUSTRATIONS:**

Your Light Shall Break Forth Like the Dawn. A sobbing little girl stood near a small church from which she had been turned away because it "was too crowded." "I can't go to Sunday school," she sobbed to the pastor as he walked by. Seeing her shabby, unkempt appearance, the pastor guessed the reason and, taking her by the hand, took her inside and found a place for her in the Sunday school class. The child was so touched that she went to bed that night thinking about the children who have no place to worship Jesus.

Some two years later, this child lay dead in one of the poor tenement buildings. The parents called for the kindhearted pastor, who had befriended their daughter, to handle the final arrangements. As her poor little body was being moved, a worn and crumpled purse was found that seemed to have been rummaged from some trash dump. Inside was found 57 cents and a note scribbled in childish handwriting that read, "This is to help build the little church bigger so more children can go to Sunday school." For two years she had saved for this offering of love. When the pastor tearfully read that note, he knew instantly what he would do.

Carrying this note and the red pocketbook to the pulpit, he told the story of the little girl's unselfish love and devotion. He challenged his peers to get busy and raise enough money for the larger building.

But the story does not end there! A newspaper learned about the story and published it. It was read by a realtor who offered the congregation a parcel of land worth many thousands of dollars. When told that the church could not pay so much, he offered it to the church for a 57-cent payment.

Church members made large contributions. Checks came from far and wide. Within five years, the little girl's gift had increased to $250,000—a huge sum for that time (near the turn of the last century). Her unselfish love had paid large dividends.

In fact, if you ever visit the city of Philadelphia, look up Temple Baptist Church, with a seating capacity of 3,300. And while you're there, go to an educational institution called Temple University, where hundreds of students are trained. Have a look, too, at the enormous Good Samaritan Hospital. And don't overlook the Sunday school building that houses hundreds of Sunday school scholars, so that no child in that area of the city will ever need to be left outside.

It is in one of the rooms of this building that you can see the sweet face of a little girl whose 57 cents, so sacrificially saved, made such remarkable history and changed the face of the City of Brotherly Love. And alongside the picture of that little girl is a portrait of her kind pastor, Dr. Russel H. Conwell, author of a book many of you have probably read, called *Acres of Diamonds*. Whenever we obey the Lord and diligently do His will, our *light shall break forth like the dawn* (Isa. 58:8).

To Hide Yourself from Your Own Kin. A story is told about a soldier who was finally coming home after having fought in Vietnam. He called his parents from San Francisco. "Mom and Dad, I'm coming home, but I've got a favor to ask. I have a friend I'd like to bring with me."

"Sure," they replied, "we'd love to meet him."

"There's something you should know," the son continued. "He was hurt pretty badly in the fighting. He stepped on a land mine and lost an arm and a leg. He has nowhere else to go, and I want him to come live with us."

"I'm sorry to hear that, son. Maybe we can help him find somewhere to live."

"No, Mom and Dad, I want him to live with us."

"Son," said the father, "you don't know what you're asking. Someone with such a handicap would be a terrible burden on us. We have our own lives to live, and we can't let something like this interfere with our lives. I think you should just come home and forget about this guy. He'll find a way to live on his own."

At that point, the son hung up the phone. The parents heard nothing more from him. A few days later, however, they received a call from the San Francisco police. Their son had died after falling from a building, they were told. The police believed it was suicide.

The grief-stricken parents flew to San Francisco and were taken to the city morgue to identify the body of their son. They recognized him, but to their horror they also discovered something they didn't know: their son had only one arm and one leg.

The parents in this story are like many of us. We find it easy to love those who are good looking or fun to have around, but we don't like people who inconvenience us or make us feel uncomfortable. We would rather stay away from people who aren't as healthy, beautiful, or smart as we are. Thankfully, there's someone who won't treat us that way, someone who loves us with an unconditional love, someone who welcomes us into His family forever, regardless of how messed up we are.

This evening before you tuck yourself in for the night, say a little prayer that God will give you the strength you need to accept people as they are, and to help us all be more understanding of those who are different from us!

Undo the Thongs of the Yoke. A nurse took the tired, anxious serviceman to the bedside. "Your son is here," she said to the old man. She had to repeat the words several times before the patient's eyes opened. Heavily sedated because of the pain of his heart attack, he dimly saw the young man in the Marine Corps uniform standing outside the oxygen tent.

The patient reached out his hand. The Marine wrapped his toughened fingers around the old man's limp ones, squeezing a message of love and encouragement. The nurse brought a chair so that the Marine could sit alongside the bed. Nights are long in hospitals—but all through the night the young Marine sat there in the poorly lighted ward, holding the old man's hand and offering him words of love and strength.

Occasionally, the nurse suggested that the Marine move away and rest awhile. He refused. Whenever the nurse came into the ward, the Marine was oblivious of her and of the night noises of the hospital—the clanking of the oxygen tank, the laughter of the night staff members exchanging greetings, and the cries and moans of the other patients. Now and then the nurse heard the Marine say a few gentle words. The dying man said nothing, only holding tightly to his son's hand all through the night.

Along toward dawn, the old man died. The Marine released the lifeless hand he had been holding and went to tell the nurse. While she did what she had to do, he waited. Finally, she returned. She started to offer words of sympathy, but the Marine interrupted her.

"That's not necessary. Who was that man?" he asked.

The nurse was startled, "He was your father," she answered.

"No, he wasn't," the Marine replied. "I never saw him before in my life."

"Then why didn't you say something when I took you to him?"

"I knew right away that there had been a mistake, but I also knew he needed his son, and his son just wasn't here. When I realized that he was too sick to tell whether I was his son, and I knew how much he needed me, I stayed."

The next time God gives you a mission, be there. Stay. You'll be glad you did.

FOR YOUTH ■ TOPIC: Get It Right

■ QUESTIONS: 1. Do you think the people had a legitimate complaint when they wondered why their acts of self-denial and repentance hadn't brought them any special favors from God? Explain your answer. 2. What is the connection between worship and compassion? 3. What might you do to *loose the bonds of injustice* (Isa. 58:6) where you live? 4. In what ways has the Lord healed you? 5. In what ways has the Lord protected and guided you?

■ ILLUSTRATIONS:

You Serve Your Own Interest. Dear Abby published this very interesting letter in July of 2000 from "Still Laughing in L.A."

Dear Abby: The letters about obscene phone calls reminded me of something that happened when I was a teenager.

A group of us would hang out at Charlie's house after school and on weekends. We'd play pingpong, cards, watch TV, or just shoot the breeze. One night, a boy named Mark began making obscene phone calls. He would dial random numbers, make a few crude remarks, and then hang up and laugh. We all wanted him to stop, afraid the calls could be traced and we'd all get in trouble. He refused. He said he was having too much fun to stop.

Another friend, Clint, said he wanted to make the next call. Mark handed him the phone. Clint dialed a number, then quickly handed the phone back to Mark, saying, "I'm too nervous. You talk."

Mark took the phone and made his usual crude remarks. His face turned white as he heard a woman say, "Mark. Mark, is that you?" Mark slammed the receiver down and asked, "What number did you dial?" "Your home phone," Clint replied.

As the rest of us howled, Mark actually burst into tears. Perhaps it was a cruel lesson, but Mark never again made an obscene phone call.

The moral of the story is that God not only knows what you're doing, but also why you're doing it!

Getting It Right. In my elementary years when I was growing up and attending church, I was taught a little song that says, "O be careful little eyes what you see. . . . There's a Father up above looking down on us with love. So be careful little eyes what you see." That song also exhorted our "little" ears to be careful what they hear and our "little" hands to be careful what they do and our "little" mouth to be careful what it says. There's a simple message in this "little" song that we seem to have too often forgotten in our present culture. And that is this: God is always with us, and God is always watching us. We neither think nor do anything outside of His presence.

GOD'S NEW CREATION

BACKGROUND SCRIPTURE: Isaiah 65:17-25
DEVOTIONAL READING: Revelation 21:1-7

KEY VERSE: I am about to create new heavens and a new earth;
the former things shall not be remembered or come to mind. Isaiah 65:17.

KING JAMES VERSION

ISAIAH 65:17 For, behold, I create new heavens and a new earth: and the former shall not be remembered, nor come into mind.

18 But be ye glad and rejoice for ever in that which I create: for, behold, I create Jerusalem a rejoicing, and her people a joy.

19 And I will rejoice in Jerusalem, and joy in my people: and the voice of weeping shall be no more heard in her, nor the voice of crying.

20 There shall be no more thence an infant of days, nor an old man that hath not filled his days: for the child shall die an hundred years old; but the sinner being an hundred years old shall be accursed.

21 And they shall build houses, and inhabit them; and they shall plant vineyards, and eat the fruit of them.

22 They shall not build, and another inhabit; they shall not plant, and another eat: for as the days of a tree are the days of my people, and mine elect shall long enjoy the work of their hands.

23 They shall not labour in vain, nor bring forth for trouble; for they are the seed of the blessed of the LORD, and their offspring with them.

24 And it shall come to pass, that before they call, I will answer; and while they are yet speaking, I will hear.

NEW REVISED STANDARD VERSION

ISAIAH 65:17 For I am about to create new heavens and a new earth;
the former things shall not be remembered or come to mind.

18 But be glad and rejoice forever in what I am creating;
for I am about to create Jerusalem as a joy, and its people as a delight.

19 I will rejoice in Jerusalem, and delight in my people;
no more shall the sound of weeping be heard in it, or the cry of distress.

20 No more shall there be in it an infant that lives but a few days,
or an old person who does not live out a lifetime;
for one who dies at a hundred years will be considered a youth,
and one who falls short of a hundred will be considered accursed.

21 They shall build houses and inhabit them;
they shall plant vineyards and eat their fruit.

22 They shall not build and another inhabit;
they shall not plant and another eat;
for like the days of a tree shall the days of my people be,
and my chosen shall long enjoy the work of their hands.

23 They shall not labor in vain,
or bear children for calamity;
for they shall be offspring blessed by the Lord—
and their descendants as well.

24 Before they call I will answer,
while they are yet speaking I will hear.

9

HOME BIBLE READINGS

Monday, January 28	Deuteronomy 10:12-22	*You Were Strangers in Egypt*
Tuesday, January 29	Deuteronomy 26:1-15	*Tithes for Aliens, Orphans, and Widows*
Wednesday, January 30	Jeremiah 7:1-8	*Act Justly and Do Not Oppress Others*
Thursday, January 31	Jeremiah 22:1-9	*Do Not Wrong Widows and Aliens*
Friday, February 1	Deuteronomy 24:14-21	*Provide for Widows and Aliens*
Saturday, February 2	Ruth 1:1-14	*Three Widows in Moab*
Sunday, February 3	Ruth 1:15-22	*Your God Will Be My God*

BACKGROUND

Of all the Old Testament prophets, Isaiah evidently saw the farthest into the future. He is thought to have begun prophesying in 740 B.C., with his ministry coming to an end around 681 B.C. During the time of his prophetic work, God gave him a vision of the fall of Israel, which occurred around 722 B.C. God also gave Isaiah a vision of the fall and exile of Judah, which occurred around 586 B.C. God further gave the prophet a vision of the rise of Cyrus and the Medo-Persian Empire, as well as the Jews' return to Jerusalem. (The first group returned under Zerubbabel around 538 B.C.) God even gave Isaiah revelations concerning the Messiah, especially His sacrificial death.

In Isaiah 65 are prophecies that extend beyond the time in which we are living today. In fact, in 65:17-25 we find a pictorial description of the time that is characterized by newness, righteousness, and peace. The passage begins with a portrayal of the *new heavens and a new earth* (65:17). Within the context of Isaiah's prophesied new heavens and new earth will be an eternity of safety, joy, and abundance that will be available to all people (Isa. 66:22-23; 2 Pet. 3:13; Rev. 21:1). In this way we are suddenly thrust forward into the celestial future of the new Jerusalem, where, according to Revelation 21:4, God will bring all weeping and crying to an end.

Seemingly within this futuristic prophecy is another prophecy. Some expositors think that Isaiah 65:20-25 paints a picture that will be a precursor to the coming of the new heavens and new earth. They differ over whether these verses refer to the heavenly state (the metaphorical view) or to a future period in which Christ will rule on earth (the literal view). In either case, Scripture clearly reveals that a new world is coming, and it will be glorious beyond imagination.

It's helpful to remember that the original recipients of this prophecy were Israelites whose hopes would have been completely dashed when they would be taken into Babylonian exile. But Isaiah offered them, through his prophecies, not only the hope of returning home and the hope of a coming Messiah, but also the hope of an everlasting kingdom in which God would be the supreme ruler. Thus their reward for enduring and persevering faith would be a new creation where the effects of sin will no longer be known. And this new creation will come at the culmination of human history.

NOTES ON THE PRINTED TEXT

Isaiah 43:19 says, *I am about to do a new thing; now it springs forth, do you not perceive it? I will make a way in the wilderness and rivers in the desert.* Later, in chapter 65, the Lord (through Isaiah) went into more depth about this matter, describing what will be, in essence, a new creation. In the Book of Revelation, a description of this new creation combines elements of Jerusalem, the temple, and even the Garden of Eden. The chief emphasis in both Isaiah and Revelation is that the earth as we know it will not last forever. After God's great judgment, He will create new heavens and a new earth (Rom. 8:18-21; 2 Pet. 3:7-13). Of course, we cannot know exactly what this new creation will look like or where it will be. But we can take comfort—along with all the saints that have gone before us—in the fact that God and all His followers will be united there.

The *new heavens and a new earth* (Isa. 65:17) that God promised will be a supernatural act of creation on His part; these new heavens and new earth evidently are not currently in existence. But at God's chosen time, He will bring them into existence. And when He does, *the former things*—the old order of things that includes pain, death, and sorrow—*shall not be remembered or come to mind.* One of the main aspects of the new creation that would bring the exiled Jews special hope was God's creation of a new *Jerusalem as a joy, and its people as a delight* (65:18). God expressly noted this creation as something for which the Jews should *be glad and rejoice forever,* for a restored community of the redeemed pointed to the ultimate victory of God and His people.

Having encouraged His people to maintain their hopes for this new creation, God, through His prophet Isaiah, next offered the people some details about this new creation. The Lord would so *rejoice in Jerusalem, and delight in my people* (65:19) that *the sound of weeping* would no longer be heard in the city. The longevity of life would be comparable to that of Adam and his early descendants in that *one who dies at a hundred years will be considered a youth, and one who falls short of hundred will be considered accursed* (65:20).

Unlike the Israelites' past in which invaders drove them from their homes and ate the produce they had tended, in the future *They shall build houses and inhabit them; they shall plant vineyards and eat their fruit. . . . My chosen shall long enjoy the work of their hands* (65:21-22). Their hopes of peace and prosperity for their children would be realized because *they shall be offspring blessed by the LORD* (65:23). No longer would they even fear that their children might be slaughtered or taken captive by invading armies.

Perhaps the richest of God's promises for His people was His commitment to be so diligent in their presence—leading them and listening to them—that He would answer their prayers before they were even offered up. What a tremendous promise God offered to His people when He pledged that *Before they call I will answer, while they are yet speaking I will hear* (65:24)!

SUGGESTIONS TO TEACHERS

Though God's people may have been at their lowest ebb emotionally during their exile in Babylon, they had from Isaiah a message of tremendous hope. The Lord told them about a new creation, setting the stage for His people to remain optimistic because He would ultimately be victorious. He would ultimately rescue and save all those who persevered in their faith, hope, and trust in Him. Believers today can draw the following from this prophecy of hope.

1. THINGS WILL GET BETTER FOR ME. Whatever pain or sorrow or hurts that we're having to face right now are merely tests of our endurance and perseverance. Our sole task is to keep our eyes on the Lord and listen to Him through His Word as He provides direction and protection for our individual lives. If we endure and persevere in our faith, we have the sure and certain hope of being rewarded—of being the recipients of God's ultimate and fantastic promises!

2. THINGS WILL GET BETTER FOR MY CHILDREN. Past generations of people have been quite concerned about "making things better" for future generations. Much of this concern has been directed toward efforts at making future generations better physically, mentally, emotionally, and (especially) financially. God puts back in the hearts of His people the desire for their children to be better off spiritually. And if this is a concern of our present generation, God promises that future generations of our children will be blessed by Him with eternal peace.

3. THINGS WILL GET BETTER FOR GOD'S PEOPLE. The supreme hope for the culmination of the future kingdom of God is that His people will be better off because the effects of sin will be eliminated. God's grace will overrule all wickedness and His goodness and righteousness will create an atmosphere of peace and prosperity, where all the spiritual members of His family will be blessed.

■ **TOPIC:** A New Creation

■ **QUESTIONS:** 1. What promises of hope did God make to His people in Isaiah 65:17-24? 2. What feelings or emotions do you think this prophecy was meant to stir up among God's people? 3. Once God creates the new heavens and new earth, what do you think life will be like for His people? 4. In what ways does this prophecy hearken back to the Genesis account of Creation and the Fall? 5. What does Isaiah's vision of the future mean for us?

■ **ILLUSTRATIONS:**

Former Things Shall Not Be Remembered. A couple of years ago, we discovered a tragedy at the parsonage that left my daughter, Gracie, in tears. I had left a little lavender-colored ceramic planter out on the deck. But this little planter was special. It had "Baby" molded into the side, and when we wound it up, a music box inside played a lullaby. This planter had been given to us 11 years before by some dear friends of ours just after Gracie was born. It must have been the rising and falling of the temperatures over several seasons that somehow shattered that little treasure into multiple pieces. Gracie glared at the pieces in her hands, tears streaming from her eyes at her sense of the loss.

We all feel saddened when an earthly treasure is taken from us. But the hope of future glory in heaven can go a long way toward helping us through a trying situation. The hope of being restored to their homeland along with the hope for new heavens and a new earth would help the exiled Jews to endure their disastrous circumstances in Babylon.

Delight in My People. Two years ago, a rabbi began urging his fellow Jews to learn from messianic Jews. Messianic Judaism is "infused with a deep sense of spirituality. It's vibrant, charismatic," said Dan Cohn-Sherbok, a Reformed rabbi and professor of Judaism at the University of Wales. "It has something to offer traditional Jews." Instead of criticizing, "come and see what goes on and learn from it," Cohn-Sherbok said, according to *The Columbus* (Ohio) *Dispatch.* "It's always better to listen to people," said Cohn-Sherbok. He made his comments at a conference of the Union of Messianic Jewish Congregations, attended by about 800 people.

Cohn-Sherbok spent eight years researching and writing the book *Messianic Judaism: The First Study of Messianic Judaism by a Non-Adherent,* which was published in June of 2000. The book's purpose was to inform the Jewish community, he said. "It doesn't mean they will embrace them or like them. But they should at least know who the messianics are." Traditional Judaism holds that the Messiah has yet to come, and so they continue in the hope of His coming. Messianic Jews believe that Jesus, referred to by the Hebrew name Yeshua, is the promised Messiah.

No More Weeping. "God, where were you in Paris?" asked a church leader named Josef Homeyer, his voice quavering with emotion as he addressed 350 people at a worship service in Hanover, Germany, after a Concorde airliner burst into flames and crashed outside Paris on July 25, 2000, killing 113 people, most of them German tourists, Reuters reported. "Why have you deserted us? Our hearts are heavy."

Homeyer then reminded the mourners of the hope in the resurrection. After him, a church leader named Horst Hirschler reminded the audience of a similar tragic incident two years earlier, when a high-speed train crashed near Hanover, taking the lives of more than 100 people. One minute vacationers were happily looking forward to the time of their lives, and the next minute they were faced with death, the pastor said. "What a tragic transformation."

The only real consolation is that even the Son of God had asked His Father in heaven, "Why hast thou forsaken me" before He died on the cross, Hirschler said. He assured his audience that Jesus Christ is with those who are feeling desperate and who mourn over the loss of their loved ones. "You will never fall deeper than into God's hand."

FOR YOUTH

■ TOPIC: Perfect World

■ QUESTIONS: 1. In your opinion, what are the best promises that God made to His people in Isaiah 65:17-24? 2. What do you think was God's purpose in making such promises? 3. When God takes away both the causes and the results of sin, what do you think life will be like? 4. What are some of the blessings associated with the newly created Jerusalem? 5. How might this prophecy of what God will someday bring about affect the way you live your life right now?

■ ILLUSTRATIONS:

Be Glad and Rejoice Forever. It was the summer of 1975. Memphis in July. I was playing on a pretty good baseball team from Germantown. It was a Saturday, and it was hot—about 102 degrees hot. The scorching humidity made it feel even hotter. We played a double-header that afternoon at a field where there was no concession stand in sight. We won both games by slim margins and were completely exhausted after 14 innings of baseball in the Memphis heat.

On the way home, Coach Norcross stopped at a little Podunk convenience store. I didn't happen to have any money on me at the time, so Coach Norcross told me to pick out a drink. Through the glass of the cooler, I saw some red drink in an ice-cold bottle. I picked it out. Never before, nor since, have I ever enjoyed a drink so much as that beverage on that Saturday afternoon in Memphis.

Through the course of that baseball season, Coach Norcross said some things that may have hurt my feelings—even though they were true—like "Wallace, you're playing second base tonight like you're sitting on your head!" or "Wallace, don't be a coward and turn your head on a hard ground ball!" But I'll never forget him for buying me that drink when I thought I might be on the verge of dying of thirst.

The Jews exiled in Babylon were dying of thirst—the thirst for hope. Through the prophet Isaiah, God gave them not only hope for the next generation, but also hope for the ultimate triumph of the kingdom of God. Such a hope would go a long way to quench their thirst for a future of peace and prosperity.

Before They Call I Will Answer. The fields were parched and brown from lack of rain, and the crops lay wilting from thirst, writes Laverne W. Hall in *Chicken*

Soup for the Christian Soul. People were anxious and irritable as they searched the sky for any sign of relief. Days turned into arid weeks, but no rain came.

The ministers of the local churches called for an hour of prayer on the town square the following Saturday. They requested that everyone bring an object of faith for inspiration. At high noon on the appointed Saturday the townspeople turned out en masse, filling the square with anxious faces and hopeful hearts. The ministers were touched to see the variety of objects clutched in prayerful hands.

When the hour ended, as if on magical command, a soft rain began to fall. Cheers swept through the crowd as they held their treasured objects high in gratitude and praise. From the middle of the crowd one faith symbol seemed to overshadow all the others—a small nine-year-old child had brought an umbrella.

Enduring Hope in God's Promises. Victor Hugo, in his story "Ninety-Three," tells of a ship caught in a dangerous storm on the high seas. At the height of the storm, the frightened sailors heard a terrible crashing noise below the deck. They knew at once that this new noise came from a cannon, part of the ship's cargo, that had broken loose. It was moving back and forth with the swaying of the ship, crashing into the side of the ship with terrible impact. Knowing that it could cause the ship to sink, two brave sailors volunteered to make the dangerous attempt to retie the loose cannon. They knew the danger of a shipwreck from the cannon was greater than the fury of the storm.

That is like human life. Storms of life may blow about us, but it is not these exterior storms that pose the gravest danger. It is the terrible corruption that can exist within us that can overwhelm us. The furious storm outside may be overwhelming but what is going on inside can pose the greater threat to our lives. Our only hope lies in conquering that wild enemy. Trusting God and believing His promises is our only hope of stilling the tempest that can harm our souls and cripple our lives.

RUTH CHOSE NAOMI'S GOD

BACKGROUND SCRIPTURE: Ruth 1
DEVOTIONAL READING: Psalm 8

KEY VERSE: Where you go, I will go; Where you lodge, I will lodge;
your people shall be my people, and your God my God. Ruth 1:16.

KING JAMES VERSION

RUTH 1:1 Now it came to pass in the days when the judges ruled, that there was a famine in the land. And a certain man of Beth-lehem-judah went to sojourn in the country of Moab, he, and his wife, and his two sons.

2 And the name of the man was Elimelech, and the name of his wife Naomi, and the name of his two sons Mahlon and Chilion, Ephrathites of Beth-lehem-judah. And they came into the country of Moab, and continued there.

3 And Elimelech Naomi's husband died; and she was left, and her two sons.

4 And they took them wives of the women of Moab; the name of the one was Orpah, and the name of the other Ruth: and they dwelled there about ten years.

5 And Mahlon and Chilion died also both of them; and the woman was left of her two sons and her husband.

6 Then she arose with her daughters in law, that she might return from the country of Moab: for she had heard in the country of Moab how that the LORD had visited his people in giving them bread.

7 Wherefore she went forth out of the place where she was, and her two daughters in law with her; and they went on the way to return unto the land of Judah.

8 And Naomi said unto her two daughters in law, Go, return each to her mother's house: the LORD deal kindly with you, as ye have dealt with the dead, and with me. . . .

16 And Ruth said, Intreat me not to leave thee, or to return from following after thee: for whither thou goest, I will go; and where thou lodgest, I will lodge: thy people shall be my people, and thy God my God:

17 Where thou diest, will I die, and there will I be buried: the LORD do so to me, and more also, if ought but death part thee and me.

NEW REVISED STANDARD VERSION

RUTH 1:1 In the days when the judges ruled, there was a famine in the land, and a certain man of Bethlehem in Judah went to live in the country of Moab, he and his wife and two sons. 2 The name of the man was Elimelech and the name of his wife Naomi, and the names of his two sons were Mahlon and Chilion; they were Ephrathites from Bethlehem in Judah. They went into the country of Moab and remained there. 3 But Elimelech, the husband of Naomi, died, and she was left with her two sons. 4 These took Moabite wives; the name of the one was Orpah and the name of the other Ruth. When they had lived there about ten years, 5 both Mahlon and Chilion also died, so that the woman was left without her two sons and her husband.

6 Then she started to return with her daughters-in-law from the country of Moab, for she had heard in the country of Moab that the LORD had considered his people and given them food. 7 So she set out from the place where she had been living, she and her two daughters-in-law, and they went on their way to go back to the land of Judah. 8 But Naomi said to her two daughters-in-law, "Go back each of you to your mother's house. May the LORD deal kindly with you, as you have dealt with the dead and with me." . . .

16 But Ruth said,
"Do not press me to leave you
    or to turn back from following you!
Where you go, I will go;
    where you lodge, I will lodge;
your people shall be my people,
    and your God my God.
17 Where you die, I will die—
    there will I be buried.
May the LORD do thus and so to me,
    and more as well,
if even death parts me from you!"

BACKGROUND

The account of familial love that takes place in the Book of Ruth probably occurred during the latter part of the period of the rule of the judges (1375–1050 B.C.). This was a time when *all the people did what was right in their own eyes* (Judg. 17:6; 21:25) and violence and chaos predominated without a central king to rule the people. The account of Ruth—with its rural setting and wholesome yet believable characters—is presented in stark contrast to these dark days for the nation of Israel.

Moab was the land east of the Dead Sea, opposite the tribal land of Judah to the sea's west. Moab was one of the nations that oppressed Israel during the period of the judges; in fact, King Eglon of Moab had forced much of Israel into being subservient to him for 18 years. And even though Israel eventually defeated Moab under Ehud's leadership (Judg. 3:12-30), there still would have been tense hostility between the two nations. Thus the famine in Israel must have been quite severe for Elimelech to make the decision to move his family to Moab (Ruth 1:1-2). The journey into Moab from their home in Bethlehem would have taken the family at least 70 miles through the Israelite tribal lands of Benjamin and Reuben, over the northern tip of the Dead Sea, and across the Jordan River.

As the head of his household, Elimelech would have maintained rights to ancestral property in Bethlehem, even after having moved to Moab. But when both he and his two sons died, the only ways Naomi could regain the property were through two legal customs: the "levirate" law and the "redemption of the land" law.

The levirate law—sometimes called the "levirate marriage"—was the custom of a widow marrying her dead husband's closest male relative, usually his brother (Deut. 25:5-10). Any offspring born from this union would carry both the name and the inheritance of the former husband. (In Naomi's case—since she was beyond childbearing years—her daughter-in-law, Ruth, became her substitute in marriage and bore a son to perpetuate the family name.)

The "redemption of the land" law was a way to get back land that had been sold because of bad crops or because the owner couldn't pay his bills. His nearest relative could redeem—or buy back—that land from its new owner. Of course, if the first owner became prosperous again, he had the right to redeem it for himself.

This enabled the Israelites to keep land in the original family. (In Naomi's case, Boaz legally cleared Elimelech's land of future claims and accepted the dual responsibility of both brother-in-law and kinsman-redeemer.)

NOTES ON THE PRINTED TEXT

This four-chapter book is named for Ruth, its chief character; but the story line is actually about how the desperate plight of Naomi and her tragic experiences and circumstances eventually ended with her gaining both abundance and happiness. After leaving her homeland and losing her husband and two sons, Naomi returned to Judah an embittered woman. But the self-giving loyalty and the tender care that Ruth showed to her mother-in-law gradually kindled a sense of courage and hope in Naomi, so that her emptiness and desperation finally turned to fullness and fulfillment.

Though Naomi and her husband, Elimelech, were from Bethlehem in Judah, severe economic conditions brought on by a life-threatening famine caused them and their two sons to relocate east of the Jordan River in Moab, where the land, people, culture, and religion were vastly different from that of Israel (1:1). They were called *Ephrathites* (1:2) because Ephrathah was a name for the area around Bethlehem.

Soon after the family had settled in Moab, Elimelech died, leaving Naomi a widow in the care of her two sons, Mahlon and Chilion. Then, sometime after Elimelech's death, both of Naomi's sons married Moabite women (1:3-4). Naomi possibly knew that Israelite relationships with the Moabites were discouraged (Deut. 23:3-6) but, of course, such relationships could not be absolutely forbidden for an Israelite living within Moabite borders. Certainly, for an Israelite to marry a Moabite would have been frowned upon under any circumstances.

When they had lived there about ten years (Ruth 1:4), both of Naomi's sons also died, leaving her alone in a foreign land with only her two childless daughters-in-law to care for her (1:5). In the ancient world, widows were often taken advantage of or ignored; they were almost always poverty stricken. With her desperate situation now at its height, Naomi made the decision to return to her homeland and try to make the best of it (1:6). She had somehow received word that the famine throughout Judah had eased, and *so she set out from the place where she had been living, she and her two daughters-in-law, and they went on their way to go back to the land of Judah* (1:7). Although Naomi was unsure whether any of her relatives in Israel were still alive, she figured she might fare better in her homeland as a widow than she would in Moab.

Knowing that she had little—and perhaps nothing at all—to offer her daughters-in-law, the desolate Naomi repeatedly urged Ruth and Orpah to return to their original homes in Moab. She thanked them for the kind way they *"have dealt with the dead and with me"* (1:8), acknowledging the loyal commitment they had made to her—freely given, though not required. But Naomi also knew they would be more likely to remarry and start their lives over in their homeland than they would in Israel. Amidst much weeping from all three women, Naomi explained that *"it has been far more bitter for me than for you, because the hand of the LORD has turned against me"* (1:13).

Orpah finally gave in to Naomi's prodding, kissing her mother-in-law and turning to go home; *but Ruth clung to [Naomi]* (1:14). Even so, Naomi still discouraged Ruth from staying with her, bidding her to do as Orpah had done and go home to her mother's house, to her own own people, and to her own gods (1:15).

It was then that Ruth burst forth with a heartfelt statement of commitment and loyalty, one that is so beautiful and expressive that it is often used in weddings to confirm the commitment between the bride and groom: *"Do not press me to leave you or to turn back from following you! Where you go, I will go; where you lodge, I will lodge; your people shall be my people, and your God my God. Where you die, I will die—there will I be buried. May the LORD do thus and so to me, and more as well, if even death parts me from you!"* (1:16-17).

SUGGESTIONS TO TEACHERS

In a very few verses, several character traits and attitudes are portrayed by one Israelite woman—Naomi—and two Moabite women—Ruth and Orpah. As we take a look at how these three women expressed these traits and attitudes, we would do well to strive to emulate them.

1. BE KIND. Naomi thanked Ruth and Orpah for the kind way they had treated her husband, her sons, and herself. Indeed, the two younger women were in no way legally bound to Naomi, but they had grown to love her and respect her, and thus they dealt with her in a kind manner. May we, too, treat others with kindness.

2. BE THOUGHTFUL. Ruth and Orpah, though widowed themselves, realized that Naomi's circumstances were more grave than their own. Naomi, in one sense, was somewhat stranded in a foreign country. Being thoughtful of Naomi's needs, they did not discourage her from returning to her homeland, but rather began escorting her on her way home. May we, too, be thoughtful of the needs of others.

3. BE CONSIDERATE. Naomi felt that it would be in the best interest of her daughters-in-law to remain in their home country. And even though she would be alone on a dangerous journey, she was considerate enough of her daughters-in-law to encourage them to stay home while she braved the trek home. May we, too, be considerate of the best interests of others—even if it means we may have to face part of our journey alone.

4. BE LOYAL. Both Ruth and Orpah expressed intense loyalty to their mother-in-law. Though Naomi was not of their native land, their native family, their native culture, or their native religion, the two daughters-in-law continually expressed their love and loyalty to their mother-in-law. May we, too, express and act upon our loyalty to our families, church, employers, friends, and (especially) our God.

5. BE COMMITTED. No amount of explanation could convince Ruth to turn away from her mother-in-law. In fact, *Ruth clung to her* (Ruth 1:14). Ruth's commitment to her mother-in-law could not be dissuaded or deterred. And even if Naomi could only offer Ruth more tragic and desperate circumstances, the young woman was committed to stay with her mother-in-law. May we, too, never be dissuaded or deterred from our commitments.

FOR ADULTS

■ TOPIC: Remaining Loyal

■ QUESTIONS: 1. What crises was Naomi facing after losing her husband and two sons? 2. In what ways was Naomi considerate of the needs of her daughters-in-law? 3. In what ways were Ruth and Orpah considerate of the needs of their mother-in-law? 4. How did Ruth go beyond expressing her loyalty to Naomi to expressing her deeper commitment to Naomi as well? 5. How does Christ's love motivate us to be loyal to other believers?

■ **ILLUSTRATIONS:**

Commitment Is the Key. "When I was a boy, my father, a baker, introduced me to the wonders of song," tenor Luciano Pavarotti relates. "He urged me to work very hard to develop my voice. Arrigo Pola, a professional tenor in my hometown of Modena, Italy, took me as a pupil. I also enrolled in a teacher's college. On graduating, I asked my father, 'Shall I be a teacher or a singer?'

"'Luciano,' my father replied, 'if you try to sit on two chairs, you will fall between them. For life, you must choose one chair.'

"I chose one. It took seven years of study and frustration before I made my first professional appearance. It took another seven to reach the Metropolitan Opera. And now I think whether it's laying bricks, writing a book—whatever we choose—we should give ourselves to it. Commitment: that's the key. Choose one chair."

Faithful to the Commitment. A young businessman was rushed to a hospital in serious condition. A doctor predicted that he might die. Not a religious man at the time, he did, however, turn on a radio and heard a Christian song being played: "God Will Take Care Of You." He said that he couldn't get that song out of his mind.

The young businessman began to pray and, as he did, he reported a sense of energy flowing in. It was near Christmas, a Sunday morning. He heard a group of nurses having a brief worship service in a nearby room and struggled up out of bed and joined them. While there, he committed his life to Christ. That man recovered. Thereafter, for the rest of his life, he remained faithful to his commitment.

That man referred every business and every personal decision to God and was resolute in his ethics, living by the teachings of Jesus. You've heard about this man, who told all about this in a book concerning his life. His name was J. C. Penney. He, too, insisted throughout his life that the apostle Paul was quite right in promising divine help for those in whom Christ's Spirit lives.

FOR YOUTH	■ TOPIC: Lifetime Commitment

■ TOPIC: Lifetime Commitment
■ QUESTIONS: 1. What type of personal disasters wreaked havoc on Naomi's life? 2. How would these tragic and desperate circumstances make you feel if you were Naomi? 3. What would you have done if you were Naomi—stay in Moab or return to Judah? Explain your answer. 4. Do you think you would have been more like Orpah, who was finally convinced to return to her own home, or more like Ruth, who could not be discouraged from her commitment to Naomi? Explain your answer. 5. When you've had to cross over to another ethnic or cultural group, were you able to assimilate or did you remain a stranger "in their land"?

■ **ILLUSTRATIONS:**

Don't Leave Home without Commitment. It has been said that "People cannot discover new oceans unless they have the courage to lose sight of the shore." It has also been said that "Conductors cannot direct the orchestra without turning their backs on the audience."

A Loyal Commitment. At 18, Marlena Thompson—who tells her story in *Chicken Soup for the Golden Soul*—left home to study history at Leeds University in Yorkshire, England. It was an exciting but stressful time in her life, for while trying to adjust to the novelty of unfamiliar surroundings, she was still learning to cope with the all-too-familiar pain of her father's recent death—an event with which she had not yet come to terms.

While at the market one day and trying to decide which bunch of flowers would best brighten up her comfortable but colorless student digs, Marlena spied an elderly gentleman having difficulty holding onto his walking stick and his bag of apples. Marlena rushed over and relieved him of the apples, giving him time to regain his balance.

"Thanks, luv," he said. "I'm quite all right now, not to worry," smiling at her not only with his mouth but with a pair of dancing bright blue eyes.

"May I walk with you?" Marlena inquired. "Just to make sure those apples don't become sauce prematurely."

The man laughed and said, "Now, you are a long way from home, lass. From the States, are you?"

"Only from one of them. New York. I'll tell you all about it as we walk."

So began Marlena's friendship with Mr. Burns, a man whose smile and warmth would very soon come to mean a great deal to her.

As the two walked, Mr. Burns leaned heavily on his stick, a stout, gnarled affair that resembled Marlena's notion of a biblical staff. When they arrived at his house, Marlena helped Mr. Burns set his parcels on the table and insisted on lending a hand with the preparations for his "tea"—that is, his meal. Marlena interpreted his weak protest as gratitude for the assistance.

After making Mr. Burns tea, Marlena asked whether it would be all right if she came back and visited with him again. She thought she'd look in on him from time to time to see whether he needed anything. With a wink and a smile Mr. Burns replied, "I've never been one to turn down an offer from a good-hearted lass."

Marlena came back the next day, at about the same time, so she could help out once more with Mr. Burn's evening meal. The great walking stick was a silent reminder of his infirmity and, though he never asked for help, he didn't protest when it was given. That very evening they had their first "heart-to-heart."

Mr. Burns asked about Marlena's studies, her plans and, mostly, about her family. She told him that her father had recently died, but she didn't offer much else about the relationship she'd had with him. In response, he gestured toward the two framed photographs on the end table next to his chair. They were pictures of two different women, one notably older than the other. But the resemblance between the two was striking.

"That's Mary," he said, indicating the photograph of the older woman. "She's been gone for six years. And that's our Alice. She was a very fine nurse. Losing her was too much for my Mary."

Marlena responded with the tears she hadn't been able to shed for her own pain. She cried for Mary. She cried for Alice. She cried for Mr. Burns. And she cried for her father to whom she never had the chance to say good-bye.

Marlena visited with Mr. Burns twice a week, always on the same days and at the same time. Whenever Marlena came, he was seated in his chair, his walking stick propped up against the wall. Mr. Burns owned a small black-and-white television set, but he evidently preferred his books and phonograph records for entertainment. He always seemed especially glad to see Marlena. Although she told herself she was delighted to be useful, she was happier still to have met someone to whom she could reveal those thoughts and feelings that, until then, she'd hardly acknowledged to herself.

After about a month, Marlena decided to pay her friend a visit on an "off day." She didn't bother to telephone as that type of formality did not seem requisite in their relationship. Coming up to the house, she saw Mr. Burns working in his garden, bending with ease and getting up with equal facility. She was dumfounded. Could this be the same man who used that massive walking stick?

Mr. Burns suddenly looked in Marlena's direction. Evidently sensing her puzzlement over his mobility, Mr. Burns waved Marlena over, looking more than a bit sheepish. Marlena said nothing, but accepted Mr. Burns invitation to come inside.

"Well, luv. Allow me to make you a 'cuppa' this time. You look all done in."

"How?" Marlena began. "I thought . . ."

"I know what you thought, luv. When you first saw me at the market, well, I'd twisted my ankle a bit earlier in the day. Tripped on a stone while doing a bit of gardening. Always been a clumsy fool."

"But . . . when were you able to . . . walk normally again?"

Somehow, Mr. Burns managed to look merry and contrite at the same time. "Ah, well, I guess that'll be the very next day after our first meeting."

"But why?" Marlena asked, truly perplexed. Surely Mr. Burns couldn't have been feigning helplessness to get Marlena to make him his tea every now and then.

"That second time you came 'round, luv, it was then I saw how unhappy you were. Feeling lonely and sad about your dad and all. I thought, well, the lass could use a bit of an old shoulder to lean on. But I knew you were telling yourself you were visiting me for my sake and not your own. Didn't think you'd come back if you knew I was fit. And I knew you were in sore need of someone to talk to. Someone older, older than your dad, even. And someone who knew how to listen."

"And the stick?"

"Ah. A fine stick, that. I use it when I walk the moors. We must do that together soon."

And so the two did. And Mr. Burns, the man Marlena set out to help, helped her. He'd made a gift of his time, bestowing attention and kindness to a young girl who needed both.

GOD'S BLESSING FOR RUTH

BACKGROUND SCRIPTURE: Ruth 2—4
DEVOTIONAL READING: Psalm 126

KEY VERSE: "May the LORD reward you for your deeds, and may you have a full reward from the LORD, the God of Israel, under whose wings you have come for refuge!" Ruth 2:12.

KING JAMES VERSION

RUTH 2:1 And Naomi had a kinsman of her husband's, a mighty man of wealth, of the family of Elimelech; and his name was Boaz. . . .

8 Then said Boaz unto Ruth, Hearest thou not, my daughter? Go not to glean in another field, neither go from hence, but abide here fast by my maidens:

9 Let thine eyes be on the field that they do reap, and go thou after them: have I not charged the young men that they shall not touch thee? and when thou art athirst, go unto the vessels, and drink of that which the young men have drawn.

10 Then she fell on her face, and bowed herself to the ground, and said unto him, Why have I found grace in thine eyes, that thou shouldest take knowledge of me, seeing I am a stranger?

11 And Boaz answered and said unto her, It hath fully been shewed me, all that thou hast done unto thy mother in law since the death of thine husband: and how thou hast left thy father and thy mother, and the land of thy nativity, and art come unto a people which thou knewest not heretofore.

12 The LORD recompense thy work, and a full reward be given thee of the LORD God of Israel, under whose wings thou art come to trust. . . .

4:13 So Boaz took Ruth, and she was his wife: and when he went in unto her, the LORD gave her conception, and she bare a son.

14 And the women said unto Naomi, Blessed be the LORD, which hath not left thee this day without a kinsman, that his name may be famous in Israel.

15 And he shall be unto thee a restorer of thy life, and a nourisher of thine old age: for thy daughter in law, which loveth thee, which is better to thee than seven sons, hath born him.

16 And Naomi took the child, and laid it in her bosom, and became nurse unto it.

17 And the women her neighbours gave it a name, saying, There is a son born to Naomi; and they called his name Obed: he is the father of Jesse, the father of David.

NEW REVISED STANDARD VERSION

RUTH 2:1 Now Naomi had a kinsman on her husband's side, a prominent rich man, of the family of Elimelech, whose name was Boaz. . . .

8 Then Boaz said to Ruth, "Now listen, my daughter, do not go to glean in another field or leave this one, but keep close to my young women. 9 Keep your eyes on the field that is being reaped, and follow behind them. I have ordered the young men not to bother you. If you get thirsty, go to the vessels and drink from what the young men have drawn." 10 Then she fell prostrate, with her face to the ground, and said to him, "Why have I found favor in your sight, that you should take notice of me, when I am a foreigner?" 11 But Boaz answered her, "All that you have done for your mother-in-law since the death of your husband has been fully told me, and how you left your father and mother and your native land and came to a people that you did not know before. 12 May the LORD reward you for your deeds, and may you have a full reward from the LORD, the God of Israel, under whose wings you have come for refuge!" . . .

4:13 So Boaz took Ruth and she became his wife. When they came together, the LORD made her conceive, and she bore a son. 14 Then the women said to Naomi, "Blessed be the LORD, who has not left you this day without next-of-kin; and may his name be renowned in Israel! 15 He shall be to you a restorer of life and a nourisher of your old age; for your daughter-in-law who loves you, who is more to you than seven sons, has borne him." 16 Then Naomi took the child and laid him in her bosom, and became his nurse. 17 The women of the neighborhood gave him a name, saying, "A son has been born to Naomi." They named him Obed; he became the father of Jesse, the father of David.

HOME BIBLE READINGS

BACKGROUND

As an account that portrays the best of kindness, faithfulness, and loyalty, the Book of Ruth also does a marvelous job of exhibiting several biblical, ethical, and theological purposes. Through this account of family solidarity and devotion, the book also provides an excellent contrast to the turbulence of the period of the judges.

The Book of Ruth provides a glimpse of a full biblical perspective in that it gives a thorough example of how God is the Redeemer of His people. In the account, Boaz emerged as the kinsman-redeemer—the person who legally cleared Elimelech's land of future claims and accepted the dual responsibility of both brother-in-law and redeemer. By doing so, Boaz saved Naomi from a life of certain poverty and destitution.

The idea of the kinsman-redeemer reached its fulfillment in Christ's giving Himself *that he might redeem us from all iniquity and purify for himself a people of his own who are zealous for good deeds* (Titus 2:14). Also, the loyalty that is exemplified by Ruth and later by Boaz is expressed in the same terms as that describing God's covenantal relationship with His people. Moreover, the genealogy at the end of the Book of Ruth is intended to reveal that Boaz and Ruth are none other than the great-grandparents of King David. This would also serve the purpose of eliciting admiration for the ancestors of the Judahite kings. Furthermore, this genealogy of David, which includes Ruth, culminates in the ancestral line of the Messiah (Matt. 1:5). Indeed, the fields near Bethlehem in which Ruth worked so diligently to glean may well have been near a later scene where shepherds first heard *good news of great joy for all the people* (Luke 2:10).

The Book of Ruth provides an ethical foundation for its readers. Naomi, Ruth, and Boaz are characters that are clearly motivated by integrity, lovingkindness, and loyalty. And it's important to note that, even as a foreigner to Israel, Ruth exemplified these qualities. These three people remained strong in character and true to God even when the society around them was collapsing.

Theologically, the Book of Ruth brings into focus God's redemptive and providential care in the everyday lives or ordinary people. These people did not have to be Israelites in order to be the recipients of His care! Not only did Ruth, a Moabite woman, clearly reflect the love of God, but she also exemplified the truth that participation in the coming kingdom of God is decided, not by blood and birth, but by the conformity of one's life to the divine will. Thus the author boldly maintained that God's covenant was not limited to national, political, or racial boundaries—an idea not easily accepted in Israel. And the fact that Ruth was introduced into the ancestry of David signifies that all nations would be represented in the kingdom of the most anticipated Son of David—Jesus of Nazareth, the Messiah.

NOTES ON THE PRINTED TEXT

As Naomi initiated her return journey to Judah, she did not know whether any of her family were still living. She had been in Moab for at least 10 years, and over that amount of time she probably lost touch with her relatives. Surely this weighed heavy on Naomi's mind as she and Ruth traveled. They arrived in Bethlehem at the beginning of the barley harvest and, in an attempt to help feed the two women, Ruth worked gleaning in *the part of the field belonging to Boaz, who was of the family of Elimelech* (Ruth 2:3) and who was also *a prominent rich man* (2:1).

When barley and other crops were ready to be harvested, the law of Moses made a provision for the poor to provide for themselves by picking up any grain that had been dropped; this was called "gleaning." Indeed, to ensure that there would be something for the poor, the law required farmers to leave a part of their harvest—usually the corners of the fields—for gleaning by the poor (Lev. 19:9-10; 23:22; Deut. 24:19-22). When Boaz—as well as his reapers—noticed how diligently Ruth worked at gleaning in his field, he called her to him and extended to Ruth special privileges above and beyond his legal obligation. For her protection, Boaz told Ruth to stay in his fields, to *keep close to [his] young women* (2:8), and *ordered the young men not to bother [her]* (Ruth 2:9). And for Ruth's health, Boaz told her to help herself to the water the young men had drawn from the well.

Amazed by these special favors extended to a Moabite woman, Ruth inquired as to why Boaz would even take notice of her (2:10). Boaz's answer expounded the reasons for his motivation: *"All that you have done for your mother-in-law since the death of your husband has been fully told me, and how you left your father and mother and your native land and came to a people that you did not know before"* (2:11). Having both seen and heard something about Ruth's character and being immensely impressed by it, Boaz then prayed a blessing upon Ruth: *"May the LORD reward you for your deeds, and may you have a full reward from the LORD, the God of Israel, under whose wings you have come for refuge!"* (2:12).

After Naomi learned that Ruth had gleaned in the fields of *"a relative of ours, one of our nearest kin"* (2:20), Naomi came up with a strategy for Ruth to gain even more of Boaz's notice. Ruth followed Naomi's instructions, and Boaz redeemed the parcel of land that had belonged to Elimelech. And *so Boaz took*

Ruth and she became his wife (4:13).

Ruth, who had not borne any children by her first husband, Mahlon (who was one of Naomi's two sons), became pregnant and gave birth to a son. *They named him Obed; he became the father of Jesse, the father of David* (4:17). "Obed" means "servant," implying that the child would serve Naomi in her later years. In addition, this son would perpetuate the name and inheritance of Naomi's husband, Elimelech, and Naomi's son, Mahlon.

Thus, as the account drew to a close, the narrative returned to its focus upon Naomi. Having endured tragic circumstances and a desperate plight, Naomi was lauded by the village women as being extremely blessed of the Lord, *"who has not left you this day without next-of-kin"* (4:14). The women saw clearly the care and protection of God over Naomi's life, and they knew that she had been rewarded for her faithfulness. Thus Boaz and Ruth's son *"shall be to you a restorer of life and a nourisher of your old age"* (4:15). And part of Naomi's reward for which the women praised the birth of Obed was that *"your daughter-in-law who loves you, who is more to you than seven sons, has borne him."*

As Obed was laid on Naomi's bosom—and as she became his nurse—Naomi's emptiness was turned to fullness, her desperation was turned to fulfillment, and her sorrow was turned to joy (4:16). Ruth, too, was lauded as heroic. Her complete loyalty to the Israelite family into which she had been received by marriage and her total devotion to her desolate mother-in-law marked her as a true daughter of Israel and a worthy ancestor of David.

SUGGESTIONS TO TEACHERS

Just as Naomi and Ruth were unaware of the larger purposes in their lives—that God was preparing for the births of David and even of Jesus—we cannot always know how God's purposes are taking shape in our lives. We certainly will not realize the importance and impact of our lives until we look back from the perspective of eternity. Therefore, it is important for us to develop certain traits that will keep us at the ready for fulfilling God's plan, direction, and will for our lives.

1. DEVELOP AN EXEMPLARY CHARACTER. Ruth had developed an exemplary character. She was consistently loving, faithful, kind, and courageous. She had formed for herself a reputation for always displaying these admirable qualities. And Boaz, the man who would become Ruth's husband, took notice of all these character traits. Developing an exemplary character takes a lot of work. To be successful in this venture, it is vital that we live out the character qualities we long for—regardless of the people around us or their land or their cultural or religious practices.

2. DEVELOP A STRONG WORK ETHIC. Ruth had developed a strong work ethic. She approached her task of gleaning—though menial, tiresome, and degrading in that it was reserved for the poor—with industriousness and diligence. Notice what the reapers said about her: *"She has been on her feet from early this morning until now, without resting even for a moment"* (Ruth 2:7). Can we develop the same kind of strong work ethic so that we approach any task put before us with diligence and devotion? God does reward a strong work ethic.

3. DEVELOP A STRATEGY FOR ACTION. Neither Ruth nor Naomi nor Boaz were the type of people who sat around waiting for something good to happen to them. Each of them are classic examples of good people who developed a strategy for action—*and then they acted.* Ruth immediately sought work gleaning in the fields, Naomi devised a plan for Boaz to further notice Ruth and become the kinsman-redeemer, and Boaz willingly provided for the needy and fulfilled his role in redeeming the parcel of land that had belonged to Elimelech. We, too, should plan to act, develop a strategy for action, and then act.

4. DEVELOP A SENSE OF ENDURANCE. Despite being hurt and bitter at times for the circumstances she found herself in, Naomi developed a sense of endurance. Throughout her dire straights, she continued to trust in God even when she thought *"the hand of the LORD has turned against me"* (Ruth 1:13). In the end, because of Naomi's sense of endurance, God brought great blessings out of her desperate situation. Jesus taught that *"the one who endures to the end will be saved"* (Matt. 10:22). Thus even as we're facing desperate situations or tragic circumstances ourselves, may we strive to develop a sense of endurance. Knowing that God is faithful, may we yearn to be faithful to Him.

FOR ADULTS	■ **TOPIC:** Showing Kindness

■ **QUESTIONS:** 1. What character traits of Ruth most impress you? 2. In what ways did Boaz fulfill the role of kinsman-redeemer? 3. In what ways did Jesus later fulfill the role of kinsman-redeemer? 4. How was the birth of Obed announced among the women of the village? 5. What opportunities do you have to act kindly toward others, especially those in great need? How might you do so?

■ **ILLUSTRATIONS:**

Demonstration of Kindness and Unity. The "blue shirts" were coming to the rescue in Fiji back in July of 2000. They were Christians from across the island nation, which had suffered because of racial strife and a failed coup in which gunmen kidnapped the prime minister and his government, according to *Outreach Magazine.*

Christians from 12 denominations in Suva, the capital, were easily identifiable wearing blue shirts as they distributed food and clothing and shared the Gospel. Some victims had lost their jobs because of the conflict or were isolated because they were afraid to travel. "People see us arriving and shout, 'the blue shirts are coming,'" Josua Mateiwai, a local church pastor, told the magazine.

It was the first time in history that Fiji churches had worked together to promote reconciliation in the nation, Mateiwai said. They were working closely with government social welfare departments, and some were giving up their incomes to support other church members who needed help.

Many of those receiving aid were Fijians of Indian origin, most of whom were Muslim or Hindu. Desperate people had tears in their eyes when relief aid arrived, church leaders said. Congregations placed a full-page advertisement in a Suva newspaper proclaiming their commitment to care for people of all races. "Christian charity between racial groups will come when the hearts of people have been changed by complete submission to Jesus Christ," the advertisement read.

Bringing People Together. Fancy moves on steaming basketball courts in Lebanon continue to open a way for the Gospel to be taught. Several years ago, eight players from Missouri conducted clinics in the summer heat of sweltering Beirut, according to *Associated Baptist Press*. The players represented Sports Crusaders, an evangelistic program supported by the Missouri Baptist Convention.

Clinics were held daily and were followed by scrimmages, giving the Lebanese an opportunity to compete against American basketball players. During halftime, team members shared their testimonies, and several Lebanese youngsters made professions of faith in Christ. One clinic took place near a church that had been bombed during the 1980s by Israeli forces, and another was conducted in a schoolyard surrounded by run-down apartments.

"Basketball is now the number one sport here in Lebanon," said Charbel Daou, a Beirut resident who helped coordinate the clinics. Sports Crusaders is "bringing together people who normally wouldn't hear the Gospel," he said. The trip had a profound impact on the Americans too. "Realizing we could share the Gospel with those kids simply because we could play basketball was amazing to me," team leader Tim Scifres, a schoolteacher, said.

Reward for Faithfulness. An anonymous poem, called "Drinking from My Saucer," continues to make its rounds through the Internet. A poem such as this may help us understand Naomi's happiness when God rewarded her for her faithful endurance.

> I've never made a fortune
> and it's probably too late now.
> But I don't worry about that much,
> I'm happy anyhow.
> And as I go along life's way,
> I'm reaping better than I sowed.
> I'm drinking from my saucer,
> 'cause my cup has overflowed.

Haven't got a lot of riches,
and sometimes the going's tough.
But I've got loving ones around me,
and that makes me rich enough.
I thank God for His blessings,
and the mercies He's bestowed.
I'm drinking from my saucer,
'cause my cup has overflowed.

I remember times when things went wrong,
my faith wore somewhat thin.
But all at once the dark clouds broke,
and the sun peeped through again.
So, Lord, help me not to gripe
about the tough rows that I've hoed.
I'm drinking from my saucer,
'cause my cup has overflowed.

If God gives me strength and courage,
when the way grows steep and rough.
I'll not ask for other blessings,
I'm already blessed enough.
And may I never be too busy,
to help others bear their loads.
Then I'll keep drinking from my saucer,
'cause my cup has overflowed.

FOR YOUTH

■ TOPIC: Faithfulness Rewarded

■ QUESTIONS: 1. Which of the characters—between Naomi, Ruth, and Boaz—do you think you are the most like? How are you like that character? 2. Which character trait of Ruth would you most like to have? 3. In what ways was Naomi's endurance and faithfulness rewarded? 4. Have you ever been rewarded for your endurance and faithfulness? If so, in what ways? 5. Why do you think the Book of Ruth concludes with a genealogy of David?

■ **ILLUSTRATIONS:**

Faithful Service. A church in Munich, Germany, provides a hatch through which mothers can place their unwanted babies. A bell alerts the ministers on the inside. Mothers can leave proof of their identity on a fingerprint pad on the outside in case they want to reclaim their child, according to the *Daily Telegraph*. The child is put up for adoption if the mother does not return in eight weeks.

The arrangement revived the practice from the fifteenth century. It is similar to others operating in Hamburg, Hungary, and South Africa.

Among the Most Despised. Eight thousand people, including many Muslims, have become Christians in Ethiopia over the past four years. Active churches have formed throughout Southeast Ethiopia, a group from mission agency Aktionskomitee für Verfolgte Christen (Action Committee for Persecuted Christians) told *DAWN FridayFax*. In one town, the Muslims "sold their small mosque to the Christians, but it is already too small." The missions agency supports 75 evangelists in Ethiopia.

Members of the missions group said they were particularly thankful for God's working in the Manja tribe, "one of the nation's most despised tribes," who live on monkey meat and roots, serve many idols, and yet live in constant fear of evil spirits. Eight churches with more than 900 members were planted among the tribe in the last three years when a former agricultural engineer evangelized in the region.

Miracles in Return for Faithfulness. A "small miracle" helped Russian children find God several years ago. Nearly 140 young people and their sponsors were on their way to a Nazarene youth camp in Volgograd when organizers learned that the building they had rented wasn't available, *Nazarene Communications Network* said.

Organizers turned for help to officials at a local school, who in the past had warned students to avoid the Nazarenes, describing the group as a "sect." But something had changed their hearts; not only did the school open its doors to the students, but also cafeteria staff provided meals and snacks during the two-day event, some giving up a holiday to serve the children.

More than 100 children became Christians at the camp, field director Chuck Sunberg said. "Do you know what that means for our church?" he asked. He described the number of professions of faith as "astonishing."

JONAH REJECTS GOD'S CALL

BACKGROUND SCRIPTURE: Jonah 1—2; Nahum 3
DEVOTIONAL READING: Psalm 40:1-8

KEY VERSE: Jonah set out to flee to Tarshish from the presence of the LORD. Jonah 1:3.

KING JAMES VERSION

JONAH 1:1 Now the word of the LORD came unto Jonah the son of Amittai, saying,

2 Arise, go to Nineveh, that great city, and cry against it; for their wickedness is come up before me.

3 But Jonah rose up to flee unto Tarshish from the presence of the LORD, and went down to Joppa; and he found a ship going to Tarshish: so he paid the fare thereof and went down into it, to go with them unto Tarshish from the presence of the LORD.

4 But the LORD sent out a great wind into the sea, and there was a mighty tempest in the sea, so that the ship was like to be broken. . . .

11 Then said they unto him, What shall we do unto thee, that the sea may be calm unto us? for the sea wrought, and was tempestuous.

12 And he said unto them, Take me up, and cast me forth into the sea; so shall the sea be calm unto you: for I know that for my sake this great tempest is upon you.

13 Nevertheless the men rowed hard to bring it to the land; but they could not: for the sea wrought, and was tempestuous against them.

14 Wherefore they cried unto the LORD, and said, We beseech thee, O LORD, we beseech thee, let us not perish for this man's life, and lay not upon us innocent blood: for thou, O LORD, hast done as it pleased thee.

15 So they took up Jonah, and cast him forth into the sea: and the sea ceased from her raging.

16 Then the men feared the LORD exceedingly, and offered a sacrifice unto the LORD, and made vows.

17 Now the LORD had prepared a great fish to swallow up Jonah. And Jonah was in the belly of the fish three days and three nights. . . .

2:1 Then Jonah prayed unto the LORD his God out of the fish's belly. . . .

10 And the LORD spake unto the fish, and it vomited out Jonah upon the dry land.

NEW REVISED STANDARD VERSION

JONAH 1:1 Now the word of the LORD came to Jonah son of Amittai, saying, 2 "Go at once to Nineveh, that great city, and cry out against it; for their wickedness has come up before me." 3 But Jonah set out to flee to Tarshish from the presence of the LORD. He went down to Joppa and found a ship going to Tarshish; so he paid his fare and went on board, to go with them to Tarshish, away from the presence of the LORD. 4 But the LORD hurled a great wind upon the sea, and such a mighty storm came upon the sea that the ship threatened to break up. . . .

11 Then they said to him, "What shall we do to you, that the sea may quiet down for us?" For the sea was growing more and more tempestuous. 12 He said to them, "Pick me up and throw me into the sea; then the sea will quiet down for you; for I know it is because of me that this great storm has come upon you."

13 Nevertheless the men rowed hard to bring the ship back to land, but they could not, for the sea grew more and more stormy against them. 14 Then they cried out to the LORD, "Please, O LORD, we pray, do not let us perish on account of this man's life. Do not make us guilty of innocent blood; for you, O LORD, have done as it pleased you." 15 So they picked Jonah up and threw him into the sea; and the sea ceased from its raging. 16 Then the men feared the LORD even more, and they offered a sacrifice to the LORD and made vows.

17 But the LORD provided a large fish to swallow up Jonah; and Jonah was in the belly of the fish three days and three nights. . . .

2:1 Then Jonah prayed to the LORD his God from the belly of the fish, . . .

2:10 Then the LORD spoke to the fish, and it spewed Jonah out upon the dry land.

BACKGROUND

What the Book of Acts is to the New Testament, the Book of Jonah is to the Old Testament. This prophetic book provides proof positive that God has always had concern for those who are foreign to His chosen people of Israel. Not only are the Gentiles without hope apart from Him, so also are the Jews. The wonderful news is that God's grace—His provision of salvation—is intended for all people to receive by faith.

The Book of Jonah is unique among all other prophetic books in that the entire prophecy is written in the third person. Though it is about Jonah the prophet, it does not contain many of his prophetic declarations. While the other prophetic books reveal some historical data and possess a fair amount of biographical information, they are overwhelmingly prophetic in content. This account of Jonah, on the other hand, is a wild tale about the prophet's call to deliver a message of warning to the Assyrians and his reaction to that call. Only a smidgen of the book contains any prophetic message at all.

The storyline throughout the short book shows both God's concern for the nation of Israel, His chosen people, and God's concern for the nation of Assyria, Israel's most dreaded enemy. While the book makes no specific mention of Israel, it is abundant in its testimony to the supernatural working of God on behalf of the nation. When God granted forgiveness and enabled the Assyrians to repent, He, in essence, guaranteed Israel's security and postponed Assyria's capture of Israel for many years. On the other hand, the book also shows God's working on behalf of the cruel and reprobate Assyrians, whom He brought to national repentance.

The Book of Jonah ends with the prophet discouraged for two reasons: one, because God was merciful to the Assyrians, whom Jonah hated, and two, because God had rebuked Jonah for his hatred. Indeed, the book's ending indicates that the prophet may have written it in his home village of Gath-hepher (a town in the territory of the tribe of Zebulun and located about three miles northeast of Nazareth), after he had returned from his evangelistic mission to Assyria and had—finally—begun to reflect on his ministry's success and his own personal failure. Whatever the case, Jonah left behind a record of God's dealing with him as an individual and with Assyria as a nation. In this unique account, Jonah magnified the power of God and obscured himself behind his message of God's love for all people.

NOTES ON THE PRINTED TEXT

The wild sense of action portrayed throughout the Book of Jonah begins with a conventional call for a prophet—*the word of the LORD came to Jonah* (1:1). Though the prophet had no doubts that the message he heard was from the Lord, he must have thought it a terrible twist of his personal destiny. For Jonah, being told to go to Nineveh, which God called *that great city* (1:2), was the same as being told to go preach in the middle of the most savage, vicious, inhuman, and barbarous people in the known world. The Assyrians had flaunted their power before God and the world through numerous acts of heartless cruelty. Thus Jonah may have also been distraught that only now had *their wickedness* come up before the Lord.

Jonah's response was immediate—he got up and left. But he did not take the northeastern land route from his hometown village of Gath-hepher in Galilee toward Nineveh. Instead, he took off in the opposite direction toward the coastal town of Joppa—at least a 75-mile journey overland—where he boarded a ship that was headed west across the Mediterranean Sea toward Tarshish. Jonah's goal was to get *away from the presence of the LORD* (1:3).

Perhaps being too frightened to go prophesy to Nineveh, Jonah slept below deck, oblivious to and unafraid of the storm that was tossing the ship and absolutely terrifying the crew on board (1:4-5). When the sailors awoke Jonah from his sleep and determined that he was the cause of the tempestuousness and tumult at sea, they asked him, *"What shall we do to you, that the sea may quiet down for us?"* (1:11). The prophet, possibly more afraid of the presence of God than of the wild, thrashing sea, responded by inviting the crew to throw him overboard. He told them that then *"the sea will quiet down for you"* (1:12). At first, the crew rejected Jonah's invitation, still attempting to row the ship back to land. But *they could not, for the sea grew more and more stormy against them* (1:13).

At that point, the entire crew prayed and pleaded with the Lord not to let them die on account of Jonah's sin. They also asked Jonah's God not to hold them responsible for following through on the prophet's suggestion that they throw him overboard. Having thus prayed, the mariners picked up Jonah and tossed him into the raging sea (1:14-15). And because the sea immediately calmed down, *the men feared the LORD even more, and they offered a sacrifice to the LORD and made vows* (1:16).

Now overboard and thrashing in the deep, Jonah next found himself swallowed by a great fish—one provided for by the Lord. Given three days and nights in the belly of the fish to reflect and with little to distract him, Jonah used the time to pray and to repent of his fleeing from God's call (2:1). The prophet was now ready to be sent on his way to Nineveh to proclaim a message of judgment. Sometime after Jonah's prayer thanking God for miraculously delivering him from drowning, God responded by causing the great fish to expectorate Jonah *out upon the dry land* (2:10).

SUGGESTIONS TO TEACHERS

Some examples show us what to do, while other examples show us what not to do. The life of Jonah provides for us an example of some things we should avoid doing.

1. AVOID THE ATTITUDE OF RELUCTANCE. Jonah hated the Assyrians and did not want them to repent. He wanted God to pour out His wrath upon them, not His mercy. As such, the prophet's attitude represented that of Israel and the nation's reluctance to share God's love and mercy with other peoples. In God's call of Abraham and thus of Abraham's descendants, God defined their mission: *"I will bless those who bless you, and the one who curses you I will curse; and in you all the families of the earth shall be blessed"* (Gen. 12:3). Perhaps like Jonah, we may not want those whom we dislike to receive God's favor and are thus reluctant to share the Gospel with them.

2. AVOID GOING YOUR OWN WAY. Jonah's instructions were to go to Nineveh. Instead, he took off in the opposite direction. Rather than following God, Jonah followed his own heart. We, too, sometimes find following our own hearts easier than following the directions of God. But we must learn to go God's way rather than our own way.

3. AVOID RUNNING AWAY FROM GOD. Running away from the presence of God only landed Jonah into worse trouble than that with which he began. It didn't take long for Jonah to come around to the understanding that he couldn't run away from God. Perhaps we, with Jonah, need to learn that we cannot seek the love and favor of God and run away from Him at the same time.

4. AVOID ENDANGERING THE LIVES OF OTHERS. By disobeying God and boarding a ship bound for Tarshish, Jonah endangered the lives of all the ship's crew. We need to understand that our sin, disobedience, and irresponsibility can hurt and actually endanger the spiritual lives of those around us.

5. AVOID TURNING A DEAF EAR ON YOUR CONSCIENCE. As the storm raged around his ship, Jonah continued to sleep below deck. It seems evident that he had turned a deaf ear on his conscience. He had willfully disobeyed a direct instruction from God, but his conscience didn't bother him enough to even disrupt his sleep in the midst of a violent storm. This reminds us that we should listen intently for what our conscience has to say to us, for God will often point out our guilt through our conscience.

6. AVOID ALLOWING HATRED TO AFFECT YOUR PERSPECTIVE. Although Jonah was willing to forfeit his life to save the crew of his ship, he had refused to even risk his life for the people of Nineveh. Why? It's because of his avowed hatred for the Assyrians. His disdain had affected his perspective, and his misdirected perspective caused him to avoid his God-given mission.

7. AVOID HIDING MISTAKES THAT CAN HELP OTHERS COME TO KNOW GOD. One thing Jonah did right was to avoid hiding his sin from the ship's crew. Because of his confession and God's answer to the crew's prayer, the sailors began to worship the Lord. God can make use of our mistakes to help others come to know Him, and admitting our sins can be a powerful example to those who don't yet know the Lord.

FOR ADULTS	■ TOPIC: Running from God

■ QUESTIONS: 1. How did Jonah's response to God's call compare to the responses of other godly prophets? 2. Why do you think Jonah chose the course of action that he did? 3. What does God's pursuit of Jonah tell you about the love and mercy of God? 4. What effect did Jonah's confession of wrongdoing have on the ship's crew? 5. How do you feel when you know you have responded favorably to God's call?

■ ILLUSTRATIONS:

Living Rent-Free in Your Head. Ann Landers penned an exquisite sentence in 1998 when she wrote, "Hanging onto resentment is letting someone you despise live rent-free in your head." Judging by Jonah's intense hatred of the Assyrians, we can easily ascertain that the Assyrians were living rent-free in the prophet's head. Of course, looking at Jonah's attitude causes us to beg the question of ourselves: *Who is living rent-free in our heads?*

Busyness of Juggling Life's Demands. In an article called "Lovin' Jesus" in *Vital Ministry* magazine, Paul Allen wrote the following:

> Whenever one of my kids does something I'm not proud of, or I find out from my wife that there's a major glitch in our finances, or someone lets me know that they'd do my ministry differently, I get this feeling that I've failed God in some way. Fortunately, God shows up; or I should say, I realize that I've left Him out of the picture. So I get back in touch with His reality. Does He get on my case or bring me major guilt for what I've dropped? Is He grading me on my juggling skills? No. He's standing there with open arms, waiting for me to embrace Him and experience His love—again.
>
> In our busyness of juggling life's demands, let's not forget the reasons we're in this profession. Our love for Jesus. His compelling love for us. Our desire to share that love with others. I think sometimes we need to stop comparing ourselves or our ministries to someone else, stop looking for that new model that will take our church to a new level, and stop expecting our families and personal business to be "ideals" for others to see. Instead, we need to reacquaint ourselves with the overwhelming love of Jesus.

Going through the Motions. Was Jonah simply going through the motions of being a prophet? In his book *The Life You've Always Wanted*, John Ortberg calls this "mindlessness," namely, a tendency toward mental drift. He tells a story about himself in which, as a college student, he was employed by the Whitney Company to make deliveries. "One morning, I completed my last delivery to Johnson Electrical Supply and was driving back to the plant in a white, nondescript pickup truck. I noticed some unusual things on my way. The gearshift indicator, which had been broken, had somehow been healed. The radio buttons were programmed to different stations than they were before. *This is odd*, I thought astutely."

Ortberg parked the truck at his plant, went to lunch, and then returned to make a run to the post office. As he left the post office, he couldn't find the Whitney truck. *Someone has stolen our truck,* he thought. Then he noticed that, although the Whitney truck was missing, there was a similar truck from Johnson Electrical Supply.

But no one had stolen the Whitney truck. He had stolen the Johnson truck—and hadn't even noticed. The keys had been in the ignition. The trucks were similar. He had mindlessly slipped into the Johnson truck and driven away. Ortberg writes, "I prayed on the way back to Whitney's that no one would have noticed yet. No such luck. Someone from Johnson's had called just after I left for the post office."

FOR YOUTH

■ TOPIC: Are You Listening?

■ QUESTIONS: 1. How do you think Jonah felt after hearing *the word of the LORD* (Jonah 1:1)? 2. What do you think was on Jonah's mind as he tried to run away *from the presence of the LORD* (1:3)? 3. Do you think Jonah was aware that he was placing the lives of the ship's crew in danger? Explain your answer. 4. If you had been Jonah, do you think your conscience would have allowed you to sleep through the storm at sea? Explain your answer. 5. What can happen if we allow a rebellious attitude to persist?

■ ILLUSTRATIONS:

Malicious Joy and Bad Fruit. In January of 2000, I preached a sermon borrowed from *Homiletics* magazine called "Schtucke in Schadenfreude." "Schadenfreude" is a German word that means "malicious joy at another person's misfortune." As I preached how Jonah was "schtucke in schadenfreude"—expounding how perfectly happy Jonah was to preach hellfire and damnation to the people of Nineveh because they deserved it—I could tell one lady in my congregation was immensely bothered by my pronunciation of "schadenfreude." Finally, Lisa, who speaks English and German along with several other languages, could stand it no longer.

"De vay you're pronouncing 'schadenfreude' would be better translated to English as 'bad fruit,'" she said in her native German accent. As I laughed along with the congregation, I realized that my pronunciation of "schadenfreude" was actually the result of "schadenfreude." For indeed, malicious joy at another person's misfortune does lead to bad fruit! And I told my congregation so.

Are we also "schtucke in schadenfreude"? While "hate" increasingly becomes newsbreaking—stories about hate crimes, hate groups, and hate web sites permeate the media—we see ourselves as innocent in the presence of such malevolence. But Jonah provided a new mirror for us to examine ourselves. Jonah presented a painfully clear reflection of slice-of-life malevolence. While war criminals and deranged zealots display glaring, colorful hatefulness for all the world to scorn, Jonah reminded us that hate also takes shape in souls that appear to be respectable and faithful—souls like ours.

Trying to Flee God's Presence. A Sunday school teacher challenged her children to take some time on Sunday afternoon to write a letter to God. They were to bring their letter back the following Sunday. One little boy wrote, "Dear God, we had a good time at church today. Wish you could have been there." Jonah, too, behaved as though he had been successful in his attempt to flee God's presence. But he hadn't.

Can't Say You Weren't Warned. Finding one of her students making faces at others on the playground at church, Ms. Smith stopped to gently reprove the child. Smiling sweetly, the Sunday school teacher said, "Bobby, when I was a child, I was told that if I made ugly faces, it would freeze and I would stay like that." Bobby looked up into the teacher's face and replied, "Well, Ms. Smith, you can't say you weren't warned."

As a prophet of the Lord, Jonah should have known that he couldn't run away from the presence of God. He, too, couldn't say that he hadn't been warned.

GOD'S MERCY TO NINEVEH

BACKGROUND SCRIPTURE: Jonah 3—4
DEVOTIONAL READING: Psalm 113

KEY VERSE: "You are a gracious God and merciful, slow to anger, and abounding in steadfast love, and ready to relent from punishing." Jonah 4:2.

KING JAMES VERSION

JONAH 3:1 And the word of the LORD came unto Jonah the second time, saying,

2 Arise, go unto Nineveh, that great city, and preach unto it the preaching that I bid thee.

3 So Jonah arose, and went unto Nineveh, according to the word of the LORD. Now Nineveh was an exceeding great city of three days' journey.

4 And Jonah began to enter into the city a day's journey, and he cried, and said, Yet forty days, and Nineveh shall be overthrown.

5 So the people of Nineveh believed God, and proclaimed a fast, and put on sackcloth, from the greatest of them even to the least of them. . . .

10 And God saw their works, that they turned from their evil way; and God repented of the evil, that he had said that he would do unto them; and he did it not. . . .

4:1 But it displeased Jonah exceedingly, and he was very angry.

2 And he prayed unto the LORD, and said, I pray thee, O LORD, was not this my saying, when I was yet in my country? Therefore I fled before unto Tarshish: for I knew that thou art a gracious God, and merciful, slow to anger, and of great kindness, and repentest thee of the evil.

3 Therefore now, O LORD, take, I beseech thee, my life from me; for it is better for me to die than to live.

4 Then said the LORD, Doest thou well to be angry?

5 So Jonah went out of the city, and sat on the east side of the city, and there made him a booth, and sat under it in the shadow, till he might see what would become of the city. . . .

11 And should not I spare Nineveh, that great city, wherein are more than sixscore thousand persons that cannot discern between their right hand and their left hand; and also much cattle?

NEW REVISED STANDARD VERSION

JONAH 3:1 The word of the LORD came to Jonah a second time, saying, 2 "Get up, go to Nineveh, that great city, and proclaim to it the message that I tell you." 3 So Jonah set out and went to Nineveh, according to the word of the LORD. Now Nineveh was an exceedingly large city, a three days' walk across.

4 Jonah began to go into the city, going a day's walk. And he cried out, "Forty days more, and Nineveh shall be overthrown!" 5 And the people of Nineveh believed God; they proclaimed a fast, and everyone, great and small, put on sackcloth. . . .

10 When God saw what they did, how they turned from their evil ways, God changed his mind about the calamity that he had said he would bring upon them; and he did not do it. . . .

4:1 But this was very displeasing to Jonah, and he became angry. 2 He prayed to the LORD and said, "O LORD! Is not this what I said while I was still in my own country? That is why I fled to Tarshish at the beginning; for I knew that you are a gracious God and merciful, slow to anger, and abounding in steadfast love, and ready to relent from punishing. 3 And now, O LORD, please take my life from me, for it is better for me to die than to live." 4 And the LORD said, "Is it right for you to be angry?" 5 Then Jonah went out of the city and sat down east of the city, and made a booth for himself there. He sat under it in the shade, waiting to see what would become of the city. . . .

11 "And should I not be concerned about Nineveh, that great city, in which there are more than a hundred and twenty thousand persons who do not know their right hand from their left, and also many animals?"

13

Monday, February 25	2 Timothy 1:8-14	*Hold to Sound Teaching*
Tuesday, February 26	2 Timothy 2:1-13	*Endure Hardship for the Sake of the Gospel*
Wednesday, February 27	2 Timothy 2:14-21	*The Lord Knows Who Are His*
Thursday, February 28	Romans 1:1-17	*The Power of the Gospel*
Friday, March 1	Acts 17:22-31	*He Will Judge the World in Righteousness*
Saturday, March 2	Romans 2:1-11	*If You Judge Others, You Condemn Yourself*
Sunday, March 3	Romans 2:12-16	*The Law Written on Their Hearts*

BACKGROUND

As a prophet, Jonah began his ministry at a very early date—probably around 785 B.C. Bible scholars believe he prophesied for about 10 years—until around 775 B.C. Second Kings 14:25 is the only other Old Testament passage mentioning the work of Jonah, indicating that he had given a prophecy that was later fulfilled during the reign of Jeroboam II: *He restored the border of Israel from Lebo-hamath as far as the Sea of the Arabah, according to the word of the LORD, the God of Israel, which he spoke by his servant Jonah son of Amittai, the prophet, who was from Gath-hepher.* This prophecy concerning Jeroboam II, a king of Israel (793–753 B.C.), would have been in regard to the nation's conflict with the Syrians.

Jonah, whose name means "dove," was the son of Amittai, whose name means "faithful." Like other prophets, most of Jonah's missions dealt with declaring a message from God, not foretelling coming events. The prophet was apparently in his hometown of Gath-hepher, in the vicinity of Galilee, when God called him to go to the great Assyrian city of Nineveh. The journey for Jonah would have been about 500 miles northeast—had he taken the direct route.

The city of Nineveh had been founded by Nimrod (Gen. 10:8-11). Several centuries before Jonah's prophetic work, the city became one of the royal residences of Assyrian kings. Nineveh was perhaps the most important city in Assyria during Jonah's day. And within several decades, King Sennacherib would make Nineveh the capital of the vast Assyrian Empire. Sennacherib greatly beautified and adorned Nineveh. The splendid temples, palaces, and fortifications made it the chief city of the empire.

When God sent Jonah to Nineveh to warn the people of His imminent judgment if they did not repent, the city was mostly renowned as a wicked place with cruel inhabitants. Though Jonah knew a lot about Nineveh's viciousness and immorality, he said little about it in the book that bears his name. However, Nahum, another minor prophet, gave more insight to the sinfulness of the city. Nahum wrote that it was guilty of evil plots against God (Nah. 1:9), exploitation of the helpless, cruelty in war (2:12), and idolatry, prostitution, and sorcery (3:4).

NOTES ON THE PRINTED TEXT

Having been rescued from drowning in the Mediterranean Sea due to being swallowed by a great fish, and having been rescued from the belly of the fish when God caused it to spit out Jonah onto dry land, the prophet may have thought that the whole horrendous ordeal was over as he sat on the sands of the shore. But Jonah's account did not end on the beach; nor was the prophet reprimanded for his poor behavior and sent back to Gath-hepher to be given another opportunity in the future. God immediately called on Jonah, again, *a second time* (Jonah 3:1), to go to Nineveh—*that great city* (3:2)—with a message that God would see to it that the city was destroyed if the people did not repent.

Just as when God called him the first time, Jonah immediately set out on a journey (3:3). But this time, the prophet followed God's instructions rather than his rebellious heart. Though the prophet obeyed the Lord's command, it seems as if he lacked enthusiasm. While traveling through the huge city, Jonah heralded a concise but hard-hitting warning to the Assyrians: *"Forty days more, and Nineveh shall be overthrown!"* (3:4).

The people of Nineveh heard Jonah's message; they listened to it. And then, what Jonah most dreaded occurred. The people responded to his message by believing what God said. Giving more than a mere intellectual assent to Jonah's message, the people of Nineveh acted on their newfound belief by declaring *a fast, and everyone, great and small, put on sackcloth* (3:5) as a visible symbol of their mourning and repentance. And once more, Jonah proved to be a successful missionary—as he had been earlier with the ship's crew—despite himself.

When God saw what they did, how they turned from their evil ways (3:10), He responded with both grace and mercy, canceling the destruction that He had warned about. *But this was very displeasing to Jonah, and he became angry* (4:1). Not only had Jonah been disobedient, but he had also been bigoted. And now his bigotry was forthrightly expressed. Jonah angrily confessed that his knowledge of God's lovingkindness was the real reason he did not want to go to Nineveh in the first place. Just as Jonah had feared, the Lord proved to be gracious and merciful, *"slow to anger, and abounding in steadfast love, and ready to relent from punishing"* (4:2).

Jonah so hated the Assyrians that he yearned for God to destroy them without warning. And once the prophet gave in to God's urging and warned the people of their impending doom, he had hoped that the people would go on practicing their wicked ways so that God would, indeed, see to it that the city was overthrown. Now that the people had believed in God and repented of their sins, and now that God had withdrawn His forewarned destruction, Jonah was distraught. His bitterness so overwhelmed him that he prayed to the Lord asking Him to *"please take my life from me, for it is better for me to die than to live"* (4:3). Jonah's attitude was that, if the Assyrians of Nineveh were allowed to live, he would just as soon die.

In an apparently most tender and gracious way, God gently chastened His defiant prophet with a simple question: *"Is it right for you to be angry?"* (4:4). The Lord hoped that His probing question for His prophet would remind him of his unholy attitude and his dire need to change. The Lord also wanted to usher Jonah into sympathy with His plan to forgive repentant people. But the bitter prophet would hear none of it. Balking at God, he *went out of the city and sat down east of the city, and made a booth for himself there. He sat under it in the shade, waiting to see what would become of the city* (4:5).

Still in no way satisfied with God's gracious and merciful response to the repentant city of Nineveh, Jonah watched. The prophet was seething in his anger, hoping against hope that God would change His mind and destroy the city for which Jonah held such hatred. The prophet's anger was further kindled when a bush (possibly the caster bean plant) that had been giving him shade withered, leaving him to roast in the sun. Again Jonah asked God to let him die. God pointed out to Jonah how he had been more concerned for a shady bush than for the 120,000 people and the countless animals of Nineveh. And thus God expressed to Jonah His concern for every living creature in the universe—even animals. In addition, He expressed His desire for all people—not just the Israelites—to come to Him, believe in Him, and accept His salvation (4:6-11).

SUGGESTIONS TO TEACHERS

Various attributes of God are put on display throughout the course of Jonah's account. For instance, we learn that God is persistent, is willing to give us additional opportunities to repent and obey, is gracious and merciful, is slow to anger, and is abounding in steadfast love.

1. GOD IS PERSISTENT. Even after Jonah had run away from God, the Lord continued prodding him, beckoning him, practically begging him, and making a way for him to go to Nineveh to tell the people there about their need to repent and believe. In being persistent with Jonah, God was also persistent toward seeing that the people of Nineveh were given an opportunity to accept His salvation.

2. GOD IS WILLING TO GIVE US ADDITIONAL OPPORTUNITIES. God could have easily allowed Jonah to drown in the Mediterranean Sea and raised up another more willing prophet to proclaim His message to Nineveh. But the Lord is willing to give His servants additional opportunities to repent and obey, even extending grace to such a hateful, bitter, and defiant prophet as Jonah.

3. GOD IS GRACIOUS AND MERCIFUL. Jonah knew all about the wickedness of Nineveh. He knew that the city deserved destruction. He yearned that the city would get what it deserved. God, too, knew all about the wickedness of Nineveh. And He, too, knew that the city deserved destruction. But God is gracious, and as such He wanted to extend to Nineveh His unmerited favor, to give them something good that they did not deserve. God is also merciful and, as such, He wanted to withhold His judgment on them. In essence, He saw the people of Nineveh as needing His love, and also longed to spare them His wrath.

4. GOD IS SLOW TO ANGER. In contrast to Jonah, who was so quickly and easily angered, God is slow to anger; His wrath is not easily attracted. It takes a great deal of sin for God to move toward punishing His people. Other than Jonah 4:2, there are five more occurrences in the Bible in which God is described in detail as being slow to anger (Neh. 9:17; Pss. 103:8; 145:8; Joel 2:13; Nah. 1:3).

5. GOD IS ABOUNDING IN STEADFAST LOVE. As the account of Jonah helps to make clear, God is abounding in steadfast love for all His people. His love is not restricted to those, like the Israelites, whom He has called to a specific mission and purpose. God feels immense compassion for all people, so much so that He devised a plan to bring them to Himself—the life, death, and resurrection of His Son, the Messiah, Jesus of Nazareth.

FOR ADULTS

■ **TOPIC:** Showing Mercy

■ **QUESTIONS:** 1. In what way did Jonah respond to God's giving him another opportunity? 2. How do you account for the people of Nineveh's response to Jonah's extra-brief message? 3. What were the real reasons behind Jonah's anger? 4. Do you think Jonah really wanted to die, or was he just bluffing? Explain your answer. 5. In what ways has God been abounding in steadfast love toward you?

■ **ILLUSTRATIONS:**

Running from God, Eluding His Rescue. In 1981, a Minnesota radio station reported a story about a stolen car in California. Police were staging an intense search for the vehicle and the driver, even to the point of placing announcements on local radio stations to contact the thief.

On the front seat of the stolen car sat a box of crackers that, unknown to the thief, were laced with poison. The car owner had intended to use the crackers as rat bait. Now the police and the owner of the VW Bug were more interested in apprehending the thief to save his life than to recover the car.

So often when we run from God, we feel it is to escape His punishment. But what we are actually doing is eluding His rescue.

Making His Mark in the New Nineveh. A great Southern novelist as well as a physician, Walker Percy, who died in 1990, was called "the moralist of the deep South" and "the doctor of the soul." By his own admission, Percy attempted to write both fiction and nonfiction that addressed the great themes of life from a Christian perspective.

In an interview with a national magazine before he died, Percy admitted that he was a believer, went to church, immersed himself in the Bible, and studied theologians. The interviewer, incredulous at such apparent naivete, asked the distinguished writer, "How is such belief possible in this day and age?" Percy replied,

"What else is there?" The reporter countered: "What do you mean, what else is there? There is humanism, atheism, materialism, agnosticism, Marxism, behaviorism, Buddhism, Sufism; there is astrology, occultism, theosophy, metaphysics." Percy said simply, "That is what I mean. What else is there?"

Mercy and Repentance. Jack took a long look at his speedometer before slowing down: 73 in a 55 zone. It was the fourth time in as many months. How could a guy get caught so often? When his car had slowed to 10 miles an hour, Jack pulled over, but only partially. He thought, "Let the cop worry about the potential traffic hazard. Maybe some other car will tweak his backside with a mirror."

The police officer was stepping out of his car, the big pad in hand. *Bob? Bob from church?* Jack sunk farther into his trench coat. This was worse than the coming ticket. A Christian police officer catching a guy from his own church, a guy who happened to be a little eager to get home after a long day at the office, a guy he was about to play golf with tomorrow. Jumping out of the car, Jack approached a man he saw every Sunday—a man he'd never seen in uniform.

"Hi, Bob. Fancy meeting you like this."

"Hello, Jack." No smile.

"Guess you caught me red-handed in a rush to see my wife and kids."

"Yeah, I guess." Bob seemed uncertain. Good.

"I've seen some long days at the office lately. I'm afraid I bent the rules a bit—just this once." Jack toed at a pebble on the pavement. "Diane said something about roast beef and potatoes tonight. Know what I mean?"

"I know what you mean. I also know that you have a reputation in our precinct." Ouch. This was not going in the right direction. Time to change tactics.

"What'd you clock me at?"

"Seventy. Would you sit back in your car please?"

"Now wait a minute here, Bob. I checked as soon as I saw you. I was barely nudging 65." The lie seemed to come easier with every ticket.

"Please, Jack, in the car."

Flustered, Jack hunched himself through the still-open door. Slamming it shut, he stared at the dasboard. He was in no rush to open the window. The minutes ticked by. Bob scribbled away on the pad. Why hadn't he asked for a driver's license? Whatever the reason, it would be a month of Sundays before Jack ever sat near this officer again. A tap on the door jerked his head to the left. There was Bob, a folded paper in hand. Jack rolled down the window a mere two inches, just enough room for Bob to pass him the slip.

"Thanks." Jack could not quite keep the sneer out of his voice. Bob returned to his police car without a word. Jack watched his retreat in the mirror. Jack unfolded the sheet of paper. How much was this one going to cost? Wait a minute. What was this? Some kind of joke? Certainly not a ticket.

Jack began to read: "Dear Jack, once upon a time I had a daughter. She was six when killed by a car. You guessed it—a speeding driver. A fine and three months in jail, and the man was free. Free to hug his daughters. All three of them. I only had one, and I'm going to have to wait until heaven before I can ever hug her again. A thousand times I've tried to forgive that man. A thousand times I thought I had. Maybe I did, but I need to do it again. Even now. Pray for me. And be careful. My son is all I have left. Bob."

Jack turned around in time to see Bob's car pull away and head down the road. Jack watched until it disappeared. A full 15 minutes later he, too, pulled away and drove slowly home, praying for forgiveness and hugging a surprised wife and kids when he arrived. *Life is precious. Handle with it care.*

FOR YOUTH	■ TOPIC: It's Not Fair!

■ **QUESTIONS:** 1. What evidences do you see throughout the account of Jonah that the Lord is willing to give us additional opportunities to repent and obey? 2. What do you think was Jonah's emotional state after he had finally delivered God's message to the people of Nineveh? 3. How did God deal with His pouting prophet? 4. In what ways is God gracious and merciful? 5. In all His dealings with you, how has God proven Himself to be merciful and gracious?

■ **ILLUSTRATIONS:**

The New Nineveh. Nineveh was a missionary priority and a prime candidate for revival in Jonah's day. But what about today? How might we pinpoint a missionary priority and a prime candidate for revival in our own day and age? Consider the following statistics released by *Homiletics* in 1991.

What is the fastest growing religion in North America today? It's Islam. What is the state in the U.S.A. that already has a Buddhist plurality? It's Hawaii. What is the century with the largest number of martyrs in Christian history? It's the twentieth century. What is the rate at which the average Christian invites someone to church? It's once every 28 years. Perhaps we should see North America and Europe as prime missionary territory today as we do Asia, Africa, and South America!

When Nineveh Came to Church. When young people in ghoulish makeup, chains, and spiked hair slip into the back rows of your church, it's not going to be a typical service. That's what happened in July of 2000 in Smyrna, Georgia, where 25 goth-style protesters politely entered the International Gospel Outreach Family Church, according to Cox News Service. One had a leather bondage mask strapped to his face, and another a T-shirt with the number 666 surrounded by the religious symbol of the fish.

The protesters sat in silence as congregants shouted, danced, and swayed during the two-hour service, according to the news service. Most of the protesters were members or fans of metal and goth bands, and said they had been told by a band promoter who once attended the church that the senior pastor had compared rock music to devil worship. Pastor Robin Hancox said he promotes godly principles but has not criticized bands in that way.

Halfway through the service, the pastor urged members to "look at your neighbor and say, 'I'm glad you're here.'" A church member crossed the aisle to give a band member a hug, which was received awkwardly. Some church members and band members spoke briefly as the service ended, then filed out.

Transformed by the Mercy of God. About 250 tough-looking bikers held a revival meeting in July of 2000 in Clinton, Illinois. The men and women, who met at a campground, were part of the Christian Motorcyclists Association (CMA), the country's largest such group with about 76,000 members, according to the *Chicago Tribune*.

Many Christian bikers are ex-motorcycle gang members who were once mixed up in drugs, drinking, and crime and had given their lives to Christ, the newspaper reported. Others are former business people who hit rock bottom, sometimes because of drugs and partying.

Members reach out to non-Christian bikers by establishing a presence at motorcycle rallies, shows, and gang funerals, where they offer to counsel anyone who wants help. Some groups hold an annual "bike blessing" at which members pray for bikers to have a safe riding season.

The Christian bikers are low-key. Sometimes they are sneered at by motorcycle toughs, but usually the bikers get along with CMA members because of their common appearance—denim jackets, aviator sunglasses, tattoos, long hair, and studded leather—and love for motorcycles.

THE POWER OF THE GOSPEL

GOD'S RIGHTEOUSNESS REVEALED

BACKGROUND SCRIPTURE: Romans 1
DEVOTIONAL READING: Psalm 34:1-8

KEY VERSES: I am not ashamed of the gospel; it is the power of God for salvation to everyone who has faith, to the Jew first and also to the Greek. For in it the righteousness of God is revealed through faith for faith. Romans 1:16-17.

KING JAMES VERSION

ROMANS 1:1 Paul, a servant of Jesus Christ, called to be an apostle, separated unto the gospel of God,

2 (Which he had promised afore by his prophets in the holy scriptures,)

3 Concerning his Son Jesus Christ our Lord, which was made of the seed of David according to the flesh;

4 And declared to be the Son of God with power, according to the spirit of holiness, by the resurrection from the dead:

5 By whom we have received grace and apostleship, for obedience to the faith among all nations, for his name:

6 Among whom are ye also the called of Jesus Christ:

7 To all that be in Rome, beloved of God, called to be saints: Grace to you and peace from God our Father, and the Lord Jesus Christ.

8 First, I thank my God through Jesus Christ for you all, that your faith is spoken of throughout the whole world.

9 For God is my witness, whom I serve with my spirit in the gospel of his Son, that without ceasing I make mention of you always in my prayers;

10 Making request, if by any means now at length I might have a prosperous journey by the will of God to come unto you.

11 For I long to see you, that I may impart unto you some spiritual gift, to the end ye may be established;

12 That is, that I may be comforted together with you by the mutual faith both of you and me.

13 Now I would not have you ignorant, brethren, that oftentimes I purposed to come unto you, (but was let hitherto,) that I might have some fruit among you also, even as among other Gentiles. . . .

16 For I am not ashamed of the gospel of Christ: for it is the power of God unto salvation to every one that believeth; to the Jew first, and also to the Greek.

17 For therein is the righteousness of God revealed from faith to faith: as it is written, The just shall live by faith.

NEW REVISED STANDARD VERSION

ROMANS 1:1 Paul, a servant of Jesus Christ, called to be an apostle, set apart for the gospel of God,

2 which he promised beforehand through his prophets in the holy scriptures, 3 the gospel concerning his Son, who was descended from David according to the flesh 4 and was declared to be Son of God with power according to the spirit of holiness by resurrection from the dead, Jesus Christ our Lord, 5 through whom we have received grace and apostleship to bring about the obedience of faith among all the Gentiles for the sake of his name, 6 including yourselves who are called to belong to Jesus Christ,

7 To all God's beloved in Rome, who are called to be saints:

Grace to you and peace from God our Father and the Lord Jesus Christ.

8 First, I thank my God through Jesus Christ for all of you, because your faith is proclaimed throughout the world. 9 For God, whom I serve with my spirit by announcing the gospel of his Son, is my witness that without ceasing I remember you always in my prayers, 10 asking that by God's will I may somehow at last succeed in coming to you. 11 For I am longing to see you so that I may share with you some spiritual gift to strengthen you— 12 or rather so that we may be mutually encouraged by each other's faith, both yours and mine. 13 I want you to know, brothers and sisters, that I have often intended to come to you (but thus far have been prevented), in order that I may reap some harvest among you as I have among the rest of the Gentiles. . . .

16 For I am not ashamed of the gospel; it is the power of God for salvation to everyone who has faith, to the Jew first and also to the Greek. 17 For in it the righteousness of God is revealed through faith for faith; as it is written, "The one who is righteous will live by faith."

HOME BIBLE READINGS

Monday, March 4	Ephesians 1:3-14	*God's Grace Is Freely Bestowed*
Tuesday, March 5	Ephesians 1:15-23	*Called to Hope*
Wednesday, March 6	Ephesians 2:1-10	*Saved by Grace*
Thursday, March 7	Ephesians 2:11-22	*We Are No Longer Strangers and Aliens*
Friday, March 8	Romans 2:17—3:8	*God Is True*
Saturday, March 9	Romans 3:9-20	*The Law Brings Knowledge of Sin*
Sunday, March 10	Romans 3:21-31	*Justified by God's Grace*

BACKGROUND

Paul's Letter to the Romans is both the deepest and most important of his epistles. Most Bible scholars agree that Romans has had more influence on the development of Christian theology and the growth of the church than any other New Testament book. Many believe that Romans presents the most systematic and comprehensive exposition of the Gospel of any other New Testament book. Indeed, we need only consider some of the important roles Paul's Letter to the Romans has played throughout the history of the church to realize its vast and continuing impact.

As Augustine struggled with his own sinfulness and lack of belief in the garden at Milan, he heard someone say to him, "Take up and read! Take up and read!" And it was the Book of Romans that he eventually took up and read, bringing about in him a personal change that would also transform the face of the church. As Martin Luther brooded over the theological beliefs and religious practices of his peers, it was his reading of the Book of Romans that enabled him to discover the truth of justification by faith. Subsequently, the Protestant Reformation was born! At Aldersgate Street, John Wesley listened carefully to a reading of Luther's preface to Romans and his heart was "strangely warmed," igniting in him a fire that would eventually spread a revival of faith across several continents. And even as late as the twentieth century, Karl Barth rocked the theological world with his first edition of *Romerbrief*, a theological treatise based on Paul's Letter to the Romans.

Like the rest of Paul's letters to first-century believers, he intended Romans to be read aloud before a congregation of worshipers. But with the exception of Colossians, Romans is unlike the apostle's other letters in that it was written to a majority of believers who had not yet even met Paul in person. This fact may help to explain why the apostle's salutation is so extraordinarily long and complex to read. (In the Greek text, the first seven verses are a single compound-complex sentence, and these verses are translated as such in both the NRSV and the KJV.) Thus, as Paul introduced himself (as well as his faith and his gospel message), he did not mince any words. With the initial words of his letter—one that would become a theological treatise for centuries to come—Paul told his readers not only about his mission, but also about the nature of the Gospel and about the one person in whom that Gospel is centered: Jesus Christ.

NOTES ON THE PRINTED TEXT

The first seven verses of Paul's Letter to the Romans comprise a one-sentence salutation, but this salutation actually makes up about half of a larger prologue section that extends through verse 15. In verses 8-15, Paul introduced the theme of his letter, which is then followed by an overall thematic statement in verses 16 and 17. Thus, whereas ancient Greek letters typically began with the names of the sender and of the recipients along with a short greeting, the apostle expanded this custom to give a detailed expression of what it meant to trust in Christ for salvation.

In the course of Paul's introduction, he began by calling himself *a servant of Jesus Christ* (1:1); in essence, Paul said that he was a slave of the long-awaited Messiah. But, as Paul would also explain in his introduction, the mission of the Messiah extended beyond that of the Jews to also include the Gentiles. Paul received his mission from God Himself. The Lord summoned Paul *to be an apostle, set apart for the gospel of God.* The apostle knew that the congregation at Rome was made up of a large number of slaves, and he also knew that these slaves were just not simple laborers. Many were highly educated and held highly responsible positions in the service of Roman civil leaders as well as in the service of the wealthy aristocracy. Because this letter would be accessible to them, Paul immediately identified himself as a slave like them—except that he was a slave of Jesus Christ, giving his total allegiance to the Messiah. (Indeed, throughout the introduction of Paul's letter to the Romans, the apostle mixed and interweaved both "slave" terminology and Jewish terminology.)

As a devout and well-studied Jew, Paul knew the Hebrew Scriptures. And though he had at first set out to persecute Christians, when he became a believer himself, he realized that God had *promised beforehand through his prophets in the holy scriptures, the gospel concerning his Son* (1:2-3). This Gospel that Paul described early in his letter is the good news that Jesus Christ has made forgiveness and freedom from sin available to all people. Through faith in Him they can be saved.

Having introduced the Gospel to his readers, the apostle next launched into a detailed, multilayered description of the Christ through whom the Gospel came into being. Paul wrote about Jesus being of the physical lineage of the great King David. The apostle also wrote about the Messiah's being *declared . . . [the] Son of God with power according to the spirit of holiness* (1:4). Paul declared that Jesus was raised from the dead and that He is Lord over all the universe. In fact, Paul called Him *Jesus Christ our Lord.*

After describing Jesus to his readers, Paul told how it was through the Messiah that *we have received grace* (1:5), namely, God's unmerited favor. It was through the Son that the Father has smiled favorably upon us all, regardless of our ancestral heritage, and has extended to us the promise of eternal life. God granted to Paul the additional grace of being called into the *apostleship to bring about the obedience of faith among all the Gentiles for the sake of his name*. Therefore, Paul's God-given purpose was to urge people from all walks of life to trust in Christ for salvation and live in obedience to His will. The people living in Rome were among those who had been *called to belong to Jesus Christ* (1:6).

In verse 7, Paul mentioned by name those for whom his letter was intended: *all God's beloved in Rome*. The apostle referred to them as those *who are called to be saints*. The apostle was stressing that they had been set apart for God and that their lives were to be marked by holiness and virtue. Also, by calling his readers saints, Paul conferred upon them a title straight out of the Hebrew Scriptures. It was one of many signals from the apostle's letter that the grace of God had been extended to all people. Regardless of birthright or nationality, all who believed in Jesus Christ, the Son of God, would be called holy (Heb. 10:10).

After all the lines of introduction, Paul sent his typical greeting: *Grace to you and peace from God our Father and the Lord Jesus Christ*. In ancient Greek letters, after the salutation usually came a short prayer of thanksgiving or a petition for those addressed. In this letter, however, Paul's prayer of thanksgiving arises because he had heard about the faith of the Romans (Rom. 1:8). As the apostle prayed for them regularly (1:9), he yearned to *somehow at last succeed in coming to [them]* (1:10). The reason for Paul's intense longing to go to Rome was *that I may share with you some spiritual gift to strengthen you* (1:11) and *that we may be mutually encouraged by each other's faith, both yours and mine* (1:12). Though it was Paul's long held desire to visit the church at Rome, he had somehow been hindered in making the journey. Nevertheless, he knew that once God had made a way for him to get to Rome, he would *reap some harvest among you as I have among the rest of the Gentiles* (1:13).

Contained within verses 16 and 17 is the theme of Paul's letter to the church at Rome. The apostle wrote that he could never be ashamed of or embarrassed to be associated with the Gospel of Christ. Paul would always be ready to preach the good news to the lost. Why did he feel this way? Paul knew that the Gospel *is the power of God for salvation to everyone who has faith* (1:16). The *power of God for salvation* removes believers from the condemnation of the law. The *power of God for salvation* enables believers to renounce sin. The *power of God for salvation* gives believers the hope of being resurrected from the dead. Faith in Christ enables us to become God's children. We receive peace with Him and a share in future glory. This is true for everyone who accepts the truth about Jesus!

It is in the Gospel that *the righteousness of God is revealed* (1:17). The Gospel unveils the righteousness of God through His plan for us to be saved, and it also discloses the righteousness of God by making us fit to spend eternity with Him. Indeed, it is through our response to the Gospel (namely, trusting in Christ) that our relationship with God is made right and whole. Paul, quoting Habakkuk 2:4, summed up this thematic statement for his letter by reminding his readers that *"the one who is righteous will live by faith"* (Rom. 1:17).

SUGGESTIONS TO TEACHERS

The theme of the Book of Romans is stated in 1:16, *For I am not ashamed of the gospel; it is the power of God for salvation to everyone who has faith.* Every word of this verse seems like an attempt by Paul to acknowledge and strengthen the faith of the believers at Rome. May we, too, do all within our sphere of influence to acknowledge and strengthen not only our own faith, but also the faith of those around us.

1. ACCEPT THE INVITATION. Paul wanted to make it clear to the believers living in Rome that the invitation to accept the grace of God was issued to all people everywhere. No matter what your cultural background, your race, your nationality, or your gender may be, the first step of your lifelong spiritual journey is to accept God's invitation to receive His grace in Christ.

2. HUMBLE YOURSELVES. Although Paul had been summoned to be an apostle, he humbly called himself a *servant of Jesus Christ* (1:1). For a Roman citizen like Paul to consider himself a slave was beyond reason. But the apostle gladly and humbly accepted his position as a slave of Christ. Paul's goal was to be completely dependent on and obedient to his Lord. As Christians, our goal—and our attitude—should be the same. Through our willingness to serve and obey Jesus Christ, we are enabled to be both useful and usable servants of our kind and loving Savior.

3. ENCOURAGE THE FAITH OF OTHERS. Paul's wish to journey to Rome centered on his desire to encourage the Roman believers in their faith. May we also look for ways to encourage other believers in their faith.

4. ALLOW THE FAITH OF OTHERS TO ENCOURAGE YOU. Paul had received news about the vibrant faith of the Christians in Rome. Although he had never met many of the believers there, Paul's own faith was encouraged by their devotion to Christ. The commitment of other believers to the Lord should not prompt us to become jealous or feel insecure. Rather, the faith of other believers should strengthen us spiritually.

5. WALK BY FAITH. Let us make walking by faith a life habit. In order for this to be true, we must continually practice walking by faith at times when we'd rather indulge our fears and doubts. But don't do it! May we practice living out our faith in the midst of disappointments, trials, temptations, and even sorrows, remembering that *"the one who is righteous will live by faith"* (1:17).

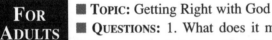

FOR ADULTS

■ **TOPIC:** Getting Right with God

■ **QUESTIONS:** 1. What does it mean to be a servant of Christ? 2. How was Paul *set apart for the gospel* (Rom. 1:1)? 3. What constitutes being a saint? 4. If the news of your faith were to be reported in your community's newspaper, how do you think the headline would read? 5. In what ways do some Christians today act as though they are ashamed of the Gospel?

■ ILLUSTRATIONS:

If Faith Had Been Encouraged. Carl Jung, the famous analytical psychologist of the twentieth century, wrote the following in his book *Memories, Dreams, Reflections:*

> Several times my father had a serious talk with me. I was free to study anything I liked, he said, but if I wanted his advice I should keep away from theology. "Be anything you like except a theologian," he said emphatically. By this time there was a tacit agreement between us that certain things could be said or done without comment. He had never taken me to task for cutting church as often as possible and for not going to Communion any more. The farther away I was from church, the better I felt. The only things I missed were the organ and the choral music, but certainly not the "religious community." The phrase meant nothing to me at all, for the habitual churchgoers struck me as being far less of a community than the "worldly" folk. The latter may have been less virtuous, but on the other hand they were much nicer people, with natural emotions, more sociable and cheerful, warmer-hearted and more sincere. I was able to reassure my father than I had not the slightest desire to be a theologian.

What might Carl Jung's assessment of the church have been had the believers encouraged each other in the faith, if they had truly lived by faith?

Passing the Faith Along. My grandmother—I called her "Mammaw"—was one of the best horticulturists that I've ever known. Her springtime and summertime flowers down in Center Point Hollow were the subject of many photographs, not to mention the number of people who slowed down or stopped just to look. She didn't know the names of all her flowers because she often made Pappaw stop along the roadside for her to dig up some wildflower that she thought was especially pretty.

And Mammaw didn't limit herself to flowers either. Her garden was always something special, too. Perhaps the most special item to ever come out of her garden was her purple-hulled green beans. These were beans that were purple until you cooked them, and then they turned green. After cooking them, you couldn't tell them from any other green beans. Mammaw gave me some seeds years ago, and we grew a fair crop at the parsonage. This year my father is growing several rows, as well as having a few rows to produce more seed.

I recently learned that those variety of beans are called Royalty Purple Pod beans, and they were developed by Elwyn M. Meader. Meader introduced more than 60 varieties—from beets to peaches to kiwi fruit to chrysanthemums. At least half of his introductions came after he "retired" from a distinguished 18-year career as a plant breeder at the University of New Hampshire. He could have gotten rich from royalties on all his releases, but instead he gave them away "as payment for his space on the planet." As a man of faith, Meader's dedication and unselfishness in sharing germplasm ideas with colleagues throughout the world may have been an even greater contribution than his varieties.

Mammaw liked to pass plants and seeds on to others, too. Several friends have recently mentioned to me, again, how Mammaw was responsible for many of the flowers in their yards and the plants in their gardens. Others throughout Stewart County still have some of Mammaw's flowers and plants growing in their gardens. Like Mammaw, Elwyn Meader passed on his ideas and his plants. By the way, Meader credited his development of the Royalty Purple Pod bean to his wife's suggestion that it would be easier to pick beans if the pod color differed from the vine color. Now you know the rest of the story!

Mammaw and Elwyn Meader were both a little like the apostle Paul. They, too, wanted to pass along their Christian faith. In that Paul desired to build up the faith of the believers living in Rome, he was "passing the faith along." May we seek to do the same!

■ **TOPIC:** Power Source

■ **QUESTIONS:** 1. Why would Paul want to consider himself a slave of Jesus Christ? 2. In what way do you think God summoned Paul to be an apostle? 3. How did Paul go about describing Jesus Christ to the believers living in Rome? 4. Do you feel like a "saint"? Explain your answer. 5. What do you think it means to *live by faith* (Rom. 1:17)?

■ **ILLUSTRATIONS:**

Live by Faith? In June of 1998, a constitutional amendment that would allow prayer in public places was proposed before the Congress of the United States. *Time* magazine reported, briefly, that the number of congressional members who voted in favor of this amendment was 224. *Time* also noted that the number of congressional members who were present on the House floor for opening prayer on the three days preceding the vote was 18, 8, and 18, respectively!

From Basketballs to Saints. For just a moment or two, think of yourself as a basketball. Think about your purpose, about what it is that you're supposed to do. Think about how you can best serve your purpose, about how big you should be and how round you should be. Also think about what your outlook on life should be.

If you are a basketball, your whole purpose for existence is first, to represent the sport that bears your name, and second, to bring enjoyment to those you were created to serve. On the one hand, if you're overinflated, you are going to bounce too high and shots will ricochet like bullets off the rim of the basket. On the other hand, if you are underinflated, you won't bounce. Either way, the game is going to suffer and the participants' enjoyment will be hampered. Also, either way, the purpose for your existence will be diminished.

So if you're a basketball, the right amount of air pressure makes all the difference in successfully achieving your purpose. If you had the ability to do so, you would do everything possible to keep yourself properly inflated. You would avoid having too much or too little air.

Well, the same is true for us as Christians. If we undervalue ourselves, we are less fit to encourage the faith of others; and if we overvalue ourselves, we are less fit to allow the faith of others to encourage us.

Okay, now you can stop thinking of yourself as a basketball. Now think of yourself as being a saint. Now think about your purpose, about what it is that you're supposed to do. Think about how you can best achieve your purpose. Finally, think about how being a saint should affect your morals, your lifestyle, your outlook on life.

GIFT OF GRACE

BACKGROUND SCRIPTURE: Romans 3
DEVOTIONAL READING: Psalm 33:13-22

KEY VERSES: Since all have sinned and fall short of the glory of God; they are now justified by his grace as a gift, through the redemption that is in Christ Jesus. Romans 3:23-24.

KING JAMES VERSION

ROMANS 3:1 What advantage then hath the Jew? or what profit is there of circumcision?

2 Much every way: chiefly, because that unto them were committed the oracles of God.

3 For what if some did not believe? shall their unbelief make the faith of God without effect?

4 God forbid: yea, let God be true, but every man a liar; as it is written, That thou mightest be justified in thy sayings, and mightest overcome when thou art judged. . . .

19 Now we know that what things soever the law saith, it saith to them who are under the law: that every mouth may be stopped, and all the world may become guilty before God.

20 Therefore by the deeds of the law there shall no flesh be justified in his sight: for by the law is the knowledge of sin.

21 But now the righteousness of God without the law is manifested, being witnessed by the law and the prophets;

22 Even the righteousness of God which is by faith of Jesus Christ unto all and upon all them that believe: for there is no difference:

23 For all have sinned, and come short of the glory of God;

24 Being justified freely by his grace through the redemption that is in Christ Jesus:

25 Whom God hath set forth to be a propitiation through faith in his blood, to declare his righteousness for the remission of sins that are past, through the forbearance of God;

26 To declare, I say, at this time his righteousness: that he might be just, and the justifier of him which believeth in Jesus.

27 Where is boasting then? It is excluded. By what law? of works? Nay: but by the law of faith.

28 Therefore we conclude that a man is justified by faith without the deeds of the law.

29 Is he the God of the Jews only? is he not also of the Gentiles? Yes, of the Gentiles also:

30 Seeing it is one God, which shall justify the circumcision by faith, and uncircumcision through faith.

31 Do we then make void the law through faith? God forbid: yea, we establish the law.

NEW REVISED STANDARD VERSION

ROMANS 3:1 Then what advantage has the Jew? Or what is the value of circumcision? 2 Much, in every way. For in the first place the Jews were entrusted with the oracles of God. 3 What if some were unfaithful? Will their faithlessness nullify the faithfulness of God? 4 By no means! Although everyone is a liar, let God be proved true, as it is written, "So that you may be justified in your words, and prevail in your judging." . . .

19 Now we know that whatever the law says, it speaks to those who are under the law, so that every mouth may be silenced, and the whole world may be held accountable to God. 20 For "no human being will be justified in his sight" by deeds prescribed by the law, for through the law comes the knowledge of sin.

21 But now, apart from law, the righteousness of God has been disclosed, and is attested by the law and the prophets, 22 the righteousness of God through faith in Jesus Christ for all who believe. For there is no distinction, 23 since all have sinned and fall short of the glory of God; 24 they are now justified by his grace as a gift, through the redemption that is in Christ Jesus, 25 whom God put forward as a sacrifice of atonement by his blood, effective through faith. He did this to show his righteousness, because in his divine forbearance he had passed over the sins previously committed; 26 it was to prove at the present time that he himself is righteous and that he justifies the one who has faith in Jesus.

27 Then what becomes of boasting? It is excluded. By what law? By that of works? No, but by the law of faith. 28 For we hold that a person is justified by faith apart from works prescribed by the law. 29 Or is God the God of Jews only? Is he not the God of Gentiles also? Yes, of Gentiles also, 30 since God is one; and he will justify the circumcised on the ground of faith and the uncircumcised through that same faith. 31 Do we then overthrow the law by this faith? By no means! On the contrary, we uphold the law.

BACKGROUND

When Paul wrote his letter to the church at Rome, he was longing to make his way to the great city of the empire. His desire was not so much fueled by a wish to see the capital as it was by a longing to meet and visit with the Christians who lived there, about whom he had heard so much.

Paul wrote Romans toward the end of his third missionary journey. It was shortly before his visit to Jerusalem, in which he carried the gift from the Gentile congregations (Acts 24:17; Rom. 15:25). Internal indications suggest that at this time Paul was a resident of Corinth. These intimations include the reference to Phoebe, a member of the church at Cenchrea (the port of Corinth; Rom. 16:1-2), the references to Gaius as Paul's host (Rom. 16:23; 1 Cor. 1:14), and the reference to Erastus (Corinth's financial officer; Acts 19:22; Rom. 16:23; 2 Tim. 4:20).

Thus, the time of writing was probably during Paul's three months in Greece, which is described in Acts 20:2-3. It is known that Gallio (before whom Paul appeared; 18:12) was proconsul (normally a one-year appointment) in Achaia in A.D. 52. Paul was in Corinth during the period of A.D. 51–53 (vs. 18). He then sailed to Ephesus for a brief visit, and went to Caesarea and probably Jerusalem as well as Antioch (vs. 22). The earliest possible date for Paul's writing of Romans would be towards the end of A.D. 54. But a later date leaves more leeway for the apostle's many activities. Thus, the epistle is best dated in the early spring of A.D. 57.

Paul perceived his ministry to be at a turning point when he wrote Romans. He sensed that he had fulfilled his evangelistic ministry in the eastern Mediterranean (15:17-23) and that the time was ripe to move west and proclaim the Gospel in Spain (vs. 24). He hoped to visit the Roman Christians on the way, fulfilling his longtime ambition. He also may have wanted to receive their assistance as a supporting church. In light of these considerations, it was essential for Paul to present his apostolic credentials so that his fellow believers in Rome might recognize the authenticity of his ministry. He may also have thought it necessary to defend his ministry from the false insinuations of his opponents (3:8).

Paul seemed deeply concerned that the church become a united fellowship of believing Jews and Gentiles. This emphasis is clear from the importance the apostle attached to the Gentiles love-gift to the Jerusalem church. This concern also surfaces throughout Romans in a consistent argument made by Paul, namely, the unity of Jew and Gentile in sin through Adam and through grace in Christ (5:12-21). The saving righteousness of God, as revealed in the Gospel, is needed by both, for all have sinned (3:23). And justification can be received by both, for it comes through faith in Christ (vss. 24-26). The outworking of God's saving righteousness in history is the clue to His ultimate purposes for both Jew and Gentile. This saving righteousness is also to be expressed in the lives of both groups, whether personally, socially, or communally.

NOTES ON THE PRINTED TEXT

Paul's Letter to the Romans contains a detailed description of the sinfulness of humanity. This includes Gentiles as well as Jews. As Paul argued in chapter 2, this was just as true for the second group, even though they had been given the Mosaic law. The apostle anticipated that some people would raise objections to his message. Therefore in chapter 3, Paul talked about *the faithfulness of God* (3:3) and *the justice of God* (3:5) in keeping His promises to the Jews.

Paul taught that the Jews were condemned along with the Gentiles. The logical question, then, was *what advantage has the Jew?* (3:1). In other words, what advantage was there in being the chosen nation of God? *Or what is the value of circumcision?* Since circumcision was the sign of Israel's covenant relationship with God, what advantage was that relationship, especially if being a Jew would not lead to salvation? Paul stressed that the Jewish people had numerous advantages (9:4-5). The apostle noted that *the Jews were entrusted with the oracles of God* (3:2). This is a reference to the entire Old Testament, especially the laws and covenants the Lord Himself had given to the nation of Israel.

The fact remained, however, that some of the Jewish people had proven themselves to be *unfaithful* (3:3) to what God had revealed in the Old Testament. Because they broke their promises, did this mean that God would also break His promises to them? Did the Jews' *faithlessness nullify the faithfulness of God?* To this question Paul responded with an emphatic *By no means!* (3:4). God's faithfulness did not depend on the faithfulness of the Jews. Even if some Jews did not believe what God had revealed in His Word, He would remain true to what He had promised (Ps. 89:30-37).

In Romans 3:5-18, Paul argued that both Jews and Gentiles were under the power of sin. Regardless of the claims that people made about how upright they were, they stood condemned by the Mosaic law. As a result, *every mouth may be silenced, and the whole world may be held accountable to God* (3:19). From this we see that the overriding purpose of the law was to make all people aware of their condition of guilt. No one would be declared righteous by doing what God required in the law, for *through the law comes the knowledge of sin* (3:20).

In this context *the righteousness of God* (3:21) does not refer to one of the

Lord's attributes. Rather, Paul was talking about an act of God in which He declared believing sinners to be righteous. This standing of righteousness was *apart from law*, though the truth was previously revealed in *the law and the prophets* (namely, the Old Testament). Paul declared that a right standing with God came *through faith in Jesus Christ* (3:22).

After all the discouraging news about our sinfulness and God's condemnation, Paul gave the wonderful news. There is a way to be declared not guilty—by trusting in Jesus Christ to take away our sins. Trusting means putting our confidence in Christ to forgive our sins, to make us right with God, and to empower us to live the way He taught us.

God's solution to the problem of sin is available to all people regardless of their background or past behavior. Paul declared that there was no distinction between the Jew and the Gentile because *all have sinned and fall short of the glory of God* (3:23). Despite this, *they are now justified by his grace as a gift, through the redemption that is in Christ Jesus* (3:24). In other words, Jesus' sacrifice on the cross is the basis for the believers' right standing before God. Jesus endured the condemnation we should have received so that, when we put our faith in Him, we can be justified in God's sight.

Paul cited two reasons why the righteousness of God came through Jesus' death. The first was to *show* (3:25) that God Himself was upright in not immediately judging the sins people had committed prior to the Cross. The second reason is that God wanted to demonstrate that He is both righteous and at the same time entirely fair and just in declaring believing sinners to be righteous (3:26). Because of Jesus' *sacrifice of atonement* (3:25), God did not compromise His holiness when He forgave sinners who put their faith in His Son.

Most religions of the world require specific duties that must be performed to make a person acceptable to the divine. Christianity is unique in that no good deed that we do will make us right with God. Paul underscored this point in 3:27 when he declared that our acquittal before God is not based on our good deeds; rather, it comes about through our faith. People are not made right with God by obeying the law but through *faith* (3:28).

If God gave salvation through the law of Moses, then He would be *the God of Jews only* (3:29). But as Paul made clear, the Lord is also *the God of Gentiles*. Since there is only one God, there is only one way of being declared righteous in His sight. He makes people right with Himself only by faith, regardless of whether they are Jews or Gentiles (3:30).

Some might have wondered whether Paul's emphasis on faith meant that believers could forget about the law. *Do we then overthrow the law by this faith?* (3:31). Paul emphatically declared *By no means!* The apostle noted that, when we have faith in Christ, we truly fulfill the law. In other words, trusting in Jesus for salvation is the first step in seeing the requirements of the law becoming fulfilled in the lives of believers.

When we understand the way of salvation through faith, we understand the Jewish religion better. We know why Abraham was chosen, why the law was given, and why God worked patiently with Israel for centuries. Faith does not *overthrow the law* (3:31). Rather, faith makes God's dealings with the Jewish people understandable. Romans 4 is where Paul expanded on this theme, explaining that even in Old Testament times justification was by faith.

SUGGESTIONS TO TEACHERS

In Romans 3, Paul contended that everyone stood guilty before God. The apostle dismantled the common excuses of people who refused to admit they were sinners. Paul then declared that every person must humbly receive by faith God's wonderful gift of salvation.

1. WHERE WE WENT WRONG. This Scripture passage shows us that one of the purposes of the Old Testament law was to reveal to us where we went wrong. The law discloses to us that we have failed to live up to God's precepts, that all of us *fall short of the glory of God* (3:23). This truth helps us understand that we must look elsewhere for our salvation, for no amount of good works or deeds can take away our sinfulness or the penalty for our sinfulness. Where shall we turn for salvation?

2. JUSTIFIED BY GRACE. We cannot turn to ourselves for salvation, nor can we turn to anything that we might do (that is, any pious deed we might perform). Not even obeying the Mosaic law would help, for through it *comes the knowledge of sin* (3:20). God, in His grace, declares sinners righteous when they trust in Christ for salvation. Salvation is a free gift that God can offer to all people because His Son died on the cross for them.

3. FREED THROUGH REDEMPTION. Though we were held captive by our own sinfulness, we have been ransomed; we have been redeemed; we have been delivered; we have been freed. We could not purchase our own freedom, but the perfect Son of God, Jesus Christ, could and did. When we put our faith in Him, He frees us from the penalty of our own sinfulness and the bondage of sin ruling and dictating our lives.

4. SALVATION BY FAITH. God's offer of salvation to us is free. The price for this gift has already been paid by someone else—Jesus Christ. All that is left for us to do is accept God's gracious offer. We do so by faith. We demonstrate our acceptance of God's grace by placing our wholehearted trust in Jesus and in His *sacrifice of atonement by his blood* (3:25).

FOR ADULTS

■ TOPIC: Admitting Need

■ QUESTIONS: 1. What did Paul declare that Jews and Gentiles have in common? 2. What did Paul mean when he said that *the whole world may be held accountable to God* (Rom. 3:19)? 3. In what ways does the law benefit us? 4. How does God's provision of justification and redemption show us His righteousness? 5. How would you describe *the law of faith* (3:27)?

■ ILLUSTRATIONS:

Christ Can Do It All! A couple of years ago, our family went on a vacation to Virginia Beach. It had been awhile since I had taken any days off, and I must confess to being at least a little tired and weary when we left. We drove across the Smoky Mountains of Tennessee and up and through the Blue Ridge of Virginia. It was a beautiful and refreshing drive.

While we were there, we stayed at the Ocean Key Resort, a beautiful and wonderful place just across Atlantic Boulevard from the beach and the Atlantic Ocean. I remember the place being so refreshing. We got to see a lot of my wife's family, and that was also refreshing. We visited the church in which my wife, Jill, grew up in Norfolk, saw a lot of wonderful people there, and that felt refreshing. My son, Nathaniel, and I got to go fishing on the Chesapeake Bay with Jill's uncle, John, and that, too, was immensely refreshing—not to mention so much incredible fun.

One night, we ate at Captain George's Seafood—a buffet about 15 yards long that had every kind of imaginable seafood served every kind of imaginable way. Wow! That was refreshing! We then went to the Virginia Science Marine Museum and actually got to pet the backs of stingrays. We also saw thousands of sea creatures and waterfowl. That, too, was incredibly refreshing. We rented bicycles and rode all up and down the boardwalk and through Virginia Beach, and that felt refreshing. We visited the beach every day we were there, and my daughter, Gracie, and I even watched the sunrise over the Atlantic one morning. It's one of those moments that will always live on as among my most special memories. Playing in that immense body of water and watching a brand-new day begin for the continent of North America was absolutely refreshing!

On the way back home, I expressed to Jill that I had been so refreshed by that vacation that I felt as though I could take on practically anything and be victorious. No task would bother me. I felt as if I could do it all! I was so refreshed, I felt like I could do anything. I was so refreshed that I thought I could write and work on several books at a time. I was so refreshed that I thought I could fulfill all my pastoral duties better than I had been doing. I was so refreshed that I thought I could counsel anybody at any time. I was so refreshed that I thought I could visit all the sick and the lonely and the needy in our area.

I was so refreshed that I thought I could study and preach and teach and pray and advise and plan and administrate and call and help and serve, and still have both the hours and the energy left to give to my family. I was so refreshed that I thought I could start back up on a running and weight-lifting program. I was so refreshed that I thought I could relearn Spanish in my spare time and maybe pick up Italian and renew my learning of sign language and Greek and Hebrew. I felt like Superman standing muscle-bound atop the tallest building in Stewart County, the "S" emblazoned on my chest and my cape gloriously flapping in the wind.

Ever since I was a child, I've had delusions of grandeur. My favorite cartoon as a little boy was Mighty Mouse! And to this day—to Nathaniel and Gracie's great humor and Jill's chagrin—I can be known to bound through the house in my boxer shorts, bursting into one of the kids's rooms, singing "Here I come to save the day!"

But as it should be, most delusions are short-lived—especially delusions built around that single-lettered word "I." "I" is not a good foundation upon which to build much of anything. *I* soon learned that *I* was not so refreshed as to be able to do what *I* dreamed of doing. Before long, I had confessed to Jill that I had previously felt like Superman. Only after a few days I felt like I'd had the "S" ripped off my chest—along with some chest hairs—which basically left me limply standing in a plain blue leotard with a red cape.

The thing that gets me into the most trouble—and maybe this gets you into trouble, too—is when I become extremely well-intentioned with my own plans and my own visions and my own tasks and my own duties and my own dreams and my own goals that I rely on my own strength to see that they all get accomplished. We can't do that with God's grace. The source of our salvation is not within ourselves. The source of our salvation is in Jesus Christ. We must accept that gift of grace by putting our faith in Him. He can do it all! We can't.

The Effects of Our Sinfulness. The story behind the painting of the Last Supper is interesting and instructive. Two incidents connected with this painting afford a most convincing lesson on the effects of thought in the life of a boy or girl, or of a man or woman.

The Last Supper was painted by Leonardo da Vinci (1452–1519), a noted Italian painter, sculptor, architect, and engineer. The time engaged for its completion was seven years. The figures representing the 12 apostles and Christ Himself were painted from living persons. The live model for the painting of the figure of Jesus was chosen first. When it was decided that da Vinci would paint this great picture, hundreds and hundreds of young men were carefully viewed in an endeavor to find a face and personality completely devoid of dissipation caused by sin. Finally, after weeks of laborious searching, a young man, 19 years of age, was selected as the model for the portrayal of Christ. For six months da Vinci worked on the production of this leading character of the famous painting.

During the next six years, da Vinci continued his labors on his sublime work of art. One by one, fitting persons were chosen to represent each of the apostles, space being left for the painting of the figure representing Judas Iscariot as the final task of this masterpiece. This was the apostle, you remember, who betrayed his Lord for 30 pieces of silver.

For weeks da Vinci searched for a man with a hard, callous face, with a countenance marked by scars of avarice and deceit, who would betray his best friend. After many discouraging experiences in searching for the type of person required to represent Judas, word came to da Vinci that a man whose appearance fully met the requirements had been found. He was in a dungeon in Rome, sentenced to die for a life of crime and murder. Da Vinci made the trip to Rome at once, and this man was brought out from his imprisonment in the dungeon and led out into the light of the sun. There da Vinci saw before him a dark, swarthy man, his long shaggy and unkempt hair sprawled over his face—a face which portrayed a character of viciousness and complete ruin. At last the painter had found the person he wanted to represent the character of Judas in his painting.

By special permission from the king, this prisoner was carried to Milan where the fresco was being painted. For six months the prisoner sat before da Vinci, at appointed hours each day, as the gifted artist diligently continued his task of transmitting to his painting this base character in the picture representing the traitor and betrayer of the Savior.

As da Vinci finished his last stroke, he turned to the guards and said, "I have finished, you may take the prisoner away." He suddenly broke loose from their control and rushed up to da Vinci, crying as he did so, "Oh, da Vinci, look at me! Do you not know who I am?" Da Vinci, with the trained eyes of a great character student, carefully scrutinized the man upon whose face he had constantly gazed for six months and replied, "No, I have never seen you in my life until you were brought before me out of the dungeon in Rome." Then lifting his eyes toward heaven, the prisoner said, "O God, have I fallen so low?" Then turning his face to the painter he cried, "Leonardo da Vinci, look at me again, for I am the same man you painted just seven years ago as the figure of Christ!"

Here was a young man whose character was so pure and unspoiled by the sins of the world, that he represented a countenance and innocence and beauty fit to be used for the painting of a representation of Christ. But during the following seven years, after a life of sin and crime, the once radiant man was changed into a person whose countenance and form had become horribly scarred by sin.

TOPIC: Equal Justice for All

QUESTIONS: 1. What advantages did Paul say there were to being a Jew? 2. How had God proven Himself to be just in His treatment of the Jews? 3. Why would God forgive those who had rebelled against Him? 4. What role does the law serve in bringing us to Christ? 5. Why do you think anyone would spurn God's offer of salvation through faith in Christ?

ILLUSTRATIONS:

Playing God. More and more computer-game users are playing God. While earlier computer games involved destroying things, new games allow users to be "the creator," designing their own universe. For instance, one game pictures the computer user as the "omnipotent hand" that can create people and "seduce worshipers by any means necessary, raining manna from heaven or unleashing lightning bolts to instill fear," the online magazine *Feed* reported. Other games allow players to merge their "god" with the deities of other players, creating a "polytheistic" world. What a far cry this is from the true God revealed in Scripture (Rom. 3:29-30).

Saved by Grace. A Japanese gangster who became a Christian is converting other criminals. Hiroyuki Suzuki takes the Christian message to railway stations and public squares, using his notoriety to grab attention, according to the *Times of London*. He has numerous tattoos and several amputated fingers attesting to his previous allegiance to the *yakuza* organized crime organization.

Suzuki, 44, is the founder of Mission Barabbas, a group of reformed gangsters who have embraced evangelical Christianity. His ministry includes fervent preaching and singing. The *yakuza,* in contrast, includes 80,000 gang members involved in extortion rackets, prostitution, and gambling, and bloody shoot-outs on the streets are frequent.

Christianity is considered a mysterious sect by most Japanese, and only 1.5 percent of the population is Christian. But Suzuki's church in Tokyo overflows on Sundays and attracts converts by targeting his former colleagues and apprentice hoodlums. In four years, he has baptized seven members of crime syndicates and persuaded them to leave the underworld.

Suzuki dates his conversion to a point when he was deep in debt, taking drugs, and plagued by illness. He put a gun to his temple but didn't have the nerve to pull the trigger. His estranged wife had been an ardent churchgoer and, out of desperation, he sought refuge in a church.

"I told the minister I was a gangster who had done time, deserted his wife and child, and was beyond redemption. But the minister talked to me about God's love and the meaning of the cross," Suzuki told the *Times*. He returned to his family and was accepted immediately. "That made me believe in the existence of unconditional love and the fact that people can start over again."

HEIRS OF THE PROMISE

BACKGROUND SCRIPTURE: Romans 4
DEVOTIONAL READING: Psalm 32:6-11

KEY VERSE: Abraham believed God, and it was reckoned to him as righteousness. Romans 4:3.

KING JAMES VERSION

ROMANS 4:2 For if Abraham were justified by works, he hath whereof to glory; but not before God.

3 For what saith the scripture? Abraham believed God, and it was counted unto him for righteousness. . . .

13 For the promise, that he should be the heir of the world, was not to Abraham, or to his seed, through the law, but through the righteousness of faith.

14 For if they which are of the law be heirs, faith is made void, and the promise made of none effect:

15 Because the law worketh wrath: for where no law is, there is no transgression.

16 Therefore it is of faith, that it might be by grace; to the end the promise might be sure to all the seed; not to that only which is of the law, but to that also which is of the faith of Abraham; who is the father of us all,

17 (As it is written, I have made thee a father of many nations,) before him whom he believed, even God, who quickeneth the dead, and calleth those things which be not as though they were.

18 Who against hope believed in hope, that he might become the father of many nations, according to that which was spoken, So shall thy seed be.

19 And being not weak in faith, he considered not his own body now dead, when he was about an hundred years old, neither yet the deadness of Sarah's womb:

20 He staggered not at the promise of God through unbelief; but was strong in faith, giving glory to God;

21 And being fully persuaded that, what he had promised, he was able also to perform.

22 And therefore it was imputed to him for righteousness.

23 Now it was not written for his sake alone, that it was imputed to him;

24 But for us also, to whom it shall be imputed, if we believe on him that raised up Jesus our Lord from the dead;

25 Who was delivered for our offences, and was raised again for our justification.

NEW REVISED STANDARD VERSION

ROMANS 4:2 For if Abraham was justified by works, he has something to boast about, but not before God. 3 For what does the scripture say? "Abraham believed God, and it was reckoned to him as righteousness." . . .

13 For the promise that he would inherit the world did not come to Abraham or to his descendants through the law but through the righteousness of faith. 14 If it is the adherents of the law who are to be the heirs, faith is null and the promise is void. 15 For the law brings wrath; but where there is no law, neither is there violation. 16 For this reason it depends on faith, in order that the promise may rest on grace and be guaranteed to all his descendants, not only to the adherents of the law but also to those who share the faith of Abraham (for he is the father of all of us, 17 as it is written, "I have made you the father of many nations")—in the presence of the God in whom he believed, who gives life to the dead and calls into existence the things that do not exist. 18 Hoping against hope, he believed that he would become "the father of many nations," according to what was said, "So numerous shall your descendants be." 19 He did not weaken in faith when he considered his own body, which was already as good as dead (for he was about a hundred years old), or when he considered the barrenness of Sarah's womb. 20 No distrust made him waver concerning the promise of God, but he grew strong in his faith as he gave glory to God, 21 being fully convinced that God was able to do what he had promised. 22 Therefore his faith "was reckoned to him as righteousness." 23 Now the words, "it was reckoned to him," were written not for his sake alone, 24 but for ours also. It will be reckoned to us who believe in him who raised Jesus our Lord from the dead, 25 who was handed over to death for our trespasses and was raised for our justification.

HOME BIBLE READINGS

BACKGROUND

The first three chapters of Romans have been devoted to proving that all people rightly fall under the condemnation of God: the Gentiles because they have rejected the revelation evident in creation (1:18-20), and the Jews because they have failed to live up to the moral standards revealed in the Mosaic law (2:17-29).

The bad news of universal condemnation (3:10-18) is overshadowed by the good news of a righteousness of God provided to all who believe in Jesus Christ (vss. 21-26). What people could not do by their own efforts, God has done in the person and work of His Son, Jesus Christ. His death atoned for our sin. And His death and resurrection provide the righteousness that people need to be acquitted in God's sight. Faith in Jesus allows people—apart from keeping the law—to be justified before God.

To the Jews the good news of salvation sounded like something entirely new. It appeared to be contrary to the Old Testament law. This objection to Paul's preaching of justification by faith is thoroughly set aside by the example of Abraham, who was regarded as the founder of the Jewish nation. If Abraham was justified by faith, then surely Paul's teaching was neither new nor untrustworthy.

Thus, Paul built his case for faith-righteousness on Abraham and David—two of the most respected figures in the Old Testament. Abraham would be particularly important as an example, for the Jews thought they had a privileged relationship with God by virtue of their physical relationship with Abraham as his descendants. Paul knew that if he could show that Abraham was justified not by works but by faith, then their false presumptions would fall like a house of cards.

NOTES ON THE PRINTED TEXT

In the Letter to the Romans, the age-old cry of people, *How then can a mortal be righteous before God?* (Job 25:4), receives an authoritative and definitive answer. Justification refers to God declaring the believing sinner righteous. It is grounded in the work of the Cross, and sinners receive the provision of righteousness by faith. Works contribute nothing to saving justification.

Paul cited the experience of Abraham and David to support his teaching concerning justification. Abraham was the ancestor of the Jews and the central person in their history. Did he become justified on the basis of obedience to some moral code (Rom. 4:1)? If this were the case, the patriarch would have had occasion to brag about his meritorious deeds, instead of God's grace (vs. 2).

Genesis 15:6 says that Abraham believed God's promise, and the Lord accepted that faith as the basis for declaring the patriarch to be justified in His sight. Abraham's faith was not the equivalent of righteousness. The patriarch received the gift of righteousness by faith, that is, by taking God at His Word (Rom. 4:3).

Even *the promise that he would inherit the world* (4:13) was received by Abraham on the basis of his faith, not through his keeping of the law. This promise was that Abraham would have many descendants and that the world would be blessed through him (Gen. 12:3; 22:18). Paul went on to explain that, if those who kept the law were the ones who would inherit God's promise, then faith in God would be pointless (Rom. 4:14).

Keeping the law in order to gain God's favor (and salvation) only produces spiritual arrogance. The purpose of the law was to reveal sin, not to bring justification. In arguing for this fact, Paul affirmed that where there is no law, there is no transgression (4:15). If people don't know right from wrong, then in one sense they cannot be held accountable for their actions. (But as Paul pointed out in 2:14-15, even those who do not have the written code of Moses have the law written upon their hearts. So all people intuitively know right from wrong, and therefore all are responsible and are without excuse.)

Because the actual purpose of the law *brings wrath* (4:15), salvation *depends on faith* (4:16). It is a free gift of God's grace. And it is offered to all of Abraham's descendants—both to those who like Abraham were *adherents of the law* and also to those who *share the faith of Abraham*. The true descendants of Abraham are those who have faith in Christ, whether they be Jews or Gentiles, and the benefits are the same for each.

Paul then initiated a description of the way Abraham exercised his faith. He had faith in a God *who gives life to the dead and calls into existence the things that do not exist* (4:17). This is a reference to Abraham's belief that God could give him a child even though his and Sarah's bodies were *as good as dead* (4:19) as far as childbearing ability was concerned. Thus Abraham was *hoping against hope* (4:18), believing God's promise that he would become *"the father of many nations."* And the patriarch's faith did not *waver concerning the promise of God, but he grew strong in his faith as he gave glory to God* (4:20). It was Abraham's faith that caused him to be absolutely convinced that God was able to do anything that He promised—even to the point of giving an old man and an old woman a child (4:21). And because of Abraham's great faith, it *"was reckoned to him as righteousness"* (4:22).

After offering this explanation of how Abraham exercised his faith, Paul wanted to make it clear that, just as Abraham's faith was accounted to him as righteousness, so it is true for those of us who come after Abraham (4:23-24). The words from Genesis 15:6—*And he believed the LORD; and the LORD reckoned it to him as righteousness*—were written not only for Abraham's benefit, said the apostle, but also for the benefit of all those *who believe in him who raised Jesus our Lord from the dead, who was handed over to death for our trespasses and was raised for our justification* (Rom. 4:24-25).

SUGGESTIONS TO TEACHERS

The historical facts in Abraham's case are not isolated and irrelevant data. They have consequences for believers today (Rom. 4:22-23). Whoever trusts in God's Word in the same way that the patriarch did will receive the same imputed righteousness.

1. FAITH: HOPE AGAINST HOPE. Faced with a desperate situation of being beyond childbearing years, Abraham nonetheless hoped against hope, believing God's promise because he believed in God, in who He is. We, too, will be hit with desperate and seemingly impossible situations. And when we are, we can hope against hope as well, putting our faith in the God who makes the impossible possible.

2. FAITH PLUS NOTHING. Abraham's faith was counted to him as righteousness. He didn't have righteousness on his own; God had to credit it to his account. It was because Abraham had faith that he pleased God, and the patriarch's faith long preceded any knowledge of the Mosaic law. Plainly put, Abraham was saved by trusting in God, not by good works. We, too, must realize that we are saved in the same way. Nothing that we can do or say or act out or work for can attain salvation. We are saved simply by putting our faith in Jesus Christ, trusting Him to forgive us and justify us.

3. FAITH LEADS TO COMMITMENT. When Abraham put his faith in God, he committed his whole life to Him. The patriarch went where the Lord sent him, did what the Lord required of him, and said what the Lord told him to say. In the same way, we must commit ourselves to the Savior in whom we have placed our trust. Our faith must move from merely believing in God to being totally committed to Him—all based on our trust in Jesus Christ, God's Son and our Savior.

■ TOPIC: Following an Example of Faith

■ QUESTIONS: 1. What was the basis for God declaring Abraham to be righteous? 2. In addition to Abraham and David, can you think of any other Old Testament characters who were justified by faith? 3. What was the basis of God's promise to Abraham that he would *inherit the world* (Rom. 4:13)? 4. What prevented Abraham from doubting God's promise? 5. How can the example of Abraham encourage us in our times of doubt? 6. How is it possible for our faith to grow in the face of seeming impossibilities?

◼ ILLUSTRATIONS:

Cost of Salvation. In his book *Be Right,* Warren Wiersbe tells how G. Campbell Morgan was trying to explain the concept of "free salvation" to a coal miner, but the man was unable to understand it. "I have to pay for it," he continually insisted. But with a flash of divine insight, Morgan asked, "How did you get down into the mine this morning?"

"Why, it was easy," the man replied. "I just got on the elevator and went down."

Then Morgan asked, "Wasn't that too easy? Didn't it cost you something?"

The man laughed. "No, it didn't cost me anything; but it must have cost the company plenty to install that elevator." Then the miner saw the truth: "It doesn't cost me anything to be saved, but it cost God the life of His Son."

Hoping against Hope. Michael Weisser, a spiritual leader in his local house of worship, is an example of a person who, like Abraham, hoped against hope. A 1992 issue of *Time* reported that Weisser had found himself the target of interest of the local Klan Grand Dragon, Larry Trapp. Trapp harassed, intimidated, and threatened Weisser with the ultimate purpose of driving him out of town.

When the late-night phone calls and the hate mail began to bombard Weisser, he knew where it was coming from, and he admitted that he was afraid. Yet his response was one that showed he was full of hope, not hate and fear. Weisser called his tormentor back and got his answering machine. After listening to its prerecorded anti-Semitic diatribe, he calmly offered to take Trapp, who is confined to a wheelchair, out to the grocery store. For weeks Weisser kept at it, leaving recorded messages of offered help for this Grand Dragon of the KKK.

Finally, Trapp called him back, complaining, "What do you want? You're harassing me." But Trapp soon called Weisser with another question; he confessed, "I want to get out of this and I don't know how." Weisser immediately responded, "I'll bring dinner and we'll talk." His wife brought along a silver ring as a peace offering. When they met face-to-face—the Klansman and the cantor— Larry Trapp burst into tears.

Eventually, Trapp even moved in with the Weissers, who cared for him as his health declined. What an example of faith in action!

Believing the Promise. In his book, *The Presence,* Bruce Larsen tells about a woman in one of his former congregations. Mrs. Chan was a tiny, energetic, and faith-filled woman. "Her daughter and son-in-law were on the verge of divorce. The problem, according to Mrs. Chan, was that her son-in-law was not a Christian. If he would just be converted, all would be well.

"She had been praying about this for some time and felt she had clear guidance. She planned to send the young man plane fare to Seattle. She would bring him to church, and he would give his life to Jesus. She was hoping he could then be baptized that very afternoon." Mrs. Chan spoke to one of her pastors about her plan. He tried to dissuade her, to help her see the foolishness of her plan. "God doesn't operate that way," the pastor told her. "You can't manipulate God or your son-in-law like that."

Mrs. Chan didn't listen to the pastor's advice. She sent the young man plane fare, and he worshiped with her the next Sunday. The invitation was issued at the end of the service for those who wanted to start the life of faith for the first time. The young man came forward and trusted in Jesus Christ for salvation. "He came, Reverend Larsen," Mrs. Chan said, beaming that Sunday, "and when you gave the invitation, he gave his life to God." Mrs. Chan was not at all surprised at the outcome.

"God spoke," Larsen writes. "Mrs. Chan acted, and her daughter's husband came into the kingdom."

■ **TOPIC:** A Treasure from the Past

■ **QUESTIONS:** 1. Why do keeping the law and doing good works fail to earn us salvation? 2. Why is our faith in God counted toward us as righteousness? 3. In what ways did Abraham express his faith? 4. In what ways is Abraham a good example of how to express our faith in God? 5. Who are some Christians today that you respect as examples of faith?

■ **ILLUSTRATIONS:**

Trusting Faith. Spencer Morgan Rice, the minister of a church in Boston, once told about how early in his ministry he was serving a small congregation in the Los Angeles basin. The sexton of the church took as much interest in those who came to pray and meditate as he did the upkeep of the church. (A sexton is a church officer or employee who takes care of the congregational property and performs related duties.)

One man in particular attracted the attention of the sexton. This man dropped by the church briefly every day about noon. He would walk down the center aisle, stand at the chancel steps, and stare at the altar for a moment. Then he would leave.

After a few days, the sexton began to worry. The man was not well-dressed. He was not the cleanest. He did not always walk steady. The sexton mentioned his concern to Rice, who suggested the sexton simply ask the man if there was anything the church could do for him.

When the sexton asked, the man said, "No, thank you. I just come in every day and stand before the altar and say, 'Jesus, it's Jim.' It is not much of a prayer, I know, but I think God knows what I mean."

Months slipped by. The sexton never again mentioned their daily visitor. Then, one morning Rice got a call from the director of a home for aged men run by a local parish. The staff ministered to men broken by life. Rice tells the rest of the story this way:

> The director told me that Jim had been admitted, and I said I would be out to see him. She met me at the door and said, "You know, Pastor Rice, he has been here for two months. He went into the most cantankerous ward we have. Every staff member here has tried their best to bring some sense of joy and calm to that ward. We failed. Jim went into that ward and the place is transformed. It is a new place. I went to him two days ago and I asked, 'Jim, how is it that you have been able to bring such joy and such a sense of peace to these men?' And he said, 'Oh, it is because of my visitor.'" And the director said, "I know he didn't have any visitors. That chair hadn't been occupied the 60 days he has been here. So I said, 'Jim, what visitors? I've never seen a visitor.' And he said, 'Ma'am, every day at 12:00, He comes and stands at the foot of my bed and says that He's Jesus!'"

Faith for the Next Generation? There's a quote in Tom Carter's book, *13 Crucial Questions Jesus Wants to Ask You,* that says, "To our forefathers, faith was an experience. To our fathers, faith was an inheritance. To us, faith is a convenience. To our children, faith is a nuisance."

Faith at Work. The renowned talk show host Larry King reported that during one of his hospital stays, he received many letters and gifts. However, the one that touched him the most was a Bible and a note sent by "Pistol" Pete Maravich, the former Louisiana State University and National Basketball Association star.

The note read: "Dear Larry, I'm so glad to hear that everything went well with your surgery. I want you to know that God was watching over you every minute, and even though I know you may question that, I also know that one day it will become evident to you . . . because He lives."

The following week, Pete Maravich died of a heart attack. Larry King says he will always remember Pete Maravich not just as a Christian, but as a caring Christian. What a wonderful legacy! What a wonderful torch to pass on!

CHRIST DIED FOR US

BACKGROUND SCRIPTURE: Romans 5
DEVOTIONAL READING: Psalm 32:1-5

KEY VERSE: Since we are justified by faith, we have peace with God through our Lord Jesus Christ. Romans 5:1.

KING JAMES VERSION

ROMANS 5:1 Therefore being justified by faith, we have peace with God through our Lord Jesus Christ:

2 By whom also we have access by faith into this grace wherein we stand, and rejoice in hope of the glory of God.

3 And not only so, but we glory in tribulations also: knowing that tribulation worketh patience;

4 And patience, experience; and experience, hope:

5 And hope maketh not ashamed; because the love of God is shed abroad in our hearts by the Holy Ghost which is given unto us.

6 For when we were yet without strength, in due time Christ died for the ungodly.

7 For scarcely for a righteous man will one die: yet peradventure for a good man some would even dare to die.

8 But God commendeth his love toward us, in that, while we were yet sinners, Christ died for us.

9 Much more then, being now justified by his blood, we shall be saved from wrath through him.

10 For if, when we were enemies, we were reconciled to God by the death of his Son, much more, being reconciled, we shall be saved by his life.

11 And not only so, but we also joy in God through our Lord Jesus Christ, by whom we have now received the atonement. . . .

18 Therefore as by the offence of one judgment came upon all men to condemnation; even so by the righteousness of one the free gift came upon all men unto justification of life.

19 For as by one man's disobedience many were made sinners, so by the obedience of one shall many be made righteous.

20 Moreover the law entered, that the offence might abound. But where sin abounded, grace did much more abound:

21 That as sin hath reigned unto death, even so might grace reign through righteousness unto eternal life by Jesus Christ our Lord.

NEW REVISED STANDARD VERSION

ROMANS 5:1 Therefore, since we are justified by faith, we have peace with God through our Lord Jesus Christ, 2 through whom we have obtained access to this grace in which we stand; and we boast in our hope of sharing the glory of God. 3 And not only that, but we also boast in our sufferings, knowing that suffering produces endurance, 4 and endurance produces character, and character produces hope, 5 and hope does not disappoint us, because God's love has been poured into our hearts through the Holy Spirit that has been given to us.

6 For while we were still weak, at the right time Christ died for the ungodly. 7 Indeed, rarely will anyone die for a righteous person—though perhaps for a good person someone might actually dare to die. 8 But God proves his love for us in that while we still were sinners Christ died for us. 9 Much more surely then, now that we have been justified by his blood, will we be saved through him from the wrath of God. 10 For if while we were enemies, we were reconciled to God through the death of his Son, much more surely, having been reconciled, will we be saved by his life. 11 But more than that, we even boast in God through our Lord Jesus Christ, through whom we have now received reconciliation. . . .

18 Therefore just as one man's trespass led to condemnation for all, so one man's act of righteousness leads to justification and life for all. 19 For just as by the one man's disobedience the many were made sinners, so by the one man's obedience the many will be made righteous. 20 But law came in, with the result that the trespass multiplied; but where sin increased, grace abounded all the more, 21 so that, just as sin exercised dominion in death, so grace might also exercise dominion through justification leading to eternal life through Jesus Christ our Lord.

Monday, March 25	Romans 6:1-14	*Alive to God in Christ*
Tuesday, March 26	Romans 6:15-23	*The Gift of Eternal Life through Christ*
Wednesday, March 27	Romans 7:4-13	*Sin Brings Death*
Thursday, March 28	Romans 7:14-25	*Thanks Be to God for Rescuing Me*
Friday, March 29	John 20:1-9	*The Stone Removed from the Tomb*
Saturday, March 30	John 20:10-18	*Mary Sees the Lord*
Sunday, March 31	John 20:19-23	*Jesus Stood among Them*

BACKGROUND

The first four chapters of Paul's letter to the Romans introduces and expounds upon the concept of justification by grace through faith. Then in chapter 5, the epistle turns a corner. In many respects, this chapter is a point of transition for the apostle's entire letter. Just as in the first four chapters Paul discussed how we are saved (the means by which God gives us salvation), in chapter 5 Paul began to write about how believers are supposed to live once they have come to salvation through faith in Christ. Thus the apostle turned his thoughts toward how to live out the spiritual life, what it means to be a Christian, and who we are supposed to be as those who have received God's gift of grace. Clearly, then, the new focus of Paul's letter to the Romans, beginning with chapter 5, is the tension between grace and good works, especially in regard to how a Spirit-filled Christian life should be lived out.

Although chapter 5 initiates a new section of this letter to the church in Rome, it continues to build on what the apostle had written in the previous four chapters. Indeed, the first four chapters provide a foundation for Paul's writing, beginning in chapter 5, about the ways in which endurance, character, and hope affect the lives of those living out the Christian faith.

In the first 11 verses of chapter 5, the apostle demonstrated how the spiritual life finds its foundation in and is lived out by the fact that we are justified by grace through our faith in Jesus Christ. Through the gracious gift of Jesus Christ, we are now able to be in a right relationship with God; and thus, our justification is the gift that provides the background for all other spiritual gifts in the Christian life.

NOTES ON THE PRINTED TEXT

Having described for his readers the concept of justification by grace through faith, Paul began in Romans 5 to describe the benefits of justification for those who believe in Christ. The apostle wanted his readers to not only acknowledge these benefits, but also to live them out in their daily lives. Paul impressed upon them that these benefits should affect every fiber of their being—physically, mentally, emotionally, and spiritually.

The first benefit that the apostle mentioned is that *we have peace with God through our Lord Jesus Christ* (5:1). Paul was not merely referring to peaceful feelings such as calmness or tranquility. Rather, he was talking about being reconciled with God. Because of Jesus' death and resurrection, God's wrath toward us because our sins has been taken away. We need no longer fear being eternally condemned because Jesus died on the cross for us and, through Jesus, we have been ushered into a peaceful relationship with God.

The second benefit the apostle referred to is that *we have obtained access to this grace in which we stand* (5:2). God has poured out to us His unmerited favor; He has granted to us something extremely good that we do not and cannot deserve. This grace is a pure gift, and it puts us in a place of highest privilege, for it has enabled us to be adopted as the sons and daughters of God.

The third benefit Paul revealed to his readers is *our hope of sharing in the glory of God* (5:2). Once again, the apostle noted what believers—whether Jews or Gentiles—should and should not boast about! Through Paul's explanation of why our justification is so desperately needed, the apostle had shown his readers that humanity had fallen short of the glorious destiny God had originally intended for it. Now, because of justification by grace through faith, redeemed humanity finds itself confidently expecting that glorious destiny, which involves, foremost, communion with God.

The fourth benefit Paul disclosed to his readers may not, on the surface, seem like a benefit at all. The apostle encouraged his readers to acknowledge and *boast in our sufferings* (5:3). Like the other benefits, these sufferings come as a result of our justification by grace through faith. Paul urged us to boast in them because they help us to realize that God is using the difficulties of life to strengthen us and build us up. When we, by God's help, face these sufferings, the trials will produce endurance*, and endurance produces character, and character produces hope* (5:4).

The fifth benefit the apostle unveiled to his readers may be considered the greatest one of all. Again, because of justification by grace through faith, *God's love has been poured into our hearts through the Holy Spirit that has been given to us* (5:5). It is because God has already shown His love toward us—through the sacrifice of His own Son—that we can be sure that He will grant us our hope of eternal life with Him. But the Holy Spirit goes beyond filling our lives with the love of God; He also enables us to live by His power.

Having told his readers about these benefits of justification by grace through faith, Paul next expounded upon the fifth benefit, giving more details about how God's love has been poured out to us. The apostle explained that *while we were still weak* (5:6)—when we were without strength to do anything good—*Christ died for the ungodly.* He took upon Himself the consequences of our own sin, and by doing so, made a way for us to be reconciled to God (5:7). It is in this way that *God proves his love for us in that while we still were sinners Christ died for us* (5:8).

The apostle reiterated that all of humanity was in a state of lostness, that it was in line to receive both the judgment and the wrath of God, that it was altogether helpless to save itself, and that we were enemies of God (5:10). But because of the sacrificial death of Jesus, *we have been justified by his blood, [and] will be saved through him from the wrath of God* (5:9). Thus, justification confirms both our salvation from God and our reconciliation with Him. Once more, the apostle returned to his theme about what believers—whether Jews or Gentiles—should and should not boast about, by saying *we even boast in God through our Lord Jesus Christ, through whom we have now received reconciliation* (5:11).

To show that Christ's saving work is extended to Jews and Gentiles alike—indeed, to all who would believe in Jesus—Paul compared the disobedience of Adam to the obedience of Christ. Whereas sinful humanity finds its demise in Adam, justified humanity finds its salvation through faith in Christ—*just as by the one man's disobedience the many were made sinners, so by the one man's obedience the many will be made righteous* (5:19). The sinful nature of humanity led to death; but those who are justified through faith in Christ receive a new life of righteousness—*so one man's act of righteousness leads to justification and life for all* (5:18).

In the midst of explaining how justification, salvation, and reconciliation come through faith in Christ, Paul further explained how and why the law came into play. The law *came in, with the result that the trespass multiplied* (5:20). The presence of the law led to an increase of sin, for the law showed clearly the wicked nature of sin. In other words, what was inherently wrong became formally and explicitly wrong once the law was revealed. Nevertheless, as people sinned more and more, God's wonderful grace became more abundant. On the one hand, sin ruled over all people and brought them to *death* (5:22). On the other hand, divine grace rules over the redeemed, giving them a right standing with God and *leading to eternal life through Jesus Christ our Lord.*

Suggestions to Teachers

Being justified by grace through faith in Christ brings us wonderful and eternal benefits. Although these benefits have been described in the previous section of this week's lesson, it would be altogether proper for us to rehearse them again. This time, however, let's apply them to how we live out our faith, especially now that we have been justified by grace.

1. PEACE WITH GOD. We have peace with God because of the reconciling work of Jesus. It is not an external peace, but rather an inner peace that comes from knowing that Jesus has made us right with God, that we are in a right relationship with Him, and that no matter what else may happen to us, our lives—and our very souls—are committed to His tender care.

2. ACCESS TO THIS GRACE. We have access to God's grace because of what Jesus did for us on the cross. He took our sin and guilt and shame upon Himself and died in our place. What a picture of divine grace! The whole human race is offered this unmerited favor from God, and those who willingly accept it—those who receive it by faith—will be eternally saved.

3. OUR HOPE. From the beginning, God has wanted us to be with Him in eternity. However, because of our sinful nature, and because He cannot allow sinfulness into His presence, we were forever separated from God. But because God loves us so much, He provided a way, through the sacrificial death of His Son, for us to be reconciled to Him. And because we are reconciled to Him, our hope of living out our destiny with Him for all eternity is assured.

4. OUR SUFFERINGS. All humanity lives through some degree of suffering. But as believers, we realize that our suffering has a purpose. God promises to use the problems and trials that we experience to help us grow in endurance, which in turn will help us to grow in character, which in turn will help us to grow in hope. Through all our experiences, God is watching over us and is ready to use those experiences to strengthen us spiritually.

5. THE HOLY SPIRIT WHO HAS BEEN GIVEN TO US. According to Romans 5:5, the Holy Spirit carries out at least a dual work in our lives. First, He convinces us of God's love for us, and the Spirit encourages us by letting us know that God's love is being *poured into our hearts*. Second, the Spirit enables and empowers us to live like people who have been justified by grace through faith. Just as we cannot live up to the standards of the law by ourselves, neither can we live as witnesses to God's love by ourselves. We must have the infilling help and power of the Spirit to truly live like Christians.

FOR ADULTS

■ TOPIC: Reaping the Benefits

■ QUESTIONS: 1. What does it mean to be justified by grace through faith? 2. In what ways does the believer have peace with God? 3. What is our role in obtaining *access to this grace in which we stand* (Rom. 5:2)? 4. What does it mean to share God's glory? 5. How would you explain to an unbeliever that you can rejoice in your sufferings?

■ ILLUSTRATIONS:

The Ladder of the Law. The *Life Application Study Bible* describes a person's attempt at keeping the law by using the analogy of a ladder that leads to God. As a sinner, separated from God, we see His law from below, as a ladder to be climbed to get to God. Perhaps we have repeatedly tried to climb it, only to fall to the ground every time we have advanced one or two rungs. Or perhaps the sheer height of the ladder seems so overwhelming that we have never even started up. In either case, what relief we should feel to see Jesus offering with open arms to lift us above the ladder of the law, to take us directly to God! Once Jesus lifts us into God's presence, we are free to obey—out of love, not necessity, and through God's power, not our own. We know that if we stumble, we will be caught and held in Christ's loving arms.

Message of Hope and Peace. Johann Sebastian Bach has struck a chord in Japan. The eighteenth-century German composer's music is conveying Christian teachings and concepts to a large and growing audience in the Asian nation, where less than one percent of the 127 million people belong to a Christian church, *First Things* magazine reported in 2000.

The nation's elite are drawn to the musical genius, and many have their first contact with Christianity through Bach's music. As many as 200 Bach choirs have started around the country in the past 10 years, and organist Masaaki Suzuki founded and conducts the Bach Collegium Japan.

Many Japanese have lost their allegiance to Buddhism and Shintoism and are attracted to the message of hope and peace they find in Bach's music. It is uncertain how many people actually have converted to Christianity.

Suffering with a Purpose. In Isaac Asimov's *Treasury of Humor*, the author confessed to having gambled only once in his life. It was, he says, "shortly after I had married; my wife left to visit her folks. I was at loose ends, and I was lured into a poker game with the boys.

"When it was all over, my conscience smote me, for I had been brought up by a puritanical father to eschew gambling in all its forms (and I had never rebelled). All I could do was confess.

"On my next trip home, I said with all the casualness I could manage, 'I played a game of poker with the boys, Papa. For money.'

"My father stared at me in astonishment and said, 'How did you make out?'

"I said, 'I lost fifteen cents.'

"And he said, 'Thank God. You might have won fifteen cents!'"

And so Asimov's father reminded him that his "sufferings" served a purpose—to discourage him from ever gambling again!

 FOR YOUTH

■ TOPIC: A Powerful Kind of Love

■ QUESTIONS: 1. What does it mean to be justified by grace through faith? 2. Why did Jesus have to die for us? 3. In what ways have you suffered in the past, and what good has God brought about because of that suffering? 4. How would you define the term "reconciliation"? 5. In what ways has the Spirit enabled you to live like a Christian?

■ ILLUSTRATIONS:

Saving Humanity. A few years ago, when the movie *Saving Private Ryan* came out, a debate arose among those who had fought in World War II. One group criticized the movie for failing to acknowledge the noble purpose of World War II. Another group praised the movie, which had as its plot a squadron of soldiers risking their lives and dying in order to pull one man out of combat to be sent home. The second group said that if the public would take Private Ryan as a symbol of the rest of us who were saved by the sacrifices of those who died in Normandy, then producer Steven Spielberg's "war is hell" message was not inconsistent with believing that this war saved humanity.

Just like the squadron of soldiers in the movie, Jesus died, shedding His own blood, to save people for all eternity. His sacrifice enables us to be justified by grace through faith.

Demonstration of Love. Writing in a 1992 issue of the *Wesleyan Christian Advocate,* Vance B. Mathis described how baseball legend Babe Ruth was playing one of his last full major league games. The Boston Braves were playing the Reds in Cincinnati. The old veteran wasn't the player he once had been. The ball looked awkward in his aging hands. He wasn't throwing well. In one inning, his misplays made most of the runs scored by Cincinnati possible. As Babe Ruth walked off the field after making a third out, head bent in embarrassment, a crescendo of boos followed him to the dugout.

A little boy in the stands couldn't tolerate it. He loved Babe Ruth, no matter what. With tears streaming down his face, the boy jumped over the railing and threw his arms around the knees of his hero. Babe Ruth picked up the boy, hugged him, set him back on the ground, and gently patted his head.

The rude booing ceased. A hush fell over the park. The crowd was touched by the child's demonstration of love and concern for the feelings of another human being. Such a story can remind us of God's love for us: *God proves his love for us in that while we still were sinners Christ died for us* (Rom. 5:8).

Live Such a Life. There's an old Indian proverb that says, "When you were born, you cried, and the whole world rejoiced. Live such a life that when you die, the whole world cries, and you rejoice."

New Life in Christ

BACKGROUND SCRIPTURE: John 20:1-18; Romans 6
DEVOTIONAL READING: Romans 6:9-13

KEY VERSE: We have been buried with him by baptism into death, so that, just as Christ was raised from the dead by the glory of the Father, so we too might walk in newness of life. Romans 6:4.

KING JAMES VERSION

JOHN 20:1 The first day of the week cometh Mary Magdalene early, when it was yet dark, unto the sepulchre, and seeth the stone taken away from the sepulchre. . . .

11 But Mary stood without at the sepulchre weeping: and as she wept, she stooped down, and looked into the sepulchre,

12 And seeth two angels in white sitting, the one at the head, and the other at the feet, where the body of Jesus had lain.

13 And they say unto her, Woman, why weepest thou? She saith unto them, Because they have taken away my Lord, and I know not where they have laid him.

14 And when she had thus said, she turned herself back, and saw Jesus standing, and knew not that it was Jesus.

15 Jesus saith unto her, Woman, why weepest thou? whom seekest thou? She, supposing him to be the gardener, saith unto him, Sir, if thou have borne him hence, tell me where thou hast laid him, and I will take him away.

16 Jesus saith unto her, Mary. She turned herself, and saith unto him, Rabboni; which is to say, Master.

17 Jesus saith unto her, Touch me not; for I am not yet ascended to my Father: but go to my brethren, and say unto them, I ascend unto my Father, and your Father; and to my God, and your God. . . .

ROMANS 6:3 Know ye not, that so many of us as were baptized into Jesus Christ were baptized into his death?

4 Therefore we are buried with him by baptism into death: that like as Christ was raised up from the dead by the glory of the Father, even so we also should walk in newness of life.

5 For if we have been planted together in the likeness of his death, we shall be also in the likeness of his resurrection:

6 Knowing this, that our old man is crucified with him, that the body of sin might be destroyed, that henceforth we should not serve sin.

7 For he that is dead is freed from sin.

8 Now if we be dead with Christ, we believe that we shall also live with him.

NEW REVISED STANDARD VERSION

JOHN 20:1 Early on the first day of the week, while it was still dark, Mary Magdalene came to the tomb and saw that the stone had been removed from the tomb. . . .

11 But Mary stood weeping outside the tomb. As she wept, she bent over to look into the tomb; 12 and she saw two angels in white, sitting where the body of Jesus had been lying, one at the head and the other at the feet.

13 They said to her, "Woman, why are you weeping?" She said to them, "They have taken away my Lord, and I do not know where they have laid him." 14 When she had said this, she turned around and saw Jesus standing there, but she did not know that it was Jesus. 15 Jesus said to her, "Woman, why are you weeping? Whom are you looking for?" Supposing him to be the gardener, she said to him, "Sir, if you have carried him away, tell me where you have laid him, and I will take him away."

16 Jesus said to her, "Mary!" She turned and said to him in Hebrew, "Rabbouni!" (which means Teacher). 17 Jesus said to her, "Do not hold on to me, because I have not yet ascended to the Father. But go to my brothers and say to them, 'I am ascending to my Father and your Father, to my God and your God.'"

ROMANS 6:3 Do you not know that all of us who have been baptized into Christ Jesus were baptized into his death? 4 Therefore we have been buried with him by baptism into death, so that, just as Christ was raised from the dead by the glory of the Father, so we too might walk in newness of life.

5 For if we have been united with him in a death like his, we will certainly be united with him in a resurrection like his. 6 We know that our old self was crucified with him so that the body of sin might be destroyed, and we might no longer be enslaved to sin. 7 For whoever has died is freed from sin. 8 But if we have died with Christ, we believe that we will also live with him.

5

BACKGROUND

Like Paul's letter to the Romans, the Gospel of John is a book about the ways Jesus has reconciled us to God. And key to our reconciliation is Jesus' resurrection. Like the other Gospel writers, John concluded his account of the life of Jesus with His resurrection. Yet John's presentation provides some unique glimpses into this event, especially in regard to the reactions of some of the people who were close to Jesus, including Mary of Magdala and Thomas. Indeed, John's Gospel shows us that Christ's resurrection was not only a decisive affirmation of Him as God and Savior, but also it left an enduring impression on the people who knew and loved Him most—those who put their faith in Him.

The biblical record of Jesus' resurrection is found not only in the four Gospels but also in the writings of Paul, especially in his first letter to the Corinthians. The apostle, writing about A.D. 55 (perhaps around the time when one of the three Synoptic Gospels was being written), declared his own knowledge of and faith in the resurrection of Jesus Christ: *For I handed on to you as of first importance what I in turn had received: that Christ died for our sins in accordance with the scriptures, and that he was buried, and that he was raised on the third day in accordance with the scriptures* (1 Cor. 15:3-4).

Paul went on to write that Jesus appeared to Peter and *then to the twelve. Then he appeared to more than five hundred brothers and sisters at one time* (15:5-6), as well as to James and *all the apostles* (15:7). In all, the Gospels and the Book of Acts record that Jesus made numerous appearances after His resurrection—solidifying and confirming not only the disciples' faith in Him but also in the fact of His resurrection.

For Paul, as for the other early Christians, the resurrection of Jesus is the foundation for our belief in Him as our Savior. Indeed, as Paul continued to write in 1 Corinthians 15, *Now if Christ is proclaimed as raised from the dead, how can some of you say there is no resurrection of the dead? If there is no resurrection of the dead, then Christ has not been raised; and if Christ has not been raised, then our proclamation has been in vain and your faith has been in vain. . . . If Christ has not been raised, your faith is futile and you are still in your sins. Then those also who have died in Christ have perished. If for this life only we have hoped in Christ, we are of all people most to be pitied* (15:12-14, 17-19).

Notes on the Printed Text

The Gospel of John begins its version of Jesus' resurrection by focusing on one woman, Mary of Magdala, not on the several other women who also had visited the empty tomb, as described by the other three Gospels. Perhaps John's focus on Mary was because she was the one who had informed him of the empty tomb, in addition to her being the first person to actually encounter the resurrected Christ.

Early on the first day of the week (John 20:1), once the Passover Sabbath had ended, *while it was still dark,* Mary Magdalene—likely accompanied by two other women (Mark 16:1)—came to the tomb to anoint Jesus' body with spices, fulfilling a Jewish custom (Luke 24:1). Mary's journey to the tomb was also in keeping with another Jewish custom, that of visiting the tomb of a loved one for three days after that person's death. (Some Jews superstitiously believed that the dead person's spirit hovered over the grave during that time and finally departed when the body became unrecognizable because of decay.) Since the Jewish law forbade people from traveling excessive distances on the Sabbath, Mary was making her way to the tomb as early as she legally and practically could.

Mary and the other women with her had been wondering how they would be able to move the massive stone away from the entrance to the tomb (Mark 16:3). Their concern vanished when they discovered that the rock had already been removed and that the body of Jesus was missing (Luke 24:2-3). Mary, undoubtedly shocked by this discovery, ran back to the place where the disciples were staying to inform them of what she had found (John 20:2).

After returning to the tomb with Peter and John (20:3-9), Mary remained nearby even after Peter and John had *returned to their homes* (20:10). Mary meanwhile wept in grief. Perhaps out of curiosity, *she bent over to look into the tomb* (20:11). *Two angels in white* (20:12) were in the tomb sitting at the head and foot of the place where the body of Jesus had been lying. The angels posed a question to Mary: *"Woman, why are you weeping?"* (20:13). Mary responded by explaining that some people had removed Jesus' body to an unknown location.

While Mary spoke, she sensed that another person was now nearby. At that point, *she turned around and saw Jesus standing there, but she did not know that it was Jesus* (20:14). Either there was something different about the risen Lord that prevented Mary from immediately recognizing Him or her eyes were blurry from her weeping; whichever is the case, Mary supposed *him to be the gardener* (20:15) even after Jesus had spoken to her. Perhaps Mary hoped that this "gardener," whom she assumed was responsible for the upkeep of the grounds, had been the one who had removed the body of her Lord. If so, Mary hoped she could find out where the body had been placed. Mary promised to go and get the body herself.

Mary's eyes were finally opened to Jesus' identity when He called her by name. *She turned and said to him in Hebrew, "Rabbouni!" (which means Teacher)*

(20:16). Jesus, speaking of His Father and His God as their Father and their God, instructed Mary to go to His disciples—*my brothers* (20:17)—to tell them about His resurrection. Now that His redemptive work was fully accomplished and the reconciliation between God and His people was completed, Jesus wanted the message of salvation to be proclaimed everywhere.

In Paul's Letter to the Romans, he affirmed the truth of Jesus' resurrection. The apostle also talked about the ramifications of that historical event for believers. Paul wrote that *all of us who have been baptized into Christ Jesus were baptized into his death* (Rom. 6:3). By the same token, *just as Christ was raised from the dead by the glory of the Father, so we too might walk in newness of life* (6:4). Thus the glory of the Father is shown by His raising Jesus from the dead and by transforming the lives of Christians! Paul then declared that, just as *we have been united with [Jesus] in a death like his* (6:5), so will we also *be united with him in a resurrection like his.*

For Paul, the death and resurrection of Christ included the transformation of our lives in the here and now. *Our old self* (6:6) refers to everything a person was before trusting in Christ for salvation, when he or she was still enslaved to sin (3:9), was ungodly (5:6), and was an enemy of God (5:10). In short, the old self is our state before being born again.

Romans 6:7-8 explains in summary fashion what Paul had already stated. Prior to trusting in Christ, the sinner was enslaved to the pull of sin. But the old self, having been crucified with Christ, is freed from this power. Sin no longer has any legal right to exercise its power in the life of the believer. The bondage has been broken. The controlling power is rendered inoperative.

SUGGESTIONS TO TEACHERS

There are three aspects of the death, burial, and resurrection of Jesus that Paul seized upon to teach his readers in Rome. Perhaps it would be beneficial if we, too, seized upon the apostle's teaching and retraced the steps in which we are justified by grace through faith.

1. BAPTISM INTO DEATH. Paul pointed out that Christians were baptized into Jesus' death (Rom. 6:3). We identify with Jesus in His death and burial so that we may also identify with Him in His resurrection, which is the key to our new life (6:4). In other words, believers—in our identification with Christ—have spiritually died to sin and have been raised to newness of life. Paul went on to say, *So you also must consider yourselves dead to sin and alive to God in Christ Jesus* (6:11). The transforming power of God's grace will help us to think of our old, sinful way of life as dead and buried; we can treat the sinful yearnings and temptations of the old nature as if they were dead.

2. WALK IN NEWNESS OF LIFE. The apostle explained that *just as Christ was raised from the dead by the glory of the Father, so we too might walk in newness of life* (6:4). Since we no longer live under sin's power, and are no longer slaves to our sinful nature, we can now choose to live for Christ *in newness of life*. Because we have been united by faith with Him in His resurrection life, we have an unbroken relationship with the Father Himself—a relationship that brings us love, joy, and peace. We are *a new creation: everything old has passed away; see, everything has become new!* (2 Cor. 5:17). We live a fresh, new life in Christ!

3. RESURRECTION LIKE HIS. Just as Christ was raised from the dead, so believers are raised to newness of life. The Greek word for "newness of life" (6:4) in this verse speaks of a life that has a fresh quality. Just as Jesus' resurrection body had a newness never seen before, so the new life of the believer is one of spiritual vitality. Since we have been united with Christ in His death, we will also be united with Him in His resurrection (6:5). Paul was not referring to our future bodily resurrection in this verse—such an idea is foreign to the context. Rather, Paul described our present identification with Christ. This is made clear in verse 6, where Paul argued that the believer's death and resurrection with Christ is to be understood as the believer's death to sin and newness of life toward God.

FOR ADULTS

■ **TOPIC:** Experiencing New Life

■ **QUESTIONS:** 1. What does Jesus' appearing first to Mary Magdalene tell you about His character? 2. In the midst of Mary Magdalene's grief and confusion, what finally breaks through to her? 3. Why do you think Jesus would refer to His apostles as *my brothers* (John 20:17)? 4. In what ways is baptism an appropriate symbol for dying with Christ? 5. How does Christ's death and resurrection transform our lives?

■ **ILLUSTRATIONS:**

Changed Lives. One of the best snapshots from the World War II era is a photograph of King George VI inspecting a bombed out section of London. In the picture, he stops to talk with a little boy who is sloppily dressed and has his cap on crooked. The king is bending on one knee and looking directly into the face of the child. And even though the picture profiles the king, you can see that he is gazing with compassion at the lad. Surely that child's life was changed. If he lived to be a hundred, he wouldn't forget that day.

The same is true of Jesus; once one truly looks into His eyes, it is difficult to turn away. "If you don't believe that," writes Brett Blair, "then ask a long parade of witnesses." Ask Mary Magdalene. She looked into Jesus' face and became a pure woman. Ask Matthew. He too looked into Jesus' face, and became an honest man. Ask Paul. When he encountered the Savior, he was changed. Paul's zeal for the law became a zeal for love. Ask Peter. Change, you ask? Oh yes, he changed. After he met Jesus, he had to wrestle with his prejudices against the Gentiles. All of these people—and all of us—represent broken men and women. Our need is to be healed, changed, repaired, and forgiven.

Born Again. In their book entitled *Born Again,* Charles Colson and Billy Graham describe what new birth in Christ really means. They note that it is literally to begin all over again, to be given a second birth.

The one who is born again doesn't all of a sudden get turned into a super-Christian. To be born again is to enter afresh into the process of spiritual growth. It is to wipe the slate clean. It is to cancel your old mortgage and start again. In other words, you don't have to be always what you have now become. Such an offer is too good to be true for many, and confusing for most; but for those who seek to be other than what they are now, who want to be more than the mere accumulation and sum total of their experiences, the invitation, "You must be born again," is an offer you cannot afford to refuse.

<table>
<tr><td>

FOR YOUTH

</td><td>

■ TOPIC: Power for Real Life

■ QUESTIONS: 1. What do you think motivated Mary Magdalene to go to the tomb so early—*while it was still dark* (John 20:1)?

</td></tr>
</table>

2. Why do you think Jesus appeared first to Mary Magdalene? 3. How do you think Mary Magdalene was affected when Jesus called her by name? 4. Why do you think some people find it difficult to believe in the resurrection of Jesus? 5. Why is it important for us to know *that our old self was crucified with him so that the body of sin might be destroyed* (Rom. 6:6)?

■ **ILLUSTRATIONS:**

No Future? While some youth have little hope for the future, apparently many more are optimistic. When polled by TIME/CNN and asked what happens after death, 61 percent of Americans felt that they would go to heaven. Joni Eareckson Tada, a quadriplegic since she was 17, trusts in full-body resurrection and the glorification of the body in heaven.

Believers around you highlight the biblical account and announcement. Jesus rose from the dead! Death has been conquered!

An Empty Egg and an Empty Tomb. Jeremy Forrester was born with a twisted body and a slow mind. At the age of 12 he was still in second grade, seemingly unable to learn. His teacher, Doris Miller, often became exasperated with him. He would squirm in his seat, drool, and make grunting noises. At other times, he spoke clearly and distinctly, as if a spot of light had penetrated the darkness of his brain. Most of the time, however, Jeremy just irritated his teacher.

One day Doris called Jeremy's parents and asked them to come in for a consultation. As the Forresters entered the empty classroom, Doris said to them, "Jeremy really belongs in a special school. It isn't fair to him to be with younger children who don't have learning problems. Why, there is a five-year gap between his age and that of the other students."

Mrs. Forrester cried softly into a tissue, while her husband spoke. "Miss Miller," he said, "there is no school of that kind nearby. It would be a terrible shock for Jeremy if we had to take him out of this school. We know he really likes it here."

Doris sat for a long time after they had left, staring at the snow outside the window. Its coldness seemed to seep into her soul. She wanted to sympathize with the Forresters. After all, their only child had a terminal illness. But it wasn't fair to keep him in her class. She had 18 other youngsters to teach, and Jeremy was a distraction. Furthermore, he would never learn to read and write. Why waste any more time trying? As she pondered the situation, guilt washed over her. *Here I am complaining when my problems are nothing compared to that poor family*, she thought. *Lord, please help me to be more patient with Jeremy.*

From that day on, Doris tried hard to ignore Jeremy's noises and his blank stares. Then one day, he limped to her desk, dragging his bad leg behind him. "I love you, Miss Miller," he exclaimed, loud enough for the whole class to hear. The other students snickered, and Doris's face turned red.

Doris stammered, "Wh-why that's very nice, Jeremy. N-now please take your seat."

Spring came, and the children talked excitedly about the coming of Easter. Doris told them the account of Jesus, and then to emphasize the idea of new life springing forth, she gave each of the children a large plastic egg. "Now," she said to them, "I want you to take this home and bring it back tomorrow with something inside that shows new life. Do you understand?"

"Yes, Miss Miller," the children responded enthusiastically—all except for Jeremy. He listened intently; his eyes never left her face. He did not even make his usual noises. Had he understood what she had said about Jesus' death and resurrection? Did he understand the assignment? Perhaps Doris should call his parents and explain the project to them.

That evening, Doris's kitchen sink stopped up. She called the landlord and waited an hour for him to come by and unclog it. After that, she still had to shop for groceries, iron a blouse, and prepare a vocabulary test for the next day. She completely forgot about phoning Jeremy's parents.

The next morning, 19 children came to school, laughing and talking as they placed their eggs in the large wicker basket on Miss Miller's desk. After they completed their math lesson, it was time to open the eggs.

In the first egg, Doris found a flower. "Oh yes, a flower is certainly a sign of new life," she said. "When plants peek through the ground, we know that spring is here." A small girl in the first row waved her arm. "That's my egg, Miss Miller," she called out. The next egg contained a plastic butterfly, which looked very real. Doris held it up. "We all know that a caterpillar changes and grows into a beautiful butterfly. Yes, that's new life, too." Little Judy smiled proudly and said, "Miss Miller, that one is mine." Next, Doris found a rock with moss on it. She explained that moss, too, showed life. Billy spoke up from the back of the classroom, "My daddy helped me," he beamed.

Then Doris opened the fourth egg. She gasped. The egg was empty. Surely it must be Jeremy's, she thought, and of course, he did not understand her instructions. If only she had not forgotten to phone his parents. Because she did not want to embarrass him, she quietly set the egg aside and reached for another.

Suddenly, Jeremy spoke up. "Miss Miller, aren't you going to talk about my egg?" Flustered, Doris replied, "But Jeremy, your egg is empty."

Jeremy looked into Doris's eyes and said softly, "Yes, but Jesus' tomb was empty, too." Time stopped. When Doris could speak again, she asked Jeremy, "Do you know why the tomb was empty?"

"Oh, yes," Jeremy said, "Jesus was killed and put in there. Then His Father raised Him up."

The recess bell rang. While the children excitedly ran out to the schoolyard, Doris cried. The cold inside her melted completely away.

Three months later, Jeremy died. Those who paid their respects at the funeral home were surprised to see 19 eggs on top of his casket—*all of them empty*!

God's Glory Revealed

Background Scripture: Romans 8; Luke 11:5-13
Devotional Reading: Romans 8:1-11

Key Verse: The sufferings of this present time are not worth comparing with the glory about to be revealed to us. Romans 8:18.

KING JAMES VERSION

ROMANS 8:18 For I reckon that the sufferings of this present time are not worthy to be compared with the glory which shall be revealed in us.

19 For the earnest expectation of the creature waiteth for the manifestation of the sons of God.

20 For the creature was made subject to vanity, not willingly, but by reason of him who hath subjected the same in hope,

21 Because the creature itself also shall be delivered from the bondage of corruption into the glorious liberty of the children of God.

22 For we know that the whole creation groaneth and travaileth in pain together until now.

23 And not only they, but ourselves also, which have the firstfruits of the Spirit, even we ourselves groan within ourselves, waiting for the adoption, to wit, the redemption of our body.

24 For we are saved by hope: but hope that is seen is not hope: for what a man seeth, why doth he yet hope for?

25 But if we hope for that we see not, then do we with patience wait for it.

26 Likewise the Spirit also helpeth our infirmities: for we know not what we should pray for as we ought: but the Spirit itself maketh intercession for us with groanings which cannot be uttered.

27 And he that searcheth the hearts knoweth what is the mind of the Spirit, because he maketh intercession for the saints according to the will of God. . . .

31 If God be for us, who can be against us?

32 He that spared not his own Son, but delivered him up for us all, how shall he not with him also freely give us all things?

33 Who shall lay any thing to the charge of God's elect? It is God that justifieth.

34 Who is he that condemneth? It is Christ that died, yea rather, that is risen again, who is even at the right hand of God, who also maketh intercession for us. . . .

38 For I am persuaded, that neither death, nor life, nor angels, nor principalities, nor powers, nor things present, nor things to come,

39 Nor height, nor depth, nor any other creature, shall be able to separate us from the love of God, which is in Christ Jesus our Lord.

NEW REVISED STANDARD VERSION

ROMANS 8:18 I consider that the sufferings of this present time are not worth comparing with the glory about to be revealed to us. 19 For the creation waits with eager longing for the revealing of the children of God; 20 for the creation was subjected to futility, not of its own will but by the will of the one who subjected it, in hope 21 that the creation itself will be set free from its bondage to decay and will obtain the freedom of the glory of the children of God. 22 We know that the whole creation has been groaning in labor pains until now; 23 and not only the creation, but we ourselves, who have the first fruits of the Spirit, groan inwardly while we wait for adoption, the redemption of our bodies. 24 For in hope we were saved. Now hope that is seen is not hope. For who hopes for what is seen? 25 But if we hope for what we do not see, we wait for it with patience.

26 Likewise the Spirit helps us in our weakness; for we do not know how to pray as we ought, but that very Spirit intercedes with sighs too deep for words. 27 And God, who searches the heart, knows what is the mind of the Spirit, because the Spirit intercedes for the saints according to the will of God. . . .

31 If God is for us, who is against us? 32 He who did not withhold his own Son, but gave him up for all of us, will he not with him also give us everything else?

33 Who will bring any charge against God's elect? It is God who justifies. 34 Who is to condemn? It is Christ Jesus, who died, yes, who was raised, who is at the right hand of God, who indeed intercedes for us. . . .

38 For I am convinced that neither death, nor life, nor angels, nor rulers, nor things present, nor things to come, nor powers, 39 nor height, nor depth, nor anything else in all creation, will be able to separate us from the love of God in Christ Jesus our Lord.

6

HOME BIBLE READINGS

BACKGROUND

After offering a description of what life propelled by a sinful nature looks like (Rom. 7:7-25), Paul began a description of what life propelled by the Spirit looks like (8:1-17). The guiding principle of life in the Spirit, according to Paul, is freedom. Overall, chapter 8 tells about freedom from sin and death. Indeed, in Warren Wiersbe's New Testament commentary on Romans entitled *Be Right*, he calls Romans 8 "the Christian's Declaration of Freedom."

Throughout the whole of the chapter, four spiritual freedoms are iterated. The first four verses talk about the Christian's freedom from judgment and guilt. The apostle wrote, *There is therefore now no condemnation for those who are in Christ Jesus* (8:1). Because the power of the Spirit enables believers to live victoriously, we are declared free from both guilt and the enslaving power of sin. Not even the law can condemn us, for we share the righteousness of God through faith in Christ.

Verses 5-17 talk about the Christian's freedom from being defeated by the carnal mindedness of our old sinful nature. The believer can live in victory over sin, for there is no obligation to the old sinful nature. Paul said, *we are debtors, not to the flesh, to live according to the flesh—for if you live according to the flesh, you will die; but if by the Spirit you put to death the deeds of the body, you will live* (8:12-13). Thus the Spirit enables us to overcome our sinful nature and to live for God.

In verses 18-30, the apostle explained that with the promise of heavenly victory will come the reality of earthly sufferings. Even in the midst of sure-to-come sufferings, Christians don't have to get discouraged and frustrated. As Paul explained earlier in this letter, when believers suffer, they suffer with a purpose (5:3-5). Beyond the present purpose of their sufferings, for Christians, *the sufferings of this present time are not worth comparing with the glory about to be revealed to us* (8:18).

Romans 8 seems to reach its full crescendo in verses 31-39. Here we have the declaration of freedom from fear. Those trusting in Christ need not fear death; we need not fear judgment; and we need not fear separation from God. Why? Because *we are more than conquerors through him who loved us* (8:37), and nothing *will be able to separate us from the love of God in Christ Jesus our Lord* (8:39).

Paul taught that those who are justified by grace through faith will face persecution, malignment, vilification, and sufferings (Rom. 8:18). Indeed, as the Christian life is lived out, it will involve hardship (as the apostle learned all too well from his missionary work). Yet Paul encouraged his readers in the midst of their painful misery by reminding them that what they were currently suffering would be nothing compared to the glory that God had in store for them later.

Even *the creation* (8:19)—including plants and animals and all of the earth—is presently being subjected to suffering *not of its own will but by the will of the one who subjected it* (8:20). Sin has caused all creation to fall from the perfect state in which God created it. Because the world is in bondage to death and decay, it cannot fulfill its intended purpose. Nevertheless, all hope is not lost, for the day is coming when creation will be liberated and transformed. Until then it yearningly waits—as if *groaning in labor pains* (8:22)—in eager anticipation of the time when it *will be set free from its bondage to decay and will obtain the freedom of the glory of the children of God* (8:21).

In the same way that the creation itself awaits being set free, so do God's children anticipate the day that they, too, will be set forever free. Like the creation, *we groan inwardly while we wait for adoption, the redemption of our bodies* (8:23). Paul pointed out that we have already been redeemed and that we already have the Holy Spirit within us. These blessings are but a foretaste of our future glory—the time when we will receive our full redemption at the resurrection. The creation itself will be delivered when the children of God are resurrected to enjoy their final salvation; at that time, the creation, too, will attain its full potential. This is the Christian's hope (8:24), and *if we hope for what we do not see, we wait for it with patience* (8:25).

We are not left to our own resources to face the sure-to-come sufferings or to develop our own patience as we anticipate this future glory. The Holy Spirit enables, empowers, and encourages us in each of these areas; *the Spirit helps us in our weakness* (8:26). Even if we don't know how to pray or what to pray for in our times of distress, the Spirit *intercedes with sighs too deep for words.* And God, *who searches the heart* (8:27) and who *knows what is the mind of the Spirit*, will act according to His own will in behalf of His saints.

With a powerful rhetorical question, Paul reminded his readers that *If God is for us, who is against us?* (8:31). Because God is on our side, no one can succeed against us. And God has shown us just how powerfully He loves us and just how much He is on our side in that *He who did not withhold his own Son, but gave him up for all of us* (8:32), will fulfill His plan to redeem His people.

Nothing can stand in God's way. No one can *bring any charge against God's elect* (8:33), for it is God Himself who has justified them by grace through faith. No one can condemn them, for *It is Christ Jesus, who died, yes, who was raised, who is at the right hand of God, who indeed intercedes for us* (8:34). **Neither can** *death, nor life, nor angels, nor rulers, nor things present, nor things to come, nor powers, nor height, nor depth, nor anything else in all creation* (8:38-39) stand in God's way or prevent Him from justifying and redeeming and saving His people. Indeed, absolutely nothing *will be able to separate us from the love of God in Christ Jesus our Lord.*

SUGGESTIONS TO TEACHERS

The reason believers will endure to the end is that they belong to God. He included them in His gracious purpose of salvation, and He is working according to His grace to bring them to the eternal glory. Romans 8 makes certain assurances to those who are justified by grace through faith. As Christian believers, we are:

1. ASSURED OF SUFFERING. Being the recipients of God's grace does not alleviate us from enduring persecution and hardships. Indeed, Paul assured his readers that sufferings would come. But he added that *the sufferings of this present time are not worth comparing with the glory about to be revealed to us* (8:18).

2. ASSURED OF GLORY. This glory is the complete fulfillment of God's plan for redeemed humanity since the inception of creation. Not only will all creation attain its fullest potential, but also all of redeemed humanity will attain its fullest potential when those who are in Christ are resurrected to enjoy their ultimate salvation.

3. ASSURED OF HELP IN OUR DISTRESS. We are never left alone in our distress. The Lord is always there *for those who love God, who are called according to his purpose* (8:28). The Spirit will bring us comfort when we need it, stamina when we need it, and direction when we need it. And even if we seem to have lost our way and don't know what to pray for, the Spirit is still with us, praying in our stead and praying in harmony with the will of God.

4. ASSURED OF VICTORY. We will be opposed. We will have spiritual battles. We will face temptations. Hardships, distresses, persecutions, famines, and perils will come. But because Christ has fought for us and won, we are already victorious in the midst of all opposition. We are already *more than conquerors through him who loved us* (8:37).

5. ASSURED OF SALVATION. Opposition will try to separate us from God, but God's hold on His own is so firm that no power of any kind has the ability to undo what Jesus has accomplished for us. What a promise we have!

6. ASSURED OF GOD'S LOVE. God has proved His eternal love for us by providing the means—through Christ—for us to be saved. God loves us so much that He yearns for us to be eternally in His presence, sharing His glory, in awe of Him, and praising Him. His love is so great and so powerful that nothing *will be able to separate us from the love of God in Christ Jesus our Lord* (8:39).

| **FOR ADULTS** | ■ **TOPIC:** Is There Hope? |

■ **QUESTIONS:** 1. What type of sufferings do you think Paul had in mind in Romans 8:18? 2. How would you describe the glory that God has in store for His children? 3. What are some of the ways that creation is in bondage to decay because of Adam's fall? 4. How has the Spirit interceded for you at a time when you didn't know how to pray or for what to pray? 5. What are some of the ways God has proven to you that He is *for* you?

■ **ILLUSTRATIONS:**

Blessed Assurance. Fanny Crosby wrote more than 8,000 hymns. The fact that she was blind apparently did nothing to diminish her productivity. She formulated an entire song in her mind and then dictated it to a friend or secretary.

In 1873, Phoebe Palmer Knapp composed a tuned and brought it to Crosby in Brooklyn. "Play it for me on the organ," Crosby asked. Knapp did so, and then asked Crosby, "What does this tune say?" She turned to see Crosby kneeling in prayer. So Knapp played it a second time—and then a third. Then the blind woman responded, "That says, 'Blessed assurance, Jesus is mine! O what a foretaste of glory divine!'"

In the vein of Romans 8, Crosby went on to add:

Heir of salvation, purchase of God,
Born of His Spirit, washed in His blood.

Perfect submission, perfect delight!
Visions of rapture now burst on my sight;
Angels descending bring from above
Echoes of mercy, whispers of love.

Perfect submission—all is at rest,
I in my Savior am happy and blest
Watching and waiting, looking above,
Filled with His goodness, lost in His love.

The refrain said:

This is my story, this is my song,
Praising my Savior all the day long;
This is my story, this is my song,
Praising my Savior all the day long.

Under the Gallows. Back in 1738, London's main prison was Newgate prison. Charles Wesley (later to be the great Christian hymn writer) frequently went there, preaching to those prisoners sentenced to death. On one occasion Charles was even locked in overnight in order to pray with and comfort prisoners.

In his *Journal*, Wesley tells about a poor man who was condemned to die. Wesley told him about "one who came down from heaven to save the lost and him in particular." Wesley led this man to faith in Christ. After Wesley served this man Communion, he accompanied the man to the gallows. The assurance of salvation was etched on the new convert's face. Because of his new friend's faith, Wesley penned, "That hour under the gallows was the most blessed hour of my life."

Accepted. As the Gospel was being presented to a woman, she explained she had tried her best to please God. Then she added, "But I'm afraid God will never accept me." The Christian talking with her said, "I agree with you. He never will." A look of astonishment came over the woman's face, for she had not expected such a response. The believer then explained, "No, He never will, but God has accepted His Son, and if you join yourself to Him through faith, you will find God's favor!"

Many people have been deceived into thinking they must somehow earn acceptance in the eyes of God. The Bible, however, tells us that there is nothing in us, nor in what we do, that can in any way merit God's love and favor (Rom. 3:28; Eph. 2:1-5). Our salvation is rooted in the Father's mercy and the Son's sacrificial death for us (Eph. 1:4-7).

Complete Salvation. John Newton, author of the well-known hymn *Amazing Grace*, was a miserable man at the age of 23. He had been involved in an immoral lifestyle and was engaged in the heartlessly cruel African slave trade. But he was fed up with his sinful way of life.

A crisis came on March 10, 1748, on board a ship that was caught in a violent storm. Thinking all was lost, Newton cried out in terror, "Lord, have mercy on us!" Suddenly the word *mercy* struck him with great force. If anybody needed it, he did. At that moment he trusted in Christ for salvation. God forgave Newton's sins and began to break the power of his wicked lifestyle.

Paul referred to both the mercy and the grace of God in salvation. The apostle declared that it is by God's grace we are justified and delivered from the guilt of our sins (Titus 3:7). But Paul also said it is God's mercy that delivers us from a lifestyle that the apostle described as *foolish* (3:3). Let's thank God daily for His grace and His mercy. Together they provide for us a complete salvation.

From Rags to Riches. During the Great Depression, a man named Mr. Yates owned a huge piece of land in Texas where he raised sheep. Financial problems had brought him to the brink of bankruptcy. Then an oil company, believing there might be oil on his land, asked for permission to drill.

With nothing to lose, Mr. Yates agreed. Soon, at a shallow depth, the workmen struck the largest oil deposit found at that time on the North American continent. Overnight, Mr. Yates became a billionaire. The amazing thing, though, is that the untapped riches were there all along. He just didn't know it!

Are you a spiritual "Mr. Yates" who is unaware of the riches you already own in Christ? When Paul wrote his Letter to the Ephesians, he revealed hidden treasure by preaching *the boundless riches of Christ* (3:8). Paul's goal was to make all Christians see how wealthy they actually are (Rom. 8:18).

FOR YOUTH	■ **TOPIC:** Does Anybody Care? ■ **QUESTIONS:** 1. Why do you think God made it necessary that

Christians suffer at least to some extent? 2. What kind of *glory* (Rom. 8:18) do you think God has in store for you? 3. Do you think it's fair that all creation has had to suffer for the sinfulness of human beings? Explain your answer. 4. How does it make you feel that God *searches the heart* (8:27)? 5. In what ways might your life demonstrate that *we are more than conquerors through him who loved us* (8:37)?

■ **ILLUSTRATIONS:**

Receptive to the Gospel. A former heavy-metal rocker saw the 2000 Olympics in Sydney, Australia, as a time to tell people about Christ. David Soesbee, who was voted in his high school as the most likely to be incarcerated or dead before the age of 30, was in Sydney to preach the message of life, Sydney's Wesley Mission reported. The then 34-year-old musician was among 230 Christians from 150 churches in the United States taking part in Reach-Out 2000 Sydney through Lay Witnesses for Christ, International.

In six hours of door-to-door evangelism during the first week of the Olympics, Soesbee prayed with 43 people who put their faith in Christ. "The people of Australia are very receptive to the gospel message," Soesbee said. "They have a yearning to fill that God-spaced emptiness in their lives."

Soesbee, a resident of Asheville, N.C., runs Touch Ministries, an organization that brings the Gospel to young people. A couple of years ago he traveled with a Christian band as well as ministered to musicians in several other bands.

The Passion in God's Heart. A Brazilian praise singer continues to donate all the proceeds of two CDs to help free child prostitutes in Bombay, India. Ana Paula Valadão, 24, and the worship team she leads, had sold more than 350,000 copies of their two CDs in the first year-and-a-half after they were released in 1999. All of the proceeds go to help rehabilitate children trapped in the illicit trade in Mubai, as Bombay is now known, Dallas-based Christ for the Nations reported. India Before the Throne, the ministry Ana and her pastor/father Marcio Valadão founded, helps get young girls off the streets and into the Bible, the singer said.

Pastor Valadão dreamed about helping the children after witnessing their plight on a 1997 missions trip to Mubai. He learned that many of the dilapidated buildings on Falkland Street were brothels for child prostitutes. He was told that more than 20,000 girls from Nepal and India's country villages live as slaves, many of them sold by their starving parents for less than $20. To pay off their bondage, the girls, some as young as six, were forced to have relations with as many as 45 men a day. Most of the girls would die of AIDS or tuberculosis before they reached 20. Many would leave behind illegitimate children with no one to care for them. The pastor was moved with compassion to help the children find better lives.

Ana Paula's dream was to see the Body of Christ grow in intimacy through worship. As her father was returning from his trip, she was returning from a music conference "with my heart burning to record our church." Ana leads congregational worship at 12,000-member Igreja Batista da Logoinha in Belo Horizonte. Because "the Lord was doing awesome things through our worship," she and the church began Exalted, a 50-member worship and orchestral recording team. Sales of their first CD, which featured original Scripture-based songs, skyrocketed and a second release sold as well. The Brazilian government music industry awarded Ana Paula for the high sales, which she said are a blessing from God.

Their visions joined in building rehabilitation homes for the former prostitutes with the musical ministry profits. "If you think that these girls are lost forever, we can tell you they're not!" Ana Paula said. Although the outreach is fairly new, already girls are finding healing for their bodies, minds, and spirits.

"We knew God wanted us to do this," Ana Paula said. "His promises were that great things would happen, but we are always amazed at what the Lord is doing through this ministry." She said they receive hundreds of letters and e-mails about their music, sales continue to climb, and more girls in India will learn about Jesus. "The mission field won't lack anything because God's people understand that reaching the nations is the passion in God's heart."

PROCLAIM THE GOSPEL

BACKGROUND SCRIPTURE: Romans 10:1-17
DEVOTIONAL READING: Romans 11:1-6

KEY VERSES: And how are they to hear without someone to proclaim him [Christ]?
And how are they to proclaim him unless they are sent? Romans 10:14-15.

KING JAMES VERSION

ROMANS 10:1 Brethren, my heart's desire and prayer to God for Israel is, that they might be saved. . . .

3 For they being ignorant of God's righteousness, and going about to establish their own righteousness, have not submitted themselves unto the righteousness of God.

4 For Christ is the end of the law for righteousness to every one that believeth.

5 For Moses describeth the righteousness which is of the law, That the man which doeth those things shall live by them.

6 But the righteousness which is of faith speaketh on this wise, Say not in thine heart, Who shall ascend into heaven? (that is, to bring Christ down from above:)

7 Or, Who shall descend into the deep? (that is, to bring up Christ again from the dead.)

8 But what saith it? The word is nigh thee, even in thy mouth, and in thy heart: that is, the word of faith, which we preach;

9 That if thou shalt confess with thy mouth the Lord Jesus, and shalt believe in thine heart that God hath raised him from the dead, thou shalt be saved.

10 For with the heart man believeth unto righteousness; and with the mouth confession is made unto salvation. . . .

12 For there is no difference between the Jew and the Greek: for the same Lord over all is rich unto all that call upon him.

13 For whosoever shall call upon the name of the Lord shall be saved.

14 How then shall they call on him in whom they have not believed? and how shall they believe in him of whom they have not heard? and how shall they hear without a preacher?

15 And how shall they preach, except they be sent? as it is written, How beautiful are the feet of them that preach the gospel of peace, and bring glad tidings of good things!

16 But they have not all obeyed the gospel. For Esaias saith, Lord, who hath believed our report?

17 So then faith cometh by hearing, and hearing by the word of God.

NEW REVISED STANDARD VERSION

ROMANS 10:1 Brothers and sisters, my heart's desire and prayer to God for them is that they may be saved. . . .

3 For, being ignorant of the righteousness that comes from God, and seeking to establish their own, they have not submitted to God's righteousness. 4 For Christ is the end of the law so that there may be righteousness for everyone who believes.

5 Moses writes concerning the righteousness that comes from the law, that "the person who does these things will live by them." 6 But the righteousness that comes from faith says, "Do not say in your heart, 'Who will ascend into heaven?'" (that is, to bring Christ down) 7 "or 'Who will descend into the abyss?'" (that is, to bring Christ up from the dead). 8 But what does it say?

"The word is near you,
  on your lips and in your heart"
(that is, the word of faith that we proclaim);
9 because if you confess with your lips that Jesus is Lord and believe in your heart that God raised him from the dead, you will be saved. 10 For one believes with the heart and so is justified, and one confesses with the mouth and so is saved. . . . 12 For there is no distinction between Jew and Greek; the same Lord is Lord of all and is generous to all who call on him.
13 For, "Everyone who calls on the name of the Lord shall be saved."

14 But how are they to call on one in whom they have not believed? And how are they to believe in one of whom they have never heard? And how are they to hear without someone to proclaim him? 15 And how are they to proclaim him unless they are sent? As it is written, "How beautiful are the feet of those who bring good news!" 16 But not all have obeyed the good news; for Isaiah says, "Lord, who has believed our message?" 17 So faith comes from what is heard, and what is heard comes through the word of Christ.

261

BACKGROUND

In his *Commentary on Romans*, the reformer Martin Luther described the contents of Romans 10 this way: "The apostle intercedes for the Jews and shows that the righteousness which makes us worthy of eternal life comes alone from . . . faith in Christ." Surely Paul was disappointed that so many fellow Jews in Rome depended solely on adherence to the law for their salvation rather than on faith in Christ. As we read Paul's words, we can sense both the sadness and the urgency he must have felt. This was based on the fact that many of his fellow Jews had not yet accepted the truth of the Gospel.

Thus Paul, building upon what he had already written in regard to the Jews' pride and boasting in their heritage, embarked on an appeal for them to understand what constitutes true righteousness. Referring to several Old Testament passages, the apostle returned to the overriding theme of the letter: justification by grace through faith. Salvation cannot be earned—not by acts of righteousness, not by correct living, and not even by adherence to the law. Salvation is a gift from God that is given because people—whether Jew or Gentile—put their faith in Jesus Christ.

Paul wanted the Jews to understand that the era of the law had come to an end, while the era of Christ had come into being. This was, in fact, the same message that the apostle had driven home in his letter to the Galatians, in which he also clarified the true purpose of the Mosaic law. Though the law could not make people righteous—and thus, could not save them—it did reveal God's will so that they might recognize their sinfulness. And once they recognized their sinfulness, they would realize their need for forgiveness and justification. Acquittal and righteousness could come only through the sacrifice of one perfect, sinless being. That person was none other than Jesus Christ.

NOTES ON THE PRINTED TEXT

Romans 10 begins with the mention of Paul's intense *desire and prayer to God* (10:1) that the Jewish people would be saved. The apostle, of course, saw faith in Christ as the only means of salvation. That is why Paul preached and taught with such intensity about the Savior. Even the Jews who possessed such a rich religious history had to turn to Jesus to be saved. Paul taught that because Jesus is the most complete revelation of God—in that He is the ful-fillment of the Old Testament Scriptures—no one can fully know God apart from Christ. We cannot come to God by any other way.

Rather than living by faith in God through His Son, Jesus Christ, many people in Paul's day had tried to make themselves acceptable in God's sight by follow-ing long-established Jewish customs and traditions. By so doing, they were *igno-rant of the righteousness that comes from God* (10:3). They had overlooked the fact that Christ's coming had marked *the end of the law so that there may be right-eousness for everyone who believes* (10:4). Righteousness does not come by our own efforts but only through the efforts of Christ, who died on the cross for our sins and rose again so that we might be the recipients of eternal life. Thus, salva-tion is His gift to us.

Moses wrote that the law's way of making a person right with God required obedience to all of its commands (10:5). However, we know from James 2:10 that the person who keeps all the laws except one is as guilty as the person who has broken all of God's laws. Since it's impossible to live a perfect life, it's also impossible to be saved by keeping the law.

In Romans 10:6-8, Paul referred to Deuteronomy 30:12-14 to underscore how readily available salvation is through Christ. For instance, one didn't need to go to heaven to find the Savior and bring Him down to help us. Likewise, one didn't have to go to the place of the dead (the abyss) to bring Christ back to life again. The salvation that Paul preached—a salvation that comes from trusting in Christ—was already within easy reach. The message was *"near you, on your lips and in your heart"* (Rom. 10:8).

Part of the Gospel message is that Christ rose from the dead, and this is living proof that He secured justification for all who believe (10:9). The saved person accepts this truth and is not afraid to publicly confess Jesus as Lord (10:10). Tragically, some people try to make getting saved a complicated process, but it's not. If we believe in our heart and say with our mouth that Christ is the risen Lord, we will be saved. It's true that the only condition for salvation is faith; but it is the kind of faith that obeys, confesses, perseveres, and works. We know from 1 Corinthians 12:3 that the only person who can really confess that Jesus is Lord is the one indwelt by the Spirit.

In Romans 10:11, Paul quoted from Isaiah 28:16 to stress that those who believed in Christ will not be put to shame. In Romans 10:13, the apostle cited Joel 2:32, which says, *"Everyone who calls on the name of the Lord shall be saved"* (Rom. 10:13). Sandwiched in between these quotations is verse 12, in which Paul declared that *there is no distinction between Jew and Greek; the same Lord is Lord of all and is generous to all who call on him.* Jesus is Lord of both Jews and Gentiles. He freely and graciously offers salvation to both and saves all who put their faith in Him. The Lord is generous in that He is always ready to save those who trust in Him for eternal life.

Clearly, God does everything necessary to bring the Gospel to the lost. He sends preachers and teachers who use His Word to explain that righteousness and reconciliation are available only through faith in Christ (10:14-15). We who have believed are among those whom God wants to use to take His great message of salvation to the lost. He can use us to encourage unbelievers to embrace the truth of the Gospel.

National Israel heard the way of righteousness explained, but by and large refused to obey the truth, just as Isaiah had foretold (10:16). Both individually and officially the Jews had rejected the truth for a lie (10:17-18). Is it possible that the Jews did not know the consequences their unbelief would bring? Absolutely not! Isaiah had foretold that Israel would be aroused to jealousy because the Gentiles had become the recipients of God's blessing, while the Jews were cut off from it (10:19-20). Israel remained stubborn and proud throughout the time that God freely offered the people mercy (10:21).

The irony is that many Jews who had been taught about the Messiah refused to believe in Him when He came. Then, when God offered His salvation to the Gentiles, many—who had previously never heard about the Messiah—heard the Gospel proclaimed and believed in Him. It's no wonder that Paul would declare in 11:33, *O the depth of the riches and wisdom and knowledge of God! How unsearchable are his judgments and how inscrutable his ways!*

SUGGESTIONS TO TEACHERS

God did not make the means of receiving His salvation complicated or difficult; rather, He made it clear and straightforward. We are saved through faith in Christ; there is no other means of salvation. Paul, knowing this, noted four unsophisticated and unpretentious steps one should follow in order to be justified by grace through faith.

1. CONFESS WITH YOUR LIPS. First comes the call to express what your mind has accepted. You've examined the facts, you've heard all the evidence you need to hear, you've realized your need for salvation, and you've recognized that Christ is your only source of salvation. Thus you express that He is the Lord who rose again, the Savior of your soul, and your Redeemer. Of course, confession made out loud represents a confirmation of what you have already accepted inside.

2. BELIEVE IN YOUR HEART. Second comes the belief that begins growing in your heart and never ceases to grow for the rest of your life. This belief becomes the center of your being; it is your complete trust in Christ and in Him alone. It is your sole hope for life that never ends. It is your conviction that God raised Christ from the dead, and that someday He'll raise you, too, to be with Him forever.

3. EMBRACE YOUR SALVATION. Third, with confession and belief comes an assurance of salvation. You have been saved from the guilt and penalty of sin.

You have been saved from the dominion of sin in your life. By embracing your salvation, you are affirming the truth of the Gospel.

4. PROCLAIM THE SAVIOR. Fourth, in return for this great gift of salvation, God asks us to love Him so much and to love others so much that we spread the Good News. Proclaim God's love for all humanity. Tell others how He has saved you—and what He has saved you from. Tell people that God gave His Son so that salvation could be offered as a free gift. Tell the lost how God yearns for all to find and accept their salvation in His Son.

FOR ADULTS	■ TOPIC: How Are They to Hear?

■ **QUESTIONS:** 1. In what ways do people still try to attain righteousness all on their own? 2. In what ways is Christ *the end of the law* (Rom. 10:4)? 3. What do you think is entailed in confessing *with your lips that Jesus is Lord* (10:9)? 4. In what ways is the Lord *generous to all who call on him* (10:12)? 5. What are some of the ways you could share the Gospel with others?

■ **ILLUSTRATIONS:**

Spreading the Gospel. Five hundred people were baptized by fire hose on a hot New York City street over an August weekend in 2000. They arrived from the neighborhood and by bus from Washington, Boston, and Philadelphia and, dressed in white, gathered in the middle of an East Harlem street to be sprayed, according to *The New York Times*.

S. C. Madison, national leader of the United House of Prayer for All People, a nondenominational church, led the ceremony, which included music from four gospel brass bands. A church official turned on the hose, attached to a city hydrant, and water shot high into the air, raining down in a cool spray for 15 minutes. Some congregants danced to music, while others dropped to the ground praying.

The church has held the mass baptisms each summer since 1937. There are 3,000,000 congregants in 28 states, and in some cities as many as 2,000 people are baptized in a river or a pool. The New York congregation uses the municipal water supply because access to rivers is limited and pools are hard to find.

Passing On a Torch. In the book *Chicken Soup for the Unsinkable Soul*, Paul Karrar tells how the tired ex-teacher edged closer to the counter at Kmart. Her left leg hurt and she hoped she had taken all of her pills for the day: the ones for her high blood pressure, dizziness, and a host of other ills. *Thank goodness I retired years ago*, she thought to herself. *I don't have the energy to teach these days.*

Just before the line to the counter formed, the teacher spotted a young man with four children and a pregnant wife or girlfriend in tow. The teacher couldn't miss the tattoo on his neck. *He's been to prison*, she thought. The teacher continued checking him out. His white T-shirt, shaved hair, and baggy pants led the teacher to surmise, *He's a gang member.*

The teacher tried to let the man go ahead of her.

"You can go first," she offered.

"No, you go first," he insisted.

"No, you have more people with you," said the teacher.

"We should respect our elders," parried the man. And with that, he gestured with a sweeping motion indicating the way for the woman.

A brief smile flickered on the teacher's lips as she hobbled in front of him. The teacher in her decided she couldn't let the moment go and she turned back to him and asked "Who taught you your good manners?"

"You did, Mrs. Simpson, in third grade."

Ultimately, we're all teachers; we're all teaching our own generation or the generation before us or the generation after us. We're all examples of something. We're all passing on a torch. The question is this: What kind of torch are you going to pass on?

Preach the Gospel. It was Saint Francis of Assisi who told his fellow believers the following: "Preach the Gospel at all times. And if necessary, use words." According to Acts 11:14, words are important, but a godly life is the attracting magnet.

FOR YOUTH

■ TOPIC: Is There an Answer?

■ QUESTIONS: 1. How is it possible to know about God and yet not to know Him? 2. Why is it that Christ can make us righteous, but we can't make ourselves righteous? 3. Does the way Paul described to be saved seem too easy to you? Explain your answer. 4. Why is it important to *confess with your lips that Jesus is Lord* (Rom. 10:9)? 5. If faith comes by hearing the Word of God, what place do dialogue, drama, feedback, and other innovations have in leading people to Christ?

■ ILLUSTRATIONS:

To Go Where the Gospel Has Never Gone Before. Native missionaries in India are taking the Gospel where it never has gone before. Workers in the Hindu strongholds of central and northern India have visited dozens of villages where people have never heard about Jesus Christ, Christian Aid Mission reported.

A Hindu leader became a Christian and has asked to be baptized, according to the Virginia-based evangelistic group. His profession of faith has caused an uproar among Hindus in the area, but many others are more open to hearing the Gospel. In another village, two Muslim young people became Christians and are facing persecution from their community.

Gold Medal Gospel. A gold medal wasn't the only prize that U.S. Olympian Sheila Taormina sought in Sydney, Australia, back in 2000. Taormina, who won a gold medal in swimming in 1996, returned to the Games because they gave her opportunities to tell others about her faith in Christ.

Taormina thought she was finished with Olympic competition after winning in Atlanta as part of the 800-meter freestyle relay swimming team, according to Beliefnet. But as she traveled afterward telling her story, she began to see her celebrity as providing an opportunity to talk about God. "The more I spoke to people, the more I began to wonder if I had stepped away from the Olympics too soon," she said.

Taormina hesitated to return to the rigorous training schedule that Olympic competition demands. She explained, "You have to become very selfish with your time. There are days when I think I could better spend my time working with the youth groups at my local church."

In Sydney, Taormina competed in the women's triathlon, involving swimming nine-tenths of a mile in the ocean, biking 24.8 miles, and running 6.2 miles. Her training regimen and enthusiasm helped her qualify for the team, and she finished sixth in Olympic competition with a time of 2 hours, 2 minutes, and 45 seconds.

"My treasure isn't another gold medal, or even returning to the Olympics again," Taormina said. "It's how I share this experience with others. It's what I bring back to them that can help them with their lives."

Your Gospel Legacy. Psychologist William James said, "The great use of life is to spend it for something that outlasts it." If you were to die today, what would be your legacy? What kind of torch would you have passed on?

Secret Service Proclamation. An advertisement in the classifieds offered a "retired" police dog for sale for $25. A woman who lived alone thought a police dog might make a good watchdog as well as a companion, so she quickly called the station and sent her check.

Later, a police officer delivered a mangy, pitiful looking creature. When the woman protested the dog's appearance and said she wanted the dog to guard her and the house, the officer replied: "Now, ma'am, don't let this dog's looks deceive you. He's in the Secret Service."

How many of us Christians are in the "Secret Service" when it comes to proclaiming the Gospel? God doesn't want secret servants!

LIVE THE GOSPEL

BACKGROUND SCRIPTURE: Romans 12
DEVOTIONAL READING: ROMANS 12:4-8

KEY VERSE: Do not be conformed to this world, but be transformed by
the renewing of your minds, so that you may discern what is the
will of God—what is good and acceptable and perfect. Romans 12:2.

KING JAMES VERSION

ROMANS 12:1 I beseech you therefore, brethren, by the mercies of God, that ye present your bodies a living sacrifice, holy, acceptable unto God, which is your reasonable service.

2 And be not conformed to this world: but be ye transformed by the renewing of your mind, that ye may prove what is that good, and acceptable, and perfect, will of God.

3 For I say, through the grace given unto me, to every man that is among you, not to think of himself more highly than he ought to think; but to think soberly, according as God hath dealt to every man the measure of faith. . . .

9 Let love be without dissimulation. Abhor that which is evil; cleave to that which is good.

10 Be kindly affectioned one to another with brotherly love; in honour preferring one another;

11 Not slothful in business; fervent in spirit; serving the Lord;

12 Rejoicing in hope; patient in tribulation; continuing instant in prayer;

13 Distributing to the necessity of saints; given to hospitality.

14 Bless them which persecute you: bless, and curse not.

15 Rejoice with them that do rejoice, and weep with them that weep.

16 Be of the same mind one toward another. Mind not high things, but condescend to men of low estate. Be not wise in your own conceits.

17 Recompense to no man evil for evil. Provide things honest in the sight of all men.

18 If it be possible, as much as lieth in you, live peaceably with all men.

19 Dearly beloved, avenge not yourselves, but rather give place unto wrath: for it is written, Vengeance is mine; I will repay, saith the Lord.

20 Therefore if thine enemy hunger, feed him; if he thirst, give him drink: for in so doing thou shalt heap coals of fire on his head.

21 Be not overcome of evil, but overcome evil with good.

NEW REVISED STANDARD VERSION

ROMANS 12:1 I appeal to you therefore, brothers and sisters, by the mercies of God, to present your bodies as a living sacrifice, holy and acceptable to God, which is your spiritual worship. 2 Do not be conformed to this world, but be transformed by the renewing of your minds, so that you may discern what is the will of God—what is good and acceptable and perfect.

3 For by the grace given to me I say to everyone among you not to think of yourself more highly than you ought to think, but to think with sober judgment, each according to the measure of faith that God has assigned. . . .

9 Let love be genuine; hate what is evil, hold fast to what is good; 10 love one another with mutual affection; outdo one another in showing honor. 11 Do not lag in zeal, be ardent in spirit, serve the Lord. 12 Rejoice in hope, be patient in suffering, persevere in prayer. 13 Contribute to the needs of the saints; extend hospitality to strangers.

14 Bless those who persecute you; bless and do not curse them. 15 Rejoice with those who rejoice, weep with those who weep. 16 Live in harmony with one another; do not be haughty, but associate with the lowly; do not claim to be wiser than you are. 17 Do not repay anyone evil for evil, but take thought for what is noble in the sight of all. 18 If it is possible, so far as it depends on you, live peaceably with all. 19 Beloved, never avenge yourselves, but leave room for the wrath of God; for it is written, "Vengeance is mine, I will repay, says the Lord." 20 No, "if your enemies are hungry, feed them; if they are thirsty, give them something to drink; for by doing this you will heap burning coals on their heads." 21 Do not be overcome by evil, but overcome evil with good.

BACKGROUND

Near the conclusion of each of Paul's letters to various churches is a discussion of practical duties that arise from the biblical truths he expounded. Though he stringently taught that justification comes by grace through faith, he also taught that grace and faith should manifest themselves in the believer's life. Salvation should affect the Christian's thoughts, actions, and behaviors. For Paul, what we believe should impact how we behave.

Just as we cannot earn our salvation on our own, neither can we perform good works on our own. Again, we need divine help. And the apostle wrote that we receive that help from the Spirit, who empowers us not only to do good deeds and follow the will of God, but also gives us special abilities to carry out our work for the Lord.

Paul was writing to a church in which there were both Jewish and Gentile Christians. As they increasingly associated together, there was plenty of room for jealousies, competition, and self-interest. Rather than these vices prevailing, Paul's desire was that there be unity and cooperation among different groups of believers. Thus the apostle told the church that God has given each of us the ability to do certain things. These spiritual gifts were to be used in service to each other and for the glory of God.

To use our spiritual gifts effectively, we should recognize that all of them come from God. Though each person in the church has different special abilities, they are all valued by the Lord and needed for the growth of His people. When we know who we are and what we do best, we will be more willing to dedicate our gifts to God's service and not to our personal success. Instead of holding back anything from God's service, we will want to utilize our gifts wholeheartedly.

NOTES ON THE PRINTED TEXT

In Romans 11, Paul declared that not all his fellow Jews had rejected God's message of salvation. There were still a faithful few. The apostle made it clear that God's plans for His people would be fulfilled, and that in the process many Gentiles would come to saving faith.

In chapter 12, Paul exhorted the Jewish and Gentile Christians living in Rome to commit themselves wholeheartedly to God. The apostle told them to present themselves—physically, mentally, emotionally, and spiritually—*as a living sacrifice, holy and acceptable to God, which is your spiritual worship* (12:1). There is no room for a self-important ego in committing ourselves to God. It involves the totality of our being. To make such an offering involves a decisive act of our own will—a positive involvement in becoming part of God's plan toward holiness. The Lord views this as an act of worship, for it is our most appropriate response to all that His Son, Jesus Christ, has done for us, having freed us from the power and presence of sin.

Paul knew that when we truly present ourselves to God, we will no longer want to be *conformed to this world* (12:2). Indeed, as Christ, through the Holy Spirit, begins living His life in and through us, we will develop an attitude of resistance to all the unsavory values of the world, especially those that pressure us to accept and live by unwholesome standards. We become transformed people because our thought patterns are changed from their old ways and renewed toward God's ways. This renewing of our minds enables us to *discern what is the will of God— what is good and acceptable and perfect.*

Within any group of people there exists the possibility for pride. Perhaps that's why Paul urged the members of the congregation at Rome *not to think of yourself more highly than you ought to think* (12:3). The apostle especially did not want any individuals or groups thinking themselves better than others within the church because of their cultural background or religious heritage. Every member of the congregation had value, and that value was based in their spiritual identity in Christ. Thus Paul told his readers to think with *sober judgment*, and to evaluate themselves honestly, humbly, and prayerfully *according to the measure of faith that God has assigned.*

After the apostle's explanation of the presence and use of spiritual gifts (12:4-8), verse 9 begins what many Bible scholars term the "practical section" of the chapter. Undergirding everything else that Paul taught in these verses is the command to *Let love be genuine* (12:9). This love is not merely an emotion; it also requires action. It is in no way hypocritical or self-serving or pretending. It is real love put into action that the apostle was writing about here. And if love is the foundation of our actions, then we will *hate what is evil, hold fast to what is good.* To further describe this love, Paul said to *love one another with mutual affection; outdo one another in showing honor* (12:10).

Where unconditional love is flourishing, other attitudes will also sprout up and prosper. For instance, Paul told his readers *Do not lag in zeal, be ardent in spirit* (12:11). Creativity, motivation, and excitement should be clear external marks of our Christian service. We are to *serve the Lord* as though it is the most important activity of our lives. In actuality, it is. To this list of Christian attitudes and characteristics, verses 12 and 13 add hope, patience, prayer, compassion, and hospitality.

In 12:14-16, Paul told his readers how they should respond to friends, neighbors, and enemies of the Gospel. In times of suffering, it is natural for believers to pray that God would afflict their persecutors with misfortune. Paul said Christians should ask the Lord to bless those who mistreated them. This reflects what Jesus taught and practiced (Matt. 5:44; Luke 23:34). It was also the practice of some in the early church (Acts 7:59-60).

When others rejoice over the good things happening in their lives, we should rejoice with them rather than be envious of them. When others grieve over some tragedy they have experienced, we should grieve with them rather than gloat over their affliction (Rom. 12:15). Regardless of whether it is the saved or the unsaved, people will see Christ in us when we respond with genuine empathy.

In trying times it is easy for believers to argue and fight with one another. Paul said God's people should promote harmony and unity, not discord and division (12:16). The apostle also said that God's people should not be swayed by one's social standing. Christians should willingly associate with others, regardless of their economic status. Believers should also freely give themselves to humble, or menial, tasks.

Paul's exhortations in Romans 12:17-21 concern how believers should relate to those who are hostile to them. He said *Do not repay anyone evil for evil, but take thought for what is noble in the sight of all* (12:17). Jesus' followers were to do their best at all times and in every circumstance to live at peace with all people (12:18). There are times, of course, when even their best intentions and efforts would fail to produce peace.

Paul urged his readers not to try to get even when others abused and exploited them. Retaliation was not the answer. Instead, Christians were to patiently wait for God to right all injustices in His time (12:19). Paul's statement agreed with Deuteronomy 32:35, which said that God would repay all wrongs and vindicate the cause of His people.

In view of this truth, Christians should heed what is written in Proverbs 25:21-22, which Paul quoted in Romans 12:20. Believers should give their hungry and thirsty enemies food to eat and liquid to drink. By doing this, God's people would heap burning coals on the heads of their opponents. In other words, it would be seen as a generous and kind act that might cause them to rethink their ways.

Paul concluded by exhorting his readers not to *be overcome by evil, but [to] overcome evil with good* (12:21). In other words, they were to resist the desire to counterattack their opponents. By showing love and kindness rather than hatred and vengeance, believers might win the unsaved to Christ.

SUGGESTIONS TO TEACHERS

One of the ways we can study and apply Romans 12 is by thinking of the chapter as a new set of "Be-Attitudes," for in these verses, Paul urged believers to exhibit certain *attitudes*. There are nine Beatitudes in Matthew 5:3-11; thus for the sake of counting, we'll list nine "Be-Attitudes" drawn from Romans 12.

1. BE A LIVING SACRIFICE. Lay aside your self-centered desires and goals and follow Jesus; put all your energy and resources at His disposal for His use, and trust Him to guide you.

2. BE TRANSFORMED. Ask yourself the question, "What would Jesus do?"; then try to think as He thinks. Be one of His vessels for His loving activity in the world today.

3. BE HUMBLE. Try to see yourself through God's eyes, and try to see others through God's eyes, too. Evaluate yourself according to heaven's values, not the values of this world.

4. BE GENUINE IN LOVE. Put your love into action. Look at those who are in need as though they were Jesus Himself.

5. BE ZEALOUS. Never view the Christian life as dull or boring. Instead, get excited about being a Christian. Develop a passion and an enthusiasm for living for Christ.

6. BE HOPEFUL. Think about all that Jesus has done for you; think about all that Jesus is doing for you right now; and think about all that Jesus is going to be doing for you in the future!

7. BE PATIENT. Learn to wait and hope at the same time. Also, remember that Jesus will guide you through your troubles. Make your trust in Him your central focus when facing difficult times.

8. BE PRAYERFUL. Keep at it; persevere; don't stop praying.

9. BE PEACEFUL. As much as possible, try to live in harmony with everyone around you. Enjoy the wholesome company of others and strive to /be nice even to mean people.

FOR ADULTS

■ TOPIC: How Are We to Live?

■ QUESTIONS: 1. In what ways did Paul connect belief and behavior in Romans 12? 2. What must we do to refrain from becoming conformed to the world? 3. How does God transform the believer's mind? 4. What must happen before we can *discern what is the will of God* (12:2)? 5. Of all the commands Paul listed in verses 9-21, which is the most difficult for you to obey? Why?

■ ILLUSTRATIONS:

So That You May Discern. A television news camera crew was on assignment in southern Florida filming the widespread destruction of Hurricane Andrew. In one scene, amid the devastation and debris stood one house on its foundation. The owner was cleaning up the yard when a reporter approached him.

"Sir, why is your house the only one still standing?" asked the reporter. "How did you manage to escape the severe damage of the hurricane?"

"I built this house myself," the man replied. "I also built it according to the Florida state building code. When the code called for 2' x 6' roof trusses, I used 2' x 6' roof trusses. I was told that a house built according to code could withstand a hurricane. I did, and it did. I suppose no one else around here followed the code."

When the sun is shining and the skies are blue, building our lives on something other than the guidance of God's Word can be tempting. But there's only one way to be ready for a storm. Heed the teachings and admonitions of our Lord.

Not to Think of Yourself More Highly. In "Letters to Rulers of People," Francis of Assisi wrote these words:

> Keep a clear eye toward life's end. Do not forget your purpose and destiny as God's creature. What you are in His sight is what you are and nothing more. Remember, that when you leave this earth, you can take nothing that you have received—fading symbols of honor, trappings of power—but only what you have given: a full heart enriched by honest service, love, sacrifice, and courage.

Let Love Be Genuine. John Wesley Zwomunondiita Kurewa, writing for *Biblical Proclamation for Africa Today,* says he actually first heard this story in a Nazarene camp meeting when he was a child. But he had forgotten it, and it seems even better now than when he first heard it.

The story is told of a young woman who had heard people talking about an interesting book that had just been published. She took the trouble to look for the book in bookshops until she secured a copy for herself. After reading the introduction and the first chapter of the book, however, she put it away. It did not seem interesting to her.

A few months later, the young woman was traveling in a foreign country. She met a handsome young man, and she fell in love with him. To her pleasant surprise, the young man was the author of the book that she had bought and put away. Upon returning home, she found the book and started reading it from the introduction to the end. This time, it was the most interesting book she had ever read in her life.

 FOR YOUTH ■ TOPIC: What Is It All About?
■ QUESTIONS: 1. According to Romans 12:1, what is the ultimate way we can worship and serve God? 2. How is God going about the renewing of your mind right now? 3. What does genuine love look like? 4. What is the proper response, according to Paul, when someone treats us badly? 5. Of all the commands Paul listed in 12:9-21, which do you consider the toughest to obey? Why that particular one?

■ ILLUSTRATIONS:

Acceptable to God. In a *Power for Living* devotional, Jamie Buckingham writes about how Fred Craddock, while lecturing at Yale University, told of going back home one summer to Gatlinburg, Tennessee, to take a short vacation with his wife. One night they found a quiet little restaurant where they looked forward to a private meal—just the two of them.

While the couple was waiting for their meal, they noticed a distinguished looking, white-haired man moving from table to table, visiting guests. Craddock whispered to his wife, "I hope he doesn't come over here." He didn't want the man to intrude on their privacy. But the man did come by his table.

"Where are you folks from?" the old fellow asked amicably.

"Oklahoma."

"Splendid state, I hear, although I've never been there. What do you do for a living?

"I teach homiletics at the graduate seminary of Phillips University."

"Oh, so you teach preachers, do you. Well, I've got a story I want to tell you." And with that he pulled up a chair and sat down at the table with Craddock and his wife. Dr. Craddock said he groaned inwardly: *Oh no, here comes another preacher story. It seems everyone has one.*

The man stuck out his hand. "I'm Ben Hooper. I was born not far from here across the mountains. My mother wasn't married when I was born so I had a hard time. When I started to school, my classmates had a name for me, and it wasn't a very nice name. I used to go off by myself at recess and during lunch time because the taunts of my playmates cut so deeply.

"What was worse was going downtown on Saturday afternoon and feeling every eye burning a hole through you. They were all wondering just who my real father was.

"When I was about 12 years old, a new preacher came to our church. I would always go in late and slip out early. But one day the preacher said the benediction so fast I got caught and had to walk out with the crowd. I could feel every eye in church on me. Just about the time I got to the door I felt a big hand on my shoulder. I looked up and the preacher was looking right at me.

"'Who are you, son? Whose boy are you?' he bellowed.

"I felt the old weight come on me. It was like a big black cloud. Even the preacher was putting me down.

"But as he looked down at me, studying my face, he began to smile a big smile of recognition. 'Wait a minute,' he said. 'I know who you are. I see the family resemblance. You are a child of God!'

"With that he slapped me across the back and said, 'Boy, you've got a great inheritance. Go and claim it!'"

The old fellow looked across the table at Fred Craddock and said, "That was the most important single sentence ever said to me." With that he smiled, shook the hands of Craddock and his wife, and moved on to another table to greet old friends.

Suddenly, Fred Craddock remembered some old state history lessons. On two occasions the people of Tennessee had elected a born-out-of-wedlock individual to be their governor. One of them, he remembered, was a man by the name of Ben Hooper.

Be Patient in Suffering. In his book *Deep Down*, Tim Riter tells how George's first job as a landscape contractor was to remove a large oak stump from a farmer's field. He also was using dynamite for the first time. With the farmer watching, George tried to hide his nervousness by carefully calculating the size of the stump, the proper amount of dynamite, and where to place it.

Finally, George and the farmer moved to the detonator behind his pickup truck. With a silent prayer, George plunged the detonator. The stump gracefully rose through the air and then crashed on the cab of the truck. George gazed in despair at the ruined cab, but the farmer was all admiration.

"Son, with a little more practice, those stumps will land in the bed of the truck every time!"

Extend Hospitality to Strangers. In Brooklyn there is a school called Chush that caters to learning-disabled children. Some children remain in Chush for their entire school career, while others are mainstreamed into conventional schools. At a recent Chush fund-raiser, the father of one of the students delivered a speech that will never be forgotten. After extolling the school and its dedicated staff, he cried out, "Where is the perfection in my son Shaya? Everything God does is done with perfection. But my child cannot understand things as other children do. My child cannot remember facts and figures as other children do. Where is God's perfection?"

The audience was shocked by the question, pained by the father's anguish, and stilled by his piercing query. "I believe," the father answered, "that when God brings a child like this into the world, the perfection that He seeks is in the way people react to this child."

The father then told a story about his son, Shaya. One afternoon Shaya and his father walked past a park where some boys Shaya knew were playing baseball. Shaya asked, "Do you think they will let me play?" Shaya's father knew that his son was not at all athletic and that most boys would not want him on their team. But Shaya's father understood that if his son was chosen to play it would give him a great sense of belonging.

Shaya's father approached one of the boys in the field and asked if Shaya could play. The boy looked around for guidance from his teammates. Getting none, he took matters into his own hands and said, "Well, we're losing by six runs and the game's in the eighth inning. I guess he can be on our team, and we'll try to put him up to bat in the ninth inning." Shaya's father was ecstatic as Shaya smiled broadly.

Shaya was told to put on a glove and go out to play right field. In the bottom of the eighth inning, Shaya's team scored a few runs but was still behind by three. In the bottom of the ninth inning, Shaya's team scored again, and now with two outs and the bases loaded with the winning run on base, Shaya was slated to bat. Would the team actually let Shaya bat at this juncture and give away their chance to win the game?

Surprisingly, Shaya was handed a bat. His teammates knew that it was all but impossible for Shaya to hit; he didn't even know how to hold the bat properly. But as Shaya stepped up to the plate, the pitcher moved in a few steps to lob the ball softly so Shaya could at least make contact. The first pitch came, Shaya swung clumsily and missed. One of Shaya's teammates ran out to Shaya, and together they held the bat and faced the pitcher waiting for the next pitch. The pitcher again took a few steps forward to toss the ball softly. As the pitch came in, Shaya and his teammate swung and together, they hit a slow ground ball to the pitcher.

The pitcher picked up the soft grounder; he could have easily thrown the ball to the first baseman. Shaya would have been out and the game would have been over. Instead, the pitcher took the ball and threw it on a high arc to right field, far beyond the reach of the first baseman. At that moment, everyone started yelling, "Shaya, run to first! Run to first!" Never in his life had Shaya run to first. He scampered down the baseline wide-eyed and startled.

By the time Shaya reached first base, the right fielder had the ball. He could have thrown the ball to the second baseman who would tag Shaya out. But the right fielder understood the pitcher's intentions, so he threw the ball high and far over the third baseman's head. Everyone yelled, "Run to second! Run to second!" Shaya ran toward second base as the runners ahead of him deliriously circled the bases toward home. As Shaya reached second, the opposing shortstop ran to him, turned him in the direction of third, and shouted, "Run to third!" As Shaya rounded third, the boys from both teams ran behind him screaming, "Shaya! Run home!" Shaya ran home and jumped on home plate. All the boys—from both teams—lifted him on their shoulders and made him the hero, just as if he had really won the game for his team.

"That day," said the father softly with tears now rolling down his face, "those 18 boys reached their level of God's perfection."

WE ARE THE LORD'S

BACKGROUND SCRIPTURE: Romans 14:1—15:13
DEVOTIONAL READING: Romans 14:14-23

KEY VERSE: Let us therefore no longer pass judgment on one another, but resolve instead never to put a stumbling block or hindrance in the way of another. Romans 14:13.

KING JAMES VERSION

ROMANS 14:1 Him that is weak in the faith receive ye, but not to doubtful disputations.

2 For one believeth that he may eat all things: another, who is weak, eateth herbs.

3 Let not him that eateth despise him that eateth not; and let not him which eateth not judge him that eateth: for God hath received him.

4 Who art thou that judgest another man's servant? to his own master he standeth or falleth. Yea, he shall be holden up: for God is able to make him stand.

5 One man esteemeth one day above another: another esteemeth every day alike. Let every man be fully persuaded in his own mind.

6 He that regardeth the day, regardeth it unto the Lord; and he that regardeth not the day, to the Lord he doth not regard it. He that eateth, eateth to the Lord, for he giveth God thanks; and he that eateth not, to the Lord he eateth not, and giveth God thanks.

7 For none of us liveth to himself, and no man dieth to himself.

8 For whether we live, we live unto the Lord; and whether we die, we die unto the Lord: whether we live therefore, or die, we are the Lord's.

9 For to this end Christ both died, and rose, and revived, that he might be Lord both of the dead and living.

10 But why dost thou judge thy brother? or why dost thou set at nought thy brother? for we shall all stand before the judgment seat of Christ.

11 For it is written, As I live, saith the Lord, every knee shall bow to me, and every tongue shall confess to God.

12 So then every one of us shall give account of himself to God.

13 Let us not therefore judge one another any more: but judge this rather, that no man put a stumblingblock or an occasion to fall in his brother's way.

NEW REVISED STANDARD VERSION

ROMANS 14:1 Welcome those who are weak in faith, but not for the purpose of quarreling over opinions. 2 Some believe in eating anything, while the weak eat only vegetables. 3 Those who eat must not despise those who abstain, and those who abstain must not pass judgment on those who eat; for God has welcomed them. 4 Who are you to pass judgment on servants of another? It is before their own lord that they stand or fall. And they will be upheld, for the Lord is able to make them stand.

5 Some judge one day to be better than another, while others judge all days to be alike. Let all be fully convinced in their own minds. 6 Those who observe the day, observe it in honor of the Lord. Also those who eat, eat in honor of the Lord, since they give thanks to God; while those who abstain, abstain in honor of the Lord and give thanks to God.

7 We do not live to ourselves, and we do not die to ourselves. 8 If we live, we live to the Lord, and if we die, we die to the Lord; so then, whether we live or whether we die, we are the Lord's. 9 For to this end Christ died and lived again, so that he might be Lord of both the dead and the living.

10 Why do you pass judgment on your brother or sister? Or you, why do you despise your brother or sister? For we will all stand before the judgment seat of God. 11 For it is written,

"As I live, says the Lord, every knee shall bow to me,
and every tongue shall give praise to God."

12 So then, each of us will be accountable to God.

13 Let us therefore no longer pass judgment on one another, but resolve instead never to put a stumbling block or hindrance in the way of another.

9

Monday, April 29	1 John 2:1-6	*Walk as Jesus Did*
Tuesday, April 30	1 John 2:7-17	*The Commandment of Love*
Wednesday, May 1	1 Corinthians 8	*Living according to the Spirit*
Thursday, May 2	1 Corinthians 10:23-33	*Do Everything for the Glory of God*
Friday, May 3	Galatians 1:1-10	*Commissioned through Jesus Christ*
Saturday, May 4	Galatians 1:11-24	*The Gospel Is Not of Human Origin*
Sunday, May 5	Galatians 2:11-21	*Crucified with Christ*

BACKGROUND

The practical portion of Paul's letter to the Romans that he began in chapter 12 continues in chapter 14. Having listed duties that arise from the foundation of faith in chapters 12 and 13, Paul next addressed a dire issue that had come before the church at Rome. The issue revolved around the same relationship that the apostle had already devoted so many of his words to—that of the relationship between the Jewish Christians and the Gentile Christians in the church.

The issues arose within the church because of the Jewish Christians' longing to continue to observe and practice the Mosaic law and their traditions. Paul's approach toward the matter was that there was nothing at all wrong with the Jewish Christians continuing to observe their dietary and festival laws and customs; he did consider it wrong, however, when the Jewish Christians tried to press the Gentile Christians to adhere to the Jewish traditions and ceremonies. Paul knew that what his readers believed would affect how they thought and acted. Thus, the apostle tried to settle the issue in a way that would be amicable to both sides, in a way that the unity between the Jewish and Gentile Christians would be preserved and solidified rather than broken apart.

Apparently, some of the Jewish Christians in the church at Rome had misgivings—due to their adherence to certain dietary customs—about eating meat, about observing the Sabbath, and about drinking certain beverages. The temptation to stress these practices that were unique to the Jewish Christians' identity was probably both immense and intense.

Paul undoubtedly knew the teaching of Jesus in Matthew 15:11, "*it is not what goes into the mouth that defiles a person, but it is what comes out of the mouth that defiles.*" That's why the apostle regarded the observance of Jewish dietary customs as being optional. He referred to those who felt bound by these rules as being *weak in faith* (Rom. 14:1), and he called those who felt free not to observe these customs *strong* (15:1).

Paul urged the weak in faith not to censure other believers who did not abide by their dietary restrictions. And the apostle cautioned the strong in faith not to look down on believers who felt obligated to observe particular Jewish customs (14:3). The most important matter was for each group to welcome and love the other unconditionally. They were to avoid causing their fellow Christians to stumble and aim for harmony in the church (14:13, 15-16).

NOTES ON THE PRINTED TEXT

Paul's words in Romans 14 make it clear that matters of food and drink and rigorously maintained schedules of prayer and fasting were issues of individual opinion. Ultimately these things did not affect the status of a believer's salvation. That's why Paul urged his readers to cultivate an attitude of acceptance and compassion for their fellow believers in Christ. The apostle realized that there were legitimate differences of opinion in the church. Not everyone in the congregation was going to agree on every lesser subject; nevertheless, these differences of opinion should not cause division within the church. Indeed, the apostle urged the church to accept Christians who were *weak in faith* (14:1). But he added an injunction—do not allow *quarreling over opinions.*

Paul referred to one group as strong and to the other as weak. Those whom he called strong thought that they could eat or drink anything served as food or beverage. They disregarded the Jewish festivals as holy days as long as these were not specifically prohibited or prescribed by Scripture. Those whom Paul called weak thought that they were bound by their traditions to eat and drink only that which was sanctioned by their customs and to observe prescribed Jewish festivals as holy days (14:2).

For the sake of unity, Paul taught that *Those who eat must not despise those who abstain, and those who abstain must not pass judgment on those who eat; for God has welcomed them* (14:3). Then Paul addressed the Jewish Christians specifically, reminding them that they were not to condemn their fellow believers who were, in actuality, servants of Christ. The apostle urged the weak in faith neither to censure nor micro-manage the lives of other Christians. Paul explained that believers were responsible to the Lord in these matters, and He would make it clear to them whether they were right or wrong in what they were doing. Paul was assured that *they will be upheld, for the Lord is able to make them stand* (14:4).

In regard to observing the Jewish festival days, Paul said, *Let all be fully convinced in their own minds* (14:5). In other words, it was alright for differences of opinion on this matter to exist within the church. While the Jewish Christians yearned to observe these days as special, the Gentile Christians tended to consider every day as being equally special to the Lord. The apostle refused to say whether one practice was better than the other; he did say, however, that whether the Christians chose to observe the Jewish festival days or chose not to observe them, they should live out their decision *in honor of the Lord and give thanks to God* (14:6). The actions of both the weak and the strong were to be an expression of service and gratitude to God.

In 14:7, Paul reminded his readers that both in life and in death they were not their own masters. The time of their birth, the course of their lives, and the end of their lives all were under God's control. And their foremost goal was not to serve themselves but rather to serve the Lord. Therefore, the apostle said, *If we live, we live to the Lord, and if we die, we die to the Lord; so then, whether we live or whether we die, we are the Lord's* (14:8). This truth is the reason why Jesus died and rose again, *so that he might be Lord of both the dead and the living* (14:9).

Paul's remarks in 14:10-13 were directed to both the weak and strong in faith. To the weak the apostle asked, *Why do you pass judgment on your brother and sister?* (14:10). This was foolish, for God was the Judge of all people. To the strong Paul asked, *why do you despise your brother and sister?* This was objectionable, for God had freely and unconditionally accepted all believers in Christ. Paul declared that God alone had the right to pass judgment on people (14:11). *So then, each of us will be accountable to God* (14:12). The apostle then summed up his instruction on how the weak and the strong were to behave toward each other: *Let us therefore no longer pass judgment on one another, but resolve instead never to put a stumbling block or hindrance in the way of another* (14:13).

SUGGESTIONS TO TEACHERS

Though Paul taught that the church should be uncompromising in its stand against activities that are specifically prohibited by Scripture, he did not want the church to be bound by additional rules and regulations of its own creation. Thus he called the church to be open-minded, compassionate, and accepting of the thoughts and opinions of those who trusted in Christ for salvation. We would do well to practice this compassionate understanding and openness in the church today.

1. SHARE IDEAS. Go beyond the willingness to share your ideas with others; also be open to encouraging and having others share their ideas with you. Listen carefully, and make the decision to respect what others say before they even say it. As we share our ideas and opinions, we will grow to have a fuller, more thorough understanding of what the Bible teaches.

2. ALLOW FOR DIFFERENCES OF OPINION. Of course, you'll never agree with all the opinions that others express to you. That would be impossible! But allow for differences of opinion even when you think others are incorrect. At least try to understand the basis for the opinions of others. And respect the person even if you can't accept his or her opinion.

3. LEARN YOUR STRENGTHS AND WEAKNESSES. We all have areas of our lives in which we are "strong Christians" and other areas of our lives in which we are "weak Christians." Therefore, it is vitally important to take inventory of ourselves to find out what are our strengths and weaknesses. Our faith is strong in an area if we can survive contact with worldly people without falling into their patterns. It is weak in an area if we must avoid certain activities, people, or places in order to protect our spiritual life.

It is important to take self-inventory in order to find out our strengths and weaknesses. In areas of strength, we should not fear being defiled by the world; rather, we should go and serve God. And in areas of weakness, we need to be cautious. If we have a strong faith and shelter it, we are not as effective for the Lord as we otherwise could be. And if we have a weak faith but expose it, we are being extremely foolish. In each case, both wisdom and caution are important to maintain.

4. BE ACCOUNTABLE TO CHRIST. It is perfectly acceptable—and even beneficial—to be accountable to other Christians who agree to talk with us about and help us work through our serving and living for Christ. Such accountability should never slip into judgmentalism of the kind the Jewish and Gentile Christians were practicing against one another in Rome. Ultimately, all of us will give a personal account to Christ for our lives. He alone knows our hearts and our motivation, and only He knows whether we are truly committed to Him.

| **FOR ADULTS** | ■ TOPIC: Who Can Judge? |

■ **QUESTIONS:** 1. What do you think was causing disunity among the believers living in Rome? 2. Why do you think Paul referred to some of the Christians as "weak" and to others as "strong"? 3. What effect can quarreling over opinions have in the church? 4. What principles should guide us when we are dealing with differences of opinion on matters that do not violate our Christian faith and morality? 5. How does the fact that we all belong to the Lord help us to stifle the temptation to judge our fellow believers?

■ **ILLUSTRATIONS:**

Weak in Faith. What is weak faith? Here's what the *Life Application Study Bible* calls it:

> [It is] immature faith that has not yet developed the muscle it needs to stand against external pressures. For example, if a person who once worshiped idols became a Christian, he might understand perfectly well that Christ saved him through faith and that idols have no real power. Still, because of his past associations, he might be badly shaken if he unknowingly ate meat that had been used in idol worship. If a person who once worshiped God on the required Jewish holy days became a Christian, he might well know that Christ saved him through faith, not through his keeping of the law. Still, when the festival days came, he might feel empty and unfaithful if he didn't dedicate those days to God. Paul responds to both weak brothers in love. Both are acting according to their consciences, but their honest convictions do not need to be made into rules for the church. Certainly some issues are central to the faith and worth fighting for, but many are based on individual differences and should not be legislated. Our principle should be: In essentials, unity; in nonessentials, liberty; in everything, love.

To Pass Judgment on Servants of Another. A frail old man went to live with his son, daughter-in-law, and four-year-old grandson. The old man's hands trembled, his eyesight was blurred, and his step faltered.

The family ate together at the table. But, the elderly grandfather's shaky hands and failing sight made eating difficult. Peas rolled off his spoon and onto the floor. When he grasped his glass, milk spilled on the tablecloth.

The son and daughter-in-law became irritated with the mess. "We must do something about Grandfather!" blurted the son. "I've had enough of the spilled milk, noisy eating, and food on the floor." So, the husband and wife set a small table in the corner. There Grandfather ate alone, while the rest of the family enjoyed dinner. Since Grandfather had broken a dish or two, his food was served in a wooden bowl.

When the family glanced in Grandfather's direction, sometimes he had a tear in his eye, especially as he sat alone. Still, the only words the couple had for him were sharp admonitions, especially when he dropped a fork or spilled food. The four-year-old watched it all in silence.

One evening, before supper, the father noticed his son playing with wood scraps on the floor. He asked the child sweetly, "What are you making?" Just as sweetly, the boy responded, "Oh, I am making a little bowl for Papa and Mama to eat their food in when I grow up." The four-year-old smiled and went back to work.

The words so struck the parents that they were speechless. Then tears started to stream down their cheeks. Though no word was spoken, both knew what must be done. That evening, the husband took Grandfather's hand and gently led him back to the family table. For the remainder of his days, he ate every meal with the family. And, for some reason, neither husband nor wife seemed to care any longer when a fork was dropped, milk was spilled, or the tablecloth was soiled.

Children are remarkably perceptive. Their eyes ever observe, their ears ever listen, and their minds ever process the messages they absorb. If they see us patiently provide a happy home atmosphere for family members, they will imitate that attitude for the rest of their lives. The wise parents realize that every day the building blocks are being laid for their child's future.

We Are the Lord's. Early in the twentieth century, Charles W. Naylor and D. Otis Teasley combined to write a beautiful hymn titled "I Am the Lord's, I Know," which reiterates the words of Romans 14:8.

Whether I live or die, Whether I wake or sleep,
Whether upon the land Or on the stormy deep;
When 'tis serene and calm Or when the wild winds blow,
I shall not be afraid—I am the Lord's, I know.

When with abundant store or in deep poverty,
And when the world may smile or it may frown on me;
When it shall help me on or shall obstruct my way,
Still shall my heart rejoice—I am the Lord's today.

When I am safe at home or in a foreign land,
When on an icebound shore or on a sunlit strand;
When on the mountain height or in the valley low,
Still doth He care for me—I am the Lord's, I know.

Nothing shall separate from His unbounded love,
Neither in depths below nor in the heights above;
And in the years to come He will abide with me;
I am the Lord's, I know, for all eternity.

FOR YOUTH

■ **TOPIC:** Who Can Belong?

■ **QUESTIONS:** 1. Why do you think maintaining unity is so essential in the church? 2. Instead of our fellow believers, what should occupy our time and energy? 3. What do you think are some of your "strengths" and "weaknesses"? 4. In what ways do you belong to the Lord? 5. How can you make sure that your decisions and actions are *in honor of the Lord* (Rom. 14:6)?

■ **ILLUSTRATIONS:**

Quarreling over Opinions. The story is told of a wise master strolling through the streets with his students. When they came to the city square, a vicious battle was being fought between government troops and rebel forces. Horrified by the bloodshed, the students implored, "Quick, Master, which side should we help?"

"Both," the master replied. The students were confused. "Both?" they demanded. "Why should we help both?" The master replied, "We need to help the authorities learn to listen to the people, and we need to help the rebels learn not to always reject authority."

Before Their Own Lord. Christians are finding a ready mission field at what has been called the country's wildest "party school." Louisiana State University (LSU), cited in 2000 for that dubious distinction by the *Princeton Review*, has ministries that are rising to the challenge. Campus groups at the 31,000-student school in Baton Rouge are serving students in practical ways and sharing the Gospel.

LSU is not much different than most universities, Campus Crusade for Christ's Charley Clary told *Religion Today*. "Drinking is a problem, but not more than at the other universities where I have worked for the past 19 years." Every school has its element of partygoers, but many who get involved are just following the crowd, said Kirk Priest of Chi Alpha, an Assemblies of God ministry. "It's key to reach [the second group] before they are sucked into the lifestyle," he said.

Chi Alpha runs a coffee shop on Chimes Street outside the north gate of LSU. Bars dot the area, and students crowd the streets on weekend nights, making the rounds. On Friday nights Chi Alpha members go into the streets telling people about Jesus Christ. "We find many people who really don't want to be there, but they just got sucked in," Priest said. He noted that a number of students become Christians every week.

Evangelism outside the bars is sometimes confrontational. "We tell them that they are not only hurting themselves, they are also offending God," Priest said. He noted that ministries aren't seeking only the partyers. They also reach out to athletes, residents of dorms and fraternity houses, and international students.

Chi Alpha helped hundreds of incoming freshman move into their dorms, Priest remarked. Volunteers helped carry furniture and boxes into the rooms, and distributed packets containing candy and information about the ministry. They formed relationships with the new students and invited them to a barbecue with a live band the next day.

Some students mistakenly think Chi Alpha is a Christian fraternity. The group held a "rush party" [RU Serving Him] with bands and free food and drink, Priest said. The ministry serves the approximately 3,000 international students at LSU. "They have direct needs, like where can they find financial aid, or furniture, or clothes," Priest noted. The group works with local churches.

There are about 1,000 Christian students actively participating in campus ministry in several groups at LSU, Priest reported. They meet in cell groups in their dorms and apartment complexes, and many take part in evangelistic activities, he added.

Despite their reputation as partyers, LSU students show more respect for religious beliefs than students at some other schools, several campus ministers said. Many students have a Christian background and politely listen to the message of the Gospel. Some haven't understood that they can have a personal relationship with Christ, and embrace that message when they hear it, Clary noted.

"In a given year we see more people come to Christ than on any other campus where I have worked," Clary remarked. "Every semester we see people trusting Christ." College students are "at a critical juncture" of life and need to hear about Christ, Clary reported. "They are away from Mom and Dad for the first time, they are choosing their vocations and, often, they are choosing their lifelong mates. We want to be there to give them the Gospel."

We Do Not Live to Ourselves. A Russian tradition that was neglected for decades is bringing families to Christ. The Supper of Love, which brought families together on holidays and weeknights to drink tea, give gifts, sing, pray, and talk about God, is being revived, the Slavic Gospel Association reports. It helped church members get to know each other better and helped new Christians learn more about God by talking with mature believers, the ministry said.

A Baptist church in Omsk revived the tradition and gave it an evangelistic twist. It invited 15 married couples, some of whom were not Christians, to attend a series of suppers at the church that included video seminars on married life and a lively discussion. Many questions about God came up, allowing the Christian couples to offer answers.

The meetings have grown swiftly because members invited their families and friends to attend. Four groups of 30 to 40 members meet weekly, and an outreach to the families of deaf people has 15 members. On Mother's Day of 2000, more than 300 people came to the church to hear seminars on family life, while their children attended evangelistic plays and concerts.

FAITH AND WORKS

BACKGROUND SCRIPTURE: Galatians 1—2
DEVOTIONAL READING: Acts 13:26-39

KEY VERSE: We have come to believe in Christ Jesus, so that we might be justified by faith in Christ, and not by doing the works of the law. Galatians 2:16.

KING JAMES VERSION

GALATIANS 1:1 Paul, an apostle, (not of men, neither by man, but by Jesus Christ, and God the Father, who raised him from the dead;)

2 And all the brethren which are with me, unto the churches of Galatia: . . .

6 I marvel that ye are so soon removed from him that called you into the grace of Christ unto another gospel:

7 Which is not another; but there be some that trouble you, and would pervert the gospel of Christ.

8 But though we, or an angel from heaven, preach any other gospel unto you than that which we have preached unto you, let him be accursed.

9 As we said before, so say I now again, If any man preach any other gospel unto you than that ye have received, let him be accursed. . . .

2:15 We who are Jews by nature, and not sinners of the Gentiles,

16 Knowing that a man is not justified by the works of the law, but by the faith of Jesus Christ, even we have believed in Jesus Christ, that we might be justified by the faith of Christ, and not by the works of the law: for by the works of the law shall no flesh be justified.

17 But if, while we seek to be justified by Christ, we ourselves also are found sinners, is therefore Christ the minister of sin? God forbid.

18 For if I build again the things which I destroyed, I make myself a transgressor.

19 For I through the law am dead to the law, that I might live unto God.

20 I am crucified with Christ: nevertheless I live; yet not I, but Christ liveth in me: and the life which I now live in the flesh I live by the faith of the Son of God, who loved me, and gave himself for me.

21 I do not frustrate the grace of God: for if righteousness come by the law, then Christ is dead in vain.

NEW REVISED STANDARD VERSION

GALATIANS 1:1 Paul an apostle—sent neither by human commission nor from human authorities, but through Jesus Christ and God the Father, who raised him from the dead— 2 and all the members of God's family who are with me, To the churches of Galatia: . . .

6 I am astonished that you are so quickly deserting the one who called you in the grace of Christ and are turning to a different gospel— 7 not that there is another gospel, but there are some who are confusing you and want to pervert the gospel of Christ. 8 But even if we or an angel from heaven should proclaim to you a gospel contrary to what we proclaimed to you, let that one be accursed! 9 As we have said before, so now I repeat, if anyone proclaims to you a gospel contrary to what you received, let that one be accursed!

2:15 We ourselves are Jews by birth and not Gentile sinners; 16 yet we know that a person is justified not by the works of the law but through faith in Jesus Christ. And we have come to believe in Christ Jesus, so that we might be justified by faith in Christ, and not by doing the works of the law, because no one will be justified by the works of the law. 17 But if, in our effort to be justified in Christ, we ourselves have been found to be sinners, is Christ then a servant of sin? Certainly not! 18 But if I build up again the very things that I once tore down, then I demonstrate that I am a transgressor. 19 For through the law I died to the law, so that I might live to God. I have been crucified with Christ; 20 and it is no longer I who live, but it is Christ who lives in me. And the life I now live in the flesh I live by faith in the Son of God, who loved me and gave himself for me. 21 I do not nullify the grace of God; for if justification comes through the law, then Christ died for nothing.

BACKGROUND

Many Bible scholars have called Paul's letter to the Galatians the "Magna Carta of Christian Liberty." What gave rise to the apostle's stringent teaching on Christian liberty was the churches' question about whether the Gentiles must convert to Judaism and observe the Mosaic law before they could be regarded as true believers. Legalistic members of these churches accused Paul of downplaying the importance of the law in order to make his message more appealing to the Gentiles.

These opponents of the apostle became known as "Judaizers." They taught that, in order for the Gentiles to become truly Christian, they had to submit to Jewish laws and customs. Heading the list for the Judaizers was the Gentiles' need to be circumcised. Paul followed the Jewish laws and customs; nevertheless, he adamantly opposed the efforts of the Judaizers to force Gentile converts to the faith to heed these requirements. In the Letter to the Galatians, the apostle repeatedly stressed that we are saved and justified by faith, not by keeping the law.

In the time of Paul, Galatia was a large Roman province located on the central plateau of Asia Minor (present-day Turkey). The name *Galatia* was introduced in 278 B.C. when a large number of Gauls migrated to the region from Europe. The area received full provincial status in 25 B.C. Paul visited Galatia on his first missionary journey, evangelizing the sophisticated, multiracial towns of Iconium, Antioch, Lystra, and Derbe (Acts 13:14—14:23). Later, Paul returned to strengthen the faith of the converts.

Paul's first mission through the province of Galatia evidently took place while he was suffering from an illness (Gal. 4:13). The circumstances created a close bond between the churches and Paul, and they treated him like an angel of God. They were his spiritual children, and with fatherly concern he longed for them to resist false teachers and grow toward spiritual maturity. That is why he was upset with them when some of them began to turn away from him and his teachings.

Certainly none of God's servants has ever held the Gospel more faithfully in his trust than Paul. In his years of seeking to be justified through observance of the law, Paul had found no salvation; but when he trusted in Christ, he received eternal life. That's why Paul became such an ardent preacher of the Gospel, stressing its great power to change people's lives.

NOTES ON THE PRINTED TEXT

As Paul introduced his letter to the churches of Galatia, he began by asserting his apostolic status. He typically did this in many of his letters. But to the churches of Galatia, Paul went a step further. In order to establish his authority for the message that was to follow, he wrote that he was *sent neither by human commission nor from human authorities, but through Jesus Christ and God the Father, who raised him from the dead* (Gal. 1:1). Having asserted such authority as a living representative of Jesus Christ, Paul fully expected the Galatians to accept what he was about to say. In mentioning that *all the members of God's family who are with me* (1:2), Paul helped to underscore his assertion of authority.

After passing along his greetings to the churches along with a synopsis of the Gospel—which, by the way, reminded the readers that justification came by grace through faith—Paul blasted the Galatians for *so quickly deserting the one who called you in the grace of Christ* (1:6). The apostle was shocked that followers of Jesus would turn away from the good news that they could be saved through believing in the saving work of Christ's death, burial, and resurrection. In one respect, the Galatians weren't so much turning away from the Gospel that Paul had preached as they were adding to the apostle's message. For the Judaizers, faith in Jesus was not enough. They added to the Gospel adherence to Jewish laws and customs.

Paul declared that these legalists were *confusing you and want to pervert the gospel of Christ* (1:7). Such a distorted message could not be of divine origin. Indeed, the apostle wrote that if anyone—including himself—*should proclaim to you a gospel contrary to what we proclaimed to you, let that one be accursed!* (1:8). Paul felt so strongly about the matter that he repeated his terse rebuke. It was his hope that God would punish anyone who preached anything different from the Gospel the believers at Galatia had already embraced (1:9).

After rehearsing his background for the Galatians and telling them about his discussions with the other apostles and his confrontation with Peter, Paul launched into a discussion about the fundamental differences between the law and the Gospel. Some Bible scholars believe that 2:15 and the subsequent verses are a continuation of Paul's confrontation with Peter. If so, then in saying *we ourselves* (2:15), Paul was likely talking about himself, Peter, and Barnabas as being born and raised as Jews. But even as Jews, they had found that they were declared right by God *not by the works of the law but through faith in Jesus Christ* (2:16). And since that was so, they should not be holding either Jewish Christians or Gentile Christians responsible for observing Jewish rules and customs.

Evidently the Judaizers thought the Gospel, when on its own, reveals one's sinfulness without revealing a way to avoid sinning. Thus, to them, the Gospel seemed actually to make Christ promote *sin* (2:17). Paul rejected this notion outright. For Christians to revert to the Jewish law is really to break the law (2:18).

Paul argued that the lawbreaker was not the one who looked to Christ for justification. Instead, it was the one who looked to the law for justification (2:18).

When Paul trusted in Christ for salvation, he was identified with Jesus' historic death, burial, and resurrection. Through spiritual union with Christ, Paul died to the law so that he could live for God (2:19). Paul, in a sense, was nailed to the cross with Christ and spiritually died there with Him. The apostle was also united with Christ in His resurrection. Thus, when Paul trusted in Jesus for salvation, He began to live in the apostle. Now as a Christian, Paul lived *by faith in the Son of God, who loved me and gave himself for me* (2:20).

Apparently the Judaizers claimed that Paul nullified God's grace in giving Israel the law, especially when the apostle taught that Gentiles did not have to obey the entire legal code. Paul rejected such an accusation. He declared that he did not set aside the grace of God. Instead, he affirmed it by teaching that justification and right behavior are established through Christ rather than through the law (2:21).

SUGGESTIONS TO TEACHERS

Paul wanted to convey to the Christians throughout Galatia—including both Jewish and Gentile Christians—the centrality of the Gospel, namely, that there is only one Gospel, and that that Gospel is the gift of salvation through faith in Jesus Christ. Any other message was a perversion of the Gospel. That's why Paul preached . . .

1. ONLY ONE WAY. Paul taught that there is only one way to be forgiven of sin, and that comes through faith in Christ for salvation. All other supposed means of salvation are insufficient. No other person, no other method, and no other ritual can redeem us or give us eternal life. The only way is through faith in Jesus Christ.

2. ONLY ONE TRUTH. Paul realized that the Judaizers had some measure of the truth; but because they were attempting to add to that truth, they were in effect twisting it. They claimed to follow Christ; but by requiring Gentiles to adhere to Jewish laws and customs, the legalists were denying that Jesus' death, burial, and resurrection were sufficient for salvation. Paul retorted that the truth of the Gospel cannot be added to or taken away from.

3. ONLY ONE GIFT. The Judaizers' argument that one had to obey the law in order to be a Christian undermined the message that salvation is a gift, not a reward for good works and deeds. Paul said that through Jesus' sacrificial death on the cross, He made God's gift of salvation available to all people—regardless of their race, nationality, or cultural and religious background. Because salvation is a gift of God, there is nothing people can do to earn it. All a person can do is accept the offer of salvation.

4. ONLY ONE REQUIREMENT. Those who were causing confusion in the Galatian churches believed that Jewish practices such as circumcision and dietary restrictions were required of all believers if they were to attain salvation. Paul reminded them that salvation cannot be attained, only received. The sole requirement is to believe in God's Son for eternal life.

5. ONLY ONE JUSTIFICATION. Paul noted that observing Jewish laws can never justify us, for the law is not able to make us acceptable to God. Because Jesus took our sins upon Himself and died in our place, our trusting in Him for salvation brings us acquittal before God. It is no longer with our own righteousness that we stand before God; rather, we do so with Jesus' righteousness. This means that believing sinners are justified by grace through faith.

6. ONLY ONE LIFE. As a result of trusting in Jesus for salvation, we have been identified with His death. We have also been identified with His resurrection and share in the new life He offers. Though we were once spiritually dead in our sins, now we can proclaim with Paul that *the life I now live in the flesh I live by faith in the Son of God* (Gal. 2:20).

FOR ADULTS

■ **TOPIC:** Living by the Truth

■ **QUESTIONS:** 1. Why do you think Paul found it necessary to assert his apostolic authority? 2. What would you say was the overriding problem in the churches of Galatia that the apostle was addressing? 3. What aspects of the Gospel did Paul stress in his letter to the Galatians? 4. In what ways were the Judaizers correct? 5. In what way were the Judaizers incorrect?

■ **ILLUSTRATIONS:**

Sermon in a Carving. While in a quaint old church outside Winchester, England, a visitor was studying a Bible resting on an old carved oak lectern. He had noticed that in nearly all old English churches, the lectern was shaped like an eagle. The pulpit in this sanctuary was also shaped like a huge eagle, except that the bird had the beak of a parrot. While examining the odd beak on the eagle, the visitor moreover noticed that a small heart was carved on the head of the eagle. The perplexed tourist asked the attendant why the lectern had the parrot's beak and the little carved heart.

"You must understand," stated the attendant, "that this ancient eagle was carved this way to remind everyone who reads the holy Word to us not to do so mechanically like a parrot, but fervently from the heart." This reminds us that when we study God's Word, we must not merely mouth the words in parrot-like fashion, but read them from the heart!

A Single Aim. Some time ago my daughter, Gracie, came in the house crying because someone had trimmed the tree she likes to climb so much. She calls it "Mytree." When I confessed that I was the culprit, she was none too happy with me. To her, it looked as though there was a good climbing branch or two that had been taken away, leaving the tree not quite as full as it had been.

Gracie was especially upset that I might have hurt "Mytree." When her anger had died down a bit, I took her outside to examine the tree. I showed her how dead branches needlessly sapped the tree of its strength. I explained that the tree's nourishment was being misdirected. I told her how I had cut the branches to help the tree, not to hurt it.

Then we walked around in the yard looking at the very hardy dogwood trees. We examined these trees with single, slender trunks and rich green leaves on every branch, just teeming with life. But then I took Gracie to a spot where about 18 dogwood shoots were growing all in one place. After all these years of living in the parsonage, I've never made the hard decision to trim back 17 of those shoots so that one could grow into a full tree. Right now these shoots are all bunched together; for years they have hardly grown at all. Some of them have already died. Most of the others look sickly and weak. Those dogwood shoots are too distracted to grow. They don't have a single aim. Their strength is divided up. Their purpose is self-reliant. They are not centered in a single source.

Those dogwood shoots were like the legalists in the churches of Galatia. To them, salvation came through believing in Christ *and* observing their regulations and customs. Paul reminded his readers that Christ—and Him alone—is the sole source of our salvation.

Deny Guilt. I heard about a woman who was at a social gathering of some ladies. When it came time to leave, she found that her car door was locked and her keys were in the ignition. Knowing that she had an appointment in an hour, the woman reluctantly went in the house and called her husband. He had to leave in the middle of an important meeting at work and drive 20 miles to the house.

While the ladies were waiting, one of them went around the car and tried each of the doors when she suddenly discovered that the passenger door was unlocked. Her friend looked at her and said, "What are you going to do?" The woman replied, "I'm gonna do what any decent wife would do." So she reached in, locked the door, and slammed it shut!

Everyone deals with guilt in different ways. You can deny guilt, attempt to minimize it, rationalize it, or blame others. But the only real solution is to repent of our sin and put our faith in Christ for salvation.

FOR YOUTH

■ TOPIC: The Only Way to Go

■ QUESTIONS: 1. Why did Paul assert that God had sent him to preach the Gospel? 2. What did the legalists say one had to do to be saved? 3. What did Paul say one had to do to be saved? 4. In what areas of life do you find it hardest to obey God? 5. In what ways do you find it hardest to love others? 6. Why do you think it is important to affirm that faith in Christ is the only way to God?

ILLUSTRATIONS:

The Main Thing. The story is told of a woman who bought a parrot to keep her company. Sadly, the woman ran into trouble, and thus she decided to return the bird the next day.

"This bird doesn't talk," the woman told the pet store owner.

"Does he have a mirror in his cage?" the pet store owner asked. "Parrots love mirrors. They see their reflection and often times that helps them to start a conversation." So the woman bought a mirror and left.

The next day the woman returned; the bird still wasn't talking.

"How about a ladder? Parrots love ladders. A happy parrot is a talkative parrot." So the woman bought a ladder and left.

But the next day, the woman was back. "Does your parrot have a swing? No? Well, that's the problem. Once he starts swinging, he'll talk up a storm." So the woman reluctantly bought a swing and left.

When the woman walked into the store the next day, her countenance had completely changed. "The parrot died," she blurted.

The pet store owner was shocked. "I am so sorry, ma'am. Tell me, did he ever say a word?" he asked.

"Yes," the woman replied. "Right before he died, he did. In a weak voice, he asked me, 'Don't they sell any food at that pet store?'"

The legalists in the churches of Galatia seem to have forgotten the main thing. Salvation through Jesus Christ and Him alone is the main thing.

Traditions Can Be Good. Traditions are a lot like habits: they can be very good. They can add to your life or take away from your life. They can help you. As a minister, I have had the wonderful privilege of sharing in many traditions—at least some of the good ones. As a church family we celebrate a few traditions, such as when we participate in the Lord's Supper throughout the year or when we have our footwashing service on Maundy Thursday and our Hanging of the Greens on the First Sunday of Advent. It's even traditional for me to greet as many folks as I can in the foyer before they leave to go home. Sweet traditions.

I've also had the privilege of participating in some people's personal traditions. For instance, Floyd has a tradition of sneaking off to the Cross Creek National Wildlife Refuge to watch the birds and sometimes to fish. A couple of springs ago Floyd took me with him to gaze with binoculars on the baby eaglets in their nest and the mother eagle feeding them food brought by the father eagle, who flew directly over our heads. It was magnificent! I'll never forget it.

Then there's Lyle and Marie's tradition of eating at Patti's Restaurant up in Grand Rivers. They introduced Jill and me to Patti's, and no matter where we've lived since—including Chicago—that has remained our favorite restaurant. And we'll never forget it.

Then there are the weddings. One of the most recent was Jeff and Jennifer's out at the Hewell farm in Woodlawn. We watched the horse-drawn carriage bring Jennifer over the gently rolling fields to where we were gathered for the ceremony. Don opened the door of the carriage, and there at Jennifer's feet in the carriage was her most incredibly loyal dog, Skeeter. And as I looked at Skeeter, I thought it was so sweet, and I had to fight back the tears to perform the ceremony. I'll never forget that either.

Or Traditions Can Be Bad. Traditions can also be bad. They can take away from your life. They can hurt you and others as well. Even our dog has certain traditions. In the last couple of months, he's even picked up a new one. We now have two dogs: Bonhoeffer, our wise and thoughtful four-year-old collie, and Oreo, our wild and crazy one-year-old mutt. Bonhoeffer has always been very good about letting us know when he wants to go outside. He will casually walk up to the door that leads to the parsonage's side yard and scratch the door three times. Whenever we open the door, Oreo shoots outside like a flying flash—way ahead of Bonhoeffer, who casually walks down the steps and out into the yard.

For the sake of this story, you also need to know that sometimes Oreo drives Bonhoeffer absolutely nuts! Oreo nips at Bonhoeffer's heals and jumps up on his head and bites his ears and steals his chew bone and steps on his tail and wakes him up while he's trying to take a nap. I'm amazed that Bonhoeffer hasn't killed that little puppy. It says a lot about the patience of that dog just by mentioning the fact that he's never even hurt Oreo.

But back to Bonhoeffer's new tradition. There are times when Bonhoeffer has taken all that he can from Oreo. (In the words of Popeye, "I've stands all I can stands and I can't stands no more!") Now when Bonhoeffer reaches the limit of his patience, he walks over to the door and scratches it three times. While Bonhoeffer stands at the door waiting to go out, we open the door. Out shoots Oreo like a flying flash. Then Bonhoeffer looks up in our eyes, breathes a sigh of relief that Oreo is outside, and walks over to the couch and lays down! He's achieved his goal of getting rid of his pest, and now he can get some rest for just a little while!

HEIRS WITH CHRIST

BACKGROUND SCRIPTURE: Galatians 3—4
DEVOTIONAL READING: Galatians 4:17-22

KEY VERSE: In Christ Jesus you are all children of God through faith. Galatians 3:26.

KING JAMES VERSION

GALATIANS 3:6 Even as Abraham believed God, and it was accounted to him for righteousness.

7 Know ye therefore that they which are of faith, the same are the children of Abraham.

8 And the scripture, foreseeing that God would justify the heathen through faith, preached before the gospel unto Abraham, saying, In thee shall all nations be blessed.

9 So then they which be of faith are blessed with faithful Abraham. . . .

23 But before faith came, we were kept under the law, shut up unto the faith which should afterwards be revealed.

24 Wherefore the law was our schoolmaster to bring us unto Christ, that we might be justified by faith.

25 But after that faith is come, we are no longer under a schoolmaster.

26 For ye are all the children of God by faith in Christ Jesus.

27 For as many of you as have been baptized into Christ have put on Christ.

28 There is neither Jew nor Greek, there is neither bond nor free, there is neither male nor female: for ye are all one in Christ Jesus.

29 And if ye be Christ's, then are ye Abraham's seed, and heirs according to the promise.

4:1 Now I say, That the heir, as long as he is a child, differeth nothing from a servant, though he be lord of all;

2 But is under tutors and governors until the time appointed of the father.

3 Even so we, when we were children, were in bondage under the elements of the world:

4 But when the fulness of the time was come, God sent forth his Son, made of a woman, made under the law,

5 To redeem them that were under the law, that we might receive the adoption of sons.

6 And because ye are sons, God hath sent forth the Spirit of his Son into your hearts, crying, Abba, Father.

7 Wherefore thou art no more a servant, but a son; and if a son, then an heir of God through Christ.

NEW REVISED STANDARD VERSION

GALATIANS 3:6 Just as Abraham "believed God, and it was reckoned to him as righteousness," 7 so, you see, those who believe are the descendants of Abraham. 8 And the scripture, foreseeing that God would justify the Gentiles by faith, declared the gospel beforehand to Abraham, saying, "All the Gentiles shall be blessed in you." 9 For this reason, those who believe are blessed with Abraham who believed. . . .

23 Now before faith came, we were imprisoned and guarded under the law until faith would be revealed. 24 Therefore the law was our disciplinarian until Christ came, so that we might be justified by faith. 25 But now that faith has come, we are no longer subject to a disciplinarian, 26 for in Christ Jesus you are all children of God through faith. 27 As many of you as were baptized into Christ have clothed yourselves with Christ. 28 There is no longer Jew or Greek, there is no longer slave or free, there is no longer male and female; for all of you are one in Christ Jesus. 29 And if you belong to Christ, then you are Abraham's offspring, heirs according to the promise. . . .

4:1 My point is this: heirs, as long as they are minors, are no better than slaves, though they are the owners of all the property; 2 but they remain under guardians and trustees until the date set by the father. 3 So with us; while we were minors, we were enslaved to the elemental spirits of the world. 4 But when the fullness of time had come, God sent his Son, born of a woman, born under the law, 5 in order to redeem those who were under the law, so that we might receive adoption as children. 6 And because you are children, God has sent the Spirit of his Son into our hearts, crying, "Abba! Father!" 7 So you are no longer a slave but a child, and if a child then also an heir, through God.

Monday, May 13	1 Corinthians 7:17-24	*Lead the Life the Lord Assigns You*
Tuesday, May 14	1 Corinthians 9:1-14	*Am I Not Free?*
Wednesday, May 15	1 Corinthians 9:15-23	*Free, but a Slave to All*
Thursday, May 16	1 Peter 1:1-12	*New Birth into a Living Hope*
Friday, May 17	1 Peter 2:11-17	*God's Servants Are Free People*
Saturday, May 18	1 Peter 3:13-22	*Free from Fear*
Sunday, May 19	Galatians 5:1-15	*You Were Called to Freedom*

BACKGROUND

The Letter to the Galatians indicates that a group of Jewish teachers insisted that non-Jewish believers must obey Jewish law and traditional roles. They believed a person was saved by following the law of Moses (with an emphasis on circumcision, the sign of the covenant), in addition to faith in Christ. In the *NIV Application Commentary* on Galatians, Scot McKnight writes the following:

> It is like telling a new convert from a Billy Graham Crusade today that he or she must also become Lutheran, Methodist, Presbyterian, etc., before the conversion process is truly complete and acceptable to God. When this sort of thing takes place, the message itself is changed; it is no longer "surrender to Christ" but "join our group." The focus of salvation shifts from Christ to a movement.

Paul opposed the efforts of the Judaizers to use the Gospel to promote their nationalistic, political, and social purposes. Part of his emotionally charged response to the Judaizers' teaching was directed not only at their misguided promotion of their religious dogma, but also at their underlying promotion of their political aspirations.

Through studying the Old Testament Scriptures, Paul realized that he could not be saved by obeying God's laws. In fact, the apostle stressed that the law served as a guide to point out our need to be forgiven. Since Christ fulfilled the obligations of the law for us, we must turn to Him to be saved. In a sense, then, Galatians is our charter of Christian freedom. We are neither under the jurisdiction of Jewish laws and traditions, nor under the authority of Jerusalem. Faith in Christ brings true freedom from sin and from the futile attempt to be right with God by keeping the law. Of course, we are not free to disobey Christ or practice immorality; rather, we are free to serve the risen Christ.

NOTES ON THE PRINTED TEXT

Abraham belonged to a family of idol worshipers living in the Mesopotamian city of Ur around 2010 B.C., when the living God called him to move to Canaan. At the age of 75, the patriarch obeyed. Abraham and the members of his clan never had a permanent home in Canaan, but rather ranged across it as nomads, and even lived for periods in neighboring areas. Yet God blessed them, and Abraham became wealthy.

God promised Abraham that he would have a son and that his descendants would possess Canaan. Finally, when Abraham was 100 years old, his son Isaac was born. The father of Israel died at the age of 175, having trusted God fully and having experienced His blessings.

It's no wonder that Paul would appeal to Abraham as an example of someone who lived by faith. The apostle noted that Abraham *"believed God, and it was reckoned to him as righteousness"* (3:6). Paul wanted to convey that only those who believe in Christ for their salvation are truly *descendants of Abraham* (3:7). Paul said this was God's plan from the time he called Abraham, noting that the Scriptures foresaw *that God would justify the Gentiles by faith* (3:8). Indeed, the provision of salvation for the Gentiles was the fulfillment of God's promise recorded in Genesis 12:3 to bless all people through Abraham.

It is our singular faith that brings us as believers together. The apostle wanted no barriers to separate those who trust in Christ for their salvation. Thus, with hopes of bringing both Jewish Christians and Gentile Christians together in a single bond of faith, despite their different religious practices and cultural backgrounds, Paul described both groups as being part of the same spiritual family: *For this reason, those who believe are blessed with Abraham who believed* (3:9).

In 3:10-22, Paul returned to the topic of the law. He explained that it revealed humanity's sinfulness and showed people their need for salvation in Christ. The apostle described us as being prisoners of sin, and in that imprisonment our only means of escape is to believe the promise of justification by grace through faith. In fact, Paul used two figures to explain how the law functions. First, it was the prison guard who kept us locked up *until faith would be revealed* (3:23). Second, the law was like a tutor who disciplined us *until Christ came, so that we might be justified* (3:24). But now that Jesus has come and enabled us to be freed through faith in Him, *we are no longer subject* (3:25) to either the prison guard or the tutor.

We have been set free from the bondage of the law. We have also been set free from the law's tendency to divide people into religious sects, *for in Christ Jesus you are all children of God through faith* (3:26). By being *baptized into Christ* (3:27), we have been united with Him and are increasingly becoming more like Him. Because we are united with Him by faith, we are also united with other believers. Issues of race, class, and gender no longer prevent us from having fellowship with any and all believers, *for all of you are one in Christ Jesus* (3:28). Because we *belong to Christ* (3:29), and therefore *are Abraham's offspring*, we are truly *heirs according to the promise*. Our equality in Christ Jesus will not permit us to hate, envy, or look down upon our fellow believers. Perhaps this is why Paul reminded his readers (both Jewish and Gentile Christians) to accept one another because they were *heirs according to the promise*.

Paul said that Israel's relationship with God could be compared to that of a child-heir during the period of adolescence. Although the children would one day receive everything their parents owned, during their minor years the children were no better off than a household servant (4:1). This is because the children were placed under the care of guardians and teachers until the time specified by their parents (4:2).

Before coming to Christ, everyone was enslaved to the *elemental spirits of the world* (4:3). Paul may have been referring to the law, to angels and demons, or to the superstitions of pagan religions. Whatever he meant by this, Paul was underscoring the enslaved status that we as people existed under before receiving the Gospel. *But when the fullness of time had come, God sent his Son, born of a woman, born under the law, in order to redeem those who were under the law, so that we might receive adoption as children* (4:4-5).

In that *God has sent the Spirit of his Son into our hearts* (4:6), the Spirit makes our adoption as the children of God a living reality. As God's spiritual children, we can call upon our Lord as *Abba*, an Aramaic word intimately referring to God as our *Father*. As the Spirit dwells within us, we become capable of the closest possible relationship with our Lord. We are promised, *So you are no longer a slave but a child, and if a child then also an heir, through God* (4:7).

SUGGESTIONS TO TEACHERS

Though Paul was addressing both Jewish Christians and Gentile Christians in the Letter to the Galatians, he took pains to make sure they understood that they were all a part of God's spiritual family. Because God adopts as His own children all who believe in His Son, *There is no longer Jew or Greek, there is no longer slave or free, there is no longer male and female; for all of you are one in Christ Jesus* (3:28). And as God's spiritual children, we have a share in all of His wonderful blessings.

1. A SHARE IN ABRAHAM'S BLESSING. As the adopted children of God, we have a great heritage that goes all the way back to Abraham. God's original promise to Abraham was that God intended to provide the means for the lost to be saved. Once Jesus Christ—the means for our salvation—had come, all those who are justified by grace through faith in Him become participants in this promise to Abraham and are eternally blessed.

2. A SHARE IN CHRIST'S SALVATION. It is actually our salvation through Christ that brings about our adoption into God's family. Through the law, we come to see our need for salvation; and through faith in Christ, we receive salvation. All who are justified by grace through faith have a share in this redemption.

3. A SHARE IN THE FAMILY OF GOD. As the adopted children of God, we are part of His family. While all of us, as believers, have a share in the family of God, none of us is better than anyone else within this family. And none of us should allow ourselves to be separated from our brothers and sisters in Christ because of differences in race, class, or gender. In fact, we would do well if we made it a point to seek out and appreciate our fellow believers who are not like us. When we do, we'll find that we have a lot in common through our faith in Christ.

4. A SHARE IN AN INTIMATE RELATIONSHIP. Because of Jesus Christ's work of salvation on the cross, He has enabled us to become the sons and daughters of God. Whereas we could not enter into God's presence with our sinfulness in tow, now that we have been forgiven, we can boldly come into the Lord's presence. Christ has opened the way for us to have a share in an intimate relationship with our heavenly Father.

5. A SHARE IN FREEDOM. Jesus' saving work on the cross not only provided the means for us to be forgiven but also redeemed us from the law. Jesus' death brought freedom for us who were enslaved to sin, and thus we also have a share in the freedom from the penalty of sin.

6. A SHARE IN CHRIST'S INHERITANCE. As the adopted children of God, we share along with Jesus—God's *only Son* (John 3:16)—all of the rights and privileges of being God's spiritual sons and daughters. We have access to God's resources; we are heirs along with Christ; and we have complete and full identity as God's children. As such, we have a share in the glory of Christ that will one day be revealed.

| **FOR ADULTS** | ■ TOPIC: God's Blended Family |
| | ■ QUESTIONS: 1. How is our faith in Christ a fulfillment of God's |

promise to Abraham? 2. How is it that all believers in Christ are *the descendants of Abraham* (Gal. 3:7)? 3. In what ways was adherence to the law like imprisonment? 4. In what ways was adherence to the law like being under the care of a disciplinarian? 5. In what ways have you *clothed* (3:27) yourself with Christ?

■ **ILLUSTRATIONS:**

Those Who Believe Are Blessed. Jenny was a bright-eyed, pretty five-year-old girl. One day when she and her mother were checking out at the grocery store, Jenny saw a plastic pearl necklace priced at $2.50. How she wanted that necklace, and when she asked her mother if she would buy it for her, her mother said, "Well, it is a pretty necklace, but it costs an awful lot of money. I'll tell you what. I'll buy you the necklace, and when we get home we can make up a list of chores that you can do to pay for the necklace. And don't forget that for your birthday Grandma just might give you a whole dollar bill, too. Okay?"

Jenny agreed, and her mother bought the pearl necklace for her. Jenny worked on her chores very hard every day and, sure enough, her grandma gave her a brand new dollar bill for her birthday. Soon Jenny had paid off the pearls. How Jenny loved those pearls. She wore them everywhere—to kindergarten, bed, and when she went out with her mother to run errands. The only time she didn't wear them was in the shower—her mother had told her that they would turn her neck green!

Now Jenny had a very loving daddy. When Jenny went to bed, he would get up from his favorite chair every night and read Jenny her favorite story. One night when he finished the story, he said, "Jenny, do you love me?"

"Oh yes, Daddy, you know I love you," the little girl said.

"Well, then, give me your pearls."

"Oh! Daddy, not my pearls!" Jenny said. "But you can have Rosie, my favorite doll. Remember her? You gave her to me last year for my birthday. And you can have her tea party outfit, too. Okay?"

"Oh no, darling, that's okay." Her father brushed her cheek with a kiss. "Good night, little one."

A week later, her father once again asked Jenny after her story, "Do you love me?"

"Oh yes, Daddy, you know I love you."

"Well, then, give me your pearls."

"Oh, Daddy, not my pearls! But you can have Ribbons, my toy horse. Do you remember her? She's my favorite. Her hair is so soft, and you can play with it and braid it and everything. You can have Ribbons if you want her, Daddy," the little girl said to her father.

"No, that's okay," her father said and brushed her cheek again with a kiss. "God bless you, little one. Sweet dreams."

Several days later, when Jenny's father came in to read her a story, Jenny was sitting on her bed and her lip was trembling.

"Here, Daddy," she said, and held out her hand. She opened it and her beloved pearl necklace was inside. She let it slip into her father's hand. With one hand her father held the plastic pearls and with the other he pulled out of his pocket a blue velvet box. Inside of the box were real, genuine, beautiful pearls. He had had them all along. He was waiting for Jenny to give up the cheap stuff so he could give her the real thing.

So it is with our heavenly Father. He is waiting for us to give up the cheap things in our lives so he can give us beautiful treasure. Isn't God good?

All the Things Written in the Book of the Law. A devout Christian athlete passed up the 2000 Olympics because the final of his event took place on Sunday. Chris Harmse of South Africa, a hammer thrower, withdrew from his country's team, the publication *Business Day* reported.

Harmse, who held the record on the African continent for the hammer throw, had qualified for the team during a pre-Olympic event. He "agonized over his decision before deciding that his faith took precedence," Sam Ramsamy, president of South Africa's National Olympic Committee, told *Business Day.*

Harmse was the second Olympian to withdraw from the games for religious reasons since 1924, when British sprinter Eric Liddell dropped out of the 100-meter race in Paris because the final took place on Sunday. Liddell, the son of a Scottish missionary, won the 400-meter gold medal but was preaching in a church on the day of the final, opening the way for Harold Abrahams to win the 100-meter gold medal. That story inspired the movie "Chariots of Fire."

All of You Are One in Christ Jesus. God speaks in the world's most difficult language. Tabasaran, spoken by a group of people living in the Caucasus region of southern Russia, is described by the *Guinness Book of World Records* as the most difficult language in the world to learn because of its complex grammatical structure, International Russian Radio/Television reports.

One ministry has started translating Christian television programs into Tabasaran, even though there are only a few Christians among the mostly Muslim people, IRR/TV's Hannu Haukka said. "There is no language so difficult that God does not speak it—that is why the Gospel of Jesus Christ must be presented to the Tabasaran people."

FOR YOUTH

■ TOPIC: God's Blended Family

■ QUESTIONS: 1. What kind of rules seem to be the most important in your peer group? In what ways are those rules good? In what ways are they bad? 2. In what ways do you see faith in Jesus breaking down racial, class, and gender barriers? 3. In what ways does the Mosaic law hold in slavery those who adhere to it? 4. What is the importance to you of being adopted as a child of God? 5. What benefits do you expect to receive as an adopted child of God?

■ **ILLUSTRATIONS:**

Guarded under the Law. There are some things that only a mother can teach you. It has been said that our mothers taught us a lot about anticipation: "You just wait until your father gets home!" They teach us logic: "If you fall off that swing and break your neck, you're not going to the store with me." They teach us medicine: "If you don't stop crossing your eyes, they're going to get stuck that way." They teach us humor: "When the lawn mower cuts off your toes, don't come running to me." They teach us about genetics: "You're just like your daddy." They teach us about the wisdom of age: "When you get to be my age, you will understand." They teach us about justice: "One day you'll have kids, and I hope they turn out just like you; then you'll see what it's like." My own mother taught me the whole gist of life and living—from the Bible, of course: *All Scripture . . . is useful for teaching, for reproof, for correction, and for training in righteousness* (2 Tim. 3:16).

The Law Was Our Disciplinarian. As kids learn lessons from their mothers, they are sometimes able to pass on to other kids what they've learned. Here's some wise advice from a few kids. Fourteen-year-old Michael has learned this: "Never tell your mom her diet's not working." Mitchell, 12, says, "Don't sneeze in front of mom when you're eating crackers." Armir has learned that "You can't hide a piece of broccoli in a glass of milk." Alyesha figured this out: "When you get a bad grade in school, show it to your mom when she's on the phone." Taylia knows that "When your mom is mad at your dad, don't let her brush your hair." And Michael advises, "When your mom is mad and asks you, 'Do I look stupid?' don't answer her."

Clothe Yourselves with Christ. A good way to judge character in people is by observing how they treat those who can do them absolutely no good. So if you want to see character, watch a loving mother with her newborn. The newborn can do the mother absolutely no good. The newborn won't even remember the care and concern offered by the mother. The mother knows this, and yet, still she showers the baby with care and warmth and concern. Why? Because love is the foundation of her character. Former UCLA basketball coach John Wooden advised his players well when he told them, "Be more concerned with your character than your reputation, because your character is what you really are, while your reputation is merely what others think you are."

CALLED TO FREEDOM

BACKGROUND SCRIPTURE: Galatians 5:1-15
DEVOTIONAL READING: 1 John 2:7-17

KEY VERSE: You were called to freedom, brothers and sisters;
only do not use your freedom as an opportunity for self-indulgence,
but through love become slaves to one another. Galatians 5:13.

KING JAMES VERSION

GALATIANS 5:1 Stand fast therefore in the liberty wherewith Christ hath made us free, and be not entangled again with the yoke of bondage.

2 Behold, I Paul say unto you, that if ye be circumcised, Christ shall profit you nothing.

3 For I testify again to every man that is circumcised, that he is a debtor to do the whole law.

4 Christ is become of no effect unto you, whosoever of you are justified by the law; ye are fallen from grace.

5 For we through the Spirit wait for the hope of righteousness by faith.

6 For in Jesus Christ neither circumcision availeth any thing, nor uncircumcision; but faith which worketh by love.

7 Ye did run well; who did hinder you that ye should not obey the truth?

8 This persuasion cometh not of him that calleth you.

9 A little leaven leaveneth the whole lump.

10 I have confidence in you through the Lord, that ye will be none otherwise minded: but he that troubleth you shall bear his judgment, whosoever he be.

11 And I, brethren, if I yet preach circumcision, why do I yet suffer persecution? then is the offence of the cross ceased.

12 I would they were even cut off which trouble you.

13 For, brethren, ye have been called unto liberty; only use not liberty for an occasion to the flesh, but by love serve one another.

14 For all the law is fulfilled in one word, even in this; Thou shalt love thy neighbour as thyself.

15 But if ye bite and devour one another, take heed that ye be not consumed one of another.

NEW REVISED STANDARD VERSION

GALATIANS 5:1 For freedom Christ has set us free. Stand firm, therefore, and do not submit again to a yoke of slavery.

2 Listen! I, Paul, am telling you that if you let yourselves be circumcised, Christ will be of no benefit to you. 3 Once again I testify to every man who lets himself be circumcised that he is obliged to obey the entire law. 4 You who want to be justified by the law have cut yourselves off from Christ; you have fallen away from grace. 5 For through the Spirit, by faith, we eagerly wait for the hope of righteousness. 6 For in Christ Jesus neither circumcision nor uncircumcision counts for anything; the only thing that counts is faith working through love.

7 You were running well; who prevented you from obeying the truth? 8 Such persuasion does not come from the one who calls you. 9 A little yeast leavens the whole batch of dough. 10 I am confident about you in the Lord that you will not think otherwise. But whoever it is that is confusing you will pay the penalty. 11 But my friends, why am I still being persecuted if I am still preaching circumcision? In that case the offense of the cross has been removed. 12 I wish those who unsettle you would castrate themselves!

13 For you were called to freedom, brothers and sisters; only do not use your freedom as an opportunity for self-indulgence, but through love become slaves to one another. 14 For the whole law is summed up in a single commandment, "You shall love your neighbor as yourself." 15 If, however, you bite and devour one another, take care that you are not consumed by one another.

Monday, May 20	Ephesians 3:1-13	*The Mystery Proclaimed by the Spirit*
Tuesday, May 21	Ephesians 3:14-21	*Be Filled with the Fullness of God*
Wednesday, May 22	Ephesians 4:1-13	*One Body and One Spirit*
Thursday, May 23	2 Corinthians 5:1-10	*Longing for Our Heavenly Dwelling*
Friday, May 24	2 Corinthians 6:1-13	*Now Is the Acceptable Time*
Saturday, May 25	Galatians 5:16-26	*The Fruit of the Spirit*
Sunday, May 26	Galatians 6	*You Reap What You Sow*

BACKGROUND

After Paul won the Galatians to Christ, they undoubtedly struggled to find their way. The new believers strained to grasp how grace had changed them. They also faced staggering social upheaval—the Gospel put Gentiles on an equal basis with Jews. In this explosive atmosphere a spark was struck. Judaizers introduced their brand of the Gospel. They believed God's grace was for Jews only. According to the legalists, if Gentiles wanted salvation, they first had to become Jewish.

Paul's message was quite different from that of the Judaizers. He taught that grace means freedom. To return to the law was to abandon grace. To use freedom irresponsibly was unloving, contradicting grace. Paul stressed to the Galatians that they needed to mature in Christ and live in the power of the Spirit, not the flesh. Many people today, of course, want to live godly lives, but they feel frustrated with their performance—particularly if they measure themselves against unrealistic standards. Some people may feel as though they dress the part on Sunday, only to blow their cover on Monday.

What happens when everyday aggravations push a person to the brink? In the stress and strain of living earthbound lives, heavenly vision can become blurred. This is what happened with the Galatian believers. Consequently, Paul stressed that their relationship to God was based on faith in Christ, not observing the law. It is only as they directed their attention to the grace of God that the Galatians would become spiritually whole once again.

In this week's lesson we will learn that Paul urged the Galatians not to give up their Christian freedom for bondage to the law. If they tried to win God's favor by obeying the law, they would be denying His grace. As long as the Galatians continued in legalism, it would hinder their spiritual growth and create division among the members of their church. That's why Paul reminded them once again of their liberty in Christ, and their freedom to serve God and others out of love.

If we want to please God and obey His Word, we must trust in Christ and live by the power of the Holy Spirit. Through the ministry of the triune God, we will realize that all that the law says can be summed up in the command to love others as much as we love ourselves. As those who are characterized by the love of God, we are encouraged by Paul not to verbally attack one another like wild animals. Instead, we should show compassion, understanding, and kindness to our fellow Christians.

NOTES ON THE PRINTED TEXT

The liberating truth the Galatians needed to embrace is that Christ had set them free from bondage to sin and the curse pronounced by the law. Although the Savior rescued His people from spiritual slavery, it was their responsibility to resist being enslaved again. The Judaizers were burdening the Galatians with a yoke of legalistic demands. Paul urged them (and us) to stand firm as *free* (Gal. 5:1) people.

Although the Galatians were flirting with legalism, they evidently had not succumbed to being *circumcised* (5:2). If they allowed this rite to be performed on them, two negative consequences would result. First, Christ would not do them any good, for they would be looking to the *law* (5:3), not Christ, for righteousness. Second, if the Galatians got circumcised, they would be a debtor to the law and obligated to obey every aspect of it. Paul's readers had not thought of this, however. In fact, by looking to the law for righteousness they alienated themselves from Christ and abandoned the *grace* (5:4) of God.

When we trust in Christ, God declares us righteous and gives us His Holy Spirit. *The Spirit* (5:5) helps us to live for God and look with anticipation to the day when the Lord will make our salvation final. *Circumcision* (5:6), by the way, has no positive effect on the outcome. From an eternal perspective, the act of circumcision does not matter with God. Rather, it is our faith in Christ demonstrating itself in sincere acts of *love*. This implies that love is the motivating force behind practical Christianity.

Paul said the Galatians had been *running well* (5:7) until the Judaizers, like unfair competitors, had cut in on them and broken their stride. The legalists had hindered Paul's readers from obeying *the truth* of the Gospel. Despite the Judaizers' claims, they and their message did not originate from God (5:8). Quoting a popular proverb, Paul said a *little yeast* (5:9) can cause a *whole batch of dough* to rise. In other words, the false teaching of the Judaizers, like yeast, was spreading through the Galatian church and poisoning the thinking of every member. Despite the grim situation in Galatia, Paul was convinced that his readers belonged to *the Lord* (5:10). The apostle was assured they would heed his words and reject the teaching of the Judaizers. Moreover, Paul believed God would punish the legalists.

The Judaizers tried to convince the Galatians that Paul affirmed the necessity of *circumcision* (5:11). The apostle, however, asked why the Judaizers *persecuted* him if he preached circumcision. If Paul insisted on the necessity of this religious ceremony, he would be nullifying Christ's work on *the cross*. The cross was an offense to the Jewish law, yet it was the source of life for all who believe.

Paul greatly disliked the confusion and distress the Judaizers had caused for the

Galatians. The apostle wished the legalists *would castrate themselves* (5:12). Paul believed that circumcision had no religious significance for Christians and that when it was forced on Gentile converts, it amounted only to bodily damage.

Paul said to his friends in Galatia that God chose them in Christ to be free. Their liberty, however, was not an excuse for living in sin, but rather an opportunity to serve God and others in *love* (5:13). The apostle declared that everything the law said could be *summed up in a single commandment, "You shall love your neighbor as yourself"* (5:14). The legalistic mentality of the Galatians had produced a critical, self-righteous spirit among them. Consequently, they were verbally biting and devouring one another like wild animals. If this continued, it would destroy their fellowship (5:15). That is why Paul wanted them to put a stop to their bickering and begin again to love one another unconditionally.

The freedom we enjoy in the West was won at the cost of many lives. It would be a tragedy if we took this freedom for granted. Yet when we relate to God in a legalistic manner, we are guilty of devaluing the freedom we have in Christ. When we try to obtain God's favor by performing a long list of good deeds, we are saying that the sacrifice of Christ was insufficient to secure our righteousness. This week's lesson has reminded us that the liberty we have in Christ is too precious to abandon or abuse.

SUGGESTIONS TO TEACHERS

Because of our freedom in Christ, we are able both to be and to refrain from being many things we weren't capable of prior to getting saved. In Galatians 5:1-15, Paul talked about at least six of these ways of existing as followers of Christ.

1. BE FREE. We are told to *Stand firm* (5:1) in the freedom that has been gained for us because of the death, burial, and resurrection of Jesus Christ. We have been set free from the constraints of the law, from our sinfulness, and from the punishment for our sinfulness. Thus we have also been set free to live unselfishly, to love others as we have been loved by God, and to obey the Savior.

2. DON'T BE CUT OFF FROM CHRIST. Seeking salvation by any other means than through faith in Christ is not only futile, but it also diminishes the significance of our faith in Him.

3. BE FAITHFUL. We are saved by faith, not by our deeds. We simply accept the gracious gift that God has offered us in Christ. In gratitude, we ought to strive to live faithfully for the one who has been so completely faithful to us.

4. BE LOVING. Compassion for others and love for God is our response for the forgiveness God offers us in Christ. Paul wrote that *the whole law is summed up in a single commandment, "You shall love your neighbor as yourself"* (5:14).

5. DON'T BE SELF-INDULGENT. In the course of living out our freedom in Christ, we are warned that our freedom is not to be exercised only for our own good. The costly freedom that Christ paid for with His own life is precious, and thus it is not to be used as we please. The apostle called upon all believers to exercise their freedom in self-sacrificing service for God and for others.

6. DON'T BE MALICIOUS. Surely we are all precious in God's sight. Therefore, we should not think of ourselves as better than or above others in the Body of Christ. When we become critical of others, when we can only see their faults, when we focus on their shortcomings, our unity as Christians is broken. Maliciousness has no place in the body of believers; it breeds destruction within a fellowship that should be operating with concern and each other's best interest at heart.

<table>
<tr><td>

FOR ADULTS

</td><td>

■ **TOPIC:** The Point of Freedom
■ **QUESTIONS:** 1. What do you think Paul meant when he said *For freedom Christ has set us free* (Gal. 5:1)? 2. What kind of *yoke of*

</td></tr>
</table>

slavery are Christians tempted to submit themselves to today? 3. How are you supposed to live out your dependence on Christ for your salvation? 4. Why would the desire to be justified by the law cut one off from Christ? 5. How is our Christian freedom sometimes seen *as an opportunity for self-indulgence* (5:13) today?

■ **ILLUSTRATIONS:**

We Eagerly Wait for the Hope of Righteousness. His name was Fleming, and he was a poor Scottish farmer. One day, while trying to make a living for his family, he heard a cry for help coming from a nearby bog. He dropped his tools and ran to the bog.

There, mired to his waist in black muck, was a terrified boy, screaming and struggling to free himself. Farmer Fleming saved the lad from what could have been a slow and terrifying death. The next day, a fancy carriage pulled up to the Scotsman's sparse surroundings. An elegantly dressed nobleman stepped out and introduced himself as the father of the boy Farmer Fleming had saved.

"I want to repay you," said the nobleman. "You saved my son's life."

"No, I can't accept payment for what I did," the Scottish farmer replied, waving off the offer. At that moment, the farmer's own son came to the door of the family hovel.

"Is that your son?" the nobleman asked.

"Yes," the farmer replied proudly.

"I'll make you a deal. Let me take him and give him a good education. If the lad is anything like his father, he'll grow to a man you can be proud of."

And that he did.

In time, Farmer Fleming's son graduated from Saint Mary's Hospital Medical School in London, and went on to become known throughout the world as the noted Sir Alexander Fleming, the discoverer of penicillin.

Years afterward, the nobleman's son was stricken with pneumonia. What saved him? Penicillin. The name of the nobleman? Lord Randolph Churchill. His son's name? Sir Winston Churchill.

Stand Firm, Therefore. On the opening day of Major League Baseball back in 1954, the Cincinnati Reds played the Milwaukee Braves. There were two rookies who started in that game. Cincinnati had a rookie who went four-for-four with four doubles. The Braves' rookie went zero-for-four.

But keep this in mind: that was just the first day. Which of these two rookies is it that people remember today? Is it the Reds' rookie who went four-for-four? I doubt it, unless you can remember the very brief baseball career of a guy named Jim Greengrass. So then it must be the Braves' rookie, the one who went zero-for-four. You've probably heard of him! His name is Hank Aaron. Hammerin' Hank surpassed Babe Ruth's lifetime record of 714 home runs, retiring with a total of 755 home runs. (Just in case you're wondering, Jim Greengrass went on to start his own lawn care company. He certainly had the right name for such a career!)

The point here is that people won't remember how you started. But they will remember how you finish. Your life may be strewn with countless mistakes and blunders and even sins, but the question for today is this: Which direction is it heading now? Face the right direction; then stand firm.

FOR YOUTH

■ TOPIC: We've Been Set Free!

■ QUESTIONS: 1. Why would anyone who had been set free want to return to slavery? 2. What exactly do you think has to happen for someone to *have fallen away from grace* (Gal. 5:4)? 3. In what ways are you, *through the Spirit, by faith* (5:5), eagerly waiting for *the hope of righteousness*? 4. How could Paul be so confident that the Galatians would accept what he had said? 5. What principles can you find in Galatians 5:13-15 to guide believers in the proper use of Christian liberty?

■ ILLUSTRATIONS:

Christ Has Set Us Free. George Thomas was a pastor in a small New England town. One Easter Sunday morning he came to church carrying a rusty, bent, old birdcage, and set it by the pulpit. Several eyebrows were raised and, as if in response, Pastor Thomas began to speak. . . .

I was walking through town yesterday when I saw a young boy coming toward me swinging this birdcage. On the bottom of the cage were three little wild birds, shivering with cold and fright. I stopped the lad and asked, "What you got there son?"

"Just some old birds," came the reply.

"What are you gonna do with them?" I asked.

"Take 'em home and have fun with 'em," he answered. I'm gonna tease 'em and pull out their feathers to make 'em fight. I'm gonna have a real good time."

"But you'll get tired of those birds sooner or later. What will you do then?"

"Oh, I got some cats," said the little boy. "They like birds. I'll take 'em to them."

I was silent for a moment. "How much do you want for those birds, son?"

"Huh? Why, you don't want them birds, mister. They're just plain old field birds. They don't sing—they ain't even pretty!"

"How much?" I asked again.

The boy sized me up as if I were crazy, and then he said, "Ten dollars?"

I reached in my pocket and took out a ten dollar bill. I placed it in the boy's hand. In a flash, he was gone. So I picked up the cage and gently carried it to the end of the alley where there was a tree and a grassy spot. Setting the cage down, I opened the door, and by softly tapping the bars persuaded the birds out, setting them free.

(Having explained the empty bird cage on the pulpit, the pastor then began to tell this story. . . .)

One day Satan and Jesus were having a conversation. Satan had just come from the Garden of Eden, and he was gloating and boasting. "Yes, sir, I just caught the world full of people down there. Set me a trap, used bait I knew they couldn't resist. Got 'em all!"

"What are you going to do with them?" Jesus asked.

Satan replied, "Oh, I'm gonna have fun! I'm gonna teach them how to marry and divorce each other, how to hate and abuse each other, how to drink and smoke and curse. I'm gonna teach them how to invent guns and bombs and kill each other. I'm really gonna have fun!"

"And what will you do when you get done with them?" Jesus asked.

"Oh, I'll kill 'em," Satan glared proudly.

"How much do you want for them?" Jesus asked.

"Oh, you don't want those people. They ain't no good. Why, you'll take them and they'll just hate you. They'll spit on you, curse you, and kill you!! You don't want those people!"

"How much?" He asked again.

Satan looked at Jesus and sneered, "All your tears and all your blood."

Jesus said, "Done!" Then He paid the price.

The Only Thing That Counts. When she learned that she was dying from cancer, Erma Bombeck wrote a column called "If I Had My Life to Live Over." In that column she recounted some of her life experiences that she wished she had done a bit differently. This is what Erma said:

> I would have gone to bed when I was sick instead of pretending the earth would go into a holding pattern if I weren't there for the day. I would have

burned the pink candle sculpted like a rose before it melted in storage. I would have talked less and listened more. I would have invited friends over to dinner even if the carpet was stained or the sofa faded. I would have eaten the popcorn in the "good" living room and worried much less about the dirt when someone wanted to light a fire in the fireplace. I would have taken the time to listen to my grandfather ramble about his youth. . . . I would never have insisted the car windows be rolled up on a summer day because my hair had just been teased and sprayed. I would have sat on the lawn with my children and not worried about grass stains. I would have cried and laughed less while watching television—and more while watching life. I would never have bought anything just because it was practical, wouldn't show soil, or was guaranteed to last a lifetime. Instead of wishing away nine months of pregnancy, I'd have cherished every moment and realized that the wonderment growing inside me was the only chance in life to assist God in a miracle. When my kids kissed me impetuously, I would never have said, "Later. Now go get washed up for dinner." There would have been more "I love yous." More "I'm sorrys." But mostly, given another shot at life, I would seize every minute—look at it and really see it, live it, and never give it back.

LIVE BY THE SPIRIT

BACKGROUND SCRIPTURE: Galatians 5:16—6:18
DEVOTIONAL READING: Colossians 3:5-17

KEY VERSE: Live by the Spirit, I say, and do not gratify the desires of the flesh. Galatians 5:16.

KING JAMES VERSION

GALATIANS 5:16 This I say then, Walk in the Spirit, and ye shall not fulfil the lust of the flesh.

17 For the flesh lusteth against the Spirit, and the Spirit against the flesh: and these are contrary the one to the other: so that ye cannot do the things that ye would.

18 But if ye be led of the Spirit, ye are not under the law.

19 Now the works of the flesh are manifest, which are these; Adultery, fornication, uncleanness, lasciviousness,

20 Idolatry, witchcraft, hatred, variance, emulations, wrath, strife, seditions, heresies,

21 Envyings, murders, drunkenness, revellings, and such like: of the which I tell you before, as I have also told you in time past, that they which do such things shall not inherit the kingdom of God.

22 But the fruit of the Spirit is love, joy, peace, long-suffering, gentleness, goodness, faith,

23 Meekness, temperance: against such there is no law.

24 And they that are Christ's have crucified the flesh with the affections and lusts.

25 If we live in the Spirit, let us also walk in the Spirit.

26 Let us not be desirous of vain glory, provoking one another, envying one another.

6:1 Brethren, if a man be overtaken in a fault, ye which are spiritual, restore such an one in the spirit of meekness; considering thyself, lest thou also be tempted.

2 Bear ye one another's burdens, and so fulfil the law of Christ.

3 For if a man think himself to be something, when he is nothing, he deceiveth himself.

4 But let every man prove his own work, and then shall he have rejoicing in himself alone, and not in another.

5 For every man shall bear his own burden. . . .

7 Be not deceived; God is not mocked: for whatsoever a man soweth, that shall he also reap.

8 For he that soweth to his flesh shall of the flesh reap corruption; but he that soweth to the Spirit shall of the Spirit reap life everlasting.

9 And let us not be weary in well doing: for in due season we shall reap, if we faint not.

NEW REVISED STANDARD VERSION

GALATIANS 5:16 Live by the Spirit, I say, and do not gratify the desires of the flesh. 17 For what the flesh desires is opposed to the Spirit, and what the Spirit desires is opposed to the flesh; for these are opposed to each other, to prevent you from doing what you want. 18 But if you are led by the Spirit, you are not subject to the law. 19 Now the works of the flesh are obvious: fornication, impurity, licentiousness, 20 idolatry, sorcery, enmities, strife, jealousy, anger, quarrels, dissensions, factions, 21 envy, drunkenness, carousing, and things like these. I am warning you, as I warned you before: those who do such things will not inherit the kingdom of God.

22 By contrast, the fruit of the Spirit is love, joy, peace, patience, kindness, generosity, faithfulness, 23 gentleness, and self-control. There is no law against such things. 24 And those who belong to Christ Jesus have crucified the flesh with its passions and desires. 25 If we live by the Spirit, let us also be guided by the Spirit. 26 Let us not become conceited, competing against one another, envying one another.

6:1 My friends, if anyone is detected in a transgression, you who have received the Spirit should restore such a one in a spirit of gentleness. Take care that you yourselves are not tempted. 2 Bear one another's burdens, and in this way you will fulfill the law of Christ. 3 For if those who are nothing think they are something, they deceive themselves. 4 All must test their own work; then that work, rather than their neighbor's work, will become a cause for pride. 5 For all must carry their own loads. . . .

7 Do not be deceived; God is not mocked, for you reap whatever you sow. 8 If you sow to your own flesh, you will reap corruption from the flesh; but if you sow to the Spirit, you will reap eternal life from the Spirit. 9 So let us not grow weary in doing what is right, for we will reap at harvest time, if we do not give up.

13

HOME BIBLE READINGS

Monday, May 27	Psalm 1	*Choose the Righteous Way*
Tuesday, May 28	Psalm 33:1-11	*God Loves Righteousness and Justice*
Wednesday, May 29	Psalm 33:12-22	*Hope in God's Steadfast Love*
Thursday, May 30	Psalm 11	*The Lord Loves Righteous Deeds*
Friday, May 31	Psalm 7	*God Is a Righteous Judge*
Saturday, June 1	Psalm 19:1-6	*The Heavens Tell of God's Glory*
Sunday, June 2	Psalm 19:7-14	*The Lord's Law Is Perfect*

BACKGROUND

Paul's letter to the Galatians is a progressive argument against the idea that people are saved by adhering to the Mosaic law; rather, justification is by grace through faith. In many respects, the first four chapters are a well-assembled succession of examples and citations about the claims of the law and the claims of the Gospel. Knowing that the Judaizers had gained considerable influence over the Gentile Christians of Galatia, Paul fiercely fought to regain lost turf. The Gospel itself had been slandered and diminished because of the Judaizers' teaching that to be saved one must not only believe in Christ, but must also heed Jewish regulations and customs.

Having led the charge to reinstate and reiterate the believer's freedom in Christ, the apostle, in the closing chapters of his letter, defined what kind of freedom the believer experiences as well as what it entails. Paul warned that Christian liberty is not a freedom toward the self-indulgence of licentiousness. Instead, he pointed to the exercise of loving service as the truest mark and measure of Christian freedom. The apostle directed his readers away from their self-interest and recalled for them that loving service is measured by the way they treated other people. Love, as demonstrated through service to others, is the fruit of Christian freedom.

Although Christians are free from the condemnation of law, the apostle said they are not free from ethical responsibility. It is possible that his teaching on Christian freedom had led some to label him as a libertine. And it is also possible that Paul intended to answer and refute those who had labeled him as such. Yet, his teaching in Galatians remains the same as that throughout his other letters. The message that we are justified by grace through faith in Christ comes through clearly, but so also do the apostle's moral imperatives for the believer.

Paul, of course, never intended for us to live up to these moral imperatives in our own strength. To do so, in one sense, was similar to attempting to attain salvation by keeping the law, for such an attempt was futile. But so was trying to live up to a good moral standard based on our own resources and strength. Paul understood that to follow God's moral imperatives, believers needed a power from outside themselves. That power, he explained, is the Holy Spirit. Only the Spirit of God can enable believers to live uprightly and serve one another sacrificially.

NOTES ON THE PRINTED TEXT

Paul made it clear that the moral life of the believer must be driven by the Holy Spirit. For if we *Live by the Spirit* (5:16), we will not be controlled by the desires of our sinful nature. Living according to our sinful human nature is diametrically opposed to our living for *what the Spirit desires* (5:17). Trapped in this conflict between the spiritual good and the selfish evil, we can consistently choose and do the good only when we yield ourselves to the Holy Spirit's leading. Thus, said the apostle (returning to the overriding theme), if we are *led by the Spirit* (5:18), we no longer try to earn our salvation by straining in vain to keep the law. Rather, the Holy Spirit enables us to live by God's law of love and therefore fulfill the purpose of the law.

As a caution to his readers not to confuse Christian liberty for license, Paul recorded a list of *works of the flesh* (5:19). In essence, these can develop from our allowing our "freedom to" to become our "freedom from." Thus our freedom to love can become *fornication*. Our freedom to worship can become *idolatry* (5:20). Our freedom to inquire can become *enmities*. Our freedom to discuss can become *quarrels*. Our freedom to disagree can become *dissensions*. Our freedom to serve can become *factions*. And our freedom to thrive can become *envy* (5:21). Such vices result from living under the control of the sinful nature.

The first three vices in this catalog—*fornication, impurity, licentiousness* (5:19)—include natural and perverted forms of sexual sin among both married and unmarried persons. The next two vices—*idolatry, sorcery* (5:20)—are perversions of worship. The next nine vices—*enmities, strife, jealousy, anger, quarrels, dissensions, factions,* and *envy* (5:21)—involve relationships that have gone awry and are the complete opposite of love for others. The final two vices—*drunkenness, carousing*—are personal offenses that emerge in social settings. The apostle said *those who do such things will not inherit the kingdom of God.*

In contrast to this list of vices, Paul also provided a list of *the fruit of the Spirit* (5:22). In that the word *fruit* is singular, the apostle signified that all nine together are the normal result of a life that is *led by the Spirit. Love* is our tender, unselfish affection toward God and others that intensely desires that God be praised and glorified and that others receive the best and the highest good. *Joy* is the intense but deep happiness within us that cannot be affected by our outer circumstances. *Peace* is the serene, inner contentment that comes from knowing that God loves us and has our best interest at heart.

Patience enables us to endure pain, difficulty, and waiting with a sense of calmness and assurance that God remains in control. *Kindness* reflects our attitude of sympathetic understanding, and *generosity* is our kindness in action. *Faithfulness* describes the integrity of our relationship with God and our trusting Him with our past, present, and future, while *gentleness* (5:23) is Christian humility, tenderness, and consideration in our relationships with other people. *Self-control* is our personal discipline under the direction of the Holy Spirit. By naming these, the apostle stressed that no law against evil could ever produce these attitudes and actions. Such a harvest can come only as *the fruit of the Spirit* (5:22).

Paul explained that *those who belong to Christ Jesus have crucified the flesh with its passions and desires* (5:24). And since we were given a new life when we professed our faith in Christ, we should stay in step with the Holy Spirit's leading and promptings throughout our lives. Even as we seek to live holy lives *guided by the Spirit* (5:25), we should *not become conceited, competing against one another, envying one another* (5:26).

Knowing that even believers would have the potential to reject the guidance of the Holy Spirit, Paul asked those who are living under the Spirit's dominion and manifesting the fruit of the Spirit to restore those who are *detected in a transgression* (6:1). Believers were instructed to do so *in a spirit of gentleness,* remembering that they themselves might fall under some temptation. They were also told to help other Christians with their weaknesses, which would strengthen the whole church, and *in this way you will fulfill the law of Christ* (6:2). When people think themselves to be morally above reproach, *they deceive themselves* (6:3). To prevent this deception, everyone must be responsible for themselves before God. True joy does not come from comparing one's moral strengths with the weaknesses of others, but rather in realizing that one measures up to God's standard with the Spirit's help (6:4-5).

Just as what we plant is what we can expect to grow, God Himself assures us that we will receive in kind according to what we have done. He cannot be mocked or outwitted by people who think they can sow evil and reap good (5:7). Paul issued a reminder that *If you sow to your own flesh, you will reap corruption from the flesh; but if you sow to the Spirit, you will reap eternal life from the Spirit* (6:8). Thus the apostle encouraged the churches of Galatia to be earnest *in doing what is right* (6:9). For though the spiritual harvest took time and was almost never immediate, God's heavenly reward was always sure.

SUGGESTIONS TO TEACHERS

Living according to our new life in the Spirit is a lot like raising a garden. There are certain little things that we need to attend to, and God abundantly blesses our efforts. From this passage in Galatians, we might create a to-do list that includes these three tasks:

1. WEED OUT THE WORKS. Paul said *the works of the flesh are obvious* (Gal. 5:19). The vices he listed in verses 19-21 should have no part in a life that is being led by the Spirit. Thus, if any of these weeds—vices—are cropping up in the garden of your life, seek God's help in weeding them out. Verse 24 tells us plainly that *those who belong to Christ Jesus have* nailed the passions and desires of their sinful nature to His cross and have crucified them there.

2. TEND TO THE FRUIT. The fruit of the Spirit that the apostle listed in verses 22-23 read like a character description of the person who is wholly committed to living by the Spirit. It is the Spirit who produces these character traits in us, and these were complete in the person of Christ. Although we don't produce this fruit, we can tend to the fruit that God is producing in us by doing our part to make sure that this fruit stays in an environment conducive to growth.

3. REAP WHAT YOU SOW. It would be ridiculous for a person to plant dandelion seeds and expect to grow an apple tree! And yet we often fool ourselves into thinking that our evil deeds will still manage to somehow reap us eternal benefits. It is a natural law that we get what we plant. Such is also true in our moral and spiritual lives. Every action, thought, and attitude has a result. Each action, thought, and attitude is like a seed we are sowing. Plant to please God, and you will reap a harvest of love, joy, peace, and everlasting life!

<table>
<tr><td>

FOR ADULTS

</td><td>

■ **TOPIC:** Choices and Consequences
■ **QUESTIONS:** 1. What evidence from your own life do you have that you are being led by the Spirit? 2. To what extent would you

</td></tr>
</table>

say that you have *crucified the flesh with its passions and desires* (Gal. 5:24)? 3. To what extent would you say that you *Take care that you yourselves are not tempted* (6:1)? 4. In what ways is *the law of Christ* (6:2) comparable to *the whole law . . . summed up in a single commandment* (5:14)? 5. What things can you do to encourage your fellow believers to make the right choices?

■ **ILLUSTRATIONS:**

Giving Thanks to God. A family returning from an August 2000 missions trip gave thanks to God after a brush with death. Henry Anhalt, who had never piloted a plane, took control of the single-engine Piper he and his family were riding in and landed it safely in Florida after the pilot, Kristopher Pearce, had a heart attack and passed out at the controls.

A part-time flight instructor in the area managed to tell Anhalt how to fly and guided him to Winter Haven airport. Pearce, 36, of Haines City, was taken to a hospital and pronounced dead. An autopsy showed he suffered from coronary artery disease.

Anhalt, his wife, and three sons were returning from the Bahamas, where they had taught vacation Bible school. They were not injured. God "sent a flight instructor—you don't get much more help than that," Anhalt said on NBC's *Today* show. Pearce, chairman of the Northridge Christian Academy school board, had taken church members to the Bahamas in his plane several times.

You Reap Whatever You Sow. In the African-American experience, the phrase "to have church" has become synonymous with "to have a good time." Zan W. Holmes, Jr., tells why, returning to an African-American adage, "If you don't put anything in, you won't get anything out." In terms of worship, says Holmes in his book *Encountering Jesus*, that means "you have to bring something to the sermon to get something out of it."

Holmes then goes on to tell the story of a "young college student who returned home for the holidays and accompanied his mother to church one Sunday. Afterward the young man said, 'The preacher was not too good today.' His mother said, 'Well, maybe not.' He said, 'I noticed that the choir was not too good today.' His mother said, 'Well, maybe not.' Then she said to him, 'Well, son, tell me, how good were you today?'"

We Will Reap at Harvest Time. Put your life in God's hands. Let Him control it through His Holy Spirit. Let Him direct it through His Holy Spirit. It will no longer be your life to live as you will, I know; but with God, your life will go on forever and it will have everlasting significance. Just as Soren Kierkegaard wrote, "The tyrant dies and his rule is over, the martyr dies and his rule begins." In many ways, Kierkegaard's words echo those of Jesus when He said, *"If any want to become my followers, let them deny themselves and take up their cross and follow me. For those who want to save their life will lose it, and those who lose their life for my sake will find it"* (Matt. 16:24-25).

FOR YOUTH	■ TOPIC: Which Way Do You Choose? ■ QUESTIONS: 1. Since we're not under the law, what would be wrong with indulging our sinful natures every once in a while?

2. How would you go about gently restoring someone who is practicing a deep, dark sin? 3. After Paul listed the fruit of the Spirit, why do you think he had to warn his readers about becoming conceited and competing with each other? 4. What are some ways that you can *Bear one another's burdens* (Gal. 6:2)? 5. What do you do for yourself to make sure that you do not *grow weary in doing what is right* (6:9)?

■ ILLUSTRATIONS:

Live by the Spirit. I used to hate it whenever my dad came home during the summer and announced that he was taking a vacation. When my dad took a vacation, it meant that I was being pulled from the teenage unemployment line and being put to work in hard, manual labor—in my dad's yard. Just when the summer heat reached its peak and the humidity readings were at a record index, I'd be out pulling weeds, hoeing gardens, and shoveling and raking manure that we had picked up from the agricultural campus at the University of Tennessee, among all the other diverse forms of yard work that my dad could concoct. We'd begin at daybreak and work into the twilight. And I never remember air-conditioning feeling so good as on those nights.

Of course, I learned a lot, because as we worked along, my dad would teach me all kinds of things about gardening, landscaping, fertilizing, and small engines—not to mention the work ethic. There were phrases I remember him using every time he took one of these "summer vacations." For example, I'll always remember getting on the riding mower, heading out into the lawn, revving it up as fast as it would go to try to generate some degree of breeze on my face, and my Dad stopping me to ask that infernal question: "Did you check the oil?" Shamefully, I'd drop my head and shake it "no," reminding him that I did fill up the gas tank. Then I'd get that brief speech that I've got well memorized now: "Son, the tractor will tell you when it's out of gas. It'll just stop running. But when it tells you that its out of oil, it's already too late. You've burned up the engine."

You know what? It wouldn't hurt us to take my dad's wise advice when it comes to our spiritual lives. When was the last time you checked the "oil" of your spiritual life? Picture yourself driving along in the car when suddenly the "check oil" light appears. What do you do? If you're smart, you would pull into the nearest gas station and add a quart of oil. Without lubrication, no engine can survive for long. And we can't survive either without God's "oil." Without the constant softening of God's anointing through the Spirit, we would dry up and become unproductive and bored. We need to be constantly refilled. So get off the tractor and check the oil. The oil for your spiritual engine, of course, is the Spirit.

WISDOM AND WORSHIP

FOR LIVING

THE WAY OF THE RIGHTEOUS

BACKGROUND SCRIPTURE: Psalms 1; 19
DEVOTIONAL READING: Psalm 19:1-6

KEY VERSE: The LORD watches over the way of the righteous,
but the way of the wicked will perish. Psalm 1:6.

KING JAMES VERSION

PSALM 1:1 Blessed is the man that walketh not in the counsel of the ungodly, nor standeth in the way of sinners, nor sitteth in the seat of the scornful.

2 But his delight is in the law of the LORD; and in his law doth he meditate day and night.

3 And he shall be like a tree planted by the rivers of water, that bringeth forth his fruit in his season; his leaf also shall not wither; and whatsoever he doeth shall prosper.

4 The ungodly are not so: but are like the chaff which the wind driveth away.

5 Therefore the ungodly shall not stand in the judgment, nor sinners in the congregation of the righteous.

6 For the LORD knoweth the way of the righteous: but the way of the ungodly shall perish. . . .

19:7 The law of the LORD is perfect, converting the soul: the testimony of the LORD is sure, making wise the simple.

8 The statutes of the LORD are right, rejoicing the heart: the commandment of the LORD is pure, enlightening the eyes.

9 The fear of the LORD is clean, enduring for ever: the judgments of the LORD are true and righteous altogether.

10 More to be desired are they than gold, yea, than much fine gold: sweeter also than honey and the honeycomb.

NEW REVISED STANDARD VERSION

PSALM 1:1 Happy are those
who do not follow the advice of the wicked,
or take the path that sinners tread,
or sit in the seat of scoffers;

2 but their delight is in the law of the LORD,
and on his law they meditate day and night.

3 They are like trees
planted by streams of water,
which yield their fruit in its season,
and their leaves do not wither.
In all that they do, they prosper.

4 The wicked are not so,
but are like chaff that the wind drives away.

5 Therefore the wicked will not stand in the
judgment,
nor sinners in the congregation of the righteous;

6 for the LORD watches over the way of the righteous,
but the way of the wicked will perish. . . .

19:7 The law of the LORD is perfect,
reviving the soul;
the decrees of the LORD are sure,
making wise the simple;

8 the precepts of the LORD are right,
rejoicing the heart;
the commandment of the LORD is clear,
enlightening the eyes;

9 the fear of the LORD is pure,
enduring forever;
the ordinances of the LORD are true
and righteous altogether.

10 More to be desired are they than gold,
even much fine gold;
sweeter also than honey,
and drippings of the honeycomb.

Monday, June 3	Psalm 42	*Hope in Distress*
Tuesday, June 4	Psalm 56:1-6	*In God I Trust*
Wednesday, June 5	Psalm 56:7-13	*I Am Not Afraid*
Thursday, June 6	Psalm 62	*My Hope Is from God*
Friday, June 7	Psalm 71:1-11	*You Are My Hope*
Saturday, June 8	Psalm 71:12-24	*I Will Hope Continually*
Sunday, June 9	Psalm 43	*God Is My Hope and Help*

BACKGROUND

Theologians have come to know that the "lived-out" part of any religion comes through most clearly in the songs that the people of that faith sing. Such is especially true of the Book of Psalms, in which those who wrote and sang these hymns expressed their dreams, fears, hopes, and troubles. As such, this is the songbook or hymnal of ancient Israel, a set of compiled lyrics that were used as prayers, petitions, and thanksgiving before God. The psalms were mostly sung in the temple by the levitical priests, but they were surely also picked up and sung by the Israelite people in their homes and on their travels. Even today, the movement to sing newly composed choruses has brought back into the worship of the church many of the psalms that had been previously relegated to reading rather than to singing.

Because it is one of the most loved books in the Bible, Psalms is also one of the most frequently read. This, too, is likely a result of the collection's unique way of expressing a wide range of heartfelt emotions. From the lowest depths of despair to the highest articulations of praise and worship, the Book of Psalms verbalizes exactly what we often feel. It has been said that the psalter not only speaks *to* us, but also speaks *for* us, drawing a vivid picture of our every mood and thought and stage of spiritual development.

The Book of Psalms is a collection of writings from different authors, and these authors come from different backgrounds and time periods. Their kinship comes from their deep desire to compose lyrics with accompanying instrumental music that would assist them in lifting up their prayers to God. Although each of these songs was composed to accompany the worship in the temple, they still fall under various categories and may be classified into the following groups:

• *Hymns.* These were songs of praise that would be suitable for any occasion. Some may be further classified as "enthronement hymns," which celebrated the Lord's kingship, while others may be further classified as "songs of Zion," which expressed devotion to Jerusalem, home of the holy temple.

• *Laments.* These were songs in which worshipers sought deliverance from ill, such as physical sickness or false accusation, or in which the nation asked for help from God in a time of distress.

• *Thanksgivings.* In these songs, the worshipers expressed their gratitude for

God's deliverance.

• *Liturgies.* These were composed for religious ceremonies, such as the initiation of a religious festival, or for historic occasions, such as the nation's renewing of its covenant with the Lord.

• *Sacred Histories.* These songs were similar to the liturgies, except that they recounted the history of God's dealings with the nation.

• *Royal Psalms.* These were also similar to the liturgies, except that they were designed to be used for occasions such as the coronation of a king or the celebration of a royal wedding.

• *Wisdom Psalms.* These songs were meditations on life and the ways of God.

• *Songs of Trust.* These songs were composed to give individuals the opportunity to express their confidence in God's readiness to help them.

NOTES ON THE PRINTED TEXT

Many Bible scholars believe that Psalm 1 was composed as an introduction to the whole psalter. It is one of several anonymously written psalms. It is also a wisdom hymn that describes in stark contrast the ways and lifestyle of the righteous alongside those of the wicked. As such, it could be referred to as the way of life and the way of disaster.

The psalm opens with a prognosis that *happy* (1:1) are the prospects of those who reject the beliefs, thoughts, and behavior of *the wicked*. In that the upright are blessed by God for following His ways, they are promised a deep-seated, lasting joy that will not be disrupted by the typical difficulties of living. Even in the worst of situations, their inner joy will remain.

The joy of the upright is won because, from the negative aspect, they reject the ways and advice of the wicked; it is won from the positive aspect in that *their delight is in the law of the LORD, and on his law they meditate day and night* (1:2). To these who put their trust in God, the law is not a burden. The law guides them, makes their lives and living better, and helps them acknowledge their dependence on God. Indeed, the upright are as blessed as *trees planted by streams of water* (1:3), and in *all that they do, they prosper*. This does not mean, of course, that they are promised health and wealth. Rather, it means that they will receive and achieve the most worthwhile things of life; they will, when they put divine wisdom into practice, reap the benefits of God's approval.

The psalmist next conveyed how the wicked forfeit these benefits because of their disregard for God. They are described as *chaff that the wind drives away* (1:4). In the threshing of grain, the crushed sheaves were tossed into the air, where the wind blew away the lighter, dryer husks, leaving only the grain to fall to the ground. In this way the eternal worthlessness of the wicked is portrayed. Being described as unable to *stand in the judgment* (1:5) tells of their instability that comes as a result of their aimless living.

The first psalm concludes with words of promise for the righteous and words of warning for the wicked. The promise is that *the LORD watches over the way of the righteous* (1:6); and the warning is that *the way of the wicked will perish*. The promise comforts those who put their faith in God, for they realize that He knows them intimately, that He cares for them actively, and that He provides guidance for their lives. Those who refuse to put their faith in God are warned of meeting dead end after dead end.

Psalm 19 is understood to be a hymn originally written by David. Having described in this psalm the general revelation of God in creation, David moved to the special revelation of God through His Word, that is, through His commandments. David did not see the law of God as a hindrance to his freedom, but rather as a guiding light for his life. Because it is *perfect* (19:7), it leads to conversion and revives *the soul*. Because the law is *sure*, it has the effect of *making wise the simple*. Because it is *right* (19:8), it brings joy to the heart. Because the law is *clear*, it gives us insight into life and living. Because the law is *pure* (19:9), it is everlasting. Because it is *true*, it institutes fairness for all our relationships.

Because to David observance of the law was a joy and not a burden, he said concerning these laws of God: *More to be desired are they than gold, even much fine gold; sweeter also than honey, and drippings of the honeycomb* (19:10). Throughout the final verses of this psalm, David claimed that the law warned him against sinning, and that in keeping the law he found the joy of a fulfilled life.

SUGGESTIONS TO TEACHERS

Both psalmists—the anonymous writer who penned Psalm 1 and David, who penned Psalm 19—affirmed the law of God because of its incredible influence and contribution to our lives.

1. GOD'S LAW REVIVES US. The mere knowledge of God's law—and therefore, His will—goes beyond helping us to distinguish between right and wrong; it also provides for us a measure of strength to do what is right and to turn away from what is wrong. David said that the law of God had a way of reviving him—physically, mentally, emotionally, and spiritually. It can have the same effect on us today.

2. GOD'S LAW MAKES US WISE. From the time when it was first given, God's law has always helped those who have learned it and studied it to discern what is true, right, and lasting. It not only reveals what God desires from His people, but also discloses much about the character and heart of God.

3. GOD'S LAW BRINGS JOY TO OUR HEART. God's law does not chain us down physically, mentally, emotionally, and spiritually. Rather, it provides for us boundaries within which we realize that it is safe and secure to work and play. That protection has the long-term effect of introducing the staying power of joy in our hearts. Just as a sheep is truly happy when it is safe within the fold of its shepherd, so too are we truly full of joy when we are safe within the fold of our Shepherd and Lord.

4. GOD'S LAW GIVES US INSIGHT. In the same way that God's law reveals much about the character and heart of God, so it also gives us insight into our own character and heart. And because it does so, it provides us the insight of our dire need for God and His love, grace, and mercy. The law's guidelines are like lights that help us see the pathway for our life's journey. The law indicates what God's ultimate will is for the lives of those who put their faith in Him.

5. GOD'S LAW WARNS US AGAINST SIN. Going beyond teaching us right from wrong, the law promises certain rewards for right living and certain consequences for wrong living. Thus it warns us of the dangers of a life of sin.

6. GOD'S LAW BRINGS US FULFILLMENT. A common thread of all humanity is the lifelong yearning for fulfillment. God's law has the capability to set us on the right path and then guide us toward a rich and fulfilling life.

FOR ADULTS

■ TOPIC: The Right Way

■ QUESTIONS: 1. What are the benefits of living the right way—according to God's law? 2. What are the dangers of living the wrong way—in rebellion against God's law? 3. How might meditating on the law *day and night* (Ps. 1:2) provide direction for your life? 4. In what way is a life obedient to God's will *like trees planted by streams of water* (1:3)? 5. What words did David use in 19:7-10 to describe the law? What do those words mean to you?

■ **ILLUSTRATIONS:**

The Way of the Wicked Will Perish. George Orwell, writing during the Second World War, tells of a rather cruel trick he once played on a wasp. The wasp was sucking jam on his plate and he cut the bug in half. The wasp paid no attention to what had happened to it, but just went on with its meal, while a tiny, stream of jam trickled out of its severed esophagus. Only when the wasp tried to fly did it realize the terrible thing that had happened to it.

What a picture of a solely consumer-oriented humanity, gorging itself, earthbound, and oblivious to its plight!

Making Wise the Simple. Sigmund Freud's favorite story was about the sailor shipwrecked on one of the South Sea islands. He was seized by the natives, hoisted to their shoulders, carried to the village, and set on a rude throne. Little by little, he learned that it was their custom once each year to make some man a king, that is, ruler for a year.

The sailor liked the idea until he began to wonder what happened to all the former kings. Soon he discovered that every year when a kingship was ended, the ruler was banished to an island, where he starved to death. The sailor did not like that idea, but he was smart and decided to remain king for a year.

Thus, the mariner put his carpenters to work making boats, his farmers to work transplanting fruit trees to the island and growing crops, and his masons to work building houses. Finally, when the sailor's kingship was over, he was banished, not to a barren island, but to an island of abundance. It is a good parable of life. We're all rulers here on earth, at least for a little while. We are also able to choose what we will do with the stuff of life.

Enlightening the Eyes. In his book, *Man's Search For Meaning*, Austrian psychiatrist Viktor Frankl documents the profound power that a life purpose exerts over an individual under even the worst of circumstances. Frankl, who survived the Nazi concentration camps, described how prisoners who felt they had nothing to live for succumbed, while those who perceived themselves as having a mission to complete, struggled to survive.

Deprived of all external supports that might give life meaning, these survivors came to realize that, in Frankl's words, "It did not really matter what we expected of life, but rather what life expected from us." Their sense of an inner purpose pulled them through the most horrible physical and emotional experiences so that they might make their unique contribution to the world.

Everyone has a purpose in life beyond one's immediate interests and gratifications, though that purpose frequently goes undiscovered. Many people devote their entire lives to the pursuit of greater ease and pleasure. Those who had not found the "why" that gives meaning to their existence may achieve material success; yet the real goodness of life will elude them. The true meaning of life lies in sharing our God-given talents and abilities with others.

FOR YOUTH

■ TOPIC: The Right Way

■ QUESTIONS: 1. According to what you see on television, what you hear on the radio, and what you encounter in advertisements, what is the world's advice for finding happiness? How does this perspective contrast with the message of God's Word? 2. According to Psalms 1 and 19, how can knowing and heeding God's Word bring us joy? 3. In what way do the destinies of the righteous and wicked contrast? 4. In what way is the Word of God perfect? How does it provide spiritual nourishment for our souls? 5. How has God's Word proven to be a source of wisdom, clarity, and truth for you?

■ **ILLUSTRATIONS:**

Does This Sound Familiar to Anyone? Richard J. Fairchild tells how he was in a church one time that had a major dispute about where the pies should be placed in the kitchen prior to serving of the annual turkey supper. One woman actually left the church community because several newcomers to the congregation had convinced the rest of the women working in the kitchen that it would be more efficient to put the pies on the counter beside the sink instead of the counter next to the refrigerator.

"It's not the right way to do it!" the woman had said. "We've never done it that way before, and I am not going to be part of doing it that way now. I won't have any part of that kind of thing. Those new people are going to ruin this church. They don't know anything. They aren't even from around here."

Does that sound familiar to you? According Luke 9:49-50, the apostle John came up to Jesus one day. *John answered, "Master, we saw someone casting out demons in your name, and we tried to stop him, because he does not follow with us." But Jesus said to him, "Do not stop him; for whoever is not against you is for you."*

The Fear of the Lord Is Pure. Christians have been aiding the poorest of the poor in the Philippines, where 218 squatters died in 2000 in the collapse of a garbage dump.

The Payatas dump in Quezon City, part of metropolitan Manila, symbolizes the wretched poverty in the country. Part of the rain-soaked mountains of garbage collapsed onto the shacks of the squatters in the early morning of July 10. The people live there and scavenge for choice scraps that can be sold to factories and junk shops.

A huge portion of one of the hills at the dump broke loose at 6:00 A.M. without warning, moved forward, then fell, according to Raineer Chu of Ministries Philippines, an outreach to the urban poor. About 200 houses were buried, he said.

Ministries Philippines has been planting churches at the Payatas dump site for six years, Chu said. It also has helped organize a cooperative of 500 scavenger families, arranging with buyers for the purchase of their trash.

On the day of the collapse, Chu said, he was praying for the people of Payatas when he got a pager call about a fire there and "was moved to tears." When he arrived home, he found his wife weeping in front of the television, which was reporting the accident.

"I believe the pain and grief of our Lord came upon us as we were praying, and God must have been so pained by the death of so many, mostly children, of very poor families," Chu said.

Some of the children attended a preschool run by a local church and lived in the area that was buried, Chu said. But "by God's miraculous intervention" only one child was missing, he remarked.

The government is blaming the squatters for refusing to move after they had been warned that the area was unsafe, Chu said. But survivors filed a $22 million class-action lawsuit accusing the government, private waste contractors, and two real estate companies for negligence, according to news reports. The complaint says the dump flagrantly violates environmental, health, and zoning laws.

Chu is trying to get capital for the squatters in the cooperative so that they can own their own trucks. That way, scraps can be removed from homes and brought to a sanitary place for sorting, then sold directly to factories, he reported.

Many Christians have helped the surviving squatters since the collapse, donating clothing and working through the night after the accident to provide assistance, Chu noted. The squatters "have seen the sacrificial response of the church, and we are confident they will also see the hand of the Lord in all this."

Chu asked for Christians to pray. "We are at our wits' end regarding the work in the dump site," he said. The city government closed the dump; thus, the squatters have no source of income, and the cooperative will close soon since it has no more scraps to sell. Chu noted, "We are now faced with the food needs of at least 500 families who are members of our cooperative." There are about 3,000 families in the dump.

2

HOPE IN GOD

BACKGROUND SCRIPTURE: Psalms 42—43
DEVOTIONAL READING: Psalm 43

KEY VERSE: Hope in God; for I shall again praise him,
my help and my God. Psalm 42:11.

KING JAMES VERSION

PSALM 42:1 As the hart panteth after the water brooks, so panteth my soul after thee, O God.

2 My soul thirsteth for God, for the living God: when shall I come and appear before God?

3 My tears have been my meat day and night, while they continually say unto me, Where is thy God?

4 When I remember these things, I pour out my soul in me: for I had gone with the multitude, I went with them to the house of God, with the voice of joy and praise, with a multitude that kept holyday.

5 Why art thou cast down, O my soul? and why art thou disquieted in me? hope thou in God: for I shall yet praise him for the help of his countenance.

6 O my God, . . .

7 Deep calleth unto deep at the noise of thy waterspouts: all thy waves and thy billows are gone over me.

8 Yet the LORD will command his lovingkindness in the daytime, and in the night his song shall be with me, and my prayer unto the God of my life.

9 I will say unto God my rock, Why hast thou forgotten me? why go I mourning because of the oppression of the enemy?

10 As with a sword in my bones, mine enemies reproach me; while they say daily unto me, Where is thy God?

11 Why art thou cast down, O my soul? and why art thou disquieted within me? hope thou in God: for I shall yet praise him, who is the health of my countenance, and my God.

NEW REVISED STANDARD VERSION

PSALM 42:1 As a deer longs for flowing streams,
  so my soul longs for you, O God.

2 My soul thirsts for God,
  for the living God.
When shall I come and behold
  the face of God?

3 My tears have been my food
  day and night,
while people say to me continually,
  "Where is your God?"

4 These things I remember,
  as I pour out my soul:
how I went with the throng,
  and led them in procession to the house of God,
with glad shouts and songs of thanksgiving,
  a multitude keeping festival.

5 Why are you cast down, O my soul,
  and why are you disquieted within me?
Hope in God; for I shall again praise him,
  my help 6 and my God. . . .

7 Deep calls to deep
  at the thunder of your cataracts;
all your waves and your billows
  have gone over me.

8 By day the LORD commands his steadfast love,
  and at night his song is with me,
  a prayer to the God of my life.

9 I say to God, my rock,
  "Why have you forgotten me?
Why must I walk about mournfully
  because the enemy oppresses me?"

10 As with a deadly wound in my body,
  my adversaries taunt me,
while they say to me continually,
  "Where is your God?"

11 Why are you cast down, O my soul,
  and why are you disquieted within me?
Hope in God; for I shall again praise him,
  my help and my God.

HOME BIBLE READINGS

BACKGROUND

Psalm 42 is the first of 12 hymns in the psalter written by the Korahites. Members of this levitical family were grouped together into two separate sets of temple duties: one group was the temple doorkeepers and guardians, and the other group was made up of musicians. As musicians, these psalm writers were hymn singers as well, in that each of the psalms they wrote, as well as others, were sung in the temple by a Korahite choir. (They also wrote Psalms 43—49, 84—85, and 87—88.)

The family was descended from a rebel leader named Korah, who conspired with Dathan and Abiram against Moses and Aaron, and by doing so, defied the Lord. Numbers 26 does not tell exactly what the conspiracy involved, but it does describe the outcome. The ground opened up and swallowed Korah along with the other leading conspirators, and 250 of their followers were destroyed by fire from the Lord on the same day as a warning to the whole nation of Israel (26:9-10). Interestingly enough, the last of the episode's description tells how Korah's children were spared: *Notwithstanding, the sons of Korah did not die* (26:11).

It was during the reign of David that a part of the Korahite family were assigned the task of being singers and musicians of the temple choir. Apparently David selected Heman to be the founder of the choir known as the "sons of Korah." Famous for his wisdom, Heman is noted as the writer of Psalm 88. Along with his fellow Levites—Asaph (who penned 12 psalms himself) and Jeduthun (who wrote Psalm 89)—Heman directed the choirs that had been drawn from the other two clans of that tribe. Thus the Korahites continued to be temple musicians for hundreds of years.

The Korahites' love for the temple and for God's presence in the temple come through quite clearly in Psalm 42. Indeed, this is a rather sad psalm as the Korahites' eloquently express the deep-felt grief and suffering that they endured while away from the temple and (thereby) away from God's presence.

NOTES ON THE PRINTED TEXT

Psalm 42 is the lament of a temple musician who was apparently exiled far away from Jerusalem. Throughout this song, he expressed his overwhelming longing to be back in Jerusalem and, more specifically, back in the temple where he could be performing his duties. As the song progresses, the Korahite writer developed a song in which his longing moved into a resolute faith and hope in God, whose presence the writer yearned to enjoy once again.

This psalm opens with the musician telling about his strong spiritual thirst during his sad experience of exile. He compared himself to a deer that had been without drink for too long a period of time, longing *for flowing streams* (42:1). Like the deer of his analogy, the psalm writer had been through a spiritual drought; he felt as though he were wilting away on a dry, barren spiritual landscape. He had known God intimately, and now being cut off from God's presence led to a spiritual desire that was just as intense as a physical thirst. Thus, being far away from the temple and God, the writer said his *soul thirsts for God, for the living God* (42:2).

The following verses further depict the psalmist's suffering, implying that even persecution and ridicule had been his experience since being far away from home. He asked the direct question, *When shall I come and behold the face of God?* (42:2). His heartfelt sorrow is expressed in that his *tears have been my food day and night* (42:3); his endurance of persecution and ridicule is voiced in that *people say to me continually, "Where is your God?"*

In the midst of thinking about his sorrows, memories of joyful temple processions flooded the psalmist's mind: *how I went with the throng, and led them in procession to the house of God, with glad shouts and songs of thanksgiving, a multitude keeping festival* (42:4). And it seems that these memories of his joining in the worship of God began to lift him out of his sorrow, restoring both his mind and soul with hope, for he posed another question: *Why are you cast down, O my soul, and why are you disquieted within me?* (42:5). The psalmist's answer to his own question pointed him back to his hope in God, as well as forward to the time when he would again praise the Lord, whom he called his help *and [his] God* (42:6). Having despaired by looking at his present circumstances, he now looked with hope to the God who had lifted him out of despairing situations—and would do so again.

The Korahite's mind then returned to his present situation—being homesick far from the temple in Jerusalem—which he described in some detail. Because his soul was *cast down within [him]* (42:6), he made himself remember again the kindness of God. This remembering occurred while he still felt an inner tumult that could be likened to tumultuous seas, raging waves, and surging tides (42:7). Yet in the midst of this inner tumult, he knew that by *day the Lord commands his steadfast love, and at night his song is with me* (42:8).

Though the psalmist acknowledged God's steadfast love, though he acknowledged the Lord as being the God of his life, and though the psalmist acknowledged God as his strength and durability, his prayer remained a hopeful cry of desperation: *"Why have you forgotten me? Why must I walk about mournfully because the enemy oppresses me?"* (42:9).

Once again the psalmist told about the taunts leveled against him by those who questioned God's presence or even His existence. Because of the psalmist's desperate circumstances, these persecutors barraged him with the question, *"Where is your God?"* (42:10), and so the hymn writer included this question in his own prayer as if to ask, "Yes, my God! Where are you indeed?" But as he had done in 42:5, so he again did in 42:11. Perhaps tempted to complete despair, he remembered that the Lord is a God of hope. The psalmist remembered that he would again be granted the opportunity to praise God, for the Lord would be at his side to help him.

SUGGESTIONS TO TEACHERS

Feeling lonely in his desperation, discouragement, and depression, the psalmist turned again and again to his hope in God. When we face situations in which there seems to be no way out, we would do well to take a cue from the psalmist, who told himself, *Hope in God; for I shall again praise him, my help and my God* (Ps. 42:11).

1. HOPE IN THE MIDST OF DESPERATION. The Korahite who wrote Psalm 42 clearly felt separated from both his home and his God. But in the midst of his desperation, he turned in hope to the Lord. Even as desperate as his situation seemed to be, the psalmist was even more fervent about his relationship with God, namely, that the relationship would be restored. We, too, face desperate situations; may we, too, turn in hope to God. May we also be fervent for our relationship with the Lord.

2. HOPE IN THE MIDST OF DISCOURAGEMENT. Exiled to a place far away from his Jerusalem home and the temple, the psalmist expressed his discouragement. It was as if all he could hold on to were his memories of serving and worshiping in the temple. But just as hope arose from the ashes of his desperation, so also hope arose from the ashes of his discouragement. By urging his soul to *hope in God* (42:5) in the midst of discouragement, he took courage in the Lord. We, too, will face discouragement; may we, too, take courage in those times by putting our hope and trust in God.

3. HOPE IN THE MIDST OF DEPRESSION. Though he mentally fought to overcome his depression, the Korahite who wrote Psalm 42 seemed to have continually fallen back into a depressed state—even in the course of writing this song. And yet he did fight his depression.

The psalmist knew that he was in a circumstance that could engender depression, but he also knew that by meditating on God's goodness and faithfulness, he could get his mind off his present situation and onto God and the hope of deliverance. We, too, will face depressing circumstances; may we, too, remember that hope will help us focus our thoughts on God's ability to deliver us and save us rather than on our own seemingly hopeless situation. *The God of all grace . . . will himself restore, support, strengthen, and establish you* (1 Pet. 5:10).

■ **TOPIC:** Live in Hope

■ **QUESTIONS:** 1. In what ways does this psalmist express his desperation? 2. In what ways does he express his discouragement? 3. In what ways does he express his depression? 4. What is the antidote for his desperation, discouragement, and depression? How would such an antidote help him in his situation? 5. In what ways do you think God commanded *his steadfast love* (Ps. 42:8) toward the psalmist?

■ **ILLUSTRATIONS:**

My Help and My God. Refugees in South Africa are being trained to carry revival to their nations. The South African branch of OMS International continues to identify and train missionaries from the ranks of refugees living there.

Millions of people living in south and central African nations have fled to South Africa since 1994, Greenwood, Indiana-based OMS International said. Ethnic conflicts, political instability, and food shortages are rife in Africa and people come to the democratic country for safety, the ministry's David Dick told *Religion Today*. Most end up in refugee camps with few prospects for the future.

The situation redirected the mission of OMS International's South Africa office. The ministry had been training and sending missionaries to go to other countries, but decided to focus its efforts on ministering to the refugees, Dick said. "They told us they would be doing better meeting the needs of the refugees in their own country rather than sending people outside."

Teams of evangelists work among the refugee communities, preaching the message of Christ and connecting new converts with local churches, Dick said. The refugees are open and receptive to the Gospel, and the results are encouraging, he said. "There are a good number of conversions, and discipleship is happening."

The outreach will fulfill the ministry's mission to send missionaries to other countries because some of the converts are expressing a desire to return to their homes and preach the Gospel, Dick reported. "Many of them are saying that they have a burden to go back. Once they receive the Gospel and it becomes a part of their life, there seems to be a calling to return."

Burundi and the Democratic Republic of Congo (DRC) are among the most dangerous countries in Africa. Burundi borders Rwanda, where 800,000 reportedly died in ethnic fighting in 1994, and many refugees from the violence still live there. Civil war and ethnic violence have torn apart the DRC for several years.

The teams are willing to go back despite the danger, Dick said. "It is amazing to me because they are putting their lives at stake to return." He said a team leader told him that he is willing to go back even if it means he will be killed. "It is humbling and inspiring to hear them talk like this."

OMS South Africa hopes to train thousands of like-minded individuals from the refugee community in the next 20 years. Workers estimate that about two out of every 100 converts accept a call to return to their homelands as missionaries, Dick said. By the year 2020, they hope refugee-based mission teams will have established 20 new ministries "from Cape Town to Cairo," he reported.

Helping Africans minister to other Africans is a crucial part of the ministry, Dick said. "It's a ministry by Africans to Africans, and that is important because it is culturally adaptable." The vision and techniques are easily transferred to others so that new ministries can be started, he reported.

Working with indigenous missionaries is the core of OMS International's ministry, Dick related. The ministry works with more than 7,000 nationals and 3,500 churches to spread the Gospel of Christ through evangelism, theological training, and church planting in Asia, Latin America, the Caribbean, Europe, and Africa.

Deep Calls to Deep. Author and lecturer Leo Buscaglia once talked about a contest he was asked to judge. The purpose of the contest was to find the most caring child. The winner was a four-year-old child whose next-door neighbor was an elderly gentleman who had recently lost his wife.

Upon seeing the man cry, the little boy went into the old gentleman's yard, climbed onto his lap, and just sat there. When his mother asked him what he had said to the neighbor, the little boy said, "Nothing. I just helped him cry."

FOR YOUTH

■ TOPIC: Don't Lose Hope

■ QUESTIONS: 1. In what ways was the psalmist plagued with depression? 2. In what ways was he plagued with spiritual doubts? 3. How did the author encourage himself in the midst of his despair? 4. How did the psalmist's enemies taunt him? 5. How can a knowledge of God's goodness and grace benefit us in trying circumstances?

■ ILLUSTRATIONS:

Hope in God. After a few of the usual Sunday evening hymns, the church's pastor once again slowly stood up, walked over to the pulpit, and gave a very brief introduction of his childhood friend. With that, an elderly gentleman stepped up to the pulpit to speak.

"A father, his son, and a friend of his son were sailing off the Pacific Coast," the speaker began, "when a fast approaching storm blocked any attempt to get back to shore. The waves were so high that, even though the father was an experienced sailor, he could not keep the boat upright, and the three were swept into the ocean."

The old man hesitated for a moment, making eye contact with two teenagers who were, for the first time since the service began, looking somewhat interested in his story. He continued, "Grabbing a rescue line, the father had to make the most excruciating decision of his life . . . to which boy he would throw the other end of the line. He only had seconds to make the decision. The father knew that his son was a Christian, and he also knew that his son's friend was not. The agony of his decision could not be matched by the torrent of waves. As the father yelled out, 'I love you, son!' he threw the line to his son's friend. By the time he pulled the friend back to the capsized boat, his son had disappeared beyond the raging swells into the black of night. His body was never recovered."

By this time, the two teenagers were sitting straighter in the pew, waiting for the next words to come out of the old man's mouth. "The father," he continued, "knew his son would step into eternity with Jesus, and he could not bear the thought of his son's friend stepping into an eternity without Jesus. Therefore, he sacrificed his son. How great is the love of God that He should do the same for us."

With that, the old man turned and sat back down in his chair as silence filled the room. Within minutes after the service ended, the two teenagers were at the old man's side. "That was a nice story," politely started one of the boys, "but I don't think it was very realistic for a father to give up his son's life in hopes that the other boy would become a Christian."

"Well, you've got a point there," the old man replied, glancing down at his worn Bible. A big smile broadened his narrow face, and he once again looked up at the boys and said, "It sure isn't very realistic, is it? But I'm standing here today to tell you that that story gives me a glimpse of what it must have been like for God to give up His Son for me. You see, I was the son's friend."

My Soul Is Cast Down within Me. In that place between wakefulness and dreams, he found himself in the room. There were no distinguishing features except for the one wall covered with small index card files. They were like the ones in libraries that list titles by author or subject in alphabetical order. But these files, which stretched from floor to ceiling and seemingly endlessly in either direction, had very different headings. As he drew near the wall of files, the first to catch his attention was one that read "Girls I Have Liked."

The man opened it and began flipping through the cards. He quickly shut it, shocked to realize that he recognized the names written on each one. And then without being told, he knew exactly where he was. This lifeless room with its small files was a crude catalog system for his life. Here were written the actions of his every moment, big and small, in a detail his memory couldn't match.

A sense of wonder and curiosity, coupled with horror, stirred within the man as he began randomly opening files and exploring their contents. Some brought joy and sweet memories; others brought a sense of shame and regret so intense that he would look over his shoulder to see if anyone was watching.

A file named "Friends" was next to one marked "Friends I Have Betrayed." The titles ranged from the mundane to the outright weird. "Books I Have Read," "Lies I Have Told," "Comfort I Have Given," and "Jokes I Have Laughed At."

Some were almost hilarious in their exactness: "Things I've Yelled at My Brothers." Others he couldn't laugh at: "Things I Have Done in My Anger" and "Things I Have Muttered Under My Breath at My Parents." The man never ceased to be surprised by the contents.

Often there were many more cards than the man expected. Sometimes there were fewer than he hoped. He was overwhelmed by the sheer volume of the life he had lived. Could it be possible that he had the time in his 20 years to write each of these thousands or even millions of cards? But each card confirmed this truth. Each was written in his own handwriting. Each signed with his signature.

When the man pulled out the file marked "Songs I Have Listened To," he realized the files grew to contain their contents. The cards were packed tightly, and yet after two or three yards, he hadn't found the end of the file. He shut it, shamed, not so much by the quality of music, but more by the vast amount of time he knew that file represented.

When the man came to a file marked "Lustful Thoughts," he felt a chill run through his body. He pulled the file out only an inch, not willing to test its size, and drew out a card. He shuddered at its detailed content. He felt sick to think that such a moment had been recorded. An almost animal rage broke on him. One thought dominated his mind: "No one must ever see these cards! No one must ever see this room! I have to destroy them!" In insane frenzy he yanked the file out. Its size didn't matter now. He had to empty it and burn the cards. But as he took it at one end and began pounding it on the floor, he could not dislodge a single card. He became desperate and pulled out a card, only to find it as strong as steel when he tried to tear it. Defeated and utterly helpless, he returned the file to its slot. Leaning his forehead against the wall, he let out a long, self-pitying sigh.

And then the man saw it. The title read, "People I Have Shared the Gospel With." The handle was brighter than those around it, newer, almost unused. He pulled on its handle and a small box not more than three inches long fell into his hands. He could count the cards it contained on one hand. And then the tears came. He began to weep, sobs so deep that the hurt started in his stomach and shook throughout him. He fell on his knees and cried. He cried out of shame, from the overwhelming shame of it all. The rows of file shelves swirled in his tear-filled eyes. "No one must ever, ever know about this room. I must lock it up and hide the key." But then as he pushed away the tears, he saw Him. "No, please not Him; not here. Oh, anyone but Jesus."

The man watched helplessly as Jesus began to open the files and read the cards. He couldn't bear to watch Jesus' response. And in the moments he could bring himself to look at Jesus' face, the man saw a sorrow deeper than his own. Jesus seemed to intuitively go to the worst boxes. Why did He have to read every one?

Finally Jesus turned and looked at the man from across the room. Jesus looked at the man with pity in His eyes. But this was a pity that didn't anger the man. He dropped his head, covered his face with his hands, and began to cry again.

Jesus walked over and put His arm around him. Jesus could have said so many things. But He didn't say a word. He just cried with him. Then He got up and walked back to the wall of files. Starting at one end of the room, He took out a file and, one by one, began to sign His name on each card.

"No!" the man shouted, rushing to Jesus. All the man could find to say was "No, no!" as he pulled the card from Jesus. Jesus' name shouldn't be on these cards. But there it was, written in red so rich, so dark, and so alive. The name of Jesus covered his own. It was written with the Savior's blood. Jesus gently took the card back. He smiled a sad smile and began to sign the cards.

The man would never understand how Jesus did it so quickly, but the next instant it seemed as if he heard Jesus close the last file and walk back to the man's side. Jesus' placed His hand on the man's shoulder and said, "It is finished." Jesus stood the man up and led him out of the room. There was no lock on its door. There were still cards to be written.

THE LORD, OUR KEEPER

BACKGROUND SCRIPTURE: Psalms 23; 80; 121
DEVOTIONAL READING: Psalm 80:14-19

KEY VERSES: I lift up my eyes to the hills—from where will my help come? My help comes from the LORD, who made heaven and earth. Psalm 121:1-2.

KING JAMES VERSION

PSALM 23:1 The LORD is my shepherd; I shall not want.

2 He maketh me to lie down in green pastures: he leadeth me beside the still waters.

3 He restoreth my soul: he leadeth me in the paths of righteousness for his name's sake.

4 Yea, though I walk through the valley of the shadow of death, I will fear no evil: for thou art with me; thy rod and thy staff they comfort me.

5 Thou preparest a table before me in the presence of mine enemies: thou anointest my head with oil; my cup runneth over.

6 Surely goodness and mercy shall follow me all the days of my life: and I will dwell in the house of the LORD for ever. . . .

121:1 I will lift up mine eyes unto the hills, from whence cometh my help.

2 My help cometh from the LORD, which made heaven and earth.

3 He will not suffer thy foot to be moved: he that keepeth thee will not slumber.

4 Behold, he that keepeth Israel shall neither slumber nor sleep.

5 The LORD is thy keeper: the LORD is thy shade upon thy right hand.

6 The sun shall not smite thee by day, nor the moon by night.

7 The LORD shall preserve thee from all evil: he shall preserve thy soul.

8 The LORD shall preserve thy going out and thy coming in from this time forth, and even for evermore.

NEW REVISED STANDARD VERSION

PSALM 23:1 The LORD is my shepherd, I shall not
    want.

2 He makes me lie down in green pastures;
he leads me beside still waters;

3 he restores my soul.
He leads me in right paths
    for his name's sake.

4 Even though I walk through the darkest valley,
    I fear no evil;
for you are with me;
    your rod and your staff—
    they comfort me.

5 You prepare a table before me
    in the presence of my enemies;
you anoint my head with oil;
    my cup overflows.

6 Surely goodness and mercy shall follow me
    all the days of my life,
and I shall dwell in the house of the LORD
    my whole life long. . . .

121:1 I lift up my eyes to the hills—
    from where will my help come?

2 My help comes from the LORD,
    who made heaven and earth.

3 He will not let your foot be moved;
    he who keeps you will not slumber.

4 He who keeps Israel
    will neither slumber nor sleep.

5 The LORD is your keeper;
    the LORD is your shade at your right hand.

6 The sun shall not strike you by day,
    nor the moon by night.

7 The LORD will keep you from all evil;
    he will keep your life.

8 The LORD will keep
    your going out and your coming in
    from this time on and forevermore.

Home Bible Readings

Background

As we read through the Old Testament, we will probably notice by the line markings just how often various ancient Hebrew books break out into poetry. Even within the narrative stories of the Old Testament are planted poems and songs—poetry describing an old wisdom saying or songs exulting and celebrating a great victory in battle. While Psalms is the main body of poems in the Old Testament, we need to recognize that they are themselves surrounded by poetry and are rooted in a long tradition of Hebrew poetry.

As a form of poetry—and because poetry readily yielded to change—the psalms lent themselves to widespread use through recitation and memorization. But first and foremost, it must be remembered that these poems were sung. In a few cases, the lyricist and the musical composer of particular psalms may have been the same person or group of persons. But certainly, at other times, the lyricist wrote the words and sent the psalm to a composer who would set it to music. Indeed, many psalms contain a prescript saying "To the leader." Although this more typically meant "to the choir director," there do seem to be instances in which it may have meant "to a musical composer." Typically, these psalms recorded in the Bible were used for hundreds of years as songs of worship and praise—some at the tabernacle and, more prominently later on, in the temple.

Of the 150 psalms in the psalter, Psalm 23 is perhaps both the simplest and the best loved. Though written by David from the perspective of a shepherd, it certainly represents the prayer and meditation of a man with a rather mature spirit. Perhaps the secret of the psalm's peacefulness is its portrayal of an intimate relationship with God at every successive stage of life. As such, among the psalms it would fall into the category of a psalm of trust. And even though Psalm 121 is also considered "a song of ascents" or a pilgrimage song, it, too, because it declares God as a source of help and strength, is thought of as a psalm of trust.

Notes on the Printed Text

Considered beautiful in its simplicity, it is actually depth and strength that underlie the distinctiveness of Psalm 23. It certainly portrays a sense of peace—a peace found only through our trusting in God. But the psalm does not provide along with that sense of peace the means of running away or escaping. It certainly portrays a sense of contentment—a contentment that comes only from being within the safety of God's "sheepfold." But the psalm does not provide along with that contentment the means of becoming complacent. Rather, in each of its six verses there is readiness on the part of the "sheep" to face whatever deep darkness or imminent attack that may come its way—as long as the Lord remains that sheep's shepherd. The goal of the psalm is to move ever homeward into the loving care of the Shepherd Himself.

Having been a shepherd in his early years, David wrote this psalm out of his own experience of loving and caring for his father's sheep. He knew that, as long as the shepherd was nearby and concerned, his sheep *shall not want* (23:1). Indeed, as a sheep obediently followed its shepherd, the shepherd would lead that sheep to peacefully graze in *green pastures* (23:2) and to securely drink from *still waters*. In essence, the shepherd would see to it that all the sheep's needs would be met. In fact, the shepherd would assure that the sheep's vitality would be constantly renewed.

In the same way, the Lord, our Shepherd, *restores [our] soul* (23:3); He provides for us the resources that will revitalize our human spirit. But He also *leads [us] in right paths for his name's sake.* By guiding and directing our lives in this manner, God has both our best interest in mind and His best interest in mind. As He leads us, He protects us from eternal harm; but also as He leads us, we grow to be walking witnesses of His love, grace, and mercy, which brings glory to Himself and to His character.

Those who have the Lord as their Shepherd need not fear evil harming them even when they're treading through the darkest valleys of their lives, for the Lord is *with me; your rod and your staff—they comfort me* (23:4). Ancient shepherds used a rod for the sheep's defense and a staff for the sheep's guidance and discipline.

In 23:5, David compared the Lord to a gracious host. The psalmist listed a series of three benefits of those whom God leads. In that the Lord will *prepare a table before me in the presence of my enemies*, He will make a provision for each of our needs even in the midst of mental, emotional, or spiritual opposition. In that He will *anoint my head with oil*, He will treat us as an honored guest at His banquet feast. In that He will cause *my cup* to overflow, He will grant us more blessings than we can count. Thus, because the Lord is our Shepherd, *Surely goodness and mercy shall follow me all the days of my life* (23:6).

Psalm 121 has been called a traveler's song, sung by pilgrims on their way over hills and through valleys to a religious feast in Jerusalem. Some Bible scholars believe this psalm was sung in the form of a conversation, perhaps between the worshipers and a priest. In essence, as the worshipers journeyed toward Jerusalem, a priest would sing out, *I lift up my eyes to the hills—from where will my help come?* (121:1), and the worshipers would answer by singing, *My help comes from the LORD, who made heaven and earth* (121:2).

Having heard the worshipers respond to his question, the priest would then respond to them by singing 121:3-8, and in this way pronounce a blessing on the pilgrims. This blessing was a promise that the Lord would guide their steps as they made their way to Jerusalem. And the Lord, who would guide their steps, *will not slumber. He who keeps Israel will neither slumber nor sleep* (121:3-4).

This God, who is always awake and who directs the pilgrims' steps, promised His people His continued protection against any perils, whether they might come by day or by night (121:4-6). Indeed, 121:7-8 expand the Lord's protection from guarding the pilgrims on their journey to Jerusalem to guarding them throughout the entire pilgrimage of their lives.

SUGGESTIONS TO TEACHERS

As the Shepherd of His people, the Lord wants us to know that we can be completely dependent upon Him. He is always on the alert, looking after His people. We can trust in Him to keep us safe and protected, and we can be completely dependent upon Him for the following:

1. FOR OUR PROVISION. Just as shepherds provide lush meadows for their sheep to graze and peaceful streams for them to drink from, so the Lord will provide for the needs of His people. God has surely proven Himself to be trustworthy in meeting our needs in the past, and He can be trusted to provide our needs in the future.

2. FOR OUR GUIDANCE. As our good Shepherd, the Lord leads and guides those of us who are His sheep. It is interesting that Jesus called Himself *the good shepherd* (John 10:11) and not "the Good Cowboy." The work of a shepherd is done out in front of the sheep, guiding them and leading them to where they should go. The work of a cowboy is done behind the cattle, driving them and pushing them to where he wants to force them to go. Thus as our Shepherd, the Lord has, in essence, paved the road before us. We need only follow Him and trust Him to guide to where we should go.

3. FOR OUR PROTECTION. Shepherds put their lives on the line to maintain their flock of sheep. To protect and rescue sheep from danger, shepherds were forced to inch out onto risky ledges and to put themselves between wild animals and their sheep. In a sense, our Shepherd has done the same for us today. Jesus put His own life on the line so that our eternal lives might be rescued, and He put Himself between us and the penalty for our sin. Thus He not only can be trusted for our protection physically, but mentally, emotionally, and spiritually, too.

4. FOR OUR CONTENTMENT. Shepherds realize that a sheep is a fearful, flighty animal that is prone to get lost or harm itself in a multitude of other ways. Therefore, shepherds sought not only to keep their sheep protected, but also to help them sense a degree of contentment in the care of the shepherd. Psalm 23 promises that God's goodness and unfailing love will actually pursue us all the days of our lives, yearning for us to find our contentment in Him.

■ TOPIC: Don't Be Afraid

■ QUESTIONS: 1. How has the Lord been a Shepherd to you this week? 2. In what ways does the Lord restore your soul? 3. What does it mean for you to be led *in right paths for his name's sake* (Ps. 23:3)? 4. What is *the darkest valley* (23:4) you think you'll ever have to walk through, and in what ways do you want to sense the Lord's presence during that time? 5. In what ways has the Lord upheld you in the past?

■ ILLUSTRATIONS:

Through the Darkest Valley. In an *Upper Room* devotional, Ellen Bergh writes how Amtrak's Coast Starlight train was filled with excited passengers, craning their necks to enjoy the Oregon scenery as the train rolled through green forests. A shining lake gleamed through the trees, and cheerful conversation filled the air.

Suddenly, the light, airy feeling was gone, like a candle blown out in a draft, as the train entered a tunnel. Expecting the sun to reappear quickly, Ellen was uncomfortable as it became even darker.

The happy sounds were a thing of the past. Everyone sat in awe of the inky blackness. The longer they traveled in the tunnel, the harder it was to remain calm without any visual cues to reassure them. Even the movement of the train seemed to fall away into pitch darkness. When they came out of the tunnel, laughter and relief filled the compartment.

"My life in Christ is like that unforgettable train ride," Ellen reflects. "Events may plunge me into darkness where I have no clues to sense the Lord's presence. Yet I can trust God is with me even when I can't see what lies ahead."

For You Are with Me. In the book, *A Window to Heaven: When Children See Life in Death*, Diane M. Komp writes how Ann and her husband were typical married baby boomers. Well-off financially, they had no time for church, and they each became busy in their respective lives. Their romance faded early, but neither wanted to give up their lifestyle. Besides, both adored their children, and their youngest son, T.J., was a special favorite of his mother.

Although the children were never sent to Sunday school and God was never mentioned in their home, one day T.J., out of the blue, said, "Mama, I love you more than anything in the world, except God. And I love Him a little bit more!" Ann was surprised but told him it was okay. *But why would he speak of God?* she wondered.

Two days later, on a bitterly cold day, while his sister was horseback riding, T.J. crossed a snow-covered creek, fell through the ice and died. Ann remembers saying, "I hate you God!" But even then she felt herself held in loving arms.

Ann's world shattered. She remembered the Christmas gift T.J. had bought her that week. He had kept trying to give it to her before Christmas. Each time she had laughed and told him to put it away until Christmas Day. When she got home from the stables where he had died, she hurried upstairs to open it. Inside was a beautiful necklace with a cross.

Ann says that Jesus made her reach out to others rather than become lost in herself. "Helping others helped me." Ann's husband also changed, and together they became new creatures in Christ. Through her ordeal, Ann discovered a gift for spiritual hospitality, bringing healing to other parents.

By now, this young mother has reached out to help hundreds of families who have lost children in accidents. She calls her efforts T.J. Ministries, not only after her T.J., but to emphasize how she's made it since then: "Through Jesus."

Your Shade at Your Right Hand. Texas media mogul Bob Buford, in his 1994 book *The Second Half*, tells of the drowning of his investment banker son, Ross, in the Rio Grande River. After 41 trackers searched for Ross, and Buford himself hired airplanes, helicopters, boats, and trackers with dogs ("everything that money could buy"), Buford walked along a limestone bluff 200 feet above the river, "as frightened as I've ever felt."

"Here's something you can't dream your way out of," Buford told himself. "Here's something you can't think your way out of. Here's something you can't buy your way out of. Here's something you can't work your way out of. . . . This is something you can only trust your way out of," Buford thought to himself while walking that river bluff.

■ TOPIC: Someone to Watch Over Me
■ QUESTIONS: 1. What *green pastures* (Ps. 23:2) has the Lord recently made you lie down in? 2. What *still waters* has the Lord recently led you beside? 3. How does God go about leading you *in right paths for his name's sake* (23:3)? 4. How have God's *goodness and mercy* (23:6) been following you around lately? 5. In what ways has the Lord been *your keeper* (121:5)?

■ **ILLUSTRATIONS:**

Even Though I Walk. Psalm 23 is perhaps the most familiar six verses of the Bible. Perhaps it has become almost too familiar. The following message was printed on a sweatshirt a few years back at the Mall of America:

"Though I walk through
The Mall of America
I shall Fear No Evil
For with Time and Plastic in my Pocket
There's Nothing to FEAR Anyway."

He Who Keeps You. Gary Smalley, popular author and psychologist, asked 100 people, "What is one specific way you knew that you had received your parents' blessing?" Here are some of those answers:

"My father would put his arm around me at church and let me lay my head on his shoulder."

"When my father was facing being transferred at work, he purposely took another job so that I could finish my senior year in high school at the same school."

"When I wrecked my parent's car, my father's first reaction was to hug me and let me cry instead of yelling at me."

"When I was 13, my dad trusted me to use his favorite hunting rifle when I was invited to go hunting with a friend and his father."

"My father went with me when I had to take back an ugly dress a saleswoman had talked me into buying."

"My father would let me practice pitching to him for a long time when he got home from work."

"Even though I had never seen him cry before, my father cried during my wedding because he was going to miss me no longer being at home."

He Will Keep Your Life. A 19-year-old student helped free 4,000 slaves in Sudan. Gerald "Jay" Williams, a sophomore at Harvard University and a member of a United Methodist church, traveled to the restricted country in 2000 with Christian Solidarity International (CSI), a Swiss-based group that buys slaves out of captivity, according to the United Methodist News Service.

Williams said he met with "hundreds of slaves in tattered clothing, dusty, no shoes, and very thin. I almost broke down." Most were Christians who had been abducted by forces of the Islamic Khartoum government and sold to Muslims, he said. "They said they had been praying to God for help. They found strength in that."

Arab Muslim "retrievers" buy the slaves with money provided by CSI, and help them return to their families. It costs about $33 to buy one person, the ministry said. The ministry also reported that 4,435 slaves were freed in September of 2000, and more than 38,000 have been liberated since 1995.

GOD OF JUSTICE

BACKGROUND SCRIPTURE: Psalms 72; 82; 113
DEVOTIONAL READING: Psalm 72:11-19

KEY VERSE: Rise up, O God, judge the earth;
for all the nations belong to you! Psalm 82:8.

4

KING JAMES VERSION

PSALM 82:1 God standeth in the congregation of the mighty; he judgeth among the gods.

2 How long will ye judge unjustly, and accept the persons of the wicked? Selah.

3 Defend the poor and fatherless: do justice to the afflicted and needy.

4 Deliver the poor and needy: rid them out of the hand of the wicked.

5 They know not, neither will they understand; they walk on in darkness: all the foundations of the earth are out of course.

6 I have said, Ye are gods; and all of you are children of the most High.

7 But ye shall die like men, and fall like one of the princes.

8 Arise, O God, judge the earth: for thou shalt inherit all nations. . . .

113:5 Who is like unto the LORD our God, who dwelleth on high,

6 Who humbleth himself to behold the things that are in heaven, and in the earth!

7 He raiseth up the poor out of the dust, and lifteth the needy out of the dunghill;

8 That he may set him with princes, even with the princes of his people.

9 He maketh the barren woman to keep house, and to be a joyful mother of children. Praise ye the LORD.

NEW REVISED STANDARD VERSION

PSALM 82:1 God has taken his place in the divine council;
  in the midst of the gods he holds judgment:
2 "How long will you judge unjustly
  and show partiality to the wicked?   *Selah*
3 Give justice to the weak and the orphan;
  maintain the right of the lowly and the destitute.
4 Rescue the weak and the needy;
  deliver them from the hand of the wicked."
5 They have neither knowledge nor understanding,
  they walk around in darkness;
  all the foundations of the earth are shaken.
6 I say, "You are gods,
  children of the Most High, all of you;
7 nevertheless, you shall die like mortals,
  and fall like any prince."
8 Rise up, O God, judge the earth;
  for all the nations belong to you! . . .
113:5 Who is like the LORD our God,
  who is seated on high,
6 who looks far down
  on the heavens and the earth?
7 He raises the poor from the dust,
  and lifts the needy from the ash heap,
8 to make them sit with princes,
  with the princes of his people.
9 He gives the barren woman a home,
  making her the joyous mother of children.
Praise the LORD!

BACKGROUND

Psalm 82 is ascribed to Asaph, a Levite and the son of Berechiah the Gershonite (1 Chron. 6:39). In ancient times, the descendants of Levi served as assistants to the priests in the worship system of the nation of Israel. As Levites, Aaron and his sons and their descendants were charged with the responsibility of the priesthood, which included offering sacrifices and leading the people in worship and confession. All the other Levites, however, who were not descended directly from Aaron were to serve as priestly assistants. They took care of the tabernacle and the temple and performed a variety of other duties (Num. 8:6).

The choice of the Levites as a people who would perform special service for God goes back to the days of the Exodus when the Israelites were camped at Mount Sinai. The people had grown restless while they waited for Moses to return from talking with the Lord on the mountain. They broke their covenant with God by making a golden calf and worshiping it (Exod. 32:1-24).

When Moses returned and called for those on the Lord's side to come forward, the descendants of Levi were the only ones who voluntarily gathered around him and showed zeal for God's honor. Even before this event, Aaron and his sons had been set apart for the priesthood; but many helpers were needed to attend to the needs of the tabernacle, which was built later at God's command in the Sinai desert. Based on what the Levites had done at Mount Sinai, they were given the honor of serving the Lord (32:25-29).

During the reign of King David, a Levite named Asaph sounded cymbals before the ark of the covenant when it was moved from the house of Obed-edom to Jerusalem (1 Chron. 15:16-19). Asaph's family later became one of the three families given responsibility for music and song in the temple (25:1-9). Twelve psalms are ascribed to Asaph (Pss. 50, 73—83). Among these, Psalms 81 and 82 are often paired together; the former deals with God's judgment over His people, while the latter concerns His judgment of world powers.

NOTES ON THE PRINTED TEXT

In Psalm 82, Asaph presented a vision of God presiding over his heavenly court, administering justice where injustice had prevailed over the poor and defenseless. Portrayed as the great King and Judge of all the earth, God called to account those responsible for oppressing the weak and downtrodden.

The first verse of the psalm shows God Himself, as the supreme Judge, arriving for the hearing and taking *his place in the divine council* (82:1). In the past, Bible scholars have thought that the *gods* mentioned in this verse referred to the many unjust rulers and judges within Israel's borders. But today, more scholars believe these *gods* refer to the kings of surrounding nations—especially those who encouraged their people to believe that they were actually or virtually divine beings. Sadly, these people typically ruled with a complete disregard for justice. These evil human leaders are confronted by the ultimate King and Judge of the world—the one true God.

Having taken His place at this grand trial, God began to level accusations against the wicked rulers for their unjust practices. The first accusation is in the form of a question: *"How long will you judge unjustly and show partiality to the wicked?"* (82:2). A typical fault of rulers in the ancient Near East was to honor justice as an ideal, but in practice to snub it. One of the first and foremost duties of any kingly administration was to protect their powerless subjects against all who might exploit or oppress them. Too often, however, it was the ruler himself who exploited and oppressed his own subjects. Thus, because of their failure to administer justice fairly, God commanded the wicked rulers to *"Give justice to the weak and the orphan; maintain the right of the lowly and the destitute. Rescue the weak and the needy; deliver them from the hand of the wicked"* (82:3-4).

Because these evil human leaders had *neither knowledge nor understanding* (82:5) of God's will and ways, *they [walked] around in darkness.* Sadly, they had no concept of the physical and spiritual order that God's rule maintains. And because they shirked their vital responsibility, the *foundations* of order upon which the whole world was based were *shaken.*

Once God had levied His accusations, He was then ready to set forth His verdict against those who practiced injustice. These kings had ruled and judged by God's appointment; as such, they had been His representatives, regardless of whether they acknowledged God. And because they had governed the earth in an unjust manner, God promised to bring them as low as any other mortal being (82:6), telling them that *"you shall die like mortals, and fall like any prince"* (82:7). Asaph then added his prayerful refrain that God would hasten His judgment: *Rise up, O God, judge the earth; for all the nations belong to you!* (82:8).

The anonymously composed Psalm 113 can be considered a continuation of Asaph's prayer at the end of Psalm 82, for the writer acknowledged that, though the Lord is gloriously exalted—*seated on high* (113:5) and looking *far down on the heavens and the earth* (113:6), He still cares for the needy, standing with and raising up the poor and the weak. Interestingly, Psalm 113 describes what the earthly kings of Psalm 82 should have done to administer justice God's way.

God raised *the poor from the dust* (113:7) and lifted *the needy from the ash heap.* In other words, the Lord came to the aid of those who were humble as well as those who were facing extremely distressful circumstances. By making *them sit with princes* (113:8), God showed that He loved the pauper just as much as the rich person. The Lord graciously lifted the lowly and downtrodden into a place of honor by making them the object of His affection. By giving *the barren woman a home* (113:9), God gave stability to those who were despised and rejected.

SUGGESTIONS TO TEACHERS

In another Old Testament passage in which there is a vision of God presiding over a court trial, the Lord again heard accusations, this time against the nation of Israel. In that trial, described by the prophet Micah, God handed down His verdict by saying, *He has told you, O mortal, what is good; and what does the* LORD *require of you but to do justice, and to love kindness, and to walk humbly with your God?* (Mic. 6:8). Just as Israel's rulers were commanded to administer justice fairly, so also believers are called upon to uphold justice in whatever way we can, whenever we can, wherever we can, and for whomever we can.

1. STOP THE INJUSTICE. The rulers mentioned in Psalm 82 not only failed to administer justice, but also failed to stop injustice. Indeed, God accused them of being the perpetrators of injustice. Perhaps the first and foremost way to begin to administer justice is to put a stop to injustice. As a participant in society and culture or in business and economics, what can you do to prevent the poor and needy from being downtrodden? What can you do concretely to take *no part in the unfruitful works of darkness, but instead expose them* (Eph. 5:11)?

2. DO JUSTICE. The rulers mentioned in Psalm 82 were accused and condemned of judging unjustly and showing partiality to the wicked. To do justice, we must assure that all people are treated fairly and equitably, regardless of their race, gender, or nationality, for to do what is right in the eyes of God is to do justice.

3. LOVE KINDNESS. The rulers mentioned in Psalm 82 were appointed by God to protect their powerless subjects against all who might exploit or oppress them; in essence, God called on the rulers to love kindness, and He provided them with Himself as an example to follow. We still have that example today. Psalm 113 says that God comes to the aid of the humble and distressed, and so should we. Psalm 113 says that God lifts the lowly and downtrodden into a place of honor, and so should we. Psalm 113 says that God gives stability to those who are despised and rejected, and so should we. By following God's example, we will learn what it is to truly love kindness.

4. WALK HUMBLY WITH YOUR GOD. The rulers mentioned in Psalm 82 failed to acknowledge that God had placed them in their positions of authority as His own representatives to carry out justice. Sadly, their arrogance and conceit led them to seek their own wealth and gain on the backs of others, and thus they failed to follow God's kingly example. To walk humbly with our God is to know and acknowledge our place. The Lord is God, and we are not!

■ **TOPIC:** Where Is Justice?

■ **QUESTIONS:** 1. Why is God so concerned about the poor, needy, and downtrodden? 2. What did God accuse the world's evil rulers and judges of? 3. Why do you think the Lord called them *gods* (Ps. 82:1) while at the same time levying His accusations against them? 4. For what reasons do you think the rulers were refusing to give *justice to the weak and the orphan* (82:3)? 5. In what ways have you seen God raise *the poor from the dust* (113:7)?

■ **ILLUSTRATIONS:**

To the Weak and the Orphan. The church in Uganda is flourishing after nearly being destroyed. A spiritual renewal is taking place in the central African nation, Southern Baptist missionary Rob Ackerman told *Religion Today*. He works with tribal people in northwestern Uganda near its borders with Sudan and the Democratic Republic of Congo. "It's been a very open climate and quite easy" to preach the Gospel, he said. Churches are growing and making an impact on society.

The spiritual climate is vastly different today from the years when Christians were horribly persecuted under dictator Idi Amin. Seeking to promote Islam, Amin tried to crush the churches, according to *Operation World*, a missions reference book. Smaller denominations were banned, churches and Christian schools were closed, key Christian leaders were executed or exiled, and thousands of lay people were killed.

The church was in a shambles. Then came a succession of civil wars after Amin's ouster in 1979 left the economy in ruins. At least 800,000 people died during Amin's rule and in subsequent wars and famines.

AIDS ravaged the country by the mid-1980s. Uganda had the highest infection rate of any African nation, and about 30 percent of the population was HIV-positive by 1992, according to *Operation World*. The disease left thousands of orphans and families without a breadwinner.

The suffering caused Ugandans to cry out to God for help, according to a ministry to the country. "A deep cry for help was born in people's hearts, a new seriousness in prayer," John Mulinede of World Trumpet Ministries said. "It was no average prayer, but the deep and lasting prayer characteristic of revival movements."

Yoweri Museveni, a professed Christian, came to power in 1986 and gradually brought political and economic stability, Mulinede said. Rebel groups in the north continue their harassment, but Museveni is firmly established; and while Uganda remains poor, the economy has seen six percent growth for the past six years, Mulinede noted.

Uganda's churches have rebuilt and are more mature, addressing topics of national interest such as the family, education, social injustice, and poverty, Mulinede told DAWN Fridayfax. "There is a notable unity between the churches.

God's Spirit is moving everywhere."

Churches have played a crucial role in the declining rate of AIDS. Christians are educating young people about moral issues involved in sexuality and encouraging them to abstain from intimate relations before marriage. Churches provide job training and biblical counseling to help young women leave prostitution.

First lady Janet Museveni, an outspoken Christian, runs a youth ministry to teach children about the dangers of AIDS. Every year thousands of teens and their families meet to discuss biblical morality as it relates to sexuality and AIDS.

Deliver Them from the Hand of the Wicked. The swashbuckling movie adventurer Indiana Jones has nothing on the Journeymen, a force of twenty-something Christians on the front lines of missionary work around the world.

Journeymen are active in developing nations, Glenn Prescott of the Southern Baptist Convention's International Mission Board told *Religion Today*. The missionaries travel by canoe and teach new Christians in the South American jungle, coordinate relief work and construction projects in Kosovo, perform Christian music in Asia, and backpack across remote areas to preach about Christ.

About 300 Journeymen are serving two-year stints in scores of countries, Prescott said. The program began in 1964 as a Christian missions version of President John F. Kennedy's Peace Corps initiative. For decades Journeymen supported traditional missionaries on the field, teaching their children and doing clerical work. But in recent years their role has expanded to take on more direct missionary activity.

"Journeymen put the legs on our long-term missionary programs," Prescott said. Traveling in teams, they identify which communities are ready to hear the Gospel and recommend ways to present it to them. They follow up on converts, helping them establish weekly Bible studies that grow into churches.

Journeymen played a major role in starting churches in Albania. The Baptist board and other Western mission and ministry groups sent workers to the country when communism fell in 1991. Thousands of volunteers showed the *Jesus* film and distributed Christian materials, and many people became Christians.

The Journeymen helped turn new Christians into committed followers of Christ. They traveled to areas where the Gospel had been proclaimed, discipling converts and starting Bible studies and churches, Prescott said. "They were the ones who were out there every day, traveling from place to place. It is incredible what they started there."

Journeymen prepare the way for evangelistic activity as part of the IMB's Rapid Advance program. They travel to remote areas where people have had little or no exposure to Christianity in order to learn about their cultures, assess their receptivity to the Gospel, and decide how to present the message of Christ most effectively.

Many are at work in nations where the Gospel is restricted. In those places, they teach school, act as farm advisers, work as nurses, and hold other secular jobs while befriending people.

One team started two churches among a group of poor families living in a crumbling hotel. Before a baptismal service, a missionary asked a boy to explain baptism to be sure he understood the commitment he was making. The boy pointed at the missionary's dirty shirt and said, "You take that shirt off and put a clean one on. That's what Jesus did to my heart."

FOR YOUTH

■ **TOPIC:** God Is the Judge

■ **QUESTIONS:** 1. Do you think the trial portrayed in Psalm 82 was conducted fairly? Why or why not? 2. In what ways had these rulers misused their power? 3. For what reasons do you think the rulers were refusing to rescue *the weak and the needy* (Ps. 82:4)? 4. If you were asked the question posed in 113:5, how do you think you would respond? 5. In what ways have you seen God lift *the needy from the ash heap* (113:7)?

■ **ILLUSTRATIONS:**

The Right of the Lowly and the Destitute. Thousands of young people cleaned up for God during the summer of 2000. Restoring a run-down community in Manchester, England, was one of the jobs taken on by 11,000 teenagers. They spent 10 days clearing brush, scrubbing graffiti, painting schools, and doing odd jobs in a low-income neighborhood as part of Soul Survivor Message 2000, Jonathan Stevens of Soul Survivor ministry told *Religion Today*. He noted that their actions spoke louder than just saying "Jesus loves you."

Housing project residents were "blown away" by the acts of love, Stevens reported. Manchester police said no crimes were committed in the Valley Housing Projects during the 10 days the volunteers were there. "It literally brought the community together. Two families that had been fighting with one another are now friends," Stevens said.

Street ministry teams performed evangelistic dramas and held sports clinics for children. Others staffed coffee houses and centers where teenagers could hang out, listen to Christian music, and talk. Manchester, a city of 465,000 people, is 65 miles northwest of London.

Large crowds gathered nightly to hear Christian bands and speakers, and the evenings ended with an invitation for people to put their faith in Christ. About 1,700 responded, including a former heroin addict who now is attending church, according to DNA, a ministry that participated in the outreach. Two young people who became Christians at an evening concert converted 22 friends.

It was the first citywide evangelistic outreach by Soul Survivor, which attracts about 5,000 people to its annual festival at the Royal Bath and West Showground near Watford. The five-day events feature music, Bible teaching, seminars, and workshops to help young Christians grow in their faith. The festivals stress worship because "that is our highest priority in Christian life," Stevens said.

The campgrounds are dotted with "cafe" areas where young people meet, listen to music, skate, watch movies, and see art in a gallery. The events help young people speak up about their faith, Stevens noted. "It fires them up to go out and make a difference." In addition to the yearly festivals, the ministry visits various cities in the United Kingdom to conduct one-day worship and teaching seminars.

From the Ash Heap. Some of Ghana's most impoverished youths are learning trades and the truth about Christ, thanks to an innovative inner-city initiative of African Enterprise (AE), a South Africa-based ministry with offices in Canada and the United States.

In Accra, thousands of young people live on the streets, penniless and parentless. African Enterprise's Street Kids project there teaches 200 of these needy children marketable skills, as well as Bible lessons, reported Executive Director Michael Cassidy. Through partnerships with local churches and communities, AE disciples them in Christianity and instructs them in dressmaking, carpentry, electronics, hairdressing, or air-conditioning repair.

Giving youths the Christian and vocational foundations they need to escape the horror of life on the streets is both "fruitful and rewarding," Cassidy said. African Enterprise has a similar rehabilitation and training program for Ghanaian prostitutes.

TEACH THE WONDERS OF GOD

BACKGROUND SCRIPTURE: Psalm 78:1-8

DEVOTIONAL READING: Psalm 135:1-7

KEY VERSE: We will tell to the coming generation the glorious deeds of the LORD, and his might, and the wonders that he has done. Psalm 78:4.

KING JAMES VERSION

PSALM 78:1 Give ear, O my people, to my law: incline your ears to the words of my mouth.

2 I will open my mouth in a parable: I will utter dark sayings of old:

3 Which we have heard and known, and our fathers have told us.

4 We will not hide them from their children, shewing to the generation to come the praises of the LORD, and his strength, and his wonderful works that he hath done.

5 For he established a testimony in Jacob, and appointed a law in Israel, which he commanded our fathers, that they should make them known to their children:

6 That the generation to come might know them, even the children which should be born; who should arise and declare them to their children:

7 That they might set their hope in God, and not forget the works of God, but keep his commandments:

8 And might not be as their fathers, a stubborn and rebellious generation; a generation that set not their heart aright, and whose spirit was not stedfast with God.

NEW REVISED STANDARD VERSION

PSALM 78:1 Give ear, O my people, to my teaching; incline your ears to the words of my mouth.

2 I will open my mouth in a parable; I will utter dark sayings from of old,

3 things that we have heard and known, that our ancestors have told us.

4 We will not hide them from their children; we will tell to the coming generation the glorious deeds of the LORD, and his might, and the wonders that he has done.

5 He established a decree in Jacob, and appointed a law in Israel, which he commanded our ancestors to teach to their children;

6 that the next generation might know them, the children yet unborn, and rise up and tell them to their children,

7 so that they should set their hope in God, and not forget the works of God, but keep his commandments;

8 and that they should not be like their ancestors, a stubborn and rebellious generation, a generation whose heart was not steadfast, whose spirit was not faithful to God.

HOME BIBLE READINGS

Monday, July 1	Psalm 136:1-9	*The Creator's Steadfast Love*
Tuesday, July 2	Psalm 147:1-11	*The Sustainer of Land and People*
Wednesday, July 3	Psalm 103:15-22	*An Eternal God Sustains His Perishable People*
Thursday, July 4	Psalm 93	*God Has Established the World*
Friday, July 5	Psalm 104:1-18	*God Set the Earth's Foundation*
Saturday, July 6	Psalm 104:19-35	*God Is the Sustainer of Life*
Sunday, July 7	Psalm 65	*God Creates and Sustains*

BACKGROUND

Psalm 78 is one of 13 hymns in the psalter that is labeled as a "Maskil." (The others are 21, 42, 44, 45, 52—55, 74, 88, 89, and 142.) "Maskil" is translated from the Hebrew word *sâkal*, which means "to be circumspect" and hence "to be intelligent." The term is also thought to mean "to make wise or prudent," or perhaps "to have success or skill." Because of the varied insights into the meaning of the word, some have translated "Maskil" to be "a psalm of understanding." And while there are some references to imparting wisdom in each of the Maskils, by no means are all the psalms in this group teaching psalms. (Conversely, there are other psalms that could easily be considered teaching psalms in which the Maskil title is not given.)

What is clear is that Psalm 78 is a teaching psalm. And the lesson that the psalm teaches is just as clear, for this hymn is a recitation of the history of the nation of Israel, beginning from the time of slavery in Egypt leading up to the reign of David. But this history is not recounted just for the sake of rehearsing history; it was sung with the purpose of searching the conscience so that it would not be history that repeated itself. It is a song of instruction that both warns Israel not to repeat its sins of the past and encourages it to recall God's saving acts. Thus, the psalm was also meant to warm the hearts of those singing it, for it tells accounts of great miracles brought about by God and of His mercy, which He offered time and again even in the midst of all of His judgments.

Psalm 78 is one of a group of psalms (along with 105, 106, 135, 136) that was composed to be sung at the nation's major festivals. It was important, while having hordes of people gathered together from the various tribes to recite their common history, to recall the account of God's dealings with His people. Of the 72 verses of the song, the first eight state the psalm's purpose; verses 9-41 retell God's care of the Israelites in the wilderness; verses 42-53 remind the singers and hearers of the Egyptian plagues; and verses 54-72 summarize the period of the Judges and culminate with the selection of David as king.

Interspersed throughout are histories of defection and disobedience as well as histories of God's miraculous guidance and protection. The desire was that new generations of Israelites would not forget the Lord and make the same mistakes as their ancestors.

NOTES ON THE PRINTED TEXT

Asaph, the lyricist and musical composer, turned historian in a sense when he wrote Psalm 78. Though the long psalm recounts the history of the Israelite nation from the time of slavery in Egypt to David's reign, the first eight verses provide a purpose statement for the whole song. And that purpose was that every generation of Israelite children would rehearse their physical and spiritual "roots." With this purpose in mind, Asaph wanted this song, in particular, to be sung over and over to each generation so that they would remain faithful to God and heed the decrees recorded in His covenant.

The initial call of the psalm is for the people to *give ear . . . to my teaching* (78:1); in other words, they were to listen to what the nation's ancestors had to say about Israel's background and history. If each successive generation of Israelites did not hear how God had intervened in and influenced the life of the nation, not only would they be ignorant of what got them to where they were, but they would also be in stark danger of losing the basis for their faith in God.

The psalmist declared that he would *open [his] mouth in a parable* (78:2); in essence, he would tell through the song an account from which the people could learn from the past lessons to apply to the present and the future. What is to be told in the parable are both the experiences of the present generation as well as what the present generation had heard from previous generations, namely, *things that we have heard and known, that our ancestors have told us* (78:3).

Psalm 78:4 stresses both a negative and a positive aspect of the same important statement: *We will not hide them from their children; we will tell to the coming generation.* Those who maintained their faith in God knew that each successive generation would be that much farther away chronologically from the events that established Israel as a nation and as God's chosen people. Therefore, it was a necessity to see to it that each generation not only learned this history, but also that they learned it well enough to recite it in its exact form to the generation that would come after them. Thus the histories were not only told in a narrative form, but were also sung and memorized through psalms like this one.

Of vital importance was that each generation would hear about *the glorious deeds of the LORD, and his might, and the wonders that he has done* (78:4). These Israelite history teachers did not want to see their children think of themselves as in any way separated from the past. Rather, they wanted their children to think of themselves as a continuation of the past—especially of what God had established in the past.

Thus Asaph brought out that God had established a covenant with the nation of Israel, and the Lord *commanded our ancestors to teach to their children* (78:5). Indeed, to pass the covenant on to the next generation was an extension of the greatest commandment: *You shall love the LORD your God with all your heart, and with all your soul, and with all your might. Keep these words that I am commanding you today in your heart. Recite them to your children and talk about them when you are at home and when you are away, when you lie down and when you rise. Bind them as a sign on your hand, fix them as an emblem on your forehead, and write them on the doorposts of your house and on your gates* (Deut. 6:5-9).

The purpose for teaching the law of God to new generations of Israelite children was *that the next generation might know* (Ps. 78:6) and obey these laws, and more specifically, from the positive perspective, *that they should set their hope in God, and not forget the works of God, but keep his commandments* (78:7). There was also a negative perspective. Throughout the psalm, Asaph would be telling portions of Israelite history that the people surely would have liked to forget. Being aware of this, the present generation did not want their children to *be like their ancestors, a stubborn and rebellious generation* (78:8). Unlike previous generations, these teachers held out hope that the coming generations of Israelites would have steadfast hearts that were faithful to God.

SUGGESTIONS TO TEACHERS

Just as Psalm 78 provided a history lesson with a purpose for those who sang it several millennia ago, it can also provide a history lesson with a purpose for those of us living today. Of course, first and foremost is the recounting of God's faithfulness along with the instruction to remember the ways in which the Lord has miraculously come to our assistance. But also added are a few details we would do well to avoid, coupled with some responsibilities we would do well to carry out.

1. DON'T BE QUIET, TEACH. We are not to be silent in regard to what God has done in our lives. This psalm practically cries out for us to tell and to teach that God has in the past, is currently, and will in the future pour out His love, grace, and mercy to those who look to Him in faith. May we *open [our] mouth* (78:2) to tell others about how God cares for His own.

2. DON'T FORGET, REMEMBER. The philosopher George Santayana said, "Those who have no knowledge of history are condemned to repeat it." Psalm 78 urges us to remember the erroneous ways of others so that we do not repeat them; but it also urges us to remember all the incredible ways God has interacted and influenced His people. To remember the sinfulness of the past will help us keep morally strong, and to remember that God's intervention in each of our lives will help us keep the faith.

3. DON'T BE STUBBORN, LISTEN. Asaph referred to the Israelites of the past as a *stubborn . . . generation* (78:8). Perhaps he was writing about their inability to learn from their own mistakes, about their unwillingness to listen to good, sound instruction, and about their hardheadedness toward applying solid teaching to their own lives. Whatever the case, a quick perusal of Israelite history reveals a stubbornness on the part of the Israelites to do things their own way and to turn their backs on God and His law and His covenant. Unlike the ancient Israelites, we have the Word of God easily and readily accessible to us today.

God's message for us and for all humanity is there. Will we listen, or will we, too, prove to be stubborn?

4. DON'T REBEL, BE FAITHFUL. Asaph also referred to the Israelites of the past as a *rebellious generation* (78:8), who were *not faithful to God*. Hoping that the present and future generations would learn from their ancestors' mistakes of the past, the psalmist encouraged the retelling of Israel's history. The point made to us is to steer clear of rebellion against God, to avoid trying to run our lives our own way. Instead, may our own generation and those who follow us find us to be faithful servants of the living God.

FOR ADULTS

■ TOPIC: Tell the Story

■ QUESTIONS: 1. What is it that Asaph wanted future generations of believers to know and not forget about God? 2. Why is it vital to tell *the coming generation the glorious deeds of the LORD* (Ps. 78:4)? 3. What *glorious deeds of the LORD*—from your own experience—would you like to tell young people about? 4. In what ways were many of the Israelites a *stubborn and rebellious generation* (78:8)? 5. In what ways might rehearsing God's mighty acts of the past help the next generation to *set their hope in God, and not forget the works of God* (78:7)?

■ ILLUSTRATIONS:

Things That We Have Heard. A few years ago, someone came up with the idea of asking people of widely varying ages what life had taught them. What follows are the ages of some of the respondents as well as their responses.

Age 6: I've learned that I like my teacher because she cries when we sing "Silent Night." Age 7: I've learned that our dog doesn't want to eat my broccoli either. Age 9: I've learned that when I wave to people in the country, they stop what they are doing and wave back.

Age 12: I've learned that, just when I get my room the way I like it, Mom makes me clean it up again. Age 14: I've learned that if you want to cheer yourself up, you should try cheering someone else up. Age 15: I've learned that, although it's hard to admit it, I'm secretly glad my parents are strict with me.

Age 24: I've learned that silent company is often more healing than words of advice. Age 26: I've learned that brushing my child's hair is one of life's great pleasures. Age 29: I've learned that wherever I go, the world's worst drivers have followed me there.

Age 39: I've learned that if someone says something unkind about me, I must live so that no one will believe it.

Age 42: I've learned that there are people who love you dearly but just don't know how to show it. Age 44: I've learned that you can make someone's day by simply sending them a little note. Age 46: I've learned that the greater a person's sense of guilt, the greater his or her need to cast blame on others. Age 47: I've learned that children and grandparents are natural allies. Age 48: I've learned that no matter what happens, or how bad it seems today, life does go on, and it will be better tomorrow. Age 49: I've learned that singing "Amazing Grace" can lift my spirits for hours.

Age 50: I've learned that motel mattresses are better on the side away from the phone. Age 52: I've learned that you can tell a lot about a man by the way he handles these three things: a rainy day, lost luggage, and tangled Christmas tree lights. Age 53: I've learned that keeping a vegetable garden is worth a medicine cabinet full of pills. Age 53: I've learned that, regardless of your relationship with your parents, you miss them terribly after they die. Age 58: I've learned that making a living is not the same thing as making a life.

Age 61: I've learned that if you want to do something positive for your children, work to improve your marriage. Age 62: I've learned that life sometimes gives you a second chance. Age 64: I've learned that you shouldn't go through life with a catcher's mitt on both hands. You need to be able to throw something back. Age 65: I've learned that if you pursue happiness, it will elude you. But if you focus on your family, the needs of others, your work, meeting new people, and doing the very best you can, happiness will find you. Age 66: I've learned that whenever I decide something with kindness, I usually make the right decision.

Age 72: I've learned that everyone can use a prayer. Age 75: I've learned that it pays to believe in miracles. And to tell you the truth, I've seen several.

Age 82: I've learned that even when I have pains, I don't have to be one. Age 85: I've learned that every day you should reach out and touch someone. People love that human touch—holding hands, a warm hug, or just a friendly pat on the back.

Age 92: I've learned that I still have a lot to learn.

That They Should Set Their Hope in God. Cyprian, before being martyred in the third century, wrote this letter to his friend, Donatus:

This is a cheerful world as I see it from my garden under the shadows of my vines. But If I were to ascend some high mountain and look over the wide lands, you know very well what I would see: brigands on the highways, pirates on the sea, armies fighting, cities burning; in the amphitheaters men murdered to please the applauding crowds; selfishness and cruelty and misery and despair under all roofs. It is a bad world, Donatus, an incredibly bad world. But I have discovered in the midst of it a quiet and holy people who have learned a great secret. They are despised and persecuted, but they care not. They are masters of their souls. They have overcome the world. These people, Donatus, are the Christians—and I am one of them.

A Stubborn and Rebellious Generation. Here are 15 reasons why God will never get tenure at any university:

1. Only published one book.
2. It was written in ancient Hebrew, Aramaic, and Greek.
3. It had no references.
4. He did not publish it in referenced journals.
5. Some doubt He even wrote it Himself.
6. He is not known for His cooperative work.
7. Sure, He created the world, but what has He done lately?
8. He did not get permission from any review board to work with human subjects.
9. When one experiment went awry, He started over by drowning most of the subjects.
10. When sample subjects do not behave as predicted, He deleted the whole sample.
11. He rarely comes to class; He just tells His students to read His book.
12. It is rumored that He sometimes lets His Son teach the class.
13. Although He only has ten requirements, His students often fail His tests.
14. He expelled His first two students for learning.
15. His office hours were infrequent and usually held on a mountaintop.

FOR YOUTH

■ TOPIC: Pass It On

■ QUESTIONS: 1. What was the main point of the writer's teaching in Psalm 78:1-8? 2. Why did the psalmist want to focus the attention of his readers on particular events from Israel's past? 3. Why did the writer emphasize the importance of religious instruction to children? 4. What were some of the *glorious deeds of the LORD* (78:4) that the psalmist had in mind? 5. How can we keep from forgetting the wonderful deeds of God?

■ ILLUSTRATIONS:

To Teach to Their Children. *The Personnel Journal* reported this incredible statistic: since the beginning of recorded history, the entire world has been at peace less than eight percent of the time! In its study, the periodical discovered that out of 3,530 years of recorded history, only 286 years saw peace. Moreover, in excess of 8,000 peace treaties were made—and broken. So what have we learned from history?

That the Next Generation Might Know Them. A father and his small son were out walking one day when the lad asked how electricity could go through the wires stretched between the telephone poles.

"I don't know," said his father. "I never knew much about electricity."

A few blocks farther on, the boy asked what caused lightning and thunder.

"That too has puzzled me," came the reply.

The youngster continued to inquire about many things, none of which the father could explain. Finally, as they were nearing home, the boy said, "Pop, I hope you didn't mind all those questions."

"Not at all," replied his father. "How else are you going to learn?"

And Not Forget. In the book, *Turned On*, by Roger Dow and Susan Cook, is the story about a room-service waiter at a Marriott hotel who learned that the sister of a guest had just died. The waiter, named Charles, bought a sympathy card, had hotel staff members sign it, and gave it to the distraught guest with a piece of hot apple pie.

"Mr. Marriott," the guest later wrote to the president of Marriott Hotels, "I'll never meet you. And I don't need to meet you. Because I met Charles. I know what you stand for. . . . I want to assure you that as long as I live, I will stay at your hotels. And I will tell my friends to stay at your hotels."

CREATOR AND SUSTAINER

BACKGROUND SCRIPTURE: Psalms 65; 104
DEVOTIONAL READING: Psalm 65

KEY VERSE: O LORD, how manifold are your works! In wisdom you
have made them all; the earth is full of your creatures. Psalm 104:24.

KING JAMES VERSION

PSALM 104:24 O LORD, how manifold are thy
works! in wisdom hast thou made them all: the earth is
full of thy riches.

25 So is this great and wide sea, wherein are things
creeping innumerable, both small and great beasts.

26 There go the ships: there is that leviathan, whom
thou hast made to play therein.

27 These wait all upon thee; that thou mayest give
them their meat in due season.

28 That thou givest them they gather: thou openest
thine hand, they are filled with good.

29 Thou hidest thy face, they are troubled: thou takest
away their breath, they die, and return to their dust.

30 Thou sendest forth thy spirit, they are created: and
thou renewest the face of the earth.

31 The glory of the LORD shall endure for ever: the
LORD shall rejoice in his works.

32 He looketh on the earth, and it trembleth: he
toucheth the hills, and they smoke.

33 I will sing unto the LORD as long as I live: I will
sing praise to my God while I have my being.

34 My meditation of him shall be sweet: I will be
glad in the LORD.

35 Let the sinners be consumed out of the earth, and
let the wicked be no more. Bless thou the LORD, O my
soul. Praise ye the LORD.

NEW REVISED STANDARD VERSION

PSALM 104:24 O LORD, how manifold are your
  works!
  In wisdom you have made them all;
  the earth is full of your creatures.

25 Yonder is the sea, great and wide,
  creeping things innumerable are there,
  living things both small and great.

26 There go the ships,
  and Leviathan that you formed to sport in it.

27 These all look to you
  to give them their food in due season;

28 when you give to them, they gather it up;
  when you open your hand, they are filled with good
    things.

29 When you hide your face, they are dismayed;
  when you take away their breath, they die
  and return to their dust.

30 When you send forth your spirit, they are created;
  and you renew the face of the ground.

31 May the glory of the LORD endure forever;
  may the LORD rejoice in his works—

32 who looks on the earth and it trembles,
  who touches the mountains and they smoke.

33 I will sing to the LORD as long as I live;
  I will sing praise to my God while I have being.

34 May my meditation be pleasing to him,
  for I rejoice in the LORD.

35 Let sinners be consumed from the earth,
  and let the wicked be no more.
Bless the LORD, O my soul.
Praise the LORD!

HOME BIBLE READINGS

Monday, July 8	Psalm 145:1-7	*Sing of God's Abundant Goodness*
Tuesday, July 9	Psalm 145:8-13	*All God's Works Give Thanks*
Wednesday, July 10	Psalm 145:14-21	*The Lord Watches Over All*
Thursday, July 11	Psalm 150	*Everything That Breathes Should Praise God*
Friday, July 12	Psalm 148:1-6, 8	*The Wonder of God's Creation*
Saturday, July 13	Psalm 75	*Give Thanks for God's Wondrous Deeds*
Sunday, July 14	Psalm 100	*Worship God, the One Who Made Us*

BACKGROUND

Psalm 104—along with Job 38 and Psalms 8 and 29—produces a magnificent poetic and musical commentary on the creation. Even the structure of the psalm draws praise in that it is modeled quite closely on the day-by-day creation events recorded in Genesis. Indeed, as the psalmist described in grandiose detail the daily acts of creation, he seemed to preach in glowing terms that what God created on each day is reason enough to praise Him!

It is clear that the psalmist used the various stages of creation as his starting points for praise. But as he developed each creation-day theme, there is a constant anticipation for more, especially for the later days of the creation. Of course, the psalmist did adhere exactly to the the day-by-day creation events recorded in Genesis 1; but he also allowed himself some poetic license. For the most part, though, he kept to the structure set out in Genesis, as the following chart shows.

Day God Created . . .   *Psalm 104:*   *Genesis 1:*

		Psalm 104:	Genesis 1:
1	Light	1-2	3-5
2	The heavens and the waters	2-4	6-8
3	Land and vegetation	5-18	9-13
4	The sun, moon, and stars	19-23	14-19
5	Fish and birds	24-26	20-23
6	Animals, people, and food to sustain them	21-24, 27-30	24-31

The opening of the psalm is a call by the singer for his soul—or whole being—to bless the Lord. Indeed, the entirety of the psalm is a beckoning to worship the Creator. Bible scholars have noted that other creation-type hymns were in existence prior to the time when this psalm was written. Many of them, like the Egyptian Akhenaten's "Hymn to the Sun," depicted the making of night and day, the providing for beast and birds, and the life-and-death dependence upon the sun.

Psalm 104, however, contrasts with this Egyptian hymn in that it makes a crystal clear distinction between worshiping the sun and worshiping the Creator of the sun. In Psalm 104, all things point to the Creator, the one true God, who is to be both worshiped and praised. *Bless the LORD, O my soul* (104:1). *O LORD, how manifold are your works! In wisdom you have made them all* (104:24).

NOTES ON THE PRINTED TEXT

Having recounted the first four days of creation and the plethora of reasons for praising the Creator, the composer of Psalm 104 erupted into a refrain in 104:24, proclaiming the vast multitude of God's creation scattered throughout both the universe and the earth! Creation is filled with a stunning array of perfectly placed substance, all of which reveal the creativity, goodness, and wisdom of God. Of course, the psalmist's focus in 104:24 was not so much on the vastness of creation as it was on the vast creativity of the Creator.

In continuing his commentary on the creation as recorded in Genesis, the psalmist next turned to the fifth day of creation, the one on which God brought into existence the fish and birds. Writing both about the seas and the creatures within them, the psalmist stood in awe of the wonders of the waters. He noted that within them are *creeping things innumerable* (104:25) and upon the waters sail great *ships* (104:26). The *Leviathan* that plays in the seas was thought to be an enormous sea creature, the proportions of which caused many to consider it a monster. Though many Bible scholars believe it to have been a giant crocodile, others consider it to be a gigantic, over-size whale-like creature.

Like the creatures that roam across the land, those that make their home in the sea and all other living things look to God *to give them their food in due season* (104:27). And God graciously meets the needs of all His creatures. As the psalmist aptly portrayed, God simply gives His creation sustenance by opening His hand, and when He does, they are all *filled with good things* (104:28). Indeed, both life and death are held within the hands of God. The psalmist said that when God withdraws His care from any living being, then that living being will *die and return to their dust* (104:29). On the other hand, *When you send forth your spirit, they are created; and you renew the face of the ground* (104:30). Essentially, all living things depend on God at every moment for their existence.

After discussing the six days of creation and providing in a song the motivation to praise and worship God, the psalmist concluded this hymn with a prayer for the restoration of the original, intended harmony of creation. He asked that the Lord *may rejoice in his works* (104:31). The psalmist ascribed to the Lord infinite power, for He alone can undo all of His creative work with a mere look or touch. Thus for these and for all the other reasons the psalmist had enumerated throughout his song, he provided himself as an example of what should be done by saying, *I will sing to the LORD as long as I live; I will sing praise to my God while I have being* (104:33).

With the hope that his hymn would be pleasing to the Lord, the psalmist reiterated *for I rejoice in the LORD* (104:34). And for those who would live their lives in open rebellion against God and against His will for His creation, the psalmist asked that the Lord would cause them to vanish *from the earth* (104:35) and *be no more*. Then the psalmist ended his song in the same way he had begun, namely, by calling for his whole being to bless and praise the Lord.

SUGGESTIONS TO TEACHERS

Even though you'll probably be reading these words sometime around the first of July, I am writing them in the middle of October. Just outside my screened window is the beautiful fall countryside. The circus of autumn is in full swing, and the sights, sounds, smells, tastes, and feelings of the season flagrantly remind me to worship and praise my loving Creator!

1. OPEN YOUR EYES! Look for those things that will remind you to focus on the creativity, goodness, and wisdom of our caring heavenly Father. Take a fresh look at the people and animals and insects and plants around you. Your God made them all! Worship and praise Him!

2. OPEN YOUR EARS! Listen for those things that will remind you to focus on the creativity, goodness, and wisdom of our caring heavenly Father. Listen like you never have before for the sounds of nature—a gentle breeze through the leaves, a gurgling stream, or even a baby's laughter. Your God made them all! Worship and praise Him!

3. OPEN YOUR NOSE! Sniff out those things that will remind you to focus on the creativity, goodness, and wisdom of our caring heavenly Father. Stick your nose in a rose; breath in deeply over a sprig of mint; or take a whiff of a freshly mown lawn. Your God made them all! Worship and praise Him!

4. OPEN YOUR MOUTH! Seek out and taste those things that will remind you to focus on the creativity, goodness, and wisdom of our caring heavenly Father. Unless you are eating something artificially flavored, your God made not only the flavors, but your taste buds as well! Worship and praise Him!

5. OPEN YOUR HANDS! Touch and feel those things that will remind you to focus on the creativity, goodness, and wisdom of our caring heavenly Father. Feel the petals of a flower, the fur of a bunny, or the bark of a tree. Your God made them all! Worship and praise Him!

FOR ADULTS

■ **TOPIC:** Let Praise Continue

■ **QUESTIONS:** 1. Why do you think the psalmist, in referring to God's creation, said *In wisdom you have made them all* (Ps. 104:24)? 2. In what ways does God's creation *look to* (104:27) Him for its sustenance? In what ways does His creation fail to look to Him for its sustenance? 3. How is God's creation renewed when He sends forth His Spirit (104:30)? 4. What do you think the psalmist meant when he wrote, *I will sing praise to my God while I have my being* (104:33)? 5. What aspects of creation help remind you to focus on the creativity, goodness, and wisdom of God?

■ **ILLUSTRATIONS:**

O Worship the King. Sir Robert Grant was acquainted with kings. His father was a member of the British Parliament and later became chairman of the East India

Company. Following in his father's footsteps, young Grant was elected to Parliament and then also became a director of the East India Company. In 1834 he was appointed governor of Bombay, and in that position he became greatly loved. A medical college in India was named in his honor.

Late in his life, Grant wrote a hymn based on Psalm 104. The progression of titles for God in the last line of that hymn—"O Worship the King"—is interesting. We know God first as our Maker. Then, even before our conversion, He is our Defender. We know Him then as Redeemer, and finally, as we walk day by day with Him, we know Him also as Friend.

> O worship the King, all glorious above,
> O gratefully sing His power and His love;
> Our Shield and Defender, the Ancient of Days,
> Pavilioned in splendor, and girded with praise.
>
> O tell of His might, O sing of His grace,
> Whose robe is the light, whose canopy space;
> His chariots of wrath the deep thunderclouds form,
> And dark is His path on the wings of the storm.
>
> The earth with its store of wonders untold,
> Almighty, Thy power hath founded of old,
> Hath stablished it fast by a changeless decree,
> And round it hath cast, like a mantle, the sea.
>
> Thy bountiful care, what tongue can recite?
> It breathes in the air, it shines in the light;
> It streams from the hills, it descends to the plain,
> And sweetly distills in the dew and the rain.
>
> Frail children of dust, and feeble as frail,
> In Thee do we trust, nor find Thee to fail;
> Thy mercies how tender, how firm to the end,
> Our Maker, Defender, Redeemer, and Friend.

Creativity and Discipline. Al Hirshfield was quoted as saying, "I believe everybody is creative, and everybody is talented. I just don't think that everybody is disciplined. I think that's a rare commodity."

From "I" to God. In Donald Deffner's opinion, one of the most dramatic and world-renowned shifts from "I" to God is the conversion of C. S. Lewis. This little man, who held the chair of Medieval and Renaissance Literature at Cambridge, sat in his study without typewriter or secretary and penned the great masterpieces that made him perhaps the most broadly read Christian writer of the twentieth century. C. S. Lewis was once an agnostic, but was *Surprised By Joy*—the title of a book in which he tells about "The Shape of My Early Life" as Christ replaced the "I" in his life.

C. S. Lewis describes the exchange between self-will and God's will in *Beyond Personality* (and his words are a challenge to us):

> Christ says, "Give me all. I don't want so much of your money and so much of your work—I want you. I have not come to torment your natural self, but to kill it. No half-measures are any good. I don't want to cut off a branch here and there, I want to have the whole tree down. I don't want to drill the tooth, or crown it, stop it, but to have it out. Hand over the whole natural self instead. In fact I will give you myself, my own will shall become yours."

■ **FOR YOUTH**

■ **TOPIC:** A Reason to Sing

■ **QUESTIONS:** 1. What do all of God's creatures have in common? 2. How do you think you would feel if God were to remove His care from you? 3. What do you think is the ultimate purpose for God's creation? 4. Does this Psalm 104 make you more or less environmentally conscious? Explain your answer. 5. What aspects of creation help remind you to focus on the creativity, goodness, and wisdom of God?

■ **ILLUSTRATIONS:**

Where God Ain't. This anonymously-written poem tells about a small boy with a big perspective:

> He was just a little boy, on a week's first day,
> He was wandering home from Sunday school, and dawdling on the way.
> He scuffed his shoes into the grass; he found a caterpillar,
> He found a fluffy milkweed pod, and blew out all the "filler."

> A bird's nest in a tree overhead, so wisely placed on high,
> Was just another wonder that caught his eager eye.
> A neighbor watched his zigzag course, and hailed him from the lawn,
> Asked him where he'd been that day and what was going on.
> "I've been to Bible School," he said and turned a piece of sod,
> He picked up a wiggly worm replying, "I've learned a lot about God."
> "Mmm, very fine way," the neighbor said, "for a boy to spend his time."
> "If you'll tell me where God is, I'll give you a brand new dime."

> Quick as a flash the answer came! Nor were his accents faint.
> "I'll give you a dollar, Mister, if you can tell me where God ain't."

The Power of Nature's God. On May 18, 1980, Mount Saint Helens in the Cascade Range of Washington state exploded with what is probably the most visible indication of the power of nature that the modern world has ever seen. At 8:32 A.M., the explosion ripped 1,300 feet off the mountain, with a force of 10 million tons of TNT, or roughly equal to 500 atom bombs. Sixty people were killed, most by a blast of 300-degree heat traveling at 200 miles an hour. Some were killed as far as 16 miles away.

The blast also leveled 150-foot Douglas firs as far as 17 miles away. A total of 3.2 billion board-feet of lumber were destroyed, enough to build 200,000 three-bedroom homes.

Where's My Ladybug? As the mother was trying to pack for the family's vacation, her three-year-old daughter was having a wonderful time playing on the bed. At one point, she said, "Mom, look at this," and stuck out two of her fingers. Trying to keep the little girl entertained, the mother reached out and stuck her daughter's fingers in her mouth and said, "Mommy gonna eat your fingers!" pretending to eat them before she rushed out of the room again.

When the mother returned, her daughter was standing on the bed staring at her fingers with a devastated look on her face. The mother asked, "What's wrong honey?" The little girl said, "Mommy, where's my ladybug?"

Once You've Experienced the Peak. Her name was Sarah Dowerday. Born with only one leg, she received national attention several years ago for climbing to the top of Mount Rainier (14,410 feet) in west central Washington state. (Mount Rainier is the highest peak in the Cascade Range.) To document this fascinating human interest story, a camera crew went along. When Dowerday finally reached the snowcapped peak, the crew asked her how she felt: "Once you have experienced the peak, your life is never the same."

THE CROWN OF CREATION

BACKGROUND SCRIPTURE: Psalms 8; 100
DEVOTIONAL READING: Psalm 100

KEY VERSE: What are human beings that you are mindful
of them, mortals that you care for them? Psalm 8:4.

KING JAMES VERSION

PSALM 8:1 O LORD our Lord, how excellent is thy name in all the earth! who hast set thy glory above the heavens.

2 Out of the mouth of babes and sucklings hast thou ordained strength because of thine enemies, that thou mightest still the enemy and the avenger.

3 When I consider thy heavens, the work of thy fingers, the moon and the stars, which thou hast ordained;

4 What is man, that thou art mindful of him? and the son of man, that thou visitest him?

5 For thou hast made him a little lower than the angels, and hast crowned him with glory and honour.

6 Thou madest him to have dominion over the works of thy hands; thou hast put all things under his feet:

7 All sheep and oxen, yea, and the beasts of the field;

8 The fowl of the air, and the fish of the sea, and whatsoever passeth through the paths of the seas.

9 O LORD our Lord, how excellent is thy name in all the earth!

NEW REVISED STANDARD VERSION

PSALM 8:1 O LORD, our Sovereign,
how majestic is your name in all the earth!
You have set your glory above the heavens.

2 Out of the mouths of babes and infants
you have founded a bulwark because of your foes,
to silence the enemy and the avenger.

3 When I look at your heavens, the work of your fingers,
the moon and the stars that you have established;

4 what are human beings that you are mindful of them,
mortals that you care for them?

5 Yet you have made them a little lower than God,
and crowned them with glory and honor.

6 You have given them dominion over the works of your hands;
you have put all things under their feet,

7 all sheep and oxen,
and also the beasts of the field,

8 the birds of the air, and the fish of the sea,
whatever passes along the paths of the seas.

9 O LORD, our Sovereign,
how majestic is your name in all the earth!

7

HOME BIBLE READINGS

BACKGROUND

In his *Tyndale Old Testament Commentary on the Psalms*, Derek Kidner writes concerning Psalm 8: "This psalm is an unsurpassed example of what a hymn should be, celebrating as it does the glory and grace of God, rehearsing who He is and what He has done, and relating us and our world to Him; all with a masterly economy of words, and in a spirit of mingled joy and awe." The hymn was authored by a former shepherd boy who surely had gazed into many a starry night and who later became king to serve as the leader of Israel for many years.

Psalm 8 extols both God's glory and the God-given dignity of human beings. Unlike the anonymously written Psalm 104, David did not draw upon the six days of creation to form the structure for his song. Rather, he wrote out of his own present experience of reality. Throughout the psalm's nine verses, David praised God, all the while referring to his own sense of wonder over the Lord's powerful ordering of creation. One senses that David composed this hymn while standing on his balcony and gazing into the sky at night—the same sky he no doubt had studied and pondered while tending his father's sheep or while on the run from King Saul. The occasion may have pushed to the back of David's mind the day-to-day affairs of administering the Israelite kingdom, while bringing to the forefront deeper thoughts such as the majesty of God and the origin of life.

Certainly two specific thoughts especially impressed David as he penned the words of this psalm. One was the magnificent glory of God as it was reflected in the clear, starry night. The other thought was the utter amazement that God, in all His glory, would even be mindful and considerate of the human aspect of His creation—so much so as to crown human beings with distinction and eminence and to give them lord-like stewardship over the rest of His creation. For the most part, David admitted that these two thoughts were practically beyond his comprehension.

Although the bulk of Psalm 8 describes humanity and its dominion over the earth, the first verse as well as the last make it clear that David wrote this psalm as an act of worship and praise to God, the Creator. Israel's king knew that the greatness of God was the basis for the worth of humankind. Thus this psalm is one of praise centering on the wonder of God Himself, especially as seen in His creation and in His treatment of humanity.

With David's reign, Israel had become a growing regional power, and the people of the nation took pride in their burgeoning strength. Though there was certainly a tendency to give God the credit for their success, many of the Israelites had grown to think of God as their own national possession, as their deity and theirs alone. Such an inclination was like those of neighboring nations, which tended to pay homage to their own national gods as well as acknowledge other national gods.

David rejected both tendencies when he opened his psalm of praise by proclaiming *how majestic is your name in all the earth!* (Ps. 8:1). David knew that God was not merely Israel's God; He is more than a national or tribal deity. David knew and proclaimed God to be Lord of all and over all.

David wrote that though God's glory is placed above the heavens, it is far more clearly seen in babies and infants. This psalmist, who apparently loved the beauty of the stars, considered human life far greater on the scale of God's creation; humanity, more than the heavens, reflected best the true nature of God's glory. In fact, out of *the mouths of babes and infants you have founded a bulwark because of your foes, to silence the enemy and the avenge*r (8:2).

David's love for the starry skies appears several times in this psalm. It is as if the poet could not help but compare any element of God's creation to the stars visible overhead. David, calling into mind the heavens as *the work of your fingers* (8:3), asked God what has become a universal human question: *what are human beings that you are mindful of them, mortals that you care for them?* (8:4). Compared to *the moon and the stars* (8:3), *human beings* (8:4) would probably seem insignificant, but not to God. The Lord is both thoughtful toward and compassionately caring for these weak and frail creatures, personally involving Himself in their welfare. David was amazed that the God who created the earth and the heavens would personally attend to the needs of human beings.

Amazingly David proclaimed, *you have made them a little lower than God* (8:5). Other versions translate this verse "a little lower than the angels." In either rendering, the significance of humankind can't be missed. God created people in His image and likeness to exercise dominion over the rest of creation (Gen. 1:26-28). This awesome responsibility uniquely rests with humanity.

David declared that God purposefully chose humans above all other created beings to be crowned *with glory and honor* (Ps. 8:5). Of course, such glory and honor have not been earned in any way. God has graciously chosen to bestow such a distinction on humanity—and this, too, awed David. He realized that his finiteness did not mean a lack of importance. God had an overarching purpose in making humanity the crown of His creation.

Of the whole of this hymn, only 8:6-8 seems to reflect any portion of the creation account in which God verbalized His intent to create humankind in His image. David rightly assumed that humanity's capacity to exercise dominion over the earth is from our being created in God's image. And as Alvin S. Lawhead has written, "What daring faith in humanity by God! What an awesome trust committed to humankind! Whatever honor belongs to humanity is only a reflection of the greater glory of God."

God has given human beings tremendous authority, namely, to be in charge of the entire earth. Nevertheless, with great authority comes great responsibility. We are stewards of God's creation and accountable to Him for our wise use of earth's natural resources.

Once David had surveyed the heavens, once he had compared the creation of the heavens to the creation of humanity, once he had reexamined the dominion given to humanity by God, he erupted again with perhaps greater appreciation than ever before with a refrain of praise: *O LORD, our Sovereign, how majestic is your name in all the earth!* (8:9).

SUGGESTIONS TO TEACHERS

Seeing God as He is has a humbling effect on a person. When Isaiah beheld God's glory in a vision, he responded, *"Woe is me! I am lost, for I am a man of unclean lips, and I live among a people of unclean lips; yet my eyes have seen the King, the LORD of hosts!"* (Isa. 6:5). When John had a vision of the risen Christ on the Isle of Patmos, the apostle *fell at his feet as though dead* (Rev. 1:17). Isaiah and John recognized their own insignificance when they witnessed God's glory. But though David did not have a vision of the Lord's splendor, Israel's king did see God's glory and majesty displayed in the created universe. David was amazed that God would be both *mindful* (Ps. 8:4) of and caring for the people whom He had created.

1. STAND IN AWE OF GOD'S MAJESTY. Just as a person can stand in awe before a great painting for hours at a time and admire its beauty—taking in every detail, observing every stroke of the brush, and appreciating every choice of color—so a Christian can follow David's example and contemplate and admire the greatness of God's universe. And just as an artist deserves praise for his or her creative work, so the Creator of the universe rightly deserves our praise, adoration, and worship in response to His magnificent creation.

2. WITH CHILDLIKE FAITH. Sometimes as we grow older, we lose that sense of childlike awe for things that are beautiful, magnificent, awesome, or huge! Perhaps we would do well to reclaim not only our childlike eyes but also our childlike faith in our Creator. Most children seem able to put their trust in God and praise Him without holding anything back. This was certainly David's approach; no one would accuse him of holding anything back in the writing of Psalm 8.

3. FOR WE ARE HIS CREATION. Psalm 100:3 says, *Know that the LORD is God. It is he that made us, and we are his; we are his people, and the sheep of his pasture.* When aligned beside the greatness of God, we pale in comparison!

Recognizing this ought to cause us to be both humble and worshipful. We are humbled because we are a tiny part of His creation. We are worshipful because we are His creation, and He has granted to us a special status—being made in His image.

4. A LITTLE LOWER THAN THE ANGELS. Not only are we stamped with the image of God, but also we have been created *a little . . . lower than the angels* (Heb. 2:7). So if you ever feel tempted to question your worth as a person, just remember how highly valuable God considers you!

5. TO EXERCISE DOMINION. God has ultimate rule over the earth, and He exercises His authority with loving care. When God delegated some of His authority to the human race, He expected us to take responsibility for the environment and the other creatures that share our planet. We should not be careless or wasteful as we fulfill this charge. After all, God was careful how He made this earth; we, likewise, should not be careless about how we take care of the planet.

FOR ADULTS

■ TOPIC: Responsible to Care

■ QUESTIONS: 1. What effect did David's understanding of God's greatness have on his view of humanity? 2. As those who have dominion over God's creation, do we have an obligation to be careful about how we use the earth's resources? Why or why not? 3. How should we go about deciding which aspects of God's creation should be used and which aspects should be protected? 4. How is your faith in God affected by observing the created universe? 5. How can knowing that God is all-powerful, all-knowing, and always present help you make it through difficult times?

■ **ILLUSTRATIONS:**

Our Lord, Our Sovereign. Louis XIV of France was the monarch who pompously called himself "Louis the Great" and made the famous statement "I am the state!" In his eyes, he had created something grand and glorious and deserved to be exalted. At the time of his death in 1715, his court was the most magnificent in Europe.

To dramatize his greatness, Louis XIV had given orders prior to his death that at the funeral, the cathedral was to be lit by a single candle set above his coffin. When that eventful day arrived, thousands of people packed into the cathedral. At the front lay Louis XIV's body in a golden coffin. And, per his instructions, a single candle had been placed above the coffin.

The congregation sat in hushed silence. Then Bishop Massilon stood and began to speak. Slowly reaching down, he snuffed out the candle and said, "Only God is great!"

Massilon recognized that even the greatest human accomplishments are insignificant when compared to the actions of the infinite Creator of the universe.

Measured against God's glory, majesty, and greatness, no human can lay claim to greatness. Louis XIV had built a government, but God had created the entire universe!

How Majestic Is Your Name. In his book *Your God Is Too Small*, J. B. Phillips pointed out that many Christians have a less-than-majestic concept of God. They seem to doubt that God is all-powerful, all-knowing, and always present. They live their lives as if God has been weakened by stress and strain. They do not rely on Him as the powerful Ruler over all the universe.

When we read the writings of such saints of the past as Martin Luther, Jonathan Edwards, and George Whitefield, we realize that these people were intimately acquainted with the mighty God who created the world. They knew the same God extolled by David in Psalm 8—the one true God whose name is majestic in all the earth. Their God was not "too small."

There is no limit to God's power, so there should not be a limit to our perception of His power. God has provided us ways to see a glimpse of His omnipotence. He has allowed us to observe His power reflected in the lives of His people as well as in the created universe.

The Work of Your Fingers. William Beebe was no armchair naturalist. His extensive knowledge of nature was gained from exploring the jungles of Asia and South America and the ocean in the world's first bathysphere.

Beebe had much in common with his friend Theodore Roosevelt, who also loved nature and exploring. Often during a visit to Sagamore Hill, Beebe recalled, he and the president went outdoors to see who could first locate the Andromeda galaxy in the constellation of Pegasus.

Gazing at the tiny smudge of distant starlight, Beebe would say something like this: "That is the spiral galaxy of Andromeda. It is as large as our Milky Way, and is one of a hundred million galaxies. It is 750,000 light-years away and consists of one hundred billion suns, each one larger than our sun."

After that thought had sunk in, Roosevelt would flash his famous toothy grin: "Now I think we are small enough." And the two men would go inside, put in their place by the limitless universe.

FOR YOUTH

■ TOPIC: Truly Awesome!

■ QUESTIONS: 1. In what ways can what comes out *of the mouths of babes and infants* (Ps. 8:2) silence the foes of God? 2. When was the last time you felt the starry sky testify to you about God's majesty and power? 3. How does creation indicate that it must have had a master designer? 4. How can some people deny God's existence while studying the details of His creation? 5. Why do you think David ended this psalm the same way he began it?

To Silence the Enemy and Avenger. Sir Isaac Newton kept a miniature replica of the solar system in his study. In the center of the replica was the sun, with the planets revolving around it.

A scientist who did not believe in God entered Newton's study one day and took notice of the replica.

"My! What an exquisite object this is!" he exclaimed. "Who made it?"

"Nobody," replied Newton to the questioner.

"You must think I am a fool," the scientist responded. "Of course somebody made it, and he is a genius."

Laying his book aside, Newton explained, "This object is but a puny imitation of a much grander system, whose laws you and I know, and I am not able to convince you that this mere toy is without a designer and maker. Yet you profess to believe that the great original from which the design is taken has come into being without either designer or maker. Now tell me, by what sort of reasoning do you reach such incongruous conclusions?"

The unbelieving scientist had offered praise to the creator of the humanly made model of the solar system. How much more deserving of praise is the majestic Creator of the universe!

When I Look at Your Heavens. David was awed by God's majesty, especially as Israel's king looked up and beheld the universe created by God's almighty hand. David was utterly astonished at the sheer vastness of what he witnessed. Perhaps you will be too when you consider the following facts.

Astronomers say that the Milky Way, the disc-shaped galaxy to which our sun belongs, is a family of more than 100 billion stars. They also say there may be as many as 100 billion other galaxies in the universe, and that the billions of stars in each of these billions of galaxies may have hundreds of millions of planets. All this came into being at God's command.

Just the size of some of the stars is enough to boggle the human mind. Astronomers tell us that our sun is so large that if it were hollow, it could contain more than one million worlds the size of the earth. There are also more stars in outer space so large that they could easily contain 500 million suns the size of ours.

The distance between planets and stars is practically unfathomable. Suppose you made a model in which the earth were represented by a ball only one inch in diameter. Using the same scale, the nearest star system—Alpha Centauri—would have to be placed nearly 51,000 miles away.

Or imagine that the thickness of this page you are reading represents the distance from the earth to the sun (about 93 million miles). The distance to the nearest star would be a 71-foot-high stack of paper. And the diameter of our own galaxy would be equal to a 310-mile stack of paper, while the edge of the known universe would be a pile of paper one-third of the way to the sun (31 million miles)!

Like David, when we ponder the incredible vastness of the universe created by God, we can only ask, *what are human beings that you are mindful of them, mortals that you care for them?* (Ps. 8:4).

That You Are Mindful of Them. When Charles Simeon, an evangelical scholar, was on his deathbed, his biographer related that "after a short pause, he looked round with one of his bright smiles and asked, 'What do you think especially gives me comfort at this time? The creation! Did the Lord create the world, or did I? I think He did; now if He made the world, He can sufficiently take care of me!'"

JOY IN FORGIVENESS

BACKGROUND SCRIPTURE: Psalms 32; 51
DEVOTIONAL READING: 51:1-12

KEY VERSE: Happy are those whose transgression
is forgiven, whose sin is covered. Psalm 32:1.

KING JAMES VERSION

PSALM 32:1 Blessed is he whose transgression is forgiven, whose sin is covered.

2 Blessed is the man unto whom the LORD imputeth not iniquity, and in whose spirit there is no guile.

3 When I kept silence, my bones waxed old through my roaring all the day long.

4 For day and night thy hand was heavy upon me: my moisture is turned into the drought of summer. Selah.

5 I acknowledged my sin unto thee, and mine iniquity have I not hid. I said, I will confess my transgressions unto the LORD; and thou forgavest the iniquity of my sin. Selah.

6 For this shall every one that is godly pray unto thee in a time when thou mayest be found: surely in the floods of great waters they shall not come nigh unto him.

7 Thou art my hiding place; thou shalt preserve me from trouble; thou shalt compass me about with songs of deliverance. Selah.

8 I will instruct thee and teach thee in the way which thou shalt go: I will guide thee with mine eye.

9 Be ye not as the horse, or as the mule, which have no understanding: whose mouth must be held in with bit and bridle, lest they come near unto thee.

10 Many sorrows shall be to the wicked: but he that trusteth in the LORD, mercy shall compass him about.

11 Be glad in the LORD, and rejoice, ye righteous: and shout for joy, all ye that are upright in heart.

NEW REVISED STANDARD VERSION

PSALM 32:1 Happy are those whose transgression is forgiven,
whose sin is covered.

2 Happy are those to whom the LORD imputes no iniquity,
and in whose spirit there is no deceit.

3 While I kept silence, my body wasted away
through my groaning all day long.

4 For day and night your hand was heavy upon me;
my strength was dried up as by the heat of summer.
Selah

5 Then I acknowledged my sin to you,
and I did not hide my iniquity;

I said, "I will confess my transgressions to the LORD,"
and you forgave the guilt of my sin. *Selah*

6 Therefore let all who are faithful
offer prayer to you;

at a time of distress, the rush of mighty waters
shall not reach them.

7 You are a hiding place for me;
you preserve me from trouble;
you surround me with glad cries of deliverance.
Selah

8 I will instruct you and teach you the way you should go;
I will counsel you with my eye upon you.

9 Do not be like a horse or a mule, without understanding,
whose temper must be curbed with bit and bridle,
else it will not stay near you.

10 Many are the torments of the wicked,
but steadfast love surrounds those who trust in the LORD.

11 Be glad in the LORD and rejoice, O righteous,
and shout for joy, all you upright in heart.

8

Home Bible Readings

Background

Psalm 32 is another of David's works, and this one is also labeled as a "Maskil." Like Psalm 78, among others, it was considered "a psalm of understanding," "a wisdom psalm," or "a teaching psalm" when it was first performed in the tabernacle and then later on in the temple. Psalm 32 is also considered one of the seven "penitential psalms" in the psalter—the others being Psalms 6, 38, 51, 102, 130, and 143. In each of these psalms, the composers expressed their deep remorse for their misdeeds and sins, their commitment to repent, and their yearning for God to forgive them.

In the way that David composed Psalm 32, it might also be considered a hymn of thanksgiving, for contained within his words are a joyful testimony thanking God for His gift of forgiveness. David has been described as *a man after [God's] own heart* (1 Sam. 13:14). For him to be in close accord with his Lord was to be truly happy. Whenever David felt that his sins had somehow broken that accord, he eventually came to God confessing his misdeeds and asking for forgiveness. David yearned to restore the relationship that brought the truest sense of joy into his life.

The composers of the penitential psalms knew, however, that though God offered His forgiveness as a gift, He did expect some changes to be made in the lives of the penitents. Therefore, in Psalm 32, David pointed out that those who are truly forgiven are those who with integrity confess their sins and remain receptive to God's rule in their lives.

Some Bible scholars see this song as a type of ceremonial conversation between David and God. Because of its being used as a liturgical hymn, this conversation would, of course, take place in the presence of the worshipers gathered at the tabernacle—and later the temple. For instance, in the first two verses and again in verse 11, David spoke to the gathered worshipers. In verses 3-7, he is recorded as speaking to God, though in the hearing of the assembly. Then in verses 8-11, David is addressed by God Himself, though likely through the voice of one of the nation's priests.

Thus the recurring theme of the psalm is this back-and-forth dialogue—David confessing his wrongdoing, God offering His forgiveness, David rehearsing the memory of his lost fellowship with God, and God offering His instructions for righteous living. The hymn is, indeed, a penitential psalm, but it is also one of understanding, wisdom, and thanksgiving.

NOTES ON THE PRINTED TEXT

By the way Psalm 32 is written, it seems that the initial words are an introduction intended for one person to announce to those assembled for worship. It may well be considered a summary statement of all that follows in the song, conveying the truth that *those whose transgression is forgiven, whose sin is covered* (32:1) are both happy and blessed. Inherent in this opening verse is the belief that only God can lift and remove the transgressions of people, and that when He does so, He somehow conceals them from His sight.

A second beatitude follows the first, saying much of the same thing except that it conveys even more of the character of God and of the reach of His forgiveness. So powerful and thorough is His forgiveness that those who receive it have *no iniquity* (32:2) counted against them, and God's regeneration so transforms their lives that in their spirit *there is no deceit.*

Having addressed the assembly with several beatitudes to introduce his song, David then turned to God, describing to Him the misery of carrying the load of his transgression alone. As long as David's sin remained undisclosed and unconfessed, his *body wasted away through my groaning all day long* (32:3). He admitted that God was dealing with him, saying that *day and night your hand was heavy upon me* (32:4). The Lord wasn't going to allow His servant to harbor sin and hide it away. Instead, God brought conviction upon David, making him sense both his guilt and his dire need for forgiveness. Thus, as long as the king resisted God, the inner struggle of his conscience drained away his vitality as if his *strength was dried up as by the heat of summer.*

After David told about the misery of trying to deal with his sin on his own, the joyfulness of the psalm begins to return in 32:5. This is the point at which David came to acknowledge his guilt and confess his transgressions. According to Israel's king, he immediately sensed God's forgiveness of *the guilt of my sin* (32:5). In this way, the psalm teaches us the way to go about seeking forgiveness for our sins, just as does 1 John 1:9—*If we confess our sins, he who is faithful and just will forgive us our sins and cleanse us from all unrighteousness.*

In the midst of David's prayer to God, he also addressed all those in the assembly of the tabernacle. Israel's king wanted them, too, to hear and learn the vital lesson that the godly should confess their rebellion against God *at a time of distress* (Ps. 32:6), long before the floodwaters of judgment overwhelmed them. David also wanted the worshipers to know about the lovingkindness of God. Thus David included in his prayer these sweet words: *You are a hiding place for me; you preserve me from trouble; you surround me with glad cries of deliverance* (32:7). By being forgiven of his sin, Israel's king had, indeed, been delivered from his miserable state.

With the end of David's prayer, God initiated His response. The Lord promised His continued guidance for all those who sought Him for forgiveness and mercy, assuring the repentant that He would *instruct you and teach you the way you should go* (32:8). But God also attached a subsequent warning to His promise. He pledged to instruct and guide; but He also wanted the repentant to have a teachable spirit in the process. Thus, He cautioned them against being *like a horse or a mule, without understanding, whose temper must be curbed with bit and bridle, else it will not stay near you* (32:9).

Before the song came to a close on a joyful note, the Lord issued one more warning. God declared that those who are wicked will face many sorrows and woes—and they'll face them without divine help. But for those who *trust in the LORD* (32:10), God will surround them with His *steadfast love*. While these people, too, will face trials and hardships, they will come through triumphant because of God's gracious provision. Because they are victorious people, God urged the recipients of His mercy to be *glad in the LORD and rejoice, O righteous, and shout for joy, all you upright in heart* (32:11).

SUGGESTIONS TO TEACHERS

Psalm 32 underscores that forgiveness brings true joy. We learn that when we ask God to forgive our sins, He brings real happiness and relief from guilt. This teaching psalm shows us four steps we can follow that lead to God's forgiveness.

1. BELIEVE, DON'T DOUBT. The first step in being forgiven is to believe that God has the willingness, the love, and the power to forgive all that we have done wrong. God's only Son, Jesus Christ, shed His blood on the cross so that our own sins would not be applied to our account. That's how great God's love is for us! We shouldn't doubt that God wants to forgive us. We shouldn't doubt how much He cares for us. We shouldn't doubt that He has provided the way for us to be forgiven and made like new.

2. CONFESS, DON'T HIDE. Trying to hide our sins from God is hopeless. He already knows everything about us. And besides, what David wrote about being miserable while keeping his silence about his wrongdoing will be true for us, too. God will continue to convict our hearts until we quit holding on to our sin and confess to Him what we've done. How do we go about confessing? Confession is admitting our sin. It is agreeing with Him, acknowledging that He is right to call what we have done sinful. It is admitting that we were wrong to do it or even to desire it. It is affirming our intention of giving up that sin so that we can follow the Lord more faithfully than we have thus far.

3. REPENT, DON'T KEEP ON SINNING. God doesn't want us to stubbornly continue on in the sin for which we have sought His forgiveness. He desires that we genuinely repent—to change directions. But we won't even be able to find the strength to repent in and of ourselves; we must get God's help.

And He gives us that help through His Holy Spirit, who *will instruct you and teach you the way you should go* (32:8). The Lord promises to empower us to overcome those sins that have hindered our relationship with Him and to transform us into people who want to be guided by His love and wisdom.

4. ACCEPT, DON'T REJECT. The final step is simply to accept the forgiveness God offers, as well as to accept the guidance He provides for our lives. In a way, to accept His forgiveness we must return to the first step and believe that He has forgiven us. To doubt God's willingness, love, and power to forgive is equal to rejecting His promise and continuing to live in rebellion against Him.

FOR ADULTS

■ **TOPIC:** Joy in Forgiveness

■ **QUESTIONS:** 1. In what way are all your sins *covered* (Ps. 32:1)? 2. When have you felt *day and night [God's] hand was heavy upon* (32:4) you? 3. In what ways do you find God to be *a hiding place* (32:7) for you? 4. In what ways lately do you think God has preserved you from trouble? 5. What are the typical results from being stubborn toward God?

■ **ILLUSTRATIONS:**

Whose Sin Is Covered? In the devotional *One with Us*, Richard Fairchild writes the following:

> I am sure most of you have seen Waterford Crystal. It is beautiful to look at. The only problem is when you drop it, it shatters into a thousand pieces, and no matter how hard you try to glue the broken pieces back together it never looks as beautiful as before it was dropped. Sometimes we get the idea that as human beings we are like leaded crystal. We are lovely until we make a mistake—and we all make them. Then life shatters into a thousand pieces and can never be put back together just right— never put back the way God meant it to be. But if we are to compare human life to any object around us, we are better compared to the children's toy Silly Putty than to leaded crystal. Like Silly Putty, we can be pulled apart, rolled into little balls, flung against the wall, or smashed flat. But like Silly Putty we can always be scraped back together again, forgiven, reworked, remolded, and reshaped into someone that is even more beautiful than before.

You Forgave the Guilt. World-famed pianist Arthur Rubinstein took aback Prime Minister Golda Meir and a national audience once when, over Israeli television, he professed faith in Jesus Christ. According to an article in the *Mount Zion Reporter,* the incident took place while Mrs. Meir was interviewing the American-Jewish virtuoso.

The prime minister asked the pianist to name the "greatest event in your life."

"When I received Yeshua Hamashiach [Jesus the Messiah] into my heart," Rubinstein replied. "Since then my life was changed. I have experienced joy and peace ever since." The report went on to state that at the comment, Mrs. Meir leaned back in her chair with an expression of complete surprise!

With My Eye upon You. Time-lapse photography compresses a series of events into one picture. Such a photo appeared in an issue of *National Geographic*. Taken from a Rocky Mountain peak during a heavy thunderstorm, the picture captured the brilliant lightning display that had taken place throughout the storm's duration. The time-lapse technique created a fascinating, spaghetti-like web out of the individual bolts.

In a similar way, our sin presents itself before the eyes of God. Where we see only isolated or individual acts, God sees the overall web of our sinning. What may seem insignificant—even sporadic—to us and passes with hardly a notice, creates a much more dramatic display from God's panoramic viewpoint.

FOR YOUTH

■ TOPIC: Forgiven!

■ QUESTIONS: 1. What is the true source of happiness mentioned in Psalm 32:1-2? 2. Why do so many people refuse to confess their sins? 3. How did you feel at a time when you were living with unconfessed sin in your life? 4. How would you explain the feeling of being forgiven to someone who is not a Christian? 5. In what ways is God instructing and teaching you *the way you should go* (32:8)?

■ ILLUSTRATIONS:

Let All Who Are Faithful. Charles Shultz, creator and author of the *Peanuts* cartoon characters, often conveyed a message in his comic strips. For instance, in one strip he conveyed through Charlie Brown the need we have to be loved and through Lucy our inability to love one another. Charlie Brown and Lucy are leaning over the proverbial fence speaking to one another:

Charlie: "All it would take to make me happy is to have someone say he or she likes me."

Lucy: "Are you sure?"

Charlie: "Of course I'm sure!"

Lucy: "You mean you'd be happy if someone merely said he or she likes you? Do you mean to tell me that someone has it within his or her power to make you happy merely by doing such a simple thing?"

Charlie: "Yes! That's exactly what I mean!"

Lucy: "Well, I don't think that's asking too much. I really don't." [Now standing face-to-face with Charlie Brown, Lucy asks one more time] "But you're sure now? All you want is to have someone say, 'I like you, Charlie Brown,' and then you'll be happy?"

Charlie: "And then I'll be happy!"

Lucy: [Lucy turns and walks away saying] "I can't do it!"

What Lucy cannot do, sinful as she was, God has done through Jesus Christ! What we need, lost and alone as we are, God supplies. God loves us and is willing and able to forgive us when we put our faith in His Son.

Offer Prayer to You. A four-year-old got confused praying the Lord's Prayer. He prayed, "And forgive us our trash baskets as we forgive those who put trash in our baskets." H.B. London says that's pretty much what Jesus meant by His words recorded in Matthew 6:12. London went on to say, "The church is simply a community of forgiven and forgiving sinners. Every individual who attends church on Sunday morning has fallen short of the glory of God. Some, however, have received God's free gift of salvation by grace."

Glad Cries of Deliverance. In his book, *An Anthropologist on Mars*, neurologist Oliver Sacks tells about Virgil, a man who had been blind from early childhood. When he was 50, Virgil underwent surgery and was given the gift of sight. But as he and Dr. Sacks found out, having the physical capacity for sight is not the same as seeing.

Virgil's first experiences with sight were confusing. He was able to make out colors and movements, but arranging them into a coherent picture was more difficult. Over time he learned to identify various objects, but his habits—his behaviors—were still those of a blind man. Sacks asserts, "One must die as a blind person to be born again as a seeing person. It is the interim, the limbo . . . that is so terrible."

To truly "see" Jesus and His truth means more than observing what He did or said; it means a complete and radical change of identity.

LET ALL THE PEOPLES PRAISE GOD

BACKGROUND SCRIPTURE: Psalms 67; 96
DEVOTIONAL READING: Psalm 97:6-12

KEY VERSE: Let the peoples praise you,
O God; let all the peoples praise you. Psalm 67:3.

KING JAMES VERSION

PSALM 67:1 God be merciful unto us, and bless us; and cause his face to shine upon us; Selah.

2 That thy way may be known upon earth, thy saving health among all nations.

3 Let the people praise thee, O God; let all the people praise thee.

4 O let the nations be glad and sing for joy: for thou shalt judge the people righteously, and govern the nations upon earth. Selah.

5 Let the people praise thee, O God; let all the people praise thee. . . .

96:1 O sing unto the LORD a new song: sing unto the LORD, all the earth.

2 Sing unto the LORD, bless his name; shew forth his salvation from day to day.

3 Declare his glory among the heathen, his wonders among all people.

4 For the LORD is great, and greatly to be praised: he is to be feared above all gods.

5 For all the gods of the nations are idols: but the LORD made the heavens.

6 Honour and majesty are before him: strength and beauty are in his sanctuary.

7 Give unto the LORD, O ye kindreds of the people, give unto the LORD glory and strength.

8 Give unto the LORD the glory due unto his name: bring an offering, and come into his courts.

9 O worship the LORD in the beauty of holiness: fear before him, all the earth.

NEW REVISED STANDARD VERSION

PSALM 67:1 May God be gracious to us and bless us
and make his face to shine upon us, *Selah*

2 that your way may be known upon earth,
your saving power among all nations.

3 Let the peoples praise you, O God;
let all the peoples praise you.

4 Let the nations be glad and sing for joy,
for you judge the peoples with equity
and guide the nations upon earth. *Selah*

5 Let the peoples praise you, O God;
let all the peoples praise you. . . .

96:1 O sing to the LORD a new song;
sing to the LORD, all the earth.

2 Sing to the LORD, bless his name;
tell of his salvation from day to day.

3 Declare his glory among the nations,
his marvelous works among all the peoples.

4 For great is the LORD, and greatly to be praised;
he is to be revered above all gods.

5 For all the gods of the peoples are idols,
but the LORD made the heavens.

6 Honor and majesty are before him;
strength and beauty are in his sanctuary.

7 Ascribe to the LORD, O families of the peoples,
ascribe to the LORD glory and strength.

8 Ascribe to the LORD the glory due his name;
bring an offering, and come into his courts.

9 Worship the LORD in holy splendor;
tremble before him, all the earth.

HOME BIBLE READINGS

BACKGROUND

Although the anonymously written Psalm 67 appears to be a thanksgiving hymn sung at the conclusion of a plentiful harvest, it actually points to a harvest of a more vital kind: a spiritual harvest. Both the form and the content of the song indicate that it was used as a part of the worship service in the temple, likely either prior to or immediately after the priest's benediction, during the nation's harvest festival. A reading of the psalm indicates, however, that the yield of the harvest is not so much the emphasis of this worship hymn as it is God's loving provision. In the end, what really matters is humanity's need for God.

The beauty of the psalm is the way that it blends the thanksgiving for a physical harvest with the thanksgiving for a spiritual harvest, for the true emphasis of the song is spiritual salvation and the harvest of souls. Indeed, to the psalmist, one harvest simply led to another. As the people of other nations took note of God's blessing of the people of Israel, they, too, would be moved to praise and worship the one true God. Thus the blessing that had reached the people of Israel would spread to all the people of the world. And in this way, God's promise to Abraham that His descendants would be both blessed and made a blessing was fulfilled. Joy came upon the people of Israel as they spread the news about their God around the world.

Psalm 67 is the third in a series of four harvest festival hymns. Its structure is purely symmetrical, with the opening two verses containing a prayer and the final two verses telling about God's answer. In the middle two verses, the Israelites sang about the worldwide praise that God's love, grace, and mercy will generate. Though also a hymn of praise, Psalm 96 concentrates on the triumphal entry of the ark of the covenant into Jerusalem rather than on a plentiful harvest. But like Psalm 67, Psalm 96 proclaims the glory of God's reign beyond the borders of Israel—throughout the world. As such, it is a call for all people to submit to God's rule.

Some Bible scholars consider this a psalm of David in that it appears with some variations in 1 Chronicles 16:23-33, which records David's song of celebration as the ark was brought into Jerusalem. In a way, Psalm 96 is an enthronement hymn celebrating God's kingship, extolling His holy presence, raising Him to the loftiest of positions, and affirming His great power.

This psalm is composed of two parts: first, the call for all nations to sing the praises of the Lord (96:1-6), and second, a call for all nations to worship the Lord and convey His righteous rule to all the world (96:7-13). The constant buildup of repeated words and phrases (such as *sing* and *ascribe*) gives the psalm a persistent, strengthening liveliness, contributing to a growing excitement at the prospect of the the Lord's coming; even the physical universe breaks out in singing as it eagerly and anxiously awaits the moment of fulfillment!

NOTES ON THE PRINTED TEXT

Although Psalm 67 is a hymn of thanksgiving, its initial verse is a prayer that God will continue to bless His people with bountiful harvests. Surely God had been *gracious* (67:1) toward His people, blessing them and making His *face to shine upon* them. But the writer of this psalm knew that the people would long for God's rich blessings to continue, and thus that request opens the song.

The people were not yearning for God's blessings simply for their own personal gain; they realized that God's blessings on their lives had an evangelistic purpose. As they received God's continuing blessings, other people of other nations would take notice and be drawn to seek out the God of Israel. Thus the psalmist also prayed in behalf of all the people of Israel: *that your way may be known upon earth, your saving power among all nations* (67:2). Then, as more and more people would begin to realize that the Lord is the one true God and the source of all their blessings and the Creator of all that exists, they, too, would join in with the Israelites in praising God.

Inherent throughout this hymn is that God's blessings on Israel is but a forerunner of His divine blessings for the whole world. Thus the appropriate desire of the chosen people of Israel—and their purpose for being chosen by God in the first place—was to be a compass pointing directly toward God and His glory. In the end all the *peoples* (67:3) would come to praise Him. The psalmist said these nations would *be glad and sing for joy* (67:4) as they witnessed how God would *judge the peoples with equity and guide the nations upon earth* (67:4). Thus the refrain of verse 5 repeats the prayer of verse 3 to *Let the peoples praise you, O God.*

Psalm 96 also has an evangelistic purpose. But rather than lauding God's blessings of a bountiful harvest, this song praises God for His kingly qualities, such as His glory, His marvelous works, His greatness, His honor, and His majesty. By pointing to these character traits of God, the singers in the tabernacle and temple of Israel attempted to reveal to the whole world that their one true God is worthy to be worshiped and praised.

Because the song was composed for a new type of celebratory occasion—the bringing of the ark of the covenant into Jerusalem—the psalmist beckoned the people of all the earth to *sing to the LORD a new song* (96:1). Of course, the purpose of this new song, which might have referred to the psalm itself, was to celebrate God's saving act, His deliverance of His people from out of the bondage of the past into a divinely ordained freedom of the present. This freedom would come as people and nations accepted God's forgiveness and submitted themselves to His rule and will. There is also a sense in the psalm that our lives should be like the song. Just as the *steadfast love of the LORD never ceases, his mercies never come to an end; they are new every morning; great is your faithfulness* (Lam. 3:22-23), so should our lives be lived as a song of praise that is ever fresh!

The psalmist made it clear that the blessings that God had showered on the nation of Israel were not to be hoarded. Rather, the poet wrote that God's people should sing *to the LORD, bless his name; tell of his salvation from day to day* (Ps. 96:2). Though this instruction surely meant for the Israelites to rehearse to each other the love and mercy of the Lord, it also meant for them to proclaim His love and mercy to the rest of the world. After all, they were told to declare *his glory among the nations, his marvelous works among all the peoples* (96:3).

As the people of Israel carried the message of God's deliverance and salvation out beyond their nation's borders, this psalm informed them of some of the resistance they were likely to face. They would certainly encounter people who worshiped other gods, and thus in the lyrics of the song their one true God was compared to these idols. When such a comparison was made, the people would see that the one true God is so *great* (96:4) that He is *to be revered above all gods.* Indeed, *all the gods of the peoples* (96:5) are mere *idols*—gods made from the materials of the earth. The one true God, on the other hand, *made the heavens.* Therefore, *honor and majesty are before him; strength and beauty are in his sanctuary* (96:6).

In 96:7-9, the psalmist instructed the people to *ascribe* three times and to *worship* once. The Hebrew verb rendered *ascribe* means to attribute or assign to God specific causes, origins, and characteristics. In this song, the psalmist probably meant to encourage the people to acknowledge God for these qualities. In essence, he urged the people to recognize and submit to God's *glory and strength* (96:7), to *the glory due his name* (96:8). The people's submission to the rule and will of God would be demonstrated to and witnessed by the rest of the world as the Israelites would *bring an offering, and come into his courts.* Furthermore, the people were instructed through the song as to the frame of mind in which to worship God. They were told to recognize His *holy splendor* (96:9), and as they did so, to recognize their own humble place before Him.

SUGGESTIONS TO TEACHERS

Both Psalms 67 and 96 are joyful hymns celebrating the kindness, goodness, and greatness of our God. By describing for us the majesty and magnificence of the Lord, they also speak to us about the type of people we ought to be in response to the love, grace, and mercy that He has poured out to us.

1. BE WITNESSES. Both psalms encourage us to recall the ways in which God has cared for us, and then to show and to tell what He has done for us. Just as the purpose of the nation of Israel was to be a witness beyond its borders of the greatness of its God, so the purpose of the church picks up where Israel's left off. We are to declare *his glory among the nations* (96:3). We are to be witnesses of God's love, grace, and mercy.

2. BE FRESH. The longer we serve the Lord—the longer we are His witnesses—the easier it is to get stuck in a rut. We show and tell the same things God did for us years ago; we show and tell in the same ways and manners what God has done for us. Many people, though, are going to ask, "What has God done for you lately?" Take note of the new ways God is being active in your life; show and tell about His activity in new and fresh ways, using new terms and new idioms and new vocabulary. *Sing to the LORD a new song* (96:1).

3. BE OVERWHELMED. Stop for a moment and think about the greatness of God. Think about His goodness. Think about His majesty. Think about His creation. Think about His splendor. The point of this exercise is to be overwhelmed! The Lord certainly does not want to become "old hat" to us. His Word makes it clear that He wants us to be amazed and awed. He truly is too marvelous for words!

4. BE CELEBRATORY. When once we've learned to be overwhelmed by God, we are not told to analyze His characteristics. We are told, rather, to celebrate Him for who He is, for all His wonders, and for all His qualities. Celebrate the Lord for who and what He has been to you.

5. BE WORSHIPFUL. Celebration and worship go hand-in-hand. But whereas celebration is more of a physical and vocal activity, worship is more of a mind and heart activity. Worship is the reverent love and devotion that we present to God. Of course, worship may include ceremonies—as well as prayer and other ways to express our ardent devotion and adoration to the Lord. But what is most important is that He be first and foremost in our minds and hearts.

6. BE HUMBLE. To get a glimpse of who God is and what He has done is to recognize our own humility. When we adore and stand in awe of God as we ought, we will naturally be humbled.

FOR ADULTS

■ **TOPIC:** Sing a New Song

■ **QUESTIONS:** 1. Why do you think a nation like ancient Israel, which had already received multiple blessings from God, was to continue to seek blessings from Him? 2. What blessings has God recently brought into your life? 3. What do you think is God's underlying purpose for bringing these blessings into your life? 4. How might you go about declaring God's glory *among the nations* (Ps. 96:3)? 5. How might you go about ascribing *to the LORD the glory due his name* (96:8)?

■ ILLUSTRATIONS:

Tell of His Salvation. Scottish evangelist John Harper was born into a Christian family in 1872. He became a Christian 13 years later and had already started preaching by age 17. He received training at the Baptist Pioneer Mission in London, and in 1896 he founded a church—now known as the Harper Memorial Church—which began with 25 worshipers but had grown to 500 members by the time he left 13 years later. When asked about his doctrine, he stated it was simply "the Word of God."

While Harper's spiritual growth followed a fairly direct uphill path, his personal life wasn't so smooth. When he was only two and a half, he fell into a well and almost drowned. At 26 he was nearly swept out to sea, and at 32 he found himself on a leaky ship in the middle of the Mediterranean. Most tragically, his wife died after only a brief marriage, leaving him alone with their daughter, Nana.

In 1912 Harper, the newly called pastor of Moody Church in Chicago, was traveling on the Titanic with his 6-year-old daughter. After the ship struck an iceberg and began to sink, he got Nana into a lifeboat but apparently made no effort to follow her. Instead, he ran through the ship yelling, "Women, children, and unsaved into the lifeboats!" Survivors report that he then began witnessing to anyone who would listen. He continued preaching even after he had jumped into the water and was clinging to a piece of wreckage. (He'd already given his life-jacket to another man.)

Harper's final moments were recounted four years later at a meeting in Hamilton, Ontario, by a man who said the following:

> I am a survivor of the Titanic. When I was drifting alone on a spar that awful night, the tide brought Mr. Harper, of Glasgow, also on a piece of wreck, near me. "Man," he said, "are you saved?" "No," I said, "I am not." He replied, "Believe on the Lord Jesus Christ and thou shalt be saved." The waves bore him away, but, strange to say, brought him back a little later, and he said, "Are you saved now?" "No," I said, "I cannot honestly say that I am." He said again, "Believe on the Lord Jesus Christ, and thou shalt be saved," and shortly after he went down; and there, alone in the night, and with two miles of water under me, I believed. I am John Harper's last convert.

This man was also one of only six people picked out of the water by the lifeboats; the other 1,522, including Harper, were left to die.

Tremble before Him. In *A Community of Joy*, Timothy Wright, who is associate pastor at a community parish in Phoenix, Arizona, wrote the following:

> I was standing in the back of our sanctuary when a tall, lanky young man approached me. He was visibly shaking and appeared troubled. I antici-pated an emergency counseling situation. Instead, he inquired about wed-

dings. He asked if he could be married in our church, even though he was not a member. We talked details for a few moments, and then he said, "Please forgive my shaking. I've never been in a church before, and I'm a little nervous." Seekers often enter our churches feeling the same way. They do not know what to expect. They are apprehensive, if not actually frightened. I am unsure what they think will happen to them, but whatever it is, they think it could be awful. Visitor-oriented congregations take those feelings seriously and design services that put guests at ease. An informal setting encourages visitors to settle in and relax. An upbeat, celebratory climate, friendly people and enthusiastic music help guests forget their fears.

FOR YOUTH

■ TOPIC: A New Song

■ QUESTIONS: 1. What do you think is really meant by the phrase *May God . . . make his face to shine upon us* (Ps. 67:1)? 2. Do you think the Lord is still judging *the peoples with equity and [guiding] the nations upon earth* (67:4)? 3. How might you go about singing *to the LORD a new song* (96:1)? 4. What do you think is the importance of rejoicing in God's superiority to all other *gods* (96:5)? 5. Why is it important that our rejoicing be based on a clear understanding of God's character?

■ **ILLUSTRATIONS:**

That Your Way May Be Known. A pastor moved from Hong Kong to Hungary to reach Chinese in Eastern Europe. Charles Hwang relocated to Budapest to minister to the approximately 10,000 ethnic Chinese in the capital city. He also has a vision to reach Chinese in the area's other metropolitan areas, *The Alliance for Saturation Church Planting*, based in both Budapest and Monument, Colorado, reported.

Hwang started several years ago with a simple home Bible study that grew into a house church. Regular attendance averages 150 people, but Hwang always has visitors. "We've baptized 100 new believers," he said, "but the church hasn't increased by 100 because Chinese people move around so quickly."

Hwang's congregation also launched a training school for church planters. It has 21 students who are training to become community outreach and cell group leaders. These targeted approaches are effective in Eastern Europe's major cities "because the Chinese are so spread out" and "have so many troubles" abroad, he said. Cell groups enable Christians to get to know Chinese people personally and pray for them one by one. "This encourages them very much," Hwang told the *Alliance*.

Few of the students see themselves as full-time ministers, Hwang said. Most are small-business owners who close their shops to attend classes late afternoons and early evenings each weekday. "I am very careful to encourage them—do your business and start a cell group," he said. "If it grows, leave your work and start a church." The strategy is working well. Several of the students are talking about returning to China to spread the Gospel.

Your Saving Power among All Nations. A "church on wheels" rolled through Russia during the autumn of 2000. Two specially designed railway cars carried pastors, seminary students, and all the trappings of the Christian faith to towns in northern Russia that do not have churches. The interior of the carriages had everything found in a traditional Russian church, including a richly decorated Bible and an area for the choir. Several small bells hung from the carriage ceiling.

Six ministers on the train conducted baptisms, weddings, and church services, traveling to towns where church buildings and public religious life had disappeared under Soviet rule. Earlier this year a prominent Russian church leader expressed his gratitude for the carriages.

Ministers hold several services during one-day stops, then travel to another town the next day. The train will visit mainly in regions with high unemployment, poverty, and alcoholism, as is the case in many northern villages. Its first stop was the Arkhangelsk region, 600 miles north of Moscow, in northern European Russia. "Most of the village churches were destroyed after the revolution," a church leader said. "People like these living in such villages are in desperate need of spiritual support." The effort followed the successful launch in 1998 of a church on a barge, which continues to serve isolated towns and villages more than 1,000 miles south of Moscow.

EMBRACE WISDOM

BACKGROUND SCRIPTURE: Proverbs 3—4
DEVOTIONAL READING: Proverbs 3:1-8

KEY VERSE: Happy are those who find wisdom,
and those who get understanding. Proverbs 3:13.

KING JAMES VERSION

PROVERBS 3:13 Happy is the man that findeth wisdom, and the man that getteth understanding.

14 For the merchandise of it is better than the merchandise of silver, and the gain thereof than fine gold.

15 She is more precious than rubies: and all the things thou canst desire are not to be compared unto her.

16 Length of days is in her right hand; and in her left hand riches and honour.

17 Her ways are ways of pleasantness, and all her paths are peace.

18 She is a tree of life to them that lay hold upon her: and happy is every one that retaineth her. . . .

4:1 Hear, ye children, the instruction of a father, and attend to know understanding.

2 For I give you good doctrine, forsake ye not my law.

3 For I was my father's son, tender and only beloved in the sight of my mother.

4 He taught me also, and said unto me, Let thine heart retain my words: keep my commandments, and live.

5 Get wisdom, get understanding: forget it not; neither decline from the words of my mouth.

6 Forsake her not, and she shall preserve thee: love her, and she shall keep thee.

7 Wisdom is the principal thing; therefore get wisdom: and with all thy getting get understanding.

8 Exalt her, and she shall promote thee: she shall bring thee to honour, when thou dost embrace her.

9 She shall give to thine head an ornament of grace: a crown of glory shall she deliver to thee.

NEW REVISED STANDARD VERSION

PROVERBS 3:13 Happy are those who find wisdom,
and those who get understanding,

14 for her income is better than silver,
and her revenue better than gold.

15 She is more precious than jewels,
and nothing you desire can compare with her.

16 Long life is in her right hand;
in her left hand are riches and honor.

17 Her ways are ways of pleasantness,
and all her paths are peace.

18 She is a tree of life to those who lay hold of her;
those who hold her fast are called happy. . .

4:1 Listen, children, to a father's instruction,
and be attentive, that you may gain insight;

2 for I give you good precepts:
do not forsake my teaching.

3 When I was a son with my father,
tender, and my mother's favorite,

4 he taught me, and said to me,
"Let your heart hold fast my words;
keep my commandments, and live.

5 Get wisdom; get insight: do not forget, nor turn away
from the words of my mouth.

6 Do not forsake her, and she will keep you;
love her, and she will guard you.

7 The beginning of wisdom is this: Get wisdom,
and whatever else you get, get insight.

8 Prize her highly, and she will exalt you;
she will honor you if you embrace her.

9 She will place on your head a fair garland;
she will bestow on you a beautiful crown."

HOME BIBLE READINGS

Monday, August 5	Proverbs 1:8-19	*Avoid Sinful Companions*
Tuesday, August 6	Proverbs 10:1-12	*Walk in Integrity*
Wednesday, August 7	Proverbs 10:13-25	*Righteousness Leads to Life*
Thursday, August 8	Proverbs 10:26-32	*Wicked Expectations Come to Nothing*
Friday, August 9	Proverbs 6:16-29	*Avoid What God Hates*
Saturday, August 10	Proverbs 16:1-9	*Fear the Lord to Avoid Evil*
Sunday, August 11	Proverbs 24:1-9	*Do Not Envy the Wicked*

BACKGROUND

As a whole, the Book of Proverbs reflects a threefold setting: general wisdom literature, insights from the royal courts, and instruction offered in the tender relationship between parents and their children. According to 25:1, a group of assistants to King Hezekiah compiled and added the proverbs of Solomon contained in chapters 25—29. Thus, while many of the wise sayings were penned during Solomon's reign in the tenth century B.C., others were not completed until the time of Hezekiah, whose reign ended in 686 B.C.

At least some of the individual sources that were collected into a whole are designated within the text of the book itself:

• *The proverbs of Solomon son of David, king of Israel* (1:1);

• *The proverbs of Solomon* (10:1);

• *The words of the wise* (22:17);

• *These also are sayings of the wise* (24:23);

• *These are other proverbs of Solomon that the officials of King Hezekiah of Judah copied* (25:1);

• *The words of Agur son of Jakeh. An oracle* (30:1);

• *The words of King Lemuel. An oracle that his mother taught him* (31:1).

The first verse of Proverbs attributes the whole of the work to Solomon perhaps because of his legendary wisdom. Others say that Solomon is the visionary behind the wisdom sayings contained in the book, while still others say the attribution is made because Solomon was the chief collector of the proverbs. Whatever the case, most believe that 1:1-6 was added to the collection to serve as an introduction to the whole book.

Proverbs consists of short pithy statements, commands, admonitions, and some long poems instructing the reader on how to live a godly life and cope with the day-to-day world. Some scholars view 1:1—9:18 as wisdom for young people, 10:1—24:34 as wisdom for all people, and 25:1—31:31 as wisdom for those in leadership.

The long wisdom poem of the first nine chapters differs in its structure from the short, crisply disconnected sayings that predominate the rest of the book. And in chapters 1, 8, and 9 is presented a personification of wisdom, in which wisdom is portrayed as a woman preaching to simple youth. Wisdom and her description of how to find *life* (8:35) stand in stark contrast to the woman who is *like a prostitute* (7:10) and to the *foolish woman* (9:13) who is *ignorant and knows nothing*.

One of the most typical mistakes made in the study of Proverbs is to view the wisdom sayings as a series of ironclad promises. Individual proverbs do make strong statements in regard to the benefits of wisdom; thus many people make the assumption that these benefits are divinely guaranteed. But they're not. The maxims in Proverbs should be seen as general statements that express a basic truth or a practical concept. A good way to analyze these adages in the back of our mind is to say to ourself, "For the most part, if I do this, then that is more likely to happen," rather than making the more assured but faulty assumption, "If I do this, then that will happen."

NOTES ON THE PRINTED TEXT

After Solomon's introduction to this collection of wisdom sayings and beginning with Proverbs 1:8, the sage personified wisdom as a motherly woman offering timely advice to her child. Then throughout the next few chapters, this lengthy poem switches back and forth from wisdom speaking to her child to wisdom being spoken of in more general terms. In 3:12, wisdom personified ends one of her brief monologues to her child, and in 3:13, wisdom is again discussed as a general topic. Throughout the following verses, the incomparable value of wisdom is shown to the reader.

This section of the poem declares that those who find wisdom and *those who get understanding* (3:13) will be blessed by God as well as enabled to live a satisfied and contented life. This happiness that is gained from growing in wisdom far supersedes the happiness that is gained from drawing a huge income (3:14) or a tremendous amount of revenue. Neither would having a great collection of jewels (3:15) be in any way near the value of wisdom. Indeed, *nothing you desire can compare with her.*

Wisdom brings with it not only its own degree of life and riches and honor, but also the good sense as to how to use those things to enhance one's own life and the lives of others. Perhaps because wisdom also brings a healthy measure of *pleasantness* (3:17) and *peace*, we find that *long life is in her right hand; in her left hand are riches and honor* (3:16). Because in Proverbs wisdom is equated with living as God commands, it is considered *a tree of life to those who lay hold of her; those who hold her fast are called happy* (3:18).

Therefore, some verses later in the poem, the young people who were hearing these words about wisdom were told to *Listen . . . to a father's instruction, and be attentive, that you may gain insight* (4:1). This appeal was meant to point out to adolescents that wisdom is the primary virtue they could gain, in that it leads to a full and satisfying life. A *father's instruction* would have his child's best interest at heart. It would be full of *good precepts* (4:2) that would improve the child's life and living.

The sage apparently slipped into reminiscence as he described being in his parents' presence, especially as his father taught him early on about wisdom (4:3). The teacher learned that keeping God's commands is the heart of being wise (4:4). Indeed, as this lengthy poem later states, *The fear of the LORD is the beginning of wisdom, and the knowledge of the Holy One is insight* (9:10). Having equated wisdom and God's commandments, the teacher again urged young people to get *wisdom; get insight: do not forget, nor turn away from the words of my mouth* (4:5).

The sage next listed a couple of wisdom's benefits. He said that wisdom *will keep you* (4:6) and *guard you*. Because of those benefits (and multitudes more), the teacher urged young people to *get wisdom* (4:7) and to *prize her highly* (4:8). He pressed upon his readers to have a resolve to go after wisdom, to make the decision and determination to commit to a lifelong search for it.

As believers continued to strive for wisdom, they would be rewarded by wisdom itself. For instance, the sage told his readers that wisdom *will exalt you* (4:8)—that it would heighten their character and effectiveness. The sage told them that wisdom *will honor you*—that it would strengthen their reputation and respectability. The sage told them that wisdom *will place on your head a fair garland* (4:9)—that it would decorate them with a victorious life. And the sage told them that wisdom *will bestow on you a beautiful crown*—that it would bring them both a measure of influence and achievement.

Thus the teacher provided for his learners two alternate ways in which to live out their lives: the way of wisdom that leads to victory and the way of the wicked that leads to destruction. The first, of course, is the far better choice!

SUGGESTIONS TO TEACHERS

Proverbs often talks about life as if there were a number of paths that lie ahead of us. The decisions that we make along the way will determine the successive paths that our lives will take. That's why the book encourages us to begin on the wise path and then to continue choosing wisdom along the way.

1. THE GREAT CHOICE. Throughout Proverbs, Solomon indicated that there are two initial paths from which to choose. One is the way of wisdom, and the other is the way of the wicked. The great choice before us is which path we will take. That decision is not a once-in-a-lifetime choice. It is a decision that must be made again and again on a daily basis.

2. THE GREAT PRINCIPLE. Once we've made the great choice, we will come to learn the great principle of wisdom. Of course, all the rewards and benefits of wisdom are too numerous to count. But the basic—and great—principle about choosing the path of wisdom is that it ultimately leads to God's blessings.

3. THE GREAT PURSUIT. Making the great choice and learning the great principle is not enough. If we are to continue to grow in wisdom, we cannot ever cease our pursuit of it. We know that there will be obstacles and discouragements in our path, but we must learn to stay the course and keep pursuing wisdom.

4. THE GREAT RESPONSIBILITY. The great pursuit should not be a solitary course. What wisdom we gain we should not harbor for ourselves or within ourselves. The sage of Proverbs 4 described how his father taught him the ways and benefits of wisdom, and thus he was now passing on to another generation that which he had learned from the previous one. Like that teacher, we have a great responsibility to encourage our children—the next generation—to be wise and to attempt to pass on the wisdom we've gained along the way.

5. THE GREAT LIFE. Having made the great choice, learned the great principle, continued the great pursuit, and exercised the great responsibility, we will have realized another aspect of the great principle, namely, that just as wisdom leads to God's blessings, so does receiving God's blessing throughout our days lead to a great and fulfilling life.

FOR ADULTS	■ **TOPIC:** Wisdom Brings Happiness ■ **QUESTIONS:** 1. In what ways does wisdom have the power to make those who possess it happy?

2. Would you agree that wisdom is more valuable than money or jewels? Explain your answer. 3. What do you think is meant by the statement, *Long life is in her right hand* (Prov. 3:16)? 4. In what ways is wisdom *a tree of life to those who lay hold of her* (3:18)? 5. Why is it so important to pass the wisdom one has gained on to the next generation?

■ **ILLUSTRATIONS:**

Happy Are Those Who Find Wisdom. A teacher by the name of John Wayne Schlatter, who writes the story "The Magic Pebbles" in *A Second Helping of Chicken Soup for the Soul*, says of all the complaints and questions he has heard from his students during his years in the classroom, the one most frequently uttered was, "Why do we have to learn all of this dumb stuff?" He always answered that question by recounting the following legend.

One night a group of nomads were preparing to retire for the evening when suddenly they were surrounded by a great light. They knew they were in the presence of a celestial being. With great anticipation, they awaited a heavenly message of great importance that they knew must be especially for them. Finally, the voice spoke, "Gather as many pebbles as you can. Put them in your saddle bags. Travel a day's journey and tomorrow night it will find you glad and it will find you sad."

After having departed, the nomads shared their disappointment and anger with each other. They had expected the revelation of a great universal truth that would enable them to create wealth, health, and purpose for the world. But instead they were given a menial task that made no sense to them at all. However, the memory of the brilliance of their visitor caused each one to pick up a few pebbles and deposit them in their saddle bags while voicing their displeasure.

The nomads traveled a day's journey and that night while making camp, they reached into their saddle bags and discovered every pebble they had gathered had become a diamond. They were glad they had diamonds. But they were sad they had not gathered more pebbles.

Schlatter goes on to say, "It was an experience I had with a student I'll call Alan, early in my teaching career, that illustrated the truth of that legend to me. When Alan was in the eighth grade, he majored in 'trouble' with a minor in 'suspensions.' He had studied how to be a bully and was getting his master's in 'thievery.'

"Every day I had my students memorize a quotation from a great thinker. As I called roll, I would begin a quotation. To be counted present, the student would be expected to finish the thought. 'Alice Adams—There is no failure except . . .' 'In no longer trying. I'm present, Mr. Schlatter.' So, by the end of the year, my young charges would have memorized 150 great thoughts. 'Think you can, think you can't—either way you're right!' 'If you can see the obstacles, you've taken your eyes off the goal.' 'A cynic is someone who knows the price of everything and the value of nothing.'

"No one complained about this daily routine more than Alan—right up to the day he was expelled and I lost touch with him for five years. Then one day, he called. He was in a special program at one of the neighboring colleges and had just finished parole. He told me that, after being sent to juvenile hall and finally being shipped off to the California Youth Authority for his antics, he had become so disgusted with himself that he had taken a razor blade and cut his wrists.

"Alan said, 'You know what, Mr. Schlatter, as I lay there with my life running out of my body, I suddenly remembered that dumb quote you made me write 20 times one day. "There is no failure except in no longer trying." Then it suddenly made sense to me. So with my remaining strength, I called for help and started a new life.'

"At the time he had heard the quotation, it was a pebble. When he needed guidance in a moment of crisis, it had become a diamond. And so it is to you I say, gather all the pebbles you can, and you can count on a future filled with diamonds."

That You May Gain Insight. Surely you've noticed that we have more to learn after we leave school than we did while we were in school? It is a true statement that it is never too late to learn. And to prove that point, you can learn some of the origins of a few familiar traditions and sayings. Many of these old traditions and old sayings come from people who lived back in the 1500s.

Most people got married in June because they took their yearly bath in May and were still smelling okay by June. However, since they were just beginning to smell not so good again, to hide their newly arising body odor, brides carried "a bouquet of flowers."

Baths were simply a big tub filled with hot water. The man of the house had the privilege of the nice clean water, then all the other sons and men, then the women, and finally the children. Last of all came the babies. By then the water was so dirty you could actually lose someone in it. Hence the old saying, "Don't throw the baby out with the bath water."

Houses had thatched roofs. Thick straw was piled high, with no wood underneath. It was the only place for animals to get warm, so all the pets—dogs, cats, and other small animals like mice, rats, and bugs—lived in the roof. When it rained, it became slippery and sometimes the animals would slip and fall off the roof. Hence the old saying, "It's raining cats and dogs."

Most floors were dirt. Only the wealthy had something other than dirt, hence the saying "dirt poor." The wealthy had slate floors that would get slippery in the winter when wet. So they spread thresh on the floor to help keep their footing. As the winter wore on, they kept adding more thresh until when you opened the door it would all start slipping outside. A piece of wood was tacked down at the entry way, hence a "threshold."

Sometimes people could obtain pork and would feel really special when that happened. When company came over, they would bring out some bacon and hang it to show it off. It was a sign of wealth—that a man could really "bring home the bacon." They would also cut off a little to share with guests, and they'd all sit around and "chew the fat."

Most people didn't eat out of pewter plates, but had trenchers—a piece of wood with the middle scooped out like a bowl. Trenchers were never washed and a lot of times worms got into the wood. After eating off wormy trenchers, people would get something called "trench mouth."

Bread was divided according to status. Workers got the burnt bottom of the loaf, the family got the middle, and guests got the top, or "the upper crust."

Lead cups were used to drink ale or whiskey. The combination would sometimes knock them out for a couple of days. Someone walking along the road would take them for dead and prepare them for burial. They were laid out on the kitchen table for a couple of days, and the family would gather around and eat and drink and wait to see if they would wake up. Hence the custom of holding "a wake."

Because England is small in land mass, the people started running out of places to bury their dead. So they would dig up coffins and would take their bones to a house and reuse the grave. In reopening these coffins, a few of the coffins were found to have scratch marks on the inside, and the people realized they had been burying people alive. So they thought they would tie a string on their wrist and lead it through the coffin and up through the ground and tie it to a bell. Someone would have to sit out in the graveyard all night to listen for the bell. Hence those that served on the "graveyard shift" would know when someone was "saved by the bell" or unfortunately, was "a dead ringer."

FOR YOUTH

■ **TOPIC:** Get Smart

■ **QUESTIONS:** 1. What do you think is the best way to *get understanding* (Prov. 3:13)? 2. Given the choice between a million dollars or a jewel-filled sunken treasure or wisdom that increases throughout one's lifetime, which would you choose? Why? 3. How are wisdom's ways the *ways of pleasantness* (3:17)? 4. In what ways will wisdom *honor you if you embrace her* (4:8)? 5. How might wisdom *bestow on you a beautiful crown* (4:9)?

■ **ILLUSTRATIONS:**

Do Not Forget, Nor Turn Away. In the eighth grade, my favorite subject was math, and my least favorite subject was English. All of that changed my freshman year at Briarcrest Baptist High School in Memphis. That year, I had an English teacher that actually convinced me to love grammar. And my sophomore year I had an English teacher that actually convinced me to love literature, especially poetry. She wanted the whole class of us to memorize "The Road Not Taken" by Robert Frost. Because of a cross-country meet, I didn't have to recite the poem like the other students before the whole class. But I distinctly remember—with great fondness now—the afternoon I stood in front of Mrs. Hilda Boyd's desk in that classroom on the second floor of the building and recited the poem just for her. . . .

Two roads diverged in a yellow wood,
And sorry I could not travel both.

I shall be telling this with a sigh
Somewhere ages and ages hence:
Two roads diverged in a wood, and I—
I took the one less traveled by,
And that has made all the difference.

When I finished reciting it from memory, Mrs. Boyd smiled at me and said, "Very good, Mr. Wallace. Now, see to it that you never forget it." Well, I have never forgotten the poem or her words of advice. *I hope I never do!*

The Beginning of Wisdom. Evangelicals are beginning to win more respect in secular intellectual circles, a sociologist says. Alan Wolfe of Boston College took a close look at Wheaton College, Calvin College, and Fuller Seminary, and discusses the trend in *The Opening of the Evangelical Mind,* an article in the October 2000 *Atlantic Monthly* magazine.

Evangelicals have ranked "dead last in intellectual stature" of all America's religious traditions, but are changing, Wolfe wrote. "Evangelical scholars are writing the books, publishing the journals, teaching the students, and sustaining the networks necessary to establish a presence in American academic life."

Wolfe says evangelicals have made progress since 1994, when Wheaton scholar Mark Noll published *The Scandal of the Evangelical Mind*, criticizing religious legalists. Noll faulted them for having what he called an unwarranted self-confidence that "casually discounted the possibility of wisdom from earlier generations." The book, Noll said later, "came very close to being my letter of resignation from the evangelical movement."

RUN FROM EVIL

BACKGROUND SCRIPTURE: Proverbs 6:16-35
DEVOTIONAL READING: Proverbs 6:6-15

KEY VERSES: My child, keep your father's commandment, and do not forsake your mother's teaching. Bind them upon your heart always; tie them around your neck. Proverbs 6:20-21.

KING JAMES VERSION

PROVERBS 6:16 These six things doth the LORD hate: yea, seven are an abomination unto him:

17 A proud look, a lying tongue, and hands that shed innocent blood,

18 An heart that deviseth wicked imaginations, feet that be swift in running to mischief,

19 A false witness that speaketh lies, and he that soweth discord among brethren.

20 My son, keep thy father's commandment, and forsake not the law of thy mother:

21 Bind them continually upon thine heart, and tie them about thy neck.

22 When thou goest, it shall lead thee; when thou sleepest, it shall keep thee; and when thou awakest, it shall talk with thee.

23 For the commandment is a lamp; and the law is light; and reproofs of instruction are the way of life:

24 To keep thee from the evil woman, from the flattery of the tongue of a strange woman.

25 Lust not after her beauty in thine heart; neither let her take thee with her eyelids.

26 For by means of a whorish woman a man is brought to a piece of bread: and the adulteress will hunt for the precious life.

27 Can a man take fire in his bosom, and his clothes not be burned?

28 Can one go upon hot coals, and his feet not be burned?

NEW REVISED STANDARD VERSION

PROVERBS 6:16 There are six things that the LORD hates,
   seven that are an abomination to him:
17 haughty eyes, a lying tongue,
   and hands that shed innocent blood,
18 a heart that devises wicked plans,
   feet that hurry to run to evil,
19 a lying witness who testifies falsely,
   and one who sows discord in a family.
20 My child, keep your father's commandment,
   and do not forsake your mother's teaching.
21 Bind them upon your heart always;
   tie them around your neck.
22 When you walk, they will lead you;
   when you lie down, they will watch over you;
   and when you awake, they will talk with you.
23 For the commandment is a lamp and the teaching
      a light,
   and the reproofs of discipline are the way of life,
24 to preserve you from the wife of another,
   from the smooth tongue of the adulteress.
25 Do not desire her beauty in your heart,
   and do not let her capture you with her eyelashes;
26 for a prostitute's fee is only a loaf of bread,
   but the wife of another stalks a man's very life.
27 Can fire be carried in the bosom
   without burning one's clothes?
28 Or can one walk on hot coals
   without scorching the feet?

11

BACKGROUND

Proverbs 6 is a continuation of the long (unrhymed) poem, attributed to Solomon, that covers the first nine chapters of the book. In the course of this poem, the teacher wanted to instruct the young people of his day in the same way that parents would give advice to their children. Although these particular wisdom sayings are aimed primarily at youth, the principles conveyed in them are beneficial to people of any age.

The proverbial sayings of this poem usually consist of two lines of parallel thought, such as is the case in 6:15.

Line 1: *on such a one calamity will descend suddenly;*

Line 2. *in a moment, damage beyond repair.*

Some of the proverbial sayings within the poem are direct commands and admonitions. As such, these typically have a motive clause explaining the reasoning behind the command or admonition, such as is the case in 6:6-8.

Command: *Go to the ant, you lazybones;*

Motive: *consider its ways, and be wise. Without having any chief or officer or ruler, it prepares its food in summer, and gathers its sustenance in harvest.*

In these and other ways, Proverbs follows much the same pattern found in other portions of wisdom literature appearing in the Old Testament. Consider the Book of Deuteronomy. Many Bible scholars have noted that the whole of the teaching and some of the form of the Proverbs is similar to that found in Deuteronomy. In that book, some of the final teachings of Moses are marked by a clear-cut view of rewards and retributions. In both Proverbs and Deuteronomy, wisdom (which is sometimes equated with righteousness) generally brings success, while folly (which is sometimes equated with wickedness) generally brings destruction.

NOTES ON THE PRINTED TEXT

Introduced in a brief but poignant section of this long poem is a list of seven vices *that are an abomination to* (Prov. 6:16) the Lord. Solomon knew these evil attributes to be poisonous character flaws, and he also knew from his own insight and wisdom that God detested them. Israel's king realized that these vices could actually appear in young people, and thus, in his teaching, Solomon hoped to steer adolescents away from such evil. He realized, too, that such sinful behavior, if allowed to persist in young people, could later result in a character that was wholly given to wickedness.

Solomon began by noting that the Lord hates *haughty eyes* (6:17), referring to the way a person may scornfully and condescendingly look down upon others. Such people would be filled with pride and arrogantly consider themselves far better than others. Second on the list was *a lying tongue,* referring to people whose deceitful approach to life makes others distrust their words. Third on the list was *hands that shed innocent blood*, referring to the type of people who would not hesitate to hurt or kill others for their own personal gain.

Fourth on the list was *a heart that devises wicked plans* (6:18), referring to people who relish not only doing evil deeds, but also take great pleasure in scheming elaborate and detailed plans to perform those deeds. Fifth on the list was *feet that hurry to run to evil,* referring basically to the kind of people who are on the constant lookout for some kind of trouble they can get into or some act that they can do maliciously. Sixth on the list was *a lying witness who testifies falsely* (6:19), referring to those who would gladly lie to bring harm to someone else. And seventh on the list was *one who sows discord in a family*, referring to people who lie or spread rumors so as to break up the unity and cohesiveness of a loving, godly relationship.

The next section of the poem is longer than the section recording *things that the Lord hates* (6:16). Rather than getting directly to the point—a warning against adultery—the sage advice seems to meander a bit. It is as if the teacher wanted first to encourage the memorization of these wisdom sayings as well as underscore the importance of living by them. To accomplish this goal, Solomon urged adolescents to *keep your father's commandment, and do not forsake your mother's teaching* (6:20). He implored them to bind these truths *upon your heart always; tie them around your neck* (6:21).

If young people would commit to remembering and living out these maxims, Solomon promised that *they will lead you* (6:22) and *watch over you* and even *talk with you.* Solomon referred to *the commandment* (6:23) as being *a lamp* and *the teaching a light.* Indeed, the correction and the discipline that these proverbs provided could be considered a *way of life.*

The main point of this section begins in 6:24, in which the teacher explained how his reproofs could serve *to preserve you from the wife of another.* Solomon warned adolescents about the seductive words that an adulteress might use to tempt them. He urged young people neither to *desire her beauty in your heart* (6:25) nor be enticed by her flirtations. Knowing that such lustful and evil behavior could become both habitual and costly, Solomon cautioned that a prostitute could reduce her victims to poverty and ruin.

Sexual immorality has the potential to do such serious harm to our lives that Proverbs spends a healthy portion of its verses warning against it. Of course, many in today's culture argue that it is all right to break God's law as long as no one gets hurt. But the truth that Solomon wanted to convey is that physical intimacy outside marriage always hurts someone. It is an affront to God because it shows that we prefer to satisfy our desires our own way instead of according to God's will. It hurts other people because it violates the commitment that is so necessary to any relationship. It hurts us because it often brings disease to our bodies and adversely affects our personalities. Sexual immorality has power to destroy families and communities because it demolishes the integrity on which these relationships are built.

God wants to protect us from hurting ourselves and others; thus, we are to have no part in sexual immorality, even if our culture readily accepts it. Perhaps Solomon put it best when he asked, *Can fire be carried in the bosom without burning one's clothes? Or can one walk on hot coals without scorching the feet? So is he who sleeps with his neighbor's wife; no one who touches her will go unpunished* (6:27-29).

SUGGESTIONS TO TEACHERS

Proverbs 6:16-28 contains practical admonitions for those who want to follow the will of God. Much of this passage is comprised of negative injunctions to avoid evil thoughts and behavior; nevertheless, a small portion is the positive injunction to pay attention to parental instruction. Having studied what Solomon said, we should consider ourselves forewarned about the following:

1. WHAT THE LORD DETESTS. Surely if God detests some thoughts and behaviors, out of our love and adoration for Him, we should strive to avoid them. Therefore may we refrain from arrogantly looking down upon others, being deceitful, hurting others, devising ways to do evil, being on the lookout for wicked activities to participate in, lying to bring harm to others, and seeking to break up the unity of a loving, godly relationship.

2. WHAT YOUR PARENTS TEACH. Even as we grow older and hopefully wiser, it would be foolish to turn a deaf ear to the sage advice that was handed down to us from our parents and grandparents. Because our parents know us so well, their advice can be tailor-made not only for our perplexing situations but also for our unique personalities. Let us not reject the wisdom of those, like our parents, who have had more time to accumulate more experience!

3. WHAT THE WARNING SIGNS LOOK LIKE. So many people who have been unfaithful to their spouses failed to see any steps or warning signs leading up to their infidelity. But the warning signs are almost always there, and it is incumbent upon all married couples to watch out for those signs so that they can affair-proof their marriages.

Infidelity rarely just happens; usually it begins with an attraction and leads to flirtations that both the man and the woman consider "innocent." But those playful come-ons can easily and quickly translate into lust. And given the right time and opportunity, lust is just as easily and quickly converted into seduction. From the point of seduction, the only barrier that stands in the way of adultery is one or both of the individuals having the moral stamina to say, "No." All these steps provide the warning signs, but Solomon urged young people to avoid even starting down the wrong path.

4. WHAT DANGERS YOU'LL FACE. Here's an old saying that is worth considering: "If you play with fire, you're going to get burned." To reject the wise advice of Solomon is to invite danger and welcome punishment. The rewards of a good moral life are enjoyed by those who adhere to Solomon's advice; painful penalties and retribution are experienced by those who spurn it.

FOR ADULTS

■ **TOPIC:** Do the Right Thing

■ **QUESTIONS:** 1. For what reasons do you think God so detests *a lying tongue* (Prov. 6:17)? 2. What kind of motivations would lie behind a person's wanting to sow *discord in a family* (6:19)? 3. In what ways have you bound your *father's commandment* (6:20) and your mother's teaching *upon your heart* (6:21)? 4. How might an adulterous affair cost a man or woman his or her life? 5. What is the overall purpose of the teacher's advice in 6:24-28?

■ **ILLUSTRATIONS:**

A Lying Tongue. There are a lot of scenes in the movie "Gone with the Wind" that are worth remembering. One that I recall is where Scarlet O'Hara is crying and pouring out all of her false guilt to Rhett Butler. Rhett's response to her is classic. He says, "Scarlet, you are not upset because you feel sorry; you are upset because you got caught." I think Scarlet is like some of us. We're more bothered by the fact that others know our mistakes than by the fact that we have disobeyed God.

The Reproofs of Discipline. In the beginning God created the heavens and the earth. Now the earth was an empty, formless mass cloaked in darkness. And the devil said, "It doesn't get any better than this!" But God said, "Let there be light," and there was light. Then sometime later God said, "Let the land burst forth with every sort of grass and seed-bearing plant." And God saw that everything He had made was good. But the devil complained, "There goes the neighborhood!"

God later on said, "Let us make people in our image, to be like ourselves. They will be masters over all life—the fish in the sea, the birds in the sky, and all the livestock, wild animals, and small animals." Thus, God created people in His own image. He patterned them after Himself. When God examined the man and woman He had made, He saw that they were lean and fit. But the devil gleefully said, "I know how I can get back in this game!"

God populated the earth with green and yellow vegetables of all kinds so that the man and woman would live long and healthy lives. And the devil created fast-food restaurants. And these restaurants brought forth the double cheeseburger. Then the devil said to man, "You want fries with that?" And the man said, "Yes!" And he gained five pounds.

Then God created the healthful yogurt, that the woman might keep her figure, which the man had found so fair. And the devil brought forth chocolate. And woman gained five pounds. God next sent heart-healthy vegetables and olive oil with which to cook them. And the devil brought forth chicken-fried steak so big that it needed its own platter. And the man gained 10 pounds and his bad cholesterol went through the roof. Then God brought forth running shoes and the man resolved to lose those extra pounds. And the devil brought forth cable television with remote control so that the man would not have to toil to change channels. And the man gained another 20 pounds!

God next brought forth the potato, a vegetable naturally low in fat and brimming with nutrition. And the devil peeled off the healthful skin and sliced the starchy center into chips and deep-fat fried them. He also created sour cream dip. And the man clutched his remote control and ate the potato chips swaddled in cholesterol. And he went into cardiac arrest. Then God sighed and created quadruple bypass surgery. And the devil canceled the man's health insurance.

God showed the woman how to peel the skin off chicken and cook the nourishing whole grain brown rice. And the devil created light beer so that the man could poison his body with alcohol while feeling righteous because he had to drink twice as much of the now-insipid brew to get the same buzz. And the man gained another 10 pounds.

Then God created the life-giving tofu. And the woman ventured forth into the land of milk chocolate, and upon returning asked the man, "Do I look fat?" And he told the truth. Then the woman went out from the presence of the man and dwelt in the land of the divorce lawyer, which is east of the marriage counselor.

And the woman put aside the seeds of the earth and took unto herself comfort food. And God brought forth weight reduction plans, but it didn't help. Then God created exercise machines with easy payments. And the devil invented the credit card with high interest rates and balloon payments. And the exercise machine went to dwell in the land of the closet, which is east of the polyester leisure suit. And in the fullness of time, the woman received the exercise machine from the man in the property settlement. But it didn't help her, either!

The point of this little story is that both God and Satan put forth commands for our lives. And we're all going to obey somebody. The vital question is *who*?

FOR YOUTH

■ **TOPIC:** Who Knows What's Right or Wrong?

■ **QUESTIONS:** 1. How does it make you feel to look into *haughty eyes* (Prov. 6:17)? 2. What kind of a person would you say has *feet that hurry to run to evil* (6:18)? 3. In what ways does your parents' teaching *lead* *you* (6:22), *watch over you*, and *talk with you*? 4. In what areas of your life do you feel like you need more discipline? How might you obtain it? 5. Who are some of the people that get hurt when a husband or a wife is unfaithful to his or her spouse?

■ ILLUSTRATIONS:

They Will Lead You. On the first day the Purple Heart Highway (which wraps around the outskirts of the nearby city of Clarksville) was opened, seven accidents occurred. Many more happened in the following weeks—most of them at busy intersections. Everyone in the region connected by the highway knew why these accidents were happening. Drivers were not obeying the signs. The signs were there, though some drivers didn't know they were there. The lesson here is that when we're driving on a new highway, we'd better watch for and obey the signs!

Once we see a stop sign, most of us recognize it and honor it immediately; otherwise we would risk a collision and physical harm. Now wouldn't it be great if we could be just as sensitive to God's "stop signs"? What if a big, bright red, octagon-shaped sign appeared every time we were about to sin? Thankfully, we already have a system like that—the Holy Spirit living in us!

The Spirit is the "sign" telling us when to stop, when to go, and when to exercise caution. He is the "sign" telling us when to yield, when to merge, and when to exit. He is the "sign" telling us when there is danger ahead, when there will be curves, and when there will be steep upgrades or downgrades. The Holy Spirit is the "sign" telling us when to speed up and when to slow down. He is the "sign" giving us direction.

A Man's Very Life. For years, the opening of "The Wide World of Sports" television program illustrated "the agony of defeat" with a painful ending to an attempted ski jump. The skier appeared in good form as he headed down the jump, but then, for no apparent reason, he tumbled head over heels off the side of the jump, bouncing off the supporting structure.

What viewers didn't know was that the skier chose to fall rather than finish the jump. Why? As he explained later, the jump surface had become too fast, and midway down the ramp, he realized that if he completed the jump, he would land on the level ground, beyond the safe sloping landing area, which could have been fatal. As it was, the skier suffered no more than a headache from the tumble. To change one's course in life can be a dramatic and sometimes painful undertaking, but change is better than a fatal landing at the end!

WATCH WHAT YOU SAY

BACKGROUND SCRIPTURE: Proverbs 15—17
DEVOTIONAL READING: Proverbs 16:16-30

KEY VERSE: A soft answer turns away wrath,
but a harsh word stirs up anger. Proverbs 15:1.

KING JAMES VERSION

PROVERBS 15:1 A soft answer turneth away wrath: but grievous words stir up anger.

2 The tongue of the wise useth knowledge aright: but the mouth of fools poureth out foolishness.

3 The eyes of the LORD are in every place, beholding the evil and the good.

4 A wholesome tongue is a tree of life: but perverseness therein is a breach in the spirit. . . .

7 The lips of the wise disperse knowledge: but the heart of the foolish doeth not so.

8 The sacrifice of the wicked is an abomination to the LORD: but the prayer of the upright is his delight. . . .

17:4 A wicked doer giveth heed to false lips; and a liar giveth ear to a naughty tongue.

5 Whoso mocketh the poor reproacheth his Maker: and he that is glad at calamities shall not be unpunished.

6 Children's children are the crown of old men; and the glory of children are their fathers.

7 Excellent speech becometh not a fool: much less do lying lips a prince.

8 A gift is as a precious stone in the eyes of him that hath it: whithersoever it turneth, it prospereth.

9 He that covereth a transgression seeketh love; but he that repeateth a matter separateth very friends.

10 A reproof entereth more into a wise man than an hundred stripes into a fool.

NEW REVISED STANDARD VERSION

PROVERBS 15:1 A soft answer turns away wrath,
but a harsh word stirs up anger.

2 The tongue of the wise dispenses knowledge,
but the mouths of fools pour out folly.

3 The eyes of the LORD are in every place,
keeping watch on the evil and the good.

4 A gentle tongue is a tree of life,
but perverseness in it breaks the spirit. . . .

7 The lips of the wise spread knowledge;
not so the minds of fools.

8 The sacrifice of the wicked is an abomination to the LORD,
but the prayer of the upright is his delight. . . .

17:4 An evildoer listens to wicked lips;
and a liar gives heed to a mischievous tongue.

5 Those who mock the poor insult their Maker;
those who are glad at calamity will not go unpunished.

6 Grandchildren are the crown of the aged,
and the glory of children is their parents.

7 Fine speech is not becoming to a fool;
still less is false speech to a ruler.

8 A bribe is like a magic stone in the eyes of those who give it;
wherever they turn they prosper.

9 One who forgives an affront fosters friendship,
but one who dwells on disputes will alienate a friend.

10 A rebuke strikes deeper into a discerning person than a hundred blows into a fool.

12

BACKGROUND

The maxims recorded in Proverbs 15—17 are part of the collected wise sayings of Solomon, which began in chapter 10 and followed the long poemlike section in the first nine chapters of the book. Many of these brief individual adages listed in chapters 10 and following tell what a wise person says, does, or thinks, and contrasts those with what a foolish person says, does, or thinks. Indeed, some of the proverbs appearing elsewhere in the book also use such contrasts.

First a positive statement is made; then it is followed by a negative statement, beginning with the word "but." Proverbs 14:35 serves as an example:

• Positive statement: *A servant who deals wisely has the king's favor;*

• Negative statement: *but his wrath falls on one who acts shamefully.*

Just as many of the newer versions of the English Bible print the Book of Psalms in poetic form, so do they also print the Book of Proverbs in poetic form. The difference between these two books is that the psalms were typically meant to be sung with musical accompaniment, while the proverbs were meant to be recited. Like most Hebrew poetry, Proverbs follows a rhythm of ideas rather than a rhythm of sound (or rhyme).

The purpose of recording these wise, poetic sayings in Proverbs was to communicate to young people in particular how to cope with life and living. These sage statements show the difference between a person who tries to please God and a person who tries only to please himself or herself; and, of course, wisdom is seeking to live a life that is pleasing to God.

Though the wisdom writers relied on observation and study, they made greater use of introspection and meditation than other Hebrew authors. The sages commented little about Israel's history, politics, geography, kings, and laws. Instead, the wisdom writers focused on the enduring aspects of the human condition. The sages examined the world around them, and under the guidance of the Spirit drew conclusions about human nature and living in a way that is pleasing to God.

A consistent characteristic of Proverbs is its practical advice and teaching on how to navigate skillfully through the twists and turns of life. From beginning to end, the advice recorded in this book is sourced in God for its ideas, methods, and morals. In His revelation through the sages, the Spirit ranged from direct and down-to-earth proverbs, to sublime poems. Though the statements recorded in Proverbs are practical, they are not superficial or external, for they contain ethical elements that stress upright living that flows out of a right relationship with God.

NOTES ON THE PRINTED TEXT

With any thoughtful reading of the Proverbs, a person will likely be impressed at how these wise sayings make perfectly good sense. Oftentimes, they seem so easy and simple to understand. But just as often, they are extremely difficult to carry out!

Consider the wise saying of 15:1, *A soft answer turns away wrath, but a harsh word stirs up anger.* It certainly does make a lot of sense. But have you ever tried to give a soft answer when you felt like harshly screaming out? The maxim is easier said than done. And yet it is true that anger is removed by a gentle response, while a severe response only seems to fuel the flame of anger.

Having introduced this section of sayings regarding the lethal or the healing power of what we say, Solomon reminded his listeners that the wise person *dispenses knowledge* (15:2) in his or her conversations, while the foolish person's time is typically consumed talking about absurd, senseless, and silly topics. Solomon wanted his pupils to know that God is so great and is so ever present that He hears every word of their mouths and knows their every thought and action. God is *keeping watch on the evil and the good* (15:3).

Once Solomon had reminded his readers of God's watchful eye, he continued with his teaching regarding our speech. Words, when used gently and appropriately, have the power to heal—to be *a tree of life* (15:4). But words also have the power, when used perversely and maliciously, to crush the feelings of another. Indeed, the inappropriate use of words *breaks the spirit.*

The teacher realized that the words we speak are generated in our minds. Thus he reviewed for his readers the most important step of considering the thoughts within their minds before those thoughts emerge off their lips. Because *knowledge* (15:7) is in the minds of the wise, the *lips of the wise spread knowledge.* Conversely, because folly is in *the minds of fools*, the lips of the foolish spread folly.

Solomon was still considering the minds of the wise and of the foolish when he offered instruction on the attitudes we should have as we come before God. The teacher said that those whose hearts are not right with God gain nothing by offering sacrifices to Him; in fact, the *sacrifice of the wicked is an abomination to the Lord* (15:8). God's greatest concern is not so much with our actions as it is with our motivations—the attitudes behind our actions. That is why the sincere prayer of the humble is more desired by God than the insincere and pretentious offering of a scoundrel who cares not for God's will or ways. *"Has the LORD as great delight in burnt offerings and sacrifices, as in obeying the voice of the LORD? Surely, to obey is better than sacrifice, and to heed than the fat of rams"* (1 Sam. 15:22).

Knowing that what is in the mind depends upon what goes into the mind, Solomon was almost as concerned with what his readers heard as he was with what they said. The teacher wanted them to guard their ears as much as they guarded their mouths. In fact, what we listen to says something about our character (Prov. 17:4).

Now turning back to consider the damage that our words can do, the teacher warned his readers against making fun of the less fortunate. Because both the rich and the poor are created in God's image, those *who mock the poor insult their Maker* (17:5). And those with the same hateful attitude who would delightfully revel at someone else's misfortune *will not go unpunished.*

Inserted among Solomon's wise sayings about the use of words is another of his general statements in regard to wisdom. When the younger generation relies heavily upon the older generation to help it obtain wisdom, *grandchildren are the crown of the aged, and the glory of children is their parents* (17:6).

Character gives rise to the type of speech we use. Thus *a fool* (17:7) cannot speak as a wise person could. This principle also carries over to those with high status or in positions of leadership. Solomon realized that the wisest among the people did not always ascend to leadership, and that there would be leaders whose characters would be marked by such vices as dishonesty and injustice.

The teacher's caution was for us not to expect to hear honest statements coming from a dishonest ruler; nor should we expect to see just actions coming from an unjust ruler. In the same way, the fact that a *bribe is like a magic stone* (17:8)—that it is so often accepted to pervert justice—is a sad commentary on the general character of most of humanity, for the *wicked accept a concealed bribe to pervert the ways of justice* (17:23).

A wise character is a forgiving character. But to harbor and dwell upon a personal verbal affront is to risk not only bitterness (which eats away at one's character just as cancer diminishes physical health), but also puts at risk a relationship. Thus, *one who forgives an affront fosters friendship, but one who dwells on disputes will alienate a friend* (17:9).

Of course, all affronts are not meant to harm or condemn. Sometimes what we may consider an affront is actually a word of correction. The teacher said that a *discerning person* (17:10) will take a word of correction to heart and act upon it; wise people will listen carefully to the correction and use it to improve both their character and life. Fools, on the other hand, can be dealt *a hundred blows* as part of their discipline, and their character would still remain unaffected.

SUGGESTIONS TO TEACHERS

Proverbs was meant to give numerous concise instructions on how to live, and this week's Scripture passages offer quite a few of their own! Because most of the wise sayings contrast what is good and righteous against what is bad and evil, the following teachings about how we use speech extol the better over the worse, and the wise over the foolish.

1. SOFTLY IS BETTER THAN HARSHLY. When talking, self-control is a must. *How* we say something reveals more about our character than *what* we say. That's why a wise person chooses to respond softly while a foolish person chooses to respond harshly.

2. KNOWLEDGE IS BETTER THAN FOLLY. When we're engaged in a conversation, do we talk about things of importance, things that relate to life and living? Or are our conversations often senseless, silly meanderings that add little or nothing to our or others' bank of knowledge and wisdom? The wise person chooses to talk knowledgeably, while a foolish person loves just to talk.

3. HUMILITY IS BETTER THAN PRIDE. The prayers of a humble person have a far greater work than the deeds of a person who desires most of all to be seen and noticed. The wise person operates from an attitude of humility while the foolish person operates from an attitude of pride.

4. TRUTH IS BETTER THAN A LIE. By living the truth, a person of character will also speak the truth. By living a lie, a person is prone to telling lies. The wise person makes a habit of telling the truth, while a foolish person makes a habit of telling lies.

5. ENCOURAGEMENT IS BETTER THAN MOCKING. Building up and encouraging the good in others' character is far better than tearing it down. That's why the wise decide to encourage others, while the foolish decide to mock them.

6. FORGIVENESS IS BETTER THAN A GRUDGE. Bitterness hurts the one who has it. The wise person knows this, and that's why he or she chooses to forgive, while the foolish person chooses to harbor a grudge.

7. CORRECTION IS BETTER THAN BLOWS. Discipline is a great teacher. Correction shows us not only what we've done wrong, but also how to do it right. The wise person listens carefully and applies correction, while the foolish person refuses to be changed and corrected even by corporal punishment.

■ TOPIC: Say the Right Thing

■ QUESTIONS: 1. In what ways have you personally seen a gentle answer turn away wrath (Prov. 15:1)? 2. What benefits can you draw from the fact that the *eyes of the LORD are in every place* (15:3)? 3. Why is it that words can break *the spirit* (15:4) of a person? 4. What effect does personal character have on the words we speak? 5. What are some ways that you can apply words of correction in your life?

■ ILLUSTRATIONS:

A Mischievous Tongue. The late Senator Adlai Stevenson was once quoted as saying, "As scarce as the truth is, the supply seems greater than the demand."

A Bribe Is Like a Magic Stone. In their statistical research published in *The Day America Told the Truth*, James Patterson and Peter Kim asked respondents, "What are you willing to do for ten million dollars?" Two-thirds of Americans polled would agree to at least one—and some to several—of the following:

- Would abandon their entire family (25%)
- Would abandon their church (25%)
- Would become prostitutes for a week or more (23%)
- Would give up their American citizenships (16%)
- Would leave their spouses (16%)
- Would withhold testimony and let a murderer go free (10%)
- Would kill a stranger (7%)
- Would put their children up for adoption (3%)

A Rebuke Strikes Deeper into a Discerning Person. On August 12, 1985, 520 people died in the crash of a Japan Airlines plane, the world's worst single plane disaster. Two months later, the president of Japan Airlines faced the relatives of the victims and bowed low and long. After turning to a wall, covered with wooden tablets bearing the victims' names, he bowed again. And in a voice that sometimes quavered, Yasumoto Takagi asked for forgiveness and accepted responsibility.

One by one, people walked up to the altar, left a chrysanthemum for remembrance, bowed, and turned away. Families, dignitaries and airline employees walked up to the altar for more than an hour, pausing to pray, wipe away a tear, or stand silently.

For Japan Airlines, this service marked the culmination of a two-month exercise in accountability. In the days right after the accident, when family members traveled to a small mountain village to identify the bodies, airline staff stayed with them, paying all expenses, bringing them food, drink, and clean clothes. Staff people stayed with the families to arrange for funerals or to block intrusive reporters. Japan Airlines set up scholarship funds for children whose parents died. It spent $1.5 million on two elaborate memorial services. Executives attended every victim's funeral, although some were turned away. The airlines will split compensation payments with the Boeing Company that will probably exceed $100 million.

The airline felt it had to perform these acts of conciliation, otherwise it would have been accused of inhumanity and irresponsibility. Naturally, the airline's self-interest was at stake. Its quick admission of responsibility and its personal help to family members created a web of gratitude and obligation that discouraged legal remedies. A cumbersome legal system in Japan also made families reluctant to sue. But how striking it is to see a corporation bowing down low, occupied with forms of penance!

■ **TOPIC:** Watch What You Say

■ **QUESTIONS:** 1. How does it make you feel when someone responds to you in a mean and harsh way? 2. Why is it better for *knowledge* (Prov. 15:2), rather than *folly*, to come out of our mouths? 3. In what ways do gentle words bring life and health—*a tree of life* (15:4)? 4. What effect does personal character have on the words we speak? 5. Why is mocking *the poor* (17:5) an insult to God?

■ **ILLUSTRATIONS:**

A Soft Answer. Pastors are patrolling part-time in police cars. More than 2,400 clergy serve police and fire departments, all but 100 as part-time volunteers. Clergy with chaplains' badges help police break the news of deaths to families, console crime victims, and defuse tense situations by appealing to criminals and mediating between groups. They also consult confidentially with police who have personal problems, *The Miami Herald* said.

Clergy who are reluctant to leave their stained-glass sanctuaries need not apply, Phineas Weberman, a minister who is helping organize "God squads" for the Miami police, told the *Herald*. "There are many clergy who just want to give a sermon and a benediction and remain apart from the individual members of their congregation. A chaplain must be somebody who has a calling and wants to relate to human emotions."

Recruits are trained to stay out of harm's way. They must pass a physical exam, criminal records check, an interview, and take CPR training. Most don't carry firearms, but are taught how to use a gun in case the officer they are riding with is shot or disabled. Some chaplains wear a police jacket instead of a full uniform to make their identity clear.

In the Name of Christ. Telemachus was a minister who lived in the fourth century. He felt that God wanted him to go to Rome. He was in a secluded parish when he put his possessions in a sack and set out for the capital of the empire.

When Telemachus arrived in the city, people were thronging in the streets. He asked why all the excitement and was told that this was the day that the gladiators would be fighting and killing each other in the Colosseum, the day of the games, the circus. Telemachus thought to himself, "Four centuries after Christ, and they are still killing each other, for enjoyment?"

Telemachus ran to the Colosseum and heard the gladiators saying, "Hail to Caesar; we die for Caesar," and he thought, "This isn't right." Telemachus jumped over the railing and went out into the middle of the field, got between two gladiators, held up his hands and shouted, "In the name of Christ, forbear!"

The crowd protested and began to shout, "Run him through! Run him through!" A gladiator came over and hit Telemachus in the stomach with the back of his sword. It sent Telemachus sprawling in the sand. He got up and ran back and again said, "In the name of Christ, forbear!" The crowd continued to chant, "Run him through!"

One gladiator came over and plunged his sword through the minister's stomach, and he fell into the sand, which began to turn crimson with his blood. One last time, he gasped out, "In the name of Christ, forbear!"

A hush came over the 80,000 people in the coliseum. Soon a man stood and left, then another and more, and within minutes all 80,000 had emptied out of the arena. It was the last known gladiatorial contest in the history of Rome!

False Speech to a Ruler. There's an old German proverb that says, "When God means to punish a nation, He deprives the rulers of wisdom."

CARE FOR THE POOR

BACKGROUND SCRIPTURE: Proverbs 19:17; 22:1-4, 8-9, 16, 22-23; 23:10-11
DEVOTIONAL READING: Proverbs 19:1-8

KEY VERSE: Whoever is kind to the poor lends
to the LORD, and will be repaid in full. Proverbs 19:17.

KING JAMES VERSION

PROVERBS 19:17 He that hath pity upon the poor lendeth unto the LORD; and that which he hath given will he pay him again.

22:1 A good name is rather to be chosen than great riches, and loving favour rather than silver and gold.

2 The rich and poor meet together: the LORD is the maker of them all.

3 A prudent man foreseeth the evil, and hideth himself: but the simple pass on, and are punished.

4 By humility and the fear of the LORD are riches, and honour, and life. . . .

8 He that soweth iniquity shall reap vanity: and the rod of his anger shall fail.

9 He that hath a bountiful eye shall be blessed; for he giveth of his bread to the poor. . . .

16 He that oppresseth the poor to increase his riches, and he that giveth to the rich, shall surely come to want. . . .

22 Rob not the poor, because he is poor: neither oppress the afflicted in the gate:

23 For the LORD will plead their cause, and spoil the soul of those that spoiled them. . . .

23:10 Remove not the old landmark; and enter not into the fields of the fatherless:

23:11 For their redeemer is mighty; he shall plead their cause with thee.

NEW REVISED STANDARD VERSION

PROVERBS 19:17 Whoever is kind to the poor lends
to the LORD,
and will be repaid in full. . . .

22:1 A good name is to be chosen rather than great riches,
and favor is better than silver or gold.

2 The rich and the poor have this in common:
the LORD is the maker of them all.

3 The clever see danger and hide;
but the simple go on, and suffer for it.

4 The reward for humility and fear of the LORD
is riches and honor and life. . . .

8 Whoever sows injustice will reap calamity,
and the rod of anger will fail.

9 Those who are generous are blessed,
for they share their bread with the poor. . . .

22 Do not rob the poor because they are poor,
or crush the afflicted at the gate;

23 for the LORD pleads their cause
and despoils of life those who despoil them. . . .

23:10 Do not remove an ancient landmark
or encroach on the fields of orphans,

11 for their redeemer is strong;
he will plead their cause against you.

BACKGROUND

The wisdom statements that relate a wise person's care for the poor are more of the sayings drawn from the pen of Solomon. He was regarded as the wisest man to have ever lived. First Kings 1—11 tells some of the accounts of his renowned wisdom. In fact, *Solomon's wisdom surpassed the wisdom of all the people of the east, and all the wisdom of Egypt* (4:30). He collected and disseminated some 3,000 proverbs—many of which were drawn from his own knowledge and experience—and more than 1,000 songs (4:32). His fame was well known: *People came from all the nations to hear the wisdom of Solomon; they came from all the kings of the earth who had heard of his wisdom* (4:34).

Solomon did not limit the topics upon which to focus his wisdom. He taught over a broad range of subjects: *He would speak of trees, from the cedar that is in the Lebanon to the hyssop that grows in the wall; he would speak of animals, and birds, and reptiles, and fish* (4:33). Indeed, the subjects covered solely in Proverbs leaves the distinct impression that Solomon's wisdom dealt with practically every area of life. Some of the topics here include discretion, eating, enemies, the family, the fear of the Lord, the fool, friendship, God, the heart and mind, the home, knowledge, labor, law, lazy people, leadership, life and death, love, neighbors, peace, poverty, prayer, pride, riches, righteousness, shame, sin, sleep, spirituality, the tongue, trust, the wicked, wine, wisdom, and words!

Although there is an ordered flow of topics in the long poem of the first nine chapters of Proverbs, the concise wise sayings that were compiled for the rest of the book defy an ordering system. Certain key emphases—such as honesty, diligence, trustworthiness, and proper attitudes—appear and reappear throughout the text.

Some of the wisdom sayings are observations, but more often a moral ideal is instilled. And if a person were to apply the moral discipline of chapters 1—9 and master the practical application of wisdom rehearsed in chapters 10—31, that person would truly have an abundant and successful life. Though these principles are not meant to be taught as doctrine, those who follow their advice will find themselves walking closely with God. As we read in 14:27, *The fear of the LORD is a fountain of life, so that one may avoid the snares of death.*

Notes on the Printed Text

Proverbs are brief, pithy maxims that communicate truths, principles, and insights about life. These adages are often practical and mostly concerned with the consequences of one's actions. Though easy to understand, proverbs can be difficult to apply.

The Book of Proverbs gives profound advice for governing our lives. For instance, Solomon said, *Whoever is kind to the poor lends to the LORD, and will be repaid in full* (19:17). In essence, when we give to the poor, the Lord considers it just as a gift we have given to Him. Jesus taught this principle as well: *"Truly I tell you, just as you did it to one of the least of these who are members of my family, you did it to me"* (Matt. 25:40).

Solomon's encouragement to choose *a good name* (Prov. 22:1) over *great riches* meant much more than just seeking to have a good reputation. The Hebrew noun rendered "name" typically referred to a person's character. As such, Solomon was urging his readers to develop a strong and upright character, for as it has been said, "Your reputation is who people think you are; your character is who you really are." Character is not based on how much wealth we have or on our earnings potential; rather, the *rich and the poor* (22:2) have the same access to character development because *the LORD is the maker of them all.*

Whether people will seek to develop their character is up to them as individuals, but the outcome of those who do and those who don't will be vastly different. For instance, the teacher said a prudent person—a wise person who is developing his or her character—foresees danger ahead and takes the proper precautions. But a simpleton—a foolish person who is unconcerned for his or her character—will go on blindly and end up suffering the consequences (22:3). Still addressing this question of character, Solomon said, *The reward for humility and fear of the LORD is riches and honor and life* (22:4).

Proverbs 22:8-9 contrasts the character of those who are generous with those who are unjust and stingy. Those who don't care about justice and even practice injustice *will reap calamity* (22:8), while those who are so generous that *they share their bread with the poor* (22:9) are truly blessed of God. Again, character is the issue. Those who are generous have and exhibit a godly character, while those who practice injustice have and exhibit a character in rebellion against the will of God. Such an ungodly character is also shown by *oppressing the poor in order to enrich oneself, and giving to the rich* (22:16), which actions, said the teacher, will lead those who practice them into poverty.

Because of God's special concern for the weak and the poor, He does not want them—*because they are poor* (22:22)—to be taken advantage of. He freely gives to them out of His own abundance and *pleads their cause* (22:23), and He desires that those who have a godly character to follow His example. In the same way, Solomon warned his pupils against cheating their neighbors—especially *orphans* (23:10) out of portions of their land. Having tillable land was the only way that many in the ancient Near East could survive. To encroach upon and deceitfully take their land could lead them into debt, which in turn, could lead them into slavery. Once in slavery, they would need a *redeemer* (23:11) to pay off their debts and set them free. Solomon said that God Himself would be the redeemer who would *plead [the] cause* of those whose land had been cheated away from them.

SUGGESTIONS TO TEACHERS

Throughout the Bible we are taught that God maintains a special concern for the disadvantaged. By the same token, He desires that we maintain a special concern for them as well. Our care and treatment of the poor is not accomplished by a single act of kindness or giving, however. It is a part of God's character to care for the poor; He wants it to be a part of our character as well. To develop this character, we need to practice the following:

1. CHOOSE A GOOD NAME. Work on your character development. Make it a high priority, if not your top priority. Remember not to worry so much about your reputation—what other people think of you. Be much more concerned about your character and about how to improve who you really are on a day-by-day basis.

2. BE KIND. Make kindness a habit. Let it be one of the main elements of your character. Practice being friendly, warmhearted, sympathetic, understanding, and considerate. Never be haughty. Never look down on someone because they have less wealth than you or less strength than you or less intelligence than you.

3. BE PRUDENT. Be concerned and careful about your own conduct. Exercise wisdom in the way you handle practical matters. Use your good judgment and put your common sense into play. Try to think things through, deciding on the best and most godly way to handle the situations that you face.

4. BE GENEROUS. Be charitable in both your giving and your sharing. Don't hold back or grow to be miserly or stingy or selfish. Think about ways you can use your wealth and your time and your efforts and your opportunities to make life better for others in addition to yourself.

5. DON'T CHEAT. Those who deceive should expect to be deceived. Those who swindle should expect to be swindled. Those who defraud should expect to be defrauded. Those who mislead should expect to be misled. Those who are dishonest should expect to be treated dishonestly. As Galatians 6:7 says, *Do not be deceived; God is not mocked, for you reap whatever you sow.*

FOR ADULTS

■ TOPIC: Who Cares for the Poor?

■ QUESTIONS: 1. How have you experienced being *repaid in full* (Prov. 19:17) by being kind to the poor and thereby lending *to the LORD?* 2. What are some ways you can develop a godly character? 3. What are some ways to promote *humility and fear of the LORD* (22:4) among believers?

4. Why do you think anyone would even want to oppress the poor? 5. In what ways today do you see or hear about the Lord pleading the cause of the poor?

▉ ILLUSTRATIONS:

Whoever Is Kind to the Poor. One day, a poor boy who was selling goods from door to door to pay his way through school, found that he had only one thin dime left, and he was hungry. He decided he would ask for a meal at the next house. However, he lost his nerve when a lovely young woman opened the door. Instead of a meal, he asked for a drink of water. She thought he looked hungry so she brought him a large glass of milk. He drank it slowly, and then asked, "How much do I owe you?"

"You don't owe me anything," the woman replied. "Mother has taught us never to accept pay for a kindness."

The lad said, "Then I thank you from my heart."

As Howard Kelly left that house, he not only felt stronger physically, but his faith in God and love for people was strong, also. He had been ready to give up and quit.

Years later that woman became critically ill. The local physicians were baffled. They finally sent her to the big city, where they called in specialists to study her rare disease. Dr. Howard Kelly was called in for the consultation. When he heard the name of the town she came from, he immediately rose and went down the hall of the hospital to her room. Dressed in his physician's gown, Kelly went in to see her. He recognized her at once. He went back to the consultation room determined to do his best to save her life.

From that day Kelly gave special attention to the case. After a long struggle, the battle was won. Kelly requested the business office to pass the final bill to him for approval. He looked at it, then wrote something on the edge and the bill was sent to her room. She feared to open it, for she was sure it would take the rest of her life to pay for it all. Finally she looked, and something caught her attention on the side of the bill. She read these words: "Paid in full with one glass of milk." It was signed, "Dr. Howard Kelly."

Tears of joy flooded the woman's eyes as her happy heart prayed: "Thank You, God, that Your love has spread abroad through human hearts and hands." Be willing to give whatever He places within your hand.

Because They Are Poor. During the waning years of the depression in a small southeastern Idaho community, a fellow named Jack used to stop by Jim Miller's roadside stand for farm-fresh produce as the season made it available. Food and money were still extremely scarce and bartering was used extensively. One particular day Jim was bagging some early potatoes for Jack. Jack noticed a small boy, delicate of bone and feature, ragged but clean, hungrily eyeing a basket of freshly picked green peas. Jack paid for his potatoes but was also drawn to the display of fresh green peas. He was a pushover for creamed peas and new potatoes. Pondering the peas, he couldn't help overhearing the conversation between Jim and the ragged boy next to him.

"Hello Barry! How are you today?"

"H'lo, Mr. Miller. Fine, thank ya. Jus' admirin' them peas. Sure look good."

"They are good, Barry. How's your Ma?"

"Fine. Gittin' stronger alla' time."

"Good, good. Anything I can help you with?"

"No sir. Jus' admirin' them peas."

"Would you like to take some home?"

"No sir. Got nuthin' to pay for 'em with."

"Well, what have you got to trade me for some of those peas?"

"All I got's my prize marble here."

"Is that right? Let me see it."

"Here 'tis. She's a dandy."

"I can see that. Hmm, only thing is this one is blue, and I sort of go for red. Do you have a red one like this at home?"

"Not 'zackley but, almost."

"Tell you what. Take this sack of peas home with you, and next trip this way let me look at that red marble."

"Sure will! Thanks, Mr. Miller!"

Mrs. Miller, who had been standing nearby, came over to help Jack while he watched the conversation. With a smile she said, "There are two other boys like him in our community. All three are in very poor circumstances. Jim just loves to bargain with them for peas, apples, tomatoes, or whatever. When they come back with their red marbles—and they always do—he decides he doesn't like red after all, and he sends them home with a bag of produce for a green marble or an orange one, perhaps." Jack left the stand smiling to himself, impressed with Jim Miller.

A short time later Jack moved to Utah, but he never forgot the story of Jim Miller, the boys, and their bartering. Several years went by each more rapid than the previous one. Twenty-some-odd years later, Jack had occasion to visit some old friends in that Idaho community, and while he was there, he learned that Jim had died. They were having his viewing that evening and, knowing that his friends wanted to go, he agreed to accompany them.

Upon their arrival at the mortuary, Jack and his friends fell into line to meet the relatives of the deceased and to offer whatever words of comfort they could. Ahead of them in line were three young men. One was in an army uniform and the other two wore dark suits and white shirts—very professional looking. They approached Mrs. Miller, standing smiling and composed, by her husband's casket. Each of the young men hugged her, kissed her on the cheek, spoke briefly with her, and moved on to the casket. Her misty light blue eyes followed them as, one by one, each young man stopped briefly and placed his own warm hand over the cold pale hand in the casket. The three of them left the mortuary together, awkwardly wiping their eyes.

When Jack's turn came to meet Mrs. Miller, he told her who he was and mentioned the story she had told him about the marbles. Mrs. Miller's eyes glistened as she took Jack's hand and led him to the casket. "Those three young men, that just left," she said, "were the boys I told you about. They just told me how they appreciated the things Jim 'traded' them. Now, at last, when Jim could not change his mind about color or size, they came to pay their debt. We've never had a great deal of the wealth of this world," she confided, "but, right now, Jim would consider himself the richest man in Idaho." With loving gentleness, Mrs. Miller lifted the lifeless fingers of her deceased husband. Resting underneath were three, magnificently shiny, red marbles.

We will not be remembered by our words, but by our kind deeds—by the way that we have kept the faith through thick and thin. Inside of every one of us is a spiritual giant, just waiting for the sunlight and rain and gentle breezes of God's love to help us grow.

■ TOPIC: Why Should I Care?

■ QUESTIONS: 1. In what ways is being generous to the poor like lending *to the LORD* (Prov. 19:17)? 2. In what ways has the Lord helped you to develop a godly character? 3. What are some of the things, from the world's perspective, that *the rich and the poor have . . . in common* (22:2)? What things do they have in common from God's perspective? 4. Why do you think anyone would even want to give *to the rich* (22:16)? 5. In what ways do you see God today acting as a *redeemer* (23:11) for the poor?

■ ILLUSTRATIONS:

Crush the Afflicted. Christians can help their suffering fellow believers, reaching into countries where the Gospel is not welcome. It doesn't take money, but it does require prayer, according to International Day of Prayer for the Persecuted Church (IDOP), a Colorado Springs-based ministry. Through an annual prayer day in November, the group focuses the attention of Christians who have freedom on those who don't.

More than 150,000 Christians die each year because of their faith, according to news reports. About 200 million live in countries where they suffer hardships for their beliefs ranging from discrimination to imprisonment, to beatings, or even death. Persecution is most severe in the Middle East, communist nations, and countries where Christians are a minority.

There is a new boldness among Christians in countries that are hostile to the Gospel, and that is evidence of the power of prayer, IDOP's Steve Haas told *Religion Today*. Haas said a Middle East church leader told him that he has grown bolder because of the intercession of Christians from around the world. "He said he could feel the prayers."

Passage of several new religious-freedom laws also shows that the prayers and advocacy of hundreds of thousands of Christians over the past four years have had tangible results, Haas said. He cited the 1998 International Religious Freedom Act (IRFA), which requires the U.S. government to respond to religious rights abuses abroad. "That's an outgrowth of the church showing up and being awake to this issue," he noted.

Imprisoned Christians in Uzbekistan were released in the latter part of 2000 because of a State Department report required by the IRFA, Haas said. "Without the law there's no report, and without the report they wouldn't have been released." His group's goal is to motivate Christians to pray and give practical support throughout the year, he noted. The ministry's web site tells how to start small groups that focus on persecuted Christians, provides daily updates on religious freedom issues, and lists organizations that suggest methods of practical help.

The Christian band *Jars of Clay* has taken up the cause. The group traveled with Haas to Vietnam and China in 2000, meeting with underground church leaders. The trip "opened our eyes and hearts to the greater picture of the Body of Christ and a tangible expression of God's gift of joy and laughter in the midst of pain and persecution," *Jars of Clay's* Dan Haseltine said. While overseas, the group performed its song "This Road," about the Christian life. As they sang for their persecuted fellow Christians, "we understood that this song was written for the world," Haseltine said.

Their Redeemer Is Strong. There was a very poor old man in a village, but even kings were jealous of him because he had a beautiful white horse. Kings offered fabulous prices for the horse, but the man would say, "This horse is not a horse to me, he is a friend. And how can you sell a friend?" So even though he faced dire poverty, he never sold the horse.

One morning, the old man found that the horse was not in the stable. The whole village gathered and they said, "You foolish old man! We knew that someday the horse would be stolen. It would have been better to sell it. What a misfortune!"

The old man said, "Don't go so far as to say that. Simply say that the horse is not in the stable. That is a fact; everything else is a judgment. Whether it is a misfortune or a blessing, I don't know, because all we have is a fragment of knowledge. Who knows what is going to follow it?"

People laughed at the old man. They had always known that he was a little off his rocker. But after more than two weeks, one night the horse returned. He had not been stolen; he had only escaped from his stable. And upon his return, he brought a dozen wild horses with him.

Again the people gathered and they said, "Old man, you were right. This was not a misfortune; it has indeed proved to be a blessing."

The old man said, "Again you are going too far. Just say that the horse is back. Who knows whether it is a blessing or not? All we have is a fragment of knowledge. You read a single word in a sentence—how can you judge the whole book?" This time the people could not say much, but inside they knew that he was wrong. Twelve beautiful horses had come.

The old man had an only son who began to train the wild horses. But a week into his training he fell from a horse and both his legs were broken. The people gathered again, and again they judged. They said, "Again you proved right! It was misfortune. Your only son has lost the use of his legs, and in your old age he was to be your only support. Now you are poorer than ever."

The old man said, "You are obsessed with judgment. Don't go that far. Say only that my son has broken his legs. Nobody knows whether this is a misfortune or a blessing. Life comes in fragments and more is never given to you."

It happened that after a few weeks the country went to war and all the young men of the town were drafted into the military. Only the old man's son was left, because he was crippled. The whole town was crying and weeping, because it appeared to be a losing fight in which few of the young men would ever come home. They came to the old man and they said, "You were right, old man—this has proved a blessing. Maybe your son is crippled, but he is still with you. Our sons may be gone forever."

The old man said, "Only God knows whether it is a blessing or a misfortune."